THE KEATS BROTHERS

THE KEATS BROTHERS

The Life of John and George

Denise Gigante

THE BELKNAP PRESS OF HARVARD UNIVERSITY PRESS
Cambridge, Massachusetts & London, England
2011

Library of Congress Cataloging-in-Publication Data

Gigante, Denise, 1965–
    The Keats brothers: the life of John and George / Denise Gigante.
        p.   cm.
    Includes bibliographical references and index.
    ISBN 978-0-674-04856-0 (alk. paper)
    1. Keats, John, 1795–1821.   2. Keats, John, 1795–1821—Family.   3. Poets, English—
19th century—Biography.   4. Keats, George, 1797–1841.   5. Keats, George, 1797–
1841—Homes and haunts—United States.   6. English—United States—Biography.
I. Title.

PR4836.G47 2011
821'.7—dc22   2011014487
[B]

Dedicated to Tom

As Tradesmen say every thing is worth what it will fetch, so probably every mental pursuit takes its reality and worth from the ardour of the pursuer—being in itself a nothing—Ethereal things may at least be thus real.

—JOHN KEATS TO BENJAMIN BAILEY,

MARCH 13, 1818

CONTENTS

Editorial Note   x

Prologue   1

Part One: 1816–1817 and Before

1. To My Brother George   11

   Margate   11

   Young Men in London   20

   The Vale of Health   34

   Cheapside Reminiscences   44

2. What Mad Pursuit?   58

   Hampstead   58

   The Isle of Wight   73

   Canterbury and Bo Peep   79

   Oxford   84

   Paris   90

   Box Hill and Teignmouth   95

Part Two: 1818

3. Man of Genius and Man of Power   111

   Emigration Fever   111

   Devonshire   124

   Brunswick Square   134

   Separation at Liverpool   148

4. The Mountains of Tartary and of Allegheny   162

   The *Telegraph*   162

   Philadelphia   166

   Poor Tom   187

   The Great Western Road   198

   Pittsburgh   206

Part Three: 1819

5. Circumstances Gathering Like Clouds   215

   The Great Odes and *The Fall of Hyperion*   215

   Down the Ohio   225

   Letters across the Atlantic   238

   Cincinnati   250

6. Backwoods and Blind Alleys   260

   Winchester   260

   Past the Falls   267

   Harmony   279

   The Red Banks Trail   285

   Audubon and the Mill   297

Part Four: 1820–1841 and After

7. Back across the Atlantic   311

    Death Warrant   311

    The *Courier*   324

    Poor John   334

    The Dark and Bloody Ground   343

    The Man from Natchez   350

8. Posthumous Lives   356

    Naples   356

    Life in Louisville   373

    Rome   381

    Poor George   390

Epilogue: Blue!   405

Abbreviations   417

Notes   421

Acknowledgments   463

Index   467

EDITORIAL NOTE

The notes in this book are intended to identify sources of information about the lives of the Keats brothers. I have clumped them together within paragraphs, and readers not pursuing further research are welcome to ignore them. Unless otherwise indicated, all quotations of John Keats's poetry are from the *Complete Poems* edited by Jack Stillinger (1982); of Shakespeare's plays, from the Arden editions; of Milton's *Paradise Lost,* from Alastair Fowler's edition; and of the Bible, from the King James edition. I have not cited specific editions of modern poetry (Thomas Gray, Thomas Moore, Lord Byron, Percy Bysshe Shelley, Mary Tighe, etc.), though I have done so in the case of prose.

For the sake of brevity, I have restricted notation of primary materials to direct quotations and specific facts. Following biographical tradition established by Walter Jackson Bate, Aileen Ward, and Robert Gittings, I cite the letters of the Keats Circle (*KL, KC,* and *ML*) without publication dates, places, or recipients. Where relevant, these are mentioned in the text. On occasion to avoid confusion I have silently corrected capitalization, spelling, and punctuation within primary materials, such as *KL, KC, Hall's Journal, Fordham's Letters.* I have retained British spelling within quotations. A list of abbreviations used in the endnotes is given at the end of the book.

I claim being the affectionate Friend and Brother of John Keats. I loved him from boyhood even when he wronged me, for the goodness of his heart and the nobleness of his spirit . . .

—GEORGE KEATS TO CHARLES WENTWORTH DILKE,

MAY 7, 1830

My brother George has ever been more than a brother to me, he has been my greatest friend.

—JOHN KEATS TO ANN WYLIE,

AUGUST 6, 1818

PROLOGUE

George Keats kept a miniature painting of his dead brother over his mantelpiece in Louisville, Kentucky. His wife, Georgiana, put some hyacinth stems in a vase in such a way that one of the bell-shaped blossoms partly covered John's face. The poet would have loved the smell. He once tossed a fresh bouquet of roses away for having no scent. What was a rose without its fragrance? Now his image was awash in the sedative scent of purplish beauty from the flower named for Hyacinth, the legendary Greek youth beloved by Apollo. Above John's picture, George hung his brother's portrait of Shakespeare with the silken tassels Georgiana had made for the frame, and above the bard, a miniature of their younger brother, Tom. The Renaissance dramatists Francis Beaumont and John Fletcher hung to either side. While not exactly the Temple of Fame that John once hoped to enter, this shrine to English literary tradition—in a wooden cabin overlooking the falls of the Ohio River on the western frontier of colonial America—had at least one devout votary in the last surviving Keats brother.

How did such things come to pass? John blamed the "Burden of Society" for driving his brother George to America; and to be sure, after the Napoleonic Wars and the War of 1812 between Britain and America, the two elder Keats brothers were at the center of global events that transformed both of their lives. George was important to John, but he was also representative of a generation of English pioneers who left the Old Country to explore the new states and territories opening up west of the Allegheny Mountains. The American and French revolutions had overthrown the imperial powers of Britain and France, and people wondered whether the system of landed power and privilege that had prevailed in Europe since medieval times would topple. Napoleon's defeat at Waterloo and the Treaty of Ghent in 1815 put an end to decades of war for Britain, as a wave of British emigrants washed over the Atlantic toward unclaimed land in the Western Country of America. George's departure from England three years later with his young bride, Georgiana, was at once a move back in time to a more primitive era *and* an imaginative leap across four thousand miles onto the tabula rasa of the American dream.

Had Charles Dickens written the story of the two older Keats brothers, George might have kept the fortune he made in America and John might have lived to marry the woman he loved. Had Shakespeare narrated it, we might have had a compelling drama of sibling rivalry and hatred, rather than fraternal affection. But the real story, in which the orphaned brothers stood together against the brutal antagonist death, and one by one lost the fight, has gone unsung. Yet John began his poetic career writing poems addressed to his brother George, and George's move to America in 1818 inspired some of John's most famous thoughts about poetry and the nature of the human condition. His most sublime verse—the Great Odes and the fragments of *Hyperion*—emerged from an abyss of loss and loneliness that opened in the wake of George's emigration and, a few months later, of Tom's death. The poet's loss of his brothers became the gain of English literary tradition.

George's experience on the western frontier of America in turn puts John's life and work in a transatlantic context, and it leads to places that critics have not previously imagined in relation to the poet. It involves steep inclines over treacherous mountain passes and a serpentine route downriver into the heart of the American continent through rough, unbroken terrain. While John delved into the dark ravines of human consciousness, and ultimately the black hole that is death, George made his way past wolves, black bears, wild pigs, and catfish weighing as much as humans. John projected his dreams onto the dark, forested vale of *Hyperion,* and George witnessed scenes of stunning beauty in America. But unlike his brother and other Romantic poets, George did not attempt to *live* in sublimity, which can be done only at enormous cost to the self. Traditionally, the painful pleasures of sublimity have hung in balance with those of the beautiful—a more social aesthetic than the solitary sublime—and aesthetically speaking, one might say that the more sociable George was the alter ego to his brother, the sublime poet.

Had George published an account of his adventures in America, the same literary journals that satirized his brother as a Cockney Poet might have mocked *him* as a Cockney Pioneer. Tory reviewers scoffed at *Endymion: A Poetic Romance,* and they considered the so-called English Prairie in Illinois no less a creature of fancy: a latter-day Land of Cockaigne, dreamed up not by medieval peasants but by middle-class pioneers like Morris Birkbeck and George Flower. In her novel *Lodore,* written after *Frankenstein,* Mary Shelley has Lord Byron, in the character of Lord Lodore, leave England to raise his daughter in the Territory of Illinois, but after a while he changes his mind and turns back. Eight years later, in *Martin Chuzzlewit,* Dickens sends *his* title character across the Atlantic and up the Mississippi to Illinois, where he finds the settlers wan and wretched, dying of destitution and disease. He returns to England disillusioned with the American dream. George Keats may have followed a dream when he followed the English pioneers to the prairielands of America, but unlike others he never turned back.

To follow George and John Keats on their bifurcated paths in life, you, dear reader, must prepare for adventure. You are advised to dress warmly and pack some calomel, for you will be walking the deck on the open seas. You may feel sick on the way from Liverpool to the Delaware Bay, but you'll be rewarded for your perseverance by the view from the mountain ridges in Pennsylvania—thousands of acres of untouched woodlands chock-full of black and red oak, blooming mountain ash, cedar, chestnut, beech, and butternut. At the fork of the Ohio River at Pittsburgh, you will board a keelboat poled by brawny boatmen, and you'll be warned about the dangers of savages and snakes. In crossing a swamp somewhere between Indiana and Illinois you will be stung by mosquitoes.

You'll spend a few months with the famous naturalist John James Audubon and his menagerie of furred and feathered creatures in the backwoods settlement of Red Banks, Kentucky, and you'll annoy Emerson by correcting him on the source of a song he quotes in "Nature." After losing all your money in a steamboat, you'll recover it slowly, accruing a fortune over many long years. You will also own slaves. You'll do many things that you never thought you would do and that George Keats, in parting from his brother, never thought he would do either.

In England, you'll explore the grounds of Carisbrooke Castle, peopled with primroses, and climb from Burford Bridge to the top of Box Hill in quest of the moon goddess, Cynthia. You'll visit the haunts of the Old Poets in the squares and quadrangles of Oxford, and, in crossing the Bay of Biscay, a Portuguese warship will fire a shot across your bow for you to stop. You will peer down into the greenish-blue sea, and join generations of readers in trying to see the world through the eyes of John Keats.

More peripherally, the story of the two older Keats brothers involves a third, star-crossed brother, doomed to die at age nineteen from the family disease (consumption), and a little sister locked away in a tower by a cruel, unfeeling guardian—or to speak less metaphorically, a brick mansion owned by a stout, middle-aged merchant in the suburbs of London. Yet the lives of these orphans do have the makings of fairy tale. As Walter Jackson Bate has written, "The life of Keats—even at first reading—has always seemed haunted by a feeling of familiarity. It reads like something we have read before, and are eager to hear again."[1] And yet again.

The biographical tradition surrounding John Keats began in 1827, a few years after his death, when his publisher John Taylor jotted down some comments by the poet's guardian Richard Abbey at a dinner sponsored by the London Company of Girdlers. In the sober light of day, Abbey's remarks appeared scandalous enough that Taylor gave up the idea of commissioning a life of John Keats. Leigh Hunt was the first to publish his memories of the poet, characterizing him, to the annoyance of his friends, as a pauper redeemed by genius. John's school friend Charles Cowden Clarke then published his "Recollections of Keats," and George Keats planned to write a memoir of his brother. But as the years rolled past, and George toiled at his sawmill and his flour-mill, he eventually gave up the task.

John's roommate Charles Armitage Brown attempted a more comprehensive life of the poet, but it was never published during his lifetime. Instead, it remained for that Victorian Man of Letters, Richard Monckton Milnes, to publish the first life of John Keats. Having met Charles Brown at a villa in Fiesole, near Florence, Milnes discovered a cache of Keatsiana and, with the energy characteristic of the age, went about gathering more. He interviewed anyone he could find who might have known the poet, and the result of his labors was the *Life, Letters, and Literary Remains of John Keats* (1848). Like most biographers, Milnes got a few facts wrong. He thought, for instance, that George was older than John and that John's friend Benjamin Bailey had died. Bailey spoke up from the grave in a pair of couplets:

> Dicky Milnes—Dicky Milnes! why what the deuce could ail ye
> When you wrote the life of Keats—to write the death of Bailey—
> The poet sleeps—oh! let him sleep—within the silent tomb-o
> But Parson Bailey lives, and kicks—Archdeacon of Colombo.[2]

By 1887, when Parson Bailey really *was* in his tomb, Sir Sidney Colvin and William Michael Rossetti (brother of the poets Dante Gabriel and Christina Rossetti) took over the biographical legacy. Their critical appreciations in the Victorian mode of life writing ensured a permanent place for John Keats in the constellation of English poets.

In the twentieth century, the American poet Amy Lowell amassed an impressive collection of Keatsiana on which she based her almost equally massive two-volume biography. Lowell's work stood as the authoritative modern biography of John Keats from the time of its publication in 1925 through the 1960s when three new major literary lives superseded her work —and at that point, George's granddaughter Alice Lee Keats felt some relief. "I did not like Amy Lowell's Keats one bit," she said. "The first volume gave me jimjams she touched too heavily and intimately at times—I do not like her any how she is so conceited."[3] Lowell died the year her biography was published (a year before receiving a Pulitzer Prize for poetry), leaving Walter Jackson Bate to win the Pulitzer Prize for his biography of John Keats. That was 1963, the same year Aileen Ward published her psychological study of the poet, and five years before Robert Gittings published his revised biography, expanded from his 1954 account of Keats's *annus mirabilis*. All three books were titled *John Keats*.

In 1997, the eve of the new millennium, English Poet Laureate Andrew Motion published an expanded study of John Keats's life and work under a condensed title, *Keats*. By a mere two years, he missed the publishing opportunity of a lifetime, the bicentennial of John's birth, publishing his biography instead on the bicentennial of George's. Filmmaker Jane Campion, touched by Motion's portrayal of the poet's love affair with Fanny Brawne, named her movie *Bright Star* after the opening line of a poem that Richard Monckton Milnes had titled "Keats's Last Sonnet." But it was *not* his last sonnet, nor will *Bright Star* be the last portrayal of John Keats's life.

As for his siblings . . . Tom died too young for us to know much about him, but Fanny Keats outlived all her brothers into old age. Marie Adami published her life, *Fanny Keats,* with Yale University Press in 1938. Around the same time, a high school teacher from Indiana named Naomi Joy Kirk tried to tell George Keats's story. She interviewed his descendants and completed her Master's thesis, "The Life of George Keats," at Columbia University in 1933. For another decade, she continued to work on the manuscript, doubling its size. But neither Yale University Press nor Harvard University Press, which published Walter Jackson Bate's biography, took an interest, and when World War II came along, it dashed her hopes for publication.

The editor Earl Balch, writing from the firm of George Palmer Putnam's Sons on July 26, 1943, prepared Naomi Kirk for another rejection: "It is only fair to tell you in advance that we are feeling considerably the war time restrictions and find ourselves with an embarrassing lack of paper, so that our list of publications for the duration is likely to be shorter than usual." Interpreting the remark and others like it, Blanche Colton Williams, author of *Forever Young: A Life of John Keats* (published that same year by the same press), wrote to Kirk: "The trouble, dear Naomi, is that the editors and publishers get certain things into their crania and you can't dislodge them with diamond pickaxes. All to whom I've spoken do not believe George Keats will 'pay,' and so believing or non-believing, they will risk nothing. Such a volume represents an outlay of from $5,000 to $10,000 and they seem averse these days to help the world by getting out any of the old-time 'back-log' books that sustain the fires of their crackling front pieces."[4] Apparently, Kirk did not crackle.

George's great-grandson Philip Speed Tuley, who had been following the progress of Naomi Kirk's manuscript since its initial stages, wrote on May 12, 1943: "I earnestly hope that the publication of your George Keats will eventuate before very long. I want to see it while I am still in the land of the living."[5] But within a couple of months, poor Mr. Tuley had died. Fifteen years later, Kirk followed him across the Great Divide, and since then, her work has sat in boxes at The Filson Historical Society in Louisville, Kentucky.

When George does show up in biographies of his more famous brother, he does not remain long—usually just long enough to disappear with John's money, leaving the poet destitute and on the brink of death, while he pursues his own fame and fortune in America. Yet despite the dramatic appeal of George as a villain, John *was* as ambitious as Caesar, and George (without the irony Shakespeare's Mark Antony would have intended) *was* an honorable man. However much it might jar with the traditional version of the story to suggest, the Cockney Pioneer deserves a place next to the Cockney Poet in the visionary company of Romanticism. While the medium of their dreams may have differed, the two eldest Keats brothers—"Man of Genius" and "Man of Power"—embodied sibling forms of the phenomenon we call Romanticism.

PART ONE
1816–1817
and before

I TO MY BROTHER GEORGE

Margate

Living in sublimity has its price. John Keats, burdened with an extraordinary mind and a sense of alienated strength, knew this. His melancholy was real as the days slipped by at the seaside resort of Margate in the summer of 1816. He was on a holiday of sorts with his brother Tom, having passed his medical exams in July and escaped the stifling air of London. He needed a break from medical school as much as Tom needed medical care, for the youngest Keats brother was sick—thin and pinched at the age of sixteen. Tuberculosis was a slow killer, and Tom, despite his bright spirit, was on the tedious road to a consumptive death.

John, too, was on the run from death. Although only twenty, he encountered it every day in the smell of sickness suffusing the claustrophobic hospital borough of Southwark in London, and in the hallways and operating theater of the United Hospitals of St. Thomas and Guy's, where he dressed wounds that quickly became infected. Breathing sickroom air in the days before antiseptics was loathsome labor. Worse than the brutal finality of death was the lingering sensation of living death that came over him in his anatomy and chemistry lectures, as he sat accruing information that he felt had no part of his being.

Without even seeming to have applied himself, John had risen to the top of his class and was on his way to becoming "John Keats, Licentiate of the Society of Apothecaries"—or, if he continued in school, a member of

the Royal College of Surgeons. He had already completed his apprenticeship as an apothecary with Dr. Thomas Hammond, a surgeon in Edmonton, where the brothers' grandmother had lived. Expectations were now
gathering for him to enter the medical practice. His future was scripted,
but in a language not his own.

John had always relied on his brothers, and particularly George, to
temper his moods. George's affability was more than a match for those dark
tormentors that besieged the poet unpredictably, but inevitably, and always
powerfully. Tom was sick and their little sister, Fanny, was far away—
though less in terms of actual distance than in terms of the psychological
distance imposed between them by their guardian Richard Abbey. The
death of their grandmother two years earlier had severed their last remaining ties to happier times, and left the orphans in the hands of a man whose
obtuse materialism, John felt, stifled every generous impulse. Ever since
Abbey had assumed a position of parental authority over the siblings, John
found that he could do little for the younger sister who so resembled Tom,
and who was now trapped in the village of Walthamstow with the Abbeys.

John always seemed to incite their guardian to opposition, but with
George things were different. A consummate people pleaser, George listened in order to understand. He was always ready with a smile—ready
with the small talk that fuels conversation and fosters social ties. Although
sixteen months younger than John, he had the aura of an elder brother, and
not only because of his extra foot in height. George's habit was to make the
best of things. Without George's congeniality, and the clever playfulness of
Tom, John knew that he would have a difficult time indeed.

While John and Tom vacationed at the beach, George stayed behind in
London, toiling in the counting house of Richard Abbey's tea wholesaling
business. Abbey had no use for a sick clerk, and at Margate Tom could take
it easy and feel some sand between his toes. And with Tom close at hand
needing attention, John felt bound to those mundane particulars that by
demanding immersion in short, disconnected moments can stave off a more
undefined despair. Life was short, his ambition lay elsewhere, and he had
lost, somehow, his independence.

Breezy Margate might seem a strange place for soul-searching, but thus
it was: two sensitive, artistically inclined young men in a town famed for its
beaches and bathing machines. At the mouth of the Thames, seventy miles
east of London, Margate had grown from a small fishing village into a fash-

ionable Regency resort—a magnet for the middle classes, who came to drink the mineral waters and enjoy the picturesque scenery. The young women dressed *à la française* in high-waisted gowns and bonnets tied with ribbons. They carried parasols and strolled through the countryside overlooking the harbor. They watched the sailors manning the small sailing vessels with their single masts rigged fore-and-aft, the old Margate hoys. In town, they visited the shops and the assembly rooms where the balls were held, the neoclassical theaters, and the libraries that circulated Gothic novels and romances to a crowd on holiday from London.

In spite of sickness and their scant stipends from Abbey, John and Tom at least had their youth, and one imagines that they also had some fun. The balmy summer air was at odds with despondence, and, as even doctors back then knew, health tends to follow the flow of good spirits. Tom, like other consumptive patients, would have been urged to try one of the curtained contraptions floating out several hundred yards from the shore that provided the signature Margate experience: a salutary dunk in the sea. These bathing machines were products of Enlightenment ingenuity and the notion that bathing was a medical procedure more than a pleasure. They would be dragged by horses to the water's edge every year and set afloat for the summer season.

Whereas books and mental application were supposed to make one vulnerable to disease, light exercise such as riding, walking, and bathing were thought to strengthen the constitution. A cold bath was the particular remedy for enervated as well as high-strung bodies, and physicians were very particular about its use. Dr. William Turton, who treated Tom for tuberculosis in 1817, explained that "the first three or four dips should be taken as hastily as possible, that the torpidity may not reach beyond the extreme capillary vessels. The merely plunging into the water and getting out again is sufficient."[1] Bathers would strip off their clothes and proceed by way of a drop-down ladder, or else be plunged by attendants through a trap door, into the sea. The sudden change in temperature was supposed to give a bracing shock to the nervous fibers, thus fortifying the system.

If the eighteenth-century Cult of Sensibility had produced persons of refined taste and delicacy, with them came a host of "hypochondriacal" and "hysterical" diseases, such as melancholy, bile, and the symptoms adding up to consumption. John's sense of creative power, which drove and kept him apart, would also have qualified as a type of "hypochondriacal" melancholy in this taxonomy of nervous complaints. Elevated reverie, sustained thought and intensity—combined with a constitutional inability to tolerate inauthenticity, either in oneself or in others—can make for great poetry, but they can also make the poet's path through life more demanding. George and Tom served as John's anchors in a world from which they had all been unmoored by the deaths of their parents and grandparents. The brothers, now alone in the world, clung together.

Whenever George was at a distance, John discovered thoughts and feelings inside himself that he might not otherwise have known. His sonnet "To My Brother George," written at Margate in August 1816, registers the deep need for human connection that the fraternal bond fulfilled:

Many the wonders I this day have seen:
    The sun, when first he kist away the tears
    That fill'd the eyes of morn;—the laurel'd peers
Who from the feathery gold of evening lean;—
The ocean with its vastness, its blue green,
    Its ships, its rocks, its caves, its hopes, its fears,—
    Its voice mysterious, which whoso hears
Must think on what will be, and what has been.
E'en now, dear George, while this for you I write,
    Cynthia is from her silken curtains peeping
So scantly, that it seems her bridal night,
    And she her half-discover'd revels keeping.
But what, without the social thought of thee,
Would be the wonders of the sky and sea?

Without the "social thought" of his brother George, the sonnet suggests, the poet would find no pleasure in the wonder of sublime experience. Transcendent vision, if one can manage to achieve it, is one thing; but without human connection, it can vanish like mist. The very thought of George, in the penultimate line of the sonnet, works against the sublime isolation of the speaker, tethering him to his own humanity.

While the speaker recognizes the beauty of the surrounding landscape, his focus is on the permanent forms of nature. As the "voice mysterious" of the sea calls out to him, its caves and hidden recesses speak of things he cannot but feel, for they are echoed in his own breast. The moon in her mythological splendor peers out through a curtained sky, not in the serenity of virgin mildness, typically associated with the moon goddess, but from the concupiscence of bridal revels. Her cloudy veils merely serve to reveal (as Percy Shelley might say) the scorn of beauty for all concealment. For all her coyness, she steps boldly into the sublime central role of John's sonnet to George, as she will do the following year in *Endymion: A Poetic Romance*. Ultimately, the sublime astral bodies in their eternal movements trump earthly beauty.

The formal highlight of the sonnet "To My Brother George" is John's apostrophe to George at the end of the second quatrain. At the expected place of the Petrarchan *volta,* or turn, where the poem typically moves toward resolution, the poet turns to his brother George; the poem "turns" formally and the subject matter shifts from sublime thoughts of "what will be, and what has been" to the present moment. That seems to have been George's effect on his brother: the presence of "dear George" signals a return from ethereal to more mundane matters.

By virtue of writing in the form of a sonnet, moreover, the poet is tethered by meter and rhyme scheme. *If by dull rhymes our English must be chain'd, / And, like Andromeda, the sonnet sweet / Fetter'd, in spite of pained loveliness. . .* John Keats was not the only poet to write a sonnet about the verse form of the sonnet. His sonnet to George abandons the rhyme scheme established by Petrarch in the two opening quatrains and shifts, in the closing lines, to the English or Shakespearean form of the sonnet: it ends with a couplet. This sophisticated move allows the speaker to emphasize the "wonders" of the opening and closing lines. And as if in uncanny prophecy, the poem ends with a rhyme of "thee" and "sea," associating George, the poet's muse, with the blue abyss of sea that was destined to come between them.

John's conversational verse to his brother George adopts the same tone of quiet confidence the young poet had found in Wordsworth. From the elder poet, too, John had learned how to take advantage of the contrast between a spontaneous overflow of powerful emotion (represented here by the oceanic passions of the sea) and the constraint provided by the form of the sonnet stanza. As in Wordsworth's "Lines Composed a Few Miles above Tintern Abbey," the speaker communicates sublime experience to a sibling, a mirror of the poet's own, best self. In Wordsworth's case, that sibling was Dorothy. In John's case, it was George. The power of sublimity lies in its unbounded nature, the challenge it poses to the mind to encompass it, or to give it formal definition, and the painful pleasure that comes in trying. George chose to leave the solitary experience of sublimity to his older brother, but the bond (indeed, band) he provided encouraged John to grasp at infinity.

George's closest bonds, too, were with his brothers, but he did not demand the same intensity of all his relationships. If his confidence did not rise to the sublime heights of John's, nor did it plummet so readily into ruminative self-doubt. John's originality, intelligence, and compassion gave him the capacity to foster social ties at the deepest level, but often he held people at a distance until he knew them well, preserving his core and letting his trust reside in his brothers. Most people who met George liked him, but those whom John let close to him loved him.

After his sonnet addressed to George from Margate, John began another poem, "To My Brother George," this time in the form of a verse epistle. It was his second known attempt at a rhymed, conversational letter in heroic meter, the first being a verse epistle to George Felton Mathew, an acquaintance from London. Whereas the verse epistle to Mathew is full of naiads, druids, laureled spirits, and fairy feet—residues of the kind of "poetic diction" that Wordsworth had condemned—the verse epistle to George, although equally fanciful, speaks more directly from the heart. One imagines that the poet is being quite literal when he describes lounging on the cliffs by the sea, trying to catch inspiration from the celestial world beyond:

> Full many a dreary hour have I past,
> My brain bewilder'd, and my mind o'ercast
> With heaviness; in seasons, when I've thought
> No spherey strains by me could e'er be caught
> From the blue dome, though I to dimness gaze
> On the far depth where sheeted lightning plays;
> Or, on the wavy grass, outstretch'd supinely,
> Pry 'mong the stars, to strive to think divinely:
> That I should never hear Apollo's song,
> Though feathery clouds were floating all along
> The purple west . . .

From the rooms he shared with Tom, John would make daily excursions to the bluffs to compose—not merely rhymes, but what Wordsworth would call "genuine poetry," the only kind that seemed worth writing. While poetry did not always have to be prophetic, it *did* have to be the utterance of a poet. As John put it in a now-famous remark to his publisher, "if Poetry comes not as naturally as the Leaves to a tree it had better not come at all."[2] One can learn the craft of poetry, but one must be born a poet.

When John addressed these poems to George a few weeks before his twenty-first birthday, he felt himself brimming with something, as yet undefined, which required an outlet. As he stretched out on the grass in the waning days of summer—at times in sun, more often in mist, usually with a book, always in the hopes of penetrating the phenomenal surface surrounding him—George provided a distant but sympathetic ear. To be sure, some self-awareness, and even irony, informs his admission that his daily labor has been to "think divinely." Yearning to see pawing and prancing white coursers, but seeing only the mild, repetitive lap of the waves, a person not naturally endowed with patience might wonder whether there were any wonders left. What if, for instance, waiting to catch ethereal strains from another world, he caught nothing? Or worse, something as banal as a cold? What if, in his case, wise passivity amounted to no more than indolence? In both of John's poems titled "To My Brother George," concerns about the idea of a poetic vocation rise to the surface.

Above all, a poet must see "through the film of death" to the inner magic of the world. Rather than water, the poet discerns in "the dark silent blue . . . all its diamonds trembling through, and through." In John's verse epistle to George, the speaker promises his brother that should he ever witness the "mysteries of night," he would translate them into lasting verse. Yet, the promise was conditional, for he already felt mortality closing in: "Fair world adieu! / Thy dales, and hills, are fading from my view: / Swiftly, I mount, upon widespreading pinions, / Far from the narrow bounds of thy dominions." At the very start of his poetic career, John was already saying his goodbyes. Another "adieu!" in the penultimate line of the verse epistle to George rhymes with the poem's final line: "'Twas but to kiss my hand, dear George, to you!" Like the personified figure of Joy in John's "Ode on Melancholy," whose hand is ever at his lips bidding adieu, either the poet or his brothers seemed ever on the verge of disappearance.

Death was stalking, and John neither could nor would stifle his ambition. "Ah, my dear friend and brother!" he exclaims. "Could I, at once, my mad ambition smother, / For tasting joys like these, sure I should be / Happier, and dearer to society." Before long, he would have to return to another, more wearying routine in the Stygian depths of the hospital borough. There, as he had written in his verse epistle to George Felton Mathew, "far different cares/Beckon me sternly from soft 'Lydian airs,'/And hold my faculties so long in thrall,/That I am oft in doubt whether at all/I shall again see Phoebus in the morning:/Or flush'd Aurora in the roseate dawning!"

The allusion to "Lydian airs" refers to Milton's "L'Allegro" (the cheerful counterpart to the more melancholy Penseroso), in which the poet casts off the malign spirits of depression in favor of the more sociable sphere of conviviality represented by the lighter, pastoral world of ancient Lydia. John would make a similar move at the start of his "Ode on Melancholy." In the meantime, he would make his way resolutely each day to the white chalk cliffs of Margate and gaze at the canvased ships as they passed. He would watch the black-winged swallows as they dropped into their nests, and the gulls as they traversed the sky. He would look down and see himself reflected in the restless, ever-changing sea.

Another poem composed in the summer of 1816 at Margate expresses the same anxiety of a youth who dissolves before he can execute—or even imagine—any noble deeds. A fragment of Spenserian romance, "Calidore" takes its name from its central character, who is summoned to the great hall of a castle for a feast. In the courtyard on the way he passes lovely maidens, clattering palfreys, and noble steeds. But before the feast begins—or any tales of heroic action can be told—the story fizzles out. The reader, like the assembled guests, is left unfulfilled, "burning/To hear of knightly deeds, and gallant spurning/Of all unworthiness." John knew that he had the skill to trick nature out in rich, Spenserian brocades, but he also knew that in the end luxurious language would not add up to the poetry he was after. The most telling thing about this early poem may be that it knew when to cease.

"Calidore" lacked the kind of irony that would ground and darken John's later work, and indeed the image of the poet whom critics would later blast as naïve and sentimental appears in it. Like the poet, the vulnerable protagonist runs the risk of being swallowed up by sweet nothings. When Calidore returns to the castle, the ladies embrace him, drowning him in "tears of languishment." Together, they represent a weepy quagmire of beauty—fair limbs, fair curves, fair eyes, all forming a soft, clingy morass into which he who steps may never escape—the predicament of the sentimental poet. "Calidore," by virtue of its status as a fragment, is an act of separation from that portrait of the artist as a young man.

Tom Keats, who breathed the very spirit of romance, copied the poem proudly into his blank, red-leather notebook, in a beautiful, sloping hand: "Lo! I must tell a tale of chivalry . . ." One imagines *him* "looking round about him with a fond,/And placid eye," like one of the characters in his brother's romance. Yet, perhaps even more than in Calidore, one finds Tom Keats in the "innocent mind" of John's first published poem, the sonnet "To Solitude," which Leigh Hunt printed under John's initials in the *Examiner* the spring before John and Tom went to Margate.

When Tom copied his brother's sonnet to solitude in his notebook, he titled it "Sonnet to Solitude." But he could just as easily have titled it "To My Brother Tom."

> O Solitude! if I must with thee dwell,
>   Let it not be among the jumbled heap
>   Of murky buildings; climb with me the steep,—
> Nature's observatory—whence the dell,
> Its flowery slopes, its river's crystal swell,
>   May seem a span; let me thy vigils keep
>   'Mongst boughs pavillion'd, where the deer's swift leap
> Startles the wild bee from the fox-glove bell.
> But though I'll gladly trace these scenes with thee,
>   Yet the sweet converse of an innocent mind,
>   Whose words are images of thoughts refin'd,
> Is my soul's pleasure; and it sure must be
>   Almost the highest bliss of human-kind,
>   When to thy haunts two kindred spirits flee.

This sonnet sounds the same dilemma as John's sonnet "To My Brother George," namely, how to attain the sublime vision made possible through solitude, and yet maintain the human connection necessary to avoid that soul-killing vacuum, solipsism?

While one might read the sonnet in the context of heterosexual romantic love, there is no reason to assume that the intimacy the speaker both feels and needs is with a lover. Tom, after all, is literally the kindred spirit who flees with the poet from the "jumbled heap/Of murky buildings" in London to the steep headlands by the sea, "Nature's observatory." Like the "so-cial thought" of George in the sonnet "To My Brother George," the frater-nal bond comes to the rescue once more in the form of an "innocent mind," which, for all we can tell about it, Tom's seemed to be. His scattered pres-ence in his older brother's letters suggests a sensitive, trusting nature.

As September advanced, John and Tom prepared to leave Margate. Rather than returning to the house on St. Thomas Street that John had shared with other medical students, near the hospitals of St. Thomas and Guy's, John would move with Tom around the corner to 8 Dean Street, an apartment on a narrow lane off St. Thomas Street. The neighborhood was "a beastly place in dirt, turnings and windings," but at least there he would be free from the constraint of un-kindred spirits.[3] And London Bridge, a mere fifteen-minute walk, would connect him and his younger brother to George. Despite the loss of sky and sea as the urban smoke and fog closed in, John, before the end of the year, would gain a clearer sense of the poetic vocation he had expressed tentatively, though explicitly, in poems addressed to George from Margate.

Young Men in London

George Keats, now nineteen, had been carrying on his daily routine of working for Richard Abbey by day, and sleeping above the counting house at 4 Pancras Lane by night, while his brothers were at Margate. "I was with my Guardian at no expense," he recalled in 1824. By contrast, for the year since John had moved to the hospital borough in central London from sub-urban Edmonton, where he had been living as a surgeon's apprentice, John and Tom, "who had been with Mʳ Abbey and left him . . . spent 3 times their income."[4] Living above the tea-house on Pancras Lane saved George money and suited Abbey's need for control.

George could remember little about his parents, but what he had heard from Richard Abbey was not flattering. Their maternal grandfather, John Jennings, whom George described as "generous and gullable," was to Abbey a mere glutton.[5] By the same yardstick, his father, Thomas Keats, was a drunkard, and his mother, Frances Jennings Keats, an exceptional woman—maybe—but a tramp. The tea dealer might not have censured the Keats family in so many words to George, but his disapprobation was plain enough. George felt the unspoken imperative to turn out different from them. Still, the Keats blood ran in his veins. Abbey kept his eye on him and remained wary.

For ten years following the death of their father, the siblings' maternal grandmother, Alice (Whalley) Jennings, had been their "discreet parent"— a legal term that in Richard Abbey's mind bore literal significance. Abbey in fact believed her to be the only discreet person in the whole misguided lot. She had been raised on a dairy farm, Doughty Pasture in Great Marsden, Yorkshire, and when she turned to Abbey for advice about her daughter's children before her own death on December 19, 1814, Abbey set her mind at ease. He took charge of her grandchildren, apprenticing John to Dr. Thomas Hammond and taking George and Tom into his tea business at Abbey & Cocks. He promised to take Fanny into his own home in Walthamstow, on the outskirts of the city, after Alice Jennings died.

George had clerked for Abbey for a few years, but Tom did not last long in the role of merchant's apprentice. Tall, narrow-shouldered, and thin, the youngest Keats brother seemed suspiciously delicate, if not androgynous. While any sensible, hardworking type knew how to soldier on through such ephemeralities as sickness, Tom only languished at his desk. And now that he had gone on summer holiday with his older brother, Abbey had no way of telling what they were up to. *There was a naughty boy, / A naughty boy was he / He would not stop at home, / He could not quiet be . . .* From the beginning, Abbey had trouble with his eldest ward. John resembled his father in bearing and had his mother's sensuous, nay downright voluptuous, features. Such a combination—even without the added extravagance of poetic ambition—was enough to make the tea dealer nervous. Clearly, the oldest boy had inherited his parents' pride, and their willfulness too.

From what Abbey could tell, the eleven-year-old Frances Mary, who had lived with her grandmother for four years since the age of seven, was dutiful and tidy. But she seemed to care for nothing so much as her pets. She kept a canary and brightly colored goldfinches in a cage, and a goldfish in a bowl. And her brothers treated *her* as a pet. John shared her fondness for "the whole tribe of the Bushes and the Brooks," and no doubt when he should have been mixing chemicals for Hammond he led her off to that slippery stream, Salmon's Brook, to look for minnows—or to that pond by

Stark's Nest, the wooded common in Edmonton where she would soil her
frock and tear her bonnet.

> There was a naughty boy,
>   And a naughty boy [was] he,
> He kept little fishes
>   In washing tubs three.
>   In spite
>   Of the might
>   Of the Maid
>   Nor afraid
>   Of his granny-good—
>   He often would
>   Hurly burly
>   Get up early
>   And go
>   By hook or crook
>   To the brook
>   And bring home
>   Miller's thumb
>   Tittlebat
>   Not over fat
>   Minnows small
>   As the stall
>   Of a glove
>   Not above
>   The size
>   Of a nice
>   Little baby's
>   Little finger . . .[6]

John knew the light in which their guardian held him. Abbey had paid
Hammond good money, about three hundred pounds, to teach his ward
the mysteries of plasters and pills. The investment was steep, but whenever
Abbey visited John in the dispensary behind Dr. Hammond's house, rather
than finding him mixing chemicals and labeling bottles he found him loll-
ing over a book, or scribbling rhymes. *There was a naughty boy / And a
naughty boy was he / For nothing would he do / But scribble poetry . . .*

Fanny Keats was not as naughty as her brother, but she was not as grateful as she could have been. Abbey prided himself on Pindars, his large brick home in Walthamstow with all the appurtenances of middle-class wealth: servants, a yard with flower and vegetable gardens, chickens to chase, horses to ride, even a high-rigged carriage. Yet the Keats girl seemed meek and miserable. His wife, Eleanor (née Jones), may have been illiterate but she *had* married into respectability, and Fanny also had the anonymous Miss Abbey, another orphan the couple had adopted, for company. Why, then, should she be so moped? Despite all he had done, she acted as if she were lonely.

But Fanny *was* uncomfortable in the big house named Pindars with the Abbeys, and she did not conceal her feelings from her brothers. In response to her complaints, John offered sympathy, while George responded pragmatically with tasks to keep her busy. He sent her some silk remnants and pasteboard to make a candle-shade for his desk. He threw in a jump rope for her to play with and suggested that she learn a country-dance called the skipping-rope hornpipe.

George was a mere six years older than his sister, but both felt the gap between them to be greater. Fanny's character, George thought, was not quite formed. In truth, conversation between her and George had never flowed as naturally as it had between her and John, who readily escaped with her into childhood, or between her and Tom, who was closest to her in age and resembled her in looks as well as personality. George often found himself going out of his way to insist on his affection for his sister. In a postscript to the letter he enclosed with the jump rope, he wrote, "I say that your Brothers love you—mind—I mean to include myself."[7]

Fanny felt cut off from her brothers, but George thought she should make more of an effort. Abbey told him that during mealtimes she stared sullenly at her plate and hardly spoke. She succumbed too easily to morbid feelings that George could not approve. When she took up the harp, he wrote to her: "I sincerely hope you may conquer it and having so powerful a restorative at command you may at pleasure drive away those melancholy fits you are subject to." George could not help thinking his sister "uncommonly serious."[8] John was no less moody, but wasn't Fanny a girl? Yet she cared not to be complaisant and made no attempt to be witty.

George had a special place in his heart for a sister, but for some reason he could never fully explain, the real-life Fanny never filled that spot. Despite the best of intentions on both sides, their communication was strained. But, having little experience with young girls or parenting, he saw no reason to doubt his guardian's policies. He would, of course, never advise her to become resigned to misery, but a change might be for the worse. "I am fully persuaded from the affectionate manner in which Mr Abbey mentions you that he is deeply interested in your happiness," George wrote, "and knowing him to be a straightforward, candid man, I feel easy while you are under his protection." Rather than focusing on "the disagreeables" of her current situation, Fanny should "cheer up and look lively."[9] By nature an optimist, George gave his sister the same advice he would have given himself. What, in any event, could he do? What could any of them do, but tough it out and make the best of things?

Fortunately, Fanny had lived with the Abbeys for only about a month before her guardian decided to place her in boarding school across the street from his house. The Misses Caley and Tuckeys' Boarding Academy was, like Pindars, on Marsh Street, the high street that led out from the village to the marshes. There, Fanny Keats studied the standard curriculum for girls: grammar, orthography, a sampling of polite literature, deportment, music, watercolor painting, French. And like her oldest brother, she worked hard. By the time John and Tom went to Margate in 1816, she had earned a school prize, *The Poetical Works of William Collins.* One of her schoolteachers had inscribed it: "Miss Keats. The reward of Merit and Industry."[10] Had Richard Abbey looked into the book, he might not have liked all that he found there: "Curst be the gold and silver which persuade / Weak men to follow far fatiguing trade!"

Susanna Tuckey was twenty-two when Fanny entered school, and judging from her tombstone in the Walthamstow Churchyard, she was an unassuming soul: "Of Gentlest Manners Unaffected Mind / Lover of Peace In Every Action Kind / Compos'd in Sufferings and in Joy Sedate / Good without Noise, Without Pretension Great." Her sister, Mary Ann Tuckey, was six years older than Susanna, and a devout scholar of syntax and grammar. Believing that a "correct knowledge of our native tongue is absolutely essential to a liberal education," she later published a textbook with a hundred pages of questions and answers, in the style of a catechism. Grammar, to her mind, was "the key which opens endless stores of intellectual treasures."[11] Fanny would remain in school with the Tuckeys for three years, until age fifteen, when despite her lamentations and John's protests she would return to the more patriarchal world under Abbey's roof.

At least, John spent less time trapped as a surgeon's apprentice in Edmonton than his sister would spend with the Abbeys. The Apothecary Act of 1815 had made it necessary for him to serve either a six-month residency at a hospital or nine months at a dispensary in order to earn his license from the Company of Apothecaries. Accordingly, he registered that very summer for a six-month term of courses at the United Hospitals of St. Thomas and Guy's. But even as Abbey supplied the money for his ward's lodging, books, surgical instruments, hospital fees, and lectures, he could tell that John's heart wasn't in medicine.

But George, who had a knack for making friends, enjoyed London. He invited his brothers to parties—dinners, dances, musical recitals, private theatricals—all harmless entertainment that Abbey himself would have approved. Ann Felton and Caroline Mathew, daughters of the merchant Felton Mathew, organized "little domestic concerts and dances" at their home above their father's business on Goswell Street in Islington to which they invited the Keats brothers.[12] Their cousin George Felton Mathew had poetic aspirations himself, and he invited John to his house on Oxford Street, off Regent's Park. His twelve-year-old sister, Mary Strange Mathew, kept a commonplace book that she titled *The Garland: Consisting of Poetical Extracts both Ancient and Modern,* and she copied poems by her brother's new friend into it.

George Felton Mathew addressed a poem to John under the title "To a Poetical Friend" in 1815, and John opened his verse epistle to Mathew that same year with the line, "Sweet are the pleasures that to verse belong." Mathew saw Keats as "a young man of promise, like a tree covered with a profusion of blossom," and John in turn saw Mathew as "a flowret blooming wild,/Close to the source, bright, pure, and undefil'd,/Whence gush the streams of song." Although the two budding poets (to borrow their own floral motif) were about the same age and both had literary interests, they were "in many respects as different as two individuals could be." John was a "faultfinder with everything established," as Mathew put it, whereas Mathew "dreaded discord and disorder" and "loved the institutions" of his country."[13]

George Felton Mathew's traditionalism fed his penchant for didactic verse. "True friends by Virtue only can be won," he wrote, in the style of

Alexander Pope; "'Love all men, trust a few, do wrong to none.'" But by the early nineteenth century the poetry of sensibility had eclipsed Augustan verse, and Mathew saw himself chiefly in the light of a sentimental poet: "Not for the palace nor the mart of trade/Were these weak nerves and trembling feelings made..."[14] The leader of the first literary clique to which the Keats brothers belonged was nothing if not a disciple of convention.

Keats and Mathew spent many evenings together reading poetry; and yet, Mathew could never discern "the tears in his eyes nor the broken voice which are indicative of extreme sensibility." He concluded that his new friend was more skeptical than tender, seduced by the superficial beauty of language from the deeper substance of moral sentiment. George Keats, on the other hand, had no trouble discerning the tears in the poet's eyes that Mathew sought for in vain: "John's eyes moistened, and his lip quivered at the relation of any tale of generosity of benevolence or noble daring, or at sights of loveliness or distress."[15] He once fought a rascal in a back alley of Hampstead who had been cruel to a cat.

Despite their differences, Mathew enjoyed having a poetical friend, just as George found it no small asset to have a poetical brother. In February 1816, George had asked John to compose a love lyric for him to give to Mary Frogley, a member of the Mathews' circle, as a valentine. The result, "Hadst thou liv'd in days of old," takes the form of a Renaissance blazon, cataloguing the attributes of the beloved: "thy lively countenance,/And thy humid eyes that dance/In the midst of their own brightness;/In the very fane [temple] of lightness./Over which thine eyebrows, leaning,/Picture out each lovely meaning." Having thus adored the subject of the poem in the act of reading, the speaker then lowers his gaze to her

> ...ankle lightly turn'd:
> With those beauties, scarce discern'd,
> Kept with such sweet privacy,
> That they seldom meet the eye
> Of the little loves that fly
> Round about with eager pry.

Like the attendant spirits that hover around Belinda in Pope's "Rape of the Lock," Keats's "little loves" go where the courtier cannot.

On another occasion, John dashed off some new lyrics for Caroline and

Ann Mathew, who had grown weary of the original verse for Reginald
Spofford's piano canzonet, "Julia to the Wood Robin."

Stay, ruby breasted warbler, stay,
  And let me see thy sparkling eye;
Oh brush not yet the pearl strung spray,
  Nor bow thy pretty head to fly.

Stay while I tell thee, fluttering thing,
  That thou of love an emblem art;
Yes! patient plume thy little wing,
  Whilst I my thoughts to thee impart....

John considered the song a trifle and did not include it in his first book
of poems. But it remained a favorite with George, who copied it, signed
his initials, and gave it to Georgiana Wylie, his future wife. She pasted it
into her scrapbook among a handful of other handwritten verse, including
John's two poems "To My Brother George."

Any exchange of sentimental tokens—poems, shells, locks of hair—
provided opportunities for romantic verse, in John's case, or romantic
speech in the case of George. When the Mathew sisters returned from vacation in Hastings, they brought back souvenirs for the Keats brothers. John's
poem, "To Some Ladies," thanks the sisters for a "curious shell," which the
poet compares to "a gem from the fret-work of heaven" bestowed by Cupid. He invokes the sentimental poet Mary Tighe, best known for her Spenserian romance, *Psyche; or, The Legend of Love* (1805). John shared subject
matter with Tighe in his "Ode to Psyche," but his early verse also shared
her predilection for, as she phrases it in the opening stanza of *Psyche,* "gentle blandishments and amorous play."

Another poem "On Receiving a Curious Shell, and a Copy of Verses,
from the Same Ladies," thanks the Mathew sisters also for a transcription
of Thomas Moore's "The Wreath and the Chain." Like his friend Mary
Tighe, Moore was a popular sentimental poet. John refers to "The Wreath
and the Chain" as a "sun-beamy tale," charming his "mind from the tram-
mels of pain." Moore was also a friend of Lord Byron, whose first collection, *Hours of Idleness* (1807), written during his college years at Cambridge,
provided further examples of poetic sensibility for the young poet. John's
sonnet "To Lord Byron," written the same month his grandmother died,

reveals that however much Keats later came to dislike Byron, he looked up to him early in his career: "Byron, how sweetly sad thy melody,/Attuning still the soul to tenderness." Byron understood the nature of pain and provided a model for turning suffering into beauty.

Not until November 1816, as John was preparing *his* first book for the printer, would Byron publish the third canto of *Childe Harold's Pilgrimage,* the poem that had catapulted him to fame when the first two cantos appeared in 1812. The third canto marks Byron's departure from the cult of sensibility by formulating the disaffected voice and character of the Byronic hero. Having shown how to make sorrow sing, Byron was now on his way to becoming that unique literary phenomenon: a bestselling poet. John followed the unconventional lord in sartorial as well as literary fashion, wearing his collar turned down *à la Byron* and a ribbon around his neck in place of a neckerchief.[16] George never tried anything so stylish.

Besides evenings spent together in mixed society, the brothers also enjoyed bachelor recreations such as billiards, boxing, and bearbaiting. The bear garden in Southwark also featured dog and cock fights. The boxing matches were held at night after the street lamps were lit, at Jack Randall's on Chancery Lane and at the Fives Court on Little St. Martin's Street. Both were large, cavernous buildings resembling modern gymnasiums, but thick with the smell of sweat and cigar smoke. The spectators milled about an elevated platform where the matches took place. The Fives Court also had courts for rackets, an early version of tennis played with a tiny white leather ball. According to John's friend William Hazlitt, literary critic and boxing aficionado, one of these balls put out the eye of the legendary boxer Jem Belcher.[17]

Those of a more imaginative cast saw the fights as epic battles and the contestants as epic heroes. Hazlitt was hardly less graphic than Homer when he described the excitement surrounding the sport: "to see two men smashed to the ground, smeared with gore, stunned, senseless, the breath beaten out of their bodies; and then, before you recover from the shock, to see them rise up with new strength and courage, stand ready to inflict or receive mortal offence, and rush upon each other 'like two clouds over the Caspian'—this is the most astonishing thing of all:—this is the high and heroic state of man!" John once described a prizefight between Ned Turner and Jack Randall, the two lightweight champions of the day, by tapping out the rhythm of blows that demolished the loser on the windowpane next to him.[18]

No small part of the allure lay in mixing with the "swells" and "slang gents" who followed the fights. These well-born young men enjoyed mixing with the boxers known collectively as "the fancy." Byron practiced sparring with John Jackson, a fighter who had made his reputation by grabbing the reigning heavyweight champion, Daniel Mendoza, by the hair and pummeling him to a pulp—a lesson to all fighters since then to crop their hair. John's school friend Charles Cowden Clarke claimed that John "would never have been a 'slang gent,' because he had other and better accomplishments to make him conspicuous." Perhaps this is true, but the poet knew how to fight. "Keats was not in childhood attached to books," recalled Edward Holmes, another friend from school. "His *penchant* was for fighting. He would fight any one—morning, noon or night; his brothers among the rest. It was meat & drink to him. . . . He was a boy whom any one from his extraordinary vivacity & personal beauty might easily have fancied would become great—but rather in some military capacity than in literature."[19]

John Hamilton Reynolds, whom John befriended in the autumn of 1816 after his return from Margate, published a volume of poetry in 1820 that drew on his experience in the world of boxing: *The Fancy: A Selection from the Poetical Remains of the Late Peter Corcoran, of Gray's Inn, Student at Law; with a Brief Memoir of His Life*. Reynolds published the book under the pen name "Peter Corcoran," drawn from a famous eighteenth-century boxer known as the First Irish Champion. His preface, styled as a memoir of Corcoran, was really a self-portrait of a twenty-three-year-old boxing fan, who, like Reynolds, hailed from Shrewsbury and studied law at Gray's Inn, London.

The preface to *The Fancy* relates how Corcoran, having witnessed a fight at Fives Court in August 1817, becomes addicted to "'the noble art of self-defence' with an ardour and a delight which knew of no repose."[20] He bets money on his favorite boxers and loses. Supported by his indulgent father (based on George Reynolds), he then arranges his own sparring match and puts a fighter into training. He feasts him on fowls and port wine, though his preparations all go for naught when his overfed favorite collapses in the ring, and loses the fight. Corcoran then takes up the boxing gloves himself and challenges the boxers. At night, he delights the fancy at the Castle Tavern ("Belcher's House") with boxing lyrics set to Irish tunes.

One poem in *The Fancy* describes Jack Randall, the "Nonpareil." Like the Greek Diomedes or Ajax, this epic hero is prepared for the fight:

> With marble-coloured shoulders, and keen eyes,
>   Protected by a forehead broad and white,—
>   And hair cut close lest it impede the sight,
>   And clenched hands, firm, and of punishing size,—
> Steadily held, or motion'd wary-wise,
>   To hit or stop,—and kerchief too drawn tight
>   O'er the unyielding loins, to keep from flight
>   The inconstant wind, that all too often flies,—
> The Nonpareil stands! . . .[21]

The fighter's fists are clenched, and his hair has been cropped short. He will not go the way of poor Daniel Mendoza. But the portrait descends from the sublime to the ridiculous when the poet describes the handkerchief drawn tight about Randall's waist to fend off flatulence: this is one poem George Keats would not have copied out under his own name for the ladies.

Another popular form of entertainment the brothers enjoyed in London around this time was bearbaiting. These spectacles, in vogue since the Renaissance, took place in large circular pits, surrounded by high fences. The hapless bear would be chained by its neck or hind leg to a post at the edge of the pit, and trained dogs would be set loose upon it. In the third part of *Henry VI,* Shakespeare—never a great canine enthusiast—portrays the cowardice of the dogs, rather than the victimization of the bear: "having pinch'd a few and made them cry,/The rest stand all aloof, and bark at him."[22] As the dogs became wounded, worn out, or killed, they would be replaced.

Unlike George, John found it hard to restrain himself at the bear garden. Charles Cowden Clarke claimed that "in his zeal to manifest and impart his knowledge, he would forget himself, and stray beyond the prescribed bounds into the ring, to the lashing resentment of its comptroller, Mr. William Soames." Soames warned the poet to keep back, but when John again ventured into the fray to cheer on the bear, he too received a

whipping. "My eyes! Bill Soames giv' me sich a licker!" Acting out the
scene for Clarke, John impersonated the bear: "his legs and arms bent and
shortened till he looked like Bruin on his hind legs, dabbing his fore paws
hither and thither, as the dogs snapped at him, and now and then acting the
gasp of one that had been suddenly caught and hugged—his own capacious
mouth adding force to the personation."[23] Yet, not all of the spectacles the
Keats brothers witnessed were so violent. They also attended concerts at
Vauxhall Gardens and plays at the two main licensed (or legitimate) theaters: Drury Lane and Covent Garden.

Throughout it all, George seems to have been a successful guide to
London sociability. "I know not how it is, but I have never made any acquaintance of my own," John later wrote to George, "nearly all through
your medium my dear Brother." Among those who entered the poet's
life through George was the solicitor-in-training, William Haslam. George
most likely met Haslam—whose father worked for Frampton & Sons,
wholesale tea dealers at 34 Leadenhall Street—through Abbey's tea business. Although Haslam met the brothers through George, he would later
become a steadfast friend to Tom—and to John at George's expense.[24]

George's chief object of attention in 1816 was eighteen-year-old Georgiana Augusta Wylie. She lived with her younger brother, sixteen-year-old
Charles Gaskell, and her mother, Ann Amelia (née Griffin) Wylie, at
3 Romney Street in Westminster. Georgiana's other brother, Henry Robert,
lived with their aunt, Amelia Millar, and their cousin, Mary Amelia Millar,
on Henrietta Street in Covent Garden. The Millar household also included
two female boarders, or "paying guests," both named Mary. One of these
was the slender and austere Mary Ann Keysell, who married Henry Wylie
two days before Christmas in 1819. The other was the "staid and self possessed" (as John saw her) Mary Waldegrave.[25] Unlike Georgiana's Aunt
Amelia, her mother kept only *unpaying* guests, among them her old gray
cat.

Georgiana was not, as George put it, "overburthen'd with accomplishments," but she had a quick wit, and the brothers never found her dull.
George considered her "*a Lady* in the best sense of the word," and "the very
spirit of candour, and generosity." John, who was as critical as anyone when
it came to women, liked Georgiana. "To see an entirely disinterested Girl
quite happy is the most pleasant and extraordinary thing in the world," he
wrote twelve days after she married his brother. Ultimately, Georgiana

would prove "a cheerful companion and persevering Friend thro' good and ill."[26]

That December, John composed a sonnet for George to give to Georgiana. The poem, beginning "Nymph of the downward smile, and sidelong glance," is Shakespearean in structure but Petrarchan in rhyme scheme, and highlights the subject's changeability.[27] Its organizing conceit is the question of what time of day, or in what mood, the beloved is "most lovely." The sonnet is marked by Spenserian turns of phrase, and when, at the start of the poem, the speaker describes the nymph as being "far astray" in "labyrinths of sweet utterance," we must understand that wandering, here as in Spenser, is tied to seduction. Later, Georgiana appears in a less loquacious, more meditative mood, "serenely wand'ring in a trance/Of sober thought." After speaking and pondering, she listens with sweetly parted "ruby lips." From the sphere of parlor conversation, the poet's gaze then pursues her into her bedchamber, where he finds her with "careless robe," in the mode of studied negligence or appealing dishabille. Ultimately, he concludes that he "can never tell what mood is best."

As time wore on, John would continue to think of Georgiana as a kaleidoscope of moods. "I wish I knew what humour you were in that I might accommodate myself to any one of your Amiabilities," he later wrote to her. Had George been as skilled with a pen as his older brother, he would have made her the protagonist of a narrative romance: "If I had the eloquence of Scott I would make her the heroine of a novel and she would make a good one for she has faults enough to take from her Character all insipidity." He swore to his sister that "to name all her good qualities would be but a vague description, since every person has some claim to all the virtues, but it is the graceful manner with which they are exercised that gives them their great charm."[28] Notwithstanding the gentlemanly code of honor captured in the compliment, it may be telling that George wrote this not during a period of courtship but six years after marriage, with a good deal of trouble along the way.

John titled the draft of his sonnet on the nymph of the downward smile "To Miss Wylie," and he gave it to George to make a fair copy for Georgiana. When Tom copied it into his notebook, he gave it the more generic title, "Sonnet to a Lady." But when John included it in his first book of poems a couple of months later, he combined such discreet anonymity with the specificity of its subject: "To G.A.W." By contrast, the poem that John wrote for George to give to Mary Frogley he published as "To ****." Georgiana later pasted John's handwritten copy of the sonnet into her scrapbook, enshrining it as a monument to her brother-in-law on a page that also contained announcements of his death.[29]

Yet Georgiana may never have mistaken the authorship of the sonnet "To G.A.W." She seems to have had few illusions about the man she would marry or about where to place her affection. No doubt she admired her suitor's attractive older brother, but she may have considered his impetuous, charismatic nature a dangerous foundation for more fervent feelings. While George was no more used to being around women than John, he did not share his brother's misgivings about women. Their mother had lavished most of her "doting fondness" on her eldest son, indulging his every whim—of which there were plenty—and John was also the favorite of their sister.[30] Fanny absorbed John's attentions and hung upon his every word. George, not expecting that kind of adoration from women, was as a result better prepared to adapt himself to a mutual partnership. If he did not pour out adulation with the same fervor as John, neither did he idealize the objects of his passion, or hoard his respect.

John admitted his own conflicted feelings with regard to women. "When among Men I have no evil thoughts, no malice, no spleen," he wrote in July 1818, "I feel free to speak or to be silent—I can listen and from every one I can learn—my hands are in my pockets, I am free from all suspicion and comfortable. When I am among Women I have evil thoughts, malice spleen—I cannot speak or be silent—I am full of Suspicions and therefore listen to no thing—I am in a hurry to be gone."[31] The poet recognized the more natural flow of conversation between his brother and Georgiana, and she became a prolific muse for his own reveries.

O come Georgiana! the rose is full blown . . . The version of the poem beginning with this line that George copied for Georgiana differs from the one John published in his first book of poems, "O come, dearest Emma!"—but in name only. When Georgiana pasted it into her scrapbook, she positioned it on a page opposite John's verse letter "To My Brother George." The poem, in tetrameter couplets, reads as a straightforward Cavalier lyric in the mode of Robert Herrick or Andrew Marvell, urging the beloved to step out of society into the natural world of physical sensation. The mood is hortatory, as the lover imagines a "bed/Of mosses and flowers" on which he invites his lady to pillow her head. In fantasy, he positions himself at her feet, and vows to keep up a steady stream of amorous lament. Yet, lest the lady think his sighs entirely spiritual, he grabs, or presses, her knee. The final stanza delivers up the expected carpe diem: "why, lovely girl, should we lose all these blisses? / That mortal's a fool who such happiness misses; / So smile acquiescence, and give me thy hand, / With love-looking eyes, and with voice sweetly bland." In writing such lyrics to Georgiana, John became a link between his brother and Georgiana, just as Georgiana would later become a link between the poet and his brother.

The Vale of Health

Notwithstanding the round of social diversion, the brothers' lives in the autumn of 1816 were not a constant party. Tom was sick, and the trip to Margate had done little to improve his health. Winter was coming, and Richard Abbey was not keen to send him on another expensive trip to the south of France. Tom had gone to Lyon only the winter before to convalesce, and what had that done? He seemed no better. Given his frailty and apparent incapacity to work, Abbey was alarmed by his ongoing requests for money. Earlier in the year, Tom had found himself with only a guinea in his pocket, having already borrowed five pounds from John at Abbey's suggestion. "Abbey is entitled to a considerable allowance on account of advances for Tom who spent at all times more than double the Interest of his money," George later said.[32]

If Tom continued his career as an invalid, he could easily run through his inheritance, Abbey feared, and then what? John and Tom seemed to be spending too much money, and too much time together when John should be studying and Tom resting so that he could return to the tea-house. While Abbey appeared a perfectly good-natured man to others, his best side did not show through with his insubordinate wards. "With so kind hearted a Man as Abbey some Children would have been very happy," John Taylor claimed; "but he was not the Man for these, especially for John Keats who seems to have given him nearly the same kind of unavailing anxiety which the Ducklings caused the old Hen who hatched them. . . . Never were there two people more opposite than the Poet & this good Man."[33] Abbey suspected that his eldest ward did not look favorably upon his profession, or on commerce in general, and he was right. Trade meant little more to John

Keats than it did to William Collins in the book his sister had won at school—the crass pursuit of wealth in a spiritless world of self-interest.

But to Richard Abbey life was no pastoral romance. He, too, had been fatherless from an early age. From a farm in the Vale of Skipwith in York-shire, he had come to London and inched his way up the social ladder. With persistence, he had advanced in business, and by the time he was in his early twenties he had made senior partner in Abbey, Cocks & Gullet—a firm sit-uated (appropriately enough, given its name) in the Poultry section of Lon-don. By 1811, Gullet had disappeared, but the Cocks remained, and the firm became, as it was now, Abbey & Cocks. By 1819, one or more Cocks would fly the coop, and the name would become Abbey, Cock, & Company. Within another six years, the partnership would dwindle to Abbey and a single Cock: "Abbey & Cock."[34]

Abbey simply could not understand how his three refractory wards, particularly the eldest, could question a man of his credentials. All the brothers seemed overly concerned with their dignity of lifestyle, a disposi-tion no doubt inherited from their father. Thomas Keats had always been inclined to act "the Man of Consequence," Abbey thought. He recalled the "remarkably fine Horse" that man would ride, and how on Sundays he would go out carousing "with others who prided themselves in the like Distinction."[35] One could spend all one's money on a horse, but in the end it could not make one a gentleman.

Richard Abbey was not the only one of the brothers' acquaintance to suspect them of aiming at something higher than their present station. Be-fore moving into Dean Street with Tom, John had lived with Henry Ste-phens and George Wilson Mackereth, medical students with whom he never felt at home. He would often sit apart, absorbed in his own reflections. At school he was similarly distracted. The speech of his medical instructors would run "from him like water from a duck's back," as his thoughts strayed "far away—in the land of Faery." John told Charles Cowden Clarke that whenever a beam of sunlight crossed the room, he would glimpse "a whole troop of creatures floating in the ray" and be "off with them to Oberon and fairyland." At home, when not reading or reflecting, John would often compose. Yet whenever Stephens showed him some of his own poetry, he felt rebuffed: "Sometimes I ventured to show him some lines which I had written, but I always had the mortification of hearing them—

condemned, indeed he seemed to think it a presumption in me to attempt
to head along the same pathway as himself, at however humble a distance."
More annoying still, was the way John's younger brothers "worshipped"
him: "They seemed to think their Brother John was to be exalted, & to exalt
the family name."[36]

John gave his roommate the impression that he considered medical
knowledge beneath him, and while there may have been some condescen-
sion involved, the poet felt trapped in a world he had not chosen. Rather
than knowledge per se, it was the specialization and professionalization of
knowledge—the dehumanizing compartmentalization of modern life—
that he resisted. Stephens interpreted his reserve as "a good deal of Pride
and some conceit," but, in truth, John was not inclined at all times to be
friendly.[37] At least in his own rooms on Dean Street with Tom, he would
offend no one by his silence.

Two miles away from the brothers, another kindred spirit, Charles
Cowden Clarke, had moved to live with his sister on Little Warner Street,
in Clerkenwell. Charles's father, John Clarke, had retired as headmaster of
the boarding academy in the village of Enfield that the Keats brothers had
attended. Charles was eight years older than John and had worked at the
school as an assistant instructor. Charles's sister, Isabella Jane, had married
John Towers, a chemist who in 1816 patented a cure for coughs, asthmas,
and other chest ailments. One imagines that Towers may have extended his
advice, if not his care, to Tom Keats. To be sure, the Clarkes were as hospi-
table to the brothers there, among the jumbled heap of murky buildings
south of the Thames, as their father, John Clarke, had been at the school by
the River Lea at Enfield. Isabella served tea with bread and homemade
jam, while her husband played the piano.[38]

Charles Cowden Clarke had been there during those black months after Frances Keats died, when John could hardly climb out of bed. Clarke
had introduced the young poet to the books that had changed his life and
had encouraged him as he read his way through the school library, spurred
on by despair. When John left school to take up his apprenticeship with Dr.
Hammond in the neighboring village of Edmonton, Clarke continued to
meet him regularly, a few times a month, for literary conversation.

John's verse epistle to Charles Cowden Clarke, also written at Margate
in the summer of 1816, opens with memories of evenings spent in spirited

discussion about rhyme, meter, and verse form. The speaker hesitates for a hundred lines or so, fearing to address a reader so familiar with "Miltonian storms, and more, Miltonian tenderness," but he eventually gives in to his exasperated muse, who exclaims: "Write! thou wilt never have a better day." The command echoes the famous opening sonnet of Sir Philip Sidney's *Astrophel and Stella,* which similarly commands: "'Fool,' said my Muse to me, 'look in thy heart, and write.'" Both poems foreground the difficulty writers find in getting started. But in John's verse epistle to Clarke, saying goodbye proved even more trying.

John once recognized the awkwardness of Englishmen at parting: "You know at taking leave of a party at a door way, sometimes a Man dallies and foolishes and gets awkward," the poet wrote to his brother George, "and does not know how to make off to advantage—Good bye—well—good-bye—and yet he does not—go—good bye and so on—well—god bless you—You know what I mean . . ."[39] John's verse letter to Charles Cowden Clarke is in the meter of heroic couplets, but its *poetry* is in its farewell. The speaker has walked with Clarke halfway home, and, after they part ways on the graveled path between their respective houses, he turns back to look after his friend:

> —your accents bland
> Still sounded in my ears, when I no more
> Could hear your footsteps touch the grav'ly floor.
> Sometimes I lost them, and then found again;
> You chang'd the footpath for the grassy plain.
> In those still moments I have wish'd you joys
> That well you know to honour:—"Life's very toys
> With him," said I, "will take a pleasant charm;
> It cannot be that ought will work him harm."
> These thoughts now come o'er me with all their might:—
> Again I shake your hand,—friend Charles, good night.

Here the poet, all uncertain about his future, deprived of any nurturing or protecting parent, finds the anxiety of separation allayed by his disinterested feelings for his friend. As in the conversation poetry of Wordsworth and Samuel Taylor Coleridge, the poem ends in a blessing that sounds like prayer. The lingering moment of separation has passed, and the comfort in the final line is palpable. *Goodnight, Friend Charles, goodnight. Sweet ladies; goodnight, goodnight . . .*[40] The poet can fold up the letter and go to sleep.

John had been hinting to his friend for months that he would like to meet Leigh Hunt, the "wrong'd Libertas," as John calls him in his verse epistle to Charles Cowden Clarke. Both Hunt and John Hunt, the brother with whom he co-edited the weekly *Examiner,* had served prison sentences in 1812 for criticizing (the charge was libel) the English Prince Regent, George Augustus Frederick of Hanover. John Hunt managed the production side of the paper that had published Keats's first poem, and his brother Leigh the editorial. In their front-page column, "The Political Examiner," the Hunt brothers had called the Prince Regent "a violator of his word, a libertine over head and ears in debt and disgrace, a despiser of domestic ties, the companion of gamblers and demireps, a man who has just closed half a century without one single claim on the gratitude of his country or the respect of posterity!"[41] The compliment earned them both two years in the clink. In 1813, at age twenty-eight, Leigh Hunt was sent to Surrey Gaol on Horsemonger Lane, in Southwark, and John Hunt went to Cold Bath Fields Prison in Clerkenwell.

Determined to show that tyrants could not conquer him, the wronged Libertas proceeded to fight off despondency by flouting the repressive nature of prison life. Rather than succumbing to despair, he obtained a pair of rooms with a garden and diffused a spirit of good cheer. His wife, Marianne (née Kent); their two young children, Thornton and John Horatio; and at one point his sister-in-law, Elizabeth, joined him. His daughter Mary Florimel was born in prison. Hunt continued his daily routine of reading, writing, playing the lute and the piano, and producing in captivity the aura of a literary salon. Amazingly, he even continued weekly publication of the *Examiner* with his brother, dispatching messengers to Cold Bath Fields and copy to the newspaper offices. Only shortly after the jailkeeper turned the key to release him from bondage, Hunt published *The Descent of Liberty: A Mask,* which was partly a celebration of the defeat of Napoleon, partly another attack on established authority. Byron called him "the wit in the dungeon," and in a letter to Thomas Moore added: "Pray Phoebus at length our political malice / May not get us lodgings within the same palace!"[42]

Hunt turned his prison quarters from a couple of dirty, spartan cells into what seemed to the world like a pleasant bower. He papered his walls with trellised roses, painted his ceiling a cerulean blue complete with drifting clouds, and hung Venetian blinds over his windows. He arranged his white, plaster busts to his liking, stacked his bookcases with his favorite books, and fenced in his garden with green palings, trellising *it* with real flowers. There was not "a handsomer room on that side of the water," he boasted. "Charles Lamb declared there was no other such room, except in a fairy tale." There certainly was none other like it in the cold reality of the penal institution. Hunt's enemies at *Blackwood's Edinburgh Magazine* would attack him in 1817 as "a vulgar man . . . perpetually laboring to be genteel": "He would fain be always tripping and waltzing, and is sorry that he cannot be allowed to walk about in the morning with yellow breeches and flesh-coloured silk-stockings. He sticks an artificial rosebud into his button hole in the midst of winter. He wears no neckcloth, and cuts his hair in imitation of the Prints of Petrarch."[43] The man parodied here as the King of the Cockneys espoused an ideal of aestheticism.

Whenever the schoolmaster John Clarke sent baskets of fruit and flowers to Leigh Hunt from Enfield (and he was not alone in showering the political martyr with sympathetic gifts), he sent his son Charles as a courier. Charles thus formed an attachment to the man Keats longed to meet. One day, as the friends were walking toward Hunt's cottage, John handed Clarke his sonnet, "Written on the Day That Mr. Leigh Hunt Left Prison" (February 2, 1815). The poem praised Hunt "for showing truth to flatter'd state" and, despite retribution, remaining as free in "his immortal spirit . . . / As the sky-searching lark, and as elate." Just as John used to project himself in fancy beyond the walls of the lecture room at Guy's Hospital, Hunt used the same means to escape his prison cell in Southwark: "In Spenser's halls he strayed, and bowers fair, / Culling enchanted flowers." When Keats gave Clarke the sonnet to take to Hunt, he did so with a "conscious look and hesitation" that signaled something momentous to be at stake in the occasion: it was the first evidence Clarke had of John's wanting to be a poet.[44]

Yet, it was John's famous sonnet "On First Looking into Chapman's Homer" that finally provided his ticket from middle-class anonymity into the more elite literary circles of his day. The story of the poem's composition is well known: Keats and Clarke sat up late one night reading George Chapman's translation of Homer, which a friend had lent to Clarke. They

admired Chapman's vigorous (as opposed to Pope's more languid) translation of the epics into English rhyme. When they parted at daybreak, John
walked home with his head full of "teeming wonderment" and contrived
to have his sonnet on Chapman's Homer on Clarke's breakfast table by ten
o'clock.

The poem opens with an echo of the start of Homer's *Odyssey,* which
canvasses the crafty hero's travels and adventures. But the perspective here
is in the first person:

> Much have I travell'd in the realms of gold,
>   And many goodly states and kingdoms seen;
>   Round many western islands have I been
> Which bards in fealty to Apollo hold.
> Oft of one wide expanse had I been told
>   That deep-brow'd Homer ruled as his demesne;
>   Yet did I never breathe its pure serene
> Till I heard Chapman speak out loud and bold:
> Then felt I like some watcher of the skies
>   When a new planet swims into his ken;
> Or like stout Cortez when with eagle eyes
>   He star'd at the Pacific—and all his men
> Look'd at each other with a wild surmise—
>   Silent, upon a peak in Darien.

John was familiar with William Robertson's *History of America* from the
school library at Clarke's school, but, as has often been noted, the history
here is muddled: Balboa, not Cortez, discovered the Pacific from the Isthmus of Darien between Central and South America. However, the effect of
abstracting the explorer from history is to emphasize the theme of explora-
tion over and above any specific discovery. When John wrote this sonnet,
George was still tied to his seat at Abbey's counting house and might thus
seem an unlikely candidate to rank among the Balboas and Cortezes of the
world. But in just a couple of years George himself would cross the Atlantic
in pursuit of the "realms of gold." Of course, the gold George sought, rather
than any Apollonian dawn or classical Golden Age, would be of the kind to
please Richard Abbey.

To Leigh Hunt, the sonnet on George Chapman's translation of Homer
confirmed not only his own good taste (in publishing the unknown poet)

but also his sense that a new age of poetry was at hand. Hunt invited John to his cottage in the Vale of Health, a clump of cottages on Hampstead Heath surrounded by hills. The sound of the songbirds and humming bees there suited the Cockney King better than the horrid cacophony of clanking chains in the dark corners of the Southwark borough, where John was still imprisoned at the hospitals. Although a mere four miles away from the urban congestion, Hampstead Heath was more rural than suburban. Hunt loved his leafy, picturesque bower and praised it for its "fine breathing prospects, its clump-wooded glades,/Dark pines, and white houses, and long-allied shades." When John brought his sick brother Tom there, Tom copied Hunt's "Sonnet to Hampstead" into his notebook and asked Hunt to sign it: the only poem in his treasured collection not written by his brother.[45]

Hunt's cottage in the Vale of Health presented a domestic scene far from what any of the Keats brothers were used to. Instead of order and propriety, one found cats, paintings, prints, urns, busts, scissors, and children, including a newborn, Swinburne Percy. "His house excels all you have ever read of," Thomas Carlyle later wrote: "a *poetical Tinkerdom,* without parallel even in literature."[46] Books were everywhere—folios, quartos, octavos, duodecimos—some uncut in drab boards, others decked out in calf, a few dressed up in marbled boards with leather corners. Freed from the task of having to perform his insouciance in public, Hunt reigned more naturally now over his idiosyncratic, and rather bohemian, household gods.

Despite, or perhaps because of, the confusion, John felt welcome. The Vale of Health quickly became a sanctuary from the unwelcome detention of medical school. Rather than walking back late at night, he often spent the night on Hunt's sofa, relaxing amid the congenial chaos and scribbling. The aptly titled "Sleep and Poetry" would become the longest poem he had written to date, and the longest in his first book of verse. After a few such visits, there could be no turning back from his dream of being a poet. Before long, he would have to muster the strength to tell Richard Abbey that he was quitting the medical profession. But the task was distasteful, and he postponed it from week to week.

Instead, as autumn stretched out into winter, the poet went about making new friends. If Hunt provided a model of genius that was convivial and uplifting, the painter Benjamin Haydon exuded grandeur and majesty. Overworked from his efforts at greatness, Haydon had also retreated from the whirl of city life, to a cottage at 7 Pond Street, in Hampstead. In an age of portraiture and landscape painting, Haydon aimed at the higher courtly genre of history painting, the visual equivalent of epic. "My great object is the public encouragement of historical painting and the glory of England, in high Art," he told John when he met him; "to ensure these I would lay my head on the block this instant." Whereas Hunt valued whimsicality, Haydon went to opposite extremes in his devotion to high seriousness and seemed ready to martyr himself to his art. John admired Haydon's uncompromising intensity and his talent, which he ranked, with Wordsworth's poetry and Hazlitt's depth of taste, one of the three things of the age in which to rejoice. Haydon added a fourth: *"John Keats' genius!"*[47]

Benjamin Haydon's vehement, self-sacrificing nature, however, came tempered with a competitiveness that spilled over into envy and suspicion. Hunt had become his current rival, and Haydon warned his young friend Keats about the delusional tendencies of the King of the Cockneys. "Beware, for God's sake of the delusions and sophistications that are ripping up the talents and morality of our friend! He will go out of the world the victim of his own weakness and the dupe of his own self-delusions." At the same time, and without the slightest hint of self-doubt, Haydon—the future suicide—confessed to having direct communication with the great luminaries of cultural tradition. "I have seen the faces of the mighty dead crowd into my room," he confided to Keats, "and I have sunk down & prayed the great Spirit that I might be worthy to accompany these immortal beings in their immortal glories, and then I have seen each smile as it passed over me, and each shake [their] hands in awful encouragement."[48] Such visionary ecstasy would have done credit to even an artist like William Blake.

Yet while the spirits of cultural tradition may have visited Haydon in his sweats at night, their patronage wasn't enough. The painter, like the young poet, craved the lifeblood of human sympathy. Trusting in Keats's genius, Haydon swore that no one else reflected his desires and ambition with the same "burning ripeness of soul." No one else had the power to "add fire, when I am exhausted, & excite fury afresh." Regardless of his own jealous streak, Haydon gushed enthusiasm for his new protégé in a dinner invitation to John Hamilton Reynolds, another young poet: "Come thou Poet!—*free* and *brown!*/Next Sunday to Hampstead Town/To meet John Keats, who soon will shine/The greatest, of this Splendid time/That e'er has woo'ed the Muses nine." To the phrase "Muses nine," he added a facetious note: "Quite original—'Muses nine' we never recollect having seen them in any Poet ancient or modern."[49] The painter, thrilled with his discovery, was well-nigh giddy.

Keats was at the start of his poetic career, but Reynolds, a mere year older than him, was nearing the end of his, as he would soon enter the profession of law. Two years earlier, Reynolds had dedicated his narrative poem *Safie: An Eastern Tale* to Lord Byron, who thought it showed "much talent, and, certainly, fire enough."[50] With support from his father, George Reynolds—and in a daring move that would serve as an example to Keats— Reynolds had given up his job as a junior clerk at the Amicable Society for a Perpetual Assurance to focus on his writing. His father taught school at Christ's Hospital, which Coleridge and Charles Lamb had attended, and his mother, Charlotte Cox Reynolds, was related to the Gothic novelist William Beckford and had literary interests of her own. Reynolds also had four sisters, and their home in Little Britain would soon open its doors to the Keats brothers.

When the young poets convened at Benjamin Haydon's cottage one week before John's twenty-first birthday, their host unleashed a torrent of inspiring speech. Welcoming them into an elite fraternity of gifted spirits, he prophesied (in a more biblical manner than Hunt would do) that the day for artistic revolution was at hand. The artist had a flair for the dramatic as well as the vatic, and his tone was catching. One finds signs of his influence in a sonnet that John sent to Haydon a month later, which begins "Great spirits now on earth are sojourning." Spirits such as Wordsworth, Hunt, and Haydon, the poem concludes, "standing apart / Upon the Forehead of the age to come; / These, these will give the world another heart, / And other pulses. Hear ye not the hum / Of mighty workings?—/ Listen awhile ye nations, and be dumb." Haydon heaped encomium on the poem and vowed to send it to Wordsworth. Wordsworth particularly liked the closing lines, which he thought "vigorously conceived and well expressed." He agreed that the poem showed "good promise."[51]

Hunt published his own prophecy, in an essay titled "Young Poets," in the *Examiner* on December 1, 1816. Wordsworth had already announced the end of the Augustan Age of poetry in his preface to *Lyrical Ballads,* but Hunt declared that the three Young Poets—John Keats, John Reynolds, and Percy Bysshe Shelley—would not only "revive Nature" but also "put a

spirit of youth in every thing." They would usher in "a new school" of poetry. The previous generation, led by Wordsworth, had broken free from
the neoclassical conventions that had been fettering English poetry since
the age of Charles II, but the new generation of "young aspirants" would
revive the Golden Age of English verse. They would "restore the same love
of Nature, and of *thinking* instead of mere *talking,* which formerly rendered
us real poets, and not merely versifying wits, and bead-rollers of couplets."
Keats took the essay to heart, showing it proudly to his friends at the hospitals. According to Henry Stephens, it "sealed his fate," and John "gave himself up more completely than before to Poetry." He used the final weeks of
the year to prepare his poems for the press.[52]

Cheapside Reminiscences

Tradition held that in order to be a true Cockney, one had to be born within
earshot of the bells that tolled every morning, noon, and evening at St.
Mary-le-Bow Church in Cheapside. George was used to the sound of the
bells, but John found them depressing—melancholy reminders of days
gone by, and other bells that had tolled. By the holidays, John and Tom had
moved out of their apartment on Dean Street and George had left his room
above Abbey & Cocks on Pancras Lane. On All Hallow's Eve, October 31,
1816, John had turned twenty-one, and together the brothers had taken
lodgings 76 Cheapside, down the street from the Bow Bells. George and
Tom were glad to have more time to spend with an older brother who
seemed to be rising into more illustrious circles.

George was only seven when his father died, and his memory of him
had shrunken down to a mere blur of dark hair, but the terrible tragedy
that had shattered the skull of Thomas Keats, Sr., and scattered their family still cast its pall over his life—and that of his siblings. Although George
could speak of him only based on hearsay, he gathered that his father had
been "a man of good sense and very much liked." Abbey remembered his
"remarkably fine Horse," but Charles Cowden Clarke recalled his "remarkably fine . . . common-sense, and native respectability."[53] Like George
and John, and probably Tom Keats as well, their father appears to have
been a natural gentleman, if not literally born to the part.

Before his death in 1804, Thomas had worked for the Swan & Hoop
inn and livery stable, owned by his father-in-law, John Jennings. Located

near the old London Wall at 24 The Pavement, Moorfields, it was a conve‐
nient place for people headed into the city from the suburbs to park their
horses. Travelers going in the other direction rented horses and carriages to
carry them to the villages north of London. When the brothers' grandpar‐
ents married in 1774, the stables had space for fifty horses and a few car‐
riages. But John Jennings expanded the premises, and with a license from
the London Company of Innholders allowing him to serve spirits, wine,
and ale, he opened a tavern. The Swan & Hoop became a full-service inn, or
house of entertainment.[54]

A few months before their sister Fanny was born, Thomas Keats had
testified at the Old Bailey against a horse thief. His recorded words, few as
they are, paint a picture of a straightforward, hardworking man. Thomas
Keats claimed that late on the morning of February 8, 1803, the thirty-year-
old defendant, Robert Mathews, presented himself at the Swan & Hoop liv‐
ery stable under the assumed name of Captain Thomson. He said that he
needed a horse to visit a friend near Somers Town, a trip that would prob‐
ably not take long. Thomas led out a large bay mare with a white stripe on
her face and let Mathews have her for five shillings an hour. The captain,
he said, could pay when he got back. When the defense attorney asked him,
"Do you let horses to any stranger?" Thomas replied, "Yes, if they give me
a good address. I would let you one."[55] No doubt, the remark provoked tit‐
ters among the audience at the Old Bailey.

As the hours wore on, Thomas became alarmed that he might not see
his horse again, and in fact Robert Mathews had no intention of returning.
At four o'clock in the afternoon, Mathews had ridden the hired mare into
the courtyard of the Red Lion Inn on Cockspur Street, Charing Cross, in‐
tending to sell her. She was limping, and her back joints were swollen, so he
must have ridden her hard. He presented himself as a Scottish cheesemon‐
ger and claimed that the mare had pulled his cheese cart from a warehouse
in the Minories for three years, covering fifty or sixty miles a day. She could
work just as well, he claimed, harnessed to a one-horse chaise. He had sold
two just like her the day before.

The hostler, James Goadby, offered Mathews five pounds for the mare,
a sum less than half her value, and they settled on six. But after Mathews
left, Goadby began to suspect that the horse had been stolen. When
the cheesemonger returned the following Friday with a brown gelding for
sale, Goadby asked a friend to detain him while he went to summon a con‐

stable. As Mathews was writing out a receipt for the horse in the back room of a tavern near the Red Lion, Constable James Bly arrested the culprit. Mathews resisted, threatening to shoot himself, but Bly got him onto a coach and into confinement at Queen Square.

Thomas Keats, meanwhile, went to seek his horse at the address Mathews had given him, but found neither man nor horse there. He then made a circuit of the neighborhood, in case the captain had become drunk and put her up at another stable by mistake. But when he could not find her, he had bills printed to advertise the theft, and two days later Constable Bly informed him that his mare was at the Red Lion. At the trial Mathews pleaded that his real purpose in hiring the horse was to go to Nottingham Place to call in a debt but that, when he could not find the debtor, he had returned to London to sell her. He would take the money, he thought, and go on a journey . . . The jury found him guilty and sentenced him to death, though he was ultimately transported to a penal colony.

Their mother, George had heard, was "a woman of uncommon talents." Abbey declared that she had more "talents and sense" than any woman besides her mother, Alice Jennings. With an attractive figure, large dark eyes, and full mouth, she aroused some uncomfortable feelings in her children's future guardian: "her passions were so ardent, he said, that it was dangerous to be alone with her." John Taylor, hearing this from Abbey himself, would later wonder whether Abbey might be the poet's father; but scrutinizing the tea dealer more closely, he dismissed the thought.[56]

Frances Jennings Keats, like her eldest son, seems to have experienced life at high speed, and in magnified dimensions. She married Thomas Keats on October 9, 1794, when she was nineteen and he a year older. To Abbey, this confirmed her pronouncement "that she must & would have a Husband."[57] Rather than settling for a wedding at any neighborhood church, she married her father's handsome employee at St. George's Church, in the more elegant neighborhood of Hanover Square. About a year later, she gave birth to John, and in two more years to George. Tom followed in another two years, and a fourth brother, Edward, two years after that. Edward died in infancy, and Fanny was born the next year, in 1803, only months before Thomas Keats died.

With their numbers growing, the Keats family moved from the Swan & Hoop to a small house on Craven Street, Finsbury, slightly north of the London Wall. It was close to the Swan & Hoop, where Thomas still worked,

and free from the noise and dirt of the city. A neighbor, Frances Grafty, remembered the rhymes that John used to make up as a young boy. From the
time he could first speak, she swore, "instead of answering questions put to
him, he would always make a rhyme to the last word people said, and then
laugh."[58] Grafty, drafty, crafty . . .

John Jennings was not getting any younger, and about a month after
Thomas Keats confronted the horse thief in the Old Bailey, Jennings decided to turn over management of the Swan & Hoop to his son-in-law.
Thomas began paying taxes on the business in March 1803, and Jennings
and his wife Alice moved out of their rooms over the Swan & Hoop to a
house ten miles away in the country—at Ponders End, a clump of houses at
the edge of Edmonton village, up the road from John Clarke's school at
Enfield. According to Abbey, Jennings then gave himself up entirely to the
pleasures of the table, becoming "a complete Gourmand." Alice Jennings
and her poor maid seemed to spend four days out of each week preparing
the old man's Sunday dinner.[59]

Yet, despite his own generous girth, Richard Abbey thought most people too indulgent. His own livery company, the Worshipful Company of
Pattenmakers (who designed the wooden platforms worn beneath shoes in
the days before the streets were paved), drank too much wine on Lord
Mayor's Day. They threw their money away by taking the whole brass
band—a noisy ensemble of French horns, clarinets, trumpet, bassoon, and
bass drum—to dinner at the London Tavern on Bishopsgate Street after
the parade. Their feasts began at four o'clock and went on all evening under wax lights and chandeliers. Abbey proposed that the pattenmakers consider "the practicability and expediency of shortening the period of the Livery Dinners on Lord Mayors days." Cowed by the moral and economic
force of his arguments, they eventually canceled their yearly election dinner
and agreed that at all future dinners, "French Wines should upon no Occasion be allowed at the expense of the Company."[60]

Frances Keats was as extravagant as the pattenmakers. If it had been
up to her, she would have spent all her money sending her sons to an elite
school like Harrow, to learn Greek, a dead language—and for what? But
the cost, rather than reason, prevented her, and so, two months after her
daughter was born, she instead enrolled her two eldest sons in school with
that dissenting freethinker John Clarke, whose boarding academy at Enfield her brothers, Midgley John Jennings and Thomas Jennings, had at-

tended. Abbey may have revealed more about himself than about the school when he told John that even if he had fifty sons, he would not have sent one of them to Clarke's school.[61]

Alas, regardless of their doom, / The little victims play! / No sense have they of ills to come, / Nor care beyond today. Thomas Gray sums up the plight of all schoolboys in his "Ode on a Distant Prospect of Eton College." John and George had been in school for only eight months when tragedy struck. Their father was, in Abbey's inimitable style of narration, "returning with some of his jolly Companions from a Carouse" one Sunday evening at a tavern; he was "riding very fast, & most probably very much in Liquor, when his Horse leaped upon the Pavement opposite the Methodist Chapel in the City Road, & falling with him against the Iron Railings so dreadfully crushed him that he died as they were carrying him Home."[62] Although it was the horse that slipped and fell, Abbey never accused the animal of intoxication. A night watchman patrolling the streets in the early hours of April 16, 1804, found Thomas Keats sprawled on the street unconscious, with the right side of his head smashed in.

Thomas died without ever having opened his eyes to witness the grief of his distraught wife. After the funeral, an Elizabeth Keats, who may have been the boys' aunt, took over management of the Swan & Hoop until one day, to everyone's surprise, a stranger stepped in. William Rawlings, a clerk at the banking firm of Smith, Payse, & Company paid the property tax for the Swan & Hoop on Midsummer Day 1804, and a week later married Frances Keats. The wedding took place on June 27, and it gave Rawlings legal claim to Thomas Keats's estate. But the marriage itself did not survive the year. Frances left her second husband, who subsequently sold the inn and took off with the money.[63]

Abbey was aghast. Not only had Frances Keats run off with William Rawlings *only weeks* after her first husband's death—a mad act that even her own indulgent mother condemned—but after marrying the gold-digger at the same church where she had married Thomas Keats, she ran off *again,* moving in with another shady character, "a Jew at Enfield, named Abraham," causing scandal in the very village where her children went to school. But her imprudence didn't stop there. She then "became addicted to drinking and in the love of the Brandy Bottle found a temporary Gratification to those inordinate Appetites which seem to have been in one Stage or another constantly soliciting her."[64] To cap off such behavior, having descended into the pit of depravity to which Abbey always thought she seemed destined, she gave up parental responsibilities for four young children to her aging parents. That poor woman: Alice Jennings.

John Jennings died one year after Thomas Keats, on March 8, 1805, and Alice Jennings moved the next summer from Ponders End to a tenement house on Church Street, Lower Edmonton, with little Tom and baby Fanny. On Sundays she took them up the twisting street to the red brick church with the stone tower, beneath the lime and elm trees. Two years after that, her son, Midgley John Jennings, a Captain in the Marines, died of what George later called the "Family Complaint." The disease had already claimed the life of their uncle Thomas Jennings, whom the brothers never knew. Midgley died in November 1808, and Frances then took to her bed in her mother's house, showing every sign of having contracted the same disease ("decline," as Thomas Jennings's death certificate read) that had claimed both of her brothers.[65]

John sat up late at night in his grandmother's home during school vacations to nurse his mother, but she died in March 1810, when John was fourteen and a half and George barely thirteen. Tom and Fanny still lived with their grandmother, but school became the only semblance of a home the older brothers had left. The school routine, and even the formality of a school uniform, provided stability. Classes began at seven in the recitation rooms of the main schoolhouse after the boys had washed, dressed, and breakfasted. Later in life, John would continue the habit of punctilious dressing in order to combat melancholy. "Whenever I find myself growing vapourish," he wrote, "I rouse myself, wash and put on a clean shirt[,] brush my hair and clothes, tie my shoestrings neatly and in fact *adonize* as I were going out."[66] Thus spoke the English Adonis.

Unlike other schools, in which the older boys tyrannized over the younger, Clarke's school managed to avoid what John called "the horrid System and consequences of the fagging at great Schools." The dormitories held only half a dozen beds, as opposed to, say, the infamous Long Chamber at Eton, where boys were packed in and sometimes had to share beds.[67] If Clarke's school wasn't as rigorous in drilling students in the classical languages as the more prestigious boarding schools—like Eton, which Shelley attended before Oxford, or Harrow, where Byron went before Cambridge—it offered security at a time when the boys' lives were marked by a seemingly endless series of calamities. And indeed it was rigorous enough: the medical exams on which John performed superlatively were as much a test of Latin as of anatomy.

John Clarke's academic focus was on the useful application of knowledge. His religious principles were dissenting, but not doctrinaire, and his politics were liberal. His pupils studied reading, writing, arithmetic, Latin, French, and the various branches of science, from astronomy to physics, geology, and botany. His pedagogical method was to use real-life examples. In a lesson that the philosopher Jean-Jacques Rousseau himself would have approved, Clarke asked his students to position themselves as planets so that they could study the solar system.[68]

The main building of Clarke's school was a brick Georgian mansion, built in the early eighteenth century by a wealthy merchant shipper, with gables and a pillared façade adorned with flowers, pomegranates, and the heads of cherubim set in niches. Charles Cowden Clarke was once scolded for leaving his sick bed to climb up and examine the angelic faces. The carriage house had been converted into the main schoolroom, and the courtyard served as a playground. Pymmes Brook, a tributary of the River Lea, ran through the school grounds into a pond the boys called a lake. Beds of strawberries surrounded the pond, and two cows that pastured in the school's two-acre paddock provided fresh milk. An old Morella cherry-tree, which the boys liked to climb, stood against a wall in the sun.[69]

During recess, the boys would choose their own sports. George liked cricket, while John preferred to fish or swim. George admitted that as children he and his brother had "quarreled often and fought fiercely," but rather than any natural animosity between them, "John's temper was the cause of all." Charles Cowden Clarke confirmed that John's "passion at times was almost ungovernable" and that "George, being considerably the taller and stronger, used frequently to hold him down by main force, laughing when John was in 'one of his moods,' and was endeavouring to beat him." Perhaps for this reason, John Clarke thought George older than John. In the end, such fights proved to be "a wisp-of-straw conflagration," for the poet "had an intensely tender affection for his brothers, and proved it upon the most trying occasions." According to George, their squabbles did not keep them from feeling "more attached than Brothers ever are."[70]

If George was protective in the manner of an older brother, John was fiercely loyal to what he loved. On one occasion after Tom had joined his brothers at school, an usher cuffed him on the ears as punishment for some

misdemeanor. "John rushed up, put himself in the received posture of offence, and, it was said, struck the usher—who could, so to say, have put him
into his pocket." Valiant if reckless at times, John "had no fears of self thro
interference in the quarrels of others, he would at all hazards, without calculating his power to defend, or his reward for the deed, defend the oppressed and distressed with heart and soul with hand and purse." He once
made an impression on the neighborhood children by challenging "a cruel,
mean-souled man who was teasing a little boy." According to one bystander,
he gave the bully "a good drubbing. . . . It was a fight that lasted an hour or
so, and the fellow went home feeling pretty cheap to be beaten by such a
little man as Mr. Keats." John later complained to George that to call him
(as a neighbor had done) "quite the little Poet" was like calling Napoleon
Bonaparte "quite the little Soldier."[71]

When his mother died, John's grief was "impassioned & prolonged."
He hid under the schoolmaster's desk and provoked "the liveliest pity &
sympathy in all who saw him." To escape from a horrid, ever-darkening
reality, he began to devour books and throw himself into translation exercises. He got up early, skipped afternoon recess, and left the schoolhouse
only when the teachers sent him out to get exercise. Even then, he would
sneak a book (one must presume) under his jacket. George was grieving
and disoriented as well, but he controlled his feelings, partly in order to be
able to console his brother. George's role was to relieve John "by continual
sympathy, explanation, and inexhaustible spirits, and good humour, from
many a bitter fit of hypochondriasm," as he put it.[72] John, in turn, showed
George that books could be a means of survival.

John Jennings died before reaching the age of seventy-five, and Alice
Jennings, now seventy-four and rightly concerned about her grandchildren's future, decided to turn over custodial responsibility for the Keats
children to two trustees, Richard Abbey and John Nowland Sandell. She
credited both men with good business sense, but in the event that something should happen to one, she needed a second. Abbey had served as a
churchwarden at St. Stephen, Walbrook, with her husband. He was also
active in parochial affairs in Walthamstow, where he volunteered as a director of the Sunday school. Yet, for all his public service—and the fact that
he was five years older than Sandell—Richard Abbey was the children's
second trustee.[73]

The first was also a merchant, like Abbey. John Nowland Sandell worked for John Schneider & Company, based at 16 Broad Street Buildings, a firm that imported goods from Russia. One of Sandell's executors, the furrier John Henry Powell Schneider, owned New Cottage farm in the village of Enfield. Ultimately, however, Sandell played a negligible role in the brothers' lives. In July 1810, five months after her daughter died, Alice Jennings legally entrusted her grandchildren to Sandell and Abbey; and "on or about" April 10, 1816, Sandell died, leaving Abbey as the sole voice of authority.[74]

Sitting by their fire in Cheapside, the brothers might well have wondered how it had all become so muddled. "I must think that difficulties nerve the Spirit of a Man," John reflected; "they make our Prime Objects a Refuge as well as a Passion."[75] The poet was determined to make something meaningful of all the pain, and however unpromising the idea might appear to Abbey, his brothers believed in his powers. So did Haydon, Reynolds, and Leigh Hunt. At twenty-one, John knew that he had the right to decide his own future. Yet he did not relish the task of telling his guardian that he had decided to quit school, his dressership at the hospital, and the medical profession in general in order to take up a position in the vanguard of a new generation of poets. He had been delaying the encounter, but when Abbey proposed that he take a job as a surgeon in Tottenham, a village adjacent to Walthamstow, John had no choice but to confront his guardian.

The dreaded interview, when it finally took place, was shocking enough for the tea dealer to recall it vividly a decade later. "Not intend to be a Surgeon! why what do you mean to be? I mean to rely upon my Abilities as a Poet—John, you are either Mad or a Fool, to talk in so absurd a Manner. My Mind is made up, said the youngster very quietly. I know that I possess Abilities greater than most Men, and therefore I am determined to gain my Living by exercising them." John's voice was steady and determined. Abbey did not know whether he was dealing with a fool or a madman. He tried appealing to reason, but when that went nowhere he dismissed his ward as "a Silly Boy, & prophesied a speedy Termination to his inconsiderate Enterprise."[76]

George was now the only one of his wards with a job. And Abbey was beginning to have suspicions in that quarter as well. The youth had deserted his room over the counting house to live with his brothers in Cheapside. Abbey feared that the idleness of the one and the professional insanity of the other might rub off on his own clerk. The family all seemed as "mad as hatters," and indeed the expression (derived from the effect of chemicals formerly used to line hats) may have entered Abbey's head in relation to his wayward charges: if the hat fits, so to speak, why not wear it? Abbey soon began to sing the praises of the hat business, the idea becoming something of an obsession for him over the next few years.

Next door to the brothers, at 74 Cheapside, a hatter named Joseph Keats was in business under the name "Keats & Company." He had been there as early as 1807, with the firm of Hammond, Stocker & Joseph Keats. John's biographer Robert Gittings has criticized the scholar Jean Haynes for assuming a connection, for which there is no evidence, between the hatters and the Keats brothers. Haynes speculated that Abbey might have "some interest of a commercial nature in the Cheapside establishment," or else "in 12 Pancras Lane, Joseph Keats's other shop, or in 14 Poultry, a hatter's run by Thomas Keats [Joseph's father]." According to George's biographer, Naomi Joy Kirk, Abbey's purpose in sending Tom to Lyon the previous winter (1815–1816) was to have him learn French hat manufacturing techniques. The claim may have been based on family tradition, for there is no evidence of that either.[77] Whether the hatter Joseph Keats was a shadowy relation or a mere namesake, none of the brothers wanted anything to do with the hat business.

John may have wondered how Abbey, sneering at the idea of a poetic career, could propose anything so ridiculous as either of his brothers, or himself, becoming a hatter. Abbey had no business trading in fashion when he was still walking around in half boots, short breeches, and white cotton socks. One business associate from the London Company of Girdlers claimed that "for a long Time there had been no other Man on the Exchange in that Dress, and he was become so conspicuous for it as to be an Object of attention in the Streets."[78] Even men who manufactured women's undergarments laughed at Abbey.

Yet if Abbey's doubts about the idea of a poetic vocation spurred his eldest ward to opposition, they also caused him misgivings. *O for ten years, that I may overwhelm / Myself in poesy, so I may do the deed / That my own soul has to itself decreed.* John was about to abandon a career in which he had already invested five years and which promised a secure future—and for what? Abbey's phantom kept asking. John knew that the road from "whining boyhood" to the place where the Poet Kings sat enthroned would be long and arduous. In "Sleep and Poetry," when he thinks about this, the enormity of the task overwhelms him:

> How much toil!
> How many days! what desperate turmoil!
> Ere I can have explored its widenesses.
> Ah, what a task! Upon my bended knees,
> I could unsay those—no, impossible!
> Impossible!

Immediately after this panic, the poet finds a familiar sort of consolation in the "social thought" of brotherhood:

> For sweet relief I'll dwell
> On humbler thoughts, and let this strange assay
> Begun in gentleness die so away.
> E'en now all tumult from my bosom fades:
> I turn full hearted to the friendly aids
> That smooth the path of honour; brotherhood,
> And friendliness, the nurse of mutual good;
> The hearty grasp that sends a pleasant sonnet
> Into the brain ere one can think upon it;
> The silence when some rhymes are coming out;
> And when they're come, the very pleasant rout . . .

Rather than a "brotherhood in song," such as the one John refers to in his verse epistle to George Felton Mathew, this fraternity is above all a circle of support. While George Keats could not claim kinship with his brother's muse, he recognized its demands, and was always ready with the "hearty grasp that sends a pleasant sonnet/Into the brain ere one can think upon it." Tom was a kindred spirit who could share the space of silence when "some rhymes are coming out." While this poem, "Sleep and Poetry," has often been associated with Leigh Hunt, in whose cottage John wrote most of its lines, in the end it was a tribute to the brothers whose presence gave him the strength to aspire.

There were others who filled out the fraternal circle at this time. One was the artist Joseph Severn, who was a couple of years older than John

but seemed younger. Having completed his apprenticeship to a copper engraver, Severn had braved paternal opposition in order to quit the more
solid career track of engraving and devote himself to painting. Severn's father, a temperamental music master, displayed about as much enthusiasm
for his son's artistic ambitions as Richard Abbey did for John's. Even more
than the predicament of unsympathetic authority, the two gifted young
men shared a stubborn belief in their own powers. George had little toler-
ance for the emotional dependency of anyone besides his brothers, and he
sometimes found Severn needy and clinging. But he would later come to
appreciate the artist's loyal affection for all it was worth.

Two and a half weeks after John's coming of age, on November 18,
1816, the poet addressed a sonnet to his younger brother on his seventeenth
birthday. Tom copied it into his notebook under the heading, "Written to
His Brother Tom on His Birthday":

> Small, busy flames play through the fresh laid coals,
>> And their faint cracklings o'er our silence creep
>> Like whispers of the household gods that keep
> A gentle empire o'er fraternal souls.
> And while, for rhymes, I search around the poles,
>> Your eyes are fix'd, as in poetic sleep,
>> Upon the lore so voluble and deep,
> That aye at fall of night our care condoles.
> This is your birth-day, Tom, and I rejoice
>> That thus it passes smoothly, quietly.
> Many such eves of gently whisp'ring noise
>> May we together pass, and calmly try
> What are this world's true joys,—ere this great voice,
>> From its fair face, shall bid our spirits fly.

The mood is quiet, even serene. In the manner of Coleridge's "Frost at
Midnight," the speaker addresses a silent auditor whose "eyes are fix'd, as
in poetic sleep." Tom is named in line 9, the apostrophe that marks the turn
in the Petrarchan sonnet, and John need not explicitly mention George, for
his presence is implied in the title he gave the poem when he published it a
few months later: "To My Brothers." As the published version indicates,
the middle brother has not been forgotten.

The closing lines of the sonnet are tinged with the same sadness and sense of mortality that starts to color John's verse from this time; yet overall, the poem bespeaks comfort. The "gentle empire" is composed of kindred spirits, or in this case, "fraternal souls." Despite the noise, congestion, and hectic pace of city life, the orphaned Keats brothers had managed to re-create a feeling of home. As the year drew to a close, they found themselves, with their damaged household gods reassembled, knit together in a spirit of mutual condolence. Only Fanny was missing to complete the domestic scene.

The Christmas holidays, as always, came with memories. On Christ-mas Eve, John drafted another sonnet, "Written in Disgust of Vulgar Su-perstition," which speaks as much about the time of year and the sym-bolic power of Christmas as it does about the forlorn bells of the Church of St. Mary-le-Bow:

> The church bells toll a melancholy round,
>   Calling the people to some other prayers,
>   Some other gloominess, more dreadful cares,
> More heark'ning to the sermon's horrid sound.
> Surely the mind of man is closely bound
>   In some black spell; seeing that each one tears
>   Himself from fireside joys, and Lydian airs.

The brothers had been to enough funerals for a lifetime. John was not in-clined to forsake the fraternal hearth for a cold church service. Although he had not yet been branded a member of Leigh Hunt's Cockney School of Poetry, his aversion to the sound of the bells with the Cockney overtones strangely forebodes his negative relation to the establishment in whose light he would appear so puny. Like the cares at the hospital ward that had sternly beckoned him from soft Lydian airs in his verse epistle to George Felton Mathew, the Bow Bells ringing out from the established Church of England disrupt more convivial pleasures. The pagan spirit of the season was in the Yuletide log. John was with his brothers, and there he wanted to stay.

Together, they were shoring up strength and confidence to do things their own way. Tom would not return to clerk for Richard Abbey, and George, likewise, would shake off the shackles of the counting house by the time spring arrived. John would leave medical school—and the surgical butchers of the human form divine—to wander in the "lovely labyrinths" of beauty. *All hail delightful hopes!*[79] While the brothers would find it hard to escape the financial clutches of Abbey, their futures, at least, in the New Year would be their own.

2 WHAT MAD PURSUIT?

Hampstead

The year 1817 was a period of mobility. George and Tom traveled to France and to the coast of Devonshire, while John made a number of short trips throughout England in an effort to write his first epic-length poem. His travels took him through the old city walls of Southampton and across the English Channel to the Isle of Wight. After a brief stay in Margate, and then in Canterbury, with Tom, he encamped at the little coastal hideaway of Bo Peep in Hastings. Later in the year, he explored the courtyards and spiked ivy towers of Oxford, and climbed to the top of Box Hill from Burford Bridge. George and Tom crossed the Channel to the coast of Normandy and found their way to the restaurants and gambling casinos of the Palais-Royal in Paris, winding up the year by the beach at Teignmouth.

The city air had done little to improve Tom's health, and John's visits to the Vale of Health had revealed a more pleasant environment than that of commercial Cheapside. The postman Benjamin Bentley had a ground-floor apartment to let at the end of Well Walk, a pretty road lined with lime trees overlooking Hampstead Heath, and the brothers decided to rent it. The air in the open meadows of gorse and heather was supposed to be healthy, and the patches of old forest provided pleasant walks. By April, the three brothers had moved from Bird-in-Hand Court to the Bentleys' home, resounding with the voices of the postman's rowdy, red-haired children—the "young Carrots," the poet called them.[1]

In a letter to his sister, John fancifully captured a day in the life of Hampstead Heath: "Old women with bobbins and red cloaks and unpresuming bonnets . . . Gipseys after hare skins and silver spoons. Then goes by a fellow with a wooden clock under his arm that strikes a hundred and more. Then comes the old French emigrant (who has been very well to do in France) with his hands joined behind on his hips, and his face full of political schemes."[2] The wars with France had ended, and despite the French aristocrat's dreams, there was no going back, anywhere in Europe, to the *ancien régime*. In Hampstead, as elsewhere in Regency England, large Georgian homes built with middle-class wealth were springing up on the rural landscape.

George had his own schemes, though less political perhaps than those of the French emigrant. Like John, the middle brother knew that he possessed abilities greater than those of most men and was determined to earn his living by exercising them. He aspired higher than bookkeeping for Richard Abbey. One day, he plucked his hat off its hook and left the counting house, never to return. According to John's friend Charles Brown, Abbey dismissed George. Brown claimed to have a copy of a letter that John had written but never sent to Abbey, in which he hoped that their guardian might consider George cured of his "carelessness and extravagant propensities." (According to Brown, John also complained "how unlucky it was for him to be the eldest of two brothers, who could not live on their incomes.") George's friend James Freeman Clarke, on the other hand, maintained that George's silence regarding why he left Abbey's was due more to honor than to shame: "he preferred to bear the accusation of being unreasonable rather than to explain the cause, which might have made difficulty."[3]

Tensions had been building at the tea-house. John's letters suggest that a dispute with Abbey's chief clerk, Cadman Hodgkinson, may have had something to do with George's departure. "George was taken into his guardian's counting-room, where he stayed a little while, but left it," Freeman Clarke reported, "because he did not choose to submit to the domineering behavior of one of the partners." Hodgkinson had recently completed his apprenticeship, earned his freedom from the City of London, and been promoted to junior partner in Abbey & Cocks. When John later heard that Abbey was thinking of retiring and selling the business, he hoped it would happen, for "if any one deserves to be put to his shifts it is that Hodg-

kinson." As for the portly, if puritanical, Abbey, "he would live a long time
upon his fat and be none the worse for a good long lent."[4] From the brothers' perspective, George, despite his role as the family breadwinner, was cut
from a different cloth than these men.

Cadman Hodgkinson had been born into a family of merchants, and
he identified with his profession. Almost five years older than George, he
had been installed at Abbey & Cocks for a couple of years before George
moved from Enfield to the Poultry. Cadman's father, Sampson Hodgkinson, a druggist in Holborn, may have sent him to the same professional day
school, the Merchant Taylors' School, to which Cadman and his wife,
Susan, would later send their sons, Cadman Junior and Harry.[5] The school
that the Keats brothers attended also had a practical approach (one of John's
school prizes was C. H. Kauffman's *Dictionary of Merchandize, and Nomen-
clature in All Languages: For the use of Counting Houses*); but Clarke's school
at Enfield did not have an explicitly vocational orientation. George saw
himself as a gentleman more than a merchant, and he carried himself accordingly.

Hodgkinson, by contrast, now having surpassed George in rank at the
tea-house, was quickly following Abbey's professional trajectory. The tea
dealer had shown what could be done in trade, importing chests of green
and black tea, cocoa, and coffee, and distributing them to retailers throughout London and the provinces. He lived among the opulent merchants in
the suburbs, and, though the lesson would come later, he was also an example of how volatile the fortunes made through trade could be. He would
ultimately run up so much debt that he would have to mortgage his warehouses and tenements on Pancras Lane and on Watling Street. By 1831, he
would no longer be able to afford Walthamstow. Perhaps inspired by his
own experience, he would develop and patent a recipe for a cheaper form
of tea, made from the common hawthorn bush: simply pluck the leaves,
steam until they turn olive, dry on a hot plate, and stir in hot water.[6]

While Hodgkinson may have earned the brothers' animosity by regarding George as his inferior in the counting house, he was an intelligent
man who would soon open his own tea wholesaling business, at 34 Dowgate Hill, a hub of commercial traffic since medieval times. Many of the
city's livery companies, or trade associations, had their headquarters on or
near the Hill in handsome neoclassical buildings with Tuscan arches and
piazzas. One wonders whether John Keats had Abbey and his chief clerk in

mind when he described the villainous merchants, those account-keeping "ledger-men," in "Isabella; or, The Pot of Basil":

> Why were they proud? Because their marble founts
>   Gush'd with more pride than do a wretch's tears?—
> Why were they proud? Because fair orange-mounts
>   Were of more soft ascent than lazar stairs?—
> Why were they proud? Because red-lin'd accounts
>   Were richer than the songs of Grecian years?—
> Why were they proud? again we ask aloud,
> Why in the name of Glory were they proud?

Why *were* they proud? The question had been plaguing John with respect to Abbey, and after George left Abbey & Cocks, he would wonder the same thing about Hodgkinson. How could men who knew more about keeping books than reading them triumph over his more noble-minded brother? Where was the glory in trade?

After his departure from Abbey & Cocks, George waited to come of age and to receive his share of the family inheritance. "He lived at home," Freeman Clarke reported, "keeping house with his two brothers, and doing nothing for some time, waiting till he should be of age, and should receive his small inheritance. Many said he was an idle fellow, who would never come to any good; but he felt within himself a conviction that he could make his way successfully through the world." Fortunately for George, Abbey, who "always predicted that George would turn out well," was not as irritated at George's leaving the tea business as he had been at John's decision to quit medicine.[7] By his steady habits and upright demeanor, George had earned his guardian's respect. Perhaps even more important, he listened when Abbey spoke of other business opportunities.

Because George at one point sent a business letter from 62 Bread Street, John's biographer Robert Gittings believes that he may have worked for the wholesale linendraper W. G. Taylor, who is listed in an 1817 London business directory at that address, along with the warehousemen Walton, Newton, & Company. But Charles Cowden Clarke's wife, Mary (née Novello), states "that Keats's lodging was in the *Poultry,* my husband is perfectly certain; and thinks it very possible that the large building 'opposite,' alluded to in his 'Recollections of John Keats,' was St. Mildred's Church," Bread

Street.[8] The church, like the address George mentions, was just above Watling Street. But George apparently did not like Bread Street any better than Pancras Lane, for he did not stay there long.

George also had business dealings with a certain Wilkinson. The man was probably a former apprentice or business associate of Abbey's. In 1825, George asked Abbey how Hodgkinson, Frith, Parker, Beilby, and Wilkinson were getting on. He also asked his sister, who replied that Hodgkinson and his partner, who ran a tea business at 27 Budge Row near Dowgate Hill, were prospering; that Beilby was living with a woman named Sarah, whom George knew from Pancras Lane; and that Frith had married and was working as a grocer on Bishopsgate Street. Wilkinson, alas, was dead. But Wilkinson's scheme for making money fell through around the time that George was at Bread Street. In May 1817, John learned from his brother that he had lost the forty or fifty pounds he had invested through George.[9]

Close to the brothers' new lodgings at Well Walk lived two young men who were soon to play a much larger role in the lives of the brothers than the Bread-Street merchants: Charles Brown and Charles Wentworth Dilke. Brown would become John's best friend, and George, even after many years abroad, would continue to think of Dilke as his best friend. Writing to Dilke and his wife, Maria, from Louisville, George would address them as "the only Spirits in existence who are congenial to me, and at the same time *know* me,—*understand* me."[10] The double-story, two-family house, known as Wentworth Place, which the Dilkes shared with Brown, would soon become a second home to the Keats brothers.

By profession, Charles Dilke was a clerk in the Naval Pay Office; by nature, he was an autodidact with literary interests. He wrote essays on the English poets and weighed in on scholarly debates like the "Junius" controversy, regarding the authorship of a series of political letters from the eighteenth century. Later, he would purchase illustrations by William Blake and edit the *Athenaeum,* a literary journal featuring work by writers from Charles Lamb to Charles Dickens. It was in relation to Dilke that John formulated the idea of *"Negative Capability,"* or the capacity "of being in uncertainties, Mysteries, doubts, without any irritable reaching after fact & reason." John saw Dilke as "a Man who cannot feel he has a personal identity unless he has made up his Mind about every thing."[11]

Maria Dilke provided a counterbalance to her more dogmatic husband. George called her a "lively, chatty being." To gaiety, she added "good sense and a large fund of disinterested good nature." She found it easier to talk to George than to John, whom she liked but did not understand. John seemed to her "a very odd young man, but good-tempered, and good-hearted, and very clever indeed." She had no reason to doubt her husband's belief in John' genius, and would later dare to stand up to his critics: "If the public cry him up as a great poet, I will henceforth be their humble servant; if not, the devil take the public."[12] The Dilkes also had a seven-year-old son, Charley, on whom they doted—at times, John felt, to excess.

Charles Brown was an eccentric man of letters who clung to his gentlemanly lifestyle by a single financial thread. In his den of literary leisure next to the Dilkes, he provided contrast. Although he could boast no ancestor as eminent as Dilke's forebear Sir Peter Wentworth, a politician and friend of John Milton, he would later amplify his own common patronymic by adopting his mother's family name, and styling himself Charles Armitage Brown. While Dilke tried to reduce the disorderly reality of life to universal truth, Brown respected complexity. Where Dilke sought method and coherency, Brown burst in with his rumpled look to shake things up. Brown was three years older than Dilke, yet his balding head and spectacles hardly crimped his style.

John would later send a few playful stanzas to George characterizing Brown:

> He was to weet a melancholy carle,
> Thin in the waist, with bushy head of hair,
> As hath the seeded thistle, when in parle
> It holds the zephyr, ere it sendeth fair
> Its light balloons into the summer air;
> Thereto his beard had not begun to bloom,
> No brush had touch'd his chin or razor sheer;
> No care had touch'd his cheek with mortal doom,
> But new he was and bright as scarf from Persian loom.
>
> Ne cared he for wine, or half and half,
> Ne cared he for fish, or flesh, or fowl,
> And sauces held he worthless as the chaff;
> He 'sdeign'd the swine-herd at the wassel bowl,
> Ne with lewd ribbalds sat he cheek by jowl,
> Ne with sly lemans in the scorner's chair;

> But after water-brooks this pilgrim's soul
> Panted, and all his food was woodland air,
> Though he would ofttimes feed on gillyflowers rare.
>
> The slang of cities in no wise he knew,
> Tipping the wink to him was heathen Greek;
> He sipp'd no olden Tom, or ruin blue,
> Or nantz, or cherry brandy, drank full meek
> By many a damsel hoarse and rouge of cheek;
> Nor did he know each aged watchman's beat,
> Nor in obscured purlieus would he seek
> For curled Jewesses with ancles neat,
> Who as they walk abroad make tinkling with their feet.

Unlike the Dilkes, who married young, Brown had no intention of giving up his bachelor lifestyle. His affair with his housekeeper Abigail O'Donhague (alternately, O'Donaghue, Donohue, Donhaugh) was no secret, for in 1820 it resulted in the birth of little Charles (Carlino). Yet it did not result in marriage. When Brown moved to Italy two years later, he took his son but left the mother behind.

Charles Brown shared literary interests with John, and he also shared the experience of having toiled at a desk in a counting house as an adolescent with George. As the sixth son of an insurance-agent-cum-stockbroker, who had moved from Scotland to London, Brown lost his father at sixteen and grew up quickly. His elder brother John Armitage Brown, a merchant shipper who had a business importing goods from Russia, hired him and sent him to St. Petersburg, where Brown made an unfortunate purchase: a batch of boar-hair bristles made worthless by an English company that had invented a cheaper whalebone substitute. He thus bankrupted the company and returned to London, hoarding his pennies and surviving on one meal a day at pothouses, or cheap taverns, where the forks and knives were chained to the tables. In 1815, his brother James, who had worked for the East India Company in the jungles of Sumatra, died. James left Charles an inheritance of £3,333, which, invested at 5 percent interest, would have yielded an income of £166 per annum; if fully invested, it was just enough to enable Brown to escape the wage mill and live as a gentleman.[13]

Poverty can be a tenacious companion, however, and it pursued Brown into the sphere of suburban respectability. His early experience had tempered his natural generosity, and he always kept a careful eye on expenses: his desk was messy, but his ledger book was neat. Since Hampstead Heath was a popular retreat for Londoners in the summer, Brown every year supplemented his income by renting his half of Wentworth Place, grabbing his walking stick, shouldering his backpack, and hiking around the British Isles. He, like Dilke, contributed verse and prose to the literary journals, and in 1814 his comic opera, *Narensky; or, The Road to Yaroslaf,* had been performed at Drury Lane Theatre. He now had a membership and connections at the theater that would serve him well when he and John submitted their tragedy, *Otho the Great,* to Drury Lane in 1819.

George, despite his predilection for puns, may have seemed too conventional to sustain Charles Brown's interest for long, but from the moment that he met John, Brown desired his "acquaintanceship, if not his friendship." A master at courtship, he knew how to play coy, and thus won his man. "I succeeded in making him come often to my house by never asking him to come oftener; and I let him feel himself at perfect liberty there, chiefly by avoiding to assure him of the fact," Brown said. An errand boy whom John once invited into Brown's parlor for a "jolly hot tea" never forgot Brown's robust, companionable nature and his obvious affection for the poet, as he put his hand on John's shoulder and laughed "in his hearty, jovial way." Anyone could tell that he was "terrible fond of Mr. Keats."[14]

At the start of the year, the three brothers were eagerly awaiting the proof sheets of John's first book. When they arrived in February 1817, they came with a note saying that if a "dedication to the book was intended it must be sent forthwith." John probably had one in mind, for "he withdrew to a side-table, and in the buzz of a mixed conversation," as Charles Cowden Clarke later recalled, scribbled out a dedicatory sonnet. John had used a line from Leigh Hunt's *Story of Rimini,* "Places of nestling green for Poets made" as the epigraph to the first poem in the collection; now, in a fond but ultimately fatal move, he dedicated the book to Hunt.[15]

The elegiac opening of John's dedicatory sonnet to Hunt echoes Wordsworth's sense, as expressed in his "Ode: Intimations of Immortality," that there had passed away a glory from the earth:

> Glory and loveliness have passed away;
>   For if we wander out in early morn,
>   No wreathed incense do we see upborne

Into the east, to meet the smiling day:
No crowd of nymphs soft voic'd and young, and gay,
   In woven baskets bringing ears of corn,
   Roses, and pinks, and violets, to adorn
The shrine of Flora in her early May.

No divinities presided over the springtime festivities at Hampstead any longer; yet (oh! to echo Wordsworth) there was still a "leafy luxury" in the presence of Hunt. The childlike Hunt was symbolically green, and in paying him homage with his "poor offerings" Keats was still greener. In dedicating his book to Hunt, he set himself up for ridicule as, to quote Byron, one of the "mock birds and bards of Mr. Hunt's little chorus."[16]

In 1817, the year that John's first volume of poetry appeared in print, the pseudonymous "Z" in *Blackwood's Edinburgh Magazine* launched an attack, "On the Cockney School of Poetry." John Gibson Lockhart, allegedly the man behind the mask of "Z," mocked Hunt in a scathing series of essays as the King of the Cockney Poets. "Mr Hunt cannot utter a dedication, or even a note, without betraying the shibboleth of low birth and low habits," sneered the Tory critic. "He is the ideal of a Cockney poet. He raves perpetually about 'green fields,' 'jaunty streams,' and 'o'er-arching leafiness,' exactly as a Cheapside shop-keeper does about the beauties of his box on the Camberwell road. Mr Hunt is altogether unacquainted with the face of nature in her magnificent scenes; he has never seen any mountain higher than Highgate-hill, nor reclined by any stream more pastoral than the Serpentine River" (the artificial lake in Hyde Park, London, made in the eighteenth century). Hunt had never been on the Grand Tour: he was a vulgar son of commerce, whose stock in trade was poetic epithets. John Wilson, another Tory critic who published under the signature "Christopher North," used the pen name "Observator" when he declared that he did not think Leigh Hunt a real poet: "at least his Sonnets to the puddles on the Hampstead heath, are no more like poetry, than if he had splashed himself in them."[17] The elitism of these reviews set the tone for articles that would soon appear about Keats.

John never published his sonnet "On Receiving a Laurel Crown from Leigh Hunt," but Hunt cemented the connection between them by including no less than three sonnets on the occasion of his having crowned Keats with laurel, and John's having crowned *him* with a wreath of ivy, in *Foliage; or, Poems Original and Translated* (1818). One would have been enough for

Lockhart to satirize them both as Cockney Poets: "There is a pair of block-heads for you! John Keats had no more right to dress up Leigh Hunt in this absurd fashion, than he had to tar and feather him—and we do not doubt, that if Leigh Hunt ever had the misfortune to have been tarred and feathered, he would have written a sonnet on his plumification, and de-scribed himself as a Bird of Paradise."[18] The mode was satire, but the dan-ger was real.

Leigh Hunt's own father (ironically a loyalist) had barely escaped being tarred and feathered on the eve of the American Revolution in Philadel-phia, and here was Hunt again flouting authority by saying that it was *in-ternal* power only that mattered: "what's within us crowned." If one could, like Napoleon for instance, snatch the crown from an authority as august as the pope and crown oneself, what might that mean for the authority of the British Crown, and the Church it commanded? Hunt's praise of an inner kingdom was about as popular among the Powers that Be in the United Kingdom as Christ's had been in Rome. It also translated all too readily into the kind of meritocracy for which the American patriots and the French *sans-culottes* had fought—in recent revolutions, whose shockwaves were still reverberating throughout the kingdom.

Hunt's preface to *Foliage* followed his December essay on the "Young Poets" by announcing a revolution in poetry: "The downfall of the French school of poetry has of late been encreasing in rapidity," he proclaimed. "Its cold and artificial compositions have given way, like so many fantastic fig-ures of snow; and imagination breathes again in a more green and genial clime."[19] Like the artificial gardens and fountains of Versailles that had flourished under the Sun King, Louis XIV, the French neoclassical school of poetry had given way, during the French Revolution, to more "natural" forms of expression. Farewell Racine, Molière, and Corneille—welcome Reynolds, Shelley, and *Keats,* the youngest of the Young Poets. As it might not be difficult to imagine, the literary establishment of Great Britain did not take any more kindly to Hunt's pronouncements about poetic freedom than Marie Antoinette had done to cries of "Liberté, egalité, fraternité!"

Yet far from initiating another revolution in poetry, John's first book of poetry was ignored when it came out a few days after George's birthday, on March 3, 1817. "Every one of us expected (and not unreasonably) that it would create a sensation in the literary world," Charles Cowden Clarke related. "Alas! the book might have emerged in Timbuctoo with far stron-ger chance of fame and approbation. It never passed to a second edition; the first was but a small one, and that was never sold off. The whole community, as if by compact, seemed determined to know nothing about it." John gave away copies of the book, as did George, who never missed an opportunity of impressing the ladies with his brother's pen. He asked John to sign a copy of the book for Georgiana, and John inscribed it "To G. A. Wylie from her Friends the Author and his Brother George." George had it handsomely bound in green leather with a gilt border.[20]

John also gave Richard Abbey a copy of his first book, and his guardian's response left no doubt about either his opinion of the poetry it contained, or his own lack of tact. "Well John I have read your Book," Abbey said, "& it reminds me of the Quaker's Horse which was hard to catch, & good for nothing when he was caught—So your Book is hard to understand & good for nothing when it is understood." The obvious anti-intellectualism of the remark notwithstanding, the verdict it contained was wounding. Abbey had crossed a line, as he himself recognized: "I don't think he ever forgave me for uttering this Opinion which however was the Truth."[21]

A few reviews did appear. One was by George Felton Mathew, who, having been superseded by other young poets in John's life, now looked askance at his verse. "There are few writers more frequent or more presumptuous in their intrusions on the public than, we know not what to call them, versifiers, rhymists, metre-ballad mongers, what you will but poets," Mathew wrote of John's 1817 *Poems*. "The attention of the public, indeed, has been so frequently arrested and abased by these exhalations of ignorance, perverted genius, and presumption, that 'poems' has become a dull feature upon a title page." Mathew did praise the poetry for its imaginative and emotional power, but he ultimately consigned it to the category of "perverted genius," finding it bereft of moral purpose. John Reynolds, by contrast, whose review appeared six days after the book itself—in the fittingly titled journal, the *Champion*—predicted that Keats would ultimately rise above moderns like Byron and Thomas Moore to the stature of Chaucer or Shakespeare. If Reynolds mixed criticism with his encomium—pointing out a certain "faultiness of measure," for example, or an exaggerated "use of compound epithets"—such censure was strategic, allowing him to make grander claims on behalf of another young poet.[22]

By the time John Reynolds's review appeared in the *Champion,* Reynolds himself had given up his own poetic ambitions. He had become engaged to Eliza Powell Drewe, his girlfriend from Devonshire, and the couple had postponed marriage until Reynolds could establish himself financially. He found the law dull, but it was a respectable profession that would enable him to marry. "I can never write anything now," Reynolds confessed to Keats on October 4, 1818. "My mind is taken the other way:—But I shall set my heart on having you, high, as you ought to be. Do *you* get Fame,—and I shall have it in being your affectionate and steady friend."[23] Reynolds was already on his way to becoming the person who would be identified on his tombstone as "The Friend of Keats."

The poet's brothers naturally assumed that the poor sales of John's book were the fault of the publishers. Perhaps Charles and James Ollier were neglecting a first-time author and not promoting the volume. Since it was hardly the author's place to complain about his own lack of popularity, George took charge of the matter and wrote to the Olliers to demand an account of the remaining inventory. While Charles Ollier was a member of the same literary clique that saw Keats as a rising star, his brother James jumped at the opportunity to unload the excess stock. From an economic standpoint, the book was a failure, pure and simple. James sent the following curt response to George Keats, signed by both Ollier brothers:

> Sir—We regret that your brother ever requested us to publish his book, or that our opinion of its talent should have led us to acquiesce in undertaking it. We are, however, much obliged to you for relieving us from the unpleasant necessity of declining any further connexion with it, which we must have done, as we think the curiosity is satisfied and the sale has dropped.—By far the greater number of Persons who have purchased it from us have found fault with it in such plain terms, that we have in many cases offer'd to take the book back rather than be annoyed with the ridicule which has, time after time, been shower'd on it. In fact,—it was only on Saturday last that we were under the mortification of having our own opinion of it's merits flatly contradicted by a Gentleman, who told us he considered it "no better than a take in."—
>
> These are unpleasant imputations for any one in business to labour under, but we should have borne them and concealed their existence from you had not the stile of your note shewn us that such delicacy would be quite thrown away. We shall take means without delay for ascertaining the number of copies on hand, & you shall be informed accordingly.[24]

This would have been a bitter pill for any poet to swallow. Reynolds suggested a move to his publishers, John Taylor and James Augustus Hessey, and George, undaunted by his previous experience with publishers, stepped back into his role as literary agent. By mid-April 1817, he had closed a deal with Taylor & Hessey to the satisfaction of all.

Their rival John Murray had made his reputation in the poetry world by publishing Byron: Why should Taylor & Hessey not hitch their reputations to another rising star? John Taylor, himself a writer, came from a publishing family. His father was a printer and a bookseller, as were his uncle and cousin. He had met James Hessey at James Lackington's bookshop in Finsbury Square, not too far from the Swan & Hoop, when the partners first came to London—Hessey from Yorkshire and Taylor from Nottinghamshire. While Taylor, like Charles Ollier, focused on the editorial end of the business, including acquisitions, Hessey, like James Ollier, handled sales and accounts. But unlike James Ollier, Hessey liked Keats's poetry. He later claimed that no single poetry collection ever gave him "more real delight" than John's 1820 *Poems.* Taylor was convinced that Keats would turn out to be "the brightest Ornament" of his age.[25]

The firm's legal advisor, twenty-eight-year-old Richard Woodhouse, while not prone to snap decisions, quickly came to believe that a poetic genius on the order of John Keats had "not appeared since Shakespeare & Milton." Industrious, serious, self-effacing, Woodhouse thought Keats "an original genius." Yet he found that genius "wayward, trembling, easily daunted," and for the rest of John's brief career, Woodhouse would back up his encouragement with financial support. "Whatever People regret that they could not do for Shakespeare or Chatterton, because he did not live in their time," Woodhouse vowed, "that I would embody into a Rational principle, and (with due regard to certain expediencies) do for Keats." When Charles Brown later took "one of his funny odd dislikes" to the attorney, John defended him in a manner that says something about the nature of their relationship: "Woodhouse likes my Poetry—conclusive."[26]

Benjamin Haydon blamed not the Olliers but Leigh Hunt, King of the Cockneys, for the failure of John's first book. John's next book, he insisted, would come like a "crash of thunder" to blast readers from their seats. The time was at hand for the Young Poet to take up "the great trumpet of nature" and make it sound with his own voice. Life was short and comfort the great enemy of genius. John's path now spread before him, and he must tear himself from all familiar associations at once by leaving Hampstead. *What! said Obstinate, and leave our Friends, and our comforts behind us! Yes, said Christian, (for that was his name) . . . I seek an Inheritance, incorruptible, undefiled, and that fadeth not away.* John Bunyan had said it before, and Haydon likewise preached from Christian tradition. "If any *man* come to me, and hate not his father, and mother, and wife, and children, and brethren, and sisters, yea, and his own life also, he cannot be my disciple," Christ explains in the Gospel of Luke.[27] The prophet must abandon selfhood in order to take up the cross of his mission.

Impressed by Haydon's dramatic speech, John informed George and Tom that he needed to leave Well Walk as soon as possible. "Banish money," he exclaimed; "Banish sofas—Banish Wine—Banish Music." Neither of his brothers shared the artist's enthusiasm for the idea, but they felt the tyranny of his fierce threat, and of the hard task proposed, like the poet in *The Fall of Hyperion*. "Now that Haydon has pointed out how necessary it is that I sho^{d} be alone to improve myself, they give up the temporary pleasure of living with me continually for a great good which I hope will follow," John wrote.[28] George and Tom supported the journey that he was to take: at once a literal journey from a land of pretty curtains and picturesque views into more remote countryside *and* a metaphorical journey from boyhood into poetic maturity.

John had already found the theme that he was about to pursue, in the lead poem of his 1817 volume, "I stood tip-toe upon a little hill." He had called that poem "Endymion" while he was composing it, and Tom copied it down under that title. But the myth of Endymion involves sublime experience, and sublimity does not sit well with the idea of a poet on tip-toes. As John related the story to his sister: "Many Years ago there was a young handsome Shepherd who fed his flocks on a Mountain's Side called Latmus—he was a very contemplative sort of a Person and lived solitary among the trees and Plains little thinking—that such a beautiful Creature as the Moon was growing mad in Love with him—However so it was; and when he was asleep in the Grass, she used to come down from heaven and admire him excessively [for] a long time; and at last could not refrain from carrying him away in her arms to the top of that high Mountain Latmus while he was a dreaming."[29] At the end of "I stood tip-toe upon a little hill," the poet stops short of imagining such transcendent love as John describes to his sister. Instead, the poem ends with the line, "My wand'ring spirit must no further soar." But he had identified the thoughtful hero of *Endymion,* whom he would now send in quest of ideal love through a symbolic landscape portrayed in exquisite language. He was ready to soar.

Percy Shelley, the third Young Poet, had met Keats at Hunt's cottage, and around the time that John's book appeared, he drew him into a friendly rivalry by proposing that they each produce a poem of epic length to ground their reputations, hitherto built on lyric. John feared being drawn into Shelley's sphere of influence, resisting on more than one occasion Shelley's overtures to friendship, but he rose to the challenge of poetic competition. And to some extent, the hero of *Endymion* resembles the protagonist of the lead poem in Shelley's recently published collection, *Alastor; or, The Spirit of Solitude and Other Poems* (1816). While Shelley recognized the futility of hoping to realize a figment of one's own imagination—particularly when that figment takes the form of a female alter ego of the narcissistic poet—in his preface to "Alastor" he praised the idealist willing to try.

Although the longest poem John had yet composed was closer to four hundred than to four thousand lines, his object was to "make 4000 Lines of one bare circumstance and fill them with Poetry."[30] In effect, what he was proposing as a test of his inventive powers was an efflorescence of lyric in the form of narrative romance. The goal, stemming from inexperience, proved his naïveté as well as his ambition. To sustain interest in a poem of that length, one needs a plot; John had no more than a kernel. He would spend the rest of the year, like his title character, chasing a dream.

While John chased Endymion around England, Shelley, who had no need to prove his ability to earn his living as a poet, would stay put in the suburb of Marlow thirty miles west of London, surrounded by devoted companions. The conclave gathered around the magnetic Shelley in the summer of 1817 included the novelist Thomas Love Peacock; Shelley's wife, Mary Wollstonecraft Godwin, who was at work on *Frankenstein;* Mary's half-sister Claire Clairmont, the stepdaughter of William Godwin; Claire's two-month-old daughter, Allegra, the natural child of Lord Byron; and the Shelleys' one-year-old son, William. Leigh Hunt, always on the run from his creditors, would join them, with his children, wife, and sister-in-law, Elizabeth Kent, who admired Hunt nearly as much as Claire Clairmont admired Percy Shelley.

Perhaps unsurprisingly given his domestic arrangements, the title characters of the poem Shelley would produce in competition with Keats, *Laon and Cythna; or, The Revolution of the Golden City: A Vision of the Nineteenth Century,* are lovers as well as siblings. According to Thomas Peacock, Shelley "carried the expression of his opinions, moral, political, and theological, beyond the bounds of discretion." The poem features a bloodless revolution against the sultan of the Ottoman Empire, a typical Shelleyan tyrant. When Shelley presented the poem to the Olliers at the end of the summer, he inspired "terror."[31] After printing only a few copies, the publishers would panic and stop the press. Keats's protagonist would likewise spend the four books of *Endymion* with his sister, but, in the end, the sibling and romantic relationships would cleave neatly, as Endymion ascends into the heavens with the moon goddess and his sister, Peona, returns home.

While Shelley sat in his favorite spot in Bisham Wood, confidently covering page after page of his notebook in pencil in the race to finish, John would drag out the painful process of poetic composition through the end of the year, moving around restlessly in search of inspiration. As the months wore on, his faith in his poem would waver, though his friends and brothers would remain loyal. Richard Woodhouse would hold fast to his belief that *Endymion,* written when Keats was twenty-two, would trump Shakespeare's "Venus and Adonis," which had been written at about the same age. "Keats's poem will be found to contain more beauties, more poetry (and that of a higher order) less conceit & bad taste and in a word," he boasted, "much more promise of excellence than are to be found in Shakespeare's work."[32] A tall order for a not-so-tall poet.

Yet, John had promised *Endymion* to his publishers, and, for better or for worse, it was time to get going. And so, on Monday, April 14, 1817, John said goodbye to his brothers, reminding them not to forget about their little sister. He did not plan to see any of them again until he had finished drafting the four books of his poem—each more than twice as long as anything he had yet written. When he stepped onto the stagecoach, he did not know that the trip would be only the first of several Keatsian junkets that he would make before the end of the year in an effort to complete *Endymion.*

The Isle of Wight

The cold ride on an outside seat of the stagecoach to Southampton triggered a sense of loneliness that John could not seem to shake. Isolation *was* his objective, and yet, as he passed places and faces that he had never seen, and might never see again, a feeling of alienation crept over him. All he could see were countless miles of desolate heaths, interspersed with woodlands. All he could recollect were vague, fleeting impressions: "dusty

Hedges—sometimes Ponds—then nothing—then a little Wood with trees."[33] He could not remember, because he did not notice, the names of the towns. Had George been with him, he might have had a better sense of his itinerary. George noticed such things.

As the sun went down, and the last "straggling Barns" and "hedge trees" faded from view, hearth fires began to light up the cottages. John's mind drifted naturally to the thought of his brothers, and he catalogued what he had seen: "lopped Trees—Cow ruminating—ditto Donkey—Man and Woman going gingerly along . . . Barber's Pole—Doctor's Shop." At times, he projected narrative onto the strange landscape around him: "William seeing his Sisters over the Heath—John waiting with a Lantern for his Mistress." When his woolen cape was no longer a match for the cold night air, he took a seat inside the carriage. At dawn, he poked his head out the window to see "an immense quantity of blooming Furze on each side [of] the road cutting a most rural dash."[34] His spirits rose with the sun, though in Southampton his disorientation returned.

The stagecoach passed into the city under the Bar Gate at the north end of the city walls, and John thought that the two lead lions flanking the turret seemed respectable guards. But the town itself seemed like any other, and all he could tell about it was that the main street was long and broad, with the usual side streets and two or three churches. After the bumpy overnight carriage ride, he was feeling "rather muzzy," and rather than attempting to make conversation at the coaching inn over breakfast, he reached into his luggage for a volume of Shakespeare's collected works. As he did so, he recalled Stephano's speech from *The Tempest* when, faced with a storm that threatens to drown him, the clown clutches his bottle and says, "here's my comfort."[35]

The strangers he saw were no more or less interesting than those he was used to seeing. He would move on, and they would vanish. "I admire Human Nature but I do not like *Men,*" he wrote to Benjamin Haydon, and no doubt he meant what he said.[36] All the same, the poet would have liked some companionship. His best response to the malaise that beset him was to head down to the wharf and make plans to depart. There, at the southern end of town, brigs and schooners lined up at the pier. Fishermen in small boats rowed out past the high walls of the city. John learned that the ferry to the Isle of Wight—a destination renowned for its beauty and more isolated than any of the southern coastal towns where Londoners vacationed—

would depart at three in the afternoon. He would have to stay awake until then.

The passage across the English Channel from Southampton to West Cowes, on the northern shore of the Isle of Wight, would turn out to be less eventful than the same trip made a couple of years later in the company of Charles Brown. That time, the rope holding the edge of the square-rigged sail at the bow of the ferry would catch the small mast of a crossing naval ship, snapping it off close to the deck. Had the mast been heavier it might have capsized the boat. John admired the stoic response of the navymen: "Neither Officer nor man in the whole Boat moved a Muscle—they scarcely notic'd it even with words." At the mouth of the Medina River on the northern shore of the island, they would see the Prince Regent's yacht, "a beautiful vessel," surrounded by other yachts and boats, passing and re-passing it, circuiting and tacking about in every direction along the coast. The ships would give the island a magical appearance: "I never beheld any thing so, silent, light, and graceful."[37] Approaching this time, John could see the sandbanks sloping gently at the mouth of the river, with the town of East and West Cowes split across it.

From the pier where the ferry docked, John could walk to the town square in West Cowes, from which the stagecoaches departed. He would board for the night in the town of Newport, in the stately shadow of Caris-brooke Castle, at the center of the island. The next day he could scout around for a place to settle. As the coach rumbled out of the central square, it passed down St. James Street, over the Carisbrooke River, and up Honey Hill. At a fork in the road, it came to a poorhouse that had been built in 1770 and that seemed strangely out of keeping with its pastoral setting: the House of Industry. But as the road approached Newport, an even more in-congruous sight, the Albany army barracks, came into view. The barracks, named for the Duke of York and Albany, Commander in Chief of the Brit-ish Army, could house two or three thousand redcoats. They had gone up a couple of decades earlier, as fortification against Britain's ancient rival, France. The wars against France had ended, but the soldiers still performed military exercises on the parade grounds by the side of the road.[38]

It was April 1817, after all, only four years after Jane Austen captured the stereotype of the dissolute redcoat in *Pride and Prejudice*. Perhaps with the perfidious Wickham in mind—a member of the royal standing army who had nothing better to do than play whist and run off with silly girls like Lydia Bennet—John cursed the "Government for placing such a Nest of Debauchery in so beautiful a place." The man sitting next to him in the coach agreed with the sentiment, complaining that the presence of the soldiers had spoiled the residents. In the room where John spent the night, a stranger had scrawled in the condensation on the window, "O Isle spoilt by the Mil*a*tary." He copied down the forlorn apostrophe, underlining the misspelling, but mulling it over in his room at night, he thought that perhaps he "did not feel very sorry at the idea of the Women being a little profligate."[39]

Through his window, John could also see the medieval stone fortress of Carisbrooke Castle, now a magnificent and comforting ruin. Like most castles in the early nineteenth century, it was in a state of picturesque disrepair, overgrown with moss and ivy. At the top of the central tower, or keep, a colony of jackdaws had built a nest. The small crows had been there many years (for all we know since the reign of King Henry I), and they can still be seen flocking above the keep in contemporary engravings of the castle. John explored his new environs, and discovered "several delightful wood-alleys, and copses," as well as (Caliban's phrase for running streams) "quick freshes." The primroses were in bloom, and there were so many that he joked: "The Island ought to be called Primrose Island: that is, if the nation of Cowslips agree thereto, of which there are diverse Clans just beginning to lift up their heads."[40] Rambling up hills, through fields, over stiles, down rural lanes, in and out of groves and thickets, kept him busy for a few days.

Exploring the coastline, he climbed to the top of St. Catherine's Hill to the old stone lighthouse shrouded in fog. He saw waterfalls and caverns. And, like other tourists, he marveled at the great wooded gap between the tall white cliffs by the village of Shanklin: "Sloping wood and meadow ground reaches round the Chine, which is a cleft between the Cliffs of the depth of nearly 300 feet at least. This cleft is filled with trees & bushes in the narrow part; and as it widens becomes bare, if it were not for primroses on one side, which spread to the very verge of the Sea, and some fishermen's huts on the other, perched midway in the Ballustrades of beautiful green Hedges along their steps down to the sands."[41] Yet for all this, John was lonely. His favorite spot was the top of Bowcombe Down, where he could look back toward the English mainland.

Hark, do you not hear the sea? Standing high on the chalky cliffs, he could visualize Edgar, disguised as poor Tom o' Bedlam, leading his blinded father, the Duke of Gloucester, to the white cliffs of Dover. In a scene of tragic futility at the end of the fourth act of *King Lear,* Gloucester literalizes the metaphoric blindness of Lear. Edgar fools his father into thinking that he is at the top of the cliffs, when he is actually on the beach, and as the old man prepares to plunge forward to what he thinks will be his doom, he kneels and addresses the gods: "O you mighty gods / This world I do renounce and in your sights / Shake patiently my great affliction off." He then leans forward, but instead of waking in the next world, Gloucester finds himself facedown in sand, an emblem of the "sublime pathetic."[42]

Those infamous "vile jellies," the Duke of Gloucester's gouged-out eyes, lurk subtly in John's sonnet "On the Sea," written at Shanklin on his visit to the Isle of Wight. The poet invokes the solace of nature for all who come, not with eyes to see, but with "eyeballs vext and tir'd." At the end of the poem, a choir of sea nymphs startles him, as he suddenly catches the ethereal, otherworldly strains he had been longing to hear at Margate in poetry addressed to George. But whereas the sonnet addressed to his brother had unleashed a flow of verse the previous autumn, in the spring of 1817, on the Isle of Wight, John could not seem to get past his sonnet "On the Sea."

The task of his long poem loomed before him, a symbol of all he had yet to accomplish. "I have asked myself so often why I should be a Poet more than other Men," he confessed to Leigh Hunt, "seeing how great a thing it is,—how great things are to be gained by it—What a thing to be in the Mouth of Fame—that at last the Idea has grown so monstrously beyond my seeming Power of attainment."[43] Keats's "Mouth of Fame," like Milton's maw of Hell, is the place where the ambitious wind up. John had set the bar high for *Endymion;* had he approached his task methodically, as George perhaps would have done, he might have been able to face the immense incoherence of unwritten epic. But despite his quantitative definition of his goal—four thousand lines—John aimed to do more in *Endymion* than write a certain quantity of verse. His true goal was to prove the *voice* behind the poetry to be that of a poet.

John was in a hurry, moreover, and rather than breaking his day into segments, he immersed himself in poetry. "I find that I cannot exist without poetry—without eternal poetry—half the day will not do—the whole of it—I began with a little, but habit has made me a Leviathan." He had left his brothers in Hampstead enjoying Shakespeare's comedies and romances, while he secluded himself with the "sublime Misery" of *King Lear*. Without his brothers to counteract his "horrid Morbidity of Temperament," his mental demons took over, and his ardor quickly turned into despair.[44]

His landlady at the boarding house in Newport had let him take a print of Shakespeare from the hallway into his room: it came closer to his idea of the bard than any other portrait he had seen. He hung it up next to a picture of Milton and his daughters and a portrait of that tragic heroine, Mary, Queen of Scots. To these inspirational heads, he hoped to add a couple more, and to that end he asked that Benjamin Haydon make him a sketch of his brothers. Surely, the artist would be willing to contribute that much to an undertaking he had promoted with such zeal. Perhaps with George's calm demeanor and Tom's sweet countenance in view, he might find some relief from the perpetual sense of feeling "rather *narvus*."[45]

But Haydon did not sketch John's brothers; nor would he produce the portrait of the poet that he promised for *Endymion*. The sacrifice he had demanded in the meantime became too much. Isolated and unable to see past the darkness filling his window at night, John could not sleep. "The Wind is in a sulky fit," he wrote, "and I feel that it would be no bad thing to be the favorite of some Fairy, who would give one the power of seeing how our Friends got on, at a Distance."[46] But no sympathetic fairy was forthcoming, and when the wind was not menacing, the silence was deafening. John's threadbare patience wore through. What was the point of staying in solitary confinement if he could not write?

Within a week of his arrival, the poet had packed up his things and given notice to Mrs. Cook, the landlady, that he was leaving. If he had accomplished nothing else on the Isle of Wight, he had proved the Satanic logic that the mind is its own place and can make a heaven of hell, a hell of heaven. George was tied up "with Wilkinson's plan," but Tom would be free to join him.[47] With his younger brother as a companion, John would no longer have to face his maddening hopes and fears alone. Maybe they could return to Margate, maybe even rent their old rooms.

The act of being in motion once again stirred John's spirits. Quite likely, Mrs. Cook also felt some relief at the departure of the young man who had seemed so sad and so full of purpose. She wished him well, insisting that he take the portrait of Shakespeare: an eminently good-natured gesture from a woman who clearly had not been spoilt by the presence of the standing army, or anything else. John gratefully accepted the gift, which he then hung up wherever he went. Georgiana would make a pair of silk tassels to hang from its frame, and, when John finally stopped moving, George would hang it over his mantelpiece in Louisville, Kentucky.

Canterbury and Bo Peep

Although Endymion had been stalled in the glens and dales of Mount Latmos, once John and Tom settled back into their old routine at Margate, he at last spread his pinions. Whenever doubts about his project assailed him, John unfolded his latest letter from Haydon. Like his speech, the artist's prose was fierce and convincing. He assured the young aspirant to the laurel that his fears were normal, not prophetic, "nothing more than the over eager anxieties of a great Spirit stretched beyond its strength, and then relapsing for a time to languid inefficiency—Every man of great views, is at times thus tormented." John should pick up where he left off, "without hesitation or fear."[48]

The painter agreed that, given John's preoccupation with his own loneliness on the Isle of Wight, John had been right to leave the island. He understood the severity of purpose that measures time only by what is achieved, and he urged John to place his trust in God, a higher genius who never fails artists in need. Whenever Haydon solicited divine assistance, he always arose "with a refreshed fury—an iron clenched firmness, and chrystal piety of feeling," which sent him "streaming on with a repulsive power against the troubles of life." From the magnetic, his metaphor turned military, as Haydon compared himself to "a cannon shot, darting through feathers." John could not help wondering, not altogether unseriously, whether Shakespeare might be *his* "good Genius."[49]

Like a genuine chameleon poet, John replied to Haydon from Margate with a bravado and hyperbolic rhetoric similar to the artist's: "Let Fame, which all hunt after in their Lives, / Live register'd upon our brazen tombs," he wrote, invoking the speech by the Spanish King Ferdinand at the opening of *Love's Labour's Lost*. Entombed side by side, Keats and Haydon would be "heirs of all eternity." Also adopting his friend's tendency for mixed metaphor, John added: "The Trumpet of Fame is as a tower of Strength."[50]

By contrast, when addressing Hunt, John's prose was shifting and unsettled, almost as if the writer were talking to himself. By this point, the poet had come to agree with Haydon that Hunt had delusional tendencies and that he no longer merited respect as one of the elect. "Perhaps it is a self delusion to say so—but I think I could not be deceived in the Manner that Hunt is—may I die tomorrow if I am to be," John vowed. "There is no greater Sin after the 7 deadly than to flatter oneself into an idea of being a great Poet—or one of those beings who are privileged to wear out their Lives in the pursuit of Honor."[51] Hunt's financial dependence on Shelley seemed to him a form of slavery. Financially insecure himself, he projected his fears onto Hunt, and swore not to turn out the same way.

Such was the status of his thinking when, in the second week of May 1817, John received word from George that Wilkinson's plan had failed. He had been counting on the return of his money, perhaps with some profit, but he now seemed to be sliding down the same slippery slope of financial insolvency that stigmatized Hunt. John recognized his own "Maidenhead with respect to money Matters," and he began to fear, as he told George, that "Money Troubles are to follow us up for some time to come perhaps for always." Before long, those "Pelican duns" (relatives of Lear's pelican daughters) would be at him too.[52] He would have to write to his publishers for an advance on the very poem in which he had lost faith.

George also felt great disappointment in the business failure, but he didn't sink into despondency. He recognized and accepted the risk that came with aiming at anything higher than a clerk's life. Even had he made partner in Abbey's firm, George told himself, he could not have produced any material change in his, or his brothers', standard of living. "If I had a starting point I am confident I should have succeeded in England," he later told Charles Dilke, "but my position was such that I could not distinguish in what way my exertions could be beneficially applied."[53] While John's connections could help *him* to advance on the road he had chosen, George lacked the infrastructure of support by which money makes money. The only hope he had of breaking free from the wage mill was to gamble. This would not be the last time he would gamble and lose.

Margate meanwhile was no longer the same. John had lost his taste for the salty sea air, and after the Isle of Wight, the place now seemed to him a sad, "treeless affair."[54] Like his hero, he needed to keep going. Canterbury was closer to London than Carisbrooke, and it had equally spectacular ruins, as well as trees. So the brothers left the beach for the city haunted by the spirit of Chaucer. While Tom explored the castle grounds, the great Gothic church, and the old Roman walls (made more interesting, perhaps, for his

time at Margate reading Plutarch), John worked to complete the first book
of *Endymion*.

Wherein lies happiness? the question appears toward the end of the first
book. The poet concludes that one must seek for happiness not in worldly
splendor, but in "that which becks/Our ready minds to fellowship divine,/A fellowship with essence." Like Endymion, John was fixed on a
"higher hope"—one that was "of too wide, too rainbow-large a scope,/To
fret at myriads of earthly wrecks." Despite its magnificence, the ancient cathedral city and its great ruined castle captured his imagination less than
the moon and the stars. He had not been in Canterbury long before he
brought the first book of *Endymion* to a close and felt that it was time, once
more, to move on. He could see the writing on the wall, however, and knew
that he would not have the poem finished by the end of the summer: Shelley would win.

John had heard—perhaps from the Mathew sisters, perhaps from Haydon, perhaps from another source—about the quaint coastal hamlet of
Bo Peep, tucked away by the sea near Hastings. The place was bucolic, but
Bo Peep also had a more dubious reputation. *Little Bo Peep has lost her sheep,
and can't tell where to find them.* Wool smugglers had been distributing wool
in contraband trade with London from the cove by the village of Bo Peep
ever since the days of Old England. Indeed, had the shepherdess of the
nursery rhyme sought her lost sheep in the secret drops, or hiding places, in
the dark labyrinth of caves and tunnels surrounding the cove, she might
have found them.

Haydon had fond memories of days spent at Bo Peep, bathing, shooting gulls, and dining at the fifteenth-century pub in 1814. At the time, the
Martello Towers, part of a larger structure of military fortifications erected
against the threat of a Napoleonic invasion, had been full of wounded soldiers from Spain. One "desperate rifleman" wrapped in flannel sitting next
to him on the coach was particularly hard to forget: "He was spare, pale,
haggard, keen, and talked all the way."[55] Now, the towers across from the
village stood empty, an unattractive blotch on the pastoral landscape.

Bo Peep might have seemed an ideal respite from the exertion of com-
pleting a thousand lines of verse, and perhaps a good place also to gather
material for the next thousand. Rather than wearing himself out with more
traveling, Tom could take the stagecoach back to Hampstead, and John,
having regained his strength, would rejoin his brothers before long. But,
O sovereign power of love! O grief! O balm! As the opening line of Book II

of *Endymion* suggests, John found something at Bo Peep that he did not expect.

Isabella Jones—beautiful, cultured, and on holiday in Hastings with an aristocratic elderly Irishman not her husband—aroused feelings in the poet that he had not experienced in previous flirtations. She was intrigued by the passionate, original youth, and he found himself entranced, if not exactly in love. Isabella might not have been what society would have called a Woman of Quality, but she was a woman of taste, wit, and intelligence. Whatever form her romance with Keats may have taken in the spring of 1817, by the time John returned to Hampstead, they had "warmed" together—one can only imagine on the windy bluffs, or out on the beach at night.[56]

John's poem "Hush, hush, tread softly," suggests that such warming may have also taken place behind the back of Isabella's consort, Donat O'Callaghan:

> Hush, hush, tread softly, hush, hush, my dear,
>   All the house is asleep, but we know very well
> That the jealous, the jealous old baldpate may hear,
>   Though you've padded his night-cap, O sweet Isabel.
>   Though your feet are more light than a fairy's feet,
>   Who dances on bubbles where brooklets meet—
> Hush, hush, tread softly, hush, hush, my dear,
> For less than a nothing the jealous can hear.

The poet here adapts the Renaissance Italian verse form of *ottava rima,* used in romance. John would use *ottava rima* again in his poem "Isabella; or, The Pot of Basil," which also suggests the influence of Isabella Jones. Here, the stanza addressed to "sweet Isabel," veers out of the standard pattern of alternating rhymes in the *ottava rima* stanza (*a-b-a-b-a-b-c-c*) into couplets two lines early (*a-b-a-b-c-c-a-a*), or as elsewhere in the poem (*a-b-a-b-c-c-d-d*). The change emphasizes the fifth and sixth lines of the stanza, which, in this case, echo the rhythm of lightly tripping feet, metrical as well as thematic: "Though your feet are more light than a fairy's feet, / Who dances on bubbles where brooklets meet . . ." In the spirit of Boccaccio (one of whose tales Keats narrates in "Isabella"), this lyric features the antics of youthful sexuality against the backdrop of aged wealth.

Bo Peep was a better place for hiding than for seeking. The smugglers knew this, and it seems John did too. As the Fool in *King Lear* sings to the king about his deceiving daughters: "Then they for sudden joy did weep/And I for sorrow sung,/That such a king should play bo-peep,/And go the fools among." In Keats's poetry, as in Shakespeare's, Bo Peep is associated with secrecy, and thus also, perchance, deception.

Another graceful lyric written around the time of John's trip to Bo Peep begins likewise with a repeated command—not "Hush, hush" this time, but "Hither, hither." In both cases, the command begins with what linguists would call a phantom consonant, which sounds, or reads, like a whisper:

Hither, hither, love,
   'Tis a shady mead;
Hither, hither, love,
   Let us feed and feed.

Hither, hither, sweet,
   'Tis a cowslip bed;
Hither, hither, sweet,
   'Tis with dew bespread.

Hither, hither, dear,
   By the breath of life,
Hither, hither, dear,
   Be the summer's wife.

Though one moment's pleasure
   In one moment flies,
Though the passion's treasure
   In one moment dies;

Yet it has not pass'd—
   Thing how near, how near;
And while it doth last,
   Think how dear, how dear.

Hither, hither, hither,
   Love this boon has sent;
If I die and wither
   I shall die content.

This poem is composed in ballad meter, the verse form popular in nursery rhyme, and here specifically balladic half measure. The light meter offers relief from the heroic meter of *Endymion* and also gives a sense of the lightness the poet seems to have felt in Bo Peep. The lyric iambic trimeter whistles away the crushing weight of responsibility he had been feeling in his attempt to write epic. Like several of his most beautiful songs, this poem did not appear in print during John's lifetime. But George held onto the manuscript, and many years later, in 1834, when he met the American poet John Howard Payne, he copied it into his scrapbook. "There is no title given to the scrap, no explanation of its bearing," Payne noted of the poem, which he found to be full of "wild beauty."[57]

Like the nymph who appears to Endymion and calls out to him, "Youth!/Too long, alas, hast thou starv'd on the ruth,/The bitterness of love," Isabella Jones might have pitied the poet in his youthful quest for greatness. But recognizing the distance he had yet to traverse, she would not stay to quench his desire. John would not "die content," as he imagines himself doing at the end of "Hither, hither, love." Instead, with his mood lifted at Bo Peep, he would head back to spend the summer with his brothers. By early June, they would be reunited beneath the old elms at the Bentleys' home in Hampstead.

Oxford

Wentworth Place became a second home for the Keats brothers in the summer of 1817. The Dilkes' maid pinned up clothes to dry among the roses and butterflies, and their dog, Boxer, ran around pestering "old Philips" the gardener. John sang the praises of Maria Dilke's vegetables—her cucumbers, cabbages, onions, radishes, beets, French beans—and pleaded guilty to a "palate-passion" for her husband's game: "the breast of a Partridge, the back of a hare, the backbone of a grouse, the wing and side of a Pheasant and a Woodcock *passim*." His culinary pleasures may have been heightened by his memory of tasteless provisions on the Isle of Wight, where Mrs. Cook, despite her promising name, failed to provide "wholesome food." Dilke himself was a bit of a bon vivant. His kitchen had a pickling tub and wine bins. The potboy delivered beer, and after dinner Dilke passed around the snuffbox, whose "gentlemanly scent" pleased his guests more than his wife.[58] Maria Dilke played the piano, and the company danced and sang.

Tom was supposed to avoid the damp night air, but John and George also spent time that summer with the Reynolds family in Little Britain. John Reynolds had four sisters: Jane was four years older than John, Marianne was George's age, Eliza (or "Lizzy") was eighteen like Tom, and Charlotte was only fifteen. Perhaps intuiting that Shakespeare's heroines often seemed more alive to John Keats than the women around him, Jane kept his attention by debating the relative merits of characters like Juliet and Cleopatra. Despite her beauty, however, John saw Jane in a sisterly light, and Marianne struck him as too plump to be attractive. He entertained the younger sisters with poetry. For Eliza, he composed a sonnet beginning, "Spenser, a jealous honorer of thine," and he set the lyrics of "Hush, hush, tread softly" to the music of a Spanish air that Charlotte would play on the piano.[59]

Charlotte Cox Reynolds, the fussy and bustling mother, presided over the "domestic homely round," as she put it: "rise, breakfast, Dine, drink Tea Sup & talk incessantly, & then to bed again." Her husband, George, usually fell into the background on social occasions, but at least he was "happy & contented with his lot," or so he *ought* to be with such a "*better half.*" The poet Thomas Hood, who later married Jane Reynolds, left a lively portrait of the matriarch ordering about her girls, her husband, and her three maids (Mary, Ann, and Lottie) at a dinner party attended by Marianne's future husband, H. G. Green:

Mary, I believ'd you quick
But you're as deaf as any beedle;
See where you have left the plates,
You've an eye, and so's a needle.
Why an't Anne behind the door,
Standing ready with her dishes?
No one ever had such maids
Always thwarting all my wishes,
Marianne set up that child—
And where's her pinafore—call Mary,
The frock I made her will be spoil'd—
Now Lizzy don't be so contrary,
Hand round the bread—"Thank God for what—"
It's done to rags! How wrong of Ann now,—
The dumplings too are hard as lead
And plates stone-cold—but that's her plan now—
Mary, a knock—now Hood take that—

Or go without—Why, George, you're wanted,
Where is that Lotte? Call her down
She knows there's no white wine decanted—
Put to the door, we always dine
In public—
Jane take that cover off the greens;
Our earthenware they play the deuce to;
Here's Mr. Green without a fork—
And I've no plate—but that I'm used to.—[60]

The original upon whom this comic soliloquy was based would later turn her critical scrutiny on George Keats—his plans for making a living, his marital intentions—but for the present she confined herself to managing her family, her servants, and her old, battered, green-eyed cat. As John depicted the last of these in his sonnet "To Mrs. Reynolds's Cat," the creature was full of mischief, stealing tidbits of food and entering the lists of local tournaments with other alley cats on a glass-bottled wall. With his "wheezy asthma" and "nicked off" tail, he can still be found chasing rats and mice, and licking his dainty wrists in John's sonnet, first published by Hood in 1830.

While John discussed Shakespeare with Jane, George entertained Marianne. "She was a favorite with me," he later admitted. "I always had a particular liking for Marianne." He thought her "worthy of almost any man" and, when he later heard that she had become engaged to H. G. Green, he hoped that her fiancé's fortunes would "enable him to pluck her from her solitary virgin stalk and engraft her on an enduring stem of never failing *Green*."[61] Competing with George for the attentions of Marianne at the time was John Reynolds's friend, Benjamin Bailey, an Oxford student preparing to take up a position in the Church of England.

Bailey had met Reynolds on vacation in Devonshire. At Slade House, near Sidmouth, they had spent time with the "Sisterhood of Slade," a social clique consisting of three sisters, Mary, Sarah, and Thomasine Leigh, the sisters' cousin Maria Pearse, and Eliza Powell Drewe, whom Reynolds would marry in 1822. The young women clipped locks of hair as keepsakes, and made watercolor miniatures and silhouettes of the young men. Reynolds and Bailey filled their commonplace books with lyrics. Thomasine titled the eighth volume of her collection, *Bailey's and Reynolds's Diamonds of Fancy and Feeling*.[62]

Although Bailey still had "now & then a few & far-between-angel-like visits of poetical feelings," once he met John Keats, he would count on him to fulfill any "golden hopes" he may have had with regard to poetry. He had read John's recently published *Poems* and considered him "a Poet of rare and original genius." In his verse, there was "something so etherial . . . that it pierces the cloud." Bailey's melancholy dispersed whenever he entered Keats's "fairy world." John in turn respected the scholarly devotion of the divinity student. Bailey was of a serious—one might say morally self-righteous—disposition. He adored "the Goddess of Truth," whom he claimed to "burn after like a man in a fever." He had a vague, Platonic notion that everything in existence was an image of the divine Logos, but he ultimately rested his faith in Jeremy Taylor, the Shakespeare of the Divines. His picture of the theologian showed him in an intimidating light, with eyes darting suspiciously to the side. John thought he looked "as if he were going to hit me a rap with a Book," and he teased Bailey for walking "in no grove but Jeremy Taylors." He imagined him courting Marianne Reynolds "with the Bible and Jeremy Taylor under his arm."[63] But Bailey stepped into John's life at just the right time.

The brothers had agreed that Tom needed a change of air greater than that which any English coastal town could provide, and since John still had half of his poem to complete, they decided that George would accompany Tom to Paris. Bailey suggested that the studious atmosphere of Oxford might be conducive to John's making progress on his poem, and in that he turned out to be right. He invited the poet to spend the rest of the summer vacation with him, and thus, in the second half of August, when the Reynolds family and the Dilkes went to Little Hampton, and his younger brothers went to France, John went to Oxford.

John Keats loved the academic ambience of the medieval university. He felt at home among the stately old buildings, with their Gothic spires and elaborate sundials. The residents walked the streets in cap and gown and seemed to converse as comfortably in Latin or Greek as in English. In a few playful stanzas, John portrayed the place as he found it in September 1817:

> The Gothic looks solemn,
>   The plain Doric column
> Supports an old bishop and crosier;
>   The mouldering arch,

Shaded o'er by a larch,
Stands next door to Wilson the Hosier.

Vicè—that is, by turns—
O'er pale faces mourns
The black tassell'd trencher and common-hat;
The chantry boy sings,
The steeple-bell rings,
And as for the Chancellor—*dominat.*

There are plenty of trees,
And plenty of ease,
And plenty of fat deer for parsons;
And when it is venison,
Short is the benison,—
Then each on a leg or thigh fastens.

From the chapel boy singing Mass for the souls of the departed, to the chancellor nodding after his midday meal in the college, the images in these stanzas addressed to Reynolds bespeak the pleasantly relaxed life that John led amid the ivory towers of Oxford for three weeks.

There, in Bailey's rooms overlooking the main quadrangle of Magdalen Hall, the poet dove, almost literally, into the third book of *Endymion,* which takes place in the aquatic world of the sea god, Glaucus. "Endymion and I are at the bottom of the Sea," John wrote to Jane and Marianne Reynolds. Recognizing the symbolic value of the plunge, he would later explain to James Hessey that in *Endymion* he had "leaped headlong into the Sea," thereby becoming "better acquainted with the Soundings, the quicksands, & the rocks, than if I had stayed upon the green shore, and piped a silly pipe, and took tea & comfortable advice."[64] He picked up his pace from the summer, and within two weeks he had completed nearly eight hundred lines of Book III.

Once he fulfilled his quota for the day, John would read his "submarine beauties" to Bailey, and the friends would go on an afternoon walk. Some days, they would explore the obscure corners of the campus; other days, the paths in the deer park. "This Oxford I have no doubt is the finest City in the world," John wrote to his sister. "It is full of old Gothic buildings— spires—towers—Quadrangles—Cloisters Groves." He marveled that such a densely built city could have so many clear streams, more than he had ever seen in one place—and more, he told John Reynolds, "than your eye lashes." Keats and Bailey christened one "particularly nice nest" in the marshes "Reynolds's Cove."[65]

Ever since his idyll by the sea at Bo Peep, John's poetry had become sexually charged. Bailey later condemned the "indelicacy" of certain passages of *Endymion* that seemed to display "that abominable principle of Shelley's—that *Sensual Love* is the principle of *things*."[66] Although Bailey could not defend the poem on moral grounds, he could divest himself of responsibility for a particularly offending passage in the second book, which had been written before John came to Oxford. "Alas!" moans Endymion, "will all this gush of feeling pass/Away in solitude? . . . Without an echo?" But, alas for Bailey, there *is* an echo, as a voice cries out, "Sweetest, here am I!" Endymion responds to the "doating cry," and the lovemaking that follows lasts for over a hundred lines.

The eroticism unleashed in the second book of *Endymion* turned out to be a prelude to a more unfortunate sexual encounter at Oxford. Symptoms of venereal disease confined the poet to his room for a couple of weeks after his return from the university town to Hampstead. They also pursued him through Scotland the next summer. "With respect to Women I think I shall be able to conquer my passions hereafter better than I have yet done," John would confide to Tom. The Reynolds sisters would worry that the disease John brought back from Oxford might have been related to Tom's illness, but as John wrote to Bailey, "you know more of the real Cause than they do." The physician, Dr. Solomon Sawrey, who treated John, had published *An Inquiry into Some of the Effects of the Venereal Poison on the Human Body* in 1802. He believed in the use of mercury as a medical treatment only in cases of venereal disease: "When it is clear that the complaint has a venereal cause we give mercury to cure it," Sawrey wrote; "But if we should be of opinion that its nature is not venereal we should of course omit it." In John's case, he did *not* omit it. Within a few weeks of seeing the doctor, John could report that the mercury had "corrected the Poison and improved my Health."[67]

On the first Thursday of October, Keats and Bailey took a slightly longer excursion, as they liked to do once a week, this time to Shakespeare's birthplace in Stratford-upon-Avon. Bailey reported that he and John had joined the "numbers numberless" who "literally blackened the walls" of Shakespeare's half-timbered home on Henley Street.[68] They also visited the

Holy Trinity Church, where the bard was baptized and buried. John admired the simplicity of the bust set between Corinthian columns on the wall above Shakespeare's grave.

Two allegorical figures adorned Shakespeare's coat of arms above his statue. On one side of the coat of arms, an allegorical figure of Labor clasps a spade. On the other side, Rest holds a torch and a skull. John had no reason, as yet, to imagine his brother George in the figure with the spade, prepared to turn up the soil. He might have had more reason, if less incentive, to see Tom in the grasp of everlasting Rest. Those things, however, came later. Now, having made his pilgrimage to the grave of the Swan of Stratford, John got off his winged horse and sat down behind some real ones on the stagecoach back to Hampstead.

Paris

George and Tom enjoyed themselves in Paris at least as much as their brother did in Oxford. George's letter to John, crosshatched, or written over at right angles, by a shorter one from Tom (as was the practice to save the cost of paper), described the many things the brothers had seen and done in France. The letter has since disappeared, but John summed up its contents in a playful catalogue of his brothers' adventures for their sister: "The French Meadows the trees the People the Towns the Churches, the Books the every thing . . . They have seen Cathedrals Manuscripts. Fountains, Pictures, Tragedy Comedy—with other things you may by chance meet with in this Country such a[s] Washerwomen, Lamplighters, Turnpikemen Fish Kettles, Dancing Masters, kettle drums, Sentry Boxes, Rocking Horses &c and, now they have taken them over set of boxing gloves . . ."[69] He did not mention the gambling halls—or the brothels—in either city.

John Scott, editor of the *Champion* (which had favorably reviewed John's first book of poems), published an account of a trip he had taken from the coast of Normandy to Paris along the same route as the Keats brothers three years earlier. The first thing Scott noticed in approaching Normandy from the English Channel were "fishwomen" in fantastic costumes: tight gray jackets over bulging red petticoats, with large gold-hoop earrings. "'For the love of Heaven,' cried an English admiral's lady, 'look at that creature in the red petticoat!'" Yet, the landscape looked much like that of England, if without hedgerows. *There he found / That the ground / Was as hard / That a yard / Was as long, / That a song / Was as merry, / That a cherry / Was as red . . . As in England . . .*[70]

John Keats never particularly liked Scott. After the New Year, having heard Leigh Hunt claim that he was "nearly sure" the series of essays "On the Cockney School of Poetry" was by Scott, John would write, "so you are right Tom!" Tom was not right, however, for Scott was not the author of the articles that he himself read with abhorrence. And Scott later lost his life defending the victims of *Blackwood's* in the *Champion*. "I know you don't like John Scott," Charles Brown wrote to John in 1820, "but he is doing a thing that tickles me to the heart's core, and you will like to hear of it, if you have any revenge in your composition."[71]

By the time Brown was writing, a former contributor to *Blackwood's,* Peter George Patmore, had provided Scott with damaging information about the staff of the magazine, which Scott then turned to advantage: "By some means (crooked enough I dare say) he has got possession of one of Blackwood's gang, who has turned King's evidence, and month after month he belabours them with the most damning facts that can be conceived;—if they are indeed facts, I know not how the rogues can stand up against them." To defend his honor, John Gibson Lockhart challenged Scott to a duel, but Scott refused to fight until the critic either took responsibility for his anonymous attacks or else denounced them. Lockhart's second, Jonathan Henry Christie, then insulted Scott, thus compelling him by the same code of honor to fight. On a cold February day in 1821, Christie put an end to *Blackwood's* nemesis with a pistol. Scott fell on the fields of Chalk Farm near Hampstead Heath, and expired three days after John Keats. Or, as John Taylor wrote, Keats died "three Days before his Defender Scott." Joseph Severn would call Scott one of the poet's "able defenders."[72]

Neither Tom nor George could have predicted any of this when they visited Scott at the Hôtel Mayence in Paris. They had crossed the English Channel, en route from Dover to Normandy, in the usual fashion. The scene of departure was chaotic. Two years after they made the crossing, the (pseudonymous) Thomas Brown left a portrait of the inns at Dover in *The Englishman in Paris*:

> I was attacked, assailed, beset, and bewildered by intruders and applicants
> of all casts, sizes, complexions, and vocations—rival masters of packet
> boats, rival boatmen, porters, custom-house officers, waiters, ostlers, *et*

cetera, sine fine; and every one had a demand: I thought I should not escape with a shilling in my pocket from these *anthropophagi,* by whom I was near being devoured alive. "The Swift, Sir," said one, "going to sail directly";—"Veri good vessel," exclaimed a Frenchman, in broken English, "mine is a veri good [ship], *faste* sailor, you SHALL go vit me *if you please,* vi *must* be over vit dis vind in *too* hour."

Across the Channel, the brothers were the ones struggling to communicate. Based on their experience, John complained to Fanny Keats that "the only end to be gained in acquiring French—is the immense accomplishment of speaking it—it is none at all—a most lamentable mistake indeed." Of course, the French language was to blame: it was the worst "ever spoken since the jabbering in the Tower of Babel." George and Tom, like other Englishmen in France, felt "a mighty preference for every thing English."[73]

By the time they arrived on the coast of Normandy, the troops had been disbanded, but there were still a number of ragtag veterans in battered overcoats and cocked hats lingering at the port towns. The streets of Dieppe where the packet boats landed were narrow, dark, and winding; the houses were tall and more elaborate than the Georgian homes back in England. They had "projecting spouts, curious signs, and elegant cornices," and came in "all sorts of shapes,—ends and fronts, pointed roofs, balconies, and clustering chimnies."[74] The paint on the doorways, ravaged by coastal weather, was peeling, and the enormous windows opened like eyes. Moss spread like a venerable beard over the slate tiles of the rooftops. The crazy buildings almost seemed alive.

To get to Paris on the stage route that passed through Rouen, travelers could purchase a carriage, but most took a stagecoach known as a diligence. The postilions had a reputation for speeding and zigzagging on roads as zany as the houses. The old feudal estates had been broken up during the French Revolution—too recently to bear remembrance—and violence still scarred the land. Most châteaux were in ruins. Children played in overgrown gardens by roofless, windowless hulks.

Yet, when George and Tom arrived, it was harvest season. The orchards in the valley between Dieppe and Rouen abounded with ripe apples and pears. Wheat, rye, and clover covered the fields, and the vineyards glowed an autumnal reddish-yellow. Dancers in the countryside still kept time to the fiddle in wooden shoes; nor had conditions at the coaching inns changed much since Laurence Sterne's Parson Yorick took a diligence to Paris in *A Sentimental Journey through France and Italy* (1768), besieged any time he stopped by beggars hoping the quintessentially English parson might spare a few sous.

Approaching Rouen, the road evened out and, within a mile of the city, was lined with regular rows of trees. Lanterns swung from ropes tied to the lower branches of the arch covering the boulevard. In the center of town, people gathered around jugglers and ballad singers; in the cafés, they took part in spirited debate. The beaux paraded, practicing their gallantry and bowing extravagantly to the ladies. Street vendors, much as they do today, displayed books, magazines, and pornography.

At Saint-Denis, just north of the medieval wall of Paris, more signs of violence remained. At the mausoleum of the Basilica of Saint-Denis, angry crowds had dug up the remains of former kings and queens and desecrated the bones, reducing the skull of Henry IV, for instance, to a football. François Girardon, architect of Versailles, had sculpted elaborate bas-reliefs for King Louis XIV on the Porte Saint-Denis that led through the old city wall into Paris, but Napoleon had replaced the inscription in honor of the Sun King with his own name; Bourbon restorers had scratched it out, but they had left the graffiti "Liberté" and "Egalité" in sympathy with the Revolution.[75]

Paris, too, was a palimpsest. Near the Louvre, exquisitely cut lawns adorned with statues, urns, and fountains spread out from the Tuileries Palace, seat of French monarchs since the day when hungry mobs dragged Marie Antoinette and her astonished husband, King Louis XVI, back from Versailles to Paris. At the Place Vendôme, the statue of Louis XIV had ceded ground to Napoleon's triumphal pillar, encased in Austrian cannon metal. Winged horses flanked the gate opening into the Place Louis XV, where the guillotine had done its bloody work.

Nearby, at Hôtel Mayence on the Rue St. Honoré, John Scott and his wife, Caroline, were in mourning. Their beloved son, Paul, had just died of a fever at the age of eight. Scott published his elegy, *The House of Mourning,* in 1817 with Taylor and Hessey:

Our little boy is dead!
Yes,—we have lost that gentle, faithful child,
Whom doating tenderness could never spoil,

So good he was in heart, so undefil'd!
He to his mother never turn'd his head,
But love, submission, and content to smile.

And to his wearied father no one knows
How much he was:—this let me now declare.
The garden of our hopes has lost its rose;
Our path leads no where;—all the view is bare!

On a hill in Père Lachaise Cemetery, Paul Conaghi's funeral pillar bore an epitaph from the Italian poet Gabriello Chiabrera. The sorrowful parents had Wordsworth's translation engraved in stone: "Not without heavy grief of heart did we,/Sojourning homeless in this foreign land,/Deposit in the hollow of the tomb/Our gentle child, most tenderly beloved./Around his early grave let flowers rise,/In memory of that fragrance which was once/From his mild manners quietly exhaled."[76] It was a dismal time for the Scotts, and this may have been why Tom Keats gave them what may have been his most valued possession.

Tom was proud of his notebook full of his brother's poems, which he often carried with him. In it he had copied (as he titled them) "Imitation of Spenser," written when John was eighteen; his "Sonnet to My Brother George," with his signature; "Calidore" and its introduction beginning, "Lo! I must tell a tale of chivalry"; his "Sonnet to Solitude"; his thank-you poem to the Mathew sisters, titled "On receiving a curious Shell and a copy of verses"; his "Sonnet on Looking into Chapman's Homer"; his sonnet "Great Spirits on Earth Are Sojourning" (whose ending Wordsworth had praised), which John also signed; Leigh Hunt's "Sonnet to Hampstead," signed by the author; John's "Sonnet: Written to His Brother Tom on His Birthday"; his "Sonnet to a Lady: Nymph of the Downward Smile and Sidelong Glance," which John had signed in December 1816; his sonnet on the Bow Bells titled "Written in Disgust of Vulgar Superstition"; a sonnet to the brothers' friend Charles Wells, and two others that are often anthologized: "To One Who Has Been Long in City Pent" and "Had I a Man's Fair Form." Caroline Scott, the bereaved mother, was sufficiently impressed that upon her return to London she sought out the company of the poet.[77] The florid calligraphy on the title page, dating the volume "July 30, 1814," also reveals artistic gifts.

Besides the Scotts, George and Tom also visited the cafés, casinos, restaurants, and shops—perhaps the baths and bordellos as well—in the galleries of the Palais-Royal. Upon entering the gambling houses on the second floor, visitors would be stripped of their hats and walking sticks and conducted into the back rooms, which contained the card and billiard tables. John Scott vividly described the scene at these "hellish tables": "Half-pay officers, private soldiers, clerks, and ex-employés, are seen in a desperate contention with treacherous fortune:—the expression of the face, as the trembling hand puts down the piece of money, is awful;—one piece follows another,—gold is succeeded by silver, and, from five franc coins, the unfortunate wretch is reduced to the risk of a single franc." Although Charles Brown could not remember the exact amount that the poet's brothers lost at the gaming tables of the Palais-Royal, he was sure that it was "far too much for their circumstances."[78]

The restaurants were another good place to lose money. In these Parisian "temples of luxury" (as Scott called them), one would be "almost struck back by their glare of decoration and enjoyment. Ladies and gentlemen in their colours, and statues in their whiteness,—and busy waiters, and painted walls, and sparkling delicacies of every kind, are mingled, and repeated, and extended in appearance, to infinity, by numerous mirrors, which add vastness to elegance." The menus, as large as newspapers, featured an array of culinary specialties for which the French were famed across the Channel. Within a few short weeks, George and Tom had disposed of their money and were ready to put an end to their "pleasure jaunt to Paris," as Brown called it.[79]

When the three brothers reconvened in Hampstead in the autumn of 1817, John had the third book of *Endymion* to show for his time, along with the disease of the *débauché*. George and Tom, with no money left, had their memories. Tom's health was no better, and George was still unemployed. Their sister was still trapped across the fields in Walthamstow, remote and lonely. But when the fraternal circle closed once again beneath the falling leaves of the old elms, they forgot all their troubles temporarily.

Box Hill and Teignmouth

John had left the medical profession, but he had enough training to tell that Tom's condition was starting to look terminal. With winter approaching, he and his brothers discussed the possibility of Tom's returning to the Continent. Richard Woodhouse had lived for a couple of years in Spain and Portugal, and he may have recommended Lisbon as a good place for an invalid. It was less expensive than France, and it had one of the mildest climates in the Mediterranean. But Tom would need a companion, and John had another book of *Endymion* to complete before the end of the year. George was glad to be back in England and would not look forward to another extended trip to Europe. The brothers cast about for a plan.

John in the meantime discovered that he had become disillusioned with his literary set. Hunt was still "infatuated" with Shelley, so much so in fact that when Hunt's fifth child was born on Lisson Grove North, where the Cockney King had moved after Marlow, he named him Percy Bysshe Shelley Hunt. Benjamin Haydon had moved next-door to Hunt, an arrangement that left them, needless to say, "jealous Neighbours." Shelley continued to torment Haydon on the topic of religion, and Hunt walked up and down Haydon's studio criticizing the faces in the crowd of his stalled magnum opus, *Christ's Entry into Jerusalem.* Where John had hoped to find the sustenance of friendship, he found only corrosive infighting: "every Body seems at Loggerheads."[80]

Haydon dragged John into the circle of gossip and bickering by warning him not to show the manuscript of *Endymion* to Hunt. Hunt, he claimed, would take credit for the best passages and disclaim the rest. Indeed, when Reynolds ran into Hunt at the theater and mentioned to him that John was approaching his goal of four thousand lines, Hunt exclaimed, "Ah! . . . had it not been for me they would have been 7000!"[81] The implication that John's verse was inflated seemed to discount everything that he had gone through to dredge up as much poetry as he had. If Hunt was so free in his criticism with John's best friend, the poet wondered, what might he say to others? Did Hunt and Shelley sit around making fun of him? O thought too horrible to imagine . . .

John was still smarting from his walk on Hampstead Heath with the taller and more socially privileged poet, who had spurned an education that Keats would have loved. While enrolled at University College, Oxford, Shelley had distributed a pamphlet espousing atheism, and, refusing to renounce it, was expeditiously expelled. Keats's encounters with Shelley always made him feel "what it is to be under six foot and not a lord."[82]

Yet Shelley knew that critics could be cruel, and he risked offending in order that John not risk his career. Recognizing talent, and with compassion for a fellow poet in the harsh world of periodical reviewing, he had tried to give John the benefit of experience when he urged him not to publish his first book of poems. But John took offense. Now that his first book had met with neglect—the worst form of censure—he had to admit that Shelley had been right. Deep down, he had his own doubts about *Endymion.*

He turned, as always, to the consolations of fraternity. The fraternal circle had expanded to include James (Jem or Jemmy) Rice, who had met Bailey and Reynolds on vacation in Devonshire. Rice invited John and his brothers to Saturday-night card games at his apartment at 50 Poland Street, near Piccadilly Circus. He served brandy, and John learned slang: hard drinking was "dying scarlet," good wine "a pretty tipple," conceiving a child "knocking out an apple," and stopping at a tavern (as it remains today), "hanging out."[83] Jem Rice—dapper in dress, Swiftian in humor—was by all accounts an amiable fellow. But he, too, was battling consumption.

Everywhere John looked, it seemed, the clammy hand of disease was gripping those he cared about. In just over a couple of weeks Tom would turn eighteen, and John had to wonder: Would his younger brother make it to *his* age? Would he even live as long as George? Jane Reynolds also was sick, and her fevered face disturbed the poet. In a few stanzas addressed to Sorrow, which John sent to Jane on October 31, his twenty-second birthday, he seems already in mourning. As included in the final book of *Endymion,* the verses read:

"O Sorrow
     Why dost borrow
The natural hue of health, from vermeil lips?—
     To give maiden blushes
     To the white rose bushes?
Or is't thy dewy hand the daisy tips?

"O Sorrow,
     Why dost borrow
The lustrous passion from a falcon-eye?—
     To give the glow-worm light?
     Or, on a moonless night,
To tinge, on syren shores, the salt sea-spry?

"O Sorrow,
    Why dost borrow
The mellow ditties from a mourning tongue?—
    To give at evening pale
    Unto the nightingale,
That thou mayst listen the cold dews among?

"O Sorrow,
    Why dost borrow
Heart's lightness from the merriment of May?—
    A lover would not tread
    A cowslip on the head,
Though he should dance from eve till peep of day—
    Nor any drooping flower
    Held sacred for thy bower,
Wherever he may sport himself and play.

"To Sorrow,
    I bade good-morrow,
And thought to leave her far away behind;
    But cheerly, cheerly,
    She loves me dearly;
She is so constant to me, and so kind:
    I would deceive her
    And so leave her,
But ah! she is so constant and so kind."

The combination of red cheek and pale visage to indicate death's fatal attraction is one the poet would use again in that haunting ballad, "La Belle Dame sans Merci." By then, the "dewy hand" of death that would soon claim his younger brother would have him, too, in its thrall. Poisoned by mercury, surrounded by sickness, having lost faith in his chances for success in this world, it was Keats who would teach a later generation of Victorian poets to aestheticize death.

He began the fourth book of *Endymion* with an invocation to a muse sympathetic to sentimental poets and others suffering those nervous disorders known collectively in the eighteenth century as the "English malady"—spleen, vapors, melancholy, lowness of spirits, and other hypochondriacal and hysterical complaints. "Great Muse," the poet cries, "thou know'st what prison,/Of flesh and bone, curbs, and confines, and frets/Our spirit's wings: despondency besets/Our pillows; and the fresh to-morrow morn/Seems to give forth its light in very scorn/Of our dull, uninspired, snail-paced lives." The noble natures that John had once admired had shown the weakness that adheres to all flesh. The world now seemed to contain "no quiet nothing but teasing and snubbing and vexation."[84] He concluded his address to the melancholy English Muse with a humble confession: "I move to the end in lowliness of heart." Without inspiration or hope, he was limping, doggedly, to the end.

By November 18, Tom's eighteenth birthday, Portugal had come to seem impractical. The cold weather had arrived, and with it danger to Tom's chance of survival. In the medical wisdom of the day, different "airs" were thought to have different effects on the body. Charles Brown later summed up the situation facing the brothers when he said that Tom's "ill state of health required a mild air." Sea air was supposed to be more temperate than inland air, and Rice, Reynolds, and Bailey had all spoken highly of Devonshire. Winters there were supposed to be warmer than elsewhere in England, and Teignmouth, sheltered by bluffs from the east wind that blew down the English Channel, was said to be particularly mild. One local guide praised "the life-giving and altogether unrivalled climate" of the town at the mouth of the Teign, which it boasted was "visited by the most genial airs only."[85]

Winter would be too chilly for Tom to take advantage of any of the sixteen bathing machines in operation at Teignmouth in 1817, but the town also had steam-driven indoor baths. Baths, like airs, were specialized provinces of medical knowledge. Dr. William Turton, a physician at Teignmouth, a specialist in consumption, and a connoisseur of the subtle element, was also a specialist in baths. In *A Treatise on Cold and Hot Baths: With Directions for Their Application in Various Diseases* (1803), Turton had written: "General directions for bathing to the invalid it is impossible to give, as they must be governed by a multitude of circumstances which can only be appreciated by a careful examination of existing appearances, and a knowledge of the causes of previous indisposition."[86] If Dr. Turton knew as much about airs as he did about baths, perhaps he was the right doctor for Tom.

A few days after Tom's birthday on November 18, 1817, therefore, John left Tom in the care of George and got off the stagecoach at Dorking, a small coaching town nestled between the Greensand Hills and the North

Downs on the old Roman road that ran southwest from London. John still had five hundred more lines of verse to go before reaching a goal that had once been a "great end" but that had since become an uninspired, snail-paced journey, made in lowliness of heart. While his brothers traveled to Devonshire, John followed the River Mole about three or four miles through fields, woods, and farms to Burford Bridge. There, he found a room overlooking the gardens at the Fox and Hounds, a Renaissance inn at the base of the path that led up Box Hill. "I like this place very much," he wrote. "There is Hill & Dale and a little River."[87] On his first evening there, he rushed up the seven hundred feet to the top of the mountain. Unlike Jane Austen's matchmaking heroine Emma, Keats experienced Box Hill by night, and in the chill air of late November—away from the fashionable Regency picnickers, who in nice weather came to enjoy the picturesque views from the hill covered with box trees.

In *Endymion* Keats shared the narrative structure of the marriage plot with Jane Austen, but in channeling his title character, he was pursuing a dreamier ideal. "His Endymion is not a Greek shepherd, loved by a Grecian goddess," quipped the *Blackwood's* critic. "He is merely a young Cockney rhymester, dreaming a phantastic dream at the full of the moon." True: insofar as John was born in the Cockney section of London and produced a rhymed poem involving a fantasy of the moon, "Z," for all his snobbery, was correct. And at the end of the poem, Endymion does dissolve with the moon goddess, Cynthia, into the heavens: "And so, like many other romances, terminates the 'Poetic Romance' of Johnny Keats, in a patched-up wedding."[88] But John imagined this wedding as a sublime, ghostly affair—far removed from the marriage market that Austen so skillfully depicts.

Before disappearing into the heavens, Endymion kisses his sister, Peona, goodbye. He has gained experience, while she, like the poet's sister, Fanny, has longer to remain in the world of innocence. In the final line of the poem, we see her heading "Home through the gloomy wood in wonderment." Home, that is, to the idyllic world the siblings had to leave at the start of the poem, so that Endymion could pursue his dream. "What the imagination seizes as Beauty must be truth," John wrote from Burford Bridge on November 22, "whether it existed before or not—for I have the same Idea of all our Passions as of Love[:] they are all in their sublime, creative of essential Beauty."[89] That which the quester pursues, and seizes, as beauty must be real.

John brought only three books with him to Burford Bridge. One of these was a volume of Shakespeare's poems. "I neer found so many beauties in the sonnets," he wrote to Reynolds: "they seem to be full of fine things said unintentionally—in the intensity of working out conceits—Is this to be borne?" He was joking that Shakespeare had left him nothing to say, but in Shakespeare's seventeenth sonnet he found an epigraph for his poem: "The stretched metre of an antique song."[90] He had certainly stretched the meter as far as it could go, and only three lines after his thousand-line goal for the last book of *Endymion,* he ended his antique song.

John had completed his poem by the end of the year, but rather than joining his brothers in Teignmouth, he returned to London and threw himself into the social whirl of the holidays. He went to parties and "hung out" with the likes of Horace Smith and John Wolcot, the satirists. He met the poet-cum-novelist Amelia Opie, and the diarist Henry Crabb Robinson. He attended a dinner party with the painters John Landseer and Peter De Wint, and visited the "Land of the Harpsicols" at the home of Vincent Novello. Mary Novello, the composer's youngest daughter who later married Charles Cowden Clarke, depicted the scene: "Keats, with his picturesque head, leaning against the instrument, one foot raised on his knee and smoothed beneath his hands; Leigh Hunt, with his jet-black hair and expressive mouth; Shelley, with his poet's eyes and brown curls; Lamb, with his spare figure and earnest face; all seen by the glow and warmth and brightness of candlelight."[91] In the culminating social event of the year, John met Wordsworth walking out on Hampstead Heath on New Year's Eve.

Since John did not know whether his brothers down in Devonshire would have access to the London papers, he sent them a copy of his review of Edmund Kean's performance as Luke Traffic in Sir James Bland Burge's comedy *Riches; or, The Wife and Brother,* published in John Scott's *Champion.* He also sent them Hunt's *Examiner* essay, "Christmas and Other Old National Merry-Makings Considered," with a detailed account of his own merrymaking with mutual friends. But George and Tom were well supplied with the papers—and anything else they might have needed—in Teignmouth. Like Margate, Teignmouth had transformed in recent years from a small fishing village into a fashionable watering hole.

An influx of money from wealthy merchant shippers and naval officers after the end of the Napoleonic Wars had enabled the expansion of the town at the mouth of the Teign in the Regency style. Edward Croydon—

printer, publisher, stationer, designer, and copperplate and lithograph engraver—had opened a splendid new library, at the widening of Regent's
Road, whose reading room stocked the London newspapers (the *Globe,* the
Star, the *Courier,* the *Examiner*) and provincial periodicals. Croydon circulated books, rented music and pictures, and sold stationery, perfume, jew-
elry, and umbrellas. The ground floor of his library served as a print gallery,
and he also had a billiards room.[92] Sergeant Winthrop Mackworth Praed of
Bitton House, Teignmouth, described the town as the odd mixture of vogu-
ish resort and fishing village that it had become around the time the Keats
brothers were there:

> The buildings in strange order lay
> As if the streets had lost their way
> Fantastic, puzzling, narrow, muddy,
> Excess of toil from lack of study . . .
> But still about that humble place
> There was a look of rustic grace;
> 'Twas sweet to see the sports and labours
> And morning greetings of good neighbours,
> The seamen mending sails and oars,
> The matrons knitting at the doors,
> The invalids enjoying dips,
> The children launching tiny ships,
> The Beldams clothed in rags and wrinkles
> Investigating periwinkles.[93]

Boulders distinguished Minnicombe from Babicombe beach, and the
looped promenade known as the Den ran west along the strip of land shel-
tering the harbor, where the fishing boats anchored. The tower of the medieval church of St. Michael the Archangel, which dominated the skyline
of East Teignmouth, was best seen from the Ness, the red sandstone prom-
ontory that rose up spectacularly in West Teignmouth. Hope's Nose protruded at the northern end of Torbay. And around the remains of an ancient Saxon church, the whole panoply of commercial Regency life had
sprung up: boot- and shoemakers, milliners, tailors, music sellers, wine
merchants, bakers, brewers, confectioners, grocers, tallow-chandlers, ironmongers, cabinetmakers, coopers, painters, perfumers, hatters, auctioneers,
druggists, general merchants, and other retailers and manufacturers.

At times, the waters flowing down the Teign River into the English Channel were placid; at other times, they raged and clashed, battling the enormous rocks strewn across the riverbed. "Fearful is the roar of the headlong waters," one guidebook declared, "as, pent up in gloomy valleys, it forces its impetuous, foamy passage to the ocean." Mrs. Stone, on French Street, rented donkeys for the trek to the top of the cliffs overlooking the Channel; and for slightly longer trips, two livery stables in West Teignmouth rented gigs. More important to George, who by the end of the year was deeply attached, if not officially engaged, to Georgiana Wylie, was the office of the postmistress Mrs. Lott, who sent out mail daily at 6:30 P.M. and distributed incoming mail (which arrived half an hour later) the next morning.[94]

Although much of the town's business was seasonal, it had four thousand residents in 1817 and rooms to rent throughout the year. George and Tom found lodging in a boarding house on the western peninsula of Teignmouth, at 20 The Strand. Their landlady, Sarah Jeffery, was a widow with two daughters. Mary Ann Jeffery, born January 11, 1798, was about a year younger than George, and her younger sister, Sarah Frances (or Fanny) Jeffery, born December 7, 1799, was nineteen days younger than Tom. George never seems to have mentioned his feelings for Georgiana Wylie to either of the sisters.

While George gravitated toward the more lighthearted Sarah for amusement, Tom discovered that Mary Ann, like his older brother, wrote poetry. It was mainly sentimental verse set in the Devonshire landscape, but Mary Ann also had a taste for the sublime:

> We stood at eve where the flashing waves,
> Rush'd down from their mountain home;
> On the dizzy brink of the time worn caves,
> In a haze of silvery foam.
>
> Ever on—ever on—how the haughty flood
> Came forth like a king in his pride;
> While we, as entranc'd, on the margin stood,
> Nor thought of the world beside.
> But our hands were clasp'd, and our voices blent,
> With the tumbling torrent's roar.
> Like the notes of some fabled instrument,
> Along an enchanted shore.[95]

Perhaps Tom stood at eve, absorbed in the crash of the flashing waves, with Mary Ann Jeffery. More likely, his brother took the girls for a pleasant walk. For George's command of French notwithstanding, he knew the language of gallantry fluently enough.

A letter sent by George to the Jeffery sisters from London in March suggests the kind of banter that took place between the young people in the winter of 1817–1818. "What think you of my impudence?" he commences (the impudence being the letter itself, which the sisters were not expecting). The letter then unfolds in the following imaginary dialogue:

> *Enter the letter—Sarah half anxious and half laughing looks enquiringly at Marianne to whom the letter is delivered, who opening it hurryingly says on looking at the signature, "From George Keats."*
>
> Sarah (quickly): I was sure he'd think of *me—correcting herself suddenly—of us,* what does he say, make haste, I'm bursting with curiosity.
> Marianne: Well you shall hear, don't be in such a hurry; what can he have to write about?
> Sarah: As if you did not know now.
> Marianne: he has already sent us word that he has delivered those drawings.
> Sarah: Do read the letter, does he say anything about my Eyes, or my hair, or my arms, or my speech, or my voice, or my manners, or, lord! Marianne how provoking you are, I never saw such a slow creature in my life.
> Marianne: he surely cannot have anything to say about the drawings.
> Sarah: why now Marianne I protest you are enough to put Job himself into a passion, read the letter or let me read it; to see what he has written is the way to ascertain what he had to write about.
>
> *Marianne reads to herself—Sarah, after a pause says—*
>
> Sarah: Well what does he say?
> Marianne: Nothing.
> Sarah: Nothing; what's the matter with the Girl, you have read through a whole page and yet he says nothing.
> Marianne: that I can understand at least.

Sarah: Let me try.

Snatches the letter—after reading some time continues,

Sarah: Well to be sure he says but very little that is at all intelligible, there's
something about being impudent—I never found him so, did you?

Marianne again takes the letter and says—

Marianne: He then goes on about Marianne & Sarah and Sarah &
Marianne; what can he mean?

*A long pause during which Marianne cons the letter, then Sarah says in an
under voice,*

Sarah: Marianne may well say he says nothing, since its so little to the
purpose, nothing at all interesting, he does not even say that he
sometimes thinks of me, he might have.

Marianne: interrupting, reads out, Oh! Sarah I cannot with all my
endeavours drive from my waking thoughts, or sleeping dreams the
image of your blue Eyes, sparkling through your long hair, and I feel
with greatest satisfaction that I have in my possession a lock of this same
hair. This is the best of all remembrances, since always beautiful, and
only valuable to the party to whom it is given. Pray Marianne send me
one by my Brothers, when they come up, let it [be] taken from a part
that you are in the habit of curling; indeed to speak properly I should
ask for a *curl* of your hair.—I shall ever remember with pleasure the
many pleasant walks we have rambled together; I fear much from the
present posture of my affairs that I shall never again pass my arm in
that of the steady, quiet Marianne, and laughing thoughtless Sarah. I
think with infinite regret that you should be obliged to look up to a
Person so every way inferior to you, however fate seems to have ordered
it, and enables you to bear with it.[96]

George's letter to the sisters was in effect a goodbye letter, written most
likely after he had proposed marriage to Georgiana Wylie.

George's "laughing thoughtless Sarah" was only seventeen, but she was
more impatient than her older sister for the ballrooms to open. Tom later
wrote to the Jeffery sisters as well, saying that he hoped that "Waltzing will
be admitted to the Teignmouth and other Town and Country Ball rooms in
Sarah's time." Perhaps reflecting her own fear, he worried that they would

not open until she had "attained the age of Fifty Six and that's no age at all." In fact, Sarah would be twenty-six when the Assembly Rooms opened in Teignmouth—although she would not find a husband in them, or anywhere else. Mary Ann would marry the wine merchant Isaac Sparke Prowse from the neighboring village of Torquay a decade after the Keats brothers left town. In the meantime, Teignmouth did have a choice of theaters. One of these was the theater in which Edmund Kean was discovered performing in pantomimes with his three-year-old son.[97]

Unlike John, who would replace George by Tom's side in March, George never got into a fight with the other theatergoers. Instead, as ever, he made friends. Among the more colorful of their acquaintance was Captain Warwick Hele Tonkin, Jr., a former navy hero. After eighteen years of active military service, Captain Tonkin had retired, though like George he could not sit still. By the end of his life, the captain would have been knighted for escorting the future Queen Victoria around Devonshire, raised a volunteer regiment of local Yeomanry Cavalry, earned a gold medal from Charles X of France for heroism during a shipwreck, and served as Lieutenant Colonel of the South Devon Artillery Brigade.[98]

During the months that the Keats brothers were in town, however, Captain Tonkin was waging a more amorous campaign. Eliza Jane Squarey Periman Mitchell, only daughter of Thomas Mitchell, Esq., and a friend of Mary Ann and Sarah Jeffery, had conquered his heart. John wondered in the summer of 1818 whether Miss Mitchell would be "stony hearted enough" to hold out for another season against the captain. He prescribed "a little love powder," observing that "it really would not be unamusing to see her languish a little." But she did surrender to the captain that summer, and the marriage took place in September, in Exeter, where Tonkin's father (Warwick Hele Tonkin, Sr., a bencher of the Middle Temple and Recorder of Plymouth and Tiverton) and mother (Letitia, née Spencer) lived. Their home was in a crescent terrace, on a graveled street lined with tall elms that had once been the counterscarp of Rougemont Castle. The captain's wife would later bequeath the boarding house run by Mrs. Jeffery to her friends Mary Ann and Sarah.[99]

The brothers' social circle in Teignmouth also included Dr. William Turton, who was treating Tom. Around the time that he published his treatise on baths, Turton had published a translation of Linnaeus's *General System of Nature* (1802–1806), thereby joining the ranks of authors, editors, and translators condemned by *Blackwood's*. He had also published a study of British fauna, and now, having narrowed his interests to aquatic inverte-brates, was at work sketching shells for his *Conchological Dictionary of the British Islands* (1819). A certain bivalve mollusk, of the genus *Turtonia*, still bears his name.

Yet, if the truth be told, George was merely biding his time with the society in Teignmouth that winter. His fixed intention, which he kept to himself and seems to have postponed telling his brothers as long as possible, was to return to London by his twenty-first birthday, claim his inheritance from Richard Abbey, and marry Georgiana Wylie. What he would do with that inheritance is another story.

PART TWO
1818

3 MAN OF GENIUS AND MAN OF POWER

Emigration Fever

All the time George was in Teignmouth, sitting with Tom or chatting with the girls at the bonnet shop, he had been turning over in his mind possibilities for the future. He had been unemployed for a good part of a year, and despite Mrs. Abbey's view "that the Keatses were ever indolent—that they would ever be so and that it was born in them," George did not like being idle.[1] Without occupation he was uncomfortable, and, like his older brother, he had ambitions for doing honor to the family name. Richard Abbey had not given up on him as a respectable tradesman, but George continued to resist the idea of himself as a hatter—or for that matter, a girdler, a draper, a haberdasher . . . He had nobler ideas than that.

Once back in London, George looked into possibilities opening up overseas. The talk of the town in March 1818 was of land in the western states and territories of America, which the federal government was virtually giving away at two dollars an acre—or, for payment in cash, a dollar and sixty-four cents. New towns were cropping up every day. All one needed to establish a township was enough money for thirty-six square miles (23,040 acres) and a surveyor to plat (or lay out) the town. George did not have the means for a Keatsville, or another American Georgetown, but he *was* thinking that he could afford fourteen hundred acres on the settlement known as the English Prairie in Illinois, which would make him master of the greater part of a township. "You know my Brother George has been out of employ some time," John wrote to Benjamin Bailey. "It has weighed very much upon him, and driven him to scheme and turn over things in his Mind. The result has been his resolution to emigrate to the back settlements of America, become farmer and work with his own hands after purchasing 1400 Acres of the American Government."[2]

To a large degree, the emigration fever that took hold of George upon his return from Teignmouth was the result of utopian promises made by Morris Birkbeck in *Notes on a Journey in America,* a bestselling book that had been published in Philadelphia in 1817 and in early 1818 in London. Writing from his fledgling settlement in the Illinois Territory, Birkbeck had portrayed glorious views and flocks of fat wild turkeys presenting themselves for dinner. He had characterized his former life in England as years wasted in the support of others, and he gave the impression that in America a hardworking man could support a family with ease.

Had he been a landholder, he reasoned, or a single person without children, he might have remained on his fifteen hundred acres of land, which he leased from Lord Oslow in Wanborough, Surrey, in order to help reform his country, "or, in pure hatred of tyranny, to stand the brunt" (as he said later). But given his circumstances, he thought it best to withdraw his family out of its reach. "A nation," he declared, "with half its population supported by alms, or poor-rates, and one fourth of its income derived from taxes, many of which are dried up in their sources, or speedily becoming so, must teem with emigrants from one end to the other: and, for such as myself, who have had 'nothing to do with the laws but to obey them,' it is quite reasonable and just to secure a timely retreat from the approaching crisis— either of anarchy or despotism."[3] George Keats's interest in emigration was prompted by his own thwarted prospects in the same system of entrenched political and economic power that Birkbeck had renounced.

Like the British colonists in America, Morris Birkbeck resented being taxed by a government that denied him a vote. "Think of a country without excisemen, or assessors, or collectors, or receivers-general," he tempted in his *Letters from Illinois,* which Taylor & Hessey were now in the process of printing, "or—informers or paupers!" Birkbeck's account of life on a fertile, unspoiled land appealed to people in the war-torn Old Country, who were now pulling up stakes to start a new life west of the Alleghenies. Writing to Percy Bysshe Shelley from Marlow on September 15, 1818, Thomas Love Peacock reported that Birkbeck's glowing account of life in the West-

ern Country of America had "fixed the public attention on that country in
an unprecedented degree. . . . Multitudes are following his example even
from this neighbourhood." Peacock described the author as "a man of vigorous intellect who thinks deeply and describes admirably. The temptation
to agriculturists with a small capital must be irresistible: and the picture he
presents of the march of population and cultivation beyond the Ohio is one
of the most wonderful spectacles ever yet presented to the mind's eye of
philosophy."[4]

A widower of thirteen years, Morris Birkbeck had left England in
1817—as it turned out, permanently—with a party consisting of his sons
Charles and Bradford, his daughters Eliza and Prudence, their friend Eliza
Julia Andrews, an orphan (Elizabeth Garton), a relation of his business
partner named Elias Pym Fordham, and (however hypocritically) a servant.
Birkbeck's partner, George Flower, was the eldest son of a brewer from
Hertfordshire. Among other things, these pioneering agriculturalists did
not like having to pay tithes to the Church of England. They shared a dissenting background—Birkbeck a Quaker, and Flower a Unitarian—and
like other dissenters, they objected to the established system of privilege in
both Church and State, in particular royal patronage and unequal parliamentary representation, or "borough-mongering." While Birkbeck wrote
the books that publicized the "English Prairie" between the Big and Little
Wabash rivers in the Illinois Territory, Flower rounded up emigrants in
London, including George Keats.

The founders of the settlement known as the English Prairie had explored farmland together in Normandy in 1814, but, given political conditions in Europe at the time, decided that the United States was "the only
country left for emigration." A couple of years later, George Flower visited
America. In Virginia, he met Thomas Jefferson, whom he noticed had
Birkbeck's *Notes on a Journey through France* (1814) on his bookshelves. At
James Madison's house in Washington, he met Colonel John Coles, whose
son Edward, an American diplomat, had told Birkbeck about wide stretches
of unclaimed land available for taking in the Western Country. "Good land
dog-cheap everywhere," as Flower put it, "and for nothing, if you will go
far enough for it."[5]

Whereas in Great Britain landholders profited from heavy taxes on
tenant farmers, the U.S. Congress had recently all but abolished the system
of land taxation. On an acre of first-rate land, the federal land tax was now

one cent, and on second-rate land, three-quarters of a cent.[6] Emigrants would have to cross the Atlantic—and travel another thousand miles over mountains and through wilderness to reach the western frontier—but there, the Land of Cockaigne, that fabled land of milk and honey dreamed about by medieval peasants, awaited.

Against a backdrop of established wealth and chartered privileges descending from the Crown, the uncharted, open lands of the American West stood for freedom. As William Blake wrote in his notebook,

> Why should I care for the men of thames
> Or the cheating waves of charterd streams
> Or shrink at the little blasts of fear
> That the hireling blows into my ear
>
> Tho born on the cheating banks of Thames
> Tho his waters bathed my infant limbs
> The Ohio shall wash his stains from me
> I was born a slave but I go to be free[7]

Blake's "hirelings" included the commercial traders—the Abbeys and Hodgkinsons of the world with ships coming and going on the Thames—weighed down with "mind-forg'd manacles" (the ideology of Church and State) and unconsciously perpetuating the same system of unequal power relations by which they were oppressed. The speaker rejects their "little blasts of fear," boldly setting out for the lands of the Ohio River Valley, where George Keats, too, would "go to be free."

Of course Blake was hardly the only poet to portray America as a land of opportunity versus an Old World in decadent decline, nourished by "the cheating waves of charterd streams." In *Laon and Cythna* (retitled *The Revolt of Islam*), which Shelley had written in competition with Keats and which the Olliers were now printing, Shelley trumpeted support for "A land beyond the Oceans of the West / Where, though with rudest rites, Freedom and Truth / Are worshipped." He prophesied that America would put the last nail in the coffin of European despotism. "Great People," he proclaimed, "Thy growth is swift as morn, when night must fade; / The multitudinous Earth shall sleep beneath thy shade." There was truth in the prophecy, if not quite in the way Shelley expected.

Among others in the Keats brothers' circle, Charles Dilke took a keen interest in the American experiment. Although no prophet, Dilke, like Shelley, believed in the idea of social progress. Dilke, "a Godwin perfectibility Man," John would write to George in America, "pleases himself with the idea that America will be the country to take up the human intellect where England leaves off." In this belief, a second generation of Romantic writers followed the first. In 1795, Samuel Taylor Coleridge and his friend Robert Southey, now the Poet Laureate, had planned to emigrate to the backwoods of western Pennsylvania. Their "Pantisocracy" would join democracy in a land freed from the clutches of a corrupt system. Wisdom would reign, supported by (as Morris Birkbeck put it) "an unshackled press."[8] Its shackled citizens were another matter.

Neither Coleridge nor Southey actually made it to America, but they helped to give the idea of emigration a philosophical dimension. By the time George decided to emigrate, "it was no longer merely the poor, the idle, the profligate, or the wildly speculative, who were proposing to quit their native country," as Henry Bradshaw Fearon wrote in his *Sketches of America* (1818), "but men also of capital, of industry, of sober habits and regular pursuits; men of reflection, who apprehended approaching evils; men of upright and conscientious minds, to whose happiness civil and religious liberty were essential; and men of domestic feelings, who wished to provide for the future support and prosperity of their offspring."[9] Many believed that civilization could begin anew west of the Alleghenies.

The British establishment had cause for concern, and it responded to the emigration fever of 1818 by satirizing the Cockney Pioneers with no less fervor than it did the Cockney Poets. The same volume of the *Quarterly Review* in which John Wilson Croker ridiculed the author of *Endymion* as a Cockney Poet also contained twenty-four closely printed pages by John Barrow and William Gifford satirizing the Cockney Pioneers. Reviewing Birkbeck's *Notes on a Journey in America* in April 1818, the Tory critics portrayed the English Prairie in the Western Country of America as a foolish concoction—a "Land of Cockaigne," they called it, a delusion the Old Country could easily dismiss.

"Whatever 'New America' may have gained by the name of Birkbeck having ceased to be found in the list of the citizens of Old England," the *Quarterly* announced, "the latter has no reason to regret the loss. Many more of the same stamp may well be spared to wage war with the bears and red Indians of the 'back-woods' of America." It parodied those considering following the Cockney Pioneers to the Illinois Territory in 1818 as odious insects, putting out their feelers to judge the prudence of advancing or retreating. "Let it be recollected that, with all our drawbacks," the reviewers concluded, "there is no country in the world where the mass of the people are so well fed, clothed and lodged, as in England; where life and property are so well protected and secured, and where real and rational liberty, the Englishman's birthright, is so fully and so effectually enjoyed."[10] So said those who enjoyed their birthright.

Frustration was growing among others. On the one hand, there was the extravagant lifestyle of the upper classes, particularly the Prince Regent, or Prince of Wales, lampooned as an overfed voluptuary: the "Prince of Whales." On the other hand, there was widespread hunger aggravated by decades of war. In 1819 Francis Jeffrey opened a review of Sydney Smith's *Radical Reform, the only Remedy for the Disorders of Our Country* in the *Edinburgh Review* by announcing it as a truth universally acknowledged that "a great deal of distress prevails in the manufacturing districts; that agriculture is far from having regained its former prosperity; [and] that the increasing evils of the poor laws have become scarcely bearable, either to those on whom they press immediately, or those whom they are intended to relieve."[11] The Poor Laws administered through the parishes of the Church of England burdened homeowners and businesses with taxes intended for public relief. The Corn Laws imposed a tax on imported grain that served landowners but drove up the price of bread for everyone else. A lack of bread had caused the French to revolt. Many believed that Britain, too, was headed for civil war.

One Surrey farmer who followed the Cockney Pioneers to the prairielands of Illinois claimed that in leaving the Old Country he had broken free "from that Aggregation of Oppression, Tyranny, Hypocrisy, & Misery" that made England look ripe for revolution: "its prisons crowded with Debtors & Criminals, its Workhouses filled with Paupers, its Road covered with Mendicants & Persons begging for employment[,] its Farmers & Tradesmen daily sinking into poverty owing to the immense burden of taxation & Labor which crushes them to the very ground while their insolent Oppressors were reveling in every Species of Luxury & treating with contempt & derision those Classes from whose Labour they derived all their means of enjoyment." Another emigrant to the English Prairie in 1818 received a letter from his father congratulating him on having "escaped from our oppressions."[12] Many had come to associate the British constitutional monarchy with *ancien-régime* absolutism.

Foreign Secretary Lord Castlereagh's aggressive tactics in putting down civil unrest two years earlier had touched a raw nerve in England in an Age of Revolution. After a dreadful harvest in 1816, thousands had gathered at Spa Fields, Islington, determined to seize control of the Tower of London. The symbolism was not lost on the Powers that Be: the Parisians had attacked the Bastille not two decades earlier as an emblem of oppression. Although the gathering had been peaceful, the British royal cavalry had dispersed the crowd, and the court sent some to the gallows, others into exile overseas. William Faux, another English writer on America, observed the effect that the Cockney Pioneer Birkbeck had on emigration: "no man, since Columbus, has done so much toward peopling America as Mr. Birkbeck, whose publications, and the authority of whose name, had effects truly prodigious; and if all could have settled in Illinois, whom he had tempted across the Atlantic and the mountains, it had now been the most populous state in the Union."[13]

By the time George Keats returned from Teignmouth to claim his inheritance, George Flower had set up operations in the counting house of a merchant tailor, James Lawrence of Hatton Garden. Lawrence was a man of property who, entranced by Birkbeck's picture of life on the prairie, had decided to emigrate. Lawrence would lead the first party of English emigrants from London to Illinois. On the way, they would be joined at the port of Bristol by another party from Surrey, and followed two and a half weeks later by Flower's own boatload of emigrants from Liverpool. In the meantime, Lawrence's counting house served as headquarters for the English Prairie. People from all ranks of life, although mainly from the lower and middle classes, flooded in to seek information about the American Land of Cockaigne.

The Cockney Pioneers' mission to recruit emigrants was succeeding beyond their wildest expectations. "The farmers of England, the miners of Cornwall, the drovers of Wales, the mechanics of Scotland, the West-India planter, the inhabitants of the Channel Isles, and the 'gentleman of no particular business' of the Emerald Isle. All were moving or preparing to move to join us in another hemisphere. The cockneys of London had decided on the reversal of their city habits, to breathe the fresh air of the prairies. Parties were moving, or preparing to move, in all directions. At one time, the movement appeared as if it would be national."[14] George Flower genuinely believed in the dream as well as the practicality of the project, and George Keats, like countless others, bought the pitch.

To give a picture of the prairielands in Illinois, Flower asked potential emigrants to imagine themselves "under a clump of oak trees, such as stand in an extensive and beautiful English park, with the sky above, the earth below, no fence, no house, and perhaps no person within twenty miles." The English Prairie bore comparison to the aristocratic English parks, but without enclosures, or hedgerows, to partition the expanse. (Of course the pioneers' first task upon settling on the prairie would be to put up wooden fences to enclose their livestock and protect their crops.) Whereas every square mile in England contained on average a hundred and eighty-one people, or in the British Isles a hundred and fifty-six, the Illinois Territory—larger than England and Wales combined—had only a single settler. Upon crossing the Wabash from Indiana into Illinois, Flower related, "a beautiful prairie suddenly opened to our view. At first, we only received the impressions of its general beauty. With longer gaze, all its distinctive features were revealed, lying in profound repose under the warm light of an afternoon's summer sun."[15]

Emigrants would need only eighty dollars for a down payment on a quarter-section of land (160 acres), the smallest claim ("freehold" in English parlance) available for sale through the United States land offices. One could pay the rest in installments over a period of four years. The register at the land office would turn the payment over to the receiver, who would report the sale to the surveyor general, who would request the commissioner in Washington, D.C., to issue a title signed by the president of the United States. The Cockney Pioneers predicted that emigrants could earn a profit of double their expenses within a year. Pessimists in the crowd shook their heads, but optimists, like George Keats, made light of difficulties. George estimated his inheritance at eleven hundred pounds, though by the time he cashed it in a couple of months later, the market would have risen and he would receive sixteen hundred. Like others, George thought that if he invested wisely and worked hard, he might return home in a few years with enough money to provide a comfortable life for his family.

The Cockney Pioneers themselves had originally hoped to purchase forty thousand acres, or several connected townships, on the English Prairie on a deferred-payment plan, but the U.S. Congress had passed a statute limiting the sale of public land. On his way back to London from the Illinois Territory, Flower had solicited Jefferson's support in asking the federal government to make an exception for them. Jefferson doubted whether Congress would waive the law intended to prevent the kind of land monopolies found in Great Britain, but he promised to put in a word with the Land Department. He praised the idea of founding "a sanctuary for those whom the misrule of Europe may compel to seek happiness in other climes" and hoped that it might encourage even those who stayed behind on British soil to expect deliverance from their many oppressions:

> This refuge, once known, will produce reaction on the happiness even of those who remain there, by warning their task-masters that when the evils of Egyptian oppression become heavier than those of the abandonment of country, another Canaan is opened where their subjects will be received as brothers, and secured against like oppressions by a participation in the right of self-government. If additional motives could be wanting with us to the maintenance of this right, they would be found in the animating consideration that a single good government becomes thus a blessing to the whole earth, its welcome to the oppressed restraining within certain limits the measure of their oppressions. . . . You have set to your own country a good example, by showing them a peaceable mode of reducing their rulers to the necessity of becoming more wise, more moderate, and more honest.[16]

Thus spoke the slave owner. But, as Jefferson had predicted, the U.S. Congress did not relent, and the founders of the English Prairie had to scale back their enterprise.

The first group of Cockney Pioneers was due to set out for the English Prairie from London in March 1818, the very month that George returned from Teignmouth. James Lawrence would lead them to Bristol, where they would be joined by a second group, led by Charles Trimmer, a young farmer from Yeatley (ten miles from Birkbeck's estate in Surrey). While Lawrence's party consisted mainly of merchants from London, Trimmer's party would be made up of farmers and manual laborers. James Peachey, one of George and John's friends from Clarke's school, knew Trimmer. Having left Enfield at the age of fourteen and a half to take up an apprenticeship in London, Peachey was now a solicitor-in-training. After George and his wife left England for America, John and Peachey would compare notes about the English settlement in Illinois.[17]

In the meantime, eighty-five men and three women would set sail from Bristol on April 6, 1818, on the packet ship *Achilles* bound for Philadelphia, whence they would proceed overland to the Land of Cockaigne west of the Allegheny Mountains. George Flower would follow with sixty-one friends and family members from Liverpool on April 23. He would take the same ship, the *Ann Maria,* commanded by the same captain, Isaac Waite, who had carried him back safely from New York the previous year, with the manuscript of Birkbeck's *Notes on a Journey in America* in his saddle-bag. Flower would also take seed, farming equipment, livestock, and a hundred thousand pounds sterling. When his ship arrived in New York, an American journalist would remark that "if gentlemen of fortune and enterprize will emigrate in the same manner, our western states will shortly be the most flourishing part of the world." Arriving in New York after only thirty days at sea despite a rough voyage, the party sailing from Liverpool on the *Ann Maria* with Flower would beat the emigrants sailing from Bristol on the *Achilles* to America.[18]

George Keats still needed to liquidate his funds and would not be ready to depart with the first boatloads of Cockney Pioneers. Nor did he know how to use a plow, a team of oxen, or even an axe. The prairie sod was tough, and George was entirely unfit for a life of labor on unbroken land. If he imagined that he could hire labor and oversee his operations in the style of an English Lord of the Manor, it was a sign of his inexperience as well as ignorance about the place to which he was going. In the Western Country of America, farmhands and domestic servants did not need to work long in order to be able to afford their own property—and then, where was the incentive to work for another? Why cross the Alleghenies, not to mention the Atlantic, to do what could be done with less trouble back home? The price of government land in the West encouraged every man to be his own master. Illinois would enter the union in December as a free state, and the Cockney Pioneers would be active in campaigning to keep it that way. The settlers on the English Prairie would have to work for themselves—and with industry, reap their own profits.

Given his resources, moreover, George's plan to purchase fourteen hundred acres on the English Prairie might appear extravagant. Yet George did not have the capital to start his own business or to support a family in England in the style to which he aspired to live. And he had a skill worth more than money or farming experience: perseverance. His future friend John James Audubon, a name well known to all bird watchers, upon observing George chop a pile of wood outside his cabin in Red Banks, Kentucky, would say: "I am sure you will do well in this country, Keats. A man who will persist, as you have been doing, in chopping that log, though it has taken you an hour to do what I could do in ten minutes, will certainly get along here."[19] George was young and confident, with a constitutionally positive outlook. Rather than following the anonymous, time-consuming route up the ranks in commercial Cheapside, he would join forces with those enterprising souls who had shifted their hopes across the Atlantic.

Yet others—and not only the conservative critics at the *Quarterly* and *Blackwood's*—were not so sanguine. The journalist William Cobbett, at the other end of the political spectrum, had built his reputation attacking "tax-eaters" and calling for parliamentary reform. He had fled from political persecution to a farm in Long Island, New York. He feared that emigrants would be disappointed by conditions in the West, and he countered Morris Birkbeck's glowing portrait of life on the English Prairie with a darker picture: emigrants would have "to boil their pot in the gipsy-fashion," with no more than a plank or a "mere board to eat on." They would have nothing but whiskey or water to drink, and they would find themselves forced "to sit and sleep under a shed far inferior to their English cowpens." The nearest mill would be twenty miles away; the nearest pharmacy, a hundred. There would be no doctor. Having spent a third of their life savings to reach the Western Country, they would find that they had purchased nothing but more suffering.[20]

George Keats knew that his brothers would go along with almost any scheme he devised, if he believed it to be for the best, but others were under no such fraternal obligations. And people much closer to him than Cobbett voiced their skepticism. Charlotte Cox Reynolds was surprised that her friend Mrs. Wylie would consider letting her daughter run off to the trackless wilds of America with such an inexperienced creature as George Keats. How could Georgiana even think of it? She had always *seemed* such a sensible girl. Mrs. Reynolds, in her wildest dreams, could never entertain the idea of the western frontier of America if it involved *her* daughters. Then again, neither Janey nor Lizzie would ever ask such a thing—of *such* a mother.

In the end, George did not heed Mrs. Reynolds's freely given advice, but her words seared into his conscience. "I frequently call to mind that M^rs R immediately before I left England in 1818 expressed the utmost astonishment that M^rs K was willing to go with me to America," he wrote in 1833, "or that her Mother would permit it." Yet, he reasoned that had Mrs. Wylie been as wise as Mrs. Reynolds, "she would have crushed in the bud a reasonable portion of human happiness, and there would not have been any little Keatses."[21] He might have been right, but this was only one of many justifications he would make in the coming decades for having taken Georgiana so far from her family.

Yet Ann Wylie, whatever her friend Charlotte Reynolds might say, was familiar enough with the idea of emigration. Her brother, Robert Griffin, had moved to North America and was doing quite well in Montreal. There, just south of the city, on a common next to a brewery and a linseed oil factory, he had set up a soap factory. The land was little more than "a swamp, flooded during the spring freshets and wet seasons," but Griffin's wife, Mary (née Carr), purchased it. Although the deal turned out to be illegal (since the man who sold it to her was only leasing it from the nuns of St. Ann for a period of ninety-nine years), the town became, as it remains today, Griffintown.[22]

A mere seven months earlier, on August 23, 1817, Robert had moved up in life, from soap maker to first cashier of the Bank of Montreal. He now had an annual salary of three hundred pounds and a staff including an accountant, two tellers, a clerk, a porter, and a bookkeeper. Whenever pigs, those roving street cleaners that cleaned up the waste that piled in the streets in the early days of colonial America, wandered into the bank, his staff would shoo them away. Griffin also had the use of the living quarters over the bank on St. Paul Street, the main thoroughfare of Montreal. In just a few years, his salary would double. His son Henry would become the bank's first notary public, and a younger son, Frederick, would become its first lawyer.[23] Frederick was Georgiana's age. The entrepreneurial spirit of the Griffins had thus far succeeded in America: Why should Georgiana not follow their path?

Besides the poetry by John that George had given her, Georgiana's scrapbook also contains two commissions, signed by King George III in October 1794, for one "James Wylie, Gentleman," the man usually assumed to be her father. The first appoints him as Adjutant to the Fifeshire regiment of Fencible Infantry in Scotland, and the second as Lieutenant to the same company. John addressed a letter to Mrs. James Wylie after George left the country with Georgiana. But while Mrs. Wylie may have been a widow, James Wylie may not have been Georgiana's father.

Georgiana's descendant from Louisville, Kentucky, Lawrence M. Crutcher, claims that the James Wylie who received his commissions from George III in October 1794 died the following year, which would have been a couple of years before Georgiana's birth in 1798 (if she was indeed forty-five at the time of her second marriage on January 5, 1843, as the marriage certificate states). This would, of course, effectively rule out the possibility of his paternity. James Freeman Clarke claimed that Georgiana left England at sixteen. George and Georgiana's future son Clarence George claimed that she was "a mother only fourteen years old." There is no record of her birth, but Crutcher proposes that another lieutenant than James Wylie, specifically a lieutenant in the First Company North Gloucester, whose commission is also in Georgiana's scrapbook, was more likely to have been Georgiana's father: Augustus Thomas Garskill. The names of Georgiana Augusta and of her younger brother, Charles Gaskell, would reflect his. A discrepancy between "Garskill" and "Gaskell" would not have been unusual in the official records, where many surnames had variants. Georgiana and Charles *were* fifteen and seventeen years, respectively, younger than their brother (one suspects half-brother) Henry Robert Wylie. Perhaps Georgiana's American descendant is correct in suggesting that her "evident illegitimacy may have contributed to her willingness to try a fresh start in America."[24]

The Wylie side of the family came from Fifeshire, in Scotland, where the old way of life was dying out and people were moving away, many of them across the Atlantic. The main activities of the region were fishing, shipping, and farming. The fishermen brought in herring, whiting, skate, salmon, sole, turbot, haddock, cod, bunnock, sparling, sprat, and sand flounders. The shippers exported stone and coal. The farmers raised oats, wheat, barley, beans, peas, potatoes, turnips, and sour grass. But in 1818 most of the landowners lived out of town, and the tenants held the land at a high price. The salt-pans on which the villages on the rocky shore of the

Firth (mouth or estuary) of the River Forth sat were going out of business. Living conditions there suggest much that the emigration literature was bringing into focus. Georgiana would try her luck with George in the New World.

The couple set their wedding day for Thursday, May 28, 1818. A few extra weeks would give them time to prepare for both the wedding and the transatlantic crossing. They would spend any time that remained with loved ones whom they were not likely to see again for a long time. Although loath to see her only daughter go, Mrs. Wylie put on a good face and went about preparing the bed and table linen. Richard Abbey, who was relieved that George had finally settled on a plan to earn a living, would see about converting George's stock into cash. George's main challenge would be to break the news about his emigration to his brothers—and *that* would not be easy.

Devonshire

"My Love for my Brothers," John wrote after George moved to America, "from the early loss of our parents and even for earlier Misfortunes has grown into a[n] affection 'passing the Love of Women.'—I have been ill temper'd with them, I have vex'd them—but the thought of them has always stifled the impression that any woman might otherwise have made upon me." John liked Georgiana, and he thought she would be good for his brother. "I have a tenderness for you," he told her, "and an admiration which I feel to be as great and more chaste than I can have for any woman in the world."[25] She was no coquette seeking a hapless wight to enslave, no fatal Cleopatra dazzling and dangerous, threatening to swallow up all honor and achievement in her own tragic splendor. John had watched a sustainable relationship develop between her and George. But none of this could cushion the blow he was about to receive.

As John lay awake at night in Teignmouth, where he had come to replace George in the middle of March, he listened to the rain pouring down and felt himself "drown'd and rotted like a grain of wheat." He may not have had the English Prairie specifically in mind (and in fact the area was not the best place to grow wheat), but he had heard the talk of emigration, and travel was on his mind as well. "If Endymion serves me as a Pioneer perhaps I ought to be content," he wrote to John Taylor on February 28,

George's twenty-first birthday. Yet, John also dreamed of escape. In Devonshire, a couple of weeks later, he was ready to "take to my Wings and fly away"—away from the salty sea spray, and the clouds closing in on the small coastal town. Away from the fishhooks and the wet ropes, slicked with tar and slime. Away from the oilcloths that covered the barnacled boats in the harbor. He would take to his wings and fly . . . "to any where but old or Nova Scotia."[26]

Ironically, Scotland would be precisely where John was headed when George sailed for America. America was on the poet's mind, and it was in the air. Every spring, ships left Teignmouth for the fisheries off the neighboring islands of Newfoundland and Nova Scotia. They returned six months later, laden with barrels of cod oil and salt fish. In the spring of 1818, when John was in Teignmouth with Tom, a local merchant made a profit of ten thousand pounds on fish from the newfound Scotland. One of the oldest inns in town was the Newfoundland Fishery, and when John wrote to Reynolds from Teignmouth, he made an attempt—taking advantage of local resources—to "be witty upon salt fish."[27]

Sometimes, between breaks in the downpour, the poet would walk out on the deserted Den. Sometimes he would hunt for caves. Most of the time, trapped indoors in the relentless rain, he would watch as life slipped slowly away from his brother. Tom had been coughing blood since January, and scattered flecks of blood-strewn mucus—harbingers of worse things to come—took their toll on both brothers. Their rooms, stale from lack of ventilation, were no more conducive to the recovery of a tubercular patient than to the health of anyone close to him. Even Tom, despite his cheerful disposition and tendency to be content whenever John was around, felt that he was living in the mouth of hell rather than on the mouth of the Teign. He called the village "*Tartarey* alias Teignmouth."[28]

John had dragged his feet in getting there. The Christmas and the New Year holidays had raced by while George and Tom waited for him in Devonshire. A few days into the New Year, he had written to them about an evening's merrymaking with Joseph Severn and Charles Wells. Having polished off a few bottles of claret and port, they became "all very witty and full of Rhyme—we played a Concert from 4 o'clock till 10." Each pretended to imitate an instrument, and in that strange cacophony, they managed to make six hours go by.[29]

Wells was an eccentric character, about Tom's age, who had been hang-

ing around the brothers for a couple of years. He was apprenticed as a solicitor, but his real talent was role-playing. His mother was an actress, and
when George and Tom were in Teignmouth, he had used his connections
at Covent Garden Theatre to bring John backstage. Yet Wells was never a
particular favorite of the poet, and when John complained, in a letter to
Reynolds from Teignmouth, of someone who had been sitting between
them at the theater, it may well have been Wells: "I thought he look'd with
a longing eye at poor Kean." Competitive and resentful, Wells no doubt
would have replaced the charismatic Edmund Kean on stage if he could
have done. His brother-in-law would call him "a most dangerous and in-
sidious person." He followed John around, perhaps as far as Devonshire,
for in his letter to Reynolds from Teignmouth John complained of "a fellow to whom I have a complete aversion, and who strange to say is har-
boured and countenanced in several houses where I visit—he is sitting now
quite impudent between me and Tom.[30]

Earlier in the summer that John and Tom went to Margate, Wells had
offended the poet somehow, and, to make amends, he sent John a bouquet
of roses. These were eloquent apologists for a lover of beauty, and they inspired forgiveness in the form of a sonnet. Tom copied it under the title,
"To Charles Wells on receiving a bunch of full blown roses." "But when, O
Wells! thy roses came to me," the poem ends, "My sense with their deli-
ciousness was spell'd: / Soft voices had they, that with tender plea / Whisper'd
of peace, and truth, and friendliness unquell'd." John signed it above the
date, June 29, 1816, and the following year he inscribed a copy of *Endymion,*
"From J.K. to his young friend Wells."[31] But the peace would not last.

John had also attended William Hazlitt's evening lectures on the English poets before joining his brother in Devonshire. Having chosen to dedi-
cate *Endymion* to the memory of the "marvellous Boy" Thomas Chatterton
(as Wordsworth calls him), John did not like Hazlitt's treatment of the impoverished genius who took his own life at seventeen. "I cannot find in
Chatterton's works any thing so extraordinary as the age at which they
were written," Hazlitt had said. "They have a facility, vigour, and knowledge, which were prodigious in a boy of sixteen, but which would not have
been so in a man of twenty. He did not shew extraordinary powers of genius, but extraordinary precocity. Nor do I believe he would have written
better, had he lived. He knew this himself, or he would have lived." John,

who was only a few years older than Chatterton, must have made his objections known, for Hazlitt began his next lecture with an apology: "What I meant was less to call into question Chatterton's genius, than to object to the common mode of estimating its magnitude by its prematureness."[32] But the speaker had made his point: Chatterton was not exceptionally talented, just extremely precocious.

John Keats was both . . . and yet, despite his growing reputation in the literary world, he had doubts about how *Endymion* would be received. His publishers may have also, for they had scaled back production of the book. Rather than a quarto, they would issue the poem in the cheaper format of an octavo. They had decided not to include an engraved portrait of the author as a frontispiece. But they did need the text, and so, while George and Tom spent the winter in Devonshire, John took advantage of his privacy to turn the draft of his poem into a finished product—cutting, slashing, and otherwise "gelding" *Endymion*.[33]

As the weeks flew past, his guilt grew about his delay in joining his brothers. He canceled an appointment with the satirist Horace Smith so that he could finish his revisions to the third book. "My Brothers are expecting me every day in Devonshire," he explained on February 19.[34] Still, he lingered. But when George showed up in time for his twenty-first birthday, and Tom wrote to say that he was feeling better and would soon be returning to see his brothers at Well Walk, John got going.

Three days after George's twenty-first birthday, or the day George thought was his birthday (March 1), John boarded the stagecoach for Devonshire. That same evening, a hurricane hit England. "The metropolis, in common with almost the whole kingdom," the *New Monthly Magazine* reported, "was visited by a hurricane more violent than has been remembered for many years past, which did considerable mischief in many places." Sitting outside the coach, John narrowly escaped being blown away with the trees and houses.[35] But that night was only the beginning of weeks of constant downpour.

"Being agog to see some Devonshire, I would have taken a walk the first day, but the rain wo^d not let me," the poet complained; "and the second, but the rain wo^d not let me; and the third; but the rain forbade it— Ditto 4 ditto 5—ditto." Waiting indoors for the rain to stop, he felt like a mussel in its shell awaiting a turn in the tide. Devonshire reminded him of

Richard Brinsley Sheridan's sentimental heroine Lydia Languish in the play *School for Scandal:* "very entertaining when at smiles, but cursedly subject to sympathetic moisture." Everywhere he looked, he saw fog, "aye fog, hail, snow rain—Mist—blanketing up" the sky. When he grumbled to Benjamin Haydon about Devonshire's "urinal qualifications," the artist, as usual, felt it his duty to cheer John up: "It has rained in Town almost incessantly ever since you went away, the fact is you dog you carried the rain with you as Ulysses did the Winds and then opening your rain bags you look round with a knowing wink, and say, 'curse this Devonshire how it rains!'"[36] But Haydon's raillery could do little to combat John's black moods, which were returning.

In the second week of March, Tom's condition took a nosedive. A blood vessel ruptured in his lung and caused violent bleeding. John sent the bad tidings to George, who had fooled himself into thinking that his younger brother was recovering. He had been telling people that Tom was doing much better. In response to John's "melancholy news," George did what might be expected of anyone feeling as responsible for others as George did, and at the same time feeling so helpless: he scolded. The invalid must be more careful: "Tom must never again presume on his strength, at all events until he has *completely* recover'd."[37] But John knew better than to count on their brother's regaining his strength.

Whenever the rain let up, John flew from the sickroom. Outdoors he at least found short intervals of relief from Tom's "countenance his voice and feebleness." The primroses now covered the meadows, nourished by "lusty rivulets" from the hills.[38] The poet peopled the woods, the waterfalls, and the grottoes along the coastline with creatures of his own imagining. The advantage of poetry, he said, was that it made everything interesting. Leaves had begun to sprout on the hedges, and, when the clouds parted, he could see the rich colors that draped the hills.

From Bishopsteignton, to Wildwood Copse, to the marshes of Newton Abbot, a few lively stanzas composed in the third week of March give a sense of what Devonshire might have been like, without all the rain, had Tom been feeling better:

> For there's Bishop's Teign
> And King's Teign

And Coomb at the clear Teign head—
Where close by the stream
You may have your cream
All spread upon barley bread.

There's Arch Brook
And there's Larch Brook
Both turning many a mill,
And cooling the drouth
Of the salmon's mouth,
And fattening his silver gill.

There is Wild Wood,
A mild hood
To the sheep on the lea o' the down,
Where the golden furze
With its green thin spurs
Doth catch at the maiden's gown.

There is Newton Marsh
With its spear grass harsh—
A pleasant summer level
Where the maidens sweet
Of the Market Street
Do meet in the dusk to revel.

There's the barton rich
With dyke and ditch
And hedge for the thrush to live in,
And the hollow tree
For the buzzing bee,
And a bank for the wasp to hive in.

And O, and O
The daisies blow,
And the Primroses are waken'd,
And the violet white
Sits in silver plight,
And the green bud's as long as the spike end.

Then who would go
Into dark Soho

And chatter with dack'd hair'd critics,
When he can stay
For the new mown hay
And startle the dappled prickets?

This speaker prefers the dappled deer to the "dack'd hair'd" (close-cropped) critics in "dark Soho," who could not appreciate Chatterton. "I cannot help seeing Hazlitt like Ferdinand," John wrote that year in a book of Hazlitt's criticism on Shakespeare, comparing the critic to the shipwrecked prince in *The Tempest:* "in one odd angle of the Isle sitting—his arms in this sad knot."[39] From such cerebral self-consciousness, the "maidens sweet/Of the Market Street" offered pleasant diversion.

   John was in no mood for falling in love, but during the few days that the sun was out and Devonshire in his better graces, his pen remained playful. If one must be wrecked in a tempest, why not amuse oneself with the local Mirandas?

Where be ye going, you Devon maid,
   And what have ye there i' the basket?
Ye tight little fairy, just fresh from the dairy,
   Will ye give me some cream if I ask it?

I love your meads and I love your flowers,
   And I love your junkets mainly;
But 'hind the door, I love kissing more—
   O look not so disdainly!

I love your hills and I love your dales,
   And I love your flocks a bleating—
But O on the hether to lie together
   With both our hearts a beating.

I'll put your basket all safe in a nook
   And your shawl I hang up on this willow,
And we will sigh in the daisy's eye
   And kiss on a grass green pillow.

These lines, one might wager, surpass any other poetry that John wrote that spring, including the rest of the sixty-three stanzas of "Isabella; or, The Pot of Basil," which John had begun on the blank leaves of his folio edition of Shakespeare in Hampstead that winter. As timeless song, this blithe lyric is certainly superior.

But the sun did not stay out long. John concluded that for all its beauty, Devonshire was "a splashy, rainy, misty snowy, foggy, haily floody, muddy, slipshod County." As fog rolled up the mouth of the Teign, the villagers scuttled along the narrow, crooked streets of the village, staring at their watches as if to hurry the season. Water streamed down in torrents from the moors, and the young women in Edward Croydon's library pored over Old Moore's *Almanack* absorbed in weather predictions as intriguing, apparently, as any Gothic romance. The air was misty, and John's pillow was damp: the Devonshire men were to blame. To him, the men of Devonshire were as limp and listless as the weather. He pitied the ladies for having "such Paramours," or rather (with a pun on impotence) "Imparamours." For the sake of his country's honor, he was glad that Julius Caesar had not landed in Devon, and he conjectured that if the Devonshire men had been doing the fighting, the Battle of Waterloo would never have been won.[40]

Yet, the soggy shire did have one thing all its waters could not wash away. Local legend held that Milton had visited a certain meadow in Devonshire that still bore his impression. Indentations in the ground at regular intervals were reputedly the result of Milton's nose, as he rolled down a hill. The exhibitor of these curious nasal concavities swore that for seven years after Milton had left his mark on the meadow, a new variety of thornless thorn had sprung up to replace the white thorns that had once grown there. John was not surprised to learn that the Devonshire men preferred the new thornless variety, which they stripped to make into walking sticks.

This Miltonic tourist attraction inspired John to leave the cottage of his own feelings (his metaphor) and indulge in some facetious metaphysics. He wondered whether the rotary motion of the Miltonic head, somehow, might have enabled the Miltonic mind to absorb all the nettles and thorns of the field in Devonshire. Perhaps, through a certain process of fermentation, the latter had converted them into the rhetorical pricks that Milton had inflicted on his enemies. In his *Defence of the People of England,* Milton had skewered the hapless Claude Saumaise (known as Salmasius), a royalist supporter of King Charles I, as "the worst of two-legged rogues," a "beast," an "ignoramus," a "dull brute," a "shameless liar," a "wretched false prophet," a "lying hired slanderer," a "French vagrant," a "mountebank," "at once a parasite and a pimp," a "gallic cock," a "moneygrabbing Frenchman," a "wife's wife," and "a talkative ass sat upon by a woman." After the publication of Milton's pamphlet, Salmasius had fallen ill and died. John wondered whether the nettles of the Devonshire meadow might claim some share of the responsibility for his "well known and unhappy end."[41]

The poet had dragged himself through the final stages of revision to *Endymion,* but his publisher was now demanding a preface. John had always spurned "a Mawkish Popularity," and now, sobered by Tom's condition, he had even less desire "to daunt and dazzle the thousand jabberers about Pictures and Books." As for critics, anything he might say to *them* would not matter. What could he possibly say in that mood of forsaken doom anyway? The sun had disappeared almost as quickly as it had come out, and everyone he loved was sick. Tom was coughing blood, Reynolds had rheumatic fever, poor Jemmy Rice was a confirmed consumptive, and John was haunted by the feeling that he, too, might soon cease to be. He felt trapped in a holding place of adolescence, having not yet explored any of the mysterious passageways that branched out from the "Chamber of Maiden-Thought."[42]

Unfortunately, he confused the sickness surrounding him with the "feverish" manner in which his poem had been written. In his second attempt at a preface (the first having been condemned by Reynolds as too negative), he portrayed the author of *Endymion* as an adolescent poet: "The imagination of a boy is healthy, and the mature imagination of a man is healthy; but there is a space of life between, in which the soul is in a ferment, the character undecided, the way of life uncertain, the ambition thick-sighted."[43] He would pay dearly for such naked honesty later.

Because the model for his poem was Spenser, John may have assumed that the few hundred words he scribbled out hastily on April 10, 1818, in Teignmouth, would be received in the mode of an apologia. But as he slipped out of the third-person narrative voice of his poem into the confessional voice of the preface, the preface slipped out of literary convention into literal apology. "The two first books, and indeed the two last," he confessed in a sentence that would damn his poem, "are not of such completion as to warrant their passing the press; nor should they if I thought a year's castigation would do them any good;—it will not: the foundations are too sandy."⁴⁴ His poem's foundations were as sandy as the Strand in West Teignmouth, the street on which he was stranded with Tom.

By the time John penned his own critical epitaph in mid-April, his friend Charles Brown had begun to plan for the summer. Brown invited John on a four-month, four-thousand-mile walking tour of Scotland, and the idea of shouldering a backpack and seeing more of the world, cheaply, appealed to the poet. His younger brother was too sick engage in any such strenuous exertion, but Tom thought perhaps he might travel south. Perhaps he could sail across the North Sea to Holland, and down the Rhine through Switzerland, thence crossing the Alps into Italy. Perhaps he could sail around Portugal and Spain into the Mediterranean, and up the Ionian Sea to some port on the Adriatic. His friend Captain Tonkin was planning a trip to Italy, perhaps to Pavia, for that seems to have been Tom's final destination.⁴⁵ But John knew that Tom could not travel alone.

Both brothers were ready to return to Hampstead as soon as Tom felt up to it. But he was still weak, time passed, the weather improved, and by the end of April they had decided to stay longer. John wrote to George to ask him to send down some more of his books. He would study Greek, he thought, perhaps Italian, and Tom would see what one of the local bathing machines might do for him. The poet had discovered some new grottoes, and the invalid had discovered the taste of Devonshire cream on Mrs. Jeffery's scones. Dr. Turton had found some new shells.

But on Saturday, May 2, their bright prospects clouded over. John sat up late with his brother, as Tom coughed up warm mouthfuls of blood. Tom's fever was alarmingly high, and neither brother got any sleep. John was not looking as well as he had when he first arrived in Devonshire. This latest episode confirmed his belief that "the World is full of Misery and Heartbreak, Pain, Sickness and oppression."⁴⁶ John had no natural gift for hiding his feelings when they were excited, and the strain of nursing Tom showed in his face. When Tom woke up from his nap on Sunday, he looked at John and said that it was time to leave Teignmouth. With no energy to resist, at a loss to propose anything better—and perhaps secretly relieved—John agreed. They would leave the next morning. In Hampstead they could make plans with George for summer travel and recovery.

The idea that George was about to get married and leave the country does not seem to have entered their minds. One does not imagine that John would have been writing to George to ask him to send down more books, as he had done only the previous week in expectation of a longer stay in Devonshire, if he had known that George had less than a month left in England. Writing to Reynolds on Sunday before Tom woke up, John asked his friend to tell George, should he see him, that he needed the stanzas from "Isabella" sent down with his books. When John did finally learn about George's imminent departure, he turned down other invitations so that he could spend the time remaining with George.

No doubt George delayed alarming his brothers. He knew that, once in America, he would no longer be able to care for Tom. Nor would he be around to cheer and steady John when his fits of melancholy descended. "Is he not very original?" George teased the Jeffery sisters. His older brother *was* original, and George was proud of him. But John burned bright in flashes. In moments of despondency, he collapsed. "I carry all matters to an extreme," he acknowledged after hearing the devastating news of George, "so that when I have any little vexation it grows in five Minutes into a theme for Sophocles."[47] John loved Tom dearly, and he doted upon his sister. But what would he do without the ballast of George?

Brunswick Square

John and Tom had not made it far on the stagecoach to London before Tom began to cough up more blood—more of it than his poor body, wasted by illness, could afford. John did not like the looks of how things were progressing. He was glad that he had not thrown his medical books away, and he intended, once he returned to Hampstead, to look into them. In the meantime, the doctors at Bridport, a coastal fishing town sheltered by bluffs on the south coast of Devonshire, drained more blood from Tom.

The old humoral theory had been abandoned, but medical practitioners continued to treat most ailments with phlebotomy (bloodletting), an ancient Galenic remedy designed to release bad spirits from the blood and to restore the body's inner balance. Physicians relegated the job of drawing blood to surgeons, who were lower on the medical hierarchy of the time, and the practice was still common enough that barbers, besides cutting hair and shaving, also drew blood from their patients. The red-and-white pole of the barbershop symbolized, for illiterate customers, the red flowing blood of the procedure. John began his ode "To Fanny" with an allusion to it: "Physician Nature! let my spirit blood! / O ease my heart of verse and let me rest."

Tom may have had the old-fashioned class of barber-surgeons in mind when he wrote to the Jeffery sisters after his return to Hampstead. Sarah had joined them for the first stage of the journey, and she had felt queasy the whole way to Honiton, the stage stop where she turned around and went back. Tom teased her through Mary Ann: "Your sister must indeed have been au desespoire [*sic*] that she could not eat a Bun—she lost her appetite and that was not all—the Bun lost an honor—instead of being masticated by a pair of *Ivory Teeth* it was destined perhaps to some hungry pityless voracious maw, or perhaps to a more fearful destiny—there are a thousand arguments for a sophist for and against." In sickness one learns philosophy, and the style of Tom's letter is mock scholastic. Continuing his conceit of the bun, he added:

> It may be cowardly to attack a poor unfortunate lumped Combination of Doe and flour—but as it has to do with a point in Philosophy I must put in this opinion: that, as material Bodies sometimes feed upon the things they nourish, so Miss S.J. may one day find herself, by the treacherous machinations of this son of paste, prematurely possessed of an unpleasant compliment of hollow teeth; which to carry on the discussion may be argued for and against—in their favour we might say—they tend to the maintenance of a very respectable class in Society the Dentists, Barber, and whatnot—the greatest objection to them is that they bring on Lisping and denote old age.[48]

Tom's jovial tone masked the gruesome turn the trip had taken after Sarah's departure. Mrs. Jeffery had developed a maternal fondness for the invalid, and she may have seen through the giddiness. A couple of weeks after the brothers' return, she sent a friend to Well Walk to check up on Tom. Mrs. Atkins, the coachman's wife, carried a letter to Tom from Mrs. Jeffery. She was supposed to pick up a copy of John's *Poems,* which the author had promised Mary Ann. But Mrs. Jeffery had been nervous about the trip, and the real purpose of her visit may have been to examine the invalid.

Dr. Turton had warned Tom to avoid painful scenes, and Mrs. Jeffery instructed her daughters not to agitate him, so the farewell scene at Teignmouth had assumed a more formal character than Tom thought natural.

Mary Ann behaved with so much composure that John had to reassure his younger brother on the coach that she would in fact regret his absence. Mrs. Jeffery loaned them money for the ride, and although she probably would have liked to go with them, she sent her younger daughter. Sarah could sustain a cheerful demeanor longer than Mary Ann.

Tom was still flirting, but George, in ending his flirtation with Sarah Jeffery, had written in a last dash of gallantry: "I would send you kisses by way of John and Tom, but I can't say I should relish your acknowledgement of them, so I'll e'en entreat you Marianne to kiss Sarah and she must fancy it is from me, she must do the same and you must use your imagination in like manner. I should like much to perform this myself, alas, it is impossible." George had no intention of returning to his "old Friends the sands and the Cliffs."[49] His plans for marriage and emigration now consumed him.

George and Georgiana were due to be married on the last Thursday of May, at St. Margaret's Church, in the parish of Westminster. Having grown up in the shadow of the soaring Gothic structure, Georgiana knew that the colonnade leading up to the altar would make any walk down the aisle an impressive event. In those days, wedding gowns did not need to be white, and Georgiana would make one she could wear again. Needlework ranked high among her domestic skills, and George never forgot how in times of trouble she offered to assist him with her needle, thus "by her noble behaviour" showing him "the best side of her character which under uninterrupted good fortune would never have been developed."[50] She might not have been prepared for all the conditions of frontier life, but Georgiana would be prepared for the wedding.

In preparing her bridal trousseau, however, Georgiana may not have gone as far as another Englishwoman who, likewise packing for the prairie in 1818, revealed the depth of her illusion about the place to which she was going: "The lady brought over her white satin shoes and gay dresses, rich carpets, and every thing but what in such a place she would require." If Georgiana didn't bring carpets, she *did* wear a silk dress and parlor slippers in a keelboat down the Ohio River to the western frontier. Neither survived the rough terrain; by the time she reached Louisville, they were shredded.[51] Georgiana may have been leaving her carpets behind, but George would one day make it up to her with a home full of imported carpets from Brussels, Scotland, and Constantinople.

As a wedding gift, John gave Georgiana a delicately wrought golden chain. It was a present he could ill afford but that someone, possibly Isabella Jones, had given him. Georgiana knew the value of practicality, and she shortened it to make a matching bracelet from the excess length.[52] Equally valuable in sentiment, John would give his sister-in-law a chain of capital letters forming an acrostic on her "golden name." Georgiana Augusta Keats was "a pretty long name," he wrote to her shortly after she set sail from England, and the acrostic was correspondingly long:

Give me your patience sister, while I frame
Exact in capitals your golden name:
Or sue the fair Apollo and he will
Rouse from his heavy slumber and instill
Great love in me for thee and Poesy.
Imagine not that greatest mastery
And kingdom over all the realms of verse
Nears more to heaven in aught than when we nurse
And surety give to love and brotherhood.

Anthropophagi in Othello's mood,
Ulysses stormed, and his enchanted belt
Glow with the muse, but they are never felt
Unbosom'd so and so eternal made,
Such tender incense in their laurel shade,
To all the regent sisters of the Nine,
As this poor offering to you, sister mine.

Kind sister! aye, this third name says you are;
Enchanted has it been the Lord knows where.
And may it taste to you like good old wine,
Take you to real happiness and give
Sons, daughters, and a home like honied hive.

The ocean was indeed a great separator, but Georgiana would be a link between the Keats brothers. John was proud of his future sister-in-law for being "of a nature liberal and highspirited enough" to follow George (American geography was never John's forte) "to the Banks of the Mississippi."[53]

Yet while John may have been unclear about where George was going, he was even less clear about where Tom was headed. This was not the first time he had seen the color of the arterial blood his younger brother was coughing up. As George went about his business, John found himself sinking back into the Moods of his own Mind. "I am now so depressed that I have not an Idea to put to paper," he confessed to Bailey a week before George's wedding. "My hand feels like lead—and yet it is [an] unpleasant numbness it does not take away the pain of existence—I don't know what to write." Accordingly, he put down his pen and did not pick it up until after the weekend. But on Monday, May 25, he was feeling no better: "I am in that temper that if I were under Water I would scarcely kick to come to the top. . . . I feel no spur at my Brothers going to America and am almost stony-hearted about his wedding."[54] The numbness was made worse by the fact that he could feel it.

George and Tom were each on separate paths out of his life—one into the American interior and the other into an abyss more profound than that—but while John was just beginning, slowly, to acknowledge the loss of Tom, he knew not how to process the sudden, unexpected loss of George. "I have two Brothers," he wrote two weeks after George's wedding; "one is driven by the 'burden of Society' to America the other, with an exquisite love of Life, is in a lingering state."[55] John's two greatest enemies—distance and disease—were phantoms one could not battle.

There was a difference, he decided, between a Man of Genius and a Man of Power. "Men of Genius are great as certain ethereal Chemicals operating on the Mass of neutral intellect," he explained, but "they have not any individuality, any determined Character." John had gained the knack of entering into and animating any object that grabbed his attention: "A Poet is the most unpoetical of any thing in existence," he wrote, "because he has no Identity—he is continually in for—and filling some other Body." The habit was foundational to his sense of self—as, precisely, *no self*. A Chameleon Poet "is not itself—it has no self—it is every thing and nothing—It has no character."[56]

Such powers of universal sympathy took the poet places that George never went, but in George's case the battlements of a consistent persona were more intact. "I feel more and more every day, as my imagination strengthens, that I do not live in this world alone but in a thousand worlds," John wrote. Yet he often had a very real sensation that his identity was flying apart. When in a room full of people, he could feel "in a very little time annihilated."[57] On such occasions, the old "social thought" of his brother helped to reel him back from the ether: George was a Man of Power. John had insight, intelligence, and imagination, mixed with a good deal of animal spirits, but he lacked the comfort George experienced in inhabiting this world. He could not, so to speak, settle down.

As both brothers knew, the Burden of Society driving George to America was closely tied to the institution of marriage. "George had only a few thousand dollars, and knew that if he remained in London he could not be married for years," James Freeman Clarke would explain. "He married a very young lady, without fortune, the daughter of a British colonel. . . . By going at once to a western State, they might live, without much society to be sure, but yet with comfort and the prospect of improving their condition. Therefore this boy and girl, he twenty-one and she sixteen, left their home and friends and went away to be content in each other's love in the wild regions beyond the Alleghanies."[58] The economic demands of social respectability were George's burden; John had the Burden of the Mystery. Neither was an Everyman who could lay his burden down.

Not knowing how long it would take to cash in his investments, George rented a honeymoon suite at 28 Judd Street for after the wedding. The rooms were near Brunswick Square, in a terraced row of newly built Regency homes embellished with porticoes and Corinthian columns. They would be an ideal setting for tea parties and other social receptions. George and Georgiana would be delighted with their new surroundings; to John, they represented all the lunacy of fashionable middle-class life that he wished to avoid. In a poem written about the time of his brother's wedding, John depicts Brunswick Square as a symbol of the commercialization of romance:

> And what is Love?—It is a doll dress'd up
> For idleness to cosset, nurse, and dandle;
> A thing of soft misnomers, so divine
> That silly youth doth think to make itself
> Divine by loving, and so goes on
> Yawning and doating a whole summer long,
> Till Miss's comb is made a pearl tiara,

And common Wellingtons turn Romeo boots;
Till Cleopatra lives at Number Seven,
And Anthony resides in Brunswick Square.

These lines present a vision of high, anguished passion reduced to cliché. The poet sees nothing noble or glorious in the world, nothing but greed that turns love itself into a commodity. The Romeo of Brunswick Square is a Bond-Street beau, who cares more about his wardrobe than about his beloved. He wears Wellington boots, a demeaned form of the military boots once worn by kings and heroes into battle that were the rage in men's footwear. Reproduced in soft calfskin leather with embarrassing heart-shaped tassels, they were better suited to sipping tea on a comfortable settee than to confronting the enemy in the mud. From the dandified Duke of Wellington to the Duke of Brunswick, the military metaphor informs John's satire of the marriage market.

The same chatterers that the poet had so much trouble addressing in his preface to *Endymion* were, to his mind, part of a larger socioeconomic picture fueling the ideology of romantic love. No regal Cleopatra lived at Number Seven Judd Street, no Mark Antony at Brunswick Square. Even the pearl that Cleopatra swallows in a magnificent tribute to Antony has been manufactured into a hairpiece. Commercialism dragged everything down. Unlike his own brother, whom John always held apart, the fashionable beaux parading down Judd Street contributed to "the miasma of London." Worse than vapors from any swamp that might once have been there, the milieu of Brunswick Square was "contaminated with bucks and soldiers, and women of fashion—and hat-band ignorance."[59]

Before the end of the year, the poet himself would fall in love, but this would not change his views about marriage. "God forbid we should what people call, *settle,*" he would write to Fanny Brawne, "turn into a pond, a stagnant Lethe—a vile crescent, row or buildings. Better be imprudent moveables than prudent fixtures. . . . Go out and wither at tea parties; freeze at dinners; bake at dances, simmer at routs."[60] Yet this is precisely what John would have to do if he wanted to spend time with his brother and sister-in-law before they left town.

Although John could hardly summon excitement to stand next to George at the wedding, when the time came, he got dressed up and did his duty. He signed the register at St. Margaret's Church as a witness, next to

Mary Ann Keysell, Henry Wylie's future wife. Georgiana was not yet twenty-one, so her mother had given her consent by signing the marriage allegation prior to the ceremony.[61] Yet for some reason hard to fathom, Richard Abbey kept Fanny Keats from attending her brother's wedding. Perhaps sickness was the excuse. Whatever the reason, it would be another decade before Fanny would meet her new sister.

In the presence of Georgiana's family, meanwhile, John felt that his family had expanded, even as it was about to contract. He and Charles Wylie looked out the window, and "quizzed," or made fun of, the people as they passed. At eighteen, Charles was a bit of a blade, and in anticipation of Victorian fashion he wore his sideburns long. They were not as long in the summer of 1818 as they would become by the following year when "his young, son of a gun's whiskers had begun to curl and curl." As John described them in a letter to George and Georgiana, they would have formed by then "little twists and twists; all down the sides of his face getting properly thickish on the angles of the visage."[62]

Charles Gaskell Wylie, unlike his sister, would not settle down for a while. In 1819, he would travel to France, and the next year to Brussels; the year after that he would go to Norway. Not until a decade after his sister's departure would he marry. At St. James's Church on Stoke Newington High Street, he would wed Margaret Roberts—and there, too, he would christen his son, George Keats Wylie. He would not be married for more than three years, however, before he would declare bankruptcy and surrender all his worldly goods to George and Charles Roberts, warehousemen and presumably his wife's relations. He would then toil at the rather incongruous trades of cheesemongering and artificial-flower manufacturing, and die before reaching forty.[63]

Henry Robert Wylie, who was in his mid-thirties, also liked to dress smartly. John preferred Henry's cook to his fiancée, and indeed Henry's figure showed the results of good living. The cook, in John's account, was thirty-something, fat, fair, and smiling, while Henry's beloved, Mary Ann Keysell, resembled a flagpole with a gown for a flag; she was a "lath with a bodice . . . fit for nothing but to cut up into Cribbage pins." John joked to his brother and sister-in-law that she would make Henry a good linchpin to fix his carriage wheel, or "his walking stick, his fishing rod, his toothpick—his hat stick (she runs so much in his head)." With her elbow resting on the table, she reminded him of the Renaissance soothsayer Mother Shipton, or rather, "a teapaper wood cut" of the wrinkled old lady. He suggested putting her out to nurse with Shakespeare's wise woman of Brentford, "an old fat woman" from *The Merry Wives of Windsor,* and he hoped that Henry would not marry her. "Non volo ut eam possideat, nam, for it would be a bam, for it would be a sham—" But he realized that it was "no uncommon thing to be *smitten with a staff.*" These were all the puns he could summon "on so spare a subject."[64]

But Henry did marry Miss Keysell, on December 23, 1819. The wedding took place at St. George Church in Bloomsbury, with the other two Marys from Henrietta Street, Mary Waldegrave and Mary Amelia Millar, in attendance. John would complain afterwards that Henry had become "wife-bound in Cambden Town" and that there was "no getting him out." Charles named his son after George, and Henry would give his daughter Georgiana's middle name: Augusta Christina Wylie. His sister would return the favor by giving her first son the middle name Henry. Despite John's insistence that his own name was "a bad name" and went "against a Man," George and Georgiana's first son was of course named John: John Henry Keats. But Augusta would die young, at twenty-six, and Henry, like other merchants including his own brother and brother-in-law, would find that fortunes made in trade were not always easy to keep afloat. He, too, would die a bankrupt.[65]

Georgiana's cousin, Mary Amelia Millar, was "a different morsel" from her skinny housemate, Mary Keysell. John parodied Cousin Mary as a coquette with a string of failed suitors: "The first tried the effect of swearing; the second of stammering; the third of whispering;—the fourth of sonnets—the fifth of Spanish leather boots the sixth of flattering her body— the seventh of flattering her mind—the eighth of flattering himself—the ninth stuck to the Mother—the tenth kissed the Chambermaid and told her to tell her Mistress." Cousin Mary had a habit of giving the poet teasing pinches he did not like and of prodding her mother along in her tedious stories, which the old lady delivered "as though her tongue were ill of the gout."[66] By the time Georgiana saw her cousin again, her talkative aunt would be dead.

George invited John Taylor as well to Brunswick Square, to meet his wife. When the publisher showed up, he brought a copy of Morris Birkbeck's *Letters from Illinois,* just off the press from Taylor & Hessey. He also brought two letters of introduction, which he thought might be helpful to

George. The first was to his cousin Michael Drury, a merchant who had recently moved from Lincolnshire to Philadelphia. Although George could not tell in advance to which port he would be heading, emigrants traveling to the Western Country of America often passed through Philadelphia. Taylor encouraged George to get in touch with his cousin and to rely upon his assistance, which he was sure that Michael Drury would render freely. The second was to Morris Birkbeck. George would carry that letter a thousand miles farther, into the heart of the unsettled West.

Yet, once George looked into the book that Taylor had given him, he discovered that the Cockney Pioneers were limiting the sale of land on the English Prairie to no more than six hundred and forty acres (a section of land) per settler. The largest lots available had less than half the acreage that George had in mind. If he were to carry through with his original plan of purchasing fourteen hundred acres on the prairie, he would have to locate his own land, and build his own house. The thought gave him pause, but with the optimism that defined his character, he decided that no worthwhile achievement came without struggle. Difficulty and inconvenience would only add to the satisfactions of independence that he would feel in America: "When I thought these things might be done the advantage seemed great, but when I consider the having to do them myself, I only feel an addition of pride to undertake and accomplish the whole task myself."[67] *This* Cockney Pioneer had already begun to think like an American.

Unlike George, John had never been swept away by the idea of America. During George and Georgiana's honeymoon period at Brunswick Square, he kept his reservations to himself; but once they had crossed the Atlantic, he would let his feelings flow more freely. "A country like the United States whose greatest Men are Franklins and Washingtons" would never fulfill its promise, he predicted. Such men could not compare with Milton and Sir Philip Sidney, politicians with poetry in their souls. Benjamin Franklin was "a philosophical Quaker full of mean and thrifty maxims," and George Washington "sold the very Charger who had taken him through all his Battles." While they might be admirable in their way, they had no sublimity. "Those Americans are great but they are not sublime Man—the humanity of the United States can never reach the sublime— Birkbeck's mind is too much in the American Style."[68] George would have to infuse a spirit of a different kind into the settlement of the Cockney Pioneers.

Leigh Hunt, whose own family was from America, saw the place in much the same way as his fellow Cockney Poet. Hunt loved Emerson, William Cullen Bryant, James Russell Lowell, and for the sake of his mother, "all Philadelphia women," but he could not help thinking that the Americans were "Englishmen with the poetry and romance taken out of them." Hunt's grandfather Stephen Shewell, Sr., a merchant shipper, represented the mercantile attitude of the Americans. When he learned that his grandson was writing—and even planning to publish—poetry as a teenager, the Philadelphia merchant became "alarmed at the fruitless consequences to which it might lead" and sent his grandson word that if he came to Philadelphia, he would make a man of him. Hunt "could not help, for some time, identifying the whole American character with his." When he thought of the American people, Hunt imagined "one great counter built along their coast from north to south, behind which they are all standing like so many linendrapers."[69]

George had not lasted long as a linendraper, and John, notwithstanding his feelings about the prosaic American spirit, would rather see him "till the ground than bow to a Customer." John believed that George was "of too independent and liberal a Mind to get on in trade" in England, where "a generous Man with a scanty recourse must be ruined." Perhaps George and Georgiana might produce "the first American Poet"—

Child, I see thee! Child, I've found thee,
Midst of the quiet all around thee!
Child, I see thee! Child, I spy thee,
And thy mother sweet is nigh thee!
Child, I know thee! Child no more,
But a Poet *ever*more
See, see the lyre, the lyre,
In a flame of fire,
Upon the little cradle's top
Flaring, flaring, flaring,
Past the eyesight's bearing—
Awake it from its sleep,
And see if it can keep
Its eye upon the blaze.
Amaze, amaze!
It stares, it stares, it stares;

It dares what no one dares;
It lifts its little hand into the flame
Unharm'd, and on the strings
Paddles a little tune and sings
With dumb endeavour sweetly!
Bard art thou completely!
Little child
O' the western wild,
Bard art thou completely!—
Sweetly, with dumb endeavour,
A Poet now or never!
Little Child
O' the western wild,
A Poet now or never!

George would hold onto the letter containing this poem, and when he later met the American poet John Howard Payne in Kentucky, he showed it to him, to the grief and humiliation of the latter: "The writer does not seem to have known that we have had, and then possessed, many poets in America." Yet Payne suspected that what John meant by "the first" was the *"greatest."* Despite the "obnoxious" remark that prefaced it, he greatly admired the lullaby-like prophecy of the little child of the Western Wild.[70]

The Cockney Poets were hardly alone in their views of the land to which the pioneer brother was moving. "Literature the Americans have none—no native literature, we mean. It is all imported," the *Edinburgh Review* reported in December 1818. "They had a Franklin, indeed; and may afford to live for half a century on his fame. . . . But why should the Americans write books, when a six weeks' passage brings them, in their own tongue, our sense, science and genius, in bales and hogsheads? Prairies, steam-boats, grist-mills, are their natural objects for centuries to come." Even Americans held such views. In a book intended to contradict negative accounts of American culture by British travel writers, James Fenimore Cooper would explain the lack of imaginative literature in America (ironically) as the result of an uninspired land: "There are no annals for the Historian; no follies (beyond the most vulgar and common place) for the satirist; no manners, for the dramatist; no obscure fictions for the writer of romance; no gross and hourly offenses against decorum for the moralist; nor any of the rich artificial auxiliaries of Poetry."[71]

Richard Abbey was concerned with not what kind of *art* George would find in America, but what kind of business opportunities. If George wanted to read books, he could stay home. But George must have convinced him that there were other possibilities overseas, for the tea dealer sprang into action and, to everyone's surprise, produced George's inheritance of £1,600 within twenty-four hours of his wedding. George does not seem to have known about the £800 he had inherited from his grandfather, a sum, tied up in Chancery, which, as Robert Gittings calculates, had accrued roughly £205 in interest. (Nor can anyone say for sure whether Abbey knew about it.) Abbey added another £75 or £100 as a wedding gift—George could not remember the exact amount. It was a good time for the pioneer brother to cash in, and for every three pounds that John had received on turning twenty-one, George received four.[72] George and Georgiana were now ready to leave in half the time anyone had expected.

After George left town, Abbey would shift his custodial anxieties onto the two remaining brothers. From what he could tell, the youngest did not seem able to work, and the oldest did not seem willing. Abbey regretted that they had failed to see the potentiality in hats. After all, didn't every house have a hat stand? Who went anywhere without a hat? But once John returned from Scotland, Abbey would hit upon a new and brilliant idea: if his eldest ward didn't want to sell hats, why not try something more up his alley? *Why not sell books?* "M'r Abbey shows at times a little anxiety about me," John informed George eight months later. "He wanted me the other day to turn Bookseller."[73] But John was about as suited to selling books for a living as his guardian was to writing them.

Meanwhile, with the money George received from Abbey, the pioneer brother set about squaring his accounts and paying his debts. On the fourth of June, he deposited £500 at Abbey & Cocks, in an account for his brothers. Later, confusion would arise about whether that deposit was a gift or a loan, but George was too caught up in his own schemes to explain his calculations to John. And John, having no taste for such details, asked no questions. As a result, the very problem that George had once hoped to avoid, namely, the brothers' being at sixes and sevens with regard to expenses, would come back to haunt them. Charles Brown would later claim that after George's departure John felt some dissatisfaction over the reckoning of accounts. Shouldn't George, John asked his friend, have given him a written record? John had spent money during Tom's sickness, "taking him to

Margate . . . and afterwards to Teignmouth."[74] Yet when George left for the United States, John was surprised to be left with so little.

Tom could not travel—in any direction—and it has be asked why, rather than remaining at home with his sick brother, John chose to accompany Brown on a trip expected to last four months. George, to be sure, considered his trip too momentous to put off, but did John really need to go hiking? "My brother Tom will I am afraid be lonely," John acknowledged when he asked Taylor to lend Tom any books he might want that summer.[75] The odds are that John knew there was little he could do for his sick brother, even if he spent the summer in Hampstead. Rallying his own spirits through a change of scene might be the best thing for all concerned. And in Brown, John would have a companion with more than backpacking experience. With his sense of humor and adventure, Brown was a bastion of strength.

There was also a professional purpose to the trip. Having produced a poetic romance, John was ready to try an epic. The majesty of the Scottish Highlands promised to fill his mind with more sublime scenes than Hampstead. "I should not have consented to myself these four Months tramping in the highlands," he would explain in July, "but that I thought it would give me more experience, rub off more Prejudice, use [me] to more hardship, identify finer scenes[,] load me with grander Mountains, and strengthen more my reach in Poetry, than would stopping at home among Books." John would see things he had not seen before, while Tom relaxed and made one "long lounge of the whole Summer."[76]

John and George planned to travel together on the stagecoach to Liverpool and separate there. George would book a passage for himself and Georgiana on one of the oceangoing packet ships anchored in Liverpool Harbor, and John and Brown would carry on north to Lancaster, where their walking tour would begin. Lighter post coaches left daily from the coaching inn where the foursome would spend their last night together. The Bentleys promised to look after Tom, and William Haslam offered to check in regularly. David Lewis, a Hampstead neighbor whom John described as "a very goodnatured, goodlooking old gentleman [who has] been very kind to Tom and George and me," would also stop by every day. Whenever Lewis couldn't visit Tom in person, he would send a messenger with a basket of fruit.[77]

John might have felt worse about leaving his sister. Fanny had a cat and chickens for companions, but outside the Abbeys' cold suburban shell, life rumbled on without her. John knew that she looked up to him for the only patches of sunshine in her otherwise Stygian existence. "I have a Sister too and may not follow them," he said, referring to his brothers, "either to America or to the Grave."[78] For Fanny, there would be no leave-taking, either at Brunswick Square or at the Swan with Two Necks, the coaching inn from which her brothers would soon depart.

Fanny would not see Georgiana with her hair pinned up under her pretty traveling bonnet. She would not see George in his high collar and jacket, nervous but smiling. Nor would she see John prepared for the Scottish Highlands with his tartan plaid and waterproofed knapsack. She would not see Brown among the men in capes brandishing whips to keep order among the horses in the courtyard of the Swan with Two Necks. She would not see the mailbags, the porters, the trunks, the portmanteaus, or the passengers crowding the inn. She would stay home and spend a dull summer with the Abbeys.

The Swan with Two Necks on Lad Lane, in Cheapside, was a mere stone's throw from the brothers' former lodgings above Bird-in-Hand Court. It must have brought back memories. Only two years earlier, they had spent evenings a-wassailing at the Queen's Head Tavern, or watching the small busy flames crackle and play over their freshly laid coal. Now, the fire lighting the "gentle empire" of "fraternal souls" was about to go out. The hearth would soon be cold, and the brothers, like ashes, would scatter.

Separation at Liverpool

The seats inside the Prince Saxe-Cobourg stagecoach that left the inner courtyard of the Swan with Two Necks on Monday morning, June 22, were hard and cramped. Georgiana was scarcely more comfortable inside the carriage than John, George, and Brown were outside it. The mail was the first priority of the coaching company. People and baggage came along for the ride. George and Georgiana had condensed their possessions to five "packages" (in this case, trunks or boxes). Furniture damaged easily on ocean voyages and could be procured more cheaply across the Atlantic. The travel guides suggested that emigrants headed to the Western Country pack, besides clothing, such useful items as cutlery, pots, dishes, and sewing boxes. On the frontier, everyday items like these were hard to find. The

1. John Keats (1795–1821), the poet.

Miniature by Joseph Severn, oil on ivory, 1819.
Copyright © National Portrait Gallery, London.

2. George Keats (1797–1841), the pioneer.

Miniature by Joseph Severn; photo by S. Manicone.
Copyright © Keats-Shelley House and S. Manicone.

3. Tom Keats (1799–1818),
the youngest brother.
Miniature by Joseph Severn, 1818; photo by S. Manicone.
Copyright © Keats-Shelley House
and S. Manicone.

4. Fanny Keats (1803–1889), the sister.
Painting of Frances Mary Llanos later in life as a married
woman by her son, Juan Llanos y Keats, c. 1860;
photo by S. Manicone.
Copyright © Keats-Shelley House and S. Manicone.

5. An eighteenth-century engraving
of St. Thomas's Hospital, where
John attended medical school.

Courtesy of Houghton Library, Harvard University,
MS Keats 10 (65).

6. James Henry Leigh Hunt (1784–1859),
editor of the *Examiner,* lampooned
as "King of the Cockney Poets."

Pencil sketch by Thomas Charles Wageman, 1815.
Copyright © National Portrait Gallery, London.

8. The poet John Hamilton Reynolds
(1794–1852).

Watercolor on ivory, by Joseph Severn, 1818.
Copyright © National Portrait Gallery, London.

7. The painter Benjamin Robert Haydon
(1786–1846) and John Keats.

Pen-and-ink sketch by John Keats, 1816.
Copyright © National Portrait Gallery, London.

9. A view of Cheapside. The Keats brothers lived at No. 76
during the winter of 1816–1817. St. Mary-le-Bow Church
can be seen in the background.

Courtesy of Houghton Library, Harvard University, MS Keats 10 (310).

10. John Clarke's boarding school at Enfield,
which all three Keats brothers attended.

Anonymous watercolor, c. 1840; photo by S. Manicone.
Copyright © Keats-Shelley House and S. Manicone.

12. Keats's Corner overlooking Hampstead Heath at the end of Well Walk, the road on which the Keats brothers lived in 1817–1818.
Courtesy of the Keats House, City of London.

11. The artist Joseph Severn (1793–1879), who accompanied John to Rome.
Self-portrait in pencil, c. 1820.
Copyright © National Portrait Gallery, London.

13. The middle of Hampstead Heath, 1818.

D. Havell, artist; John Hassell, engraver. Courtesy of the London Metropolitan Archives, London.

14. Wentworth Place, home of Charles Armitage Brown and Charles
Wentworth Dilke, near Hampstead Heath. Later, John lived in the
smaller part of the house with Brown, and Fanny Brawne's family sublet
the part formerly owned by Dilke. The seal in the lower-right
corner is from one of John's letters.

Etching by W. Goodride Beal. Courtesy of Houghton Library,
Harvard University, MS Keats 10 (256).

15. Charles Wentworth Dilke (1789–1864), critic and Man of Letters.

Anonymous portrait, c. 1825.
Courtesy of the Keats House, City of London.

16. Maria Dover Walker Dilke, wife of Charles Wentworth Dilke.

Portrait by Sears Gallagher after a miniature.
Courtesy of Houghton Library, Harvard University,
MS Keats 10 (527).

17. Charles Armitage Brown (1787–1842), critic, poet, adventurer.

Photo of bust by Andrew Wilson, 1828.
Courtesy of the Keats House, City of London.

18. John Keats at Wentworth Place,
with John's portrait of Shakespeare in the background.

Painted from memory by Joseph Severn in 1821. Oil on canvas.
Courtesy of the National Portrait Gallery, London.

19. Fanny Brawne (1800–1865),
John's beloved.

Miniature by unknown painter, c. 1833.
Courtesy of the Keats House, City of London.

20. The Bar Gate, Southampton. John thought the two lions flanking the turret
"respectable guards" when he passed through on his way to
the Isle of Wight in 1817.

Courtesy of Houghton Library, Harvard University, MS Keats 10 (260).

21. Carisbrooke Castle, Isle of Wight. The colony of jackdaws that John saw
when he stayed at Newport can be seen flocking above the keep.

Engraving by George Brannon, 1823, from *Vectis Scenery: Being a Series of Original and Select Views,
Exhibiting the Picturesque Beauties, Local Peculiarities, and Places of Particular Interest in the Isle of Wight.*
Courtesy of Harvard College Library, Widener Library, KF 1058.

22. Hastings, Sussex, near the hamlet of Bo Peep.
John met Isabella Jones there in the spring of 1817.

Engraving by W. B. Cooke, 1816.
Courtesy of Houghton Library, Harvard University, MS Keats 10 (110).

23. John Scott (1783–1821), editor of the
Champion, whom George and Tom
visited in Paris in 1817.

Portrait engraving, c. 1814. Courtesy of Houghton
Library, Harvard University, MS Keats 10 (600).

24. Edward Croydon's Public Library on Regent's Road in
Teignmouth, Devonshire.

Aquatint engraving by N. Shury, 1817.
Courtesy of the Westcountry Studies Library, Exeter, SC 2826.

25. View of Teignmouth, Devonshire, as seen from the Ness, the red sandstone headland across the mouth of the Teign River from the Den (the circular promenade).

Aquatint by J. Strutt, Jr., c. 1828. Courtesy of the Westcountry Studies Library, Exeter, SC 2917-2.

26. The Bathing Place at Teignmouth, on the English Channel.

Illustration by R. Speare, Esq., engraved by J. Baily, 1816. Courtesy of the Westcountry Studies Library, Exeter, SC 2839.

27. John Taylor (1781–1864),
John's publisher and cousin of the
English emigrants Michael and
Mary Drury, whom George and
Georgiana met in America.

Wax medallion by unknown artist.
Courtesy of the National Portrait Gallery,
London.

28. George and Georgiana Keats.

Anonymous silhouettes, c. 1828. Courtesy of Lawrence M. Crutcher.

29. The Swan with Two Necks, Lad Lane, in London.
The stagecoach carrying John and George to Liverpool left
from the courtyard of this inn.

Aquatint by James Pollard, engraved by F. Rosenberg, 1831.
Courtesy of the London Metropolitan Archives.

couple would also need bedding and featherbeds for their berths in the ship's cabin, but these could be readily obtained at the docks in Liverpool.

John and Brown had packed even more lightly: a change of shirt, a towel, a nightcap, a hairbrush, a comb, and, in John's case, a three-volume pocket edition of Dante's *Divine Comedy* just out from Taylor & Hessey. John called it his book full of vowels, to rhyme with "towels" in the verse catalogue of his knapsack that he sent to his sister from Scotland:

He took
In his knapsack
A book
Full of vowels
And a shirt
With some towels—
A slight cap
For night cap—
A hair brush
Comb ditto
New stockings
For old ones
Would split O!
This knapsack
Tight at 's back
He rivetted close
And followed his nose
To the north
To the north
And follow'd his nose
To the north—[79]

To Abbey, John and Brown, with their walking sticks and tartan capes, looked as ridiculous as a pair of Don Quixotes. In the Highlands, they would be taken for other things: peddlers, spectacle vendors, razor sellers, jewelers, traveling linendrapers, even excisemen. One old man in his cups would suspect them to be French spies in disguise. Yet, whatever they were about to become, once they pulled out of the inner courtyard of the Swan with Two Necks, they were young men on their way to adventure.

John was looking forward to meeting his old roommate Henry Stephens at the Black Bull Inn in Redbourne, Hertfordshire, to break up the journey. The trip to Liverpool would be a bumpy, thirty-two-hour stage-coach ride in the rain. The coaching road passed through the main street of Redbourne, where Stephens had taken a position as a surgeon-apothecary. John hadn't seen much of him since medical school. Although they had once been at odds about Pope, whom Stephens liked, and Spenser, whom John championed, time puts things in perspective, and they would be glad to see each other again.

John sent Stephens a note, and he joined them for an early-afternoon dinner. Stephens found himself enchanted by Georgiana. "Somewhat sin-gular & girlish in her attire," he recalled, she was "not what might be strictly called handsome." But like her new gifted relation, she had an "imagina-tive poetical cast." Stephens's description resembles John's own view of his sister-in-law as "unearthly, spiritual and ethereal." The apothecary sensed that "there was something original about her," and by the time the party was ready to resume its journey, he had decided that she was "a being whom any man of moderate Sensibility might easily love."[80]

Somehow the ephemerality of the moment—the feeling of youth quickly passing away—contributed to the poignancy of the imminent sepa-ration. The meal seemed to end before it began, and the travelers climbed back on board the coach. The weather was wet as they pursued their course along the old Roman road through the moors toward old Stony-Stratford. There, they passed The Cock and The Bull, the coaching inns on opposite sides of the street that gave their names to the phrase "cock-and-bull story." What do travelers who find themselves stuck waiting in such places for a change of horses *do* anyway, but entertain each other with a tall tale or two, over a pint . . . or two?

As the Prince Saxe-Coburg stagecoach rattled on in a northwesterly direction through the Chiltern Hills, the sky stayed overcast. Occasionally, it showered. That evening, the coach crossed the Great Ouse River into the landlocked counties of Northamptonshire and Warwickshire, with their spires and squires. After passing through Coventry, the traveling compan-ions could see the Welsh mountains, as they descended the hills toward the open plains of Cheshire. Not until the next day would they cross the River Mersey into the bustling port city of Liverpool.[81]

The harbor was crammed with masts and sails. Pilot boats shuttled be-tween the ships at anchor and the shore. Horse-drawn carts dragged boxes and barrels from the docks to the warehouses. Particularly in summer, the place was in a tumult: sailors shouting, children crying, pigs squealing, chickens clucking, geese squawking, cows mooing, goats bleating and stamping—impatient, or so it seemed, to be gone. "All is hurry, bustle, and confusion!" cried William Amphlett, an English emigrant who sailed to the United States a month before George and Georgiana did from Liverpool. The scene of departure was a spectacle worthy of Noah's Ark:

> The passengers running to and fro; some taking an affectionate, an ever-lasting farewell of their kindred and friends; others without a friend to take leave of, standing with a strange mixture of joy and grief in their countenances, looking a last adieu to the land of their fathers! Others arriving too late, are making to the vessel in boats, with their last articles of luggage hastily packed up—a strange medley of clothing and provisions—band-boxes, and bags of potatoes, legs of mutton, hampers of porter, salt herrings, and barrels of biscuit.[82]

Like other places in England, Liverpool had grown quickly since the end of the Napoleonic Wars, and a large percentage of the world's trade now passed through the port. At night, the street lamps lit up the town, and the lighthouse shot forth its beams to guide the incoming ships. Lanterns dangling from the bowsprits of schooners looked as if they were indeed the spirits—*sprits*—of the ships. Weary from travel, the brothers and their respective partners put up at the Crown Inn, on Red Cross Street, run by Samuel Henshaw.

Again, it has been asked why John Keats, if not to see more of the city, at least to find out where his brother was going, did not stay longer in Liverpool. Travelers bound on oceangoing voyages sometimes had to wait weeks to depart, but John and Brown would be gone before daybreak. John would direct letters to George and Georgiana at the Crown Inn after their departure for lack of better information. As John fretted to Tom on July 26, he had no idea where George had gone: "I in my carelessness never thought of knowing where a letter would find him on the other side."[83] But John's ignorance in this case was not carelessness.

Why prolong the inevitable? The anxiety, the feeling of abandonment, the sense of isolation and loss, had been welling inside the poet. George, this time, could provide no consolation, for he was the source of the pain. Having already explored England by foot, Brown was eager to be off to the North. John, equally restless, always felt better being on the move. Both of them, perhaps even more so Brown, wished to avoid what was shaping up to be a melancholy farewell. *O horrible! to lose the sight of well remember'd face, / Of brother's eyes, of sister's brow, constant to every place.* John's "Lines written in the highlands after a visit to Burns's Country" expressed the sentiment he may have been feeling during the wet ride to Liverpool. He could "play at cut and run as well as Falstaff."[84]

George dealt with matters as the need arose, but John had in fact been experiencing the pain of separation from his brother for weeks. "My brother George has ever been more than a brother to me," John explained to Georgiana's mother; "he has been my greatest friend."[85] The symbolic content of leave-taking had been spent, and the scene of forced sociality with Stephens at Redbourne in the end only made things worse. Compared to the trials of anticipation John had already faced, the act of leaving would no doubt have come as a relief. The actual goodbye was empty ceremony. Reality was in the harbor, and it was in the salty air.

From George's perspective, it was not the end of the world. The pioneer brother was in the empowered position of having decided to leave, and he planned to return. He would see John again. He would not be leaving England if he did not think the move was in everyone's best interest. "If I did not feel fully persuaded that my motive was to acquire an independence to support us all in case of necessity," he later insisted, "I never should forgive myself for leaving him[;] some extraordinary exertion was necessary to retrieve our affairs from the gradual decline they were suffering—that exertion I made whether wisely, or not, future events had to decide."[86] A Man of Power made choices and stuck to them—for better or for worse.

Just as John had once consoled himself for the absence of his brothers by wandering down to the wharf at Southampton to catch the ferry to the Isle of Wight, George set about making plans to sail. The American packet ships were the fastest on the ocean at the time, and George discovered that an American ship, the *Telegraph,* bound for Philadelphia, had already been cleared to depart and that it still had first-class cabin space available. The ship had been built near Boston and registered, four years earlier, by its owners, Wiggin & Whitney, of Philadelphia. It had been afloat long enough, in other words, to have a track record; and yet, not so long as to not seem new.

The company boasted that it was "a very superior built ship, a fast sailor" with "excellent accommodations," and, like most top-of-the-line packet ships, it was smartly coppered and copper-fastened. In the case of the *Telegraph,* its very name announced modernity, the telegraph being a wooden device used to communicate signals from shore. The ship had been cleared to sail on the day that George and Georgiana left London and was now at anchor in the River Mersey, awaiting a favorable wind.[87] George quickly reserved first-class cabin space for him and Georgiana.

The ship's captain, Hector Coffin, had one of the best reputations on the North Atlantic. He had commanded the *Telegraph* on the eastbound leg of the round-trip journey from Philadelphia on April 11, or twelve days before George Flower and his party of Cockney Pioneers set sail for Philadelphia from Liverpool. The ships crossed each other in passing. The *Telegraph* swung past the Saltee Islands off the southern coast of Ireland on May 11 and sailed up the Irish Sea, docking in Liverpool after a voyage that lasted one month. Within twenty-one days, the ship had been reloaded to capacity with puncheons of rum, bales of cotton, and other hampers, bundles, chests, casks, barrels, rolls, and quantities constituting packages. Most of its three hundred and ninety-one tons of cargo consisted of iron—in bars, squares, hoops, and rods—to be wrought into saws that would cut down the trees and nails that would hold up the houses in the New World—as well as shovels, spades, sockets, hoes, ploughshares, and other farming equipment intended to tame the land.[88]

Traversing the Atlantic was a risky business. Despite Captain Coffin's ill-boding name, he knew the route backwards and forwards, and his record of speedy and safe ocean crossings was reassuring. After depositing George and Georgiana in Philadelphia at the end of August, he would sail the *Telegraph* on the same route from Philadelphia eight weeks later, on an eastbound crossing that would take five days longer than George and Georgiana's forty-seven days at sea. He would sail the *Telegraph* back from Liverpool to Philadelphia in late January. He had made the same westbound trip from Liverpool to Philadelphia in stormy seas the previous January, while George and Tom were in Teignmouth. The ship had been caught in a hurricane and the bowsprit had sprung, so that it could no longer support the headsails. The *Telegraph* veered off-course, but Captain Coffin finally brought her into harbor, after forty-six hard days at sea, with a full cargo of human freight and dry goods: rolled sheet lead, copper rods and bolts, chests of tea, hogsheads of porter and ale, hampers of potatoes and cheese, stones, and shrubbery, among other bales, cases, and barrels. Included in these packages were twenty-five addressed to Taylor's cousin Michael Drury, in Philadelphia.[89]

Traveling in the cabin with George and Georgiana would be a Mr. Walter Conyers and a Miss Rebecca K. West. Conyers was probably the boot manufacturer who in 1818 worked at 40 South Third Street, Philadelphia, with the shoemaker John Conyers. In December 1819, Walter Conyers would press charges against a customer for failing to honor a promissory note of $85.92—a case "of general importance . . . as containing a caution to men of business in the payment of debts, to take adequate vouchers." This would be one of many cautions that emigrants like George would have been advised to heed. The female passenger may have been Conyers's daughter, for seventeen years later a "Miss Rebecca," described as the only daughter of Walter Conyers, Esq., married a Dr. T. M. Jones in Philadelphia.[90]

Cabin passengers spent weeks in close quarters with the captain, and in this respect, George and Georgiana were fortunate. Captain Coffin, now in his mid-thirties, had the social aptitude as well as the maritime skills necessary to be a successful shipmaster. His English ancestor Tristram Coffin, Jr., had built a house on High Street in Newburyport, Massachusetts, in the seventeenth century, which Coffin and his wife would inherit. His father, Dr. Charles Coffin, was a physician in Newburyport, and his elder brother, the Reverend Charles Coffin, Jr., was president of Greenville College in Knoxville, Tennessee. Both were Harvard graduates, and Captain Coffin himself had attended Phillips Exeter Academy. He had also, like James Wylie, served as a lieutenant in a company of fencibles: the Newbury Sea Fencibles, a company of eighty volunteer privates who had defended their country against the British in the War of 1812. His armorial bookplate bore the motto *Exstant recte factus praemia*: "Rewards await those who have acted well."[91]

Although captains did not usually take their wives to sea, Captain Coffin was a family man. The previous summer, he had taken his wife, Mary Caswell (née Cook), from Philadelphia to Liverpool. After they left, his father, Charles Coffin, Sr., wrote to his brother, Charles Coffin, Jr.: "Pray for him that while they see the wonders of the Lord in the deep they may be constrained to put their trust in him." The captain and his wife had been married ten years, and while their son, Francis Vergnies, apparently did not survive childhood, Coffin had also raised a local Newburyport lad, Frederick William Comerford (fatherless since the age of four), as a shipmaster. Captain Comerford was now twenty-seven, and later that same year, on November 2, 1818, after returning to Boston from India, his ship, the *Pekin*, would be condemned off Gibraltar as unseaworthy. Captain Coffin would write to the ship's owner, Captain William Sturgis, that very day to seek information about the *Pekin*, politely asking him to forgive the inquiry, "caused by the regard I have for the young man who commands her, who I brought up, together with a small adventure in her, under his care."[92]

While Captain Coffin's father and brother prayed for him and his wife, a party of American craftsmen, led by the inventor Jacob Perkins, joined the Coffins in the cabins of the *Telegraph*. Perkins spent his time at sea studying the compressibility of water on a machine of his own invention called a pyometer. After eight days at sea, Captain Coffin would report that "Mr. Perkins . . . had succeeded in his experiment." The party carried twenty-six cases of machinery that they would use to compete for the Royal Commission to redesign banknotes for the Bank of England. Captain Coffin offered to invest £25,000 in the project, though nothing in the end came of it.[93]

Notwithstanding the romance that later became attached to the idea of an ocean cruise, travel in the days of the early oceangoing packet ships was hardly luxurious. The cabins were tiny and cramped, and the rolling of the sea was felt more there than down in the steerage: the cargo hold below deck, named for the control lines that steered the rudder, where a second class of less fortunate souls spent their time at sea. The *Telegraph* had twelve state-rooms and two "second cabins," though in many cases the latter often had little to recommend them beyond a clear demarcation between *their* occupants and those thrown together in the steerage.[94] Bilge water contaminated the air contributing to sea-sickness. Even on a top-of-the-line ship like the *Telegraph*, conditions at the best of times were Spartan. Freight was easier to ship than human beings, and it paid about the same.

Charles Dickens crossed the Atlantic two decades after George and Georgiana, on a steam packet from Liverpool to Boston, and his experience led him to burlesque the very idea of a state-room at sea:

That this state-room had been specially engaged for "Charles Dickens, Esquire, and Lady," was rendered sufficiently clear even to my scared intellect by a very small manuscript, announcing the fact, which was pinned on a very flat quilt, covering a very thin mattress, spread like a surgical plaster on a most inaccessible shelf. But that this was the state-room concerning which Charles Dickens, Esquire, and Lady, had held daily and nightly conferences for at least four months preceding: that this could by any possibility be that small snug chamber of the imagination, which Charles Dickens, Esquire, with the spirit of prophecy strong upon him, had always foretold would contain at least one little sofa, and which his lady, with a modest yet most magnificent sense of its limited dimensions, had from the first opined would not hold more than two enormous portmanteaus in some odd corner out of sight (portmanteaus which could now no more be got in at the door, not to say stowed away, than a giraffe could be persuaded or forced into a flower-pot): that this utterly impracticable, thoroughly hopeless, and profoundly preposterous box, had the remotest reference to, or connexion with, those chaste and pretty, not to say gorgeous little bowers, sketched by a masterly hand, in the highly varnished lithographic plan hanging up in the agent's counting-house in the city of London; that this room of state, in short, could be anything but a pleasant fiction and cheerful jest of the captain's, invented and put in practice for the better relish and enjoyment of the real state-room presently to be disclosed:—these were truths which I really could not, for the moment, bring my mind at all to bear upon or comprehend. And I sat down upon a kind of horsehair slab, or perch, of which there were two within; and looked, without any expression of countenance whatever, at some friends who had come on board with us, and who were crushing their faces into all manner of shapes by endeavouring to squeeze them through the small doorway.[95]

As bad as things were in the cabins, they were worse below deck. Cabin fare cost forty or forty-five pounds, while steerage fare cost about seven. Most working-class emigrants had to spend weeks at sea in the dark bowels of the ship. And until 1819, when the law limited packet ships to two passengers for every five tons, conditions were unregulated—often overcrowded and unhealthy.

According to the numbers that the law would enforce, the *Telegraph* could have handled about seventy-eight people in the steerage. When George and Georgiana sailed, there were fifty—most of them traveling in groups, and particularly families. There were two families of seven (Mills and Liddell), one family of six (Harman), one of five (Wall), three families of four (Smyth, Winn, and Thompson), two of three (Slater and Drew), one couple (Sarah and William Nuttall), and a handful of others (Joseph Dodgson, Hannah Savage, Margaret Saunders, Hannah Stockdale, and Horace Cody). Some of the larger families brought fewer packages with them than George and Georgiana. The Mills family—who numbered seven—brought, besides the necessary bed and bedding, only two packages (as compared to George and Georgiana's five).[96]

While the ship's cook prepared meals for those in the cabins, the steerage passengers had to fend for themselves. Normally, this involved packing about eighty pounds of food, calculated to last seventy days at sea. Such staples as salted meat, potatoes, biscuit, suet, fowls, flour, eggs, onions, rice, and grits were advised. One Englishman on his way to the English Prairie with his wife and nine children ran low on provisions, and the captain sent down a pig.[97] Steerage passengers boiled food in net bags and competed for space among the clanging pots and saucepans in the ship's kitchen, or caboose.

Cabin passengers were expected to wash and dress for dinner, but those in the steerage simply sat down to their makeshift board. No steward descended to serve wine, porter, or rum. Water was provided, but the water casks were easily polluted—particularly in summertime, when George and Georgiana were traveling. The captain would provide a filtering device for the cabins, but steerage passengers either had to bring their own filtering stones or detoxify their water by mixing in charcoal powder or alum. A teaspoonful per pint was supposed to clear the water in a quarter of an hour.[98]

The sailors set up temporary privies over the sides of the ship, but in bad weather these devices became unusable. Yet, given the lack of privacy and ventilation below deck, they were preferable to the chamber pot. Often after only a short time at sea the steerage (one must say it) stank like a cesspool. Many sought escape from such conditions in sleep, but between the clanging in the caboose, the creaking of the berths, and the crash of the waves against the sides of the ship, the environment was hardly soporific. All shared the ordeals of ocean travel, regardless of station.

Furniture that was not made fast would roll when the waters were rough, and below deck, the wooden planks attached to the sides of the ship

as sleeping berths echoed the groans of the sick. Since these planks would
be taken down once the ship reached port, the berths were rickety affairs,
quickly slapped together. Rather than attempting to sleep on these precarious perches, some travelers slung hammocks, or threw down bedding
wherever they could find space. Some brought straw mattresses. In bad
weather no one could sleep. "The reeling and tumbling of the vessel," wrote
the Englishman Emanuel Howitt in 1819, "the waves dashing over the
forecastle—the tremendous thunder of the sea along the sides of the ship—
the shrieks of the passengers and the indifference of the seamen—taught us
in a moment the terrible majesty of a storm."[99]

Charles Dickens left another memorable account, of trying to calm the
ladies in the cabin during a storm with a tumbler of brandy-and-water:

> It being impossible to stand or sit without holding on, they were all
> heaped together in one corner of a long sofa—a fixture extending entirely
> across the cabin—where they clung to each other in momentary expecta-
> tion of being drowned. When I approached this place with my specific,
> and was about to administer it, with many consolatory expressions to the
> nearest sufferer, what was my dismay to see them all roll slowly down to
> the other end! And when I staggered to that end, and held out the glass
> once more, how immensely baffled were my good intentions by the ship
> giving another lurch, and their all rolling back again! I suppose I dodged
> them up and down this sofa for at least a quarter of an hour, without
> reaching them once; and by the time I did catch them, the brandy-and-
> water was diminished, by constant spilling, to a teaspoonful. To complete
> the group, it is necessary to recognize in this disconcerted dodger, an indi-
> vidual very pale from sea-sickness, who had shaved his beard and brushed
> his hair, last, at Liverpool: and whose only articles of dress (linen not in-
> cluded) were a pair of dreadnought trousers; a blue jacket, formerly ad-
> mired upon the Thames at Richmond; no stockings; and one slipper.[100]

Brandy-and-water might have helped to dull the senses, but the typical
medicine kit for an ocean crossing would also include fainting salts; calomel, milk of magnesia, castor oil, and rhubarb to help digestion; cream of
tartar to treat the aches and pains of rheumatism; laudanum, used as a
cough suppressant and painkiller; and powdered bark, to make poultices
for wounds and swellings. In Liverpool in 1818 there were forty-four druggists prepared to equip travelers against the array of hazards that bedeviled
ocean journeys. George sometimes took calomel to clear his stomach of bile,

but on the *Telegraph* his stomach would resist all such conciliatory measures. At times, he may have felt, quite literally, the sentiment that Benjamin Bailey had once expressed to Reynolds: "We are two beings in the bosom of dark and stormy waters."[101]

Captain Coffin expected passengers to be on board the *Telegraph* by two o'clock in the afternoon of Thursday, June 25.[102] George and Georgiana would have just enough time to pick up any last-minute supplies for the trip. When not life-threatening, ocean travel could be tedious, and the newlyweds would have been advised to bring books, newspapers, checkers, chess pieces, a playing board, and playing cards. The grocers in town sold a variety of snacks: plum cakes, fruit preserves, cider, soda powders, and fresh fruit rolled in paper. Liverpool also had hundreds of public houses providing liquid pick-me-ups and calm-me-downs, from coffee and tea, to wine, punch, ale, and porter. The taverns served more substantial fare as well. A virtual surfeit of wild fowl, ham, giblet pie, breads and puddings, sweetmeats, jellies, and flummery (that Welsh specialty made from stewed fruit) filled the menus. One hopes the couple indulged any culinary whims they may have had before boarding, for their ship would be stuck in the harbor for another two and a half weeks awaiting a wind.

Had George been prescient, he also would have gotten out of the inn with Georgiana to stretch his limbs before crossing. George was tall, an inch or two shy of six feet, and given the low ceilings in the cabins, he would have little room to turn around for the next seven weeks. Liverpool had public parks with graveled walks, and a botanic garden with tropical orchids and gingers. A popular stroll from the Doric temple at the top of St. James Mount took in picturesque views of the harbor, the Irish Sea, and the Welsh mountains. The Theatre Royal on Williamson Square, designed by Sir William Chambers, architect of the Royal Botanic Gardens and the Royal Academy, was playing Hannah Cowley's *The Belle's Stratagem,* followed by a fittingly titled musical farce: *The Day after the Wedding; or, A Wife's First Lesson.*[103] Sir Richard Westmacott, who had made the town's equestrian statue of George III (and whose son Richard would later attend John's funeral in Rome), had painted scenes.

While the packet ships carried plenty of sail, there had to be a wind to catch. For the next seventeen days the passengers on the *Telegraph* would have to wait. The sailors, called "packet rats," knew all the mysteries and subtleties of sail—from the lower to the topmast and topgallant sails, to the studding sails ("stuns'ls"), to the skysails on sliding gunter masts. The sailors spoke the language of sails, and, like rats, they scurried up and down the masts in all kinds of weather. To manage the crews, the captains and mates often had to display as much discipline on deck as politeness in the cabins. One Englishman who traveled shortly after George and Georgiana saw his ship's cook knock out three teeth of a sailor with a wooden club. For his pains, the angry cook earned the punishment known as "cobbing": he was tied to the windlass and given two or three whacks with the flat side of a carpenter's saw by each of the crewmembers.[104] The captain also had the legal right to clap irons on unruly passengers.

After what seemed like endless delay, Captain Coffin finally gave the command to weigh anchor, and on July 12, 1818, the *Telegraph* sailed majestically from its berth in the River Mersey toward the Irish Sea. Excitement took turns with despondency, as the coastline began to recede and the panorama of the Old Country faded from view. Most of the travelers were saying a permanent farewell to family, friends, and all the local attachments that bind a person to his or her native land. Sailing from Liverpool a few weeks earlier, George Flower described the experience: "Standing alone on the stern of the vessel, or surrounded by unsympathizing strangers; carried on by an irresistible power into the wide waste of waters, the land of his birth receding and sinking out of sight; desolation and gloom oppress the soul, relieved only by sea-sickness, substituting physical for mental suffering."[105] Flower's ship, the *Ann Maria*, had been full of family and friends, but on the *Telegraph* George's only companion—and he was lucky to have her—was Georgiana.

In 1819 Washington Irving portrayed the sense of alienation that overcame many seagoing travelers in an essay called "The Voyage," published in the same collection as "Rip Van Winkle": "A wide sea voyage severs us at once. It makes us conscious of being cut loose from the secure anchorage of settled life, and sent adrift upon a doubtful world. It interposes a gulf, not merely imaginary, but real, between us and our homes—a gulf subject to tempest, and fear, and uncertainty, rendering distance palpable, and return precarious. . . . Who can tell, when he sets forth to wander, whither he may be driven by the uncertain currents of existence; or when he may return; or whether it may ever be his lot to revisit the scenes of his childhood?"[106] George Keats had every hope of seeing his native country again, but his brother, at the foot of Helvellyn Mountain in Cumberland, had darker forebodings.

Nine days before the *Telegraph* set sail, John sat down by Derwent Water in the Lake District and scribbled out a few lines, in which he imagined a reunion with his brother and sister-in-law in America:

> Sweet sweet is the greeting of eyes,
> And sweet is the voice in its greeting,
> When adieux have grown old and goodbyes
> Fade away where old time is retreating.
>
> Warm the nerve of a welcoming hand,
> And earnest a kiss on the brow,
> When we meet over sea and o'er land
> Where furrows are new to the plough.

When John sent these lines to George and Georgiana, in the letter that also contained his acrostic on Georgiana's name, to the Crown Inn in Liverpool, it came back to him. The couple had already departed. John would not see Georgiana again, and when he fleetingly saw George in the winter of 1819–1820, their lives would have completely changed.

Still, the poet dreamed. Should he live another three years, John thought, perhaps he would spend a year with George and Georgiana on the American frontier. A veil of uncertainty shrouded his future. Enveloped in cloud, seated on stones a few feet from the edge of a perpendicular precipice, he looked down from the summit of Ben Nevis and wrote: "mist is spread/Before the earth beneath me; even such,/Even so vague is man's sight of himself."[107] As John and Charles Brown faded away into the northern landscape, becoming creatures of rivers, lakes, and mountains, George and Georgiana sailed south and faded with their ship into the sea.

The low-lying coastline of Lancashire gave way to the rounded hills of the Welsh mountains, and the couple could see the gulls and cormorants nesting in the craggy cliffs of Great Ormes Head. Then, Holyhead jutted out from the coastline in a great bulge of limestone, patched over with mold-like green. As the ship made its way through St. George's Channel into the Irish Sea, the crew continued to sound the depths off the eastern coast of Ireland. The waters still retained their greenish hue. Not until the *Telegraph* was out on the vast expanse of the Atlantic would the liquid element lose its translucence and transform into a dark, fathomless blue.

4 THE MOUNTAINS OF TARTARY
AND OF ALLEGHENY

The Telegraph

George had a special place in his heart for Cervantes's hero. John and Charles Brown may have looked more obviously the part of Quixotes, but George, who seemed to everyone to be endowed with the family store of common sense, was no less a romantic idealist. John predicted that George's ultimate downfall in business would be his generosity, a trait with no value in the cutthroat world of commercial capitalism, and he was right. George was no "scheming financier"—even he himself recognized this—but as he sailed toward America, he brought whatever skills he had to what was, essentially, a visionary quest.[1]

To Richard Abbey and likeminded critics, Don Quixote was a fool tilting at the windmills of poetic illusion. But George imagined the Spanish visionary as an impressive character with striking features: "a handsome intelligent melancholy countenance, with something wild but benevolent about the eyes, a lofty Forehead but not very broad, with finely arched eyebrows denoting candour and generosity." With the possible exception of the wildness, and the arch of the eyebrows, the portrait resembled George. To him, Don Quixote spoke with as much "sound sense, elevated morality and true piety, as any divine who ever wrote." He thought it a shame that minds so much inferior to Quixote's should laugh at his eccentricities. Were he to meet such a man, he would almost hate himself for doing the same. People who knew George in Kentucky would find him "an honourable, high-minded gentleman," and indeed the same chivalric spirit that drove the ingenious Knight of La Mancha on his comic adventures tinged the character of this Cockney Pioneer.[2]

The Spanish squire's library of romances is usually blamed for curdling his brain to make him see giants in windmills on the plains above the Sierra Morena, and courtly ladies in country peasants. George's Quixotic adventures on the prairielands of Illinois would be blamed on a different kind of romance. Hearing his brother's account of the English Prairie, John would compare Morris Birkbeck's *Notes on a Journey in America* to Thomas Campbell's poem about the American Revolution, *Gertrude of Wyoming: A Pennsylvanian Tale* (1809), complaining that one is "almost as poetical as the other."[3] But George admired the author's spirit of fearless enterprise as much as Quixote's as he read Birkbeck's *Letters from Illinois,* the book Taylor had given him, on the ocean crossing.

George had always thought of himself as his brother's safety valve, to release pressure when his passions threatened to explode, and as he sailed west—reading, chatting, napping—he also could not stop worrying. He had left John with full responsibility for Tom, and emotional responsibility for Fanny. The price of John's genius, he knew, was a nature "sensitive and hypochondriacal": his brother's "nervous morbid temperament," like other complaints stemming from sensibility, was as variable as the English weather. John's extreme sensibility made him unusually "devoted and affectionate," but to the same degree, he was often "melancholy and complaining." He was not exactly "peevish," like those the Cockney Pioneer advised to stay home in the book that George was reading, but he *did* dwell on present evils more than George thought that he should.[4] Was it right to leave him for so long?

In response to such doubts, George reminded himself that John had an uncanny knack for attaching people to him. Didn't his brother have Bailey? Haslam? Reynolds? Rice? Dilke? And that boisterous itinerant Brown? For all George knew, Brown was leading his brother in some spirited highland jig at the very moment that he sat worrying. Yet again, George asked himself: Wasn't he the only person in the world who knew his brother "well enough, who was fitted to relieve him of its friction, who was qualified to make things go easy with him"? Perhaps, without George's sympathetic ear, John would allow too "many things to prey upon his mind and his health."[5] Try as he might to suppress such disturbing thoughts, they always seemed to drift back to the surface of consciousness—like those tentacled jellyfish the sailors called "sea blubbers" that floated up with the waves. George would just have to have patience: the brothers would hear from each other soon enough.

The ocean voyage, in the meantime, followed the typical pattern: birds cawing and crying overhead in the sails and the rigging, the wind whistling, the waves splashing against the hull of the ship . . . the usual nautical cacophony. The sailors gave lessons in maritime hygiene by tying their clothes to old rope, dragging them along the sides of the ship, spreading them out on the deck to dry, and in this manner producing stiff shirts for Sundays. Adlard Welby, another Englishman who made the transatlantic crossing one year after George, summed up the voyage this way: "Some risk,—little comfort,—a total inversion of all accustomed habits,—a feeling of insecurity,—irritability,—a longing to be ashore; in short, a total *be-blue-devilment* at times, with a few hours of pleasanter colour just to keep hope alive."[6] Conversation on deck consisted mainly of winds, weather, and, inevitably, speculation about how much longer the trip would last.

Yet, it was summer, and the sea held its own magic. Shoals of charismatic porpoises tumbled and sported in the waves, and, in deeper waters, pods of gray dolphins swam by. By day, the water sparkled with the glittering silver scales of fish skimming the surface of the water. At night, spiral-shelled nautiluses rose up to feed. The ocean sunfish, like giant floating fish heads with fins, feasted on the jellyfish. And even the largest ocean creatures were not free from predators. The thresher shark, spotting a whale, would raise itself on its victim's back until its tail was nearly upright and thrash it repeatedly on the head, as Adlard Welby was amazed to witness. Meanwhile its hunting companion, the striped pilot fish, would stab at the whale's belly with its sword-like snout. Aroused by the ardor of battle, this carnivorous mackerel would lose its stripes, gain some spots, and transform from dark blue into a silvery white. Sharks circled the bow of the ship, and at the top of the feeding chain, the fearsome black-and-white killer whale chased the pursuers. Like his brother, George "saw / Too far into the sea; where every maw, / The greater on the less feeds evermore . . . an eternal fierce destruction."[7]

At last, after three thousand watery miles, and forty-seven days at sea, the scout of the *Telegraph* spotted land from the masthead, and the cry of "Land-ho!" echoed among all hands on deck. Passengers flocked up from the steerage and crowded the sides of the ship. They passed around the spy-glass and started to come to life again at the sight of the lively panorama of Delaware Bay. The pilot boat approached, carrying the helmsman who would steer the ship through the mouth of the Delaware River and up-stream to Philadelphia. Boarding the ship, he appeared like a Virgil to a suffering Dante: a guide from the oceanic netherworld to paradise. An august personage in the eyes of all.

Except for a few months in winter, when ice blocked the river, thousands of ships made their way upstream from Delaware Bay to Philadelphia every year. At the coastal town of Port Penn, fishermen caught shad from the river, much as their Dutch and English ancestors had done for a century and a half. Farther upstream, past more woods and orchards, the steeples and brick buildings of Newcastle came into view, followed by the mill town of Wilmington, on the Brandywine Creek, surrounded by swelling hills.

Across from the shipbuilding town of Chester was a small island that served as a lazaretto, or quarantine station, for ships coming from international waters. There, health inspectors, including a physician and the quarantine master, would board the ship, and the captain would line the passengers up on deck for inspection. Any ships refused passage would be quarantined. Once cleared to proceed, those passengers who wished to debark could take with them any luggage they could carry. The rest would have to be registered with the Customs Office in Philadelphia.

High up on a bluff at the mouth of the Mercer River just outside the city was Fort Billings. One day after declaring independence, the Continental Congress had purchased the fort, and Benjamin Franklin had hired General Tadeusz Kosciusko to take command and protect the nascent capital during the Revolutionary War. Having been moved by the language of the American Declaration, Kosciusko put his men to work building parapets, sharpening logs and positioning them in the underbrush and the bed of the river, and pointing cannons against the threat of imperial onslaught. But things had changed since the days when the subjects of King George III approached Philadelphia as enemies.

In December 1816, when the Keats brothers were living in Cheapside, John had written a sonnet, "To Kosciusko," which praised the Polish-Lithuanian war hero. Coleridge had also written a sonnet to Kosciusko, as had Leigh Hunt, who praised him as a man who dared to stand up to kings and emperors: "To Kosciusko: Who Took Part Neither with Bonaparte in the Blight of His Power, nor with the Allies in the Height of Theirs" (1815). Having fought on behalf of the American patriots, Kosciusko had gone on to lead Poland in a struggle for liberty against the combined might of Prussia and Russia. But John admired him perhaps most of all for his fame: "in worlds unknown,/The names of heroes, burst from clouds concealing,/Are changed to harmonies, for ever stealing/Through cloudless blue." By the time John was writing, the "great man," as Hunt called him in the *Examiner* on January 12, 1817, was old and "covered with scars, but still inflexible of heart." By the time George passed the fortress where he had defended the rebellious young nation, Kosciusko had died.[8]

John might have liked to sail endlessly through "cloudless blue" with the immortal heroes, but George, like others on board the *Telegraph,* was ready to exchange the limitless blue of sky and sea for the leafy green squares of Philadelphia. The weather was inviting: the day George and Georgiana's ship docked in Philadelphia (Wednesday, August 26) was a balmy seventy degrees. The temperature stayed comfortable all day, rising only a couple of degrees by noon and another in the mid-afternoon. The previous day had been much the same, reaching a high of seventy-six, and the next day it would stay in the low seventies. The same would hold true for the day after that, and the day after that . . . and so on into early September.[9]

George might have been uncomfortable in the ship's cabin, but luckily he and Georgiana had missed the midday blasts of ninety-six-degree heat that had assailed earlier boatloads of emigrants—causing some who were unused to such weather to drop in the streets in their overcoats. The beautiful weather brightened the couple's spirits as they finally arrived after nine weeks afloat—more than two in Liverpool, and almost seven at sea—in Philadelphia. The *Telegraph* tacked and maneuvered its way over the bar and pulled up, with its weary load, to the pier owned by Wiggin & Whitney.[10]

Philadelphia

Most visitors were delighted with their first view of Philadelphia. While there were no turreted castles or Gothic church spires to dazzle the onlooker—no spectacular buildings on the scale of St. Paul's Cathedral or

Westminster Abbey—there were also no beggars. "No dark alleys, whose confined and noisome atmosphere marks the presence of a dense and suffering population," observed Frances Wright, a British visitor, in October 1818: "no hovels, in whose ruined garrets, or dank and gloomy cellars, crowd the wretched victims of vice and disease, whom penury drives to despair, ere she opens to them the grave."[11] The extremes of wealth and poverty in Philadelphia were less readily apparent in the regularity of brick Georgian (or in America, "Federalist") homes and wide streets lined with green.

The white marble steps of the two-story homes stood out against the red brick. The chimneys reached up in unison above the slate-shingled roofs. Compared to the crooked, irregular plan of London and other English cities—eclectic medleys of Roman circuses, thin medieval lanes, and Regency crescents—the alternating pattern of red-and-white rectangular buildings and green squares gave Philadelphia an orderly, even geometrical appearance. The streets crossed each other at right angles, rather than crisscrossing, winding about in curves, or slicing across the city in diagonals.

Visitors were impressed that the streets were washed every day and that the plants seemed so healthy. Water, propelled by steam pumps, filtered down from a domed neoclassical building in Center Square, the reservoir at the highest point in the city, through wooden pipes to water the trees and keep the streets clean. The low, columnar branches of the Lombardy poplars lining the streets provided a maximum of green, but their roots reached menacingly close to the ground, perpetually threatening to come through the pavement that, among other things, distinguished Philadelphia from American cities out West.

Some found the urban design monotonous. William Amphlett, on approaching Philadelphia from the Delaware River a couple of months before the Keatses, remarked that "the paucity of public edifices, and the perfect regularity of the streets, contribute to give a kind of plain dulness to the whole, which soon abates curiosity and tires the stranger of taste." Sir Augustus Foster, a British diplomat, thought the architectural uniformity lacked aesthetic appeal, for the city was "built too much in the shape of a chess board to be beautiful."[12]

Rather than a square, however, Philadelphia took the shape of a parallelogram. The Delaware River bounded the city to the east, and the Schuylkill River to the west. The streets running parallel to the Delaware were numbered, starting with Front and then Second Street, up through Seventh. Broad Street divided the grid down the middle, and the streets descending on the other side toward the Schuylkill River began with Eighth and proceeded, through Thirteenth, to River Street. Seven on the east. Seven on the west. Depending on their position relative to High (later Market) Street, which crossed Broad Street at a right angle in Center Square, the streets were designated North or South. Those that ran parallel to High Street took the names of indigenous trees: to the north, Mulberry, Sassafras, and Vine; to the south, Chestnut, Walnut, Locust, Spruce, Pine, and Cedar.

The city plan had its ideological appeal. With wide sidewalks to protect pedestrians from carriage wheels and splashing, the streets "might with justice be termed *rues démocrates,*" as opposed to the *rues aristocrates* of European capitals, Frances Wright remarked. Although the residents practiced various religions, a Quakerish atmosphere suffused the town. "The comfortable, substantial, straight-streeted city of Philadelphia," George Flower observed, "has a peculiar tone of quietude, a sort of *drab-colouredness* thrown over it, indicative of its quaker origin." The Scottish cartographer John Melish, who drew the map of the English Prairie for Birkbeck's *Letters from Illinois,* said of the Philadelphians: "They do not conduct their business in the same *dashing* style which is done by some commercial cities; but confine themselves within bounds, and secure what they gain."[1] Philadelphia, as the birthplace of the United States, bespoke a thoroughly middle-class mentality.

Racial hypocrisy and exploitation persisted, but emigrants who had been prepared to find independence and equality found just that. The Act for the Gradual Abolition of Slavery had made Pennsylvania a free state in 1780, but those who were slaves before the act passed remained slaves until death. No new slaves could be imported into the state, but those born to existing slaves were slaves until twenty-eight. Of the roughly 7,500 African Americans living in Philadelphia in 1818, there were still a few slaves in the city and its environs.[14]

On the day the *Telegraph* docked, Philadelphia's daily paper, the *Franklin Gazette,* posted a "One Cent Reward" for the return of a sixteen-year-old runaway slave named Olympe. She was of mixed-race origin and had made her escape in a striped gingham frock, with a handkerchief on her head, a red-bead necklace, and no shoes. On the previous day, the paper in which Taylor's cousin Michael Drury advertised his wares had posted a six-cent reward for the return of a male slave of the same age. A few doors up from Drury, at 49 South Front Street, the tobacco-and-snuff dealers Daniel Dick & Company advertised the products of slave labor: Maccouba and Rappee snuff; plug, pigtail, and Virginia twist; and black Prime Cavendish tobacco. The company logo featured a young, half-clothed African puffing a long clay pipe by a giant tobacco flower: an emblem of the strange, black-and-white world that George and Georgiana had just entered. Family legend has it that George's first impression of America was the sight of a black man on the Philadelphia dock eating a watermelon.[15]

As usual, the appearance of the packet ship from Europe caused no small commotion. Ticket-porters (licensed baggage carriers with tin nameplates bearing their names and addresses) thronged Wiggin & Whitney's pier at 19 South Front Street. Many were black refugees from the slave states who had fled to Philadelphia after the War of 1812. Others were working-class British emigrants. Representatives from the city's hotels and boarding houses came carrying business cards. Fruit sellers hawked cherries, peaches, apples, and melons. Relatives and friends looked for those they had come to greet. Some with no particular purpose came to gawk at the spectacle, as the crew made the ship fast to the pier.

George and Georgiana saw no familiar faces. Even their family back in the Old Country did not know where they were. George would have to rely on Taylor's letter of introduction and his own personality, which never failed to make friends. Captain Coffin recorded George's destination vaguely, as the "United States," and while George intended to travel to the English Prairie in Illinois, the fact that he was not specific may testify to his unsettled purpose. Nor did he specify a profession. "Georgianna" joined the ranks of emigrants with misspelled names. But to the benefit of posterity, the Customs officials recorded their sexes correctly.[16]

Most of the boarding houses in Philadelphia charged about five dollars a week for room and board, which included three generous meals a day. The hotels cost up to three times that amount. The Washington Hall on South Third Street, reputedly the best hotel in the country, charged two dollars per day—the price of an acre of public land. For sentimental reasons, one might prefer to imagine George and Georgiana at Judd's Hotel, on South Third Street opposite the post office. The name would have conjured fond memories of their honeymoon days on Judd Street, near Brunswick Square.

Given that Philadelphia was fifty or sixty feet above the river, and that one had to go nearly a mile uphill to a place even as close as South Third Street, George would have hired a coach to carry him and Georgiana from the pier into town. And he would have had a hard time fending off the porters eager to help with their bags. The retail stores along the road from the wharf to the center of town exhibited their wares *à l'américaine* on the sidewalks. "What is called a store in America, is a shop or place where all kinds of commodities intended for consumption are to be found, and sold by retail," S. H. Collins explained in a guide published for English emigrants. "Nothing is excluded from it. Train oil and candles, stationery wares, hardwares, and cloth, together with distilled spirits, sugar, wines, and coffee, are all kept in it, in the same manner as in the shops of some of the remote villages in Scotland."[17] George, like his brother in the Scottish Highlands, quickly gained familiarity with the idea of the general store.

If New York was famed for its commerce, Philadelphia was known for its manufactures. The city, in 1818, produced virtually every species of commodity. Watchmakers made clocks and watches, hat-makers (Abbey might have noted *how*) made hats, and broom-makers fastened bristles to the ends of satinwood, bird-eye, walnut, and cherry poles. At the factories, ironmongers forged andirons, buckets, plates, measuring cups, coffeepots, spouts, and other farm and household items to be loaded onto wagons and sent down High Street on the trail of westward migration.

Philadelphia, now with 120,000 residents, no longer resembled the place where William Hazlitt had lived as a six-year-old boy. Nor did it seem the same place it had been when two of Leigh Hunt's seven siblings were buried there. As a child, Hunt had visions of returning. Philadelphia was once a city, as he told his aunt Lydia Shewell when he was six, that he would have been "very happy to visit as it was the place where my dear good mama was born, and . . . Grandpapa, Grandmama, and all my relations and friends, whose Health and Happiness I pray for every night and morning." Benjamin Franklin had once offered to teach his mother the guitar. But she had other, more vivid memories of colonial America that "had shaken her soul as well as frame." Hunt's father had narrowly missed being tarred and feathered on the eve of Revolution, and his brother Stephen had been kidnapped by Native Americans and carried across the Delaware River. "It is thought, they intended to carry him into their own quarters, and bring him up as an Indian; so that . . . we might have had for a brother the Great Buffalo, Bloody Bear, or some such grim personage." But Hunt's Uncle Stephen intervened to reclaim the boy.[18]

Many, including Hunt's grandfather Stephen Shewell, Sr., had found it impossible to maintain a complete neutrality during the American Revolution. Shewell's sympathies had lain with the British, and when an escaped British prisoner-of-war showed up at his house on Front Street one night in the pouring rain, Shewell hid him in the attic. The Patriots burned one of his ships laden with cargo to keep it from the British, and they made free with his botargoes (cured fish roe). They also "despatched every now and then a file of soldiers to rifle his house of everything that could be serviceable: linen, blankets, &c. And this, unfortunately, was only a taste of what he was to suffer; for, emptying his mercantile stores from time to time, they paid him with their continental currency, paper-money; the depreciation of which was so great as to leave him, at the close of war, bankrupt of everything but some houses, which his wife brought him."[19] By 1818, Hunt had lost touch with the American side of his family.

George's first item of business, after settling his wife, was to post a letter to England to let their families know they had arrived. Transatlantic communication was hardly reliable, and when writing from the Western Country George would always worry that his letters would get lost. But sending mail from Philadelphia was easy, and sailing to England took less time than sailing in the other direction. George's letter would reach home in less time than George had spent at sea.

Rather than dwelling on the trials of the nauseous ocean crossing, George, in keeping with his character, deflected attention onto his future prospects for happiness. He had married a woman whose wit rivaled his brother's, and he could not accept John's skepticism about marriage. "Though the most beautiful Creature were waiting for me at the end of a Journey or a Walk," John wrote to George in October, after receiving his brother's letter, "though the carpet were of Silk, the Curtains of the morning Clouds; the chairs and Sofa stuffed with Cygnet's down; the food Manna, the Wine beyond Claret, the Window opening on Winander mere, I should not feel—or rather my Happiness would not be so fine, a[s] my Solitude is sublime."[20] Married people often wish others to marry, and George in this respect seems to have been no different.

An undated poem titled "On Woman" that George composed probably around this time, or months after his trip to France when marriage was foremost on his mind, responds cleverly to John's professed aversion to matrimony. George attached a key to the poem in French: "Ceux qui sont plus favorablement enclin[és] vers les dames, qu'ils lisent la première & troisième ligne & ensuite la seconde & quatrième de chaque Vers" ("Those favorably inclined toward women should read the first and third line and then the second and fourth of each stanza"):

> Happy a man may pass his life,
> If freed from matrimonial chains,
> If he's directed by a Wife,
> He's sure to suffer for his pains.
>
> What tongue is able to unfold
> The falsehoods that in Women dwell,
> Virtues in Women you behold,
> Are almost imperceptible.
>
> Adam could find no solid peace,
> When Eve was given for a mate
> Till he beheld a Woman's face,
> Adam was in a happy state.
>
> For in this sex you'll see appear
> Hypocrisy, deceit, and pride,
> Truth, darling of a heart sincere
> In Women never can reside.
>
> Distraction take the men, I say,
> Who make the Women their delight,
> Who no regard to Women pay;
> Keep reason always in their sight.

The poem reads as a straightforward condemnation of marriage, until one reads the even-numbered after the odd-numbered lines. Like any skilled rhetorician, the speaker expresses sympathy with an opposite point of view in order to insinuate his own perspective more effectively. This is one of the few surviving instances in which George's cleverness found its way into written form. Georgiana would later call him "the most inveterate punster" in the state of Kentucky.[21]

George's other pressing item of business in Philadelphia was to pay a visit to Michael Drury at 14 South Front Street. Drury had come over from Liverpool on the ship *Lancaster* the previous October, at age twenty-five. Like his cousin John Taylor—whose father, James Taylor, was a bookseller in Lincolnshire—Michael Drury had grown up in a publishing family. His father, John Drury, Sr., had been a bookseller on High Street, Lincoln. His aunt Sarah (née Drury) was Taylor's mother. Of his nine siblings, two had moved, or were about to move, to the United States.[22]

Michael's younger brother Edward Bell Drury also followed the family trade. He had set himself up as a bookseller and printer at the New Public Library on High Street, Stamford, and around the time that Michael was hosting George Keats in Philadelphia, Edward stumbled upon another impoverished genius. The poet John Clare, employed in the lime-pits at Ryhall about two miles north of Stamford, and finding himself unable to pay a shoemaker's bill of three pounds, scribbled out a prospectus for a volume of poetic "Trifles" in order to raise money through subscription. Along with the prospectus, he printed a few sample poems as "offsprings of those leisure intervals which the short remittance from hard and manual labor sparingly afforded to compose them." Edward Drury read these poetic "trifles" and saw in them original genius and a romantic outlook on rural life. He tracked down the author in a cold, damp cottage in Helpstone (now Helpston, Northamptonshire), which James Hessey would call a "comfortless village."[23]

Edward Drury would give John Clare the money he needed to pay the shoemaker and send Clare's manuscript to John Taylor. In 1820, Taylor & Hessey would publish Clare's *Poems Descriptive of Rural Life and Scenery,* announcing the author on the title page as "John Clare, a Northamptonshire Peasant." The volume would catapult Clare into fame as the English Burns. One Philadelphia magazine, reviewing the book based on excerpts from the London *Quarterly,* remarked: "This is a very extraordinary instance of the triumph of talent over untoward circumstances. The poet is a real peasant, poor, uneducated and friendless; much more destitute of the means of improvement than [Robert] Bloomfield, [Robert] Burns, or [James] Hogg; and yet the author of verses, which neither of the three need to have blushed for his own." Shortly after the book's publication, Taylor wondered whether Michael Drury might profit from an American edition. Two years later, he would still be grateful for the "kind Attentions" that his cousin had shown to George Keats.[24]

Unlike his brother Ned, Michael Drury traded not in books, but in dry goods, typically quilts, shawls, veils, merino wool, Irish linens, cotton, flannel, prints, muslins, lace shawls, and other similar items, which he and his business partner, James Tallant, stocked in their warehouse on the Delaware River. In January 1818, they advertised a wholesale shipment of veils, dresses, tippets, suspenders, brown Holland boots, handkerchiefs, angora, silk, cotton, and worsted stockings. Within three weeks came another shipment, this time of bed ticks, twilled woolen cloth, hogsheads of Muscovado sugar, crates of blue printed earthenware, and eighty tons of sheet lead. On the twelfth of June: "Satin Hair Seating . . . suitable for Chairs, Sofas, Lounges, &c. to be had cheap."[25] Michael lived above the warehouse at 14 South Front Street, and his partner resided nearby, at 71 Walnut Street.

Two days before George and Georgiana arrived in Philadelphia, James Tallant had become Michael Drury's brother-in-law, as well as his business partner. On August 23, 1818, in the village of Sculcoates, just north of Hull, James married Michael's youngest sister, Mary. The same issue of the *New Monthly Magazine* that contained John Gibson Lockhart's attack "On the Cockney School of Prose Writers" (October 1818) also announced the marriage of "Mr. J. Tallant, merchant, of the firm of Drury and Tallant at Philadelphia and New York, to Mary, youngest daughter of the late Mr. Drury, printer and bookseller, of Lincoln." (The firm of Drury & Tallant was based in Philadelphia, though the partners may have also received shipments through New York.) Two other Drury sisters also married Tallants. Elizabeth Jane Drury married John Tallant in 1813, and stayed in England to raise twelve children. Jane Drury married James's older brother William Tallant in 1811 and moved with him to the United States. By 1820, Jane and William had moved to Cincinnati, where James and Mary Tallant would join them.[26]

"The Change since I last saw her, seems more like a Dream than a Reality," Taylor wrote of the bride, Mary Drury, who like Georgiana seems to have become a woman all at once. He regretted the loss—or, more poetically, the "far-away Wanderings"—of his cousins, Michael and Mary, but he hoped that they would retain their "Affection for Old England" and be "Absentees for a Season" only. Like other English emigrants, the Drurys and Tallants may have come to America with the dream of making money and returning to the Old Country. Mary Drury would later send Taylor "favorable Accounts" of George and Georgiana's "health and Comfort and

Domestic Happiness" in the Western Country. But James Tallant would not return to England, and when Mary Drury Tallant did, it would not be in the manner she, or anyone else, expected.[27]

Fortunes in nineteenth-century America were not always easy to make or to keep once made. A few weeks after George and Georgiana left Philadelphia, the firm of Drury & Tallant would move from 14 South Front Street to number eleven; within six months, it would move again up the street to 43 North Front. By September 4, 1819, the partnership would be dissolved by mutual consent. James Tallant would leave Philadelphia to try his fortunes in Cincinnati, and Michael Drury would take over the business, calling in debts and requesting claimants to liquidate their accounts. Since the end of the War of 1812, the American economy had been running on credit, and when it crashed in 1819 Drury and Tallant were not the only losers. When Adlard Welby traveled west that same year, he "met everywhere grave, eager, hungry looking faces; and could perceive, as well as hear complaints of, a general want of employment."[28]

In picking up and moving west, James and William Tallant would be following the pattern of many merchants. Their move would be in keeping with the tendency of "small and middling tradesmen," as Henry Bradshaw Fearon explained: "If they find business getting bad, they do, what is called, 'sell out,' and pack up for the 'back country.'" Profits in the Western Country were supposed to be greater than they were in the east, and the cost of living lower. James Tallant would establish himself as a dry goods merchant near the wharf in Cincinnati at 36 Main Street, and William, if not in the same building, would work nearby on Main Street between Second and Third streets.[29] There, at the public landing place on a bend in the Ohio River, they would watch the boatmen unload the dry goods, millstones, and other cargo that floated downriver in flatboats from Pittsburgh.

To Michael Drury, neither George nor Georgiana Keats would have appeared particularly equipped for the western frontier. The brother of a butcher from Lincolnshire, "who accompanied a Mr. KEATS and his wife from England to Philadelphia," reported after the couple left Philadelphia that they had "gone westward to join BIRKBECK's settlement in the Illinois; they were a complete Bond-street beau and belle, and shockingly unfit for their destination, for that is a miserable place of Birkbeck's, who is a notorious fibber!" The same article claimed that many English emigrants had not "found the 'better life' they sought to gain" in America.[30]

Yet, contradictory claims were circulating about conditions west of the

Alleghenies, and Michael Drury himself probably did not know what to think, or what to tell George. Sometimes, even in a single breath, the newspapers gave conflicting reports. In the *New York Evening Post,* for instance, an anonymous "Friend to Humanity" described land on the English Prairie as "not so desirable," while "An Illinoian" insisted in a note that "the water and land in most of those settlements are extremely good." A day after the *Telegraph* arrived at the Philadelphia dock, the *Franklin Gazette* reported an anecdote about one emigrant who had traveled to Kentucky and immediately found work at two dollars a day. His employers gave him a small plot of land with "a pretty snug little house," and within three weeks he had purchased a cow. When asked how he was doing, he replied, "Main well, zur. Why, zur, hies gotten a cow, and it cost me nothing to feed her; and she and three dollars a week gives us all as much good victuals as ever we can eat,—and we've got money 'forehand!" The man and his wife estimated that back in the Old Country it would have taken them a year and ten weeks to afford the cow alone. An editorial comment following the anecdote made plain the moral of the story: "The labor and economy exerted in some places to *live,* will soon make a man rich in another, if persevered in."[31]

George Flower himself would later caution emigrants that "to remove to the interior of America with a notion of making a fortune, and then returning to England to spend it, is a most delusive fallacy. . . . America generally, and the Western country particularly, although the easiest countries in the world to live in, are the worst in the world to make a fortune in. If a man comes to Illinois, he must come with a singleness of purpose, with an intention and desire of finding some occupation by which he can support his family in happy mediocrity of circumstances."[32] Flower's *Errors of Emigrants,* in which this warning appeared, did not come out until the year George Keats died, and George, anyway, had not crossed the Atlantic to raise a family in "happy mediocrity of circumstances."

He could not have known that while he was discussing his shining prospects with Michael Drury in brightly lit Philadelphia, the emigrants on the English Prairie were making do without candles. Cockney Pioneers who had at least been used to warm chimneys and wallpapered rooms had arrived in the summer of 1818 to find themselves crammed on the dirt floor of a few log cabins: "a fermenting mass," as Flower put it, with nothing but whiskey, cornbread, and salt pork to ensure survival. "Some laughed and

joked; some moped and sulked; some cursed and swore." With the help of
some backwoodsmen, Birkbeck had erected a few "barracks," but he had
sown no crops and dug no wells for the settlers. As people continued to
trickle into the settlement, some would make do, others would drop back
to more populous states, the more enterprising would forge ahead to unclaimed land in the Missouri Territory, and those who could afford it would
return whence they had come.[33]

An Englishman named J. Filder, who traveled to America from Liverpool with George Flower and his family, gave up on the English Prairie
without reaching his destination. After having been tossed by stormy seas,
Filder then encountered "bad roads, swollen streams, bad cooking, buggy
beds—altogether enough to put an elderly gentleman a little out of sorts."
At Vincennes, Indiana, he found that he could take it no longer. The settlement of Vincennes sat low on a swampy plain, and its "narrow crooked
streets, ruined fences, roofless houses, and unglazed windows, gave it the
appearance of poverty and wretchedness," one contemporary observed:
"All seemed idle. Sickness had closed the doors, unnerved the arm of industry, and subdued the desire of display." Filder was now only forty miles
from the English Prairie, but he heard that he would have to sell his horse
and purchase a canoe to get there—and that once there he would find the
other English settlers without water, shaking with fever and ague. Filder
was in his fifties and worth £40,000: just the sort of man the Cockney Pioneers were hoping to attract. But he had grown attached to the animal that
had carried him so far in safety, and he gave up on the American Land of
Cockaigne, retracing his steps back to the Old Country.[34]

Charles Cowden Clarke's sister, Isabella Towers, later published a
novel, *Perils in the Woods; or, The Emigrant Family's Return* (1835), based on
the experience of English emigrants in America. One of the characters
blames the emigration literature for disappointments such as Filder's:

> The "Guides" and encouragements to emigration, give the bright side of
> the picture only;—the difficulties are kept back, or so few of them are
> described, that a man with the very least share of mental energy would
> rather meet with them than not. They are represented to be merely pleas-
> ant varieties in the happy state of the settlers!—I consulted many books
> on emigration, and found them all favourable, and as I now find, all par-
> tial. I was not so fortunate as to meet with men who had tried the scheme

of settling, nor can I wonder; for the poor deluded creatures flock over full of expectation and false hopes,—are disappointed—cheated—injured by the worthless and desperate of their fellow-countrymen—are unsuccessful and reduced to poverty; and are then obliged to remain in the country, for want of money to bring them home again. I do not intend to assert that *all* who emigrate are disappointed: no, for the greater number—after undergoing excessive hardships, which they would have shrunk from the idea of having to endure before they left home—settle, and in the course of time, contrive to procure a few of those blessings, and to create some of those comforts around them, which in England were thought nothing of, because they were as common as the sun at noon-day. In the lapse of years, too, other settlers join the first—villages spring up, and are scattered over the wide surface of that beautiful country. It appears to me, that no benefit which the back-settlers may possess—excepting that of freedom from heavy taxation—can compensate them for the numberless privations and inconveniences to which they are, and will be exposed, for many years to come.

Rumors had spread about some of the English emigrants who, upon arriving to find no accommodations ready for them on the prairie, slept in the woods wrapped in blankets, clutching their guns for protection. Some got sick, and this became the source of reports about unhealthy conditions in the West. Welby claimed to have met one group returning in disappointment from the English Prairie after having lost eight of its members to dysentery, fever, and ague.[35]

William Cobbett, writing from his farm in Hyde Park, Long Island, expressed sentiments similar to those fictionalized by Isabella Towers. "I see Cobbett has been attacking the Settlement," John wrote to George six months after George's arrival, "but I cannot tell what to believe—and shall be all out at elbows till I hear from you." John had seen the letters addressed to Morris Birkbeck in *Cobbett's Weekly Register,* accusing the Cockney Pioneer of inspiring false hopes, if not of direct false dealing. When Henry Bradshaw Fearon visited Cobbett around the time George and Georgiana were in Philadelphia, he was surprised to find the journalist who had such scathing things to say about the English Prairie living in ramshackle conditions himself: "a path rarely trod, fences in ruins, the gate broken, a house mouldering to decay . . ." Except for a chair and a few trunks of clothes, Cobbett's front parlor was empty. Despite his radical politics, some suspected him of being in the pocket of eastern land sharks. Birkbeck would accuse him of as much in his address to "British Emigrants Arriving in the Eastern Ports" (1819).[36]

In truth, the prairielands of Illinois were no less healthy than the eastern states, but settlers were more isolated and conditions more primitive. Rival colonists, moreover, had incentive to broadcast any bad news from the West. Writing from the English settlement in western Pennsylvania in 1818—and adopting the high-sounding rhetoric of the Declaration of Independence—Charles Britten Johnson compared conditions in Susquehanna County to those in the Western Country and declared:

> That the produce of the farmer in Susquehanna county, would sell for double the amount it will bring in the Western states.
> That the work of the mechanic is proportionally more valuable.
> That all imported articles, are cheaper than in the Western states.
> That the settlement is removed from all danger, in case of war.
> That it has the advantage of provisions, already raised within itself.
> That materials for building, and for furniture, are abundant and cheap.
> That taxes are scarcely worth naming, and that there are no poor.
> That the situation is particularly eligible, from its vicinity to good markets; the soil of a good quality, the water excellent, and the climate healthy . . .[37]

Ultimately, emigrants could not know what to think until they inspected matters for themselves, as George Keats, despite all the rumors, was determined to do.

Although Michael Drury could not provide George with first-hand knowledge of conditions out West, he *could* give him information about how to get there. George and Georgiana were not traveling with a large family, and so they had the option of taking a stagecoach and sending their belongings to Pittsburgh by stagewagon. The going rate was six to eight dollars per package or a hundred pounds of weight. Professional movers lined up on High Street every morning to load furniture, boxes, trunks, barrels, and other goods onto wagons for conveyance to the Western Country. Most of these movers owned their own teams, but some were farmers who hauled merchandise in the off-season. Some had warehouses in Pittsburgh to store the merchandise once it arrived. They had a reputation as a rough, unpolished set, but they were not known for losing packages entrusted to their care since they would be financially responsible for anything that was lost, damaged, or destroyed.

If George and Georgiana chose to travel by stagecoach, George would not have to worry about horses or about trying to maneuver a carriage on pitted, unfamiliar roads over the mountains. But the coachmen stopped at the inns that paid a commission, and to meet their schedules they often drove through the night. Typically, the mountain inns were little more than a house, not always well provisioned, whose owners had hung up a wooden sign to designate it a public house. They rarely provided the fare or comfort most Englishmen expected. The food was notorious, and the beds infested by "that ugly and sleep-destroying insect" (as George Flower's father called bedbugs). To ford muddy streams and rivers, stagecoach passengers often had to disembark and wade across. Sometimes carriages overturned. When John James Audubon's bride, Lucy, was crossing the Alleghenies, her carriage overturned and she was badly bruised. Birkbeck called stagecoach travel "a necessary evil" in his *Letters from Illinois.*[38]

To make it over the Alleghenies, most families took covered wagons designed for mountain terrain. The floors of these Pennsylvania, or Conestoga, wagons curved upward to prevent their contents from shifting. Tall, iron-enforced wheels carried them high over the tree stumps that had been left in the way by the soldiers who blazed the road. The wagons' tough main frames, usually of hickory or oak, could support up to twelve thousand pounds. Elias Pym Fordham, George Flower's cousin, dragged a piano over the mountains for Birkbeck's daughters in one of these wagons.[39]

If George and Georgiana traveled by wagon with a camp kettle and provisions, they could avoid both the inconveniences of stagecoach travel and the mountain inns. But the wagons were awkward to manage and overturned easily. The road through the mountains ran through sloughs, over rocks, and up steep precipices. It was not uncommon to see drivers whipping their horses while passengers tugged at ropes to drag the wagons uphill. "The getting these waggons and families over the mountains," Henry Fearon observed, "appeared little less than a continuance of miracles."[40]

In the end, George chose the most expensive option. He purchased a carriage and a team of horses and sent his trunks to Pittsburgh by stagewagon.[41] This course of action cost him several hundred dollars, and when he sold the carriage at Pittsburgh, where most emigrants exchanged their overland conveyances for flatboats, he would expect to receive only half of what he paid for it. But Georgiana was now pregnant, and her health was a paramount concern. The carriage would be of little use to George in the Western Country, but he could hire riders to take the horses to Princeton, Indiana, the post station for the English Prairie, where they would come in handy. There were always emigrants on the lookout for cheap transportation to the West. The going would be rough under the best conditions, but at least in their own carriage the couple could travel at their own pace, and slow down to appreciate the scenery. They could stock up on provisions at the farms in the Great Appalachian Valley on the way to the mountains, and even picnic.

The travel guides advised against staying too long in the port cities. "So many emigrants arrive at all the principal ports in the United States," wrote John Bradbury in a guide for emigrants published in London in 1817, "that there is very little chance of employment, and almost the whole of the distress that has been reported to exist in America, has arisen from the number of emigrants who have foolishly lingered in the cities until they have spent all their money."[42] George did not intend to stay long in Philadelphia, but he and Georgiana had been cooped up in a ship's cabin for weeks, and they were now facing a three-hundred-mile trek across the state of Pennsylvania. Before going any farther west, he and his bride would step out on the town.

Unlike the muddy settlement of Washington D.C., which had taken over as the nation's capital, Philadelphia had all the appurtenances of culture: theaters, libraries, bookshops, panoramic exhibitions, restaurants, oyster cellars, art galleries, billiard rooms, circuses, museums, a scientific institution, and a philosophical lecture hall. Behind a marble statue of Benjamin Franklin on Fifth Street, the public library loaned books to anyone for a small fee and a deposit. Subscribers did not have to pay, and all were welcome to read in the library, which was open every day but Sunday from two o'clock, when the markets closed, until sunset.[43]

Philadelphians were proud of their humanitarian heritage. The prisonkeeper led tours of the prison, comparing it favorably to prisons in London. "Here, instead of the prisoners passing their time in idleness, or in low debauchery and gaming, all was sobriety, life, and activity," Fearon wrote. "A complete manufacturing town was in fact collected within the narrow precincts of these otherwise gloomy walls."[44] A model institution devoted to reeducating and training criminals, the prison made white prisoners and black prisoners work together, but they did not eat together at the same tables.

Even the hospital was a tourist attraction. Benjamin West's painting, *Christ Healing the Sick in the Temple* (1817), hung in its own specially constructed lobby, and, during its first year on display, received thirty thousand visitors. A bronze statue of William Penn stood in the hospital gardens, amid groves of lemon and orange trees. Inscriptions on the four sides of the pedestal told his story—from his birth in 1644, to his arrival in Philadelphia forty years later, to his death in 1718. The front panel bore his family coat of arms and the motto "Mercy and Justice." The statue's hand held a scroll of the Charter of Privileges from King Charles II, guaranteeing (in the plaque's abbreviated version) "that no person who shall acknowledge one Almighty God, and profess himself obliged to live quietly under the civil government, shall be in any case molested." Another inscription somewhat dubiously praised Penn's "just and amicable arrangement with the natives for the purchase of their lands."[45]

At the statehouse, or Independence Hall, the Liberty Bell made to commemorate the fiftieth anniversary of Penn's Charter of Privileges hung in the steeple. In 1776, the bell had summoned the townspeople to Independence Square (between Fifth and Sixth streets and Chestnut and Pine) to hear independence proclaimed. Nine years later, in the upper floor of the statehouse, Charles Willson Peale had opened the nation's first public museum on the model of the "imperial Museums of Europe." There, where the Continental Congress once met, he hung paintings by himself, his daughter, and other painters, of historical figures and scenes from the American Revolution. For twenty-five cents, visitors also gained admission to Peale's natural history collection, which included specimens of more than twelve hundred birds from around the world and hundreds of fish, snakes, lizards, insects, tortoises, turtles, and shells—including a three-hundred-and-fifty-pound Indian oyster. In glass cases, he had stuffed grizzly bears, hyenas, porcupines, an orangutan, an anteater, a lion, a five-legged cow, a giant Madagascar bat, and an elephant seal from the Pacific. He had corals, minerals, fossils, and scientific displays: optical devices, Isaiah Lukens's model of perpetual motion, and an "electrifying machine." He also had anatomical specimens of biological deformities, prompting Frances Wright to call the museum "a mausoleum of dead monsters."[46]

The *crème de la crème* of Peale's collection was a mammoth skeleton that a farmer had dug up in Ulster County, New York. On Independence Day, while George and Georgiana were waiting for a wind in Liverpool Harbor, thirteen men, representing the thirteen colonial governors, had dined at a table beneath the ribcage of the skeleton. Leigh Hunt would compare the "gigantic fragment" of John's *Hyperion* to "the bones of the Mastodon." John himself, having seen a similar awe-inspiring skeleton in the British Museum, referred to his Titans as a "mammoth-brood." Other skeletons like the one in Charles Willson Peale's Museum had been excavated in Big Bone Valley, Kentucky, at the mouth of the River Licking. The stiff blue clay of the Big Bone salt lick, across from Cincinnati, held more than five tons of prehistoric remains: spine joints, feet, femurs, upper jaws, giant molars, horns . . . all waiting to be put back together.[47]

Daniel Boone had raised his cabin there, in the Valley of Big Bones, to hunt the deer, bear, elk, buffalo, and other game drawn to the same salt lick that had attracted the ill-fated mammoths. Native Americans had a tradition, communicated by the chief of the Delaware Nation to the governor of Virginia during the American Revolution, about the fate of the mammoths. They believed—never imagining that these tusked hairy creatures were herbivores—that the Great Man above, seeing the mammoths devour game intended for humans, had seized his lightning bolts and descended to earth in a rage. He then seated himself on a nearby mountain, where the imprint of his feet could still be seen, and hurled his bolts at the beasts until he had slaughtered all but one defiant bull. The last mammoth parried the angry shafts with his forehead, shaking them off one by one, until one of them finally penetrated his side. He sprang away, bounding over the Ohio River and across the Great Lakes to a land where he was still living.[48]

By 1818, the Native Americans had mostly been pushed back to the fringes of the Northwest Territory and beyond the western frontier, but people still spoke about "the hostile state of the Indians" on the banks of the Wabash River between Illinois and Indiana. Peale's Museum kept such fears alive by exhibiting waxwork figures of Native Americans brandishing instruments of war—bows, arrows, axes, spears, tomahawks, and clubs. Dressed in native costumes, they were arranged in groups evoking scenes from the French and Indian War. Leigh Hunt's mother could still recall the "war-whoops of the Indians which she heard in Philadelphia."[49]

Although Peale did not have William Penn among his portraits, to his credit he did have Penn's curtains. His other relics included Prince Talley-

rand's oath of allegiance to the United States, quart bottles filled with ashes
of Continental money, a cake of dried soup sent from England to the British army in 1775, and the last stanza of *The Cow Chase,* an epic poem by
Major John André, the British officer caught conspiring with Benedict Arnold.[50] In lines penned a few hours before his execution, André had written: "And now I've closed my epic strain,/I tremble as I shew it,/Lest this
same warrior-drover,/Wayne, should ever catch the poet." But General
Anthony Wayne did turn out to command the soldiers at André's execution.

Standing on the site where the principles of American democracy had
been forged, George Keats had his own opinions. "The great fault of the
really patriotic men who framed the constitution was, that they presumed
that the American people would always elect an intelligent and honourable
man for President," he later complained. The Founding Fathers had given
the chief executive "power on this fatal presumption, with the feeling that
he was responsible to the People, never thinking that it is the people that
make the worst tyrants, or if they did think so, that the *American people*
were superior to all other *people.*"[51] Neither George nor Georgiana would
ever succumb to a similar delusion.

George did not object, in theory, to the idea of equal rights, but he believed that a monarch limited by a constitution was preferable to "a mob
President." When it came to the franchise, he was wary: "universal suffrage
is the Demagogues staff. Shake off the Law of Primogeniture, reduce the
patronage of the crown, but keep the King, and enact a general system of
qualification for voters . . . the qualification to be reduced as the intelligence
of the people may increase."[52] By "intelligence" George also meant knowledge; an uninformed public with political power was dangerous.

In 1818, the president of the United States was James Monroe, who
with his powdered wig and knee breeches represented the last of the old-
guard republicans. Once the presidency shifted to Andrew Jackson, a Dem-
ocrat, George would find demagoguery rearing its ugly head in earnest. He
would watch his adopted country "getting blacker and blacker in political
villainy, until all is fair in politics," and he would be "astonished to see how
shamelessly the press is carried on; lying, slandering blackguarding, changing opinion with every change of circumstances." The state elections in
Kentucky would entail "an unusual portion of drunkenness, fighting, foul

voting and buying of votes."[53] For the moment, however, George was still enjoying his freedom away from the Old Country.

A popular ramble in Philadelphia at the time ran up the Schuylkill River through an "enchanting vale" to a waterfall four miles north of the city. While the falls themselves were not much to speak of, especially to an Englishman, they were surrounded by scenery that, as Emanuel Howitt put it in 1819, was "highly romantic and picturesque." Willow trees shaded the river, and in August raspberries were in bloom. Above the falls, a wobbly covered bridge of planks held together by wire was suspended over the river, from a tree on one side and the window of a mill on the other. The view from the middle of the bridge was supposed to be worth the risk of stepping onto it. *Alone by the Schuylkill a wanderer rov'd / And bright were its flowery banks to his eye; / But far, very far, were the friends that he lov'd, / And he gaz'd on its flowery banks with a sigh!*[54] George Keats may have shared the sentiment expressed in these lines by Thomas Moore.

Among the great estates overlooking the Schuylkill River was Fatland Ford, the paternal seat of some young people who were soon to play a leading role in George and Georgiana's lives in the West. Their father, William Bakewell, Sr., a fifty-seven-year-old English squire, lived in the columned stone mansion where George Washington and his officers had dined on occasion during the bitter winter of 1777-1778, while his bedraggled Continental Army was encamped in the snow across the way at Valley Forge.

In England, Squire William Bakewell and his brother Benjamin had formed part of a radical circle of intellectuals that included Joseph Priestley and Erasmus Darwin (grandfather of Charles Darwin), chemists and Unitarians who renounced the divinity of Christ. Having barely escaped the angry crowds that burned down his house and chemical laboratory, Priestley fled to the United States in 1794. He founded the First Unitarian Church of Philadelphia, and from his settlement on the banks of the Susquehanna continued to preach and to champion the cause of freedom until he died ten years later. Squire Bakewell and his brother were also Unitarians and chemists, and when the squire was asked to resign his position as magistrate, a hereditary honor that came with the title, he followed his friend Priestley, and his own brother, to America.

Unlike Samuel Taylor Coleridge, a quondam Unitarian preacher, who never came up with the money to settle with his friend Robert Southey on Priestley's land, Squire Bakewell did purchase land near Priestley in Susquehanna County. But when the brewery he ran with his brother Benjamin in New Haven, Connecticut, burned down in 1802, rather than settling in western Pennsylvania, Squire Bakewell returned to the life of a gentleman farmer on the banks of the Schuylkill.⁵⁵ The squire's sons, Thomas Woodhouse Bakewell and William Gifford Bakewell, would both become George's business partners in Kentucky. Tom was nine years older than George, and Will was the same age as Tom Keats.

Mill Grove, next to the Bakewell estate at Fatland Ford, was the former home of John James Audubon, the squire's son-in-law. Lucy Green Bakewell, the squire's eldest child, had married Audubon and moved with him to Kentucky in 1808. Eight years later, her sister Eliza had married Audubon's friend Nicholas Berthoud, and the Berthouds now lived in Shippingport, a few miles downriver from Louisville, which was where Tom Bakewell lived, and a hundred miles upriver from Red Banks (or Henderson), which is where the Audubons lived. Will Bakewell also lived in Kentucky with his siblings. The squire's two younger daughters, Sarah and Ann, would also marry friends of the Audubons, Berthouds, and Bakewells in the West.⁵⁶ George and Georgiana would become part of the same circle.

In Philadelphia, meanwhile, the days were growing shorter. The trip across the state of Pennsylvania to Pittsburgh, where emigrants exchanged wagons for flatboats at the head of the Ohio River, could take from ten days to three weeks. The leaves in the orchards were starting to change color, and the view of the woodlands from the mountains would be spectacular. The best times to travel were autumn and spring, though the former was preferable since the roads tended to be drier, and provisions more plentiful. *Season of mists and mellow fruitfulness, / Close bosom-friend of the maturing sun, / Conspiring with him how to load and bless / with fruit the vines . . . / And fill all fruit with ripeness to the core.*

Many people were on the move in 1818. "Old America seems to be breaking up, and moving westward," Morris Birkbeck wrote when he crossed the Allegheny Mountains the previous year. "We are seldom out of sight, as we travel on this grand track, towards the Ohio, of family groups behind and before us." Henry Fearon, traveling about the same time as George and Georgiana, counted passers-by on the road from Chambersburg to Pittsburgh and came up with a hundred and three stagewagons, two hundred people on horseback, twenty on foot, a beggar, and "one family, with their waggon, returning from Cincinnati, entirely disappointed."[57] To take into account the full length of the road from Philadelphia to Pittsburgh, one would need to double those numbers.

With their belongings packed and their goodbyes said, George and Georgiana Keats, like so many pioneers before and after them, clattered west down High Street toward the Schuylkill River. The Schuylkill Bridge would spill out into the Great Western Road, which led across the Great Appalachian Valley to the mountains the young couple had heard so much about. One can only guess at what must have been their feelings as they passed through the covered wooden bridge—that symbolic nexus between east and west—on their way to the Land of Cockaigne. They would not be alone in chasing what John, in *Endymion,* had called "a hope beyond the shadow of a dream."

Poor Tom

Back in Hampstead, things were about as bad as they could be. Tom's spirit and body were exhausted, and he would not live more than a few weeks. No longer could the brothers pretend that his "illness was all mistaken Fancy." The sight of his pale, emaciated visage haunted all who saw him. When Benjamin Bailey wrote to John Taylor at the end of August—three days after George and Georgiana landed in Philadelphia—he hoped that John would make it back from Scotland before Tom died. He feared, however, that Tom might already be dead. A month later, Haydon expressed his sympathy for Tom in a letter to John: "Poor fellow—I shall never forget his look when I saw him last."[58] Despite the posthumous tone of Haydon's remark, Tom's suffering was not yet over.

John himself was sick. Physically worn down from traveling, poisoned by the mercury he had taken as a treatment for venereal disease, emotionally exhausted from losing a brother he considered his best friend, he now had a sore throat that he had picked up in the Scottish Hebrides while "bog trotting in the Island of Mull." Compounding the sore throat was "a confounded tooth ache." When John fell sick with a fever, he took a packet ship from Inverness back to London two months ahead of schedule, while his friend Charles Brown stumped off on his ten toes to the North.[59]

On his way back to Well Walk, on the evening of Tuesday, August 18,

John had stopped at Wentworth Place. Maria Dilke remarked that he had come back from his travels "as brown and shabby as you can imagine; scarcely any shoes left, his jacket all torn at the back, a fur cap, a great plaid, and his knapsack." She had been worried that John would not make it back to see Tom alive, but now she was worried about *him*. John himself accurately predicted that, like his brother, he would "never be again secure in Robustness." He now had within him a "core of disease" that, putting it mildly, would be "not easy to pull out."[60]

Mercury, which has a half-life of fifteen to thirty years in the central nervous system, can cause psychological, neurological, and immunological complications: tremors, insomnia, emotional volatility and irritability, neuropathy, headaches, weakness, blurred vision, numbness, and tingling or pricking skin. Physicians, even at the time, recognized the negative side effects that could result from the various forms of mercury (pills, vapors, ointments, plasters, injections) that were used to treat disease. "To give mercury to a young and irritable person, who is probably constantly exposed to vicissitudes of temperature, and for a disease which does not require it (thus exposing the health and even the life of the patient to danger) is in the present state of our knowledge perfectly unpardonable," wrote Sir Astley Cooper, who, unlike Dr. Solomon Sawrey, did not believe in the use of mercury for venereal disease: "At the present time a surgeon must be either grossly ignorant or shamefully negligent of the duty which he owes to the character of his profession and to the common dictates of humanity if he persists in giving mercury for [venereal] disease." John was now living "in a continual fever," but he recognized that "it may be a nervousness proceeding from the Mercury."[61]

George would later recognize the effect of John's having been cooped up with Tom at Well Walk after the summer. After George left, there was no one who understood John's "character perfectly but poor Tom and he had not the power to divert his frequent melancholy, and eventually encreased his disease most fearfully by the horrors of his own lingering death." John's school friend Edward Holmes suggested that the poet's "premature death may have been brought on by his performing the office of nurse to a younger brother, who died of decline, for his attention to the invalid was so anxious and unwearied, that his friends could see distinctly that his own health had suffered in the exertion." Indeed, by releasing infected mucus from the lungs, the coughing of the consumptive patient proved highly contagious. John's close confinement with Tom in the autumn of 1818 virtually ensured that he, too, would die of the family disease.[62]

John had been waiting three and a half months to hear from his brother in America. "I have your Miniature on the Table George the great," he wrote to him in November: "its very like—though not quite about the upper lip." It may have been growing faint, but John still had a clear image of George in his mind. "I remember your Ways and Manners and actions; I know you[r] manner of thinking, you[r] manner of feeling: I know what shape your joy or your sorrow would take, I know the manner of you[r] walking, standing, sauntering, sitting down, laughing, punning, and every action so truly that you seem near to me."[63] But Tom was fading, and John found himself in a blur of fatigue and emotional and physical discomfort. By the time that John finally received George's letter from Philadelphia, he wasn't sure how to reply. There was little that he could say to his brother that he would want to hear. George would never see Tom in this life again.

As an escape from the horrors of impending death, the poet turned to those epic "abstractions" that he had begun to formulate among the sublime scenes of the Highlands. *Instead of thrones, hard flint they sat upon, / Couches of rugged stone, and slaty ridge* . . . Like his Titans, cast down into a scene resembling Milton's underworld by the Olympian gods, John felt himself in the mouth of hell. "The Mountains of Tartary are a favourite lounge," he joked to George, "if I happen to miss the Allegany ridge."[64] Even more than he let on to his brother, John identified with the profound pathos of the fallen Titans, in their timeless, barren world. The "thunderous waterfalls and torrents hoarse," the "Crag jutting forth to crag, and rocks that seem'd / Ever as if just rising from a sleep," made a "fit roofing" to his own "nest of woe."

Deep in a vale as still and silent as death, the Titans, like no one else, shared the same grim reality John was inhabiting with Tom. Saturn's reign of power has ended, and the giant god finds himself at the start of *Hyperion* in much the same position as Satan, lying sprawled on the burning lake, at the start of *Paradise Lost*. Yet Satan recovers more quickly than Saturn, who finds it difficult to summon the energy necessary for epic struggle:

> Deep in the shady sadness of a vale
> Far sunken from the healthy breath of morn,
> Far from the fiery noon, and eve's one star,
> Sat gray-hair'd Saturn, quiet as a stone,

Still as the silence round about his lair;
Forest on forest hung above his head
Like cloud on cloud. No stir of air was there,
Not so much life as on a summer's day
Robs not one light seed from the feather'd grass,
But where the dead leaf fell, there did it rest.

The challenge the melancholy protagonists of *Hyperion* face is to rouse themselves to battle once more, and it may be telling that John gave up on the poem shortly after the second book had ended: the place in *Paradise Lost* where Satan exits hell to conquer the world. The ending of Book II of *Hyperion* recognizes that the time for wavering has passed: "all the Gods / Gave from their hollow throats the name of 'Saturn!'" Yet Saturn, unlike Satan, remains defeated. Rather than rebelling against his miserable fate, he seems to resign himself to it, sinking back into the shadow of his own faded glory and enduring the profound pain that must motivate any epic endeavor.

Saturn's successor, the Apollonian ascendant god, has his own struggles to face when he wakes up in the epic world of *Hyperion.* At the start of the third book, Apollo receives what is at once the gift and the burden of prophecy: "Knowledge enormous makes a God of me. / Names, deeds, gray legends, dire events, rebellions, / Majesties, Sovran voices, agonies, / Creations and destroyings, all at once / Pour into the wide hollows of my brain, / And deify me." Compelled by the acute pain of such omniscient, transcendent vision, Apollo shrieks—and the poem breaks off. By the start of the sequel, *The Fall of Hyperion*—or rather, John's second attempt at the epic story of the fallen Titans—Apollo will have become a merely human poet.

In *Hyperion,* the central concern is not mortal suffering so much as the sublime, immortal agony of the eternals. The poet projected onto those forms so much larger than life the fevered-out eyes and numbed, palsied limbs of mortal sickness. Now the once invincible Titans

Were pent in regions of laborious breath;
Dungeon'd in opaque element, to keep
Their clenched teeth still clench'd, and all their limbs
Lock'd up like veins of metal, crampt and screw'd;
Without a motion, save of their big hearts
Heaving in pain, and horribly convuls'd
With sanguine feverous boiling gurge of pulse.

Unlike Milton's angels in *Paradise Lost,* Keats's Titans are *sick.* The "sanguine" or bloody "feverous boiling gurge of pulse" of the consumptive patient may be even more horrific than Milton's distant infernal regions, where, in *Paradise Lost,* "a black bituminous gurge/Boils out from under ground, the mouth of hell." Their teeth are clenched. Their breath is labored. Liquid mercury, which John believed "must be poisonous to life," locks up their veins like metal.[65] Their big hearts heave in pain in their chests. Their limbs are convulsed. And more dreadful than the dark, tartareous dregs vomited up by the Miltonic "mouth of hell" are the dark, viscous mouthfuls of blood that turns blacker as the sufferer—too close for comfort in this case—approaches his end.

Yet, in epic as in romance, Thanatos is shadowed by Eros. While "poor Tom" (to borrow a phrase John used repeatedly) lay dying, the poet found himself, quickly and irreversibly, falling in love. Mrs. Frances Brawne, whose husband had recently died of the same disease that was torturing Tom, had rented Charles Brown's half of Wentworth Place during the summer that he and John went to Scotland. Liking the open air by the heath, and not wanting to lose any more family members to consumption, she had moved to a nearby cottage when her sublet from Brown expired. She had a fourteen-year-old son named Sam, a little girl named Margaret, and a daughter, Fanny, who had just turned eighteen, on August 9.

Fanny Brawne may have been new to society, but she had an affinity for it. She liked attention, especially the reluctant attention of a young man as intriguing and charismatic as John Keats. Literally as well as figuratively, John and Fanny saw eye to eye. They were about the same height, and both held their heads high. Fanny had a flair for fashion, which John claimed to hate, though he could not help admiring its disciple. When George Keats met Fanny in 1819, he heard her being complimented on having revived a "tasty headdress" from the age of Charles the Second. Fanny had creativity, wit like Georgiana, and resolve. John described his new neighbor's appeal in a string of oddly matched adjectives to George and Georgiana: "beautiful and elegant, graceful, silly, fashionable and strange."[66] Fanny turned the poet's head by taking him off guard and offering a different kind of challenge from any he had previously encountered.

Fanny also seems to have intuited that John was battling a deeply entrenched suspicion of women. He adored them, and he hated them. They meant everything to him, and nothing. He was, in short, skittish. Fanny captured his attention, as Charles Brown had done, by not being overly solicitous. She showed no shame about her taste for sentimental fiction, going so far as to prefer it to lyric. But she did like narrative poetry, and the couple at least had Shakespeare, if not Byron, in common.

Fanny Brawne was certainly different from Isabella Jones, who reappeared suddenly in the poet's life that autumn. One night, on the way to the opera, John ran into her, and his first impulse was to keep going. But he quickly regretted his behavior and turned back. She showed no sign of having taken offense, and they walked together toward Islington, where she invited him up to her apartment on Queen Square. Her rooms stacked with books and glimmering in candlelight with mirrors and pictures reflected the refined taste of the occupant. She had an Aeolian harp, a bronze bust of Napoleon, a parrot, and a red-breasted finch in a cage. She offered her guest a choice of fine liqueurs and a grouse for his sick brother. She wrote down his address, to send more game.

Perhaps more out of gratitude than affection, John attempted a kiss; but, recognizing the emptiness of the gesture, she refused it. "She contrived to disappoint me in a way which made me feel more pleasure than a simple kiss could do," John wrote to George. "She said I should please her much more if I would only press her hand and go away." John respected Isabella for her knowledge and cultural sophistication. But his feelings for her never deepened into romantic love. He placed her in a category with Georgiana as the only women, about his own age, whom he felt "content to know for their mind and friendship alone."[67]

John's strange new feelings for Fanny Brawne also differed from what he had felt for Jane Cox, a cousin of John Reynolds, whom he met after his return from Scotland. Jane Cox had "a rich eastern look" and "the Beauty of a Leopardess." But like a sonata by Mozart, or a sunset, her grandeur did not touch him. He could raise her up—not as high as Cleopatra, perhaps, but at least as high as her charming maid, Charmian—and worship her from afar. "I dont cry to take the moon home with me in my Pocket," he explained to George; nor did he "fret to leave her behind me."[68] One admires sublimity; one does not love it.

Jane Cox's appeal was of a kind to diffuse the poet's insecurities and at the same time "to make women of inferior charms hate her." Jane and Marianne Reynolds, gossiping behind their cousin's back, exasperated John by trying to draw him into their tête-à-tête. John complained to George that the majority of women appeared to him "as children to whom I would rather give a Sugar Plum than my time . . . a barrier against Matrimony

which I rejoice in." Whether protesting too much or too little one cannot know, but John claimed to discern little difference between the "Dress
Maker," the intellectual "blue Stocking," and the "charming sentimental-
ist."[69] The first knew nothing, the second claimed to know more than she
did, and the third knew too little to support her opinions.

Another undated poem by George, titled "The Influence of Tea upon
the *Ladies,*" captures his older brother's attitude toward women as he found
them in the Reynolds' establishment in the autumn of 1818:

Dear Tea, that enlivener of Wit and of Soul,
More loquacious by far than the draughts of the Bowl
Soon unloosens the tongue, and enlivens the mind,
And enlivens the eyes to the faults of mankind,
It brings on the tapis their neighbours defects,
The faults of their Friends, or their wilful neglects,
Reminds them of many a good-natured tale,
About those who are stylish, or those who are frail;
In harmless Chit Chat an acquaintance they roast,
And serve up a friend, as they serve up a toast,
. . . . .
And by nods inuendoes and hints and what not
Reputation and Tea send together to Pot,
While Madam in Cambrics, & Laces array'd
With her plate and her liveries in splendid parade,
Will drink in *Imperial* a friend at a sup,
Or in *gunpowder,* blow them by dozens all up.[70]

George clearly had a knack for satire. As in his puzzle-poem "On Woman,"
these lines are taut and intelligent. Instead of empathy, the speaker displays
wit, as secure in his parody of society ladies, as any satirist. In August, John
Gibson Lockhart had defended that master satirist, Alexander Pope, by
comparing him, as a Man of Power, to the Cockney Poets: "it is most piti-
ably ridiculous to hear men, of whom their country will always have reason to be proud, reviled by uneducated and flimsy striplings, who are not
capable of understanding either their merits, or those of any other *men of
power.*"[71] George was not yet the wealthy civic leader he would become
later, but he too was a Man of Power. He wrote clever poetry like the poem
above and left the genius to John.

If John knew little about his brother's changed reality overseas, George knew even less about the changed status of his brother's heart. Georgiana would have been more likely than George to notice that, in the same letter in which John was making up reasons *not* to be married, he kept swerving back to the same fascinating subject.

> Shall I give you Miss Brawne? She is about my height—with a fine style of countenance of the lengthen'd sort—she wants sentiment in every feature—she manages to make her hair look well—her nostrils are fine—though a little painful—her mouth is bad and good—her Profile is better than her full-face which indeed is not full [but] pale and thin without showing any bone—Her shape is very graceful and so are her movements—her Arms are good her hands badish—her feet tolerable—she is not seventeen—but she is ignorant—monstrous in her behaviour flying out in all directions, calling people such names—that I was forced lately to make use of the term *Minx*—this is I think not from any innate vice but from a penchant she has for acting stylishly. I am however tired of such style and shall decline any more of it—[72]

As this passage in John's letter to George and Georgiana reveals, love has little to do with perfection. John might denounce stylish behavior, but he could not renounce Fanny Brawne. In the midst of describing a party he had attended, he shifts to this description of Fanny with no more transition than a dash. Love has more to do with timing, and Fanny Brawne entered John Keats's life at just the right time. George was gone, Tom was dying, and John was vulnerable: Fanny provided more than a breath of fresh air from the cloistered sickroom.

Poor Tom found no such relief. Adding to the sorrow of sickness was a failed love affair that was never real in the first place. During the summer while his brothers were away, and Tom found himself alone in Hampstead, Charles Wells seems to have taken advantage of his illness to address a series of sophomoric love letters to Tom under the pen name "Amena Bellefila." Tom fell for the deception, taking seriously the mysterious French lady's teasing speech. At one point, adopting the role of a courtly lady to address Tom as a chivalrous knight, Wells wrote: "Now would dame Fortune, Fickle Jade, grant me but my request this Instant, would I bind about thy Loins a Cuirass, a Shield, & Sword," like "a mass of Shining Adament." The writer then tops off her fantasy by crowning her lover with a helmet, emblazoned with a dove, a symbol of her own virgin modesty.[73] Trusting such chimeras to be authentic, Tom honorably kept the epistolary love affair secret.

But late one night, as John was nursing Tom, the story spilled out of the invalid in a gush of fevered speech. Tom cried that he was dying of a broken heart, and John, discovering the deception, never forgave Wells. "I shall say, once for all, to my friends generally and severally, cut that fellow, or I cut you," he had written from Teignmouth ("cut" meaning to snub or disrespect), but now that the prankster's emotional manipulation of Tom had been uncovered, John cut Wells himself. Wells knew better than to send John a bouquet of roses this time. But he would later confess to having written the biblical drama, *Joseph and His Brethren,* to impress the poet: "I wrote it in six weeks to compel Keats to esteem me and admit my *power,* for we had quarreled, and everybody who knew him must feel I was in fault."[74] Wells, however, compelled nothing but comtempt.

The dying invalid now looked up to his brother as his only consolation, and they both knew the end would come soon. John could not bring himself to ask Tom whether he had any last words to send to George. "His heart speaks to you," he wrote instead. "Be as happy as you can." Suffering was part of the human condition, and death was inevitable. George must go on with his life after their terrible loss, as John would try to do. Their sister had seen Tom only once since John's return from Scotland. "He says that once more between this and the Holydays will be sufficient," John wrote to Fanny of their guardian on November 5. "What can I do?" Yet, as the month wore on, John became the one delaying his sister's visit to Hampstead: "it would be so painful to you both."[75]

John considered his ties to his siblings to be sacred, a gift from "providence to prevent the deleterious effects of one great, solitary grief." At times, he felt that George was so far away, so lost "in the Wilds of America," that they no longer shared the same world. "Have you some warm furs?" he asked George in December, imagining him like Daniel Boone perhaps, or one of the early French explorers. While the poet pursued tomtits, tiny brown birds no bigger than a hummingbird, on Hampstead Heath, the pioneer brother (or so John imagined) pursued the horned American bison into the sunset. "Have you shot a Buffalo?"[76] John Keats had no reason to know that the buffalo had disappeared from the prairies of Illinois, as the last mammoth had fled from the Big Bone Valley in Kentucky.

Other times, John felt "a direct communication of spirit" with George. By writing to him as he would write in a journal, he found that he could be more emotionally forthright than if he had been speaking to his brother face to face. He proposed that at ten o'clock on Sundays (notwithstanding the time difference), they each read Shakespeare. He thought that in this manner the brothers would at least be as close as two people reading in the same room ever are. "My Thoughts are very frequently in a foreign Country," John wrote to George in December. "I live more out of England than in it."[77]

Yet, for all their metaphysical closeness, when Tom died at eight o'clock in the morning on Tuesday, December 1, George was not there. Where, exactly, we do not know, but he was far away, most likely at a cabin in the woods of Kentucky with John James Audubon, Audubon's tall and elegant English wife, their two young sons, Victor Woodhouse and John Gifford, and a menagerie of woodland creatures. A wild turkey nested on the roof of the cabin, and the family's eccentric pet swan, Trumpeter, chased the children.[78] John was alone with his grief.

Worn out from his grueling vigil by Tom's side, John stumbled over to Wentworth Place and awoke Brown with a press of the hand. Without needing to be told, Brown realized why his friend was standing over him so early in the morning. He joined John in silence for a few moments, but then he turned to the practical: John must not stay at Well Walk. He should leave the awful place where he had endured so much grief and where his younger brother now lay, a corpse. The trip to Scotland had shown that they could live together: John should move in with Brown as soon as possible. They would "keep house" together, and the poet would feel less alone. Perhaps he might also feel less anxiety about money and be able to get back to writing, the best way to work through the pain.[79] This may have been Charles Brown's finest moment as a friend.

But at the same time as Brown came to the rescue of the poet, he became confirmed in his animosity to George. A willful person whose instincts were at once possessive and protective, he resented the pioneer brother for his absence, and he proceeded to take the fraternal role upon himself, shielding the poet from anything and anyone he judged to be a threat, including the people John loved best. Brown was ready and willing to lend a shrewd eye and strong hand to support his friend, but the price for this was unconditional loyalty. Brown would never look anything but contemptuously upon George Keats again.

George, in turn, would find fault with Brown for his behavior. Yes, Brown had been generous in taking John into his home, but hadn't Brown also profited from the arrangement? "No Man who ever lived was more impatient at being under an obligation than John, as long as I knew him," George insisted, "and he misled me himself if he did not divide with Brown the expences of House Keeping at Hampstead." Brown was "close, painstaking and calculating," and his actions were no doubt self-interested. John "was open, prodigal, and had no power of calculation whatever." George had little doubt that Brown thought highly of his brother, but George also thought that Brown believed John's character needed tempering with more judgment than he credited John with having. Brown misjudged his brother, laughing at "the foolery" of his very best qualities, as Don Quixote's smug detractors laughed at his idealistic exploits.[80]

John had always taken the lead role in his brothers' lives, but the extroverted Brown had taken the lead during their tour of Scotland, putting on his best brogue to communicate with people they met and attaching the poet permanently to him. John took longer to warm up to strangers. The Scottish tour had brought out Brown's best side and now, just as George had "little George" (as John called Georgiana), and John had his little sister, Brown had "little Keats"—as the schoolboys at Clarke's school once called the poet.[81]

But Charles Brown at least appreciated John as a Man of Genius. Society often interprets social discomfort as ineptitude, and the poet "did not generally make the most favorable impression upon people where he visited. He could not well unbend himself & was rather of an unsocial disposition, unless he was among those who were of his own tastes," his friend Henry Stephens said.[82] A better phrase might have been "those who were of his own choosing." Sympathy came in many forms, and the poet's range of friends suggests that a taste for Milton or Spenser was not a requirement for his friendship. In the presence of kindred spirits, John left his shell. In the company of dissonant souls, he shriveled up like a snail in salt.

Most people, the poet explained, "do not know me not even my most intimate acquaintance—I give into their feelings as though I were refraining from irritating a little child—Some think me middling, others silly, others foolish—everyone thinks he sees my weak side against my will; when in truth it is with my will—I am content to be thought all this because I have in my own breast so great a resource. This is one great reason why they like me so; because they can all show to advantage in a room, and eclipse from a certain tact one who is reckoned to be a good Poet."[83] John's reserve was an effective shield against the intimacy of anyone who proved a threat to that which he held most dear. To have held himself superior to those around him would have been a gross failure of empathy on the part of the chameleon-poet. Yet, John also realized that to blend in would be to betray his gift.

While society in Regency England was not as formally patterned as it had been in prior eras, when a fixed symbolic language of gesture and manner ruled courtly life, it did not look kindly on idiosyncrasy either. Percy Shelley might perform his freaks and larks in public, or out on the heath as the spirit moved him, but John Keats was too precariously perched in the middle ranks of society for such eccentric behavior to be an option. Recent critical reviews of *Endymion,* which focused more on the poet's social status than on his poetry, heightened any existing social sensitivity. The essay "On the Cockney School of Poetry" in the August issue of *Blackwood's* advised that it was "a better and a wiser thing, to be a starved apothecary than a starved poet," and concluded: "So back to the shop Mr John, back to 'plasters, pills, and ointment boxes.'"[84]

Writing to George on December 31, 1818, on the eve of the New Year he would be facing alone, John concluded that the present moment had no claim on him. Through the powers of imagination, he explained, "manners and customs long since passed whether among the Babylonians or the Bactrians are as real, or even more real than those among which I now live." Neither time nor space was an accurate measure of reality. Tom had been dead for a month, but his presence in eternity was real. When John and George opened their Shakespeare at the same time, they might encounter each other, if not on Hampstead Heath perhaps on the stormy heath of *King Lear,* where "poor Tom" might still speak his whims. "Bless thy five wits!" their lost, madcap brother might have said. "Tom's a-cold."[85]

The Great Western Road

The town of Chambersburg, at the foot of the North Mountain in the Great Appalachian Valley, was the last stop before the first major ascent up the Alleghenies—and the last bastion of anything as civilized, to English eyes, as brick. Although the road getting there had been littered with rocks and sun-baked clumps of clay, this would be nothing compared to the challenges that George and Georgiana would face for many miles as they crossed the mountain ridges. George Flower had left his young bride, Eliza (Andrews), at a "comfortable and quiet tavern" in Chambersburg when he returned to England to recruit more settlers for the English Prairie, and the people there remembered him as bubbling with enthusiasm and bragging about land that was fifty to a hundred times less expensive than land in the Great Appalachian Valley.[86] And fertile! Not rocky and unkempt.

The road through Chambersburg linked the stage roads from Baltimore, Washington, and Philadelphia to Pittsburgh. A hundred feet from the road, on the eastern branch of Conecocheague Creek high up on a hill, sat a stone church. The grassy ravine sloping down from the church had once, until beavers diverted the current of the stream, served as the bed of the creek. Charlotte Chambers, a granddaughter of the town's Scottish founder, Benjamin Chambers, recalled that once people had come "from town, from hamlet, and from country wide" to worship in the old log cabin that had been there before the stone church:

> Blest sight it was to mark that Godly flock,
>   At intermission, grouped through this wood.
> Each log, each bench, each family upping-block,
>   Some granddame held amidst her gathered brood.
>   Here cakes were shared, and fruit, and counsel good;
> Devoutly spoken, 'twas of crops and rain.[87]

The members of the small Presbyterian congregation no longer needed the upping blocks to mount the horses that would take them back into the woods after services. A town of a couple of thousand residents had since grown up in the immediate vicinity.

Among the buildings that made up the town of Chambersburg were several mills situated on the brown muddy waters of the creek: Chambers's Mill, Weaver's Mill, and Hettick's Mill among them, the last presumably belonging to some relation of Mrs. Hettick, who ran the inn where George Flower's wife spent the winter.[88] The mills ground grain, pressed oil, spun wool, and made the paper that in the old days pack animals, and then covered wagons, had hauled from the East. The embankment on the far side of the creek covered the bones of the town's first settlers beneath gray gravestones.

In Chambersburg in 1818 people lived in houses made of brick or of wooden boards, but in the mountains people still lived in log cabins. These structures foreign to European eyes consisted normally of a single room covered by a wood-shingled roof, the American backwoods equivalent of the thatched country cottage in Great Britain. The floors were composed of packed dirt, or of split logs laid against each other with the flat sides facing up. The chimneys attached to the outer walls of the cabins, like the furniture inside them, were also made of wood, plastered inside and outside with mud. To keep out wind and insects, the spaces between the logs were "mudded," or else "chuncked"—that is, filled with wood chips. Some cabins had windows to let in light; others, only doors.

The first mile up the North Mountain would be relatively easy. After that, the road would narrow and become more steep and rugged. Ascending vehicles were supposed to signal their approach with a horn, so that the wagons and carriages on the descent could stop and wait wherever passing seemed feasible. At the top of the mountain, the stage road turned into the turnpike road made by General John Forbes and his army during the French and Indian War. The view from the top made the haul up the mountain seem worthwhile: tens of thousands of untouched acres of spectacularly colored trees—black, red, and white oak, cedar, chestnut, beech, butternut . . . William Tell Harris, another Englishman passing through at this time, waxed poetic about the stunning array of foliage seen from the top of the Allegheny Mountains: "The dogwood, the locust, and the mountain ash, with their gay and varied bloom," he said, offered "handsome reliefs to the sombre oak, whose sturdy arms protect him from the blast."[89]

From the summit of the North Mountain, one could also see a quaint cluster of log cabins known as McConnellsville, surrounding a wooden church with an octagonal spire. This hamlet, located in "a Sweet Valley" before Scrub Ridge and Sidling Hill, inspired even Henry Fearon to put aside his signature irony: "This apparently delightful little town appeared secluded from the rest of the world, and one might have imagined it another Eden, cut off by means of woods and trackless wilds, and mountain snows, from the vices and the corruptions which, in every other quarter, visit and torment mankind." Of course, once he entered the village, it turned out to be all too human. Prices were inflated and the service "cold, friendless, unfeeling, callous, and selfish."[90]

In reading contemporary English accounts of the mountain inns, one must keep in mind the perspective of John Bull in a nation that was similar enough to the Old Country to make any difference stand out. Taverns and inns on opposite sides of the Atlantic often had the same names, and on the road from Philadelphia to Pittsburgh there was even a Swan with Two Necks. The privations English writers in America complained of in the central Appalachian Mountain Range were similar to those Keats and Brown experienced in the Scottish Highlands. Brown described the kind of discourse that took place that summer as the friends stumbled, soaking and weary of struggling with a map, into a long-awaited inn: "What have you for Dinner? 'Truly nothing.' No Eggs? 'We have two.' Any loaf bread? 'No, Sir, but we've nice oat-cakes.' Any bacon? any dried fish? 'No, no, no, Sir!' But you've plenty of Whiskey? 'O yes, Sir, plenty of Whiskey!'"[91]

Henry Fearon complained similarly, if with more annoyance and less genuine humor, of the fare at the Fountain Inn in the Alleghenies, "a miserable log-house, or what you would call a dog-hole." When he requested something to eat, the owner replied, "I guess whiskey is all the feed we have on sale." Fearon had grown used to the drill:

Have you any meat?
No.
Either cold or hot will make no difference to me.
I guess I don't know.
Have you any fowls?
No.
Fish?
No.
Ham?
No.
Bread?
No.
Cheese?
No.
Crackers (biscuits)?
No.
I will pay you any price you please.
I guess we have only rum and whiskey feed.

There was almost a sense among English writers in America that the innkeepers were holding back the plenty promised by the land. Emanuel Howitt claimed in September 1819 to have seen clusters of fox grapes hanging in luxurious profusion outside a tavern that provided neither sheets nor blankets. He spent the night on the floor between two beds, wrapped in a rug.[92]

A few weeks before George and Georgiana crossed the mountains, William Amphlett arrived at one mountain inn to discover the proprietor in the lap of her daughter, undergoing a treatment for lice:

> It was now dark, when we approached the first tavern on the summit. We groped our way to the door, to behold our hostess sitting upon the ground, with her head in the lap of her daughter, who was hunting up her vermin by fire-light! She did not attempt to rise on our entrance; and to our demand, if we could have beds and supper, after a dignified pause, she replied, "I guess so.—Bess, go and make some candles!—You should have come before sun-down. The stable is behind the house.—Jack, get up, and give the movers some hay." We had now to attend to the horses in the dark as well as we could, and then wait about an hour and a half while our supper was procuring. The broiled chicken was alive long after our arrival; and the cakes unbaked, that we were to eat with our coffee. The coffee also was roasted in our presence, and the candles making by the same hands that attended to it. Our supper-table was furnished with chicken, ham, cake, coffee, butter, sugar, eggs, apple-butter, apple-pye, cyder, cherry-bounce, milk, and whiskey.
>
> Of these articles, the coffee only was not the produce of their own land! What people, therefore, can be more independent? To complain of delay, or express any kind of impatience, is not only futile, but impolitic. Patience is the only remedy, and complaisance your best recommendation. On being shown to our room, (for one only could we procure, and the two sash-windows of that contained three panes of glass,) we felt an involuntary shuddering at the sight of our beds; so contrasted with former indulgences. Our new-made candle was brought up in the girl's hand, as the house only afforded one candlestick; and she, by dropping a little of the tallow on the floor, stuck it up: fortunately it soon fell down and went out, which induced us to lie down in our clothes: but, alas! these could not long protect us! "Forth from their calm retreats" came a most innumerable host, and, with simultaneous fangs, began the work of blood! We could console ourselves neither with
>
> _____ "Scraps of verse,"
>
> Nor "Sayings of philosophers"
>
> but, after a few shrugs and shakings, were absolutely obliged most cowardly to run for it, and beg the favour of being allowed to sleep in our

own waggons, and recline upon our own beds! We had to wait two hours in the morning for our breakfast, which was just a counterpart of our supper; and on our departure from this *hotel,* were modestly charged seven dollars for myself and wife, five children and two servants, including the hay and corn for the horses! This was certainly one of the worst places we met with in our route to Pittsburg; but many are very little better, and the worst inns in England are far before the *best* here.[93]

There was no disputing that amid the sublime scenery of the Alleghenies there was poverty. But a hearty meal of chicken, ham, homemade apple pie, and cider—all gleaned from the bounty of the land—was enough to restore anyone to rights. Just imagine, such accounts imply, what someone from the Old Country could accomplish with the same means. Arcadia was at hand for those willing to work, and nature promised a ready return.

Yet beneath the contempt, one discerns respect, if not envy, for the American ideal of self-sufficiency. The Americans might be lazy and slovenly, but they didn't seem to know it. They displayed no shame, either for their behavior or, as the case may be, their own lowly existence. Adlard Welby was shocked at the role reversal that took place when he landed in New York and entered a boarding house: "A young woman who was sweeping the floor slip-shod, desired us to walk into a room she pointed to; where, she said, we might wait for further orders!!" In another guide for emigrants, S. H. Collins warned readers that the profession of innkeeper in the United States was "perfectly respectable" and "often carried on by persons of distinguished character."[94]

As opposed to the Old Country, where the inheritance of land entailed political, religious, and military might, in America the people were selling their land more cheaply than they were renting their rooms. Titles did not impart the same social status, and travelers were often surprised to discover colonels, brigade generals, majors, and state representatives pouring whiskey at the bar and serving meals. "Let no one here indulge himself in abusing the waiter or hostler at an inn," John Bradbury counseled. "That waiter or hostler is probably a citizen, and does not, nor cannot conceive, that a situation in which he discharges a duty to society, not in itself dishonourable, should subject him to insult."[95] Most proprietors owned the land their establishments sat on, and they did not expect to be treated as servants. If guests were not satisfied, they could continue on down the road.

After McConnellsville, the road to Pittsburgh crossed the winding and rocky Juniata River, a branch of the Susquehanna that reminded more than one Englishman of the Wye. In the Juniata Valley, streams crossed the road, and to make it over some of the mountain cascades travelers had to improvise bridges by throwing down planks and logs, or piling large flat stones. "A London coachman would in half an hour have dashed the strongest English stage to pieces," Henry Fearon observed of one particularly difficult mountain pass, "and probably broken the necks of his passengers."[96]

On the far side of the Juniata River sat the village of Bloody Run, named for a battle fought between settlers and Native Americans on the steep, rugged banks of the river—a "massacre," the residents called it. The only predators lurking now in the area were the red foxes and the raccoons that fished in the river. Besides its gruesome moniker, the village of Bloody Run also had a blacksmith and a wheelwright to fix carriages and wagons that made it over the mountains.[97] After Bloody Run would come yet more rugged terrain: North Ridge, Cove Ridge, Dry Ridge, Allegheny Ridge, and the South or Southern Ridge, with many smaller elevations and sharp inclines in between.

At times, the road became vertical for several feet at a stretch. Progress was excruciatingly slow, and it often seemed more efficient to get out and walk. "Many a traveller tugs his weary way, and with frequent gasp, turns him round to view the progress he has made," Harris recounted in 1818, "but far he cannot see: behind, before, appears the mountain covered with wood." The trees, as one traveled west, seemed larger, and richer in variety, the hollow ones occasionally filled with colonies of bees. In the undergrowth, whortleberries and blackberries abounded. From the summit of Dry Ridge, one could see the Blue, Cove, Laurel, and Chestnut Ridges, and at the foot of Chestnut Ridge, the woods thinned out. By that point, travelers had broken the back of the Allegheny Mountains, the "great barrier between east and west America."[98]

The steep and stony road then approached the fertile valleys of western Pennsylvania. The road improved as it wound through orchards and farms, nourished by springs and rivulets branching off the Yohogany River. Trout swam in the streams and the creeks. The goldenrod and purple violets were no longer in bloom, but lavender, yellowish-pink columbines, and other wild flowers graced the hilly farmlands: the beautiful riposte to the mountains' sublime.

To most travelers coming down from the mountains, the cows and sheep grazing in the fields looked like beef and mutton. The hens and pigs took on the appearance of fried chicken and spare ribs. In fact, the inns in western Pennsylvania behind the mountains laid more plentiful tables than their peers up in the mountains. For breakfast, one might find buckwheat pancakes, corncakes, poached eggs, bacon, sliced cheese, bread and butter; for dinner, turkey, pheasant, partridge, pork, beef, pickled cabbage, cucumbers, beets . . . ; for dessert, fruit topped with cream, or blueberry, apple, peach, and cherry pies. The rest of the journey promised to be relatively easy.

Across from Turtle Creek, about a mile up Turtle Hill, the turnpike road passed the fields where General Edward Braddock had met his infamous defeat in the summer of 1755 during the French and Indian War. Having marched thousands of redcoats up from Virginia, and hauled British cannon artillery through the mountains in an effort to capture the French garrison at Fort Duquesne, General Braddock and his troops found themselves unprepared for backwoods combat. They fell to the rifles and tomahawks of the Iroquois and the French, who hid in the forests by the Monongahela River. The bones of the massacred battalion could still be seen bleaching in the sun. But not those of General Braddock: young George Washington, then serving under the British as Braddock's volunteer aide-de-camp, buried his commander's bones beneath the army's path of retreat so they could not be found. When the British captured Fort Duquesne from the French three years later, they changed its name to Fort Pitt.

Past Brownsville, also known as Old Fort, the Monongahela River meandered toward Pittsburgh. Harris noted in 1818 that "at every turn of the river, farms, towns, bold and impending rocks, and fertile slopes, successively presented themselves to my delighted eyes." Estwick Evans, in *A Pedestrious Tour of Four Thousand Miles, through the Western States and Territories, during the Winter and Spring of 1818,* observed "a silent grandeur" in the confluence of the Allegheny and Monongahela rivers at the head of the Ohio. Steam navigation was in its infancy then, but fourteen years later in his *Manual for Emigrants,* Calvin Colton recorded his surprise at the sight of "the majestic steam-boats . . . coming and going, as if by concert they had assembled from unknown regions to sport among the mountains, and assist in the creation of this vision of enchantment."[99]

Whatever George and Georgiana Keats might have thought on their approach to Pittsburgh at the fork of the Ohio, it is to their credit that, de-

spite all the difficulties, the ups and downs of inexperience and the naviga-
tional challenges of the mountains, they made it to this place: the gateway
to the West. George would resign his riding whip to the keelboatmen, who
would take over with poles and oars. Georgiana would finally get out of
the jolting carriage. The trip downriver would be a luxury as well as a necessity.

Pittsburgh

The streets of Pittsburgh, like those of Philadelphia, were laid out in
straight lines between two rivers that crossed each other at right angles. But
whereas Philadelphia took the shape of a parallelogram, Pittsburgh was
formed like a triangle. At the tip of the city, two rivers converged: the Allegheny flowed in clear and transparent from the north; the Monongahela,
thick and muddy, flowed from the south. Two covered wooden bridges on
stone piers were under construction across each of them. The Monongahela
Bridge, which was designed to be higher and longer than London Bridge,
was nearly complete. Pedestrians crossed in a separate lane from the wagons and carriages. Gaps in the sides of the bridge let in light. One could see
that the usual cautions applied: "Keep to the right as the law directs," and
"A penalty for smoking segars while passing over."[100]

Because Pittsburgh held the key to the West, the British and the French
had fought for control of the fort at the fork of the Ohio in the French and
Indian War. Only one day after George and Georgiana docked in Philadelphia, the *Franklin Gazette* made clear that the battle for the western market
was still going on: "Much of the prosperity and future growth of Philadelphia depends upon the exertions used to retain the trade of the Western
Country. To supply the wants of a vast territory daily increasing both in
population and wealth, in a ratio hitherto unexampled, will be, in a commercial point of view, a priviledge [sic] of no trifling importance."[101] Old
Fort Pitt, like Cincinnati, and Louisville farther downriver, was a middle-
man.

Pittsburgh now had roughly ten thousand residents—mostly of Irish,
English, Scottish, French, Dutch, and Swiss descent—and the various languages could be heard on the streets. The city had grown from a military
garrison into a busy manufacturing city, and the Native peoples in the area
had moved away. The few that remained had settled nearby and "adopted

the manners of the Americans."[102] People now seemed to pay less attention to each other than to their work, and the streets resounded with the clang of industry. The main products were iron, tin, and glass, but the city also shipped a profusion of other colonial wares—flax, saddles, bridles, cabinets, grindstones, lumber, livestock, bacon, flour, corn, cider, porter, and whiskey, to name a few—down the river.

In 1818 Pittsburgh had masons; stone cutters; carpenters; brick, cabinet, clock, watch, and button makers; coopers; turners; ship builders, machine makers; wheelwrights; nailors; brass founders; copper, tin, silver, gun, and lock smiths; cutlers; wire workers; screw and hinge makers; glass blowers; tanners; curriers; saddlers; bootmakers; glovers; butchers; bakers; brewers; distillers; cotton spinners; weavers; dyers; tailors; printers; paper and ink makers; rope walkers; tobacconists; soap boilers; candle, brush, and comb manufacturers; potters; painters; and that was not all. When Thomas Hulme visited Pittsburgh on his way to the English Prairie in 1819, he noted that there was "scarcely a denomination of manufacture or manual profession" not represented.[103]

Yet while the city at the fork of the Ohio may have had banks and taverns, churches, stores, a market, a small public library, even a couple of weekly papers (in which George could have checked the going rate for gigs), it lacked bookstores. John Keats would have found himself at a loss in Pittsburgh. "You will perceive that it is quite out of my interest to come to America," he wrote to George. "What could I do there? How could I employ myself?"[104] George, on the other hand, whose explicit aim in moving to America had been to make money, would have seen the potential in the commercial activity of the city and in the market of the quickly expanding West.

A cultured disdain for commerce, in any event, would have had little to feed on in nineteenth-century America. The newspaper in which Michael Drury and James Tallant advertised their wares quoted Joseph Addison in defense of trade: "There is not, says Addison, a more useful class of Society than *Merchants*. They knit mankind together in mutual intercourse of good offices, distribute the gifts of nature, find work for the poor, augment the wealth of a nation, and increase the comforts and conveniences of life." Just in case the authority of the English prose master was not enough to combat any lingering cultural prejudice against commerce, the editors added a few lines from another literary source from the Old World, the Welsh poet,

John Dyer: "To censure trade,/Or hold her busy people in contempt/Let none presume."[105]

Since most of Pittsburgh's industry was coal driven, the city had a smoky appearance. The miners digging out the rich deposits of coal across the rivers contributed at once to its wealth and filth. While it might not have lived up to its reputation as the Birmingham of the West to all who saw it, Pittsburgh *was* enveloped in smoke: "Even the complexion of the people is affected by this cause," Estwick Evans noted. The cheapness of coal (only six cents a bushel) might have helped to account for the city's "black and dismal appearance." The coal from the surrounding mountains was heavier, of a more bituminous quality, than English coal. When Lucy Audubon visited Pittsburgh a decade earlier, she remarked that it was "really the blackest looking place I ever saw."[106]

George had gained his brother's knack of seeing the world through the lens of literature, and no one can say that he did not see the parallel between the dark, bituminous appearance of Pittsburgh and Milton's hell: *He with a crew, whom like ambition joins/With him or under him to tyrannize,/Marching from Eden towards the west, shall find/The plain, wherein a black bituminous gurge/Boils out from under ground.*[107] Ambition drove Satan and his rebel angels on their path of westward migration in *Paradise Lost,* and ambition likewise caused English emigrants like George Keats to travel west. If the picturesque valleys the pioneer brother had just seen in western Pennsylvania seemed anything like Eden after the trials of the mountains, the black, bituminous appearance of the Pandemonium at the fork of the Ohio suited his commercial ambition.

A major category of export to the Western Country was glassware, and Benjamin Bakewell, the brother of the Squire of Fatland Ford and the uncle of the young generation of Bakewells in the West, dominated the business. His factory on the Monongahela River had become a showcase of British industry, producing everything from wine decanters and tumblers to glass frames. When Fearon saw cut-glass chandeliers and egg-cups in Benjamin Bakewell's warehouse, he marveled that "the demand for these articles of elegant luxury lies *in the Western States!* . . . What interesting themes of reflection are offered by such facts to the philosopher as well as to the politician! Not thirty years since the whole right bank of the Ohio was termed the 'Indian side.' Spots in Tennessee, in Ohio and Kentucky, that within the life-time of even young men, witnessed only the arrow and the scalping-knife, now present to the traveler articles of elegance and modes of luxury which might rival the displays of London and Paris." English merchants in America were creating a market for luxury products that seemed out of keeping with the primitive, survival conditions of the West. The stores, according to Fearon, were "literally stuffed with odds of English manufacture, consisting of articles of the most varied kind, from a man's coat or lady's gown, down to a whip or an oyster knife."[108]

The market required versatility as well as ingenuity to survive, and Benjamin Bakewell had both. After his brewery in New Haven burned down, he had opened a shipping business in Manhattan, near the South Street Seaport. His business partner at the glass factory, Benjamin Page, used to run another shipping firm opposite him on Pearl Street. Together, they had become the two most prominent agents for English goods in post-revolutionary America. But then Jefferson's Embargo Act of 1807 devastated the merchant shipping business. A poet in the Ohio River Valley wrote on July 4, 1808:

> Our ships all in motion
> Once whiten'd the Ocean
> They sailed and returned with a cargo;
> Now doomed to decay
> They have fallen a prey
> To Jefferson, worms, and embargo.[109]

But while Benjamin Bakewell may have fallen a prey to the schemes of politicians—and his cargo to the natural instincts of worms—he was not doomed to decay. Declaring bankruptcy in December 1807, Benjamin moved to Pittsburgh and, in the mode of the successful emigrant, reinvented himself.

He purchased a glass factory on the Monongahela River with his partner Benjamin Page and another business associate, Thomas Kinder, and set about learning how to make glass. But the furnace, he soon discovered, was poorly made and the workmen inexperienced. Supplies were costly and difficult to transport. Pittsburgh's yellow sand was not suited to flint glass, and pearl ash, red lead, and pot clay all had to be dragged over the mountains at enormous trouble and cost. By 1811, Kinder had lost faith in the company and pulled out. But Benjamin Bakewell, together with his sons,

Thomas Bakewell and John Palmer Bakewell, located better materials, replaced the furnace, and imported skilled glassworkers from England and Belgium. Through his "untiring industry & chemical knowledge" (in the words of his nephew, Tom Bakewell), the factory thrived. When Thomas turned twenty-one, he became a senior partner, and the company changed its name from Benjamin Bakewell & Company to Bakewell, Page, & Bakewell.[110]

Benjamin Bakewell is remembered today for the cameo encrustation technique he developed to make silvery glass casing for ceramic portrait medallions. Josiah Wedgwood had invented the paste that was used to make these mass-produced portrait "gems" in vogue during the early nineteenth century. William Tassie turned them into a fad at his shop on Leicester Square, and Benjamin Bakewell spread that fad to the United States by inventing glass frames to encase them. Charles Cowden Clarke's wife, Mary, remembered walking through Leicester Fields with her mother to Tassie's shop, a "fascinating place," where she would kneel on a high chair and "peer into the glass cases full of lovely gems." Fanny Keats also loved these gems. John would send them to her as special gifts, and he himself owned at least nine, including heads of Milton, Shakespeare, and King Alfred.[111]

John once planned to write a series of Shakespearean sonnets on some of Tassie's portrait medallions. His sonnet "On a Leander Which Miss Reynolds, My Kind Friend, Gave Me" (1816) is an ekphrastic poem, in the mode of his more famous "Ode on a Grecian Urn," of the drowning Grecian hero depicted on one of Tassie's gems. But the gem that John chose to seal his first letter to his brother in America bore an image of a different nature: a Grecian lyre, surrounded by the motto, "Qui me néglige me désole," or, as Tassie's 1820 catalogue translated it, "By neglect, thou ruinest me."[112] The message would have been hard to miss.

George Keats had less knowledge about what *he* might do in the West than hope for what could be accomplished. "They are no dreamers weak," the goddess Moneta tells the poet in *The Fall of Hyperion,* of those who dare not risk the unknown. "They have no thought to come— /And thou art here, for thou art . . . a dreaming thing." Readers have not missed the phonetic echo of "money" in "Moneta," and the same goddess who addresses the poet in these lines could just as easily have risen up as the moneyed spirit of the Ohio to chastise his pioneer brother. While one would not want to compare the trials that the two brothers, each in his own way, had to face, George was no less willing than John to imagine the impossible. The medium of their dreams may have differed, but in the final months of 1818, as the brothers drifted ever further apart, they were both what the goddess Moneta might call dreaming things. "God bless you," John wrote to George. "I whisper good night in your ears and you will dream of me."[113]

PART THREE
1819

5 CIRCUMSTANCES GATHERING LIKE CLOUDS

The Great Odes and The Fall of Hyperion

Circumstances, John said, were gathering like clouds. He had been unable to shake the ominous sore throat he had contracted in Scotland; his money had run out; and his second book, far from initiating a new dawn in poetry, had been panned as fast as the first one had sunk dead in the water. John was seriously considering other career options. Perhaps he should go back to medical school, maybe in Scotland? Or perhaps, take a position as a ship's surgeon on one of the packet ships plying the East India trade? Perhaps join a whaler bound for the South Seas—or South America? "His mind was then all in a ferment," as Charles Dilke explained. "He was in love & saw the impossibility of maintaining a wife, and, as I suspect, for the first time & *consequent,* the impossibility of maintaining himself."[1] But quitting poetry, as Benjamin Bailey and John Reynolds had done, was never really an option for John Keats. His authenticity would not allow it.

It was Keats, after all, who believed that nothing is real until it has been "proved upon our pulses," he who taught the Victorians that in this life there are only a limited number of pulses given and that we must make the most of them.[2] John knew that his days on the couch in Brown's front parlor were numbered. Brown suggested that they spend the summer on the Isle of Wight and co-author a tragedy about the Holy Roman Emperor Otho the Great. Brown would supply the plot, the characters, the action; all John would have to do would be to measure the story into verse.

John thought about it. A successful opening night at Drury Lane Theatre might put him back on the map of the literary world and at the same time restore his flagging finances. While a book of poetry priced at nine shillings (like *Endymion*), with an average print run of five hundred copies, could not keep an author in silk waistcoats, a single evening at Drury Lane Theatre could provide an audience six times that size. The fact that his other friends scoffed at the idea of his writing for the stage, predicting that he would not make it through a single scene, only fired his determination to try. Hadn't he nursed himself on Shakespeare? A historical drama might be just the thing to save him from the reputation he had earned in the Vale of Health with Leigh Hunt as a self-crowned Apollo. And in tragedy, too, there was dignity.

John was done with his "Poetic Romance." It was time to try a more masculine genre. *For I would not be dieted with praise, / A pet-lamb in a sentimental farce!* No longer would he strut with Hunt in his green leafy bowers. In a letter to George and Georgiana in the spring of 1819—the spring of his Great Odes—John included a brilliant parody of himself as an impoverished Cockney Poet that suggests the degree to which the reviews of *Endymion* from the previous year were still on his mind. Adopting the voice of a fictional "Count de Cockaigne" to beg succor from a cynical Richard Abbey, he produced the following burlesque, in legalese: "forasmuch as the undersigned has committed, transferred, given up, made over, consigned, and aberrated himself, to the art & mystery of poetry; for as much as he hath cut, rebuffed, affronted, huffed, & shirked, and taken stint, at all other employments, arts, mysteries, & occupations honest, middling & dishonest; for as much as he hath at sundry times, & in diverse places, told truth unto the men of this generation, & eke to the women, moreover . . . he prayeth your Worships to give him a lodging—witnessed by R^d Abbey & Co. cum familiaribus & Consanguiniis (signed) Count de Cockaigne."[3] The same obscurantist legal language that John uses here to communicate with Abbey was filling the paperwork in the Court of Chancery, where his inheritance was tied up. He was broke, and his mock-status as Count de Cockaigne (the word, after all, is French) in Hunt's Cockney kingdom motivated his decision to try a new, hopefully more lucrative, genre.

In August 1818, in the fourth installment of "On The Cockney School of Poetry," John Gibson Lockhart had belittled him with the class-inflected diminutive "Johnny Keats." George would later fume that his brother, "the very soul of courage and manliness," was "as much like the *holy Ghost* as *Johnny Keats.*" George vowed that had the anonymous "sneaking poacher" from *Blackwood's* been within his reach, "a good cudgelling should have been his reward." George "could have walked 100 miles to have dirked him à l'Américaine, for his cruelly associating John in the cockney school, and other blackguardisms." The reviewer who inflicted the mortal blow of disgrace either knew his brother "well and touched him in the tenderest place purposely, or knew nothing of him and supposed he went all lengths with the set in their festering opinions."[4] But in the spring of 1819 George was not around to dirk, scalp, or inflict any other punishment on his brother's critics.

John himself never shrank from a fight, but the challenge he now faced was to summon the steady, quiet determination necessary to stand alone on the rock of his own powers. His brothers were gone. Tom was no longer in the background enlivening the scene with his quick, unchecked bursts of humor. No one could say any longer, as they had done when John and Tom returned from Devonshire, that they were all mad in Hampstead. "George is in America and I have no Brother left," John wrote to Mary Ann Jeffery on the last day of May. "My Brother George always stood between me and any dealings with the world—Now I find I must buffet it—I must take my stand upon some vantage ground and begin to fight—I must choose between despair & Energy—I choose the latter."[5] As John knew from Spenser, the Cave of Despair was a sinful place. Better to follow Wordsworth's example and seek compensation for the ravages of time in the philosophic mind.

The excitement and breathless urgency of youth were gone; so be it. The poet would "substitute a more thoughtful and quiet power." Since the loss of his brothers, the world seemed to have taken on a gray, "quakerish look." John was used to seeing the world in black and white. A "violence & vehemence" had characterized him ever since boyhood, Edward Holmes claimed; at school he was always "in passions of tears or outrageous fits of laughter always in extremes." Everything in extremity might be a recipe for "poetic ardour and fire," but after the trauma of George's departure and Tom's death, John's verse had taken a more sober, meditative turn.[6]

Charles Brown claimed that every poem that John was moved to compose in the spring of 1819 "was scrawled on the first piece of paper at hand." The practice had always been a habit, but when combined with depression and doubt about his poetic vocation, it meant that he treated such scraps with unwonted indifference, using them as bookmarks, giving them away, or shoving them carelessly into any corner at hand. Brown asked his friend's permission to copy any fugitive pieces that he might dismiss as trifling. Without this effort, Brown claimed, John's "Ode to a Nightingale" would have been lost.[7]

The mood of the odes written that spring—Nightingale, Grecian Urn, Melancholy, Indolence, "mournful" Psyche—was melancholy. While John could not hear George's voice from across the blue abyss between them, or Tom's from out of the heavenly vault, he *could* hear Procne, that wronged Greek maiden turned into a nightingale, mourning her tragic fate in song. *And hark! the Nightingale begins its song, / "Most musical, most melancholy" bird! / A melancholy bird? Oh! Idle thought! / In Nature there is nothing melancholy.* But those words belonged to Coleridge. And they were written in the youth of Coleridge's own frustrated poetic career.

John Keats had a different nightingale. Beneath the plum tree in Brown's backyard, the plumed lyric songster poured forth her tale of rape, mutilation, and murder from across the sea of time. As the poet listened to her sorrowful, strains, he wrote:

> My heart aches, and a drowsy numbness pains
>   My sense, as though of hemlock I had drunk,
> Or emptied some dull opiate to the drains
>   One minute past, and Lethe-wards had sunk . . .

Lethe, river of forgetfulness. Souls of the dead drank from its water to re-enter the land of the living. But how, when there can be no forgetting, is one to begin again? *What can I do to drive away, / Remembrance from my eyes?*[8] The answer: precious little, perhaps.

Sitting a stone's throw from Well Walk, John might indeed have wondered whether he waked or slept. He wished, as he confessed to the immortal bird, to "Fade far away, dissolve, and quite forget / What thou among the leaves hast never known, / The weariness, the fever, and the fret / Here, where men sit and hear each other groan; / Where palsy shakes a few, sad, last gray hairs, / Where youth grows pale, and spectre-thin, and dies." The youth depicted on the Attic shape of the Grecian Urn may remain perpetually young, but in the real world, youth withers and dies. Tom's passing had shaken John to the core, and he knew that he, too, was dying.

The previous spring, as George was tied up with his move to America and John was coming and going with friends, Tom had thought of himself as "the only idler." But in the months following Tom's death, John came to realize that there was a difference between idling and wasting time. *My idle days? Ripe was the drowsy hour.*[9] Despite all the doubts, the grief and sickness, the loneliness and pain of unfulfilled desire, this would turn out to be John's great year of poetry: his *annus mirabilis.* Almost as if in a dream, without labor, it would seem, the Great Odes spilled out of him in the spring after Tom's death.

They toil not, neither do they spin. The epigraph to John's "Ode on Indolence" provides the context for understanding the Great Odes of the spring of 1819. The line derives from the Gospel of Matthew, in which Jesus, preaching from a mount beside the Sea of Galilee to crowds who come bearing their afflicted—demoniacs, epileptics, blind men, paralytics— teaches that *real* ills are a disease of the soul. "No man can serve two masters," Christ says, "for either he will hate the one, and love the other; or else he will hold to the one, and despise the other. Ye cannot serve God and mammon."[10] These words address the central issue of John's brief career. How to serve both the self-concentrating force of selfhood *and* the divinity, or genius, within, whose tendency is to expand and ultimately annihilate that self? Christ's message is that one cannot.

For all his newfound Quakerish perspective, John was an extremist who believed that the choices available to him that spring pulled in opposite directions. He was either to embrace solitude and lead "a fevrous life alone with Poetry"—sacrificing himself to his genius—or else sacrifice that genius to the spirit of material self-interest. To become a Man of Power demands self-concentration. The Man of Genius must annihilate selfhood. "Take no thought for your life, what ye shall eat, or what ye shall drink; nor yet for your body, what ye shall put on. Is not the life more than meat, and the body than raiment?" In answer to his own questions, Christ says: "Consider the lilies of the field, how they grow; they toil not, neither do they spin. And yet I say unto you that even Solomon in all his glory was not arrayed like one of these."[11] A life of spirit requires self-sacrifice. Yet the alternative to a Man of Genius cannot be endured.

One does not gain popularity by speaking the truth unto the members of one's own generation, as John himself suggests in the voice of the Count de Cockaigne. Poisoning and crucifixion are a more likely result. He recognized that much of the wisdom of the ancient and the modern worlds, the Christian and pre-Christian, stemmed from two disinterested fonts: "I have no doubt that thousands of people never heard of have had hearts completely disinterested," John wrote to George in America. "I can remember but two—Socrates and Jesus—their Histories evince it." Neither Socrates nor Jesus wrote down his own words. Each died so that his words would live on. But the lives of Socrates and Jesus were mythic: in the real world, "the greater part of Men make their way with the same instinctiveness, the same unwandering eye from their purposes, the same animal eagerness as the Hawk." Were the hawk to show a disinterested attitude toward the robin, it would lose its breakfast. Were the robin to do the same with the worm, it, too, would lose its meal.[12]

Yet for the poet to whom nothing was real until proved on the pulses, none of the speculation about love and death in the Great Odes in the spring of 1819 remained at the level of abstraction. The Dilkes had moved to town to be closer to their son at Westminster School, and Fanny Brawne's family had moved back into Wentworth Place. John feared, as he confessed to Fanny that same year in a distraught sonnet, "I cry your mercy," that by living on her "wretched thrall," he might "Forget, in the midst of idle misery,/Life's purposes,—the palate of my mind/Losing its gust, and my ambition blind." The poet toys with the idea of giving up Love, together with Poetry and Ambition in his "Ode on Indolence," where the three driving forces of his life parade past him like allegorical figures in a masque. He orders them to be gone at the end of the poem, but there is no indication that they have heard his final "Farewell!" The reader suspects that they will come around again, like those dark and mysterious figures in an endless loop on a Grecian urn.

In Western literary tradition, love has never been compatible with duty, and to John Keats in the spring of 1819, Fanny Brawne was a trap. Just as Odysseus renounces the luxury of Calypso's island to return to the rocky shore of Ithaca, Aeneas strips off his Phoenician robes and deserts Dido on the shores of Carthage. The same epic imperative required John to leave Fanny at Hampstead in order to pursue his epic quest. Segueing from his

Great Odes to his great, unfinished epic, John began *The Fall of Hyperion* in the summer after leaving Hampstead.

In *The Fall of Hyperion,* he recast the fragment of *Hyperion* as dream vision. He switched mentors from Milton to Dante, and left Satan's halls for the hellish circles of the Inferno. He changed the "books" of the poem into "cantos," and refashioned Apollo as an all-too-human poet. Above all, he withdrew from the cover of the tragic Titans to face vision in the first person. Yet, how to tell the difference between vision and fantasy? *Fanatics have their dreams, wherewith they weave / A paradise for a sect.* So begins the second version of *Hyperion. The savage too / From forth the loftiest fashion of his sleep / Guesses at heaven: / . . . / Who alive can say / "Thou art no poet; may'st not tell thy dreams"?* The fanatic has his dreams, and writes them down on the prairielands of Illinois. The Indian has his dreams, and wears them proudly when they drop out of the sky like a feather from the Great Spirit above. Who alive can say that they are not poets?

What distinguishes belief from delusion? To an acute literary ear, it might sound dissonant to drag the Cockney Pioneers Morris Birkbeck and George Flower into the sublime world of *The Fall of Hyperion,* but they, like the poet and his brother, were dreamers. "Lo, the poor Indian! whose untutored mind / Sees God in clouds, or hears Him in the wind," writes Pope.[13] What *is* the difference between a poet and a dreamer? The question has particular urgency for anyone, like John Keats, willing to take beauty seriously as an object of worship. To reframe the question: To a poet of enormous powers who knew he was dying, who had just lived through the death of one brother and who harbored fears for the other, as well as for himself, who would dare to say that beauty is not divine? Without orthodoxy to chain one down to the tenets of established religion, might one not, like Keats or Shelley, choose to worship the Spirit of Intellectual Beauty?

John had no answers to such questions. But, writing from the height of his accrued powers, he knew enough to ask. The Native American may pick up his sharpened thunderbolts on the prairie and chase the buffalo into the sunset, but he does not tell his dreams: "pity these have not / Trac'd upon vellum or wild Indian leaf / The shadows of melodious utterance / . . . / For Poesy alone can tell her dreams, / With the fine spell of words alone can save / Imagination from the sable charm / And dumb enchantment." Like papyrus, vellum and palm leaf both preceded paper. The poet is speak-

ing of all oral tradition: all myths and religions from the dawn of time that
have not been handed down in the form of scripture. William Blake was
not the only Romantic poet to believe that all religions are one, and the
"dumb enchantment" of the Indian on the plains of the Far West would
bear up here just as well as the "sable charm" of the African.

Like Socrates at the end of his trial, or Jesus in the Garden of Geth-
semane, the poet of *The Fall of Hyperion* knows that he must quaff the cup
he has been handed. At the start of the poem, when he drinks the "full
draught" that is the source of his song, he symbolically takes up the mission
for which he has spent a lifetime preparing—and suffers as only a man can
do. To experience vision beyond the mundane, one must die and be born
again. This speaker struggles hard against the domineering potion, but in
vain. When he starts up again, it is "As if with wings."

The cup has been passed. Each generation must have its prophet. It is
no easier for a Man of Genius to run from vision than it is for a Hebrew
prophet to run from God. As Jonah found out in the belly of the whale, it is
not merely futile but shameful to try. For all of his worries about what was
to be the "great end" of his poetry, John Keats acknowledged his vocation
early, and to his credit he never ran away.

Yet, the challenge to the anointed man is immense. "If thou canst not
ascend / These steps, die on that marble where thou art," a voice commands.
"Thy flesh, near cousin to the common dust, / Will parch for lack of nutri-
ment—thy bones / Will wither in a few years, and vanish so / That not the
quickest eye could find a grain / Of what thou now art on that pavement
cold." A grim prognostication. If the speaker who hears this command does
not take up what seems like an impossible task, the poet inside him will
sink into the common man, and his vision, as well as his dreams, will disappear.

Feeling "the tyranny / Of that fierce threat, and the hard task proposed," the speaker does the same thing as Apollo at the end of *Hyperion,*
and perhaps what anyone, in such a situation, might reasonably do: he
shrieks. The cry, stinging his ears, propels him into motion. "I strove hard
to escape / The numbness," the speaker relates, "strove to gain the lowest
step. / Slow, heavy, deadly was my pace: the cold / Grew stifling, suffocating,
at the heart; / And when I clasp'd my hands I felt them not." The epic simile
that follows is important to understanding what is happening here. As the
speaker touches the lowest step, new life rushes into his frame, and he

mounts the stairs "As once fair angels on a ladder flew/From the green earth toward heaven." He does not say *that* he approached heaven, *for he is a modern poet and does not know where he is going.* Instead, he drags himself up the steps *as if* he were one of the angels that flew up the ladder toward the gate of heaven in Jacob's dream.

Having mounted, he might as well see. "'High Prophetess,' said I, 'purge off/Benign, if so it please thee, my mind's film.'" The request harks back to the penultimate book of *Paradise Lost,* when the archangel Michael purges the veil from Adam's eyes so that he can see as a god sees, and the collective past and future of the human race—in all its dying generations —rushes into his brain in a moment of synthetic vision. Similarly, at the end of *Hyperion,* the goddess Mnemosyne grants Apollo the burden of prophecy:

> Knowledge enormous makes a God of me.
> Names, deeds, gray legends, dire events, rebellions,
> Majesties, sovran voices, agonies,
> Creations and destroyings, all at once
> Pour into the wide hollows of my brain,
> And deify me, as if of some blithe wine
> Or bright elixir peerless I had drunk,
> And so become immortal.

Yet whereas Apollo is a god, and Adam mythic, the speaker of *The Fall of Hyperion* is merely a man. Perfect knowledge is the province of the immortals; interpretation, the task of the living. The disembodied voice of the goddess Moneta in *The Fall of Hyperion* does not deny so much as deflect the speaker's request, as well as his questions. The dialogue that ensues between them is one in which questions are posed and answers given in the form of more questions, as in the Gospels and the wider tradition of wisdom literature: parables, epigrams, Socratic dialogues, all requiring interpretation and teasing the mind out of its established patterns.

The first thing *this* speaker wants to know is why he is alone. Keats wrote *The Fall of Hyperion* in the void opened by the loss of his brothers, and it should perhaps come as no surprise that the poet should ask the goddess for an explanation of his solitude: "I sure should see/Other men here: but I am here alone." The poet learns that those who find a haven in the world must in that world remain. Only "those to whom the miseries of the world / Are misery, and will not let them rest" can enter the sublime world of existential doubt, which alone leads to knowledge enormous. They who have no thought to go where the speaker has gone, who "thoughtless sleep away their days" in the material world, are no visionaries. As the goddess puts it:

> —"They are no dreamers weak,
> They seek no wonder but the human face;
> No music but a happy-noted voice—
> They come not here, they have no thought to come—
> And thou art here for thou art less than they.
> What benefit canst thou do, or all thy tribe,
> To the great world? Thou art a dreaming thing;
> A fever of thyself—think of the earth;
> What bliss even in hope is there for thee?
> What haven? Every creature hath its home;
> Every sole man hath days of joy and pain,
> Whether his labours be sublime or low—
> The pain alone; the joy alone; distinct:
> Only the dreamer venoms all his days,
> Bearing more woe than all his sins deserve."

Without a doubt, this speaker is a demanding presence. Like Socrates with his stubborn, unceasing interrogation, or Jesus with his puzzling parables, he disturbs the complacency of those around him. The human race, ever since Eve, has been punished for seeking to know more than it ought, but its heroes are those who ask questions.

And questions motivate Keats's *annus mirabilis*. The speaker of the most famous of the Great Odes from the spring of 1819 pesters the Grecian Urn: "What men or gods are these? What maidens loth? / What mad pursuit? What struggle to escape? / What pipes and timbrels? What wild ecstasy?" After five stanzas of interrogation from such a speaker, the "silent form" of the urn finally yields up its immortal response: "'Beauty is truth, truth beauty,'—that is all / Ye know on earth, and all ye need to know." Another enigma.

Just as the speaker of the "Ode on a Grecian Urn" wrestles with the "Attic shape" of the urn—or perhaps in a more apt analogy, as Jacob wrestles with the angel of God in Genesis—the speaker of *The Fall of Hyperion* wrestles with the goddess Moneta. And like Jacob, this wrestler demands a name: "What am I then? Thou spakest of my tribe:/What tribe?" As usual, the question turns back on him: "Art thou not of the dreamer tribe?" Rather than defining the dreamer, Moneta goes on to make clear that, whatever a dreamer and a poet might be, a dreamer is not the same thing as a poet: "The poet and the dreamer are distinct,/Diverse, sheer opposite, antipodes./The one pours out a balm upon the world,/The other vexes it." But if a dreamer, *quid ergo?* Fanatics have their dreams, and savages do too: Why not the poet? *Poesy alone can tell her dreams . . .*

If there is to be a difference between a poet and a dreamer, it seems that one must not rest content with their formulation as opposites. *The lunatic, the lover and the poet/Are of imagination all compact.*[14] A symbolic holy Trinity—for Shakespeare. In *The Fall of Hyperion* the poet is opposed to the fanatic. And there can be, after all, only two opposites: a magnet has only two poles. The opposite of a positive electric charge is a negative. Is not what is true in physics true in poetry? *Beauty is truth, truth beauty . . .*

Or, poet, fanatic, dreamer: of imagination all compact. While it might seem simple to conclude that John Keats was a poet and that his brother George was a dreamer, John recognized in George a man with poetry in his soul, or enough of it to infuse another kind of spirit into the English Prairie. And George did not need the goddess Moneta to tell him that his brother was a dreamer. Insofar as there can be no stab at greatness without zeal, moreover, both brothers were fanatic. Throughout the *annus mirabilis* of 1819, the two older Keats brothers, having lost the third member of their triad, would continue to find themselves in shifting roles that were, if not interchangeable, at least—and most certainly—not opposite.

Down the Ohio

Native Americans called it "Ohiyo," meaning, "it is beautiful." The French called it "La Belle Rivière." While the poet was wrangling with his Muse, the pioneer brother was pursuing the serpentine course of the Ohio River into the Western Country. The sloping banks of the river rose and fell in alternating patterns of hills and valleys, and clusters of pink and red rhododendrons peeped out from the undergrowth. Grape vines twisted overhead in purple profusion, forming "large canopies, festoons, arbours, grottoes, with numerous other fantastic figures" in the branches of trees.[15] And as the foliage of Indian summer burned bright in the autumn of 1818, George and Georgiana might have called it sublime.

James Freeman Clarke—the Transcendentalist, Unitarian minister, who befriended the pioneer brother when he moved to Louisville in 1833 —described George and Georgiana's honeymoon ride down the Ohio River:

> Day after day they floated tranquilly on, as through a succession of fairy lakes, sometimes in the shadow of the lofty and wooded bluff, sometimes by the side of wide-spread meadows, or beneath the graceful overhanging branches of the cotton-wood and sycamore. At times, while the boat floated lazily along, the young people would go ashore and walk through the woods across a point around which the river made a bend. All uncertain as their prospects were, they could easily, amid the luxuriance of nature, abandon themselves to the enjoyment of the hour.

Whether the portrait represents fact or fantasy makes little difference. It is how the young couple remembered it. The flatboats followed the lazy drift of the current, which rarely exceeded two to three miles an hour, and passengers did have time for an occasional scenic stroll. At one point, as Clarke describes, George and Georgiana decided to walk across a thin isthmus as their keelboat swung around the bend. Georgiana "wore a silk dress and parlour slippers, both of which were thoroughly torn to pieces before they reached the other side."[16] A pretty picture of youthful inexperience.

Parakeets roosted in the trunks of the cottonwood trees, and yellow birds, red birds, and blue jays animated the sky. The larks seemed larger than those in England, and in the evenings the cry of the brown whippoorwill rang out. The mockingbirds echoed the whole woodland chorus. Following the custom of Native Americans, who strung hollow gourds in the trees for black martins to nest in, the settlers made birdhouses by mounting boxes on poles. The martins kept away the vultures that preyed on the meat the settlers hung on racks to dry outside their cabins. The most common bird was the woodpecker, which hammered at the tree trunks with no less energy than the settlers hacked at them.

From its headwaters at Pittsburgh, the Ohio flowed down clear and serene, drawing sustenance from many tributary streams, until falling, at last, after a thousand miles, into the Mississippi. When the river left Pennsylvania, it became the boundary that separated the state of Virginia (not yet divided into Virginia and West Virginia), and then Kentucky, on the south, from the state of Ohio, and then Indiana, on the north. The distance from Pittsburgh to Louisville was six or seven hundred miles, at which point a rugged limestone bed interrupted the flow of the river, causing it to crash down in rapids. In April 1818 one English emigrant in Marietta, Ohio, counted nearly a thousand boats floating down the Ohio River on the current of westward migration, most of them headed for the new states and territories in the West.[17]

The river towns that lasted the longest sat on high bluffs, a couple of hundred feet above the low water mark. The "bottoms," or flood plains, extended anywhere from several yards to a mile from the river. Their alluvial deposits were extremely fertile, but the river could rise suddenly, and sickness spread quickly when the floods came, usually in March. Below Pittsburgh, the first town of note was Beaverstown, which looked down from a stony plain on the north side of the river, just below Beaver Creek. The town consisted of a few dozen log houses, a jail, a post office, some taverns and shops. Twelve miles farther down, on the southern side, also high on a bluff, came Georgetown, the last stop before the Ohio River left Pennsylvania.[18]

Most boats gravitated to the northern side of the river, where slavery was illegal. "The improvements do not seem to keep pace on the Virginia side, with those in the state of Ohio," John Melish observed; "the existence of slavery is a damper upon the operations of the white people." The white inhabitants in Virginia scarcely seemed to lift a finger on their own behalf, and things appeared, "as might be expected, 'miserable, and wretched, and poor, and almost naked.'" The Nottinghamshire farmer John Woods, who settled on the English Prairie with the Cockney Pioneers, noticed that on the southern side, where "every thing is done by the negroes, while the whites look on," conditions seemed dismal.[19]

The Ohio side gave a better impression, but racial exploitation persisted. The state had outlawed slavery, though its residents continued to employ "coloured people, which they call *their property,*" Henry Fearon reported. "The mode in which they effect this perpetuation of slavery, in violation of the spirit of the Ohio constitution, is to purchase blacks, and have them *apprenticed* to them. Some are so base as to take these negroes down the river at the approach of the expiration of their apprenticeship, *and sell them at Natchez for life!*"[20] Natchez, which sat high on a bluff just below the confluence of the Ohio and Mississippi rivers, was a center for cotton and tobacco plantations—and the home of at least one businessman whom George would have done better to avoid.

The Indian and buffalo trails leading down to the Ohio River were no longer in use, and travel conditions differed greatly from those of a former era, when Europeans descended the river in barges and canoes armed with muskets, rifles, and enough ammunition to make dangerous landings unnecessary. The Iroquois and other Native peoples had considered the Europeans enemies of America, and, indeed, as settlers flooded into the Ohio River Valley, they chopped down the trees, tore up the undergrowth, killed the animals, and blackened the skies with smoke. John James Audubon compared the Ohio River Valley as he had seen it ten years before George and Georgiana first saw it to the place it would become ten years after the couple had moved West:

> When I think of these times, and call back to my mind the grandeur and beauty of those almost uninhabited shores; when I picture to myself the dense and lofty summits of the forest, that everywhere spread along the hills, and overhung the margins of the stream, unmolested by the axe of the settler; when I know how dearly purchased the safe navigation of that river has been by the blood of many worthy Virginians; when I see that no longer any Aborigines are to be found there, and that the vast herds of elks, deer and buffaloes which once pastured on these hills and in these valleys, making for themselves great roads to the several salt-springs, have ceased to exist; when I reflect that all this grand portion of our union, instead of being in a state of nature, is now more or less covered with villages, farms, and towns, where the din of hammers and machinery is constantly heard; that the woods are fast disappearing under the axe by day, and the fire by night; that hundreds of steam-boats are gliding to and fro, over the whole length of the majestic river, forcing commerce to take root and to prosper at every spot; when I see the surplus population of Europe coming to assist in the destruction of the forest, and transplanting civilization into its darkest recesses;—when I remember that these extraordinary changes have all taken place in the short period of twenty years, I pause, wonder, and, although I know all to be fact, can scarcely believe its reality.[21]

Having dispensed with the elk and buffalo, the settlers now hunted down the smaller creatures that raided their fields, orchards, and gardens. The rabbits, which were smaller than their English brethren, with thinner skins and darker flesh, hid in the hollows of trees, rather than burrowing, making the farmers come after them with axes.

But the most persistent threat when George and Georgiana traveled west was the squirrels. The settlers would form posses of six to ten men who, armed with rifles, competed in a macabre festivity known as a squirrel frolic. They would place bets on who would claim the more victims, and at the end of the day they would celebrate their triumph over the squirrel kind by dressing and roasting a hog in Indian style—in a hole covered with hot stones. The whiskey would flow freely, and the event would culminate, as most frolics did, with a target-shooting competition. Hundreds of chipmunks, woodchucks, and squirrels were killed at every such hunt, though it never seemed to lessen their numbers.

Barges had been around since the early days of river navigation, carrying armaments and supplies to the forts in the Ohio River Valley, but by 1818 these massive rivercraft had given way to slightly smaller, though no less clunky, flat-bottomed riverboats called arks, alternately "broadhorns" or "Kentucky flats," which carried most emigrants west. Allegedly named for their resemblance to Noah's Ark, they were essentially long, floating boxes maneuvered by poles. Thomas Hulme, who followed the same route as George and Georgiana Keats to the English Prairie, described the ark as "a thing by no means pleasant to travel in, especially at night. It is strong at bottom but may be compared to an orange-box, bowed over at top, and so badly made as to admit a boy's hand to steal the oranges: it is proof against the river, but not against the rain." Like the covered wagons, their overland equivalent, these broad flatboats would broadcast their comings and goings with tin horns; hence the name "broadhorn." *O, boatman! Wind that horn again . . .*[22]

Because progress by land was slower and more expensive than by river, families often disposed of their wagons at the head of the Ohio River and pooled their resources to travel together in an ark. The boats could typically hold three or four families and thirty to fifty tons of cargo. The shipyards in Pittsburgh (and other towns along the river) sold them, but some emigrants also built them from scratch, of pine or oak boards. The arks came in various sizes, the most common being fifty feet long by fourteen feet wide, a width determined by the rocks on either side of one of the channels through which the boats had to pass at Louisville. At those dimensions, each ark could accommodate a cargo of horses conveniently tethered in two rows. Since they were intended for travel downriver only, they were rudely made; once they reached their destination, they would be torn apart, and sold or used as lumber.

Some flatboats had brick fireplaces, others only sandboxes for camp-fires. Passengers often slept on deck among the bales and barrels. Two years after George and Georgiana, an American, James Hall, wrote about his adventures in the Western Country, describing his improvised "state room" on one of these arks:

> My state room is in the bow of the boat, and is formed by leaving a vacancy, large enough for a bed and chair, among the boxes and barrels which encompass me. I have an excellent bedstead, composed of packages and parcels, so disposed as to receive a comfortable mattress, and here I snore among British goods and domestic manufactures. . . . The ample surface of a huge box is devoted to the functions of a table, and my fare is drawn from a small store provided by myself, and consisting of such articles as are easy of preparation. Of the culinary department, I cannot speak in high praise.[23]

The flatboats were the most common species of rivercraft afloat, but there were other contraptions on the river vying with them for space. Hall also saw two large rafts lashed together, each about eighty or ninety feet long, carrying several families headed toward "the land of promise in the western woods." Each raft supported a small house, and a haystack

> around which several horses and cows were feeding, while the paraphernalia of a farm-yard, the ploughs, waggons, pigs, children, and poultry, carelessly distributed, gave to the whole more the appearance of a permanent residence, than of a caravan of adventurers seeking a home. A respectable looking old lady, with *spectacles on nose,* was seated on a chair at the door of one of the cabins, employed in knitting; another female was at the wash-tub; the men were chewing their tobacco, with as much complacency as if they had been in "the land of steady habits," and the various family avocations seemed to go on like clock-work.

The place of "steady habits" that Hall alludes to is New England. The Western Country, by contrast, was the land of the lazy. George would later claim to work "with industry and perseverance that astonishes the lazy Kentuckians."[24] Yet when he first traveled down the river, he left the poling to others.

Keelboats, the other major option for emigrants headed west, came equipped with professional boatmen, and this is the option George Keats chose. About the same size as arks, the keelboats were longer and narrower, with pointed instead of square ends. In shallow waters and narrow passages, keelboats were easier to manage. Still, maneuvering them around bends in the river required strength and skill, as well as practice. The boatmen's talk was mainly of "riffles" (shallow ripples) and "shoots" (rapids). One could earn a place at the head pole of the boat—the place of honor— only by steering safely through a rapid.

The boatmen also knew best how to avoid such common river hazards as "floating islands" (made of matted driftwood) and "sawyers," "planters" and "snags" (all trees that fell along the side of the river and got stuck in perilous positions). When they fell, they took with them masses of sod that would fasten to the mud of the river and hold them fast. When a tree fell in such a way that the upper end of its trunk lodged in the riverbed near a strong current, it would rise and sink like a saw; hence the name "sawyer." The oscillatory motion could last several minutes before the tree disappeared from view, only to spring back up unexpectedly, menacing the bows of oncoming boats with its huge branchy arms. Sometimes the sawyers would stay submerged, wreaking more havoc through their concealment. Many a steamboat sank in this manner.

Unlike sawyers, "planters" did not saw; they stayed planted. The force of the current would pull one end of the toppled tree down and raise the other to a sharp, deadly point facing downstream. Collision with planters could be fatal, although they were usually less feared than sawyers, whose unpredictability increased their danger. "Snags" were fallen tree trunks that snagged in the riverbanks and jutted out into the current. Between the sluggish pace of the water, and the care needed to avoid the various obstacles in the river, flatboat progress was slow.

Among boatmen, a "Kentuck" was considered the best man at a pole, and a French Canadian, or "Canuck," the best man at an oar. To direct the keelboat through swift waters, the helmsman would use a small oar called a "gouger" at the prow. Most of the time, the long steering oar at the stern of the boat sufficed. Usually this was a board fastened to a pole, extending forty to fifty feet from handle to blade and balanced on a forked stick. To propel the boat, the boatmen would use shorter side oars called "sweeps." Six to ten men (two per sweep), plus a steersman, made up a crew.

> Some rows up, but we rows down,
> All the way to Shawnee town,
>   Pull away—pull away!

Timing their strokes to the cadences of river songs, the crew would divide into two groups and position themselves on running boards along the sides of the boat. When the steersman gave the command, they would set their poles at the head of the boat and walk back toward the stern with their shoulders braced against the pole. In a single sweep, they could push the boat a distance equal to its length.[25]

No keelboat was complete without a whiskey barrel to reward arduous struggles against the current. The boatmen alternated swigs of whiskey with river water. They fueled themselves with biscuits, potatoes, beef and pork jerky, and coarse bread made of Indian corn. They wore red linsey-woolsey shirts and made coats from blankets in the wintertime. In summer, they dispensed with the inconvenience of shirts altogether.

> The boatman is a lucky man,
> No one can do as the boatman can,
> The boatmen dance and the boatmen sing,
> The boatman is up to everything.
>
> Hi-O, away we go,
> Floating down the river on the O-hi-o.
>
> When the boatman goes on shore,
> Look, old man, your sheep is gone,
> He steals your sheep and steals your shote,
> He puts 'em in a bag and totes 'em to the boat.
>
> When the boatman goes on shore
> He spends his money and works for more,

I never saw a girl in all my life,
But what she would be a boatman's wife.[26]

Strong and proud, the boatmen had a reputation for mischief—drinking, fiddling, singing, swearing, wrestling, yarn spinning, coon hunting, and making free with the ladies by the side of the river. George Flower's cousin Elias Pym Fordham, who traveled to the English Prairie with the Cockney Pioneers two years before George and Georgiana came west, suggested taking adequate precautions against the boatmen. One would be wise, he counseled, to hire a servant and carry a dagger or brace of pistols, "for there are no desperadoes more savage in their anger than these men. Give them your hand,—accost them with a bold air,—taste their whisky,—and you win their hearts. But a little too much reserve or haughtiness offends them instantly, and draws upon you torrents of abuse, if not a personal assault. They are a dauntless, hardy set; thoughtless, and short lived from intemperance."[27]

The keelboats, like the arks, traveled only downstream, and in the days before steamboats became the best means of traveling upstream, the bargemen poled and dragged the barges loaded with cargo against the current. The towing ropes, known as "cordelles," were several hundred to a thousand feet long; they would be fastened to the top of the mast and passed through a ring to the boatmen on shore. A short rope, called a bridle, would be lashed to the bow to keep the boat from swinging. Audubon had recourse to these towing ropes many times, and he portrayed the progress of the barges upstream:

The men, who have rested a few minutes, are ordered to take their stations and lay holds of their oars, for the river must be crossed, it being seldom possible to double such a point and proceed along the same shore. The boat is crossing, its head slanting to the current, which is, however, too strong for the rowers, and when the other side of the river has been reached, it has drifted perhaps a quarter of a mile. The men by this time are exhausted, and, as we shall suppose it to be 12 o'clock, fasten the boat to a tree on the shore. A small glass of whiskey is given to each, when they cook and eat their dinner, and after resting from their fatigue for an hour, recommence their labors. The boat is again seen slowly advancing against the stream. It has reached the lower end of a sandbar, along the edge of which it is propelled by means of long poles, if the bottom be hard. Two men, called bowsmen, remain at the prow to assist, in concert with the steersman, in managing the boat and keeping its head right against the current. The rest place themselves on the land side of the footway of the vessel, put one end of their poles on the ground and the other against their shoulders and push with all their might. As each of the men reaches the stern, he crosses to the other side, runs along it and comes again to the landward side of the bow, when he recommences operation. The barge in the meantime is ascending at a rate not exceeding one mile in the hour.[28]

The bargemen were used to fighting their way through brush and wading through water with guns strapped to their backs. They had a reputation for being more dangerous than the keelboatmen. Their fearlessness had served them well in the days of early river travel, when backwoodsmen and Indian braves hid in the woods to plunder the boats.

This was no longer the case, and George and Georgiana hadn't gone far before they realized that it was going to be a pleasant ride. The river brimmed with schools of fish. Most English emigrants were familiar with sturgeon, but there were also rockfish, buffalo fish, and yellow and white perch, which made strange rumbling noises beneath the boats. The whiskered catfish slapped the water with their huge tails before disappearing from view, and when they did, they made quite a splash. It was not unusual to see an eighty-pound catfish pulled out of the river with a hook and a line.[29]

In 1818, there were about four hundred thousand settlers living on land in Ohio that had originally belonged to the Ottawa, Chippewa, Shawnee, Delaware, Potawatomie, Sac, and Wyandot Nations, the latter being the most ancient inhabitants. Repeated attempts to extinguish their claim to the land, assisted by a flurry of paperwork including congressional, patent, and tax titles, finally resulted, in 1817, in a treaty that abolished the last boundary demarcating Indian Territory, a hundred miles north of the river. Three thousand Native Americans remained in the state, but most had disappeared with the larger game to the northern and western territories. Every so often a wolf would snatch a pig, an ewe, or a ram, but the wolf packs, too, had retreated.

Since much of the land in Ohio was already occupied and "improved," it cost four to fifteen times more than unclaimed land farther west. Often such improvements amounted to little more than a few log cabins, and a dozen or more acres of cultivated ground. Gilbert Imlay, who is best remembered as Mary Wollstonecraft's lover, described the western states and territories of America, praising the land of the Ohio River Valley in particular for its richness: "Nature in her pride has given to the regions of this fair river a fertility so astonishing, that, to believe it, ocular demonstration becomes necessary." John Melish judged the soil in Ohio to be fertile enough to feed the entire nation.[30]

The farmers who worked the land broke down into three classes. "Squatters" occupied land that was not theirs until they earned enough money to purchase their own land, or else became dissatisfied with their situation and moved on. Small, or "weak-handed," farmers could afford a small plot of land (a quarter-section, or 160 acres), but they usually could not afford to hire farmhands. They would raise large families and cultivate enough to survive "in a condition which, if compelled *by legislative acts, or by external force to endure,*" Fearon wrote, "would be considered truly wretched." Independence seemed to compensate them for the challenges of subsistence farming, and they did not complain.[31]

The "Strong-handed" farmers, the American version of English country squires, could afford as many as twelve hundred acres and plenty of farmhands. According to Fearon, the strong-handed farmer was "always a man of *plain business-like sense,* though not in possession, nor desirous of a very cultivated intellect; understands his own interest, and that of his country; lives in sufficient affluence, and is possessed of *comfort,* according to the American acceptation of the term, but to which we *'old country'* folks must feel inclined to take an exception: but in conclusion, and a most important conclusion it is, the majority of this class of men were, ten or fifteen years ago, inhabitants of the eastern States, and not worth, upon their arrival in Ohio, twenty dollars."[32] Unlike the English country squire, the strong-handed farmer in America was a self-made man.

The original crop in the Ohio River Valley was Indian corn: a plant at once hardy enough not to spoil after ripening and beautiful enough to impress successive waves of emigrants. Horses, pigs, and cattle ate it raw from the stalks in the fields, thus saving the small-handed farmers extra labor. Yet to dine al fresco in this manner, the livestock often had to compete with raccoons, deer, and squirrels for their share. When roasted or boiled, it tasted, William Tell Harris thought, "very similar to young peas."[33]

To clear the land for planting, farmers either cut down the trees or girdled them. Girdling involved cutting them around the middle just enough to kill them and then clearing away the undergrowth to plant crops. On the prairies, one did not have to worry about the nuisance of trees, but the sod was so thick that even with teams of yoked oxen, farmers found it hard to cultivate. Morris Birkbeck was not the only Cockney Pioneer to break his plow on the tough prairie turf. At rolling frolics, the farmers in the Ohio River Valley would cut the trees into sections of ten or twelve feet, roll them into giant pyramids, and set fire to them using brushwood and roots as kindling. Sometimes, after lopping the trunks into sections, they would forgo the bonfire and stack them into a cabin or barn. On such occasions, another group would be employed to make shingles. "The builders generally worked hard by day," George Flower remarked, but at night "they gathered around the whisky-barrel, as bees around a favorite flower."[34] During harvest season, the farmers held husking and reaping frolics.

Standing proudly above the farms of Ohio, the town of Steubenville came into view as George and Georgiana's keelboat floated downstream. One could hear "the music of its ponderous steam engines" several miles before seeing the town. Named for Friedrich Wilhelm Augustus von Steuben, the eccentric Prussian officer who helped Washington train his Continental Army at Valley Forge, Steubenville now had about four hundred buildings and could "rival the finest cities of the west." Black billows rose from the chimneys, darkening the sky but delighting the eyes of emigrants who sought business opportunity out West. To Thomas Hulme, the smoke was positively enchanting. America, he wrote, "might save almost all her dollars if she would but bring her invaluable black diamonds into service," for it was coal that would enrich the young nation.[35]

The wool factory in Steubenville claimed to be the first in the West. Although wool frequently got torn in the thick underbrush in the Western Country, sheep out West were raised exclusively for their wool since Westerners did not consider them fit to eat. Englishmen noted with surprise that Americans in general held mutton "in the utmost contempt." Some considered mutton eaters no better than a "family of wolves." In Kentucky, Morris Birkbeck reported, "even the negroes would no more eat mutton than they would horse-flesh." The Cockney Pioneer himself had introduced the breeding of Merino sheep to England, but, he noticed, "Merino mania seems to have prevailed in America in a degree exceeding its highest pitch in England." John Keats chose an appropriate metaphor when he warned his pioneer brother to be careful: "Those Americans will I am afraid . . . fleece you."[36]

Between Steubenville and Wheeling, twenty-three miles downriver on the Virginia side, the land was thickly wooded. James Freeman Clarke thought that the forests during Indian summer "seemed to belong to fairyland, and not to reality. The majestic sycamores leaning their vast trunks and massive limbs over the shallow streams which we often forded, the beautiful gum tree carrying up a tower of foliage toward the skies, the enormous tulip trees, and the cottonwood with its leaves always in motion, were unlike anything with which I was familiar."[37] On the river bottoms grew crabapple, plum, spicewood, dogwood, and pawpaw; above them, beech, black walnut, honey locust, buckeye, and hackberry. The more robust trees, from hickory to sugar maple, towered in arboreal splendor in the hills. Woodcocks and snipes fed farther inland in the smaller rivers and streams branching off the river, while the geese, ducks, grouse, pheasants, turkeys, and quail came to feed in the shallows.

After passing a ripple known as Letarts Rapids, on the Virginia side, the keelboat approached the French settlement of Gallipolis, or Alexandria, at the mouth of the Big Scioto River. To judge from the fossils of the plants, fish, and mollusks that littered the shores, the waters possessed minerals with a petrifying quality. As everywhere else in the West, however, dissipation and indolence seemed to characterize the inhabitants. In 1817, in a guidebook titled *Western Gazetteer; or, Emigrant's Directory,* Samuel Brown characterized Alexandria as "fifteen old buildings, and a tavern well supported by the votaries of Bacchus."[38]

Although many of the original French colonists had fled during the French and Indian War, their gardens, orchards, and vineyards remained. The pumpkins grew easily enough that at a dollar per wagonload they made good food for livestock. They grew up to a couple of hundred pounds. The "motley flock of sheep" belonging to the town may have "had a rotten appearance" (if John Woods can be believed), but a cornucopia of watermelons, muskmelons, squash, sweet potatoes, cucumbers, beans, peaches, and apples piled up at the market. Since change for a dollar was not always easy to come by on the banks of the river, the fruit vendors compensated by chopping dollars, half-dollars, and quarters into smaller pieces, with an axe or a chisel, to make (literally) "cut-money." Some were "so expert and *honest,* as to make five quarters out of a dollar."[39]

Cincinnati was now only hours away. Should conditions prove favorable, perhaps George might still follow through with his original plan of settling with the other Cockney Pioneers. But he had seen more of what it took to be a farmer out West, and like his brother back home, he was probably confused by the conflicting accounts he had heard about the English Prairie. "I cannot put faith in any reports I hear of the Settlement," John wrote to George in the spring of 1819. "Some are good some bad."[40]

Perhaps George had begun to think that trade might, after all, prove the most practical application of his skills in the Western Country. He had not yet purchased land on the prairie or broken his back on the tough prairie sod, and Georgiana (one imagines) had not yet taken off her silk slippers. George's money was still in his pocket to spend, and he was fairly sure that by investing it wisely, he would do well. James Freeman Clarke met George when George, at thirty-six, was already a successful businessman, but he claims to have seen signs of an inborn prosperity: "The heavy bar of observation over his eyes indicated the strong perceptive faculties of a business man."[41]

While George was eager to invest and to get established, he knew that there were dangers in proceeding too quickly. Others besides his brother warned him about the scheming Americans. Speculators of all stripes, foreign and domestic, prowled around with tempting opportunities—often the more tempting, the more dishonest. In an *Emigrant's Guide to the United States of America* (1818), Thomas Smith urged newcomers to "avoid precipitancy in the choice of a situation" and to "be extremely cautious in the investment of their money." He proposed the prudent step of depositing one's money in a bank or investing it in public stock.[42] George was on his guard, but he was also a novice at business. His lessons in American commercial enterprise would come soon enough.

Letters across the Atlantic

In 1818, mail going in both directions across the Atlantic often got delayed, stolen, or lost, and John would later find that four of his letters, one of them containing a hundred-pound remittance from Abbey, had piled up in transit, forcing his brother to the desperate step of re-crossing the Atlantic. The mail system hadn't yet been centralized as a government operation in the United States, and George would send his letters to England, as John did to America, through private merchant shipping companies that sent mailbags along with their merchandise. The sea-captains took responsibility for the mail, recording delays and transfers, and newspapers posted the names of people who had letters waiting to be picked up at the postal offices. Coffee houses also distributed the mail. Captain Coffin would deposit more than one mailbag from Liverpool at the Merchant's Coffee House in Philadelphia.

Within a few years, the U.S. Postal Service would standardize the cost of a single-page letter, traveling up to four hundred miles, at twenty-five cents (about an English shilling); or for a two-page letter, twice that cost. Before such rates were established, however, the cost of postage varied based on weight and distance. Following British protocol, the recipient had to pay the cost calculated by the receiving office. George would later assure his sister from Louisville that while he was happy to pay for any letters she cared to send, *he* refrained from writing more frequently so as not to impose on her. "To be sure our health might be communicated from time to time," he explained in 1822, "but when we feel ourselves well it seems thinking much of ourselves to put you to the expense of letters to inform you of it, when we are sick we delay writing until we can send better news."[43] Letters in the nineteenth century often began with a catalogue of excuses. Richard Abbey, on the other hand, would complain that Fanny Keats was receiving too many letters from her other, scribbling brother.

"You may fairly accuse me for not writing so frequently as I ought to have done," George wrote to Fanny six years later, "but I am persuaded you have not received several letters that I have sent[.] I hope in future that our correspondence will be attended with better fortune." George was realistic, perhaps too realistic, about the difficulty of maintaining intimacy with his siblings through the mail. The posts were "uncertain and dilatory," and it was futile to imagine that they could keep up regular communication: "the space of 6 months between question and answer is enough to freeze the most interesting subject." Another time, he described how procrastination feeds on itself: "having delayed writing six months another delay of a month seems nothing."[44] George, like his brother, spoke the truth to his sister, but he was also more remote and his silences lasted longer.

Writing from Louisville, George would sometimes rush to catch the
next steamboat headed upriver to Pittsburgh—or downriver to New Orleans. The system did not inspire confidence, and George was at times
"obliged . . . to adopt a somewhat precarious mode of conveyance." On
other occasions, he counted on friends to convey his letters from the Western Country. Charles Briggs, a friend from Clarke's school at Enfield,
was one of these. Briggs always seemed to show up where he wasn't expected. In 1816, when John and Tom were in Margate, George "most fortunately" ran into Briggs in London. He considered him "a very agreeable
man."[45] And he was even more surprised when he ran into Briggs in Kentucky.

Explaining his delay, George once wrote to Charles Dilke that he had
spent most of his time since receiving Dilke's last letter "in endeavouring to
arrange a sure channel to convey letters" through Briggs. By that point,
Charles Briggs was working as an insurance and commission agent at Gordon, Forstall, & Company in New Orleans. Tom Bakewell, George's future
business partner, had learned about the cotton trade from Major William
Gordon of Natchez, a former officer in Washington's Continental Army
and a sugar planter who did business with Benjamin Bakewell in New
York. In 1823 Tom's sister Ann would marry Alexander Gordon, the major's son who ran the shipping firm in New Orleans with the banker Edmond Jean Forstall.[46] Briggs sent George's mail on Gordon's ships.

John likewise arranged for communication with George through mutual friends. William Haslam could always be counted on for such practical
assistance, and John sent the letter he concluded on his twenty-third birthday to George and Georgiana in the Western Country through Haslam.
(Seeing its size, Haslam would give the poet some thin blue paper for his
next marathon epistle, and John would economize in his own way by
squeezing eight hundred words onto each sheet.) Haslam relayed the first
bundle of papers sealed with John's Tassie gem—there were, as yet, no en-
velopes: letters were simply folded and sealed with wax—to the merchant
shippers John Capper and William Haslewood. The letter was already
bulky, but after Haslam left, John added an extra page, which he then sent
to Haslam through the two-penny post, the mail system internal to London
that charged two pence for a standard letter—thus getting in his last "two
cents."

Capper & Haslewood did not have a ship sailing for Philadelphia for another six weeks, so they put John's letter in their postbag headed for Boston. Their agent in Boston would forward it by stagecoach to John Warder, a merchant shipper in Philadelphia, who would send it on to George in the West. Warder was the son of Jeremiah Warder, a shipping tycoon who owned land throughout Philadelphia. His mansion sat behind an imposing brick wall on the north side of Sassafras Street, near the dock, and he ran John Warder & Sons with his sons Jeremiah, Jr., and John, Jr. His eldest son, Jeremiah Junior, ran another shipping firm, Warder & Brothers, at 371 North Front Street with two of his brothers, William and Benjamin. Besides the twenty-five packages for Drury & Tallant that Captain Coffin had brought from Liverpool in March 1818 were eleven for Warder & Brothers.[47]

After George settled in Louisville, John would continue to rely on the Warders to convey his letters to George. On November 12, 1819, John warned his brother that he would "be much disappointed at the smallness of the Sum remitted to Warder's." He was referring to the letter containing a hundred-pound remittance from Richard Abbey, which was part of George's share of Tom's estate and which could have saved George another transatlantic crossing. But there was an inevitable time lag in communication between the brothers. "The distance between us is so great, the Posts so uncertain," John sighed. "We must hope."[48]

The market, with its propensity for boom and bust, was always a risky proposition, and during the American Revolution, John Warder had moved to London, where he met his wife, Ann (née Head), through their mutual friends the Cappers. They returned to Philadelphia, and on July 3, 1794, Ann recorded the suicide of Harry Capper, a Philadelphia merchant whose "improvident speculations" had left him bankrupt. When the sheriffs came to take possession of his house, Capper's "Frantic mind could not contain itself," and he "tore the back of his head all to pieces." Like the Warders, the Cappers were Quaker, and the affair was shameful enough that Harry's sister Mary either did not know of, or did not admit, the manner of his death. One month after Harry Capper's suicide, Mary Capper reported that his "illness was short" and that he had "left a young wife for whom I feel much." Harry Capper's wife had recovered from the faint caused by the arrival of the sheriffs just in time to hear the shot of her husband's pistol.[49] In a country built on speculation, fortunes were lost as quickly as they were made, and the Philadelphia Capper's response to financial insolvency was no lesson for George.

The same day that George and Georgiana's ship docked in Philadelphia, the paper in which Michael Drury advertised his wares protested the frequency of suicide, a "dreadful and irremediable crime" in America. The editor quoted Robert Blair's gloomy long poem, *The Grave:* "If there is an *hereafter,* / And trust there is / . . . / Then must it be an awful thing to *die;* / More horrid yet to die by one's own hand. / *Self Murder!* name it not; our nation's shame, / That makes her the reproach of neighboring states!" Harry Capper's suicide may not have been unusual, but George believed that in a country "where business, productions, industry, and of course wealth, is ever on the encrease there is no fear that misfortune or accident will *altogether* crush a persevering intelligent man, unless an accumulation of untoward circumstances break his spirit, or drive him to the bottle—many, very many fall victims to the latter, very few to a broken spirit."[50] George never thought of turning to the bottle, and his spirit would prove hard to break.

John's journal-letter to George and Georgiana from the spring of 1819 made it through various hands to the Western Country of America, and in it the poet reveals just what a strange place the land west of the Alleghenies seemed to him. At one point, in a playful series of questions, he teases his sister-in-law about life on the prairie:

> Now you have by this time crumpled up your large Bonnet, what do you wear—a cap! do you put your hair in papers of a night? do you pay the Miss Birkbeck a morning visit—have you any tea? or [do] you milk and water with them—What place of Worship do you go to—the Quakers the Moravians, the Unitarians or the Methodists—Are there any flowers in bloom you like—any beautiful heaths—Any Streets full of Corset Makers. What sort of shoes have you to fit those pretty feet of yours? Do you desire Comp^ts [compliments] to one another? Do you ride on Horseback? What do you have for breakfast, dinner and supper? Without mentioning lunch and bever and wet and snack—and a bit to stay one's stomach—Do you get any spirits—now you might easily distill some whiskey—and going into the woods set up a whiskey s[h]op for the Mon-

keys—Do you and the miss Birkbecks get groggy on any thing—a little
so so ish so as to be obliged to be seen home with a Lantern—You may
perhaps have a game at puss in the corner—Ladies are warranted to play
at this game though they have not whiskers. Have you a fiddle in the Settlement—or at any rate a jew's harp—which will play in spite of ones
teeth . . .

Presumably, John was joking about the monkeys, but one can never be sure.
He was writing shortly after Andrew Jackson's aggressive military campaign against the Seminole Nation, which forced Spain to relinquish its ter-
ritorial rights in east and west Florida, and the story was in the news. "I
want very much a little of your wit my dear sister," the poet wrote in the
same letter containing his questions about Illinois, "to bandy back a pun or
two across the Atlantic and send a quibble over the Floridas."[51] Whether
John thought his quibble would fly over the Floridas on its way to George
and Georgiana in Illinois, or whether he thought there were monkeys on
the prairie, he stretched his imagination to share his brother's experience.
One suspects—as his confusion of Balboa and Cortez, or the Ohio and the
Mississippi suggests—that the poet was thinking of America more meta
phorically than literally.

As for his curiosity about western shoes and corsets, one would not
want to guess at Georgiana's response, for it was her wit the poet was seeking to engage, but Georgiana knew enough about fashion in the Western
Country by this point to know that there was not much to tell. The streets
were not paved, and women often went without shoes and stockings, even
when fully dressed. For the most part, ladies out West followed the London
fashions, many months in arrears. Georgiana would later complain to Maria Dilke that "it would only be an act of charity if you were to write us a
letter sometimes, giving us some idea how you in the fashionable world are
going on."[52] She probably already missed the more fashionable world she
had left behind.

Yet, for all the playfulness of John's letter to George and Georgiana, the
poet was still deep in a grief about which George may, or may not, have
heard. William Haslam had offered to send word to George about Tom's
death, but it is not clear whether George had received the news by the time
John's letter reached him. After his lighthearted queries about life on the

prairie, the poet switched to a different discursive register in an attempt to make sense of their loss. None of the brothers had been raised to any strong faith, but John had come away from Tom's deathbed with "scarce a doubt of immortality of some nature o[r] other."[53] He was interested in the idea of a soul; but, unlike many of his contemporaries, he wasn't concerned with the metaphysics of the soul's materiality. Nor was he interested, like his professors in medical school, in its precise location in the body, whether pineal gland, nervous fibers, or brain. He was more concerned with its genesis and development.

In Psalm 84, the Hebrew people, in "passing through the valley of Baca, make it a well" with their weeping—"in valle lacrimarum" is the Vulgate translation. Revising the idea of life as a "Vale of Tears," John proposed that life was instead a "Vale of Soul-making."[54] Having had his share of pain, misery, and heartbreak, he was not proposing to pretend that sorrow, in this life, does not exist, but a Vale of Tears offers no redemption. There are intelligences, he posited—atoms of perception, sparks of divinity—in human beings that become souls only through the pains and pleasures of experience. Nothing is real until it is experienced, he believed: "Even a Proverb is no proverb to you till your Life has illustrated it."[55] This belief led him to articulate a deeply original, experiential theory of soul. In terms of Enlightenment empiricist philosophy, he drew on John Locke's explanation of the mechanics of human understanding to formulate an idea of the human soul as a spiritual blank slate on which experience inscribes the contours of identity. Only embodied human existence gives intelligences a distinct identity.

In the Vale of Soul-making, sensibility translates not into meaningless pain but rather into spiritual growth. "Do you not see how necessary a World of Pains and troubles is to school an Intelligence and make it a soul?" John asked his brother. "A Place where the heart must feel and suffer in a thousand diverse ways!" He was perhaps not far off when he called the Vale of Soul-making "a system of Spirit-creation."[56] More than metaphysical hairsplitting about the distinction between souls and intelligences, John's discussion of the Vale of Soul-making reveals his bold willingness to think through fundamental human questions from an individual, undoctrinaire perspective. One might defy all of Benjamin Bailey's theological treatises combined to offer as much wisdom about something so basic to human understanding as the soul—a concept to which every culture has

30. The Water Works designed by Benjamin Henry Latrobe (1764–1820) in Centre Square, Philadelphia, at the intersection of Broad and High streets.

Drawn and engraved by William Russell Birch & Son, 1800; courtesy of the Stanford University Library.

31. The back of the State House on Independence Square, Philadelphia. Charles Willson Peale's museum was on the second floor.

Engraving by William Russell Birch, 1800.

32. William Bakewell of Fatland Ford, Philadelphia (1762–1821). English emigrant and father of George's business partners in Kentucky, and of John James Audubon's wife, Lucy Green Bakewell.

Courtesy of the Princeton University Library, Department of Rare Books and Special Collections.

33. A stagecoach on High Street, Philadelphia. The road led west to Schuylkill Bridge, which spilled into the stage road across the Great Appalachian Valley, on the way to Pittsburgh.

Aquatint, c. 1807, from Seymour Dunbar, *A History of Travel in America* (1915).

34. Covered wooden bridge spanning the Schuylkill River, which George and
Georgiana crossed on their way to the Western Country.
Aquatint by Carl Fredrik Akrell, from *Atlas til Friherre Klinkowstroms
Bref om de Forenta Staterne* (Stockholm, 1824).

35. "I am going to Illinois!" "I have been!!" Wood engraving satirizing
the English Prairie in Illinois.
From Major Walter Wilkey, *Narrative of a Tour to, & One Year's Residence in "Edensburgh"* (1839).
Courtesy of the Beinecke Library, Yale University.

36. The Cockney Pioneer Morris Birkbeck (1764–1825)
at his writing desk in Wanborough, Illinois,
on the English Prairie.

Anonymous pencil sketch, c. 1825.
Courtesy of the Chicago Historical Society.

37. George Flower (1780–1862), Morris
Birkbeck's business partner and the founder
of Albion, Illinois, on the English Prairie.

Painting by D. Roster, 1855.
Courtesy of the Chicago Historical Society.

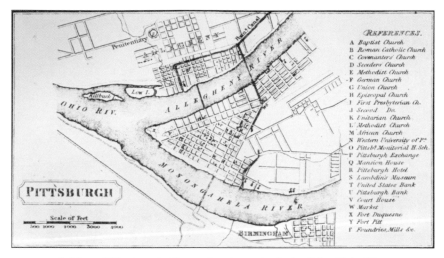

38. Map of Pittsburgh, Pennsylvania, at the fork of the Ohio River.

Copper engraving from Robert Baird, *View of the Valley of the Mississippi; or, The Emigrant's and Traveller's Guide to the West* (1834).

39. View of Pittsburgh from the Ohio River, below the confluence
of the Monongahela and Allegheny rivers.

Steel engraving, c. 1840, from Seymour Dunbar, *A History of Travel in America* (1915).

40. Benjamin Bakewell (1767–1844), brother of Squire William Bakewell and owner of a glass factory in Pittsburgh.
Courtesy of the Princeton University Library, Department of Rare Books and Special Collections, Rare Books Division.

41. A flatboat, the type of vessel that carried most emigrants west, steering past a snag on the Ohio River.
Illustration from Walter Whipple Spooner, *The Back-Woodsmen; or, Tales of the Borders* (1883).

42. A Kentucky flat, also known as a broadhorn, loaded with cargo and
heading downstream with a "sawyer" in its path.

Wood engraving, c. 1860, from Seymour Dunbar, *A History of Travel in America* (1915).

43. Flatboat interior.

Illustration by Charles-Alexandre Lesueur, c. 1826,
from *Les Voyages du Naturaliste Charles-Alexandre Lesueur en Amérique du Nord* (1904).

44. Keelboat propelled by professional boatmen, the type of vessel
George and Georgiana took down the Ohio River.

Anonymous wood engraving, c. 1850, from Seymour Dunbar, *A History of Travel in America* (1915).

45. Pioneer log cabin in the West, with a wood-shingled roof and a cat-and-clay
chimney made from sticks and slats of wood plastered with mud, c. 1840.

Lithograph from Seymour Dunbar, *A History of Travel in America* (1915).

devoted its best minds—as does this section of John's letter to George and Georgiana, written around the time as his Great Odes in the spring of 1819. Alone and without a compass, the intuitive and timelessly wise young poet devised a theory of human identity that made sense of the suffering he had experienced—and a concept of salvation that did not affront, as he put it, his reason or humanity.

The pith of the Keatsian cosmology is that painful human experience ultimately contributes to the triumph, if not delight, of the soul. There can be no real pleasure detached from pain. "Circumstances are like Clouds continually gathering and bursting," John wrote. "While we are laughing the seed of some trouble is put into the wide arable land of events—while we are laughing it sprouts i[t] grows and suddenly bears a poison fruit which we must pluck." The character of a people is expressed in its art, and the English poets endured lives that were all clouded over. One reason the English "produced the finest writers in the world; is, that the English world has ill-treated them during their lives and foster'd them after their deaths. They have in general been trampled aside into the bye paths of life and seen the festerings of Society." Moody Hamlet best expressed the race. The comical Italian Boiardo "was a noble Poet of Romance; not a miserable and mighty Poet of the human Heart," like Shakespeare or Wordsworth.[57]

Haslam had just lost his father, and this gave John further opportunity to formulate thoughts that had been brewing inside him about the purpose of suffering in relation to Tom's death. "I began by seeing how man was formed by circumstances—and what are circumstances?—but touchstones of his heart—? and what are touch stones?—but proovings of his heart?—and what are proovings of his heart but fortifiers or alterers of his nature?"[58] Contingencies leave their impression on the *heart* of an individual as well as the mind. By a sort of spiritual chemistry, these two elements combine with soulish substance to produce an eternal identity.

In the spring after Tom's death, John had also been brooding over the affair of the "degraded Wells and Amena"—"a wretched business," he called it. He had been re-reading the letters that Charles Wells had sent to Tom in his illness while his brothers were away and concluded that the "diabolical scheme" had been provoked *not* by good-natured waggishness, but rather by "vanity, and the love of intrigue." Wells had used Tom to feed his own ego: "It was no thoughtless hoax—but a cruel deception on a sanguine

Temperament, with every show of friendship." John did not think death too severe a punishment, and he vowed to be "prudently revengeful."[59] Indeed, Wells found being "cut" by John Keats punishment enough.

The other circumstances gathering like clouds around John in the spring of 1819 were financial. John Jennings's will had been causing dissension ever since the time of its execution, and that dissension had spilled out from behind closed doors into the Court of Chancery: a self-perpetuating machine of bureaucracy and greed that ground down plaintiffs and defendants alike with as much efficiency as any mill. Jennings had hired a land surveyor, rather than a solicitor, to draft the will, and it contained mistakes that had caused complications that the legal experts were still debating.

In brief, John Jennings had bequeathed half of his estate (£13,187) to his wife, Alice, and a third to his son, Midgley. He had also set aside enough capital to provide a fifty-pound annuity for his daughter, Frances, and a thirty-pound annuity for his sister, Mary Sweetinburgh. And he left a thousand pounds to be divided evenly among the Keats children. But Midgley's wife, Margaret, had been pregnant at the time the will had been drafted, and it neglected to make any provision for *their* children. Midgley's portion included £1,900 in government funds and stock in the British East India Company, valued at £1,000; but when John Jennings died, the stock turned out to be worth half the estimated amount. And when Midgley died, according to the terms of the will, his wife could retain only five hundred pounds, the balance reverting to Alice Jennings, and ultimately to the Keats children. Midgley petitioned the court that his family be allowed to retain the full amount (£2,900) of his father's bequest after his own death. But when Midgley died in 1808, the filing and counter-filing were still going on.[60] Over a decade later, the case was *still* grinding through the Chancery machinery, with no end in sight.

To make matters worse, Margaret Jennings was now threatening further legal action on behalf of her three surviving children—Mary Ann, Midgley John, Jr., and Margaret Alice—the Keats cousins, who ranged in age from twelve to fourteen. "You do not understand the business," John told his sister on June 17. "I trust it will not in the end be detrimental to you." A vague sort of evasion. But the truth is that John did not understand it either. Who could? The essential point as far as the poet was concerned was that when he showed up at Abbey's counting house in June 1819 to withdraw his remaining share of his deceased brother's estate for his summer expenses, Abbey fended him off with the letter from his aunt's solicitor. Even if she did not win her lawsuit, the tea dealer explained, John and his siblings would still be responsible for legal expenses. "Before this Chancery threat had cut [off] every legitimate supply of Cash from me I had a little at my disposal," John wrote to George three months later.[61]

John's pockets were now emptier than even Benjamin Haydon's, and he forced himself to the unpleasant task of writing to the artist to ask for the return of a loan he had made him. The request went nowhere, and John had to borrow more money from Brown. He was now sinking into debt. He planned to "retire to live cheaply in the country and compose myself and verses as well as I can," taking Brown's advice to give his writing one last chance; but, he explained to his sister, he could not spare the coach fare to see her once more in Walthamstow before leaving for the Isle of Wight for the summer.[62] On the third of May, he had walked through the fields to see her, and the visit had sapped his strength—emotionally, perhaps, as well as physically, for Fanny detailed to him her many grievances against the Abbeys. The slightest chill now flew to his throat, and John did not think it wise to repeat the visit.

Given his precarious health, his insecurity about his future, his dejection following Tom's death, George's absence, and his hopeless love for Fanny Brawne, it is perhaps hardly surprising that John's letters to his brother and sister-in-law should dwell so much upon death. Continuing the deeply reflective mood that inspired the Vale of Soul-making, he posed an existential—hence unanswerable—question in the opening line of a sonnet: "Why did I laugh tonight?" One cannot say whence, in this world of trouble and pain, comes such a laugh. "No voice will tell:/No God, no Deamon of severe response/Deigns to reply from heaven or from Hell." In the second quatrain of the sonnet, the poet restates the question and, giving up on both heaven and hell, asks his own heart: "Heart! thou and I are here sad and alone;/Say, wherefore did I laugh? O mortal pain!/O Darkness! Darkness!"[63] The laugh, however, dominates the sonnet, which in the end turns out to be as much about the resiliency of the human spirit in the face of death as about death itself.

It did cross John's mind while copying the sonnet for George that its morbid tone and closing tribute to death might frighten his brother. "Verse, fame, and Beauty are intense, indeed," the poem concludes, "But Death intenser—Death is Life's high mead." John worried that George's anxiety on

his behalf would lead him to "fear for the violence of my temperament continually smothered down." But he asked his brother (and sister-in-law) to
look over the previous two pages of his letter, and decide whether he had it
in him to "bear the buffets of the world." His own probing thoughts about
life and death were to be the best commentary on his poems. "Give me this
credit—Do you not think I strive—to know myself?" This was the goal of
"divine Philosophy," as he knew, quoting Milton: "Not harsh and crabbed
as dull fools suppose/But musical as is Apollo's lute." John's sonnet "Why
did I laugh tonight?" grew out of the same crisis that had inspired him to
put the heart at the center of his system of spirit-creation: "I wrote with my
Mind," he assured George, "and perhaps I must confess a little bit of my
heart."[64] A conscious understatement. As his meditations on the Vale of
Soul-making reveal, the heart was at the center of John's philosophy as well
as his poetry in the spring of 1819.

And Fanny Brawne, living next to him at Wentworth Place, was at the
center of his heart. Following his redemptive laugh in the face of death, the
poet recounts a dream that became the basis of another poetic meditation
on the afterlife: "A Dream, after Reading Dante's Episode of Paulo and
Francesca," or, as Hunt published it in the *Examiner,* "As Hermes Once
took to his Feathers Light." Hunt himself, in *Story of Rimini* (1816), had
narrated the ill-fated loves of Paolo and his sister-in-law Francesca da Rimini, from Canto 5 of Dante's *Inferno.* When John took up the subject, he
put himself in the place of Paolo, and Fanny (Frances) Brawne in the place
of Francesca.

The speaker of Keats's sonnet imagines himself in Dante's hell, specifically the Second Circle of *The Inferno,* where Paulo and Francesca, like
other adulterers, spend eternity whirling about in a "melancholy storm" of
unsatisfied desire. John described the dream to George as "one of the most
delightful enjoyments I ever had in my life."[65] With their lips pressed together, the lovers—like figures frozen on a Grecian Urn—represent desire
inflamed to its greatest pitch, an exquisite, painful form of pleasure that is
eternal in art but ephemeral in life. In the real world, love sated kills desire,
and youth grows spectre-thin and dies.

John began his journal-letter to George and Georgiana on Valentine's
Day, and, not knowing when the mail would go out, kept adding to it week
after week throughout the spring of 1819, until the start of May. On the
morning of Wednesday, May 5, the poet learned from his publisher that he
must wrap up the letter. Richard Birkbeck, the eldest son of the Cockney

Pioneer, was ready to sail for the English Prairie. The younger Birkbeck had remained behind in Wanborough, Surrey, to wrap up family business, but he was now ready to join his father, brothers, and sisters in the *new* Wanborough, Illinois.

John had originally planned to send his letter with another group of pioneers, who were traveling to the English Prairie at the end of February. Like Charles Trimmer, they were acquaintances of James Peachey, whom John knew from Clarke's school. But when the poet heard that Richard Birkbeck would be sailing a few weeks later, he held on to the letter so that he might (as he told Georgiana) do more in it than gossip. The extra time gave him a chance to include not only his tongue-in-cheek queries about life on the prairie but also his more profound musings on the nature of the soul, which otherwise would have been lost to posterity. On April 15, expecting Richard Birkbeck to leave within the week, John wrote to his sister to ask her for some lines to send George.

But still, the young Cockney Pioneer lingered, giving John time to copy his "Ode to Psyche"; "La Belle Dame sans Merci"; his sonnet on "Paulo and Francesca"; his Spenserian stanzas on Charles Brown; a sonnet "To Sleep"; two sonnets "On Fame"; and his sonnet about the form of the sonnet, "If by dull rhymes . . ." Despite his feeling that he was at a standstill in his writing, he also improvised a "Chorus of Fairies" and several pages of blank verse. The latter contain a truncated narrative about a princess, a dwarf, an ape, a fool, and a mule that escapes from a prince and, pretending to be asleep, tricks some "thievish Monkies" into filching his bridle so that he can be free.[66] Monkeys were on John's mind more than once in his letter to George and Georgiana on the English Prairie.

Besides learning that Richard Birkbeck was about to depart with the mail, when John spoke with Taylor on May 5, he also learned that the mailbags on the way from Illinois to England had been robbed. He guessed that this was the reason he had not yet received any word from George in the Western Country. He confessed that while he had "never been very uneasy" about his brother's silence after leaving Philadelphia, he did have to reassure Georgiana's mother more than once to keep her from "any despondence about it."[67] John concluded his letter on a sheet of paper that ultimately traveled down through George's family on a different path from the rest of the letter, making its appearance too late for Hyder Edward Rollins to include in *The Letters of John Keats* (1958).

The fugitive page contains a request for George to spare no detail about life on the English Prairie: "You must let me know every thing—how parcels come and go—what Papers Birkbecks [*sic*] has and what newspaper you want and other things." He reported that their sister was well, but that she had sprouted up recently and that now, just shy of sixteen, she was quite thin. He found her "very sensible," but he did not think that she was growing up to be "very pretty." For sentimental reasons, he hoped that he would meet the young Cockney Pioneer at Taylor's place to give him the letter, and he signed off with a blessing, "Your ever affectionate Brother."[68]

Having disposed of the weighty packet, containing his even more weighty thoughts, he then turned to his neglected correspondence. He informed Mary Ann Jeffery that he had decided to forge ahead with his writing career that summer, but that he would be going farther south than Devonshire, to the Isle of Wight. She had been kind enough to make inquiries on his behalf about cheap lodging. *She nurs'd / Romantic fancies, till her soul became / The very home of love.* Mary Ann, too, was a poet. *Her love was adoration: her sole life,—/ The spring of her existence—not so, his;—/ She was his pride, his sister, confidant—/ But not—his love—*[69] One wonders whether those readers who have assumed that Mary Ann Jeffery fell for John Keats are correct.

John thanked Mary Ann for supporting his plan to keep writing, but in response to her comment that his having taken a position as a ship's surgeon would have sapped his mental powers, he begged to differ. "To be thrown among people who care not for you, with whom you have no sympathies forces the Mind upon its own resources," he wrote, "and leaves it free to make its speculations of the differences of human character and to class them with the calmness of a Botanist."[70] Throwing oneself into the unknown only strengthens character. George now had such open fields of opportunity before him. Although John had finally let go of his long journal-letter, and was, in this instance, writing to Mary Ann Jeffery, his thoughts were still far away, not infrequently with his pioneer brother in the West.

Cincinnati

On approaching Cincinnati from the Ohio River, one could see the "hill" rising gradually to a height of fifty feet from the river, bounded by the highlands to the north. Below the hill, between the mouth of Deer Creek and Mill Creek, sat the "bottom." Cincinnati was built on plains of unequal elevation, but like other cities George and Georgiana had seen, it was laid out on a grid of streets that intersected each other at right angles. Proceeding west from Broadway to Western, and stretching back in columns from the river, came the streets named for the indigenous plants (and in this case, people and animals): Sycamore, Miami, Walnut, Vine, Race, Elm, and Plum. Horses were not indigenous to the West (the wild horses of the Indians having escaped from colonial settlements), but they raced down Race Street. From Water Street, the streets proceeded back toward the hill in rows: Front, Second, Third, Fourth, Fifth, Sixth, and Northern. The brick and white-frame buildings along Front Street announced health and prosperity, yet here, as elsewhere in America, it also seemed that little energy had been expended on pleasing the eye. When Frances Milton Trollope, the English novelist, visited Cincinnati in 1828, she remarked that "it is by no means a city of striking appearance; it wants domes, towers, and steeples." Rather than handsome, the city was "neat."[71]

Yet no one could deny that business was booming. "Gain! Gain! Gain!" Morris Birkbeck exclaimed upon visiting Ohio the previous year, "is the beginning, the middle and the end, the *alpha* and *omega* of the founders of American towns." In the space of two decades, Cincinnati had transformed from a muddy settlement built around a fort into a hub of commerce—the main port for trade in the Western Country. One could scarcely walk a block without seeing a wagon full of brick or stones trundling by to a construction site. In 1818, Cincinnati had 9,120 inhabitants, enough to qualify as a city, although it would not officially become one until the following year. From a population of 960 people in 1805, it had grown to almost ten times that size.[72] Travelers coming from Pittsburgh could not tell which of the two cities was larger.

Cincinnati was not yet facing the repercussions of over-speculation. The average mid-sized shop kept twenty to thirty thousand dollars' worth of stock and took half its profit in the form of credit, payable in six to eighteen months. English merchants extended credit to get their goods across the sea, and bankers in the eastern states extended credit to transport supplies to the West. Farmers purchased merchandise on credit until the harvest season, and then sent crops back in the opposite direction, balancing accounts and keeping the whole circuit running on credit. When Henry Fearon visited Cincinnati about the same time as George and Georgiana, he observed the effect of overexpansion in "an universal and most important error in all the stores—too large a stock: by this means, tradesmen, in every country, are exposed to lose as much as by bad debts."[73] As the Panic of 1819 proved, he was correct.

Until then, Cincinnati was thriving. Masons piled stones. Bricklayers stacked bricks. Millworkers cut and planed boards. Carpenters nailed them together. One made wire sieves, another hand-mills, to grind coffee. More than one made guns. An engraver made copper plates to advertise the guns, and the printers reproduced the engravings with paper and ink from the manufacturers who made those items. The bellows makers supplied the smiths, who hammered copper, tin, and silver into useful and sometimes decorative shapes. Leatherworkers tanned hides for the saddler and the whip-maker, and one woodworker made saddletrees. Nail cutters fed flat metal strips into machines, coopers beveled barrels, and turners rotated wood on lathes to make the wheels that the wheelwrights then mounted on axles. Mechanics set timepieces in ivory and wood, while bakers baked, painters painted, dyers dyed, spinners spun, weavers wove, and the whole town kept time to the sounds of commerce.

In 1818, Cincinnati was importing one-and-a-half million dollars' worth of goods annually, and exporting a similar amount. "In the main street," Fearon marveled, *"English goods abound in as great profusion as in Cheapside."* When Oliver Farnsworth printed the city's first business directory a year later, he commented on the changes that the average Cincinnatian had witnessed:

> He has seen adventurers from almost every part of the habitable globe come and settle around him. He has seen the forests prostrated by the hand of industry, and fields, meadows and pastures occupy the regions where they stood. In the course of a few years, he has seen a little village of cabins transformed, as if by magic, into a populous, active and commercial city. He has seen the canoe give way to the barge, and the barge to the steamboat. In short, he has seen hills torn down, marshes filled up, streets laid out, graduated and paved, public buildings erected, manufactories established, and every part of the country around him improved and beautified by the active spirit of enterprize and civilization.

But colonization comes at a cost. Charlotte Ludlow, one of Cincinnati's original settlers, also noted how greatly things had changed since her husband, Israel, first laid out the town. Back in 1797, when she first approached the landing place in a canoe, she found only "a garrison of soldiers, with a few scattered houses and muddy streets."[74]

The main building at that time was Fort Washington: the first in a chain of government forts extending west that also included Fort St. Clair, on the eastern branch of the Great Miami River, and Forts Jefferson and Greenville, on its western branches. Ludlow Station, a quadrangular fort of log cabins, was the closest military station to Fort Washington, five miles from the settlement in the valley of Mill Creek. "Now the streets of the busy city are crowded; hills are levelled; valleys are raised; and crooked ways made straight," Ludlow wrote on January 29, 1819. "Deep mire is succeeded by adamant and brick, and cabins give place to great houses." Native Americans no longer came to take their meals and a pipe on the lawn of Ludlow Station, and "the thin blue curl of smoke" from their fires had disappeared. Restrained by treaty from killing cattle, burning cabins, and kidnapping or scalping settlers, the original occupants had given up their claim to the land and moved on. "What I have often told you, is now come to pass," a Piankashaw chief told his council near the Miami River in 1784. "This day I received news from my great chief, at the falls of Ohio. Peace is made with the enemies of America."[75] Native Americans were now on the run, rather than on the warpath.

While tensions with Native Americans had subsided, traces of a troubled past remained. The Newport army barracks, across the Ohio at the mouth of the River Licking, had replaced Fort Washington. They housed a garrison of blue-coated state troopers and an arsenal of firearms and gunpowder against the threat of a Native American uprising. The town of Coverly, across the mouth of the River Licking, extended in a continuous pattern from Newport. The streets of both towns mirrored those of Cincinnati. John Filson, one of Cincinnati's founders, had named it "Losantiville," a linguistic hodgepodge consisting of L (for "Licking"), os (Latin, "mouth"), anti (Greek, "opposite"), and ville (French, "town"); hence, "town opposite the mouth of the River Licking." But when General Arthur St. Clair came out West to subdue the Indians, he renamed the town after George Washington: the American Cincinnatus. After a battle known locally as "St. Clair's Defeat," General "Mad" Anthony Wayne replaced St. Clair and continued to wage war against the Native Americans. Eventually, conflicts were resolved by means of a treaty. "Emigration then again commenced, and new towns and farms spread through the yielding forest."[76]

Yet if the original inhabitants of Ohio sought refuge farther west, such sanctuary was bound to be short lived. "On the road, every emigrant tells you he is going to Ohio," Fearon reported. "When you arrive in Ohio, its inhabitants are 'moving' to Missouri and Alabama; thus it is that the point for final settlement is for ever receding as you advance, and thus it will hereafter proceed and only be terminated by that effectual barrier—the Pacific Ocean."[77] The forecast was clear, and it did not take a prophet, or even a poet like Shelley, to predict Manifest Destiny.

An imposing monument to mercantilism in the West—a "stupendous edifice," Farnsworth called it, ten stories high, with stone walls ten feet thick and ninety windows—sat on a bed of limestone on the Ohio River near Broadway. The massive millstones were six feet in diameter and churned out roughly a hundred barrels of flour per day, twelve thousand annually. The mill also had machinery for carding, fulling, and dressing wool. For the previous four years, it had been producing an average of four thousand dollars' worth of cloth per year. While his brother might have preferred—like the lilies of the field—not to toil or to spin, George Keats, in coming to the West, had accepted the promise that George Flower held out to British emigrants: "They come, they toil, they prosper."[78]

Logs floated downriver in rafts to a three-story sawmill on the riverbank just below Cincinnati. Instead of horses, a twenty-horsepower steam-engine hauled logs from the river and drove the saws that cut the wood. The mill's four saws working simultaneously could produce eight hundred feet of boards per hour, or four thousand feet per day, 1,460,000 feet annually. Nearby, on the mouth of Mill Creek, the Cincinnati Manufacturing Company turned out fifty to sixty yards of broadcloth daily and consumed 6,500 bushels of coal annually. The city's three cotton factories had a combined total of twelve hundred spindles producing carpets, blankets, diapers, denim, and other fabrics.[79] British writers in America were obsessed with measurement, for when it came to business, the magic was in the numbers. Efficiency translated into profit as the land gave up its resources in the form of commodities.

The architect George Evans, who designed the ten-story stone mill on the river, had hired his father, the steam engineer Oliver Evans, to build the steam-engine that drove the millstones. The elder Evans had written the most widely read text in the nation on steam engineering—as applied to forging, distilling, papermaking, lathe turning, flour milling, plaster grinding, lumber cutting, water pumping, sugarcane pressing, metal rolling, coal raising, and steamboat and carriage propulsion. His foundries in Pittsburgh cast, forged, and built boilers, gearing, and power-driven machinery. He had invented a high-pressure steam engine to lift water to the reservoir in Center Square, Philadelphia, and a steam-powered flour-mill for George Washington. Perhaps, had Morris Birkbeck accepted Washington's offer to supervise his agricultural operations at Mount Vernon, he might have joined an industrial rather than a social revolution, for Oliver Evans's self-automated mill system revolutionized a process that human beings had been toiling at for millennia.[80]

Oliver Evans believed that the science of mechanics introduced a certainty into commerce that guaranteed success. Had he lived longer, he might have realized his dream of seeing an American railway system propelled by steam locomotion. Steam had this advantage over other sources of power: it was predictable and could be calculated mathematically. "Waterfalls are not at our command in all places, and are liable to be obstructed by frost, drought, and many other accidents. Wind is inconstant and unsteady: animal power, expensive, tedious in the operation, and unprofitable, as well as subject to innumerable accidents," Evans explained. "But steam at once presents us with a faithful servant, at command in all places, in all seasons; whose power is unlimited; for whom no task is too great nor yet too small; quick as lightning in operation; docile as the elephant led by a silken thread, ready, at our command, to render asunder the strongest works made by the arts of man."[81] Of course, steam boilers could explode unexpectedly, killing the people they served, and investments in steam engineering could blow up also.

More than one English emigrant, including the unfortunate James Tallant, discovered this truth. After his business split with Michael Drury, Tallant entered the dry-goods business in Cincinnati, near Yeatman's Cove. (Griffin Yeatman, the county recorder for births, deaths, and marriages, ran a tavern, the Square & Compass, on the public square by the cove.) Tallant partnered with William R. Foster, a merchant from New York, at Foster & Company, importing and exporting goods by the river, at 36 Main Street. Foster boarded at Andrew Mack's Hotel in the northeast corner of Yeatman's Cove, while Tallant lived up the street from the store, at number ninety-six. Eventually, Foster partnered with Charles Foster and Cornelius S. Bradbury, dry-goods merchants at 81 Main Street, while Tallant stayed on at the general store.[82]

   Yet James Tallant, like other people in the West, believed in the power
of steam to revolutionize industry, and he, like George Keats, aspired to
something greater than spending his life behind a counter. Steamboats
freighted with goods and people had been coming and going on the Ohio
and the Mississippi rivers since 1811, and they had nearly replaced the
barges that came up the Mississippi River from New Orleans. They would
eventually replace the flatboats that carried emigrants and supplies down
the Ohio River from Pittsburgh. Tallant was thinking ahead when he borrowed money from the Ohio Insurance Company (on whose board he
served as a director) to load a steamboat named the *Walter Scott* with cargo
and send it downriver to New Orleans. (Ironically, this is the same name
that Mark Twain would give the sinking steamboat in *The Adventures of
Huckleberry Finn.*)

   "Know all men by these presents, that I, James Tallant, of the city of
Cincinnati, Ohio, owner of the good steamboat called the Walter Scott,
now lying on the stocks at Cincinnati (to be launched at my risk as soon as
the water will permit,) and necessitated at this time to borrow and take up
upon the adventure of said steamboat, the sum of six thousand dollars, for
the profitable and advantageous sailing of said boat for the period of one
year from the date hereof . . ." This legal soliloquy bound Tallant to repay
money borrowed at the exorbitant rate of sixteen percent interest, or nine
hundred and sixty dollars on a loan of six thousand dollars, within a year.
Joseph Pierce, a foundry owner and fellow director of the Ohio Insurance
Company, ensured Tallant's bond, as did two other sureties: the real estate
broker Thomas Carneal and the merchant William D. Jones, who shared a
pew with Tallant's family in the Episcopal Christ Church.[83]

   The *Walter Scott* set sail for New Orleans, but by the end of the year
Tallant found himself unable to pay back the loan to the Ohio Insurance
Company. The company demanded a seizure of the boat, and the sheriffs
in Louisville carried out the legal order from the Chancery Court. After
sixty days had passed and no claimants appeared, the sheriffs put the *Walter
Scott* up for sale at a public auction. Francis H. Edmonson purchased the
boat for $1,500, which was four or five times under its market value. The
insurance company sued Edmonson to recover their $6,960, and, when
the case came to trial, Supreme Court Judge Alexander Porter, Jr., ruled
that the defendant had known about the lien when he purchased the boat,

and that Edmonson therefore should pay back the company. The gavel came down.

But Edmonson appealed, and when the judge reconsidered, he decided that since the boat had been in Kentucky for sixty days prior to the sale, the creditors had had ample time to present their claim. The sale was legal in the state of Kentucky, moreover, and the insurance company had provided no proof that James Tallant had actually received the six thousand dollars. The judge ordered the Ohio Insurance Company to pay back Edmonson, and a few others involved in the appeal. The gavel came down.

James Tallant had been doing well enough before the *Walter Scott* set sail. The General Assembly of the Ohio state legislature appointed him to oversee the distribution of half a million dollars in capital stock for the Commercial Bank of Cincinnati. But within two years of his scheme involving the *Walter Scott,* James Tallant and his brother William had disappeared from the Cincinnati business directory. James's wife, Mary, instead appeared in it as a schoolmistress at a boarding school for girls, on Seventh Street between Vine and Walnut. James's niece, Alice Drury, would later report that James and Mary Tallant had left Hull in England for Cincinnati, "where Mr. Tallant engaged at a later date, in an attempt to perfect a high-pressure steam-boat engine, during the trial of which both he and his boat disappeared and neither was ever heard from."[84] Steamboats were a high-stakes game for all involved.

Mary Drury Tallant in the end gave up her life as a pioneer in the American West. She took her youngest children, Sarah Tuxford, John James, and Alice Gwynne, back to England. Her oldest son, Julius Ferdinand, remained behind to follow the path blazed by his father and uncles, William and Joseph. Mary would open a boarding school for girls in the town of West Haddon, Northamptonshire. Her daughter Alice and her niece Helen Drury would be among her students. Nearby, in the village of Nortoft, the brothers John and Isaac Edmonds ran a boarding school for boys, where Mary would send her son John. A decade after her husband's disappearance, Mary Tallant would marry her son's fifty-year-old schoolmaster, John Edmonds.[85] One wonders whether James Tallant went the way of poor Harry Capper, the suicide.

Down the river from Cincinnati, in Red Banks, Kentucky, John James Audubon and his brother-in-law Thomas Bakewell had applied the wonders of steam engineering to a steam-powered grist- and sawmill, with an engine on Oliver Evans's model. The engineer David Prentice, a Scottish emigrant who had built a steam-powered threshing machine for Squire Bakewell at Fatland Ford, had studied Evans's engines before building the engine for the Henderson mill. George would later open a steam sawmill in partnership with David Prentice and Tom Bakewell in Louisville. By the time Tom moved to Cincinnati in 1824 to design his own steamboats, George would be grinding seventy barrels of flour a day—only thirty percent less than the mill that was the boast of Cincinnati.

As yet, however, George and Georgiana had gone only half the length of the river. Primitive as Cincinnati might have seemed to them, they had not fully experienced the reality of life in the West. In the states and territories farther downriver, rather than merchants and manufacturers, they would find a "rough set of men, much given to drinking whiskey, fighting and gouging." Gouging was a style of fighting common in the Western Country in which combatants competed for the distinction of putting out "each others eyes with their fingers and thumbs, and sometimes biting off each others noses or ears." Gouged eyeballs would hang down the loser's cheeks from their sockets, and on occasion the victor would snatch and pocket them as trophies. John Woods had a neighbor on the English Prairie, who had "the top of his nose bitten off, in one of these brutal frays." William Tell Harris complained that "the sight of one or two victims to the brutal practice of gouging is sufficiently sickening to stifle the wish for any intercourse with a people capable of, or even winking at, such a practice." While Kentucky discouraged gouging with a prison term of two to ten years and a fine of up to a thousand dollars, Illinois had taken no such measures.[86]

Even the Cockney Pioneer Birkbeck admitted that, in the West, "thousands on thousands perish through intoxication, and the frantic broils which it continually occasions." He described one fray in which "a Cado bit off the under lip of a Choctaw, both young men; the latter was so drunk, that he did not know who had been his antagonist; he lost his lip, got sober, and returned to the chase as usual." Some backwoodsmen in Illinois claimed to have no more qualms about shooting an Indian than they would a wildcat or a raccoon. "You hear of desperate characters in London," Emanuel Howitt remarked during his tour of the United States in 1819, "but these men beat them hollow, in all species of crime." In Louisville, people enjoyed gander-pulling: a sport that involved tying a goose to a tree, greasing its neck, riding past it on horseback, and trying to pull off its head.[87]

The inns along the river were packed with drinking, swearing, spitting, tobacco-chewing, and cigar-smoking Westerners. The gambling room of one tavern on Main Street in Louisville was "kept going night and day, without intermission; and the *gentry* who occupied it spoke as if they had been obliged to *depose every word upon oath*." To this description, John Melish added that he "could not stand the scene a minute, for it became immediately associated in my mind with the horrible idea I had formed of hell, when I was at school." Like the damned in the Book of Revelation, these backcountrymen "would roar, curse, and blaspheme," and "the fumes of tobacco, with which they were enveloped, wanted only a sprinkling of brimstone to bear a very lively resemblance to 'the smoke of their torment ascending up for ever and ever.'"[88]

Whereas the future Queen City at least had pretensions to culture, the places to which George and Georgiana were going at present had no such ambitions. The leisure time of the Louisville residents amounted to "the most senseless and comfortless mode of killing time" that Fearon had ever seen. Indeed, after leaving Philadelphia, he had failed to find any "man who appear[ed] to have a single earthly object in view, except spitting and smoking segars." Nor, since that time, had he "seen a book in the hands of any person."[89] In 1818, most people on the western frontier of America had other things than poetry on their minds.

6   BACKWOODS AND BLIND ALLEYS

Winchester

The old stone cottage at the south end of High Street, which John and Charles Brown had rented for the summer to work on *Otho the Great,* was five minutes from the windy shore and the white-capped waves. From his window, John could see the ships in the distance, blown about by a multitude of sails. When they passed the chimneys on the shingled roofs of the village (or seemed to do, from his perspective), they looked like weathercocks spinning on poles in the wind. The neighboring cottages, covered with eglantine, honeysuckle, and roses, seemed to him fitting abodes for old maids and naval widows living on comfortable stipends. He imagined them in their sitting rooms, beneath low-beamed ceilings, at their card tables, or sipping tea from porcelain tea sets and reading poetry.

Had John been feeling better, his rambles through the hilly countryside might have been pleasant. His friends Jem Rice and John Martin (the bookseller who had printed Reynolds's first book of poems) had visited. They had stayed up late, as John and George had once done at Rice's Saturday night Boys' Club, smoking and playing cards. They feasted on lobster and drained more than one bottle of claret. They teased Brown for his sexual exploits: "Open daylight! he don't care." Each morning, when Brown came downstairs in his robe and nightcap, refreshed from a good night's sleep and ready for breakfast, John prepared to hitch himself back to their "dog-cart," as John called *Otho the Great,* dragging it along from scene to scene.[1]

While Brown paced the room, waving his arms and dictating events dredged up from the annals of history—a fury of plots and speeches, complicated by counter-plots and counter-speeches—John struggled to translate the story into verse. They had made it as far as the fourth act when Brown suggested introducing an elephant onto the stage for dramatic effect. John thought he was joking. But Brown spoke so eloquently and fervently on the elephant's behalf that John agreed to think about it. He'd have to check whether Otho, like the Carthaginian Hannibal, had ever driven elephants into battle.

Every night, as John retired from castles and conspirators to his solitary chamber, Fanny Brawne drifted in, unbidden. Her soft white hand, her lips, her laugh . . . He was "not one of the Paladins of old who lived upon water grass and smiles for years together." He wanted Fanny—he wanted her badly—but he knew he could not have her outside marriage. *Give me those lips again! / Enough! Enough! it is enough for me / To dream of thee!* The next day he would project his madness onto Ludolph, his fiery protagonist. "My life!" says Ludolph. "Long have I loved thee, yet till now not loved." Yet as night descended, images of beautiful, flirting Fanny returned. "Thank God for my diligence!" he wrote to her: "were it not for that I should be miserable. I encourage it and strive not to think of you—but when I have succeeded in doing so all day and as far as midnight, you return as soon as this artificial excitement goes off more severely from the fever I am left in—Upon my soul I cannot say what you could like me for."[2]

John's love for Fanny Brawne had always been haunted by a sense that their relationship was doomed. He could not see his way past his own financial insolvency to a future that would not compromise his ambitions. The young women at Shanklin, in their summer gowns and bonnets, the tourists who came panting after the picturesque, reminded him of the "literary fashionables" in London. He wished he had a guinea for every spyglass in that wooded ravine between the cliffs.[3]

John had been counting on *Otho the Great* to rescue him from financial embarrassment, but it was no longer certain whether Edmund Kean, the tragic actor he had been counting on to play Ludolph, Otho's rebellious son, would remain in London or spend the season in America. John had created the role specifically with him in mind. There was no one else who could do it. The effect of the whole depended on Kean's performing the part. John's future depended on it, for he was now living on borrowed money—and, he feared, on borrowed time.

When the fog rolled in and clouds blanketed the sky, John decided to leave Shanklin. Brown would cross the Channel to Bedhampton, where Dilke's sister Letitia lived with her husband, John Snook, and their two young sons (Henry and John, Jr.). Brown would stay with the Snooks at the big mill on the tidal stream, watching the swans drifting by, plucking at the rushes. John would take the stage road past Southampton to the cathedral city of Winchester, which had a good library, and read up about elephants. The temporary break from *Otho the Great* might also give him a chance to finish some other poems he had been writing.

John was hoping that his next book of verse would be more marketable than the first. He had written *Lamia,* a narrative poem in two books, ultimately published as a fragment, in the heroic couplets of Pope, the Augustan Man of Power. He had also begun to revise *Hyperion* into *The Fall of Hyperion.* "I am in a train of writing now I fear to disturb it," he wrote to Fanny Brawne in the first week of August, partly by way of explanation for why he had not come to see her; "let it have its course bad or good—in it I shall try my own strength and the public pulse."[4]

In the meantime, John liked living in Winchester. It was statelier, with a deeper weight of history than Shanklin. Its foundations were solid, not sandy. Its somber atmosphere of donnish sequestration suited him. He liked standing by the gate to the city watching the evening light fall against the buildings. He liked the grassy squares shaded by trees that seemed as if they had been made for the musings of deans and prebendaries. Beneath the old archways, and down the side alleys of the city, he poked around, past dark—one might now say Dickensian—doorways. The brass knockers in the shape of lions' and rams' heads had "a staid serious, nay almost awful quietness about them."[5]

"This Winchester is a place tolerably well suited to me," John wrote to George in September. "There is not one loom or anything like manufacturing beyond bread & butter in the whole City. . . . It is a respectable, ancient, aristocratical place—and moreover it contains a nunnery." He had decided, for the present, to spin nothing but text, but he was determined to prove that he was more than a "weaver boy."[6] The textile metaphors that enter his letters at this time were, in fact, topical.

The newspapers had been broadcasting the dissatisfaction of unemployed textile workers throughout England ever since the Luddite riots of 1811. But on August 16, 1819, when John was in Winchester, things reached a breaking point. Sixty thousand unemployed textile workers from the manufacturing towns of northern England gathered for a meeting at St. Peter's Field in Manchester. Low wages and chronic unemployment, the same problems that had been driving British emigrants overseas, had caused widespread hunger. Although the gathering was peaceable, the royal cavalry intervened, using violence to disperse the crowd. Eleven people were killed, hundreds more wounded, and the event became known as the Peterloo Massacre. Now that the wars with France and America had ended, the British government, it seemed, was waging war on its own people.

Leigh Hunt began his column "The Political Examiner" on Sunday, August 22, in indignation at the outrage. "The long irritated sufferings of the Reformers, and the eagerness of power to avail itself of the first opportunity to attack them, have at length given rise to a disturbance at Manchester," he wrote. Those who perpetuated the "monstrous and anticonstitutional inequalities" the reformers had been trying to change had good reason to fear the specter of revolution in reform.[7]

Shelley, meanwhile, from his self-imposed exile in Tuscany, sent irate poems attacking the "leech-like" rulers who starved and pillaged the people. He urged the men of England to stand up against oppression:

> Men of England, wherefore plough
> For the lords who lay ye low?
> Wherefore weave with toil and care
> The rich robes your tyrants wear? . . .

Questions such as these, the poet knew, had resulted in more than one recent revolution. Yet, whereas Shelley, the rebel aristocrat, might have plunged into the crowd himself to lead the revolt, Keats, whose brother had fled the country with the Manchester weavers, preferred his sanctuary in Winchester.

John liked the walk that led out through the cathedral yard, through the arched stone portal, to the nearby monastery of St. Cross. Like a wayfarer seeking alms from the cloistered monks, he went in pilgrimage

through the countryside surrounding Winchester. Across from the meadows by the River Itchen, in the valley beneath St. Catherine's Hill, he took
the winding country lane to the Hospital of the Brethren of St. Cross. The
crusading Knights Hospitaller, who besieged the Holy Land in red coats
blazoned with white crosses, had vowed to serve the poor and the sick. But
while they crusaded, the monks stayed home, raised hops and grain, and
doled out beer and bread—to the poor and the sick.

There, among the remains of Britain's feudal past—ancient hall, Norman church, Tudor cloister, Gothic tower—John wove images on his own
"sombre loom":

> I look'd around upon the carved sides
> Of an old sanctuary, with roof august,
> Builded so high, it seem'd that filmed clouds
> Might spread beneath, as o'er the stars of heaven;
> So old the place was, I remembered none
> The like upon the earth; what I had seen
> Of grey cathedrals, buttress'd walls, rent towers,
> The superannuations of sunk realms,
> Or nature's rocks toil'd hard in waves and winds,
> Seem'd but the faulture of decrepit things
> To that eternal domed monument.
> Upon the marble at my feet there lay
> Store of strange vessels, and large draperies,
> Which needs had been of dyed asbestus wove,
> Or in that place the moth could not corrupt,
> So white the linen; so, in some, distinct
> Ran imageries from a sombre loom.

It *was* a somber loom at the end of that summer. Staring at such scenes of
colossal, superhuman loss through the eyes of the speaker in *The Fall of
Hyperion* was draining. By candlelight, in his room by the cathedral, the
poet would often find himself fevered and weak from mental exertion. Yet,
the intensity of his solitude was itself a form of compensation. If there were
now no kindred spirit to share his space of solitude, at least he did not have
to chatter. Instead, he wrote furious letters to his brother and sister-in-law
in America, his lover in Hampstead, his sister in Walthamstow, his editor,

his friends . . . Sometimes he hardly knew what he was saying. Fanatic, dreamer, poet: Who could tell?

There among venerable monuments of Britain's past, John steeped himself in Chaucer's Middle English, and in the fantastic archaisms of that marvelous boy, Chatterton, the "sleepless Soul that perish'd in its pride." John nourished his *own* "Pride and Obstinacy," measuring his worth not against nameless, carping reviewers but rather against English literary tradition. "Who would wish to be among the commonplace crowd of the little-famous? he wondered: Is this worth louting or playing the hypocrite for? To beg suffrages for a seat on the benches of a myriad aristocracy in Letters?" Yet Taylor, who had been advancing John money for his next book—the book to follow *Endymion*—was perhaps even more disturbed to hear his author *answer* his own questions thus: "so much as I am humbled by the genius above my grasp, am I exalted and look with hate and contempt upon the literary world."[8] Expecting, or perhaps not caring, to be understood, John added to these imprecations a request for more money.

Taylor forwarded John's letter, expressing contempt for the very readers who kept Taylor & Hessey in business, to his friend Woodhouse. Although prostrate with sickness, Woodhouse raised himself from his sickbed to explain that what Keats meant by "pride" was not personal pride or egotism, but a "literary Pride,—that disposition which arises out of a Consciousness of superior & improving poetical Powers, & which would keep him, even in his present state of comparative imperfectness, from writing so as to minister to the depraved taste of the age."[9] The poetic pride John Keats spoke of was akin to the pride Milton displays in *Reason of Church Government* when he scourges the corruption of the Anglican prelates, another "myriad aristocracy." Woodhouse agreed that the public was more indebted to Keats for his poetry than Keats was to them, and he enclosed a fifty-pound note for Taylor to send to the young poet in his pride.

John was debating which of his poems to include in his next book. "Isabella; or, The Pot of Basil" and "The Eve of St. Agnes" both seemed too inexperienced, too Gothic. Rather than admiring Porphyro for his boldness, readers would laugh at him, call him a silly boy, and say that he had piled Madeline's table with as many sweets and delicacies—and as insubstantial—as the poet had stuffed his book with. John was less worried about *Lamia,* whose heroine is undoubtedly his best. She is also, despite all her magic, the most profoundly human—perhaps of *all* his characters, with the exception of the poet? dreamer? fanatic? in *The Fall of Hyperion.*

John identified with Lamia's raw vulnerability. She, too, was a loner in need of human connection, a creature of self-transformation, and a chameleon. Had the poet's attitude toward French been better, he might even have said, in the spirit of Gustave Flaubert, "Lamia, c'est moi." Lamia, having filled the world around her with beauty, meets her death at the hands of a merciless public who cannot appreciate her genius. Woodhouse recognized *Lamia* as a poem in which Keats "wipes the Cits"—the bourgeoisie, or "gossip rout," as Keats calls them, who in failing to perceive the sublimity of the heroine destroy her.[10] Her wealth is not theirs, and they cannot understand "whence all this mighty cost and blaze of wealth could spring."

In some lines that Keats toned down in the published version, the narrator chides the title character's lover, Lycius, for subjecting her to public censure. "O senseless Lycius! Dolt! Fool! Madman! Lout! / Why would you murder happiness like yours, / And show to common eyes these secret bowers?"[11] When his guests show up at his palace for his marriage feast, they do not know what to make of what they find there: Lamia has transformed every nook and crevice of the palace into a thing of stunning beauty. "The herd approach'd; and each guest, with busy brain, / Arriving at the portal, gaz'd amain, / And enter'd marveling." The hoi polloi in *Lamia* are an image of the poet's own audience.

John wrote *Lamia* in the summer of 1819 in light of the cynical attitude expressed in recent reviews of *Endymion.* Girding his loins for his next book of poems, he not only crafted the poem in the Augustan verse style of Pope, but he also infused it with the skepticism of writers like Lord Byron and Jane Austen, who countered sentimentality with the economics of the marriage market. *Love in a hut, with water and a crust, / Is—Love, forgive us!— cinders, ashes, dust.* So says the narrator of *Lamia* at the start of the second book. One cannot live on love. But Lamia herself is a dreamer, and she does not hear the narrator—any more than the allegorical figures of Love, Poetry, and Ambition hear the speaker in John's "Ode on Indolence."

Brilliant as Lamia is, she lacks the emotional sophistication to know that she cannot be everything to her lover. Her effort to imprison him in love and to gratify his every desire inevitably results in the destruction of their love affair. "Pleasure and pain are so intimately connected," Bailey once said, "that the sweets of the one cannot be tasted without a dash of the bitters of the other." Lamia is mistaken in the assumption that, when it comes to love, more bliss is better. What she discovers in trying to "unperplex bliss from its neighbour pain" is that removing pain from the intoxicating brew of love does not increase, but rather diminishes, love's power. *Oh! the sweetness of the pain!*[12] John's passion for Fanny Brawne only flamed the brighter for every pang that she caused him. Lycius shares responsibility with Lamia, though, for killing love with a wedding.

If John hoped that *Lamia* would appeal to a wider audience, he was also counting less on his poetry than on his tragedy to save him. He needed *Otho the Great* to redeem his reputation and his purse. Perhaps Brown's elephants would do the trick. Perhaps they would dispose their audience more favorably toward those giants he cared more about, the Titans in the *Hyperion* poems. But then, at the end of August, John received the bad news that Edmund Kean would spend the season in America.

John and Brown would submit their drama to Drury Lane Theatre anyway, and although the theater would accept it for production, it could not be staged there until the following season, or the next. John could not wait that long. He and Brown would revise and send the play to Covent Garden, where it would be speedily rejected. Brown would learn that it had never been "unrolled." *Otho the Great* would not be staged until November 26, 1950.

Life was a seesaw. And by September 1819 John had fallen to the ground. He described to George the feeling of being stuck there, "in that uneasy position where the seat slants so abominably." He still had unpaid bills from the previous season and a "very long standing" debt to Dr. Solomon Sawrey, who had treated him for venereal disease. He hoped that Haslam would pay Dr. Sawrey, for "My Character with him must be so low that I really should not like to meet him." John, now living on the charity of Brown, did not imagine that his finances could get much worse. But on Friday, the tenth of September, a letter arrived from George that sent him flying back on the night coach to London, with an urgent message to deliver to Richard Abbey.[13]

Past the Falls

Things were not looking as promising for George and Georgiana once they passed the falls of the Ohio. The cabins were more primitive than the ones they had seen coming downriver. Some had no windows. Some had only holes in the roof to let out smoke. Most had cats-and-clay chimneys made of twigs that caught fire and clay that crumbled onto the hearth. The couple may have wondered what kind of a place they had gotten into—if not into the heart of darkness, then certainly the heart of the wild, unbroken West.

Boys on the banks of the river smoked cigars, and mothers nursed their infants while puffing on white clay pipes. "Every log Cabin is swarming with half-naked children," Elias Pym Fordham noticed in 1817. "Boys of 18 build huts, marry, and raise hogs and children at about the same expence." Many came down to the river to bathe. On his way to the English Prairie, John Woods observed: "They do not appear healthy; but they look happy, rolling in the water and dirt. We often saw very little boys swimming in the river, sometimes leading others that could not walk."[14]

Perhaps, had Georgiana known what pioneer life in the Western Country would be like, she might not have left Westminster. She had begun to despair of finding any cultured, even well-mannered people in the West. Men stabbed at their meat in the taverns with knives as if they were still in the Dark Ages. Whiskey was cheap, brawls and duels common. It was not unheard of for men in Kentucky to conceal dirks, or daggers, in their walking sticks. Georgiana had given up trying to keep the hem of her skirts clean. In some respects, the falls of the Ohio resembled *the* Fall: from Eden into a rude and rugged reality.

When Charles Dickens took a steamboat up the Mississippi to Illinois in 1842, he fictionalized his experience in *The Life and Adventures of Martin Chuzzlewit,* whose narrator describes the disorientation of the experience of advancing farther and farther from all things familiar:

> At first they parted with some of their passengers once or twice a day, and took in others to replace them. But by degrees, the towns upon their route became more thinly scattered; and for many hours together they would see no other habitations than the huts of the wood-cutters, where the vessel stopped for fuel. Sky, wood, and water all the livelong day; and heat that blistered everything it touched.
>
> On they toiled through great solitudes, where the trees upon the banks grew thick and close; and floated in the stream; and held up shrivelled arms from out the river's depths; and slid down from the margin of

the land, half growing, half decaying, in the miry water. On through the weary day and melancholy night: beneath the burning sun, and in the mist and vapour of the evening: on, until return appeared impossible, and restoration to their home a miserable dream.

They had now but few people on board, and these few were as flat, as dull, and stagnant, as the vegetation that oppressed their eyes. No sound of cheerfulness or hope was heard; no pleasant talk beguiled the tardy time; no little group made common cause against the dull depression of the scene. But that, at certain periods, they swallowed food together from a common trough, it might have been old Charon's boat, conveying melancholy shades to judgment.

At length they drew near New Thermopylae; where, that same evening, Mrs. Hominy would disembark. A gleam of comfort sunk into Martin's bosom when she told him this. Mark needed none; but he was not displeased.

It was almost night when they came alongside the landing-place. A steep bank with an hotel like a barn on the top of it; a wooden store or two; and a few scattered sheds.

"You sleep here to-night, and go on in the morning, I suppose, ma'am?" said Martin.

"Where should I go on to?" cried the mother of the modern Gracchi.

"To New Thermopylae."

"My! ain't I there?" said Mrs. Hominy.

Martin looked for it all round the darkening panorama, but he couldn't see it, and was obliged to say so.

"Why that's it!" cried Mrs. Hominy, pointing to the sheds just mentioned.

"*That!*" exclaimed Martin.

"Ah! that; and work it which way you will, it whips Eden," said Mrs. Hominy, nodding her head with great expression.[15]

Martin Chuzzlewit is on his way to Eden, a settlement modeled on the Looking Glass Prairie, thirty miles south of the Cockney Pioneers, which Dickens had visited in Illinois. Although Dickens approached the much-vaunted prairielands from the south, while George and Georgiana Keats traveled west, their destination was ultimately the same. Another cartoon of the English Prairie, which appeared a few years before Dickens's satire of Eden in *Martin Chuzzlewit,* depicts a family in a broken-down covered wagon, returning from "Edensburgh." An emigrant headed west toward the very place they have left says, "I am going to Illinois!" The man on the nag pulling the wagon back in the other direction replies that, alas, "I have been!!" So much for Eden after the falls.

Dickens's fictional river town of "New Thermopylae"—like the French settlement of Alexandria, located at the mouth of the Big Scioto River on the Ohio—symbolized the dreams of European emigrants who hoped to start civilization anew in the Western Country of America. Dickens continues:

A flat morass, bestrewn with fallen timber; a marsh on which the good growth of the earth seemed to have been wrecked and cast away, that from its decomposing ashes vile and ugly things might rise; where the very trees took the aspect of huge weeds, begotten of the slime from which they sprung, by the hot sun that burnt them up; where fatal maladies, seeking whom they might infect, came forth at night in misty shapes, and creeping out upon the water, hunted them like spectres until day; where even the blessed sun, shining down on festering elements of corruption and disease, became a horror; this was the realm of Hope through which they moved.

At last they stopped. At Eden too. The waters of the Deluge might have left it but a week before: so choked with slime and matted growth was the hideous swamp which bore that name.

There being no depth of water close in shore, they landed from the vessel's boat, with all their goods beside them. There were a few log-houses visible among the dark trees; the best, a cow-shed or a rude stable. But for the wharves, the market-place, the public buildings!

"Here comes an Edener," said Mark. "He'll get us help to carry these things up. Keep a good heart, sir. Hallo there!"

The man advanced toward them through the thickening gloom, very slowly: leaning on a stick. As he drew nearer, they observed that he was pale and worn, and that his anxious eyes were deeply sunken in his head. His dress of homespun blue hung about him in rags; his feet and head were bare. He sat down on a stump half-way, and beckoned them to come to him. When they complied, he put his hand upon his side as if in pain, and while he fetched his breath stared at them, wondering.

"Strangers!" he exclaimed, as soon as he could speak.

"The very same," said Mark. "How are you, sir?"

"I've had the fever very bad," he answered faintly. "I haven't stood upright these many weeks. Those are your notions I see," pointing to their property.

"Yes, sir," said Mark, "they are. You couldn't recommend us some one as would lend a hand to help carry 'em up to the—to the town, could you, sir?"

"My eldest son would do it if he could," replied the man; "but to-day he has his chill upon him, and is lying wrapped up in the blankets. My youngest died last week."[16]

Yellow fever, typhoid, and ague (the catchall phrase for any sickness with symptoms of fever and shivering) afflicted all the river towns. In his *American Notes,* Dickens described Cairo, Illinois, at the junction of the Ohio and Mississippi rivers, as built "on ground so flat and low and marshy, that at certain seasons of the year it . . . lies a breeding-place of fever, ague, and death." Cairo was not too far from Shawneetown, whose land office sold sections of the English Prairie. In reality, Dickens suggests, Eden was a "dismal swamp, on which the half-built houses rot away."[17] The account might seem exaggerated, but it is not too far from what other travel writers had described.

During the seasonal floods, people climbed to the top of their homes, or else retreated to higher ground inland, only to see their belongings floating away down the river. "This place I account as a phenomenon evincing the pertinacious adhesion of the human animal to the spot where it has once fixed itself," Morris Birkbeck claimed of Shawneetown. "The Ohio with its annual overflowings is unable to wash away the inhabitants."[18] Sickness would also be a problem in Louisville. In 1819, a few months after the birth of George and Georgiana's first child, both mother and daughter would contract a bilious fever that almost put an abrupt end to George's American experiment.

At Louisville, a bed of limestone obstructed the river current, causing the water to swell and shoot down through gaps in the stone. When the water was low, sharp edges of rock sliced through the surface of the river. At high water, one could hear the crashing of the rapids from six miles away. The declivity itself was not much—twenty-three feet over the two miles from Louisville to Shippingport at the bottom of the falls—but given the gradual descent of the river up till then (about five inches per mile) the sudden surge of water, combined with the jutting and menacing rocks, proved a threat.

> As we go—as we go
> Down the O-hi-o,
> There's a tight place at Louisville,
> You know, boys, know.[19]

The channels through which the boats needed to pass were called "chutes" (or "shoots"). In 1818, there were three main chutes: the Kentucky chute, the Indiana (or "Indian") chute, and the Middle chute. The width of the flatboats on the Ohio River was standardized at fifteen feet so that the boats could make it through the two large rocks that protruded at either end of the Indiana chute. The Indiana was of course on the Indiana side; the Middle chute lay between Rock and Goose islands; and the Kentucky chute lay between Goose Island and the Kentucky shore. Most pilots preferred the Indian chute, since it did not have any steep, sudden falls. *Its* danger consisted in the sharp spines of limestone that cut through the water as it shot, spewed, and spurted out between the rocks.

The law required that all vessels descending the Ohio stop at Louisville, or at Jeffersonville (a mile across the river on the Indiana side), to pick up a pilot. These boatmen were familiar with the treacherous terrain of the riverbed by the falls. Most boats stopped at Louisville to unload passengers and cargo; at Shippingport, two miles downstream on the Kentucky side, the boats would reload and drop off the pilots. The dock owners charged a fee for loading, based on weight. John Anthony Tarascon's wharves at Shippingport and at Rock Island charged a docking fee of twenty-five cents per day for vessels under fifty tons, and up to a dollar and twenty-five cents for steamboats. He charged a penny for every hundred pounds of cargo that his dockworkers loaded or unloaded. People could fish for free on Rock Island with a pole, but to fish with a net he charged ten dollars a day.[20]

Whoever controlled the falls controlled the river trade. The towns on either side of the river were planning to dig canals to circumvent the rapids. The Kentucky legislature had incorporated a company to dig a canal, starting a little below the mouth of Beargrass Creek, just above Louis-

ville, to come out below Shippingport: a project they estimated would require $252,638. Across the way, the people at Jeffersonville would hold a
lottery to raise money for the Ohio Canal Company. One writer in the *Louisville Public Advertiser* would compare the two rivals for river business to
the Guelphs and the Ghibellines, warring factions in medieval Italy that
figure prominently in Dante's *Inferno* and provide the subject for Mary
Shelley's *Valperga; or, The Life and Adventures of Castruccio, Prince of Lucca*
(1823).[21]

When George and Georgiana first saw Louisville, it was a bustling
river town with a population of five thousand. The printer James Francis
Moore, on Main Street, issued checks for the Bank of Louisville that depicted a woman in a high-waisted gown, seated before a schooner on a pile
of crates and barrels. Yet the Ohio snaked too much for sails to be of use,
and one suspects that the printer was either using an imported stamp, or
that the emigrant had not yet mentally adapted to the reality of her new life
in the West. "Here I met with many English families," William Tell Harris
wrote when he visited Louisville in September 1818, "some whose views
were directed to St. Louis and the Missouri, others to Illinois, and some
who being disappointed in their expectations of [the] English Prairie, are
undecided where to settle, or whether to return."[22] George was not ready to
return; nor had he decided where to settle.

Shippingport, next door to Louisville, was the home of James Berthoud,
formerly Hervé de Belisle, Marquis de Saint-Pié, a refugee from the French
Revolution. He had purchased the town fifteen years earlier, and he now
presided over the shipyard and docks with his son, Nicholas Augustus.
Ever since 1816, when Nicholas married Eliza Bakewell, Nicholas and
John James Audubon (who likewise anglicized his given name, Jean-
Jacques Fougère Audubon) had been legally related. Eliza's older sister,
Lucy Green Bakewell, was Audubon's wife. As European society started to
thin out past the falls, the network of relations among the Berthouds, the
Audubons, the Bakewells, and the Keatses would start to thicken.

Nicholas Berthoud and his father shipped dry goods on commission,
mainly between Louisville and New Orleans. A typical inventory at their
warehouse in Shippingport would have included: cases of claret; clay pipes;
Madeira wine; prime whiskey; sugar; puncheons of fourth-proof Jamaica
rum; kegs of spiced salmon; gunpowder; cut nails; Spanish whiting; casks
of bottled London porter; tons of Swedish iron; white and pig lead; barrels

of rosin used in glues, soaps, and varnishes; bacon; beef; lard; flour; and that colorless astringent, alum, used to purify water, size paper, cure leather, and make dyes, fireproofing, and medicine.[23]

Before moving to Shippingport, the elder Berthoud had worked for Louis Anastasius Tarascon and John Anthony Tarascon, wealthy French shippers who had fled France for America during the French Revolution, and who also owned wharves in Shippingport. After working for the Tarascon brothers in Philadelphia, Old Berthoud had opened the firm "John A. Tarascon Brothers, James Berthoud, & Company" in Pittsburgh. There, he built boats and shipped merchandise down the Ohio River into the interior of the country. Eventually, he carried his expertise into the Western Country and built his docks at Shippingport. By the time George and Georgiana had arrived, Old Berthoud was, as Thomas Hulme remarked, "indeed, a great shipper, though at a thousand miles from the sea."[24]

The Berthouds' home in Shippingport may not have compared with the Berthouds' French château, but it was richly appointed. Old Berthoud and his wife, Marie-Anne-Julia, former *dame d'honneur* to Marie Antoinette, liked to entertain as much as did their French relation, Audubon, a hundred-and-some-odd miles down the river in Red Banks, Kentucky. The settlement at Red Banks was also called Henderson, after Colonel Richard Henderson, who had purchased most of Kentucky, and parts of Tennessee, from the Cherokee Nation at the start of the American Revolution. Henderson had hired Daniel Boone to blaze the Great Wilderness Road to the West. Henderson was the name associated with the mill.

Audubon, who drifted downriver from Shippingport to Red Banks at the same time of year as George and Georgiana, tended to view landscape through the highly romantic—and highly aestheticized—lens that tinted his entire outlook on life. His description may say more about the man George and Georgiana were soon to encounter than about the river or its surroundings:

> It was in the month of October. The autumnal tints already decorated the
> shores of that queen of rivers, the Ohio. Every tree was hung with long
> and flowing festoons of different species of vines, many loaded with clus-
> tered fruits of varied brilliancy, their rich bronzed carmine mingling
> beautifully with the yellow foliage, which now predominated over the yet

green leaves, reflecting more lively tints from the clear stream than ever landscape painter portrayed or poet imagined.

The days were yet warm. The sun had assumed the rich and glowing hue which at that season produces the singular phenomenon called there the "Indian Summer." The moon had rather passed the meridian of her grandeur.

As night came, sinking in darkness the broader portions of the river, our minds became affected by strong emotions, and wandered far beyond the present moments. The tinkling of bells told us that the cattle which bore them were gently roving from valley to valley in search of food, or returning to their distant homes. The hooting of the Great Owl, or the muffled noise of its wings as it sailed smoothly over the stream, were matters of interest to us; so was the sound of the boatman's horn, as it came winding more and more softly from afar. When daylight returned, many songsters burst forth with echoing notes, more and more mellow to the listening ear. Here and there the lonely cabin of a squatter struck the eye, giving note of commencing civilization. The crossing of the stream by a deer foretold how soon the hills would be covered with snow.

Many sluggish flat-boats we overtook and passed: some laden with produce from the different head-waters of the small rivers that pour their tributary streams into the Ohio; others, of less dimensions, crowded with emigrants from distant parts, in search of a new home.[25]

Evansville, Indiana, where Audubon ends his account, sat high on a bluff, on the northern side of the river, at the mouth of Pigeon Creek. From Evansville, the river sagged south in the shape of a noose toward Red Banks, Kentucky, on the southern side at the bottom of the noose—and the image is not inappropriate. Flocks of wild turkeys, pigeons, and other birds drawn to the creek attracted the turkey buzzards that cleaned up the carrion, which otherwise could cause disease. For this reason, along the Mississippi, it was a crime to shoot the buzzards. In the forests of Indiana slightly north of Evansville, dozens of English emigrants who had originally planned to settle with the Cockney Pioneers in Illinois had begun a separate settlement. What had happened?

The demon of discord had entered Eden. The Cockney Pioneers Birkbeck and Flower had laid out separate towns, about a mile and a half to three miles (depending on who is telling the story) from each other. Morris

Birkbeck, on the west side of the divide, named his settlement Wanborough; and George Flower, on the east, named his Albion. When George Keats wrote to his brother about the rift between the Cockney Pioneers, John vaguely remembered having met a friend of Eliza Julia Andrews, the young woman who seemed to be at the center of things. "Any third person would think I was addressing myself to a Lover of Scandal," John wrote to Georgiana after hearing about the squabble from George. "But we know we do not love scandal but fun, and if Scandal happens to be fun that is no fault of ours. There were some very pretty pickings for me in George's Letters about the Prairie Settlement, if I had had any taste to turn them to account in England."[26] Unfortunately, John did *not* make use of his brother's version of the story about what had happened on the English Prairie, and since Birkbeck never wrote about it, we must rely on Flower.

Flower claimed that when he showed up in the summer of 1818 with his party of emigrants, he was surprised to find no cabins, no gardens, no squares, no wells, no orchards—nothing that the partners had discussed Birkbeck's preparing while Flower rounded up settlers in London. Birkbeck had his shoddily constructed "barracks," which he hired backwoodsmen to put up while he built his fences, but Flower found nothing for himself and his family beyond an isolated cabin, without doors or windows, standing in the midst of a prairie, on dirt. After unloading their bedding, utensils, bridles, saddles, and other objects hauled over from England, Flower mounted his horse and rode over to see his partner. He found him sitting beneath the shade of an oak tree outside his cabin.

As Flower was preparing to dismount, Birkbeck got up and crossed in front of his partner's horse, looking "pale, haggard, and agitated." He was about to go into his cabin. Flower tried to speak to him, but Birkbeck shook his head and said, "No, we can not meet, I can not see you." Staring in wonder, Flower protested: they *had* to talk! Their affairs were unsettled, their plans, their investments . . . But Birkbeck was resolved. "'Stop, stop,' said he, 'let a third person arrange all.'" Flower rode off, thinking, "So be it." The two men never spoke again. Flower's father would thereafter avoid seeing Birkbeck, "because, if I came near, I must lay violent hands on him; I must knock him down. . . . a reconciliation is impossible."[27] What had happened?

Eliza Julia Andrews, second daughter of the Reverend Mordecai Andrews and Elizabeth Rutt of Eigeshall, Essex, had met Birkbeck at Richard

Flower's estate, Marden, in Hertfordshire, while the Cockney Pioneer was trying to convince the elder Flower to emigrate. Andrews was in her mid-twenties, and Birkbeck twenty-eight years older. Birkbeck's daughters, Elizabeth and Prudence, were around Eliza Andrews's age, and they invited her to join them on their American adventure. She came, and in Virginia, the party met up with Flower. The Cockney Pioneers then traveled over the mountains and west along the Ohio River on horseback.

On July 15, 1817, Flower shocked his partner by asking him to stand in as father of the bride at his wedding in Vincennes, Indiana. In the belief that Flower, who was twenty-nine and separated but not divorced from his wife, Jane Dawson, *was* in fact divorced—and wishing to avoid scandal should Flower carry out his threat to live with Andrews on the English Prairie out of wedlock—Birkbeck agreed. But he had covert, perhaps not so covert, romantic feelings for Andrews himself, and when Flower returned to London to recruit more settlers, leaving a pregnant Andrews in Chambersburg, Pennsylvania, Birkbeck brooded over the changed state of affairs. He discovered, or decided, that Andrews was the reason Flower had left his wife, and that his partner was therefore an adulterer—and now, *with Birkbeck's own support,* a bigamist.[28]

The partners did not quarrel outright, but the split between them was a fact, and the result was not good for either. The smith at Wanborough had no iron, and the settlers at Albion had no water. The wheelwright, disappointed with his diet of "reasty" (rancid) bacon, spent his afternoons hunting and drinking whiskey. The saddler and the collar-maker took orders, but gave the products of their labor away to anyone who showed up with cash. "Precious miserable people at the Prairie," John wrote to Georgiana after hearing George's account of the English Prairie.[29]

Before the dispute between the Cockney Pioneers, Birkbeck had planned to profit from the sale of his land, at the rate of twenty-five or fifty cents an acre, but he had learned better and lowered his price. By the time George and Georgiana arrived in the Western Country, he had been reduced to giving away lots of land that seemed unsalable. His first lesson came in the form of Saunders Hornbrook, Jr., the son of Saunders Hornbrook, a wealthy English manufacturer from Devonshire. When Hornbrook Junior arrived to purchase land for his family, he learned what George Keats had already discovered in the book Taylor had given him: the Cockney Pioneers were limiting the sale of land on the English Prairie to a

single section of land (640 acres). To make matters worse, Birkbeck was as-
signing spots on the prairie to settlers, rather than giving them a choice of
where to settle. He had selected a spot for the Hornbrooks that was twenty
miles from the nearest village. Hornbrook Junior decided to find his own
land, and after "fourteen days of constant fag, sometimes one and sometimes two meals a day, sleeping in a barn or cabin at night," as Saunders
Senior reported, he located 960 acres of land (six sections) near Evansville,
which he registered with the land office in Vincennes.[30]

Hornbrook Senior then sold his foundry and woolen mills, and headed
with his family to "Saundersville," Indiana. On the way there, he met James
Maidlow, Jr., a farmer who had been unable to turn a profit back in England and was now traveling alone to the English Prairie. Maidlow's wife
had refused to leave England. Hornbrook Senior and his family traveled
together with Maidlow Junior to Wheeling, Virginia, where they fitted up
an ark and floated downriver to Evansville, Indiana. They arrived around
the same time that George Flower landed at Shawneetown with his party
of Cockney Pioneers. Maidlow then purchased 960 acres of land adjacent to
the Hornbrooks. Another man of means, John Ingle, Jr., who had traveled
with his family in the *Ann Maria* (with Flower) from Liverpool, had purchased more land in the woods of Indiana near Saundersville.[31]

Forty miles east of Saundersville, in a windowless cabin with a bear-
skin door, on Anderson's Creek, a man and his wife had been living in the
area for two years, girdling trees, grubbing roots, and dropping pump-
kin and corn seeds into the earth. It was hard to make a go of it, but the
man, Thomas, and his wife, Nancy, had their nine-year-old son to help. His
name was Abraham Lincoln, future president of the United States.[32]

Girdling trees was the easiest option for clearing the land in the timber
belt of Indiana. The trees were enormous, often twenty-four feet in cir-
cumference, and John Ingle, Jr., for instance, working with more skill and
energy than most, found that he had cleared only seventeen acres by November. The "barrens" of Indiana, by contrast, while barren of trees, had
soil that was "as thin as a clap-board or bear-skin" (to quote one local
inhabitant). It was difficult for even an experienced farmer working a
quarter-section of land to grow enough food to maintain a family.[33] Making
a fortune that way seemed out of the question.

George and Georgiana knew little about all this when they snaked
down on the river from Evansville to Red Banks. In the distance, they could

see Audubon's grist- and sawmill looming high on the river, hissing steam from its exhausts and puffing black smoke. Its whipsawed yellow weatherboarding sat on rough joists above a thick foundation of stone. Yet, Red Banks, which was not a wheat-growing area, could not provide much grist. Nor did the small backwoods outpost, of about a hundred buildings, have much use for lumber. It already had a jail, a courthouse, at least one tavern (all necessary in the West), and, next to Audubon's mill, a warehouse stocked with hogsheads of stemmed, dark-leaf tobacco from the neighboring plantations.

Before the steam-powered grist- and sawmill reared its jaundiced head in Red Banks, Audubon had been successful. He was a charismatic and convincing salesman, and he sold real estate as well as dry goods. But he had been struggling at the mill, and his wealth had disappeared. He had sold off his property, exhausted his liquid resources, and borrowed money from friends and family. He hated the dark, Satanic mill and all that it stood for, and he was sorry that he had let his brother-in-law Tom Bakewell talk him into building it. When George and Georgiana saw the mill from the river, they, too, were far from imagining the devastating role it would play in their futures.

Harmony

George's daughter Emma Frances later claimed that when her father first arrived in the Western Country, he traveled to Harmony, Indiana, with George Flower, and then returned to Red Banks, where he and Georgiana lived for a while with the Audubons. Although Emma could have been confusing Harmony with Albion, it is also possible that she was accurately describing George's overland travels—visiting the Cockney Pioneers on the English Prairie and then riding back down to the Ohio River with Flower, through Harmony, to Red Banks. George and Georgiana would, indeed, spend a few months with the Audubons, while George pondered how best to invest his money.[34]

The Cockney Pioneers on the English Prairie depended on the German settlers at Harmony, who sold them bushels of corn and flour, barrels of whiskey, yards of cotton cloth, hardware, and other supplies. "The Government, Arrangement, & results produced at this Place are truly astonishing," said William Hall, one of Birkbeck's neighbors, in 1821. "All their

operations are conducted with uncommon Order, Industry, & Neatness."
Harmony, Indiana, was just across the Wabash River from the English settlement in Illinois, and was reputed to be, in Richard Flower's words, the
"wonder of the west."[35]

George Flower claimed that the Harmonites' prices were inflated, that
his first bill from them amounted to eleven thousand dollars, and that in
the six years from 1818 to 1824 the pioneers on the English Prairie paid the
Harmonites $150,000 in cash.[36] And they did not provide a delivery service:
the Cockney Pioneers would have to row the supplies up the Wabash River
in canoes or in skiffs to the Bon Pas River, where they would unload, and
then drag or cart them about a dozen miles across the prairie. The canoe
trip was only twelve miles, but it could take as many hours. The goods had
to be hauled in batches from the riverbank, and while it was being carted,
the remaining supplies had to be disguised, or guarded from wild animals
and hunters.

Like the Cockney Pioneers, the Harmonites were driven by social ide-
als, but there was one key difference between them: Harmony was a religious colony. Johann Georg Rapp, a minister from Württemberg who had
split off from the Lutheran Church, had led his followers across the Atlantic to America in search of the Promised Land. In imitation of Acts 4:32,
they had pooled their resources: "And the multitude of them that believed
were of one heart and of one soul: neither said any of them that aught of the
things which he possessed was his own; but they had all things common."
In 1805, they purchased land across the Monongahela River from Pittsburgh, and named their town Harmony, after the ideal they hoped to embody. They shared ovens and brewed beer for common use. They ate at the
same time of day in the spirit of community. And around a small domed
temple, which was rough outside but smooth within, they planted a symbolic labyrinth of hedgerows: the inner temple represented at once the difficulty of arriving at harmony and its beauty once achieved.[37]

Embracing celibacy, the Harmonites then began channeling their energies into work—plowing fields, raising sheep and cattle, grinding wheat,
brewing beer, distilling wine, curing leather, dying broadcloth, pressing
pumpkin-seed oil, and otherwise preparing for the coming millennium. Johann Rapp did not require sexual abstinence, but his religious creed encouraged it. "People see the fine fields of the Harmonites, but, the prospect
comes damped with the idea of bondage and celibacy," Thomas Hulme re-

marked of the German settlers after they had moved to Indiana. The colony imposed certain restrictions so that when babies came, they came only every few years, "in little flocks, all within the same month, perhaps, like a farmer's lambs."[38] From an initial nine log cabins, Harmony grew quickly, and before long, the Harmonites were filling their storehouses for the winter with thousands of bushels of rye, wheat, Indian corn, potatoes, barley, and oats, and thousands of pounds of flax and hemp. Some left the group to try their luck as independent farmers farther west, but others came to replace them.

When Johann Rapp sold Harmony in 1814 at a nine-fold profit, the Harmonites drifted downriver to the banks of the Wabash. From a small brush camp, their settlement grew, and by 1818 rows of Lombardy poplars lined the Main Street. Every home had flower as well as vegetable gardens, which made Harmony stand out against its more prosaic neighbors. "A garden is the last thing that is thought of by the generality of the Americans," John Woods observed.[39] On the town common, fruit trees enclosed vegetable gardens, which in turn enclosed a botanic garden that the doctor had arranged according to the Linnaean system. Besides a garden, each family kept chickens and a cow. The bells could be heard tinkling as the cows ambled back from the fields in the evenings.

While most of the Harmonites spoke only German, the innkeeper, who kept a tavern at the southern end of town, catered to English clients. When Hulme visited, he and his family found "every thing we wanted for ourselves and our horses, and all very clean and nice, besides many good things we did not expect, such as beer, porter, and even wine, all made within the Society, and very good indeed." Across from the tavern, a general store sold merchandise that Harmonites could purchase with money withdrawn from the bank—at certain times and under certain conditions. Frederick Rapp, the minister's son, handled the town's finances and kept all accounts in his name. Anyone who deposited money at the time of joining the community could demand it back upon leaving, "but *without interest*."[40]

Every evening, the white-haired pastor held divine service in the church at the north end of town. "The old man's face beamed with intelligence," John Melish observed when he met Johann Rapp in Pennsylvania, "and he appeared to have a consciousness of having performed a good work."[41] Wearing a plain blue cap and linsey-woolsey coat, Rapp would sit behind a table on a raised stage, and preach to the assembly. Despite his modest demeanor, he delivered his sermons with passion, holding his congregation in rapt attention, sometimes for hours. The Harmonites would occasionally kneel in prayer, but most often they bent forward in an attitude of submission. After the service, Rapp would dismiss the assembly with a short benediction.

At night, a pair of men would keep watch over the town on a rotating basis. Every hour, from ten until two, they would cry out, "Again a day is past, and a step made nearer to our end; *our time runs away, and the joys of Heaven are our reward.*" At three, they would cry, "Again a night is past, and the morning is come; our time runs away, and the joys of Heaven are our reward." The Harmonites liked music as much as flowers, and during harvest season they would awake to the sound of French horns and march out to the fields in costumes like those of peasants on the Rhine. The men came first, followed by married women, and then unmarried women, who wore hair ornaments of striped cedar-wood. Richard Flower witnessed such a procession on the prairie, led by a band of musicians.[42]

Special groups of laborers carried out the town's main industries under the supervision of senior foremen. Tanners, distillers, hatmakers, millers, tinners, turners, blacksmiths, carpenters, masons, and other manual laborers answered to the foremen, who in turn answered to Johann Rapp, who made all final decisions on behalf of the townspeople. "Here is a large body of people, active, industrious, possessed of much physical strength," William Harris remarked, "yet unanimously resigning all their individual energies to the despotic control and government of one man, whose word and nod are as imperative as the mandate of the Russian autocrat; yet he has no life-guards, no armed force, no bastile, no executioner, to give efficacy to his command."[43] From the observatory at the top of his brick house by the church, Rapp monitored the goings-on in the town.

In the end, Harmony would fare better than its English neighbors on the prairie. In 1824, having shown how social harmony (and, Freud might add, sexual restraint) can translate into economic profit, Rapp would move the colony back to Pennsylvania, changing its name to "Economy." Richard Flower would help Rapp to negotiate the sale of the town to Robert Owen, a textile manufacturer and father of the more famous social reformer Robert Dale Owen. One year after that, on June 4, 1825, as Birkbeck was riding back from a visit to Robert Owen in "New Harmony," the Cockney Pioneer, at age sixty-one, slipped on his horse and drowned at the confluence of the Fox and the Wabash rivers, bringing his own social vision to a tragic, unexpected end. William Hall described "the melancholy Catastrophe" of the Cockney Pioneer whom he had followed to Illinois:

> On his arriving at Fox River with his third Son (Bradford) they found the Flat in which they expected to be ferried over had been taken away & entered the water on their Horses with the intention of Swimming over. Bradfords Horse plunged & threw him in the water being a good Swimmer he altho' incumbered with a great coat & very weak from recent illness had nearly reached the opposite shore when he heard his Fathers voice calling for assistance & turning himself round saw him struggling in the middle of the stream & returned to his assistance. Upon reaching him his Father caught hold of him & they both sunk together upon rising again he desi[red] his Father to take hold of his coat in another place which he did & both sunk again but Bradford alone rose & throwing himself upon his Back he floated & quite exhausted reached the Bank where after some time his cries bro[ugh]t a person to his assistance who endeavoured to recover the Body of his Father but in vain. It was not found till the day following when it was brought up with an Umbrella firmly grasped in the right hand.[44]

As his umbrella suggests, Morris Birkbeck, for all his enthusiasm about the English Prairie, remained an Englishman to the last. If he had any regrets about having left Wanborough, Surrey, for Wanborough, Illinois, he did not make them known. At the time he died he still had every expectation that within a few years he would be able to live in the style to which he had been accustomed, away from borough-mongering, pensioned aristocrats.

Until then, the Cockney Pioneer had his books, and his newspapers came in weekly, through Princeton, Indiana. True, the papers arrived from the east coast one month late, and from Europe even later than that, but Birkbeck was not holding his breath for significant change during his lifetime in the Old Country. While he turned out to be correct in his expectations, he did not know that his time would be cut short so soon, or that change would come so quickly. Birkbeck would drown a few years before the passing of the Reform Act in 1832, the political watershed in Great Britain.

The Harmonites may have proved what could be accomplished through a unified social vision, but the settlers on the English Prairie found it harder to corral their disparate beliefs. At first, an indifference to religion obviated any form of common worship. "When I arrived at Albion, a more disorganized, demoralized state of society never existed," Richard Flower lamented. The settlers spent Sundays target shooting and playing cricket. Often the Lord's Day ended "in riot and savage fighting." The elder Flower began to read scripture in the dissenting style in the marketplace himself, while his son enlisted an Englishman to read the Episcopalian service (the American version of the Anglican) to the settlers at Albion. On Sunday, April 25, 1820, Birkbeck, the Quaker who had left England to avoid paying tithes to the Church of England, would begin reading the Episcopal service at Wanborough. Flower Senior would observe, sarcastically (and before his son recruited "the gentleman from Guernsey" to do the same), that Birkbeck had turned Wanborough into "the seat of *orthodoxy*," leaving Albion "in the ranks of *heresy*."[45]

Taking a cue from Richard Flower, the London *Quarterly,* in a combined review of Birkbeck's *Letters from Illinois* and of other "Views, Visits, and Tours in North America," informed the British reading public that the settlers on the English Prairie scoffed at religion. The Cockney Pioneers "acknowledged no God but *interest,* no worship but that of *self*"; and beyond that, it was "a matter of perfect indifference to Mr. Morris Birkbeck whether he officiated as an 'orthodox divine,' or as an Imaun, Bonze, Lama, Fetish-man, or Mumbo-Jumbo." With thirty thousand acres of land to unload, he did not care what lies he promulgated to lure Englishmen to the American "land of Cocaigne."[46]

John wondered where George and Georgiana would find to worship in the West. Like the poet, Georgiana had been raised in the Church of England, and she would later keep a miniature red-leather Book of Common Prayer in a little tin box in her home in Louisville. George, who had been christened at St. Leonard's Shoreditch and confirmed by the Archbishop of Canterbury, would later become one of the original hundred and eighty-two subscribers of the first Episcopalian Christ Church in Louisville, which he provided the lumber to build in 1823.[47] Ultimately, George and Georgiana would both convert to Unitarianism, the faith common to English freethinkers with an interest in the American experiment—like Hazlitt, Coleridge, Priestley, and the Bakewells.

Unitarianism was also the faith of American Transcendentalists, from Ralph Waldo Emerson to James Freeman Clarke, and the latter would come to admire George Keats for being "too honest not to leave the popular and fashionable church for an unpopular faith, since this was more of a home to his mind." George's great-granddaughter Emma Speed Simpson left an account of how her pioneer ancestor had chosen the Unitarian religion: "George Keats was walking along the street when he came upon a group of little children playing on the sidewalk. Informed that there was a Sunday school picnic taking place in the woods near Louisville and that children of all denominations were included, he stopped when he saw some children: 'Why are you little children not at the picnic?' 'Oh, we are Unitarians and weren't invited.' George Keats was interested immediately. He made it his business to find out what Unitarians stood for, what they believed, and was so impressed by their doctrine that he soon became an ardent Unitarian."[48] Many of George's closest friends in Louisville would belong to the Unitarian faith. At the end of 1818, however, finding a place of religious worship was probably the last thing on George's mind. All uncertain about where he would wind up or what he would do, he had other, more immediately pressing concerns.

The Red Banks Trail

Audubon's cabin had shuttered windows and a wide front porch. It was set back from Second Street between Green and Elm in the center of Red Banks. The naturalist liked to spread his table with the bounty of the land, and in the pond behind his cabin, he kept wing-clipped geese, prairie hens, ducks, and turtles for his specialty, *soupe à la tortue*. He had a smokehouse, a pasture, a stable, and a game preserve. His ice-house provided ice to keep the water jug and the butter plate chilled, and in summer, his orchards provided cherries, peaches, and apples. Lucy made preserves and pies. *This* Frenchman liked cream with his strawberries.

When Flower's cousin Elias Pym Fordham visited Red Banks from Albion in the summer of 1818, he learned that Audubon would not hear of guests from the English Prairie putting up at the local tavern. He led him home and sent for his horses. Fordham had already eaten, but his gracious host handed around iced fruit and hot toddies. These ceremonies performed, he summoned a slave performing in the role of footman to usher the astonished guest to his room. The slave then stood in attendance, while another, serving as a maid, took Fordham's shirt and cravat to be cleaned.

Rather than being pestered by insects, Fordham spent the night in a bed with fresh linen, beneath mosquito nets. He marveled at the contrast between the Audubon cabin and "the dirty Ohio houses, and the Indiana and Illinois pigsties, in which men women and children wallow in promiscuous filth."[49]

The Audubons were used to hosting displaced emigrants at their tasteful cabin in the wilderness. The English Prairie, north of the river, was in no condition to accommodate new arrivals, and the Audubons had carpeted floors, furniture of walnut and cherry-wood, and bookshelves stocked with more than a hundred and fifty books, which was no small supply for a pioneer cabin on the western frontier. Lucy served tea from a silver tea set and displayed silver candlesticks on a linen tablecloth. She read books and played the piano, while Audubon drew, told stories, and played the flute and fiddle.[50]

No doubt, Audubon warned George Keats not only about conditions north of the river in Indiana and Illinois, but also about the dangers in getting there. Wolves, bears, panthers, and polecats prowled the woods on the road to Princeton, Indiana, a small settlement about the size of Henderson thirty miles east of the English Prairie, across the Wabash River. The road that led north from the Ohio River to Princeton was an Indian trail, the Red Banks Trail, which continued farther north to the old fur-trading outpost of Vincennes, Indiana. At places, the trail was merely a blazed path through the woods, marked by notches on the towering trees.

When William Faux stayed at Evansville in the autumn of 1819, he cowered in his bed as "the wolves . . . howled horribly and prowled into town." John Woods met one settler at a cabin in the woods of Indiana who claimed to have killed more than a hundred bears in his lifetime.[51] Hogs and pigs roamed the forests wild, feeding on nuts and acorns, and occasionally, the less fortunate among them would return to their sty with a pound or two of flesh torn away. There were so many wild animals in the woods that hunters took only the hides and hindquarters of game, leaving other predators to dispose of the rest. Whenever livestock wandered off, Native hunters, or the backwoodsmen who had learned their ways, were available to track them. They might disappear for days at a time, but they invariably returned with the errant stock.

"Regulator justice" ruled the West in 1818, and it was not advisable to carry off another man's pigs or chickens. "Law and justice," Faux observed, "extend not thus far at present." Even if acquitted by a jury, an accused thief could not always escape justice at the hands of his neighbors. Most often, such "justice" involved tying the accused to a tree and whipping him to within an inch of his life. One woman living near Evansville in 1818 lost her husband in precisely this manner. Sometimes, a suspected thief was simply shot down, or "rifled." An unsettled country "is always a place of retreat for rude and even abandoned characters, who find the regulations of society intolerable," Birkbeck explained, but "such, no doubt had taken up their unfixed abode in Indiana."[52] Often, the law was the most merciful form of punishment.

Chief among the dangers besetting the Red Banks Trail during Indian Summer were the prairie fires. During October and November (when George was traveling), the grass was dry and caught fire quickly. Native hunters purposely set fire to the undergrowth, to scare out the game. Until the winter rains came to wash the fires away, smoke obscured the sun, the moon, and the stars for days at a time. Bathing, typically performed on Saturday nights in colonial America, was impossible when the prairie fires raged, and men, women, and children worked around the clock to put out the flames. Like the sky above them, they too became covered in black.

"A Prairie fire when seen under favorable circumstances is a most sublime spectacle," William Hall claimed. Toward evening, thick clouds of smoke would obscure the horizon as the flames and darkness came on. The flames would advance rapidly in a bright jagged line, stretching for miles into the distance. A creek might give the flames a temporary check, but a gust of wind would carry them across, "roaring, crackling, thundering" with pent-up fury. They would dart up a nearby hill and tear into the woods, consuming dry leaves and everything else in their path. They would then run up the trees in pillars of flame, to illuminate the forests—like beacons of apocalypse. According to William Faux, one could see "millions of acres, for thousands of miles round, being in a wide-spreading, flaming, blazing, smoking fire, rising up through wood and prairie, hill and dale, to the tops of low shrubs and high trees, which are kindled by the coarse, thick, long, prairie grass, and dying leaves."[53] Of course, fires or no fires, George Keats had not traveled four thousand miles carrying his letter to the Cockney Pioneer for nothing.

Being a determined person who liked to see things through, he intended to inspect the prairielands for himself. But because there was no easy way to get there, he did not need to drag Georgiana along on his re-connaissance mission. Better for her to avoid the perils besetting the Red Banks Trail and remain with Lucy Audubon in Red Banks. Like Georgiana, Lucy was expecting a child, and she would be glad for the company. George could then make the exploratory circuit more quickly. Audubon always kept excellent horses, and he may have been willing to lend one to George for his trip north of the river. He may have even offered to come, all or part of the way, as an excuse to get away from his mill. The woods inevitably held unexpected treasures. Yet whether Audubon traveled north with George, or followed the crimson crest of a bird in an opposite direction, George Keats ultimately found his way to the Cockney Pioneers.

Besides the Red Banks Trail, the only other viable route for George to have taken to the English Prairie would have been the more indirect route through Shawneetown—a setting-off point much farther south, with even less to recommend it. George would have to float a hundred miles out of his way, or ride an equivalent distance across the state of Kentucky, to reach Shawneetown. He would then have to travel another sixty miles over swampy land, and cross the Little Wabash River. Driving any vehicle around tree stumps across the wetlands was not easy: one constantly ran the risk of getting stuck in the mud. It was better to walk or to ride. The land office at Shawneetown would be of little use, unless George planned to purchase land he had not seen—and this, at least, George had the good sense not to do. He still had most of his money in his pocket, and with each passing day he was gaining a better sense of the lay of the land.

The Red Banks Trail commenced a few miles upstream from Red Banks at a place where sandbanks made it possible to ford the Ohio River at low water, by foot or on horseback. George could walk or ride there, or ferry across from Henderson, and then travel east along the Indiana side of the river toward Evansville, where the trail cut north across the river from Kentucky. At Princeton, another trail cut west at a right angle across the Red Banks Trail. That trail led to the Great Wabash River, which divided the state of Indiana from the Illinois Territory farther west. George would have to cross a marshy area known as the Coffee Island Swamp, and, between the Wabash and the Bon Pas rivers, traverse seventeen miles of boggy wetlands known as the Big Prairie. He would also have to fight his way through tall, mosquito-ridden grasses to the Bon Pas, and then ferry over to another blazed trail that led through the woods to Albion. To get to Wan-

borough from Albion, he would have to hike across the unmarked grass-
lands. But George did all this more than once.

At the western edge of the Big Prairie, where one crossed the Bon Pas
River to the English Prairie, it was easy to get lost. Even after many years of
living out West, George would still lose his way:

> Once, when he was taking a journey on horseback, to visit some friends
> on the British Prairie, in Illinois, he approached the Wabash in the after-
> noon, at a time when the river had overflowed its banks. Following the
> horse path, for there was no carriage road, he came to a succession of little
> lakes, which he was obliged to ford. But when he reached the other side it
> was impossible to find the path again, and equally difficult to regain it by
> recrossing. The path here went through a cane-brake, and the cane grew
> so close together that the track could only be distinguished when you
> were actually upon it. What was to be done? There was no human being
> for miles around, and no one might pass that way for weeks. To stop or to
> go on seemed equally dangerous. But at last Mr. Keats discovered the fol-
> lowing expedient, the only one, perhaps, that could have saved him. The
> direction of the path he had been traveling was east and west. He turned
> and rode toward the south until he was sure that he was to the south of
> the track. He then returned slowly to the north, carefully examining the
> ground as he passed along, until at last he found himself crossing the path,
> which he took, and reached the river in safety.[54]

There can be no saying that George Keats was not clever. Approaching the
prairie from the Princeton side would also have given George a chance to
inspect the splinter settlement of the English pioneers in Indiana, for the
Red Banks Trail passed directly in front of John Ingle Jr.'s cabin. Conditions inside the cabin were typical of pioneer life in the West.

The only light filtered in between the logs, and wind, rain, and snow
came in through slats on the roof above the loft where Ingle Junior and his
six children slept. Beneath them, in the main room of the cabin, Ingle's wife
and their English maidservant made up their beds. One morning, when
Ingle's friend William Faux was staying with the family, the ladder to Ingle's loft gave way, leaving the head of household dangling from the floor of
the loft. "Such are the miserable shifts to which people here submit without
grumbling," Faux noted.[55]

Like farmhands, domestic servants on the western frontier were difficult to find, or to keep once found. For every woman in the area, there were several men, and those who came over with their employers from Europe soon found other situations preferable to servitude. In the meantime, they lived as de facto members of the household. "Here is no servant. The maid is equal to the master," Faux commented, shaking his head.[56]

Even when hired hands *could* be found, they were not always reliable. Ingle once hired a man dressed as a clergyman to help him clear some land. Trusting to the cloth, he paid the man forty dollars in advance; but while the man kept the money, he did not finish the work. Ingle, stranded without legal recourse, resorted to insult, calling the idler "a right reverend rascal and thief." When the man's son took affront, Ingle threatened to chop *him* into rails. One wonders what Ingle's father, the Reverend John Ingle, Sr., of Somersham, Huntingdonshire, would have said. In October 1818, about the time that George Keats was passing his son's cabin, the Reverend Ingle cautioned his son: "Remember it is a sinful world, and much imperfection remains in the best state, of such a state."[57] Indiana at that time was basically in a state of nature.

Brick was inconvenient and expensive in the forests around Saundersville, and everything in the cabins, including the chimneys, was made of wood. Pioneers used horses to drag logs to their cabins, and they yoked carts to horses to drag water from Pigeon Creek. Ingle found that he could haul twelve gallons at a time in this manner, though the effort cost him hundreds of valuable hours.[58] There were no mills, and to buy boards for tables, bedsteads, and chairs, settlers had to travel to Princeton. Hauling them back was another challenge. George had as yet no skill with an axe, but he may have begun to think that a sawmill, anywhere in the Western Country, would prosper.

Outside Harmony, iron was scarce, and most English pioneers were making do without the luxury of nails, hinges, or even pothooks to retrieve food from their fires. Families cooked in a single skillet, called the "cook-all." Yet while the Cockney Pioneers around Saundersville survived in the woods without such luxuries as sugar for months at a time, at least the trees in the forests had plenty of maple syrup. On the path to Princeton, George would have seen the trees channeling sugary sap, a drop at a time, into wooden pails or troughs, through tubes that hung down from the trunks, about three feet above the ground. When the pail was full, the pioneers would pour the sap into large pots and boil it into a substance of thicker consistency. Birkbeck estimated that it took forty gallons of the "limpid and slightly sweet liquor" to yield one gallon of more condensed sap. The latter would then be placed in a tub or barrel to undergo the process of graining. Eventually, maple syrup would seep out through holes between the crystals.[59]

The sun didn't penetrate the tops of the trees in Indiana, and it was hard to see farther than a few hundred yards. Like others, including his former partner, Morris Birkbeck, George Flower "shrank from the idea of settling in the midst of a wood of heavy timber, to hack and hew [his] way to a little farm, ever bounded by a wall of gloomy forest." The road climbed out of the forest along some tall ridges north of Evansville. From the summit, one could see the prospect open up to reveal a settlement of about a hundred wooden cabins and nineteen streets, built around a square: that was Princeton. The settlement may have been no town for a prince (and, indeed, it was named after a friend of Ingle's, who was a lawyer), but the village of Mechanicsville, seated in a valley between the hills south of Princeton, did have its manual laborers. Faux found it to consist of "a few English mechanics regretting they had left England, where they think they could do better."[60]

While Birkbeck and his two younger sons, Bradford and Charles, prepared a home for their family on the English Prairie, Birkbeck's daughters, Eliza and Prudence, boarded at a tavern in Princeton. According to Eliza, the young Cockney Pioneers had gone off to the prairie "with their rifles and their dogs in true backwood style." On April 17, 1818, she wrote: "I believe their highest ambition is to kill a deer, a wolf and a bear, all of which are found in abundance on our wild estate." The tavern where Eliza and "Prue" boarded charged two dollars per day—or, as much as the best hotels in Philadelphia. But on the frontier such accommodation was a luxury. As Eliza explained to an uncle back in England, "emigrants of all sorts and sizes from all parts of the globe are constantly roaming through this western country in quest of land, or employment, or for the sake of travelling."[61] One of these was a garrulous Irishman staying at the tavern with the sisters. Eliza portrayed him in a manner worthy of Jane Austen's Emma:

> The business of his life is—talking; his only pleasure in life is—talking—
> the greatest punishment to be inflicted on him is silence, so that when he
> meets with people who like to speak as well as listen, his company be-

comes rather irksome. We, whom you know are all *chatterboxes,* avoid him like a pestilence, but the other day could not refuse his *self invitation* to accompany a party of us in a charming ride to the river Patoka; the weather was beautiful, the roads in excellent order; and everybody enjoyed the day extremely except poor Prue, who being the greatest talker in the family we thought would be the best match for our Irish friend, so Bradford and I contrived to make him her constant and only companion for the day. It was amusing to see her scowl to us from under [her] bonnet then turn to him all suavity and smiles and nod gracious assent to all his absurd speeches, without listening to a word he said. He is a square-built man with a big head, turns in his toes, wears his hair in a crest and we call him *'Cockatoo.'*

Unlike their brothers, who at the respective ages of fifteen and seventeen liked frontier life—sending their sisters the occasional rattlesnake tail or squirrel skin as trophies from the prairie—Eliza and Prue did not like their new environment. They tried to keep up their social accomplishments, riding their horses, painting landscapes, and playing the piano that Fordham had dragged over the mountains for them, but most of the time they felt "very far removed from the refinements of polished society." Eliza swore that she would never get used to "the dingy complexions and slatternly dress of the women in these back settlements," and added: "they have a great taste for what Prue and I call *'savage finery'* and though you see them on working days dawdling about their cabins in dirty 'homespun,' on Sundays they spader forth in white dresses and colored ribbons, spangled combs and green or red shoes."[62] Her verb "spader" (and she does seem to have coined it) conjures an image of the pioneer women being tossed from their cabins with a spade, as dirt was thrown on the prairie.

The word in Princeton about prospects on the English Prairie, whatever the young Cockney Pioneers might have thought, was not good. One shopkeeper who had visited recently had found Birkbeck "very much embarrassed" and Flower likewise "very short of cash." By the same token, Thomas Hulme did not think much of the lazy backwoods settlement at Princeton. He was shocked to find so little going on: "They cannot *all* keep stores and taverns!" One storekeeper told him that he did not turn over more than $10,000 worth of merchandise a year: "He ought, then, to manufacture something and not spend nine tenths of his time lolling with a segar in his mouth." English writers, here too, seemed to attribute the poverty they found to an almost willful neglect. The inhabitants of the Northwest Territory, whether they came up from Kentucky, or over from Ohio, seemed to have degenerated. William Faux called on an acquaintance from Somersetshire, who had moved to Princeton, and found him at a dingy cabin, "very shabby, wild, and dirty." The man apologized for his dishabille, and said: "Sir, if a stranger like you had found me in this plight in England, and I could have seen you coming up to my door, I should have hid myself."[63] On the frontier, standards were more lax.

In 1818, the Territory of Illinois, across the Wabash River from Indiana, had about forty thousand residents and was larger than the state of Indiana. It had obtained a good portion of its thirty-five million acres the previous year from its Native occupants. Small numbers of Delawares, Miamis, Kaskaskians, Piankashaws, Hurons, Weeaws, Shawnees, Mascontins, Kickapoos, Ouitanans, and Pottawattamies still roamed the prairies, though here as elsewhere, they were disappearing as the land became settled. The Miamis decorated their guns the way they did their tomahawks, and rode pure-blood ponies. Fordham, an expert hunter, admired the skill of one young Delaware whom he saw hold a heavy rifle motionless for several minutes without moving a muscle.[64]

Tensions between the settlers and Native Americans still ran high, and the English Prairie was not free from them. Jeremiah Birks, the first pioneer anyone could remember in the area, owned four thousand acres, three miles west of the English Prairie, and in 1817 he chased from his land, but did not shoot, three Indian hunters because they were with their wives. But at the southern edge of Birkbeck's property, a party of backwoodsmen shot and buried all six Indians. The following year, while in Red Banks, Fordham heard that a party of backwoodsmen had gone to drive some Native hunters from his property line. He stated flatly, "If the Indians resist they will be murdered."[65]

The backwoodsmen led a vagabond existence. When necessary, they would live on raccoons and squirrels and sleep in blankets in the hollows of trees. Some squatted and raised log cabins resembling the dens of the Highland clansmen in Sir Walter Scott's novels. Yet game was abundant on the prairie, and poaching did not present the same problem that it did in Great Britain, where the game laws severely restricted hunting. If the backwoodsmen in Illinois and Indiana were outlaws (like Walter Scott's bandits) they were outlaws for other reasons. Fearon, for one, found their character and behavior "extremely wretched" and claimed to prefer "the genuine *uncontaminated* Indian" to these "half-civilized and half-savage" backwoodsmen.[66]

At one rough-and-ready backwoods barbecue that Fordham attended, those present simply cut off the part of the game he or she liked best from the spoils the hunters brought back—a buck this time, but on less bounteous occasions, a prairie hen, or a wild turkey—and stuck it on the end of a sharpened wooden spit to roast in the fire. After the feast, primed with wild-honey liquor, one of the backwoodsmen pulled out a broken fiddle and inaugurated the "dances, songs and mirth" that lasted until well past midnight. With no regular schedules or commitments, Fordham complained, "night and day are alike to them."[67] The women did not seem to mind dressing and undressing in front of the men; they had no curtains in the cabins for privacy.

To cross the Wabash River on the way from Princeton to the Big Prairie, one took a ferry. But the ferryman's specialty was not hospitality, and, rather than welcoming strangers into his cabin for refreshment, he sent them down the road on the Illinois side. The only service he provided was the crossing. Thomas Hulme was happy just to have made it to the ferry: "We were obliged to lead our horses, and walk up to the knees in mud and water," he recounted: "Before we got half across we began to think of going back; but, there is a sound bottom under it all, and we waded through it as well as we could."[68] Across the Wabash River on the Illinois side was the soggy Big Prairie that one crossed to reach the Bon Pas River.

In Illinois, as elsewhere in the West, there were both upland and bottom prairies. The latter, as in the Big Prairie, consisted of rich, poorly drained alluvial soil that swarmed with mosquitoes. The insects that came out in autumn to feed seemed "more muscular and sprightly" than their spring brethren. They had "a good appetite and sharp teeth." The upland prairies, on the other hand, fifty to a hundred and fifty feet higher, were wooded and hilly. After being mired in swamps and scourged by mosquitoes, one needed sustenance. In 1819, John Woods bolted down a lunch of pork and Indian cornbread at one of the farms between the two rivers. William Harris struck the jackpot with a certain Judge Thompson: wild turkey, French beans, ham, potatoes, wild grapes, and cherries topped with honey and cream.[69] On the western side of the Big Prairie, another ferry would shuttle travelers across the Bon Pas River to the woods, where one followed a blazed trail to George Flower's Albion, now the rival to Birkbeck's Wanborough, a couple of miles farther west.

As the woods opened up, George would have seen the hayricks piled for the winter on the English Prairie, where the Cockney Pioneers were still putting up rails and constructing fences to enclose their livestock. Flower had a few oxen and a flock of four hundred mismatched sheep, acquired at different places. Children stacked cobs of Indian corn into miniature log cabins. Birkbeck joked that these "cob houses" resembled the proverbial houses of cards, "whose chief merit lies in their tumbling down before they are finished." He also compared them to "castles in the air, which are built by most people in every country *under the age of fifty.*"[70] By his own logic, though not by others', the Cockney Pioneer was safely past the age when *he* could be accused of building such castles in air.

Still, some tried to build them. Fordham saw one cabin on the Village Prairie near Albion elaborately fitted up with carpets, gilt-frame mirrors, and a hickory four-poster bedstead. "It looked like a fairy bower in the wilderness," he said. Elsewhere, Faux found two brothers from Lincolnshire, living on their quarter-section of land, who did not look anything like fairies: "Both were more filthy, stinking, ragged, and repelling, than any English stroller or beggar ever seen; garments rotting off, linen unwashed, face unshaven and unwashed, for, I should think, a month." Faux was shocked that they were expecting their siblings to join them in such abject squalor, where they were "fast barbarizing, in a most miserable log-cabin, not mudded, having only one room, no furniture of any kind, save a miserable, filthy, ragged bed." One had cut his leg on a plowshare and lay on the floor unable to move. He refused to see a doctor, and his brother shook his head: "Here (says he) a man learns philosophy and its uses!"[71]

Even a Cockney Pioneer as committed to the idea of emigration as Fordham, who vowed that he would never return to England until he became a rich man, and who laid out the town of Albion by improvising a surveyor's chain from a grapevine, ultimately gave up the dream of seeing "*ab initio* an English settlement in the wilderness of the Illinois." In the time he spent in Illinois, he planted crops, dug wells, constructed sawpits, put up a windmill, built a bridge over the Bon Pas, and ran a general store. In Princeton, he even raised an American flag. But in the end, "dirt, bad cooking, and discomfort of every kind" got the best of him. "You ask me, can a farmer with a capital of £250 live comfortably in this country?" he wrote to a friend in England. "Certainly much more comfortably than he can in England, if he has only £250, and no friends to lend him £2,000 in addition to it, or his friends are unwilling to help him. It is only a matter of choice then between servitude and independence." The impoverished English farmer could do well enough in Illinois or Indiana, he suggested, but the English country gentleman should not venture west. Genteel farmers, who could afford a plantation and slaves, should try Kentucky. Skilled workers could find work in the Ohio River Valley, but merchants and manufacturers of luxury items "should never cross the mountains." The Western Country, as Birkbeck himself cautioned, was "not the country for fine gentlemen or fine ladies of any class or description."[72]

George Keats was no genteel farmer or country gentleman. And until he met Audubon he was not poor. By the time he reached the English Prairie, he had seen his share of dirt floors, dirty clothing, and plain food. "Seeming short roads to wealth most frequently terminate in blind alleys," he discovered, as he later expressed it to Dilke. George had come far from the Old Country, and far from his brother. "The goings on of the world make me dizzy," John wrote. "There you are with Birkbeck—here I am with Brown." Hearing George's account of the English Prairie, John would quip that Birkbeck's *Notes on a Journey in America* should be bound together with Thomas Campbell's *Gertrude of Wyoming*, "like a Brace of Decoy Ducks—One is almost as poetical as the other." Birkbeck, the Cockney Pioneer, like the Cockney Poet of *Endymion*, had published "a poetical romance."[73]

There, in the meantime, in the northwest corner of the English Prairie, he sat, a long-stemmed clay pipe in his mouth: the American Kurtz at the end of George's river journey into the heart of the American West. Rather than plowing, harrowing, or planting, Birkbeck had spent his time on an infrastructure of barns, fences, and corncribs. He had a few horses, cows, and pigs, but his land was not yet under cultivation. Even his friend Hulme remarked that "*any* American settler, even without a dollar in his pocket, would have *had something growing by this time*."[74] Whatever the Cockney Pioneer may have said to George Keats when the latter finally delivered up his letter from John Taylor, it was not enough to keep him on the prairie. George would not stay to see Birkbeck's Indian corn come up, or his beans sprout. At the end of his quest, he knew his destination to be elsewhere.

On the way back to Red Banks, George thought of Georgiana, and he thought of his unborn child. He could not think of bringing a future generation of Keatses into the world under such conditions as he had seen north of the river. He also thought of his brother, most likely in the same terms in which his brother thought of him. "Sometimes I fancy an immense separation, and sometimes," John wrote to George, "a direct communication of spirit with you."[75] The poet, by then, had seen the sublime wonders of the North, and the pioneer brother had seen his share of wonders in the West. Experience had changed them both, and it would not be long before, at their next reunion, they would register that change.

Audubon and the Mill

The only members of George's immediate circle who had supported his scheme of emigration, besides his brothers and Georgiana's mother, were the Dilkes. Charles Dilke was following the news about the English Prairie, but not having gone the lengths that George had to see the place, he thought that George should have stayed there. George had a unique opportunity to help found a new society based on principles of equality and justice. John did not have the same universalist attitude as their friend, and, taking the pulse of the situation from his brother's letter, concluded that George had "done perfectly right" in giving up the idea of settling on the English Prairie.[76]

George was now ready to put the idea of dirt farming behind him and turn to more lucrative pursuits, but the problems he faced once he crossed the Ohio River back into Kentucky were inexperience and the quagmire of insolvency he stepped into in Henderson. Fortunes in the West seemed to rise and fall with the river. And currency, prior to the Panic of 1819, was inflated. The American economy was headed for a crash. One resident of Cincinnati explained that "a desire to become suddenly rich had led too many into wild speculations, on borrowed money, from the United States and other banks. They were willing to lend to almost anyone who could get two indorsers. This was no difficult matter, for it had got to be a maxim, 'You indorse for me, and I indorse for you.'"[77] George likewise endorsed for others.

According to George's grandson John Gilmer Speed, "Audubon, the naturalist, sold to George Keats a boat loaded with merchandise, which at the time of the sale Audubon knew to be at the bottom of the Mississippi

River."[78] George *did* invest money in a steamboat, but the version of the story handed down by Speed, and generally accepted as true, probably has little basis in actual fact. At the same time, insofar as Audubon lived in a world of endlessly deferred credit—and involved George Keats in that credit economy—the spirit of the remark holds true. Audubon did borrow money from George to keep his various operations afloat, but there is no reason to suppose that he expected to lose the money. If he exaggerated and bent the truth, it was part of a lifelong habit of half-perceiving and half-creating the world, which a Romantic poet like Wordsworth would have approved. Audubon had grown up on the bounty of a wealthy father, and his own interests lay far from any bank. Perhaps the worst one might say of him is that he was careless, even reckless, with regard to money.

In the end, however, all casuistry regarding Audubon's conscience turns out to be irrelevant, for before he could pay George back, he went bankrupt. That symbol of mercantilism—the mill between First and Second on Water Street in Henderson, Kentucky—was what broke him financially. However much George may have come to suspect Audubon's intentions later, he did not accuse him of duplicity at the time, as John's letters of 1819 indicate. And until then, the Audubons and the Keatses lived happily enough for a while at a cabin in the woods near the mill.

Like George, Audubon had spent time as a clerk in a counting house. But his position at Benjamin Bakewell's shipping firm in New York had suited him no better than the position at Abbey's tea-house had suited George. After a visit to speak with his father in France, Audubon had decided to try his luck in the American West. In 1807, he and his partner, Ferdinand Rozier, the son of his father's friend, Claude François Rozier, borrowed $3,647.29 from Benjamin Bakewell (just before his shipping business collapsed), a sum payable within eight months, which the partners used to purchase shot, tackle, whiskey, and other dry goods to set up a general store in Louisville. They loaded crates and casks onto a flatboat and drifted, occasionally dragged the boat through shallows, down the Ohio.

When Lucy Green Bakewell came of age the next year, Audubon married her and brought her to Kentucky. They boarded above the bar at the Indian Queen Tavern on Main Street, Louisville. While Rozier tended the store, Audubon disappeared into the woods to hunt. Their clerk, Nathaniel Wells Pope, a local Kentucky lad, would help beat the bushes and flush out the birds. Sometimes they would be gone for days at a time. A hawk once led Audubon on a three-day chase over creeks and through the underbrush, until he finally brought down the majestic creature with a ball from his rifle.[79]

Sales at the store were slow, and in 1810 Rozier convinced Audubon to pull up stakes and move farther downriver: the settlement at Red Banks needed a general store. The move turned out to be a good one for Audubon, who now had more space to fish, hunt, ride, and swim across the river with his tall, athletic wife. But Ferdinand Rozier remained discontented. He decided to move farther west, to Ste. Geneviève, a French colony on the Mississippi, in Missouri. Lucy Bakewell Audubon did not want to move another hundred and sixty-five miles into the wilderness. So, when Audubon, using Rozier as an excuse to explore new terrain in the Mississippi River Valley, left for Ste. Geneviève, Lucy boarded at Meadow Brook, a plantation three miles outside Henderson, with Dr. Adam Rankin and his (third) wife, Elizabeth Speed Rankin. The Audubons paid five dollars a week, and Lucy taught Rankin's ten children, and her own, their school lessons.

On a keelboat loaded with supplies from the store, Audubon and Rozier took off down the Ohio for the land where Daniel Boone was still hunting and trapping. But ice blocked the river, and after a few weeks spent at an Osage camp at Tawapatee Bottom, wrapped in blankets and living on bear sandwiches greased with bear fat, the partners decided to part ways. Rozier bought out Audubon's share of their stock at Ste. Geneviève, and Audubon turned back with a party of Osages, whom he had impressed by his skill with a red pencil and his aptitude for their language. Those who guided him through the woods of Kentucky were, according to Washington Irving, "stern and simple in garb and aspect. They wore no ornaments; their dress consisted merely of blankets, leggings, and moccasons. Their heads were bare; their hair was cropped close, excepting a bristling ridge on the top, like the crest of a helmet, with a long scalp lock hanging behind."[80] Back in Red Banks with Lucy, Audubon reopened his store, supplied his table once more with rod and rifle, and went back to sketching the wildlife around him.

Then, Tom Bakewell entered their lives. Like Audubon, Tom had clerked for his uncle Benjamin Bakewell in New York, and on his way to New Orleans, to open a branch office for some merchants from Liverpool —his mission, to set up operations shipping cotton on consignment—Tom convinced Audubon to join him in another business venture trading pork, lard, and flour. But when, in June 1812, the United States declared war on Britain, both businesses failed. Tom made his way up through the woods from New Orleans to Red Banks, where he found his brother-in-law sketching an otter.[81] He moved into the Audubons' cabin and went to work at the general store.

But the ambitions of the man who would later become George's business partner in the West could not rest there. Tom Bakewell's father and his uncle were both chemists, and Tom's scientific interests lay in mechanical engineering. "As a finished scholar and theoretical mechanic in iron and wood," one person who knew Tom attested, "Mr. Bakewell had no superior. His early mathematical training gave him a love for that science, and his mind was constantly engaged in solving abstruse problems relating to the power of steam and its application to machinery." When Squire Bakewell died in 1821, Tom told his mother-in-law, Rebecca (née Smith), that he wanted nothing in particular besides the scientific books, articles, and instruments his father had used to instruct him.[82]

In Henderson, Tom's brainchild was a steam-powered grist- and saw-mill, which he designed on a scale out of keeping with the small frontier outpost—and "in a country then as unfit for such a thing," Audubon said, as it would have been for Audubon "to attempt to settle in the moon." Tom himself would later admit that the mill was "unsuited to the *non* wheat growing section of Country." The project ultimately cost fifteen thousand dollars, but Tom calculated an initial investment of ten thousand. He convinced his father and Audubon to invest a "moderate amount" each, about four or five thousand dollars.[83] But the firm of Audubon & Bakewell still needed money, and so Tom targeted another former clerk of Benjamin Bakewell's.

Thomas Pears had married Tom's English cousin, Sarah Palmer. Her mother, Sarah White Palmer, had a sister named Anne, who was Benjamin Bakewell's second wife. Sarah Palmer's grandfather, the Reverend John Palmer, was a Unitarian preacher associated with Joseph Priestley. Sarah did not want to move to Kentucky. But the combined powers of Thomas Woodhouse Bakewell and John James Audubon proved impossible for poor Pears to resist. Forking over the final three or four thousand dollars needed to commence construction of the mill, Pears moved his wife and four young children (Maria, John Palmer, Sarah Ann, and Benjamin) into the Audubons' cabin. "Oh, if you could see some of the rough uncouth creatures here, I think you would find it rather hard to look upon them exactly in the light of brothers and sisters," Sarah wrote on a later occasion to her uncle Benjamin from Indiana. In much the same terms, she complained of Henderson.[84]

Tom Bakewell also convinced David Prentice, the steam engineer who had built a steam-powered thresher for his father, to construct a sixteen-horsepower steam-engine for the mill at Red Banks. Squire Bakewell had been delighted with the thresher, and Prentice, with money advanced by the squire, had opened a foundry named Eagle Works, in Pennsylvania. But the War of 1812 had ruined his business, and so David Prentice agreed to build the engine for the Henderson mill. Audubon & Bakewell were to provide four thousand dollars, as well as timber, masonry, manpower, and travel-expenses. Also, for three dollars a day, Prentice and his wife would board with the Audubons.[85]

David Prentice was an excellent theoretical engineer, Tom Bakewell said, but he found him, as a millwright, to be baffled by practical matters. "Mr. Prentice has an excellent head, but no hands," Tom wrote. "We have a very good Engine put up in a very slovenly imperfect manner which we are remedying by degrees ourselves. He is a capital man to prescribe, but not to administer—his *advice & opinion* in matters of his profession are invaluable but his execution worthless."[86] Tom would make similar complaints about Prentice, after joining him at an iron foundry in Louisville, which Prentice purchased with money from the mill.

With credit from the Bank of Kentucky, meanwhile, Audubon & Bakewell leased two hundred feet of riverfront property for a period of ninety-nine years, at twenty dollars a year. The town trustees approved construction of the mill, which began immediately. But Thomas Pears, giving in to pressure from his wife, sold his share of the mill at a loss and moved back to Pittsburgh, going to work for Benjamin Bakewell at the glass factory. On July 27, 1816, Tom Bakewell married the daughter of Benjamin Bakewell's business partner, Elizabeth Rankin Page. But Tom's wife, like his cousin Sarah, hated Red Banks. After a few months, and before the Henderson mill was finished, she moved to Louisville, where Tom would soon follow her.

Tom Bakewell strategized about how to extract himself from the Henderson mill. By this point, he considered himself an expert in steam engi-

neering, having "complete knowledge" of any mill system powered by a
steam engine. He would not "thank even Mr. Prentice for his opinion on
that subject." All that Tom Bakewell needed was "a *good workman*" to execute his orders. Since Audubon and Bakewell were both responsible for the
debts their company incurred, however, Tom agreed to stay on at the Henderson mill until July 1, 1817. "This place never having had any allurements
for me, & still less *endearments* since I was married," he explained in December 1816, "I have dissolved partnership with Mr. Audubon, he taking
all the property and debts due to A&B, & agreeing to pay all their debts, for
which I take loss to about $5000, & he is to pay me $5500. . . . I consider him
to have the best bargain." Audubon, stuck at the mill, may have thought
otherwise. *How I labored at that infernal mill! from dawn to dark, nay, at times
all night . . .*[87]

These events all transpired before George and Georgiana arrived in
Kentucky—indeed, before they were married. But they triggered a downward spiral of debt that would sweep the young couple away with the
Audubons. After Tom's departure, Audubon changed the name of the business from Audubon & Bakewell to John James Audubon & Company, and
sought new investors. David Apperson (the branch manager of the general store in Shawneetown) purchased some shares, as did Nathaniel Pope
of Ste. Geneviève (the uncle of Audubon's former clerk, Nathaniel Wells
Pope); Tom's father-in-law, Benjamin Page; and the ever-reliable Nicholas
Berthoud. But the business floundered, and Audubon, out of his element at
the mill, considered himself (to use his own bird metaphor) to have been
"gulled by all these men." Yet whether he was gulled, or gulled others in
turn, Audubon swore to his sons that "the building of that accursed steam-
mill was, of all the follies of man, one of the greatest, and to your uncle and
me the worst of all our pecuniary misfortunes."[88]

Tom Bakewell joined David Prentice in Louisville at the iron foundry
the latter had purchased, which had formerly been used to cast gudgeons
(the tubular pieces of a hinge used in mills), along with equally glamorous
objects, from oven lids to clothing irons. With Prentice's money, Tom drew
up more blueprints, hired blacksmiths, and set about transforming the old
dusty foundry into a modern steam-engine factory.

The partners at the foundry produced their first steam-engine to
power a cotton mill, and then went on to construct a steam-engine for a
hybrid vessel, a keelboat equipped with a paddlewheel. They named it the

Pike, after the Mississippi explorer Zebulon M. Pike. Prentice steered it up-river from Henderson to Louisville, and farther upstream toward Pittsburgh. He made it as far as White's Ripple before the *Pike* foundered in shallow waters. Benjamin Bakewell came down to help dislodge the boat, which Prentice then steered back to Louisville and sold to a man who fitted it out for trade. But in March 1818, the *Pike* sank on a sawyer in the Red River.[89]

Tom and his partner next constructed a steamboat capable of carrying eighty-five tons, which they named the *Henderson* and sold to the Henderson Company. This was most likely the boat that sank George's fortune. "We also took it into our heads to have a steamboat," Audubon (still partnered with Bakewell) related, "in partnership with the engineer [Prentice] who had come from Philadelphia to fix the engine of that mill. This also proved an entire failure, and misfortune after misfortune came down upon us like so many avalanches, both fearful and destructive."[90] Samuel Adams Bowen, of the Henderson Company, gave Tom Bakewell a promissory note for $4,250, payable within a year, and took possession of the *Henderson.* Tom then used Bowen's promissory note to withdraw from the Henderson mill, by signing it over to Audubon on February 13, 1819, in exchange for $5,500 in cash, which Audubon raised, evidently, through George Keats.

When Samuel Bowen's promissory note came due a couple of months later on April 1, 1819, however, Bowen failed to honor the note. When Audubon tried to cash it in, he could not. Bowen then took the *Henderson* downriver in order to sell it in New Orleans. Audubon found himself headed upstream without a paddle—or, to speak more accurately, downstream with several paddles, pursuing the fugitive at breakneck speed with the help of two of his slaves. Audubon reached New Orleans on May 12, 1819, one day after Samuel Bowen had resold the *Henderson.* James Freeman Clarke later reported that George, after living with the Audubons, settled in Louisville and "invested a large part of his property in the first steamboat which went down the river to New Orleans, and lost it all, in consequence of the death of the Captain at that place."[91] The *Henderson* may not exactly have been the first steamboat to go down the river to New Orleans, but it *was* the first steamboat built in Louisville to do so.

Having pursued the *Henderson* to New Orleans, Audubon demanded that Samuel Bowen turn over either the money he owed him, or the boat. When Bowen failed to do either, Audubon appeared before Judge James

Pitot of the New Orleans Parish Court to swear that the defendants, Samuel Bowen and his partner James Wilson, owed him $4,250 for a steamboat anchored within the jurisdiction of the court. The judge, making Audubon sign a bond for $8,000 to guarantee that his statement was true, issued an attachment ordering seizure of the boat.[92] But the boat had already been sold.

Accusing Samuel Bowen of fraud, Audubon pleaded that a legal attachment be plastered to the boat while it was still within the jurisdiction of the court. The court demanded a second bond, for $8,500, and the judge issued the attachment. But it soon became clear that Audubon had lost the case: the sale was legal in the state of Louisiana. Audubon took revenge by decrying Bowen all over the French-speaking town, and, by the end of May, he had done enough damage to Bowen's reputation that Bowen determined to kill him.

The sequence of events suggests that Audubon borrowed the money from George Keats around the time the buyout took place in mid-February. This was roughly six weeks before Samuel Bowen failed to honor his promissory note. George wrote to John on July 24, 1819, the same month that Audubon declared bankruptcy, with news of the loss of his money, and a request for an immediate remittance from Abbey.

John had little doubt that his brother had been swindled. "I cannot help thinking M‍ʳ Audubon a dishonest man," he wrote in September. "Why did he make you believe that he was a Man of Property? How is it his circumstances have altered so suddenly? In truth I do not believe you fit to deal with the world; or at least the American world—But good God—who can avoid these chances—You have done your best—Take matters as coolly as you can and confidently expecting help from England, act as if no help was nigh."[93] John found it hard to conceive how Audubon's affairs could have met with such a sudden reversal in such a short span of time. But Audubon *himself* was shocked by the quick succession of events that had left him a bankrupt.

After his return from New Orleans, Samuel Bowen had stirred up resentment among the townspeople at Red Banks. Together with his brother William Russell Bowen and a handful of friends (Robert Speed, Obadiah Smith, George Brent, and Bennett Marshall), he sued Audubon for ten thousand dollars in damages. But punishment for personal insult in Kentucky rarely waited for the long arm of the law, and Bowen's "violent and ungovernable temper was too well known." One day, as Audubon was going to work, Bowen approached carrying a club. "I stood still, and he soon reached me," Audubon related. "He complained of my conduct to him at New Orleans, and suddenly raising his bludgeon laid it about me. Though white with wrath, I spoke not nor moved not till he had given me twelve severe blows, then, drawing my dagger with my left hand (unfortunately my right hand was disabled and in a sling, having been caught and much injured in the wheels of the steam-engine), I stabbed him and he instantly fell."[94] Bleeding, Audubon staggered back to his cabin, while James Berthoud and Will Bakewell, Tom and Lucy's younger brother, carried the assailant home on a plank.

At the time George invested his money with Audubon, he had already begun construction of a lumber mill near the falls in Louisville. "Had the Mill been finished within *a year* of the time agreed upon in my contract with the Builders you should not have wanted money now," George later explained to John; "it was not finished within 21 mos, such a disappointment driving me to every shift to live, rent and servant hire unpaid, will weigh heavy upon me some time." George identified his partners at George Keats & Company as "the principal Iron founders in the western Country," or in other words, Tom Bakewell and David Prentice. Tom would maintain his partnership with George Keats until February 1, 1823. Prentice would do so for another three years, until April 29, 1826. When David Prentice died, George would become his executor.[95]

George lost his investment also at the very time the American economy collapsed in the Panic of 1819. Writing to Fanny Keats in September, shortly after hearing from their brother, John summed up George's situation accurately enough (if also trying to mollify the news for his little sister): "The whole amount of the ill news is that his mercantile speculations have not had success in consequence of the general depression of trade in the whole province of Kentucky and indeed all America." The Bank of the United States had been extending credit to the state banks in a massive recovery effort that had produced a bubble of overspeculation after the War of 1812. When the federal bank called in its notes, the Panic broke out and caused eighty-five banks, or roughly a quarter of the national total, to fail. Currency in circulation dropped to less than forty percent of what it had been three years earlier, as mortgages foreclosed, stores shut down, and notes of credit became as worthless as Samuel Bowen's.[96]

In the long term, George Keats, like Audubon, would overcome the crisis. But in the summer of 1819, when George wrote to his brother, nobody knew this. A couple of months earlier, John Quincy Adams had described the state of the American economy as "alarming": "The bank bubbles are breaking. The staple productions of the soil, constituting our principal articles of export, are falling to half and less than half the prices which they have lately borne, the merchants are crumbling to ruin, the manufactures perishing, agriculture stagnating, and distress universal in every part of the country." Speculators up and down the river, fearing arrest by the sheriffs, began (in the words of one Westerner) to "scatter like rats from a submerged flour barrel."[97] George's private panic was swallowed by an even larger one.

Audubon had chastised the boat thief, Bowen, and a group of Kentuckians determined to give the artist a "regulator" whipping in retribution showed up at his cabin. James Berthoud, who was staying with the Audubons at the time, recognized that armed resistance would be useless, and bravely stepped out onto the porch to address the angry crowd. With white hair flying in the wind, with a flood of conciliatory speech—and no doubt with images of French revolutionary mobs flashing through his mind—he harangued the regulators. This turned out to be a valiant last stand, for Old Berthoud would be dead within a few months of dispersing the belligerents.[98]

Audubon now faced trial for assault with a deadly weapon. But the plaintiffs failed to appear at the Jefferson County Court, and legend has it that after Judge Henry P. Broadnax dismissed the case, he said gruffly, "Mr. Audubon, you committed a serious offense, an exceedingly serious offense, sir—in failing to kill the damned rascal!" But killing Samuel Bowen would not have produced Audubon's—or George Keats's—money. Audubon could no longer continue his operations at the mill, or pay his creditors. *The once wealthy man was now nothing.* Audubon kept only the clothes on his back, his portfolio of bird drawings, and his gun, or "Long Tom."[99]

Lucy Bakewell Audubon left the cabin at Red Banks and went back upriver with her two sons to Shippingport, where her sister, Eliza Bakewell Berthoud, lived. Judge Fortunatus Cosby, Jr., later an executor of George's estate, advised Audubon to file a petition of voluntary bankruptcy. And in a safekeeping measure that could not prevent misery, Nicholas Berthoud purchased the remainder of Audubon's estate, forking over $4,450 for his slaves, $14,000 for his share of the mill, and $7,000 for his household effects, from the bedposts down to the candlesticks.[100]

Before the mill had entered his life, Audubon, between his real estate, his slaves, and his store, had been worth about fifty thousand dollars, which by contemporary standards made him wealthy. He had lost a fortune, but he still had that within him which no amount of money could buy: his genius, with its capacity for self-renewal. Reduced to penury, Audubon would soon reestablish himself in Louisville with a piece of black charcoal, sketching portrait heads for five dollars each. His reputation would spread quickly. One grieving clergyman would go so far as to disinter his recently buried son so that Audubon could take his likeness. Audubon would hand over the "fac-simile of his face . . . to the parents as if still alive, to their intense satisfaction."[101]

The loss of George's fortune ended the friendship between the Audubons and the Keatses. Georgiana complained of Lucy Audubon's "affectation of fashion and politeness" to John, who sympathized: "Give my Compliments to Mrs Audubon and tell her I cannot think her either good looking or honest." George had to borrow money. "'T is an extraordinary thing," John wrote. "How could you do without that assistance?" George did not name the source of the assistance, and although George was in partnership with Tom Bakewell and David Prentice, Hyder E. Rollins adds a note in his edition of John Keats's letters to say that the assistance came from William Bakewell.[102] His hunch may be correct, for William Bakewell, Jr., seems to have been as good at lending money as his older brother was at borrowing it, and William Bakewell, Sr., had money to lend.

George was broke, but, in June 1819, the month President James Monroe and General Andrew Jackson came riding into Louisville, Georgiana Emily Keats was born. The people of Louisville hosted a ball for these two worthies—symbols of the Old America and the New—while George worried about whether he would ever again see his money. In July, when Audubon declared bankruptcy, George wrote to John, thus commencing more weeks, and then months, of anxious waiting. As time wore on, George knew, without having to be told, that his brother would petition Richard Abbey for help on his behalf, but ineffectively. John had never been a successful negotiator with their guardian. And despite his best efforts to help, John was perplexed by George's affairs. Their aunt, Margaret Jennings, was still threatening legal action, and Abbey did not want to dispose of more of Tom's stock at a loss for George. "You urg'd me to get Mr Abbey to advance you money—that he will by no means do," John explained. "He will never be persuaded but you will lose it in America." John admitted to having the same fear himself. "I am afraid you are no more than myself form'd for a gainer of money," he confessed to George.[103]

John *did* send a hundred pounds to George through the Warders in Philadelphia, but the remittance was stalled in transit. George knew nothing of it. He began to fear that his own letter to his brother had gotten lost, or that, even if it had not, Abbey would not understand the urgency of releasing money to help support his family that winter in Louisville. Stocks were down, and the tea dealer was conservative, habitually unwilling to sell at a loss. George was not yet drawing a salary, and he could not afford to hire help. His expenses were outstripping his income. He was left with no other choice: he would have to go back to England. "He will not see the necessity of a thing till he is hit in the mouth," John said of Abbey in September, and if anyone should do the hitting in this case, it should be George.[104] So, borrowing money for the trip, George kissed his wife and his baby daughter goodbye, and headed back in the opposite direction across the Atlantic.

PART FOUR

1820–1841

and after

7 BACK ACROSS THE ATLANTIC

Death Warrant

John had always thought that mental grief was his worst enemy. George's calamity, rousing him from his summer reveries, had scared away all his "blue devils." George and Georgiana needed him, and John vowed to do something about it. Accordingly, he asked Charles Dilke to help him find a place to live in Westminster, and, in October 1819, left Winchester to move a few doors down from the Dilkes. Perhaps Dilke could also help him find work reviewing for the journals to which he contributed. "Even if I am swept away like a Spider from a drawing room I am determined to spin," John announced. "Home spun any thing for sale. Yea I will traffic. Any thing but Mortgage my Brain to Blackwood. I am determined not to lay like a dead lump."[1] The lilies of the field toil not; but it was time to spin. For a while, John would be a weaver boy.

Richard Abbey suggested an alternative. He told John that he was thinking of retiring. He was in his mid-fifties and ready to turn the tea business over to someone younger—someone capable, someone he could trust. His chief clerk, Cadman Hodgkinson, wanted his own tea business; perhaps John could take over the firm. The English would always want tea: there was a good future in the business. John considered his guardian's offer and decided that, temporarily, it might work. Perhaps he could hold the position for George. But when he returned to Abbey to ask about the details, the tea dealer got nervous.

There were difficulties, after all. It had taken Abbey years to learn the tea trade. John would have to start from the ground up. What did he understand, for instance, about excise taxes? He knew none of the suppliers, and every little country buyer and city retailer tried to dictate his own terms. One needed to take stock, make entries, keep track of orders. It was easy to be cheated, and those dockworkers down by the Thames could be trouble. Chests of tea were complex affairs, riddled with possibilities for disaster. There was more to it than poundage. The permit offices were packed with different kinds of permits. And if the leaves weren't packed tightly enough, they could spoil . . . After several hours of such talk, John decided that his only hope lay with *Otho the Great.* "Whether I shall at all be set afloat upon the world depends now upon the success of the Tragedy I spoke of," he told George.[2]

Ever since Tom's death, John had felt adrift; martyring himself to George's chances for happiness might give him a grip. George had a family and a disposition to enjoy life. When good things came his way, George knew how to enjoy them. His mild pleasures had always provided a reliable meridian between the shifting poles of John's more extreme moods. Sometimes up, sometimes down, the poet had always tethered himself to his brother. Now the anchor had pulled loose, and the roles were reversed. "I have no meridian to fix you to," he confessed to George in September, "being the Slave of what is to happen."[3]

And yet, for all his resolve to help George, he did not last long living in Winchester. A single visit to Fanny Brawne in Hampstead in mid-October, a couple of weeks before his twenty-fourth birthday, was enough to make him flee back to the heath, the pole star of his adult existence. "The time is passed when I had power to advise and warn you against the unpromising morning of my Life," John wrote to Fanny: "My love has made me selfish. I cannot exist without you—I am forgetful of every thing but seeing you again—my Life seems to stop there—I see no further . . ."[4] He had tried to warn her away from the foundering ship, but it was now too late. His principles gave way to his passion, and in mid-October John moved back to Wentworth Place. He did not know what would come of it.

Besides the poverty complicating his hopeless romance—and now the financial burden of his brother in America—he had been sick on and off since the start of the year. And given his family history, the prognosis did

not look good. Several months spent in the sickroom with Tom had exacerbated the persistent sore throat he'd contracted in Scotland. In April, when
John was writing his Great Odes, he had met Coleridge walking north of
the heath by Highgate with Joseph Henry Green. John had known Green,
an instructor of morbid anatomy, from the hospitals. Green introduced
John to Coleridge, though without naming his former pupil, and they
walked together for a couple of miles at the elder poet's leisurely, after-
dinner pace. John had admired the bold associative sweep of oratory for
which Coleridge was so justly famed, and Coleridge, in turn, felt a twinge
of interest for the slackly dressed youth who had such a striking countenance.

Like his own Ancient Mariner, Coleridge was known for holding lis-
teners spellbound with his twinkling eye, and yet, when he looked into
John's face *he* saw a strange glint there, as if from another world. When
they'd parted, John had turned back to shake Coleridge's hand, and Coleridge never forgot the feeling. He had been eloquent enough until then, but
when he looked down at the hand that Keats had shaken, he could only
mutter, "There is death in *his* hand."[5] When pressed by Green, who took an
interest in morbid matters, to explain himself, Coleridge could hardly say
what he meant. The hand was chalky somehow, and damp. It was hard to
describe the ghostly feeling that had come from that wan, pasty grip.

John seems to have intuited its strange effect. On some blank space of a
page on which he was drafting "The Cap and Bells," a poem he had begun
toward the end of the year with Brown's encouragement, he wrote:

> This living hand, now warm and capable
> Of earnest grasping, would, if it were cold
> And in the icy silence of the tomb,
> So haunt thy days and chill thy dreaming nights
> That thou would wish thine own heart dry of blood,
> So in my veins red life might stream again,
> And thou be conscience-calm'd. See, here it is—
> I hold it towards you.

If John's feelings for Fanny Brawne had anything to do with these lines,
they are certainly an anguished love lyric. Yet one suspects that this brief

and chilling meditation on the poet's "living hand" might have had more to do with his critics, and his yet-unrealized imaginary world that was receding farther every day into the distance.

To say, with Shelley and Byron, that the reviews of *Endymion* killed John Keats was, as Coleridge claimed, "absurd." Yet Coleridge also recognized the profound effect they'd had. "It is very well for those who have a place in the world and are independent to talk of these things," Coleridge explained; "they can bear such a blow, so can those who have a strong religious principle; but all men are not born Philosophers, and all men have not those advantages of birth and education. Poor Keats had not, and it is impossible I say to conceive the effect which such a Review must have had upon him, knowing as he did that he had his way to make in the world by his own exertions."[6] Until he could prove otherwise, John was what "Z" had made him: a Cockney Poet.

John Gibson Lockhart, whom generations of literary critics have believed to be the "Z" behind the Cockney School of Poetry, was well equipped for his task of cultural demolition. His precocious learning in Greek had qualified him to enter Balliol College, Oxford, at the age of fourteen, the same age that George found himself consigned to Abbey's counting stool while John was following the surgeon on his rounds at Edmonton. Lockhart's grasp of literature was imperial: having mastered the classics he had gone on to read in French, Italian, German, and Spanish. He took an interest in heraldry, the artistry of rank, and, ensconced in a circle of Tories and cultural aristocrats in Edinburgh, he leveled his assaults on the raw enthusiasm of genius. John did not resent the reviews of *Endymion* as much as his friends did. Attention, even negative attention, was better than the neglect his first book had received. And if there were any truth in the reviews, he was to blame. But to bar the Temple of Fame from him because of his social status was a low blow.

At times, John felt that he might rise to the challenge of producing a more virile, less mawkish volume of poetry that might actually sell. At times, while revising *Otho the Great* with Brown, he counted on their drama to redeem his reputation and his purse. More often than not, he felt a studied indifference, bordering on misanthropy, to the world's opinion. From the time George had left England, John felt that he had "altered completely." He had drifted away from friends they once shared. Poor Jem Rice was frequently too indisposed to venture out to Hampstead, where John

and Brown always promised him a bed. John Reynolds, having taken lodgings near Rice, was on his way to becoming the "broken-down, discontented man" he would reputedly become by the end of his life. William
Haslam was ensconced in Deptford below the river with his new wife and
had his hands full with his deceased father's estate. The life had gone out of
their Saturday-night Boys' Club.[7]

To the degree that John had opened his heart to Fanny Brawne, moreover, he had closed it proportionally (though no doubt unintentionally) to
George. "When I returned in 1820 he was not the same being," George later
said. "Altho' his reception of me was as warm as heart could wish, he did
not speak with his former openness and unreserve, he had lost the reviving
custom of venting his griefs."[8] When George showed up unexpectedly at
Wentworth Place at the holidays, John may have felt like Antony in the
arms of Cleopatra in Alexandria: stunned by the intrusion of an emissary
from a former life.

Neither brother was the same person he had been eighteen months before. By the time George reappeared, John and Fanny had reached a private understanding. An official engagement was as yet out of the question,
but their love for each other (if nothing else) was secure. John, in the final
months of the year, had developed a surrogate fraternal bond with Charles
Brown and become something of an older brother to the adolescent Sam
Brawne, next door. He and Fanny's little sister ("Toots") had their own language of teasing. George had a half-erected sawmill near Beargrass Creek
in Louisville, a steam-engine whose boiler and cylinders he was struggling
to figure out, and a newborn daughter.

Secure of a warm welcome, George had raced back to London as soon
as he landed in Liverpool. But at Wentworth Place he found himself, with
Brown on the one side and Fanny Brawne on the other, an awkward fit.
John did not share with George what was closest to his heart, in part because his feelings for Fanny were at odds with his commitment to help
George. Preoccupied with his own affairs, George knew little of Fanny
other than what he had read in John's letters: she was a flirt—of the type
John had vowed to have nothing more to do with. Brown saw George as a
lesser being, and Fanny may have seen him, proud father and failed businessman with a head full of schemes, as self-important. He did not seem to
register her presence.

John was caught awkwardly between his mismatched loved ones. Negotiating the rapids between Brown and Fanny had been an ongoing chore, albeit a labor of love, and now George had risen up like another obstacle to smooth-flowing relations. In the weeks that the brothers spent together in the winter of 1819–1820, they felt vaguely estranged. Each sensed that the distance looming between them was of a more profound nature than the four thousand miles between London and Louisville. "I dare say you have altered also," John had written to George in September. "Every man does— Our bodies every seven years are completely fresh-materiald. . . . This is the reason why men who had been bosom friends, on being separated for any number of years, afterwards meet coldly, neither of them knowing why— The fact is they are both altered—Men who live together have a silent moulding and influencing power over each other—They interassimilate. 'T is an uneasy thought that in seven years the same hands cannot greet each other again."[9] Such detachment *might* be overcome by a strenuous exertion of mind, but the effort would have to be constant, for time with its relentless militia marches on.

At one point during George's visit, Maria Dilke invited the brothers to "a piano forte hop." There, John met to an American whom George had invited. The man's name was Hart, and John liked him, "in a Moderate way." By this point, perhaps, if George hadn't been his own brother, John might have liked *him* in a moderate way. Hart could have been John de Hart, a steamboat captain who plied the waters between New Orleans and Louisville. "I saw Cap^n John Dehart in the streets," Audubon wrote later from Louisville, "and he looks just the same as he was 20 years ago." Or, he could have been the Samuel Hart whose steamboat, the *United States,* was under construction at Jeffersonville, across from Louisville. Once it had issued forth from its berth, a local inhabitant would call it "the finest merchant steamboat in the universe."[10] Its engine came from England. For all one knows, Hart came to England with George to make the purchase. But if speculation of the commercial sort dominated the New World economy, based increasingly on steam power, John was involved in speculations of a darker, more personal nature.

The Reynolds sisters had begun a "not very enticing row," and John asked Hart to look closely and form his own opinion of the difference between British and American women. He had grown weary of the endless round of gossip, and the Reynolds sisters now appeared to him as petty as Elizabeth Bennet's sisters appear to Mr. Darcy in *Pride and Prejudice*. Among other rivals, the Reynolds sisters disliked Fanny Brawne, and they may have been the ones to provide George with his information that she was "an artful bad hearted Girl." John almost thought that if he had the means he would return with George to Louisville and spend a few weeks with the three "Georges." But "almost" was John's word.[11] He had no desire to leave Fanny Brawne.

George, however, had not come to London to make social calls. His first priority was to sort out the eleven hundred pounds left from Tom's estate. From that amount, John had withdrawn £100 for his own use, and he had sent another £100 to George, which was the draft George had not received. Putting aside another £100 for their sister, to keep the accounts even, eight hundred pounds remained, to be divided equally among the three siblings (£266.66 each); or, as George estimated, there were about £540 between the brothers.[12]

George would have to subtract return fare across the Atlantic (about £80) and round trip travel from Liverpool to London, and from Louisville to New York. Between those and other travel expenses, he would not have much left. Yet without money, as one Louisville resident remarked, little could be done: "Now you'll own without money man *here* has less chance/Than Don Quixote in combat, deprived of his lance." George may have resembled Cervantes' hero in other ways, but he had lost his lance. Real estate in Louisville was expensive, and he could not afford to purchase a house. Boarding his family in the meantime was "a very considerable item of expence."[13] There was no telling when he could begin operations at the mill, or when his business would begin to yield enough profit to build a home, even with lumber from the mill. The Panic of 1819 had devastated the American economy. George would need to raise more money.

When George left London in 1818, he had deposited £500 at Abbey & Cocks for his brothers, an amount that he considered a loan, which he would not have called in under other circumstances. From that account, John had withdrawn £140 to pay his and Tom's expenses, and Abbey had deducted £31.9.2 for tea, chocolate, and cocoa that the three brothers had consumed. John saw at least part of the £336 pounds remaining as his. George and Tom had spent money in France that belonged to all the brothers, but that John had not kept track of, counting on George to keep things

fair. John may also have seen in George's honeymoon deposit moral compensation for George's happy prospects—*and* the fact that he was leaving
John with full responsibility for Tom and emotional responsibility for their
sister. John had withdrawn money from Abbey & Cocks probably not expecting George to ask for it back, but in January 1820 that is precisely what
George did. "George had need of all the money he could scrape together for
his American scheme," Brown explained.[14]

Ever since the summer, John had been living on Charles Brown's
money. In August, when John had requested a loan from his publisher, and
Brown had given his name as a surety, Brown had explained: "I am fully
acquainted with his circumstances,—the monies owing to him amount to
£230,—the Chancery Suit will not I think eventually be injurious to him,—
and his perseverance in the employment of his talents,—will, in my opinion, in a short time, place him in a situation more pleasant to his feelings as
far as his pocket is concerned." Like John, Brown hoped that a production
of *Otho the Great* at Drury Lane Theatre might help to fill that pocket. Most
of Brown's property was "locked up" in investments that yielded "quarterly
& half yearly driblets, insufficient for the support of both of us."[15] He did
not foresee George's reentering the picture in this manner.

When Brown later asked Abbey how much John had given George to
take back with him to America, Abbey replied "about £350 to £400 . . .
something like that amount." Brown performed his own calculations and
came up with £640. By the time reports of the transaction reached John
Taylor, the sum would have grown to £730. George did indeed take back
about £700 to Kentucky, but the money did not all come from John. George,
as Dilke put it, had "to borrow & scrape money in every direction."[16] As on
the occasion of his previous departure, George did not go into details with
his brother, assuming that it would all come out right in the end.

"John himself was ignorant of the real state of his funds," George later
claimed: "it was so painful a subject and in our private communications he
was so extremely melancholy that I always had to shew him the pleasing
side of things; when I left London I had not courage to say that the 700£ I
had obtained was not all ours by right; he therefore imagined it was, but he
never thought and never could have informed any one of his Friends that
the whole was his." George never considered it necessary to let his brother
"know the rights of it" because once he returned to America he planned to

send back as much money as he could, not merely what he owed his brother but whatever he could afford.[17]

Yet, all this left Brown empty-handed. Brown would later insist that "it took nothing from the charge against George, in a moral point of view," *how* much John had loaned him. If George was innocent of cheating his brother, he "took the best means to show himself guilty." Poverty can be a stern teacher, and Brown had learned her lessons well, having climbed his way out of pennilessness. He was not about to go back to dining in cheap pothouses. He had offered the poet a place to stay, never making him feel a debtor, but he always kept "a running account" of expenses . . .

1819	Decr. 22	Balance	£ 6.4.1
1820	Jan. 1	Examiners.	2.10.10
	. . . . . .	Half Wine and Spirits bill.	5.9.6
	. . . 8	Boot-maker's bill.	3.6.6
	March.	Dr. Bree	4.4.0
	. . .	Coach hire.	.3.0
	. . . 22	Board 3 months.	15.0.0
	May 4	Sundries.	.6.6
	. . . . . .	One week's rent in advance at Kentish Town	1.1.0
	. . . 6	Board 1 1/2 months.	7.10.0
	. . . . . .	Loan	50.0.0
	. . . . . .	Half wine and spirits bill.	5.18.0
1821	March 6	Mr. Rodd's bill.	13.11.0
			115.4.5
		Less received of J.K., 6th Feby. 1820.	40.0.0
			£75.4.5

John might have mistaken the exact amount that should have been his share of the family inheritance, but Brown did not think that John was incompetent in "money affairs." Uninterested, yes—even indifferent—but on one occasion when Brown had been balancing accounts, John had looked over his shoulder and pointed out an error "of such a nature as required a merchant's eye." When Brown expressed surprise, John responded, "I detest my own accounts, because they are bad; but I have learnt accounts, and, when mine are worth looking into, I shall be a good accomptant."[18]

The critical point as far as Charles Brown was concerned was that, when John returned from saying goodbye to George on Friday, January 28, he had less money in his pocket than he owed Brown. "John, after taking leave of him in town, came to me at Hampstead, pulled out a packet of notes from his pocket, placed them in my hands, and told me that was all George had left him. I counted them instantly; they amounted to £40. He and I then sat down to calculate how much he owed, and we found it to be about £60: so he was left by George about £20 in debt." Whether or not George had left his brother "worse than destitute—in debt," he *had* left him dependent on Brown.[19]

Yet George was not thinking this way. From his perspective, when he left London for Louisville in 1820 he was "more miserably distressed than John, being as pennyless or more so and having a wife and child to partake of my miseries. I could at the time have exhibited a picture of distress that would have brought tears and forgiveness from John, the reasons why I did not are manifest, he had troubles enough and this would have capped them all." But Brown, in his frustration, would turn the settling of the brothers' accounts into a tale of highway robbery on the part of George, the dastardly, dishonest brother. "O Severn," he exclaimed, "nothing on my part could stop that cruel brother's hand."[20]

Hearing the rumors that had been circulating about him after his departure, George would wonder where his brother could have found the fortune that he was supposed to have robbed from him. To explain himself, he flooded Dilke with facts and figures, and Brown responded with more facts and figures. Ultimately, despite Dilke's efforts to mediate, George did not forgive Brown for smearing his reputation, and Brown remained unconvinced by George's self-defense. "I hate him more than ever," Brown wrote to Dilke. "Once or twice I was on the point of throwing this paper in the fire; but I wished to prove the knave a knave; and I am anxious to disprove any idea that may be entertained of my having either rashly or wantonly spoken against him."[21]

Abbey, meanwhile, performed his part, lecturing both brothers about the dangers of taking money to America. After George's departure, he discovered that, due to an error on Hodgkinson's part, George had escaped with an extra fifty pounds from the counting house.[22] Abbey would swallow the loss, but he would refuse to advance any more money—to either brother, even when John needed money to go to Italy as his doctors ordered. Abbey had his own troubles. And besides, hadn't he warned John? Hadn't he told him not to give his money to George? Abbey no longer believed that the pioneer knew any more about business than the poet.

Yet both brothers considered living at home an advantage that John had, which George did not. "It is better in ill luck to have at least the comfort of ones friends," John would write to Georgiana's mother, "than to be shipwreck'd among Americans." The metaphor of shipwreck was becoming a favorite. When John sent George the £100 remittance from Abbey, he had cautioned him "not to sink it," though George *did,* as Dilke said, suffer "shipwreck on his return." If George must be shipwrecked among the Audubons and Bakewells of the world, John at least had long-standing, devoted friends and a publisher willing to serve as a banker. He also had proximity to Abbey, for whatever that might be worth. "You, John, have so many friends," George said in parting; "they will be sure to take care of you!"[23] He did not know how his words would later ring in John's ears.

John had always relied on his brother's honesty; but now, as on their previous separation, he had misgivings. "That was not, Brown, fair—was it?" he asked his friend. Brown remembered the question as negatively rhetorical, and by the time it reached Richard Woodhouse, it had become a positive assertion: "Brown, he ought not to have asked me." According to Brown, John thought that George "did not act rightly in leaving him so."[24] Honor required John to keep his promise to help his brother, but it also compelled George to recognize John's circumstances and not to hold him to that promise.

George, now alone, endured a cold ride to Liverpool. The winter of 1819–1820 was bitter in Europe, and particularly so on the British Isles. At Deptford, where Haslam lived, the ice on the Thames was so thick that people had set up booths on the river and were ice-skating. The trees in Hampstead were covered with ice, and the eaves of the houses dripped with icicles. "This is a beautiful day," John wrote to Georgiana on January 15. "I hope you will not quarrel with it if I call it an American one. The Sun comes upon the snow and makes a prettier candy than we have on twelvth [Twelfth Night] cakes."[25] But the snow did more that winter than glitter like sugar.

It fell heavy and thick, blocking the roads and waterways. "In our Grain market an almost total suspense of business has been experienced," reported one Liverpool paper that George's ship carried back to America: "The state of the winds has kept out all supplies, and the severity of the weather has cut off all communications by lands with the interior." In some places in England in mid-January the temperature had dropped to nineteen degrees below freezing. The weather in Paris was colder than it had been in twenty years, and the Seine itself had frozen over. Fishermen *even in Lisbon* were freezing to death.[26]

One story from a London paper reprinted in the *New York Evening Post* chronicled the misfortune of the Reverend R. Keats, who in crossing the border from Wiveliscombe to Tiverton in Devonshire, on Wednesday, January 5, fell with his horse into a ditch full of snow:

> Mr. K. then dismounted, but was immediately precipitated into the snow, to a depth that confined him to the spot. A few minutes only had elapsed, when a labourer appeared, who had been sent thither to render that part of the road passable; but Mr. K's hopes of relief were baffled by the deafness of the man, to whom calls for assistance were ineffectually made. In this predicament an ingenious resource suggested itself: Mr. K. supplied himself with snowballs, which he threw towards the labourer, and thus attracted the attention of which he stood so much in need. The man came to the spot, and with his spade successfully applied himself to the liberation of the snow-bound prisoner, who with his horse, completed the remainder of the journey in safety.[27]

The paper might have been confusing the resourceful clergyman, "Rev. R. Keats," with his more newsworthy son, Sir Richard Goodwin Keats, a military hero who had served under Lord Nelson in the Napoleonic Wars. The register of Peter Blundell's school in Tiverton records that the Reverend Richard Keats, headmaster of the school from 1775 to 1797, died in 1812, and was buried beside his wife, Elizabeth, in Kings Nympton Church beneath a tombstone erected by his son. Perhaps the Reverend R. Keats of Tiverton, as Sidney Colvin thinks (though without reference to this event), bore no direct relation to the brothers. Perhaps they did not see the story. Yet the mishap in Tiverton, about thirty miles north of Teignmouth, known for its mildness, illustrates the severity of the weather that winter.[28]

The royal family also suffered its ravages. In January, while the Prince Regent was confined to his bed with a cold and a sore throat, his younger brother, Prince Edward—Duke of Kent and Strathearn and father of the future Queen Victoria—caught a cold coming home in wet socks. His doctor prescribed calomel and Dr. James's powders, a popular cure-all, and the prince went to sleep thinking that rest would cure him. But he woke up feeling worse, and his cold turned into pneumonia. Within a few days, he died, a victim of snow.[29]

One week after the death of Prince Edward, King George III—the old, mad, blind king who had ruled Britain for more than fifty-nine years —followed his son to the grave. The king had been confined to an asylum as unfit to rule since 1811, and some believed his madness to have been caused by the loss of his American colonies. For the American revolutionaries, George III had served as a symbol of political and religious tyranny, and the American Declaration of Independence has an ignominious place reserved for him: "He has plundered our Seas, ravaged our Coasts, burnt our Towns, and destroyed the Lives of our People . . ." It was in listing their grievances against King George III that the people of the United States had declared their freedom.

The king died one day after George Keats left London, on Saturday, January 29, 1820. The Privy Council met at Carlton House the next day to pronounce his son, George Augustus Frederick of Hanover, who had ruled as Prince Regent for nine years, the next king of the Hanoverian dynasty, George IV. Two days after ringing out the old king, the bells of St. Paul's pealed again to ring in the new. But George IV's health was precarious, for the prince had been confined to his bed with a severe head cold for more than a week prior to becoming king.[30] When George Keats sailed to New York from Liverpool, he brought with him the news about the death of the monarch against whom the Americans had rebelled.

Like the royal family, George had been feeling under the weather. But sea air was supposed to be restorative, and John hoped that it would be George's "Physician in case of illness." John himself was sick, and before they parted, he may have given George the same advice he would give to John Reynolds in February: "if you travel outside have some flannel against the wind. . . . Should it rain do not stop upon deck though the Passengers should vomit themselves inside out. Keep under Hatches from all sort of wet." John worried about George during their intervals of separation. But on the last day of the three-day mourning period for George III, the poet himself received his own "death-warrant."[31]

Milder weather had set in on Thursday, February 3, producing a thaw. John had been ill since December, and he took the opportunity of warmer weather to go to town. He did not think he needed to take his bulky winter coat, but sitting outside the coach on the way back to Hampstead from

London, he realized his mistake. He caught a chill, which quickly turned into a fever. By the time he staggered through the door of Wentworth Place, he looked bad enough for Brown to ask: "What is the matter?—you are fevered?" John's response came out confused: "Yes, yes," he said, "I was on the outside of the coach this bitter day till I was severely chilled,—but now I don't feel it. Fevered!—of course, a little."[32] Brown sent his friend up to bed and went for a cordial.

When Brown entered the bedroom, John had climbed in between the cold sheets and was leaning forward to stare at a drop of blood on his pillow. "That is blood from my mouth," he said. "Bring me the candle, Brown; and let me see this blood." After examining it carefully, he looked up at his friend, and with a steadiness that Brown never forgot, said, "I know the colour of that blood;—it is arterial blood;—I cannot be deceived in that colour;—that drop of blood is my death-warrant;—I must die."[33] Brown rushed for the local doctor, who came and drained some more blood from the patient. When John finally dropped off to sleep, he looked ghastly. The family stigmata had passed from "poor Tom" to "poor John."

The Courier

George was on a fast-sailing packet ship back to New York when his brother received his death warrant. The *Courier* was the first in a regular line of packet ships, the Black Ball Line, sailing the North Atlantic. The ships had been keeping up a continuous loop between New York and Liverpool since 1817. Like clockwork, on the first day of each month—foul weather or fair, fully loaded or not—a Black Ball ship was due to leave from the River Mersey on the westbound journey to New York. On the tenth of each month, another ship would leave the Fulton Street wharf in downtown Manhattan, and sail east to Liverpool. Because of the prevailing westerly winds, the trip took, on average, just over twenty days on the eastbound journey, and forty days going back across the Atlantic. With more room for cargo and smaller crews, the Black Ballers were the fastest ships on the ocean.

A large black ball affixed to the foretopsail of each ship announced their comings and goings, and each ship also flew a pennant crimson flag with a black ball at the center. The merchants Francis Thompson and Isaac Wright who owned the Black Ball Line shared the dissenting profile common to English emigrants in America. Francis Thompson was a Quaker from the woolen-manufacturing district of West Riding in Yorkshire, and Isaac Wright was a Quaker from Sheffield. The four ships in their line— the *Amity,* the *Albion,* the *Courier,* and the *James Monroe*—were all built at the shipyards in New York.[34] George Keats crossed the ocean on the *Courier* on its second run.

Cabin passage, fixed at forty pounds, included not only wine and food, but bed and bedding, so George would not have to worry about that. The Black Ball ship captains were "men of great experience and activity," and the company insured cargo "at the lowest rates." In the roundabout style of the era, the company boasted: "These several recommendations, and the dependence which may be placed upon the periods of their departure, afford, it is thought, to these conveyances, advantages of considerable importance, both to passengers, and to the shippers of goods."[35]

The *Courier*'s sister ship, the *Albion,* which had cleared to sail from New York on November 9, 1819, and arrived in Liverpool less than a month later (by December 8), may have been the one George took to England. He seems to have timed his departure from Hampstead to arrive in Liverpool by February 1, when he knew the next Black Ball ship would sail for New York. Unlike the Delaware River leading to Philadelphia or Chesapeake Bay outside Baltimore, which were both locked up with ice during part of each winter, the Bay of New York was always accessible from the Atlantic. The Black Ball ships had the advantage of sailing all through the year. When Georgiana returned to England eight years later, she took the Black Ball Line.[36]

The *Albion* had sailed back to New York on New Year's Day loaded with dry goods and a handful of passengers, under the command of Captain John ("Kicking Jack") Williams, a man who has become legendary in song for snapping his daydreaming sailors back to work with the toe of his boot:

'Tis when the Black Baller is clear of the land,
    Yo ho, blow the man down!
The boatswain then bawls out the word of command,
    Oh, give me some time to blow the man down!

"Lay aft," is the cry, "to the break of the poop,
    Yo ho, blow the man down!

Or I'll help you along with the toe of my boot."
   Oh, give me some time to blow the man down!

To larboard and starboard on deck you will sprawl,
   Yo ho, blow the man down!
For "Kicking" Jack Williams commands that Black Ball,
   Oh, give me some time to blow the man down![37]

"Lay aft" in effect meant, "What in God's name are you doing?" The "break of the poop" was the forward end of the deck at the stern of the ship. If George did take the *Albion* to England in 1819, he would have been wise not to get in the way.

   He was certainly lucky not to have sailed with Kicking Jack two years later. On the same route from New York to Liverpool on April 1, 1822, the *Albion*—loaded to capacity with bales of cotton, bushels of rice, turpentine, beeswax, silver, gold, and fifty-four people—got caught in a gale after twenty days at sea. Just twenty miles off the southern coast of Ireland, the foreyard sail tore away, the topsail split, and the main mast toppled into the waves. The ship filled with water, and seven people were thrown overboard. The crew and twenty-eight desperate passengers lashed themselves to the pumps, as the ship was driven on a collision course toward Fastnet Rock. "It is barely possible to conceive the horrors of their situation," one report stated; "the deadly and relentless blast impelled them to destruction—the ship a wreck—the raging of the billows against the precipice on which they were driving, sending back from the caverns and the rocks the hoarse and melancholy warnings of death—dark, cold, and wet."[38] A few survived by clinging to the wreckage of the famous poop, but Kicking Jack went down with his ship.

   George's ship, the *Courier,* was due to sail on February 1 under the command of Captain Jonathan Eldridge, another prominent figure on the high seas. Like its sister ships, it had a capacity of nearly four hundred tons, and was loaded with three hundred and eighty-one tons of dry goods and coal. Seventeen passengers were registered to sail with George: three merchants (John Molsom, Robert Williams, and Samuel Grundy), three carpenters (James Robb, Thomas Wood, and John Wood, Jr.), two weavers (Andrew and Walter Kitchen), two unskilled laborers (Cuthbert Landreth and Henry A. Launey), a manufacturer (William Ridgeway); a gardener (Andrew Ure), a musician (John W. Clark), and a cotton spinner (Molly

Clark) with her three-year-old son (William) and eighteen-month-old baby (Charles). One passenger (William Jones) proclaimed himself a gentleman. George this time threw in his lot with the merchants.[39]

One can almost see George on deck telling the twenty-five-year-old mother about his own "little Emily," as George and Georgiana called their first daughter (no doubt to distinguish her from Georgiana, though they would later give up on that and go back to "little George," or "Georgy"). John had teased his brother while he was in town for following "the common beaten road of every father" and bragging about his daughter. Perhaps for this reason, in writing to his sister, George prefaced his remarks by acknowledging that all fathers "talk of their darlings in the same strain, she cannot be otherwise than beautiful the most obvious recommendation to a baby . . ."; yet, surely, his little girl *was* "both beautiful and intelligent for her age." People told him that she was *too intelligent* to live long: "This is a sort of flattery intended to be believed, and to create pleasure at the same time, would you suppose it possible?" John also teased Georgiana: "There is no Child like his Child—so original! original forsooth. However I take you at your words; I have a lively faith that yours is the very gem of all Children—Aint I its Unkle?"[40]

Just as George had once imagined the Jeffery sisters reading the letter he had sent them in Teignmouth, John depicted George and Georgiana, the latter with little Emily on her lap, reading his letter to them in Louisville:

> *Georgiana:* Haydon—yes . . . here is a sum total account of Haydon again I wonder your Brother don't put a monthly bulletin in the Philadelphia Papers about him—I wont hear—no—skip down to the bottom—aye and there are some more of his verses, skip (lullaby-by) them too.
> *George:* No, let's go regularly through.
> *Georgiana:* I wont hear a word about Haydon—bless the child, how rioty she is!—there go on there . . .

[John complains about Haydon's not repaying his money]

> *Georgiana:* Hunt—there . . . there's another of those dull folks—not a syllable about my friends—well—Hunt—what about Hunt pray—you little thing see how she bites my finger—my! is not this a tooth . . .[41]

With his wife and child waiting for him at home, his prematurely receding hairline, and his American venture in jeopardy, George may have felt older than his twenty-three years. Captain Eldridge identified him with the other merchants on board the *Courier,* who were older than the average passenger and ranged in age from thirty-two to fifty, when he listed George's age as twenty-eight.[42] The additional five years could have been a transcription error. The numeral 3 can look like an 8, and ship manifests were full of mistakes: ink smudged, people were illiterate and spelling inconsistent, and many guessed at ages. George himself mistook his own birth-date. But he also carried himself in such a way that he seemed older.

Writing to say goodbye to his sister from Liverpool, George likened himself to the old "bald Pate" in his brother's poem, "Hush, hush, tread softly." He had seen his sister only once during his business trip to London. Abbey had permitted her one visit to Hampstead, and George had never made it across the fields to Walthamstow. He had promised to visit her before he left town, but he was busy and did not get around to it. Yet, when it came to his sister, George always found excuses for procrastination. The tricks he used to cheer up John never seemed to work with Fanny—now seventeen, and estranged from George by temperament as well as distance. It would have been fitting for him to have borrowed a sentiment from John's letter of the previous November to address his sister: "I should, in duty, endeavour to write you a Letter with a comfortable nonchalance, but how can I do so when you are in so perplexing a situation, and I not able to help you out of it."[43]

George knew that Fanny disliked the Abbeys. But George also trusted more in Abbey's good nature than John or Fanny. Abbey was strict, but at least he was honest (or so George thought) and reliable. More to the point, under the present circumstances, George had no alternative to offer. "M͗ Abbey behaved very kindly to me before I left for which I am sure you will feel grateful," he lectured his sister from Liverpool. "He is attentive in his commerce with his fellows in all essentials. He observes with pleasure, the pleasure communicated to others; he says you sometimes look thin and pale, but he thinks that you have been better since you have run about a little feeding chickens, attending your little Cat &c. A man of coarse feeling would never notice these things."[44] George was leaving England, but John would keep in touch with her and let her know how George was doing.

After George's return to Louisville, John would inform his brother that Fanny was feeling neglected, but there was little else he could do. He did not attempt to invalidate her feelings, or to defend George's behavior. He

agreed that George's "troubles, anxieties and fatigues are not quite a sufficient excuse."[45] He nudged George to send some words for Fanny for him
to relay, but in the end George had a way of undoing whatever progress
John could make on his behalf. When George learned of Fanny's wounded
feelings, he scolded her mildly: with so much time on her hands, she could
not appreciate the many demands a businessman—and head of household
—like George had to face. Whether he was right or wrong was not the
point. Fanny read his heart in his tone, and his perceived neglect of her at
this juncture bred resentment that would take years, and much persistence
on George's part, to overcome. Even then, the siblings would never become
close, and Fanny would never visit Louisville. When she needed George,
he was not there, and as a result, when things settled down for George, and
he sought a more intimate bond with his sister, it would be too late.

Writing to Fanny from Liverpool, meanwhile, he did what guilty parties do best. He rationalized his behavior. "I considered not taking a final
leave of you a misfortune," he wrote, "and regretted very much that constant occupation detained me from coming to Walthamstow; but now I
look upon the pain attending the last good bye, and shake of the hand as
well spared, and reflect on the pleasure of seeing you again at however remote a period; when you will be a *Woman* and I a *'bald Pate.'*"[46] The self-
deprecating tone of his letter hardly detracts from the chill recognition that
George and his sister might not see each other again until many years had
passed—perhaps not ever again, as the case turned out to be.

Yet George *had* been busy, and he needed rest. At the coaching inn in
Liverpool, he fell asleep on a comfortable featherbed, but within a few
hours he awoke to find himself drenched. The tap to a cistern on the floor
above him had been left open, and water had leaked through the boards of
the ceiling. As George retailed the story for his sister:

> In this said English Feather bed I was in a greater risk to lose my life than
> thro' all my journey from Louisville to London. Before going to bed I
> thought it prudent to clear my stomach of bile, and took calomel; a cold
> taken while this is operating on the system frequently proves fatal, it
> opens the pores of the skin, and allows the inflammation to lay complete
> hold of one. Not having slept for two nights, I remained dead asleep while
> water was dripping thro' the ceiling until it had penetrated through all
> the clothes, the feather bed and the mattrass. The instant I awoke I

jumped out of bed, called the Servants and was put into a fresh bed, fully expecting to be laid up, but this morning to my astonishment I find myself well; you see if I can stand water when it nearly floats me in my bed without any injury, I cannot be born to be drowned.

George Keats, unlike the Cockney Pioneer Birkbeck, or Percy Shelley, was not born to drown. He worried that he might suffer the ill effects of the accident later, and his brother was worried that he might be facing a more "fatal attack."[47] But the family disease would not pass to George for another two decades.

His resistance was, no doubt, lowered. George had been running himself ragged, trying to prove that he, too, had talents superior to those of most men and that he could make a living by exercising them. In his few weeks in London, he had done as much, it seemed, as man could do. He had sorted out his accounts with Abbey and borrowed money from friends like William Haslam. Haslam had a friend, a man named Kent, who wanted to sell goods on commission in America. George was not optimistic about the man's chances for success in the Western Country, but he promised to look into it. The Panic had left everyone short of cash. By the end of the year he would have to report that Kent's merchandise would be "totally unsaleable" in the West.[48]

George had also spent time with Georgiana's family. He had taken his mother-in-law to Covent Garden to see Shakespeare's *Comedy of Errors* and the pantomime *Harlequin and Don Quixote*—a fitting enough double feature for George at this point in his life. But George assured Mrs. Wylie that he had run aground only temporarily. His sawmill was going up, and in no time at all, he would bring Georgiana and little Emily back for a visit. (Eight years later, he would still be talking about Georgiana's "long promised visit" to her mother in England.) His prospects for the future looked bright. Great George . . . "George the great."[49]

Although he had been worried about his family back in Louisville, George had never seriously considered that they might not be there when he got back. "Occupation will drive away the mumps until I get on board," he wrote to John from Liverpool, "and I hope favorable gales will keep them away when on board. When arrived at New York and the remainder of my journey[,] occupation and the near approach to George and our darling, the mumps will be to me antipodes."[50] Yet George had an uncanny knack for escaping the onset of sickness in his loved ones. He had hardly left Kentucky before a bilious fever that could have been cholera, malaria, or that "slow fever" typhoid, ravaged his family. Georgiana and little Georgiana had survived, but just barely.

George, for his part, survived the ocean crossing. After thirty-seven days at sea (to his great relief, nine fewer than his previous passage from Liverpool), the *Courier* entered the Bay of New York. He had expected to arrive about the middle of March, and in fact the *Courier* came in ahead of schedule, entering the Bay of New York by Tuesday, March 7, 1820. But the ship had to wait for a few days before it found a pilot who could guide it through the neck of the bay to the harbor. Farther inland, toward the north of the bay, the eastern tip of Staten Island and the western tip of Brooklyn formed a channel known as the Narrows, which all ships had to pass through to reach the harbor. "The packet ship *Courier,* Eldredge, arrived off the Hook on Tuesday last, and has been beating about for three days, and firing for a pilot," the *New-York Gazette and General Advertiser* reported.[51] At the southern edge of the mouth of the bay, the barrier spit known as Sandy Hook jutted up from New Jersey, proudly bearing the lighthouse that guided the incoming ships.

The *Courier* crept west along the southern shore of Long Island, and George could see the schooners, brigs, steamers, skiffs, and pilot boats animating the bay. It was crowded with ships from virtually all ports of call in the navigable world. Six rivers fed into it, including the Raritan, which led inland to New Brunswick, a post stop on the stage route to the Western Country. As the *Courier* drifted about, signaling for a pilot, its sister ship, the *Albion,* with Captain Kicking Jack Williams once more in command, coursed by on its eastbound trip to Liverpool. Later that same day, Friday, March 10, the *Courier* entered New York Harbor.[52]

Before passing through the Narrows, a customs officer and health inspector boarded the ship. The previous year, yellow fever imported from the West Indies had ravaged the city. The quarantine ground now had a separate pier, though many worried about diseases that might be festering in the wooden planks of the pier itself.[53] Smaller craft approached to ask the news from Europe, and while normally such talk involved winds and weather, the length of the voyage, and other maritime concerns, this time the *Courier* carried a more newsworthy story.

When Captain Eldridge turned over the mailbag to the pilot boy, he delivered the news about the death of King George III to the very nation that had allegedly driven him mad. Starting with the New York dailies, which printed the story headlined "Death of the King" from the *London Gazette,* the American papers would spread the news about the historic event to the other states and territories. The *National Advocate* would report that "the fast sailing packet ship Courier" had brought back news of the death of "the oldest King that ever sat on the English throne." The journalist added: "His reign was intimately connected with the most interesting events of the American revolution—he lived to wage war twice against us, and twice, for us, to make peace on honorable terms." Upon hearing that King George IV was dangerously ill and likely to die also, the *Louisville Public Advertiser* remarked a couple of weeks later that while the English might weep at the death of another king, "we should not be among those, who on hearing of it, would be disposed to mourn, or cover ourselves with sackcloth and ashes."[54]

The flag of the young nation now waved high, high on a bluff of Staten Island a few miles north of the Narrows. There, opposite the wooded bluffs of Brooklyn at the western end of Long Island, the fort known as Flagstaff Fort guarded the harbor that the British had seized at the start of the American Revolution. Not too much time had gone by since the cannons of the world's leading navy had exploded there in a show of military might intended to crush the upstart colonials with terror. But what George Washington, then Commander in Chief of the Continental Army, had learned most from the spectacle was the tactical use of retreat, and the Stars and Stripes now waved proudly from the fort.

Perhaps not literally. It was raining when George's ship entered New York Harbor, and about six and a half miles across the harbor from the Narrows, the dockworkers had thrown down planks across the mud for passengers to disembark. The piers, made of logs and filled with dirt and loose stone, fringed the coast of Manhattan. Francis Thompson of the Black Ball Line ran the warehouse at 10 Beekman Street, parallel to Fulton Street, across from the Fulton Street Wharf, where the Black Ball ships docked. The harbor was densely spiked with sails, but the neighboring ships made way with a bustle of yards and rigging as the pilot guided the *Courier* toward its slip. As if with perfectly orchestrated symmetry, the *James Monroe,* another Black Ball ship, docked at Liverpool at about the same time that the crew of the *Courier* made the ship fast to the pier in New York. One month later, on April 10, 1820, Captain Eldridge would sail the *Courier* out of the mouth of the bay, on the eastbound trip back to Liverpool.[55] In the meantime, porters ready to carry crates, trunks, and other luggage to nearby boarding houses crammed the pier.

From the harbor, George could see the Battery of lower Manhattan. It had originally served as an artillery battery defending the settlement behind it. But the population of New York City had been doubling about every fourteen years since then, and the Battery had lost its military mien and become a civic center with a marble City Hall. Rows of poplars demarcating the lines of the streets in the tight triangular grid of streets by the seaport could be seen above the rooftops. This dense concentration of buildings in lower Manhattan had become the main hub of commercial activity in the United States.

George was about to be released from more than five weeks of seasick captivity, and a frustrating few days beating about the bay, and he was glad to see the commotion. "Do not fret yourself," he remembered John saying, "on account of any immediate opportunity being lost: for in a new country whoever has money must have opportunity of employing it in many ways."[56] George had made the most of his trip, and was carrying back the banknotes he would need to get started again. Despite the Panic of 1819, it was still the "Era of Good Feelings" under President James Monroe's administration.[57] The spending spree after the War of 1812 had produced those good feelings, and the Monroe Doctrine, announcing an end to European imperialism in North America under the second term of Monroe's presidency, would sustain them.

From lower Manhattan, regular lines of stagecoaches and stagewagons ran along the stage route west. Before leaving the island, George had promised to let his mother-in-law know when he arrived, and he must have posted his letter right away, for it would reach London in about five weeks. "Louisville is not such a Monstrous distance," John assured Mrs. Wylie: "if Georgiana liv'd at York it would be just as far off. You see George will make nothing of the journey here and back. His absence will have been perhaps a fortunate event for Georgiana, for the pleasure of his return will be so great that it will wipe away the consciousness of many troubles felt before very deeply. She will see him return'd from us and be convinced that the separation is not so very formidable although the Atlantic is between."[58] In the ledger book of feelings, their loss would be Georgiana's gain. In the long run: debit London, credit Louisville.

Most of the coaches that left from lower Manhattan carried mail. Some saved time by skipping the post stops. George would be in for a wet ride either way. The same day the *Courier* dropped anchor in the New York Harbor, one local paper announced the postponement of a concert in "consequence of the inclement state of the weather." The ship arrived late Friday night, and on Saturday, March 11, another reported: "the weather has been so stormy that few persons venture out."[59]

Yet George had not completed three-quarters of his journey back to Louisville to let rain, sleet, or gloom-of-night deter him. With a necessary infusion of cash, he was ready to start over. He would leave the Battery of New York for Louisville. His brother, on the other hand, hemorrhaging life-blood, was facing a battery of a more threatening kind. Before the end of the year, John would find himself preparing to travel south to Italy "as a soldier marches up to a battery."[60] He knew, better than any of his friends, where that march would end.

Poor John

Neither doctor who attended John Keats following the receipt of his bloody "death-warrant" diagnosed his disease as tuberculosis—or, as it was called then, *phthisis* (its Greek name). Dr. George R. Rodd, a Hampstead surgeon, attributed his fever to mental anxiety. Dr. Robert Bree, a consulting specialist who had treated Charles Brown's brother James, agreed that to some extent the disease was nervous, but he believed that it was centered in the stomach, rather than the brain.[61] The doctors ordered rest, and John spent the rest of the winter under a blanket before the fire in Charles Brown's front parlor.

Although John placed little trust in his physicians, he felt justified in sending their opinions to his sister. "The Doctor assures me that there is nothing the matter with me except nervous irritability and a general weakness of the whole system which has proceeded from my anxiety of mind of late years and the too great excitement of poetry," he wrote to Fanny Keats on April 21, a day after he learned from Georgiana's mother that George had landed.[62] John was always strictly honest with his sister. It says much that he reported the status of his health through the voice of medical authority.

Brown, on the other hand, chose to place his bets with the medical professionals. After the hemorrhage at the start of February, he was fierce in enforcing the doctors' orders. Above all, he deemed it crucial to keep the patient from anything that might produce excitement. Fanny Brawne had to make do with seeing her lover through his window, or waiting until Brown went to town to sneak in and sit by John's side. John invited her to bring her needlework, but only when Brown was not there.

After ten weeks of vigilant guard, Brown was relieved to find his rigor paying off, as the invalid began to attempt short walks to the heath. As spring approached, the mood in the front parlor lifted and Brown began to make plans once more to follow his nose to the North. *When the weather / Was warm— / Och the charm / When we choose / To follow one's nose / To the north / To the north, / To follow one's nose to the north!* But things had changed drastically since John sent those lines to his sister from Scotland.

The doctors cautiously suggested that a change of air might be beneficial, but they would have liked to send the patient south, rather than north. Brown knew that John did not want to go to Italy, or anywhere else for that matter, but why not, he urged, pack a light knapsack and come along? They had seen no sickly wights in the Highlands. The mountains were good for body as well as soul. Of course, in reality, Brown doubted that his friend could make the trip. He would have loved John's company, but he remembered the sore throat and fever that had sent him back to London two months ahead of schedule in the summer of 1818. Brown did not expect John to accept his offer to join him. John knew better than to test the strength he did not have, and Brown knew better than to push him.

Yet, by renting his half of Wentworth Place for the summer, Brown was in effect leaving his best friend homeless. He borrowed money (fifty pounds, with interest) to lend John for his summer expenses. On May 4, 1820, he gave him a pound and a shilling to use as a deposit for the room where John would spend the summer, at 2 Wesleyan Place. It overlooked a noisy street in Kentish Town, but the rental did have one advantage over Hampstead: it was cheap. Leigh Hunt and his family would be around the corner, at 13 Mortimer Terrace. And should John feel up to it, it was still within walking distance of the old neighborhood.

John parted with Brown on the first weekend in May, at Gravesend, a port town twenty-five miles downriver from London with an ominous, in

John's case, prophetic, name. When he next docked at Gravesend, he would be at the start of his death march to Rome. He and Brown would cross paths there once again, but they would do so unawares. When they took leave of each other, in May 1820, it was for the last time. Brown turned north in a packet ship at the mouth of the Thames into the Irish Sea, and John traveled back up the river toward Kentish Town.

John would have to bear up as best he could for the next few months. The purgatory in Kentish Town would not last forever. Brown would return, and John could then return to Paradise, alias Hampstead. But while he tried work on "The Cap and Bells; or, The Jealousies: A Faëry Tale," a lighthearted Spenserian romance he had begun in the winter, he could not focus. He had lost his taste for the abstract amours of Emperor Elfinan and the fairy princess Bellanaine. He was too far from Fanny Brawne to be at ease, and in place of his fictional "Jealousies," the demons of real jealousy crowded his hot summer prison.

John no longer had the nightly comfort of goodnight notes from Fanny to put under his pillow to assure himself of her affection, and throughout May and June he produced a series of anguished love letters that reveal a terrible agony of mind. He could not walk much, and etiquette of the early nineteenth century did not permit a young, unmarried lady to pay social calls to a man in his own apartment. Fanny Brawne was no Cressida, as John feared she might turn out (like the Trojan Troilus's unfaithful love), but neither did she shut herself up at Wentworth Place while John was in Kentish Town. Such behavior would not be good for her, and she did not see how it could help him.

Yet, sick and lonely at a further remove, John wondered whether any woman could be faithful. His ode "To Fanny" asks: "Must not a woman be / A feather on the sea, / Swayed to and fro by every wind and tide?" The poem was written about the same time as his anguished love letters to Fanny, which, luckily, she knew how to handle; she informed him that by doubting her character, he had insulted her in word, thought, and deed. The tormented invalid relieved himself in more verse:

> I cry your mercy—pity—love!—aye, love,
>   Merciful love that tantalises not,
> One-thoughted, never wand'ring, guileless love,
>   Unmask'd, and being seen—without a blot!

O, let me have thee whole,—all,—all—be mine!
   That shape, that fairness, that sweet minor zest
Of love, your kiss, those hands, those eyes divine,
   That warm, white, lucent, million-pleasured breast,—
Yourself—your soul—in pity give me all,
   Withhold no atom's atom or I die . . .

Such sentiments were enough to embarrass the Victorians. Clearly, John's nerves were frayed. Matthew Arnold later complained that the posthumous publication of John's love letters to Fanny Brawne, written as they were "under the throttling and unmanning grasp of mortal disease," was "inexcusable." With no brothers or other fraternal confidants on hand, John turned the full force of his passions on Fanny. "I cannot brook the wolfsbane of fashion and foppery and tattle," he told her. "You must be mine to die upon the rack if I want you."[63] His statement reflects his belief that women like to be told to do a thing by a fine-looking fellow, and while, under certain conditions, this might be true, in the summer of 1820 John was in no shape to enforce his commands.

Yet, he did find some consolation in the company of Joseph Severn. Severn had escaped the paternal roof and now lived with his sister on Goswell Street, in Islington. He had painted the miniature portrait of George that John kept beside him, and the miniature painting of John that George hung in his home in Louisville. Unlike other people in the poet's life, Severn had not gone away for the summer—or disappeared into legal papers, marital commitments, or backwoods America. The congenial artist had been floating in and out of the brothers' lives since 1816, and after Brown left for Scotland, Severn secured his own position as a friend. He attached himself to the poet less by virtue of his artistic gifts than by his steady devotion. While John did not open his heart to Severn in the same way that he did to George or to Brown, he would do so soon enough when Severn assumed the leading role in the drama of John's life, and death.

Severn and Keats had a few things in common. Severn had not enjoyed etching copperplates for the engraver William Bond any more than John had liked mixing medicines for Dr. Thomas Hammond in Edmonton. And both found inspiration in Shakespeare. Shakespeare's head in profile appears on the title page of John's first book of poems, and Shakespeare provided the subject for Severn's first oil painting, *Hermia and Helena,* based on the characters from *A Midsummer Night's Dream*. "Whatever may be the merits of this case about your picture," George had encouraged Severn when he submitted his painting to a competition at the Royal Academy of Arts, "you may depend on victory, since Shakespeare will be sure to side with one who so well illustrates the pictures of his imagination."[64] Both Keats and Severn had ambitions exceeding the positions for which their apprenticeships had prepared them, ambitions worth fighting for.

And Severn understood John's moods. Both men suffered the side effects of a sensitive nature. In 1817, having felt neglected by John, Severn complained to George, who in turn reprimanded the artist: Severn was an "unconscionable fellow" for assuming the worst about John's behavior "without knowing the 'how'—and the 'why.'" George assured Severn that John had *not* forgotten him, and he ordered him to stop complaining. But when Severn next accused *George* of neglect, George burst out in exasperation:

> Have the goodness never to complain again about being forgotten. How many invitations have you received from me? How many have you answered? To the former question may be answered "a dozen"; to the latter, "not one"! Has Sampson done more execution than the Jews ever wished, or Joseph Severn intended? . . . If you are completely disabled I can do no more than pardon your right hand, throw pardon to ours. You shall be executed, tortured till your hair turn grey, or I'll pray the fates to direct a thunder-bolt through the broken roof of your Philistine temple, making a destruction of your canvas more dreadful than was the actual event. Unless you behave better I'll do such deeds, what they are I know not.[65]

No more Hermia and Helena. The mood was now Samson Agonistes. Shakespeare to Milton, the comic to the tragic: Furious George. George was, of course, teasing, but he also had little time or patience for reassuring anyone besides his brothers.

John had expected his lodgings in Kentish Town to serve him through the end of the summer; but in the third week of June 1820, those plans changed. On Thursday, June 22, he left his boarding house intending to pay a long overdue visit to his sister. But as he was walking, his mouth filled with blood. Another blood vessel had ruptured in his lung. Nauseous, dizzy, fearing that he might suffocate, John stumbled back in the direction he had come. Rather than passing under the rounded arch above the door-way to Wesleyan Place (an arch perhaps too much in the shape of a tomb-stone), and dragging himself up the stairs to his room, he kept going. He knew that a more dreadful deluge was coming, and he could not face it alone. So he turned the corner to Mortimer Terrace and lifted the knocker on Leigh Hunt's door.

As usual, Hunt had guests. John had to sit politely with the terrible taste of death in his mouth, listening to Maria Reveley Gisborne, an English expatriate who had befriended the Shelleys in Italy, expound her opinions about opera. Henry Reveley, her son, was a steamboat engineer, and Shelley described the contents of his study in a verse letter of July 1, 1820: "calculations much perplext,/With steam-boats, frigates and machinery quaint/Traced over them in blue and yellow paint./Then comes a range of mathematical/Instruments, for plans nautical and statical."[66] But John cared as little at the moment for steamboats as he did for opera. Maria Gisborne would note in her journal that she had met the young poet she had heard so much about, but that he had hardly spoken at all. When he did, he was barely audible.

Leigh Hunt could be oblivious to many things, but he could tell that his friend was in terrible shape. John now seemed a ghost of his former self. His skin was pale, tired-looking, and his clothing hung upon him. His hand was clammy. Hunt had almost expected something like it when John's landlady came rushing over from Wesleyan Place later to say that the young man upstairs was vomiting blood. When Hunt arrived, he found John in a condition little better than that of his own Titans, "Heaving in pain, and horribly convuls'd."

Hunt sent for Dr. William Lambe, Shelley's physician, who, like Shelley, was a vegetarian. His treatise on consumption and other chronic diseases claimed that "under the regimen of vegetables and pure water, the chest takes a more perfect and expanded form." He came not only to draw more blood from the patient but to prescribe a diet so strict that John would suffer, all summer, from hunger. His hemorrhage had weakened him, and Lambe's good intentions notwithstanding, the doctor's medical practices weakened him further. Even without those aggravating factors, convalescence after such a copious loss of blood was bound to be slow. "Poor Keats has been still nearer the next world," Severn wrote to Haslam. "His appearance is shocking and now reminds me of poor Tom—and I have been inclined to think him in the same way—for himself—he makes sure of it—and seems prepossessed that he cannot recover."[67]

John needed nursing, and he could no longer live alone, so Hunt had a bed made up for him in one of the upstairs rooms of his house on Mortimer Terrace. But even if recovery had been in his stars, the place where John would spend the next seven weeks was not conducive to the recovery of a consumptive invalid. Byron later described Hunt's six children in 1822 as "dirtier and more mischievous than Yahoos. What they can't destroy with their feet they will with their fingers." The "little blackguards" seemed to come "out of the Hottentot country." Marianne Hunt revealed something of her child-rearing philosophy in response to Byron's complaints when she wrote in her journal: "Can anything be more absurd than a peer of the realm—and a *poet* making such a fuss about three or four children disfiguring the walls of a few rooms—The very children would blush for him, fye Lord B.—fye."[68] Physically and emotionally drained, John did not make a fuss.

He slept much of the day. When not asleep, he would stare in the direction of Hampstead, thinking of Fanny. Normally, he preferred to look out the window, but the streets were "very much pester'd with cries, ballad singers, and street music," whose merrymaking jarred with his own mood.[69] Although it was summer, the clamor on the street, rather than striking a note of festivity, combined with the fracas of Hunt's household to make John feel perhaps as if he had fallen farther than from Paradise into Purgatory—from Purgatory into Pandemonium. Illness can heighten sensitivity, and heat can produce irritability. John's attitude toward Hunt had softened, but in Hunt's home he felt trapped.

Whenever John attempted to escape to the fields, Hunt offered to go with him. One day, when the friends were out walking on the path toward Highgate, John said that he would like to visit the room in which his brother Tom had died. Hunt tried to discourage the melancholy expedition, but John was determined. They went, and, after visiting the Bentleys' house, sat down on a bench beneath the elm trees. No longer able to restrain his emotion, John covered his face with his hands and through his tears cried that he was "dying of a broken heart."[70] Hunt later confessed that he was shocked. He had always considered the poet extremely private, even proud. He didn't know what to say.

But it was clear that the doctors were not making progress, and that

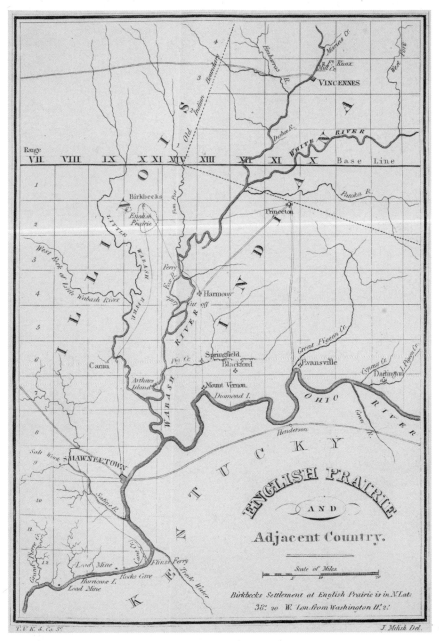

46. Map of the English Prairie, Illinois, between the Big and Little Wabash rivers.
Drawn by John Melish and published with Morris Birkbeck's *Letters from Illinois* (1818).
Courtesy of the Department of Special Collections and University Archives,
Stanford University Libraries.

47. Church at Harmony, Indiana, the German settlement
on the Wabash River near the English Prairie founded
by Johann Georg Rapp (1757–1847).

Illustration from Adlard Welby, *A Visit to North America and the
English Settlements in Illinois* (1821).

48. View of the mouth of the Fox River, Indiana, where
Morris Birkbeck drowned on June 4, 1825.

Courtesy of the Library of Congress.

49. John James Audubon (1785–1851), the American Woodsman, who hosted George and Georgiana in Red Banks (Henderson), Kentucky.

Portrait by Henry Inman, 1832, engraved by H. B. Hall. From Lucy Audubon, *The Life of John James Audubon, the Naturalist* (1875).

50. Lucy Green Audubon (1787–1874), enduring wife of the bird artist, and daughter of Squire Bakewell.

Based on a miniature by Frederick Cruikshank, 1831; from Francis Robert Herrick, *Audubon the Naturalist* (1917).

51. Audubon cabin in the woods.

Illustration by Peer; from Lucy Audubon, *The Life of John James Audubon, the Naturalist* (1875).

52. Maple sugar camp.

Illustration by Charles-Alexandre Lesueur, c. 1826, from *Les Voyages du Naturaliste Charles-Alexandre Lesueur en Amérique du Nord* (1904).

53. Log tavern in Indiana, 1820.

Engraving from Adlard Welby, *A Visit to North America and the English Settlements in Illinois* (1821).

54. Thomas Woodhouse Bakewell (1788–1867), George's business partner in Louisville.

Portrait by John James Audubon, 1820; from *The Cardinal* (Audubon Society of Sewickley Valley, Sewickley, Pennsylvania), July 1934.

55. Wreck of the *Albion,* commanded by Captain John (Kicking Jack) Williams, on Fastnet Rock, April 22, 1822. One of the Black Ball Line of packet ships on which George sailed.

Anonymous illustration from *Tales of Shipwrecks and Adventures at Sea* (1846).

56. Georgiana Emily Keats (1819–1855), George and Georgiana's first-born child.

Courtesy of Houghton Library, Harvard University, MS Keats 10 (489).

57. Louisville, Kentucky, as seen from the Indiana shore across the Ohio River.
Drawing by T. A. Evans, c. 1836, engraved by Doolittle and Munson. Courtesy of the
Filson Historical Society, Louisville.

58. Bas-relief from the Cemetery Gate of the Church of St. Stephen's,
Coleman Street, where Tom Keats was buried in December 1818.
The church no longer stands.

Wood engraving, c. 1850. Courtesy of the London Metropolitan Archives.

59. Pier at Naples, Italy, where John Keats and Joseph Severn were
quarantined for ten days in October 1820.

Engraving, c. 1820. Courtesy of Houghton Library, Harvard University, MS Keats 10 (642).

60. Capuan Gate, Naples. John admired the gusto of the Italians
eating spaghetti with their hands, as he made his way
back to the city through the gate.

Illustration from *American Architect and Building News* (1891).

61. Georgiana Augusta Wylie Keats (1798?–1879) on the beach.
Undated photograph. Courtesy of the Filson Historical Society, Louisville, Kentucky.

62. Georgiana Keats Jeffrey, as an older woman, remarried to the civil
engineer and Scottish emigrant John Jeffrey.

Undated photograph. Courtesy of the Filson Historical Society, Louisville, Kentucky.

63. John Keats on his deathbed at 26 Piazza di Spagna, Rome.
Sketch by Joseph Severn, 1821. Courtesy of the Keats House, City of London.

64. Design for John Keats's funeral monument. Sketch by Joseph Severn, 1826. Severn eventually honored the poet's request for anonymity, keeping only the lyre with the broken string for John's tombstone in the Protestant Cemetery, Rome.

65. The "Englishman's Palace." George Keats's mansion on Walnut Street, Louisville, between Third and Fourth streets. It no longer stands.

Undated photograph (HJC-73). Courtesy of the Filson Historical Society, Louisville, Kentucky.

colder weather was coming. John Taylor sent his own physician, Dr. George Darling, to examine the patient, and the verdict was then unanimous: John must leave England. His only chance for survival was to escape the cold weather posthaste. Shelley issued a warm invitation for Keats to join him and his family for the winter in Pisa. "This consumption is a disease particularly fond of people who write such good verses as you have done," Shelley sympathized on July 27, adding that he did not "think that young & amiable poets are at all bound to gratify its taste; they have entered into no bond with the Muses to that effect."[71] Hunt was delighted. Despite any darker forebodings he may have had, he mustered an attitude of blithe jocularity, praising the wonders of Shelley's hospitality, the beauty of Tuscany, the genius of Ariosto—anything that might appeal to his sick houseguest. He even began to call John by his Italian name, Giovanni, and to pepper his conversation with bits of Italian.

But John did not want to leave Fanny Brawne, and he regretted leaving his sister. "We have been so unfortunate for so long a time," he wrote to the latter five days before receiving Shelley's letter, "every event has been of so depressing a nature that I must persuade myself to think some change will take place in the aspect of our affairs."[72] Change did come, just over a couple of weeks later, but it was nothing he had been expecting. On Thursday, August 10, Marianne Hunt, busy with her baby, asked her housekeeper to carry a letter up to Mr. Keats. John may have been sleeping, for the housekeeper put it aside and forgot about it. Before she left the next day, she gave it to Thornton Leigh Hunt, the eldest boy, who was not yet nine, asking him to hand it over to his mother on Saturday. He did so, but by the time he did, the letter had been crumpled and soiled—and its wax seal broken. There was nothing of moment in it, but the letter was from Fanny Brawne. And two days to *this* invalid were a lifetime. John was entirely capable, as the hours dragged by with no message arriving from Hampstead, of imagining the worst.

Hunt apologized profusely, but John packed up, blind with frustration and rage, and left the house. In that distracted frame of mind, he made his way to Hampstead, where he had the vague idea of taking his old room at the Bentleys' home until Brown should return. At Wentworth Place, he paused. When Mrs. Brawne came to the door, she was shocked at what she found there. At the sight of the distraught and dying young man, her maternal instincts took over: John must go no farther. She knew that taking him into her home with an unmarried daughter would be a major breach of etiquette, perhaps a minor scandal. But John needed nursing. He seemed headed in the same direction as her late husband. Just as, two years earlier, Ann Wylie had ignored whispering tongues to let her daughter marry George Keats, a man bent on emigration, Frances Brawne now defied social convention to let her daughter nurse John. Both were single mothers of three. Both have taken their place in English literary tradition as surrogate mothers to the orphaned Keats brothers.

But the invalid could not stay for long. "He is advised—nay ordered— to go to Italy," Reynolds reported, "but in such a state it is a hopeless doom." By the third week of August, the cold winds had started to blow. John, left with no alternative, picked up his pen to address Taylor. How much money would be needed to go to Italy? Could the publisher help him to find out? John's latest book, *Lamia, Isabella, The Eve of St. Agnes, and Other Poems,* had been out for some weeks, and it had met a better critical response than his previous books. Perhaps Taylor & Hessey could advance him money against the proceeds? On a convenient scrap of paper, he scratched out a last will and testament to enclose with his letter. He asked that his trunk of books be divided among his friends and that any extra profit from his poems be used to pay an outstanding bill from his tailor. "This Journey to Italy wakes me at daylight every morning and haunts me horribly," he confessed . . . but he had to stop.[73] With every word that he wrote, the tightness increased in his chest.

In response to negative reviews of *Endymion,* John had said that he believed his name would be "among the English Poets" when he died. But now that he was dying, he did not know how quickly his name and fame would spread in the few months he had left. On September 1, while he was staying at Wentworth Place with the Brawnes, the *New Monthly Magazine and Universal Register* announced that his new poems were "very far superiour to any which their author has previously committed to the press." They had "nothing showy, or extravagant, or eccentric about them," but were, rather, "pieces of calm beauty, or of lone and self-supported grandeur. . . . There is a fine freeness of touch about them, like that which is manifest in the old marbles, as though the poet played at will his fancies virginal, and produced his most perfect works without toil."[74] They toil not. But neither, any longer, could this poet spin.

Taylor & Hessey sent copies of John's latest volume to booksellers in

America, and on November 1, the *New York Literary Journal,* in an essay entitled "Modern Periodical Literature," informed American readers that "Mr. Keats now happily has attained the vantage-ground whence he may defy criticism." In mid-December the *Norwich Courier* of Connecticut reprinted some stanzas from "Isabella; or, The Pot of Basil," which its editor felt displayed "a wild and affecting simplicity." Having read Francis Jeffrey's review, the editor understood that the author was "a very young man, gifted with powers, which, if properly directed, will obtain for him an elevated and a lasting station among the English Poets." About a month later, the *Rhode-Island American* quoted some lines from *Hyperion* that exhibited "a striking picture of Saturn in his solitude."[75]

These were among the first of countless times that John Keats's poetry would be reprinted, anthologized, and circulated to an admiring international audience. On New Year's Day, 1821, a couple of months before he died, a New York reviewer proclaimed: "Keats, whose *Endymion* was so cruelly treated by the critics, has just put forth a volume of poems which must effectually silence his deriders. The rich romance of his *Lamia*—the holy beauty of his *St. Agnes' Eve*—the pure and simple diction and intense feeling of his *Isabella*—the rough sublimity of his *Hyperion*—cannot be laughed down, though all the periodical critics in England and Scotland were to assail them with their sneers." Yet, by the time such commentary began to appear in the American press, John's sublime portrait of the defeated Saturn in his solitude would present a disturbing counterpart to Severn's picture of the defeated, solitary poet in Rome—one that would be depicted in a series of desolate letters, written with a less practiced, if no less "wild and affecting simplicity."[76]

The Dark and Bloody Ground

George began a letter to John four days before his brother's second major pulmonary hemorrhage with the question, "Where will our miseries end?"[77] George had only just heard from Brown about the *first* hemorrhage, which had taken place in Hampstead just after George had left London. Brown claimed that John was recovering, but George could not help feeling more sad than relieved. He found it unnerving that such a short span of time could suffice to deprive him of nearly everything that made life worth living. The same mail that contained the news of his brother's fatal sickness also contained a letter from Henry Wylie, with the news that Georgiana's aunt, Amelia Millar, had died. Everywhere George went now, it seemed, death and disease followed. Tom had died less than six months after George had left England the first time, and George could not help wondering: Would John survive the year? Would the brothers ever see each other again?

George also had to wonder whether his own family would survive Louisville. The mill was unfinished, and Georgiana was miserable. The town, which sat relatively low on the river, was rife with sickness. He shuddered to recall that while he was away his daughter had become "so ill as to approach the Grave dragging . . . dear George [Georgiana] after her." Typhus, pneumonia, rheumatism, scrofula, consumption, dysentery, scarlet fever, yellow fever, and other diseases were common. While germs had not yet been identified as the cause of disease, it was clear that the large pools of standing water that accumulated during the wet season in and around Louisville were pestilent. "When I landed here," one inhabitant recalled, "This town was not handsome, and living darned dear,/The streets were all ponds, and I'm told the Trustees/Had sooner wade thro' them, quite up to the knees,/Than incur the expense to have them drained off." In 1818 it seemed that every tenth house in Louisville contained a physician.[78]

Georgiana had been raised among the spires of Westminster, and she found the scenery in Kentucky as dull as the society. People never seemed to walk when they could ride, and the same utilitarian mentality accounted for the lack of trees and pleasant walks. Dogs barked, men shouted, and on market day the auctioneer rode up and down Main Street crying, "Forty dollars for the horse!" There was Jacob's Woods, a last patch of native woodland owned by John Jacob (a future neighbor of the Keatses); but for the most part, large stumps here and there were all that remained of former arboreal grandeur. Near the falls, "one solitary majestic sycamore" remained.[79] Nature, ever self-renewing, could do little to combat the axe. George himself was in the business of turning trees into dead wood.

Compared to the richly draped hills that Georgiana had seen coming down the Ohio, the flatlands surrounding Louisville seemed desolate. The town was in a valley between two higher plateaus, the Bluegrass and the Knobs. There were no shrubberies, no gardens, no ornamentation of any sort to vary the dreary sameness. Plain, unadorned houses of brick and of wood sat on dirt, without grass. The streets were washed only when the rain came down, and then the showers turned the dust back into mud. The inhabitants seemed determined to cut down every tree they could find, and in the evenings they swept the wood shavings into the street and set fire to them, spreading more dust. It was "a hardish fate," John commiserated, "to be settled among such a people.[80]

The taverns in Louisville provided virtually the only form of entertainment. On the south side of Main Street, between Second and Third under a painted wooden sign of George Washington, was Archibald Allan's "Washington Hall." Two blocks down, on the corner of Fifth and Main, was John Gwathmey's "Indian Queen." Little Georgiana Emily would later marry Alfred Gwathmey, the nephew of the proprietor of the Indian Queen (although the year she was born, John Gwathmey sold it to his rival across the street, and Allan changed the name to Union Hall). Around the corner, on Fifth Street, Harmony Hall served meals, coffee in the coffee room, ice cream in summertime, and whiskey at all times at the bar. By the end of 1820, the Exchange Coffee House would add more billiard tables, a bowling alley, and another reading room to the local culture. Occasionally, the taverns held balls, such as the one commemorating the ninetieth anniversary of George Washington's birth at Washington Hall in 1822, but more often, whiskey flowed, a fiddler fiddled, and men in the barroom showed their approval by stomping, clapping, and spitting tobacco through air thick with cigar smoke.

The daily routine at the taverns began with the bell that announced breakfast. Another bell rang half an hour later, and the doors to the dining room would fly open to reveal tables heaped with flesh: pork, beef, fish, and fowl baked in pies, roasted, or fried in grease. Breakfast came also with eggs, bacon, cornbread, milk, tea, and coffee. Henry Fearon noted that "some activity, as well as dexterity" was necessary to secure a seat at a table once the scramble for breakfast began. Meals were consumed "with a rapidity truly extraordinary." Fearon was surprised to find himself alone, even before he had finished his first cup of tea, in a room that only minutes before had been "crowded to suffocation." William Tell Harris described a similar scene in neighboring Virginia: "Negroes are stationed at each door of the dining-room, and when the second bell announces that all is ready, they turn the key, and escape as for their lives,—a general rush is made by the hungry company who were eagerly waiting outside, and without ceremony they commence a general attack upon the smoking board."[81] The same drill would be repeated at two o'clock for dinner; and again, at six o'clock, for supper. By ten, most guests had retreated to their beds, ushered into the regions of Morpheus by soporifics taken at the bar.

For a night's stay, one applied to the barkeeper. Each room held four to eight beds, each bed made up with patchwork quilts and calico sheets. There were no bed curtains or featherbeds, but at least the bedposts did not sprout leaves, as they had been known to do on the wetlands of Illinois. Guests washed at a large wooden cistern in the courtyard, and a slave stood in attendance with towels.[82] Some preferred their own handkerchiefs. Others used the private baths at the Louisville Bathing House, which stayed open from five in the morning until ten at night.

In the "newsroom" of the taverns, men would read the papers, and pace back and forth as if walking the deck of a ship. In the "boot room," or bar, they would sit and drink whiskey. Guests could help themselves from a tub of drinking water on the bar. For anything stronger, the bartender handed over a decanter with a glass. Fearon noticed that people in Louisville drank their "eye openers," "toddy," and "phlegm dispersers" in relative silence. The billiard table in the adjoining room had upstaged the art of conversation. Elias Pym Fordham remembered entering the boot-room of Washington Hall dressed like a backwoodsman. He wore a blanket over his shoulders pinned under his chin in Indian style, a hunting knife strapped to a leather belt, and Kentucky leggings. Fifteen years earlier, he said, the outfit had been as common in Kentucky as it still was in Indiana and Illinois. But in 1818 it raised eyebrows. "Mercantile adventurers," Fordham complained, had "introduced the fashions of London and Paris."[83]

Of course not everyone would have agreed that the merchants had spoiled Louisville with fashion. Georgiana felt cut off from the polite world she had left behind. She was doomed to raise her daughter in a place that was known, and for good reason, as the Dark and Bloody Ground. In 1769, when Daniel Boone arrived in Kentucky with a party of explorers, he discovered the fertile valleys and bountiful hunting grounds that the Native inhabitants were not keen to relinquish. "The state of Kentucky was the darling spot of many tribes of Indians, and was reserved among them as a common hunting ground," Frances Trollope observed. "It is said that they cannot yet name it without emotion, and that they have a sad and wild lament that they still chaunt to its memory."[84]

Boone, the only survivor of the original scouting expedition, had been warned by the Native people never to come back, but he came back with a vengeance, leading a group of about fifty pioneers from North Carolina in covered wagons and carving out the Great Wilderness Road through the forests along the way. For years, the road that Boone and his loggers hacked through the Great Cumberland Gap between the mountains of Virginia, Kentucky, and Tennessee had funneled hundreds of thousands of emigrants into Kentucky. By the time George Keats returned to Louisville from London, however, the stream of westward migration had been diverted from the Great Wilderness Road to the Great National Road (alternately, the United States Road), now the best overland route into Kentucky.

At the time of year that George traveled back from New York to Louisville, land travel was more efficient than river travel. The stage road from New York connected with the stage road to Somerset, New Jersey, in New Brunswick. From there, the route led west to Union Town, Pennsylvania, at the start of the Great National Road: "the great thorough fare of the people, in which there is incessant travelling from different parts to the Atlantic States, and from these States into the western country."[85] At Wheeling, Virginia (now West Virginia), the Ohio River dropped south, and a ferry shuttled travelers from the Great National Road across to Zane's Trace: the road opened by Colonel Ebenezer Zane across the state of Ohio, to Chillicothe, where another ferry crossed over to Limestone (or Maysville), Kentucky.

Like the Great Wilderness Road, the Great National Road at that time was unpaved and deeply rutted. In places, it consisted of little more than logs positioned side by side over swampy terrain, called corduroy crossings. The logs rocked back and forth as they shifted position, cracked, broke, sank, or suddenly rose up, making overland travel treacherous. When James Freeman Clarke took a stagecoach to Louisville in 1833, his carriage overturned going downhill on a road gullied by rain. "Inconvenient as it was to be overturned in the day," he claimed, "it was still worse in the night."[86] Passengers usually escaped with bruises, but broken limbs and even deaths could also result.

Thirty-eight miles west of Zanesville, Ohio, on the eastern bank of the Muskingum River, the stage road to Kentucky passed through the German settlement of New Lancaster. From the road, one could see a granite rock towering several hundred feet in the midst of a plain, a mile north of the town. In the early nineteenth century, there was much speculation about a Welsh tribe under the command of Madog ab Owain Gynedd (in English, "Madoc") that was supposed to have sailed to America several centuries before Columbus. In the preface to his epic, *Madoc* (1805), composed to help finance "Pantisocracy," Robert Southey claimed that there was strong evidence that Madoc not only reached America, but that his descendants were still living "on the southern branches of the Missouri, retaining their complexion, their language, and, in some degree, their arts." William Tell Harris surmised that the chamber hollowed out at the top of the rock near New Lancaster was a legacy of Madoc and his men.[87]

Yet, if these reputedly primitive remains looming large on the plains of Ohio *were* linked in an odd, poetic sort of way to the history of the Old Country, George did not have time for sightseeing on his way back to Louisville in 1820. He estimated that one could make the trip from New York to Louisville in a week. Since the *Courier* docked in New York on March 11, George was no doubt home more than two weeks later when, on Saturday April 1, a snowstorm hit Kentucky. Like another grim trick by the April Fool, the same one who, when Samuel Bowen's note came due on April 1, 1819, had swallowed his fortune, the snowstorm blighted the young buds that had begun to sprout.[88] Frost covered the ground for a couple of days, and the apple and peach blossoms in the orchards were destroyed. George's stubborn optimism notwithstanding, he may have seen these bleak events as evil omens.

His mother had made it to the age of thirty-five before being blighted by the same complaint that had carried away her younger brothers, Midgley John Jennings and Thomas Jennings. Midgley had died a couple of years younger than she, and Thomas, the phantom uncle whom John could not remember and who died before George and Tom were born, died at fourteen.[89] George's own brother Tom, not two weeks shy of his nineteenth birthday, had gone the way of his mother and uncles. When the snowstorm blighted the young buds in Kentucky, John Keats was twenty-four.

Every spring at this time, George would find himself thinking of his brother's lines from the start of *Endymion:* "'Tis now the early budders are just new / And spread in mazes of the youngest hue / About old Forests." In April four years later, he copied these lines for his sister and added:

This season never comes round without reminding me of these lines and many others equally appropriate, and beautiful of our dear John; the Horse chestnut Trees or as they are here called the "Buckeyes" (named I presume from the resemblance of its fruit to the beautiful large dark brown eye of the deer) are now so large in leaf as to tint the woods with green, the orchards which are so numerous and extensive are in the richest blossom, pink and white, Peaches Apples and Cherries, some blue grass we have down round the House and along the walks of the Garden is about an inch out of the Ground, and our vegetables are coming forward rapidly, keeping pace with your spring, we are generally about a month earlier. With the exception of the blue bird resembling in shape and habits the robin, we have nothing musical in the feathered tribe to usher in the spring, no blackbird, thrush, linnet Goldfinch, or earliest Cuckoo; our woods ring with the harsh cries of innumerable woodpeckers of gaudy plumage and ungraceful form, but no tender Nightingale sings his melodious song. We sometimes see at an enormous height a flight of Swans, flying in the form of a wedge, after the manner of ducks and Geese; Storks and cranes of very large size frequently fish in the shallow water of the falls within sight of the House, and when hunting in solitary places I have seen most noble eagles.[90]

The eagles in Kentucky were grand—to be sure they were grand—but *Endymion* was not his brother's only poem, nor were these, for George, the only eagles. In three short years, John had made the circuit of the traditional poetic career, from pastoral to epic. In his sonnet "On Seeing the Elgin Marbles," he had imagined each pinnacle and steep of godlike hardship telling him he must die, "Like a sick eagle looking at the sky." Three years later, the morbid "eagle brood" of Titans in the *Fall of Hyperion* seemed fit for nothing *but* to die. Even in *Hyperion,* when they had not yet changed from a "mammoth-brood" into eagles, they seemed as ill-fated as the giant beasts in the Big Bone Valley, by the River Licking.

George could not shake off an amorphous sadness. While in London he had copied out John's recent poems, and he could not help noticing that they had grown darker.[91] Somehow, the weeks that he had spent with his brother at Wentworth Place had left him feeling more estranged than he had before the visit. He remembered when John used to avoid "teazing any one with his miseries" but himself and Tom, always regretting his behavior afterward and contritely begging their forgiveness.[92] But this was no longer the case. George guessed that John's new roommate did not like him, and in fact, ever since the walking tour of Scotland in 1818, Brown did *not* like George. His indifference to the stiff, formal brother with the bad puns had turned to disgust. George told himself that the situation was temporary. Any distance that had arisen between the brothers was only the natural result of daily habits and routines sundered. All would be well once George returned to England with their fortunes made. But still, Brown made him uneasy.

And Tom was gone. He was buried in the family vault at the Church of St. Stephen's on Coleman Street. George had seen the bas-relief carving above the cemetery gate countless times. God, naked from the waist up, a white sheet draped over his lap, sits on a cloud surrounded by angels. In one hand, he holds a pennant flag bearing the British cross; the other rests on a globe, emblazoned with a matching cross. Souls of the living aspire, some more desperately than others, toward heavenly redemption in the realm above the clouds. Satan falls, at the center of the image, as an angel of resurrection blows a trumpet into his ear. It was a disturbing image, meant to be monitory.

At the bottom of the sculpture, two coffins flank a solitary, seated human figure. The coffin to the left contains a skeleton; the other, a fully fleshed mortal reclined on his side, eyes open, pensive. George could hardly picture Tom in his coffin—a skeleton, lifeless, skinless, sightless . . . *O horrible! to lose the sight of well remember'd face.* Yet it took a still greater effort of mind to imagine the inside of the second coffin, where, except for the belly, the reclined figure looks for all the world like John Keats. Could George have made *that* leap of imagination, he would have had to see *himself* in the solitary figure between the two coffins, reaching out with his left arm toward the freshly buried corpse.

The Man from Natchez

"Since your health requires it," George wrote to John on June 18, 1820, some time after the receipt of Brown's letter, "to Italy you must and shall go."[93] But George no longer had any cash. On his return from London, he had sunk most of the money he brought back from London into his saw-mill. He went to work every day at George Keats & Company, where he oversaw the felling of trees and the cutting of logs. He acquired some skill with a circular saw, and learned how to plane wood to a uniform thickness. He learned about the grooving and tonguing of planks, how to fit the edge of one into the groove of the next to produce a smooth surface. He took orders for pine and hickory boards, fencing, shingles, joists, and scantling. He had regained his lance and begun to strike out around him, like a chivalrous knight on behalf of his family, when Charles Brown's letter arrived, saddling him with the job of raising money to send his brother to Italy.

George's future was the mill, but he had also invested money in another steamboat. The fact might seem surprising, but George, like most people in Louisville, saw steamboats as the future. The steamboat business was the premier industry in the West, and Tom Bakewell and David Prentice, George's partners at the sawmill, cast steam-engines at their foundry in Louisville. A man from Natchez, Mississippi, who owned a fifth of the steamboat in which George had invested, had offered George two hundred pounds for his share. After thinking it over, George had decided to accept the offer, but now he would have to wait until a third party who had conveyed the offer returned from an upcountry trip. The man could then relay George's acceptance to the man from Natchez and close the deal. Since George could not sell his mill, he would have to sell his share in the boat. "I have no other means of raising anything like that Sum," he explained to John; "scarcely a Man in the Town could borrow such a sum."[94]

There was always a chance, George warned, that the man from Natchez would change his mind, but he did not think that would happen since the man seemed eager to increase his share. The deal would go through. George would send two hundred pounds to John through his agent in New Orleans. "I know not what comfort to give you under these circumstances," George remembered his brother writing the previous year. "Our affairs are in an awkward state." They were *still* in an awkward state, but the roles were now reversed. The brothers were back in their accustomed positions: John needed help, and George would provide it. "Make your mind easy and place confidence in my success," he wrote. "I cannot ensure it, but I will deserve it."[95]

Having formulated his plan, George returned to his sawmill. In the evenings, sitting by his fire next to Georgiana, he wondered how his brother was doing. During mealtimes, little Emily would pretend to offer "bread and buttée" and "Apple-tootie" to her absent Uncle John.[96] Georgiana

urged George to invite his brother to Louisville. Her nursing would restore him to rights. But as the weeks rolled past, and the leaves on the
trees began to change color, George did not hear back from the man from
Natchez.

High on a bluff of the Mississippi River three hundred miles upriver
from New Orleans, Natchez was the receiving port for the surrounding
plantations. Jervis Cutler observed in 1812 that "after entering the Mississippi from the Ohio, the whole prospect is so much changed, as to exhibit
the appearance of a different country." During harvest season, the streets of
the town were crammed with bales of cotton and hogsheads of tobacco on
their way to the ports at both ends of the river. Normally, the planters cultivated anywhere from four hundred to a thousand acres, and brought in up
to thirty thousand dollars per year. They kept elaborate houses in town,
with piazzas, balconies, and gardens brimming with figs, white plums,
grapes, and oranges. Like New Orleans, Natchez was notorious for the
"*open* profligacy" of its saloons, gambling houses, and brothels.[97]

In 1820, however, things looked different. A severe drought had wiped
out the crops. A diminished harvest of cotton and tobacco, combined with a
reduced market for cotton (caused in part by the fact that Britain's agriculture was recovering), added up to an enormous loss for the planters around
Natchez—the bigger the plantation, the greater the loss. In many cases, the
crops were not worth the cost of shipping. The sale of public land that year
dropped to a quarter of what it had been two years earlier. Many rushed to
cash in their investments. Some took a loss; others found their investments
to have no worth at all. Speculators along the river crammed the jails.
"Though hard times are plenty, and hard money scarce, let us not complain
while we have whisky for our friends and gunpowder for our enemies,"
toasted the men of Shawneetown on the Fourth of July.[98]

"The spring of 1820 was a gloomy time," a resident of Cincinnati wrote.
"All business was brought to a sudden stand. No more brick wagons, stone
wagons, or new cellars were to be seen in the streets. The mechanics lately
so blithe and cheerful had gone in different directions in search of work, at
any price, to keep themselves and families from starving. Almost any mechanic could be hired for fifty cents a day, working, as was then the custom, from sunrise to sunset; few could get employment at that." Formerly
wealthy men of the city had resorted to chopping logs, riding them to market, and selling them from a wagon at the going rate of a dollar and a half

per cord. Farmhands outside the slave states were now working for five dollars a month—and glad to find work at even that rate. A resident of Indiana counted close to fifteen hundred men seeking employment since the start of hard times. Lumber prices had fallen. In this, George, too, was affected.[99]

Because of the drought, the Ohio River was lower than it had been in many years. "Both the steam boats which usually ply between this place and Cincinnati, have been laid up for want of sufficient water to pass and re-pass," the *Louisville Public Advertiser* reported on October 4, 1820. "Nature seems to have laid an embargo on our trade both from above and below; for there are now at this place, Shippingport and Portland, nineteen or twenty steam boats which cannot depart until a swell takes place in the river. Business appears therefore, to be at a stand."[100] The steamboat business was at a complete standstill but George had sunk a large sum in a steamboat, and he needed to recover that money.

His partners at the sawmill, Tom Bakewell and David Prentice, were also struggling at their foundry in Louisville. Tom had commissioned Jacob Beckwith, another Louisville entrepreneur, to produce hulls for the steamboat engines that he and Prentice produced. But orders had dropped, and some of their engines had broken. Others had floundered midstream, unable to propel the steamboats back up the river. The company was facing lawsuits and bad debts that it could ill afford. Tom held Prentice accountable for design flaws in the engines that had caused the problems. When he dissolved his partnership with him the next year, he would calculate the company's losses at forty thousand dollars.[101]

When George accepted the offer from the man from Natchez, it was planting season. Days, and then weeks, slipped by, and still, no word from the man from Natchez. The trees in the orchards began to bow their branches to the ground, as every day, George rose and went to work at his mill. When the leaves began to blow, he worried about the onset of cold weather. How was John holding up? Whatever others might think, George considered himself "more nearly allied to poor John in feeling," as he was "more closely connected in Blood than any other in the whole circle of his Friendships."[102] It was not pleasant for him to have no money to send his brother.

George had always tried to be the reassuring voice in John's life, but by November all he could offer was a plea to hang on: "If you fail us we lose the most material object for which we now toil and save, in fact the goal to which we stretch is a future residence in England, and a communion once more with those who understand us and love us, you are the most prominent in our minds as one of those, your distress is ours. . . . All we want at present is your health and happiness."[103] Georgiana sent her love.

The cotton bolls began to burst, and the Choctaw children and squaws came to Natchez to harvest the cotton. The men did not come. The slaves drove carts loaded with bales and barrels down to the river, whipping the mules as they themselves had been whipped: "thus these much-injured men revenge upon the dumb animal the wrongs they themselves receive from their common owner," Fearon remarked on his visit to Natchez.[104] Women in Kentucky and Mississippi held picking frolics to pick out the seeds from the cotton. They held quilting bees to make quilts. And still, George did not hear back from the man from Natchez.

Before the snowstorm in Kentucky blighted the early budders, John James Audubon moved from Louisville to Cincinnati. Dr. Daniel Drake had offered him two hundred dollars a month to draw and stuff animals for his Western Museum. But although Audubon produced his sketches, Drake did not produce the salary. Audubon gave up on Drake and headed back down the river. On November 2, 1820, stopping just a couple of miles upstream from Henderson, he noted in his journal: "I can scarcely conceive that I stayed there eight years and passed therein comfortably, for it is undoubtedly on the poorest spot in the country, according to my present opinion." The next day at sunrise he passed the Henderson mill, and "with thoughts that made my blood run almost cold, bid it an eternal farewell."[105] Yet while Audubon may have said goodbye to the mill, its tentacles were still reaching after him.

On April 1, the day of the April Fool's snowstorm, Tom Bakewell filed a bill of complaint in the Jefferson County Circuit Court against his brother-in-law Audubon to recover the money he had lost in the Henderson mill. He estimated that amount to be forty thousand dollars—or with the money invested by his father, forty-four thousand. But when the sheriffs showed up at Nicholas Berthoud's house in Shippingport to summon the bird artist to court, they found that he had escaped to Cincinnati. Berthoud legally demurred on Audubon's behalf, but Tom Bakewell obtained a restraining order against his other brother-in-law, petitioning the court to prohibit Berthoud from delivering or paying over to Audubon any money, goods, effects, or credits in his possession pertaining to the latter. Tom also got his brother Will involved, and on May 10 Will signed a bond for $2,500, payable to Audubon should Tom's charges prove false.[106]

Eventually, George came to realize that the man from Natchez had changed his mind, or else that the deal had fallen through for another reason. George did not want to lose money in another steamboat, and he does not seem to have lowered his price. Perhaps he figured that it would make little difference. During the summer he had a consignment of goods that he had hoped to sell on commission, but he does not seem to have realized a profit sufficient to send to his brother. "Rest in the confidence that I will not omit any exertion to benefit you by some means or other," John had promised George the previous year. "If I cannot remit you hundreds, I will tens and if not that ones."[107] But George may have thought that sending tens or ones when his brother needed hundreds would be pointless, if not insulting. What, for instance, would Brown think?

Perhaps, in the end, George could have done better. Perhaps, he could have felt the urgency more. Perhaps had he been able to foresee how things would turn out, he might have even returned to London a second time. "M^rs K can bear witness, how much I suffered from my inability to remit," he would later plead; "I did not willingly add one pang to the sorrows of poor John." Yet, if he added no pangs, he also provided no relief. On November 8, 1820, the day Tom Bakewell's restraining order against Nicholas Berthoud and John James Audubon lodged in Chancery—and after John had already spent a week in Italy—George wrote to say that he had failed to raise the money that John needed to go south. "Again, and Again I must send bad news," he began . . . *Ah, bitter chill it was!*[108] The weather had grown cold, and no help was nigh.

8 POSTHUMOUS LIVES

Naples

As John waited at Taylor's house for the departure of the *Maria Crowther*, the brig that would take him to Italy, he tried to think of reasons *not* to dash back to Hampstead. Parting with Fanny Brawne had surely been the most difficult thing he had ever done. He could still see her—her gesture, her expression, her figure—eternally fading. *The day is gone, and all its sweets are gone!* Had he known that the small merchant ship would not sail for another four days, he would have remained in Hampstead. Instead, on Wednesday, September 13, 1820, he began what he called his "posthumous existence."[1] The break with Hampstead and all it contained had been made, and could not be undone.

John was now stuck in the purgatory of Fleet Street, in the publishing district, watching everything happen at a distance. As in a vision from one of his Great Odes, Taylor had conjured up a five-o'clock dinner to which he had invited William Haslam. Yet although the friends did their best to distract him, John felt himself to be, at core, a walking corpse. *They pass'd, like figures on a marble urn . . . And they were strange to me.* He could no more banish his devoted friends from his presence than he could Love, Ambition, or Poetry, those shades returning in ceaseless revolution like figures on a Grecian Urn.

Leigh Hunt had helped haul his trunks to the city. The light touch that the King of the Cockneys worked hard to maintain against all kinds of odds

made him a good companion for the coach ride from Hampstead, just as
Sarah Jeffery had once made a suitable companion for Tom when he left
Teignmouth in a similar condition. Hunt's life may have fallen short of his
own dreams, but he never let his disillusionment show. He now understood
the meaning of John's broken heart, and he let John keep quiet inside the
carriage on the stage ride to London. He could almost feel his chest tighten-
ing inside him. His stomach sickness was legible in his face. When Hunt
dropped the invalid off at Taylor's place, he delivered a burden he could not
have sustained much longer.

John had clearly steeled himself for the trial of separation. There had
been no histrionics or open displays of emotion between him and Fanny
Brawne at parting. Having already said everything needful to say, they
handled themselves with sober decorum. An errand boy recalled seeing
Fanny later that afternoon at Wentworth Place: "I coud n't resist going
around to the kitchen door to ask after Mr. Keats, for I had n't seen him for
a long time tramping around. It was September, and the back door was half
open, and just inside was Miss Brawne herself talking to one of the maids. I
stammered out my words, not feeling sure of my welcome, some way. Her
answer was curt enough, but I have always fancied she'd been crying. She
said that Mr. Keats had that very morning gone to London to sail for Italy."
Everyone knew the purpose of the trip. After a while, "any one with half an
eye could see Mr. Keats wasn't long for this world."[2]

Saying goodbye to John Keats also took its toll on Hunt. Too thin-
skinned to bear much more, he stumbled home and collapsed in a sympathetic "sickness and melancholy." The sickness would stretch out into
weeks, and then into months. "Judge how often I thought of Keats, and
with what feelings," Hunt later wrote to Joseph Severn. "But he knows it
all already, and can put it in better language than any man. . . . Tell him—
tell that great poet and noble-hearted man that we shall all bear his memory
in the most precious part of our hearts, and that the world shall bow their
heads to it, as our loves do."[3]

But the doctors had decided that John must go, and go he must. Who
could say the voyage wouldn't be for the best? From Mrs. Brawne's perspective, allowing the invalid to remain at Wentworth Place for the winter
would be akin to sealing his fate. Even her own headstrong daughter—
who cherished hope that her lover might recover, despite his own repeated
warnings to the contrary—would leave no remedy untried. Charles Brown

had not returned from Scotland, but when he did, John knew what to expect: he would join the chorus of exhortation, barking and thundering that there was nothing wrong with Keats that some good Italian wine, or Italian women, could not cure.

During their final days together, Fanny had made every effort to pretend that the couple would be seeing each other again in the spring. John had always been drawn to her positive outlook, and he was hardly surprised to find that she braved those last, difficult days with grace and good humor. In preparation for the journey, she clipped a lock of her hair for him as a keepsake, and she lined his traveling cap with silk. If he must go, he would go in style. Soon that silk lining would sear his scalp with the pain of recollection.

John packed nothing as heavy as his own memories. Besides his sentimental gifts from Fanny and his Shakespeare, which he never went anywhere without, he selected a few original copies of his poems to take with him—among them, his sonnet "To My Brother George," and his sonnet on Tom's seventeenth birthday, "To My Brothers." He was now following Tom, whither he knew not. He no longer had the same conviction in an afterlife that he had experienced at the time of Tom's death. The trip to Italy was a ruse, and he knew it.

John's one consolation was the knowledge that by leaving England he would be shielding his lover from the horrors he knew to be coming. He had seen it all before: the gradual wasting of features and of limbs, the fevered sleepless nights, the sheets and nightshirts drenched in sweat, the constant hacking cough and heart palpitations, the spewing of bloody mucus. Then would come the chattering teeth, the glassy stare of eyes gazing out past the sickroom walls, the phlegm that clumped like clay in the throat, blood that poured up from the lungs ever thicker and darker, and that final degradation, the diarrhea that would wash all sustenance from his system until—pale, parched, and fevered, like his own Endymion—he would expire in a fit of convulsions. Even were he to die more calmly, the end would not be pretty, certainly nothing for Fanny to see. Her father had already fallen victim to the dreadful disease, and John did not want to expose her to a similar fate. For her sake, therefore, he dragged himself—bare, forked creature that he was—from her embrace.

The day before his departure John made over the copyright of his three books to his publishers. He hoped that the latest would turn out to be worth more than the cotton rags it was printed on. Richard Woodhouse and Haslam were there to witness the legal transaction. Although Woodhouse was presently low on cash, he planned to recover shortly, and would be happy to honor any bank drafts that might come from Rome. "What is the value of Pelf after the supply of one's own wants?" None for him, he assured the poet. His own mission was to make a difference in the world, and through John Keats, he had a chance to do so. There were many others like himself, he assured John, who took "more than a brotherly Interest" in his welfare. The attorney might not have realized that the phrase might strike a chord he did not intend.[4]

The *Maria Crowther* was docked at the bridge by London Tower, and on Sunday morning, September 17, Taylor, Woodhouse, and Haslam accompanied John to the pier. Severn met them with his "jolly" brother Tom; but in the trauma of escaping from an overbearing father who did not want Severn to make the trip, and who struck his son to the ground as he was on his way out the door, Severn had forgotten his passport. Haslam, who had persuaded him to go, would have to go back for it. The *Maria Crowther* would dock overnight at Gravesend, and Haslam could have the passport delivered first thing in the morning. In the meantime, the small group of friends would spend a last day together, traveling down the river to Gravesend—and postponing their goodbyes until after dinner.

For the next six weeks, Keats and Severn would share cabin space with the captain, Thomas Walsh, and two women. The first of these, a salty matron named Mrs. Pidgeon, boarded with the other passengers by the Tower Bridge. The second, Miss Cotterell, was a fragile adolescent, also in the advanced stages of consumption, who would join them at Gravesend. Mrs. Pidgeon would soon begin to feel that five people in a cramped ship's cabin, two of them afflicted with what was obviously a terminal disease, was a less-than-ideal arrangement. Her politeness would wear off as soon as she met Miss Cotterell. She had not signed on as a nurse; and for all anyone knew, the disease might be contagious.

Once the traveling party had assembled, the skipper gave the command to weigh anchor, and John, with the sea wind in his face, felt again the old relief of motion. Recognizing how much trouble his friends had gone through on his behalf, he roused himself to show a companionable spirit, and even managed a few witticisms that Woodhouse neglected to record. But as the boat approached the tall wooden pier at Gravesend, Haslam felt *his* chest clenching inside him. Sundays can be depressing, and the place seemed provincial, and final: *Grave send. Graves end. Gravesend.* Haslam regretted that he could not make the trip to Italy. Severn may have had an illegitimate child, but Haslam had a legitimate wife, and a pile of paperwork waiting for him.[5] But he made Severn promise to keep a daily journal. As it turned out, when Severn sent the first installment of that journal, Haslam would find it so painful that he would have to put it aside for several days before showing it to John's friends.

Since the poet did not have the energy to disembark at Gravesend, the friends took dinner and afternoon tea on board the ship with the captain and Mrs. Pidgeon. At four o'clock, Taylor, Woodhouse, and Haslam undertook their awkward goodbyes. Haslam would look forward to seeing John, fattened up by spaghetti, in the spring; Woodhouse would wait to hear from his bankers; Taylor would be in touch with his doctor, James Clark, the best there was in Rome . . . And Keats and Severn, wiped out from the day, would pass out as soon as their friends left. Severn's dreams were troubled, though, and he woke up imagining himself trapped in a wine cellar. But the dark subterranean space was only the cabin. Severn fell back asleep, menaced by fears of an overprotective father, and dreamt himself in a shoemaker's shop.

Between his troubled dreams and his chronic liver complaint, Severn did not look well the next morning. When Miss Cotterell showed up bright and early, she could not tell which of the two young men was the one who was supposed to be dying. But she revealed her ignorance, as well as her imprudence, by asking. As soon as she discovered that John understood her symptoms better than her own doctor, she began to turn every conversation inevitably their way. Severn reported to Haslam, "We find sick people insisting and quarrelling about being worse than each other. . . . Now here we are better of[f]—for the Lady who is a very sweet girl about 18 but quite a martyr to the complaint—she insists on [being] better than Keats—and Keats feels she is certain[ly] worse than himself."[6] But he broke off there, overwhelmed by the pathos of the situation.

After breakfast, Severn decided to stretch his limbs and calm his stomach. He offered to pick up some last-minute supplies for the trip, and came back bearing fifty apples and a dozen biscuits, to supplement the captain's diet of ham, beef, and tongue. The captain seems to have experienced that strange personal interest that Taylor once described as the poet's peculiar effect on strangers, for he searched all over town for a goat to provide the invalid with fresh milk. John also gave Severn some prescriptions to fill at the chemist. Among them was a vial of laudanum, the liquid form of opium, used as a painkiller. In the early nineteenth century, this was sold regularly over the counter. Severn did not think twice about it. A good Christian, he did not imagine that he was bringing back material for the destruction, as well as the preservation, of life. But John had no intention of subjecting Severn to the trials that he had endured while nursing Tom; nor did he want to subject himself to the pains poor Tom had suffered.

From Gravesend, the *Maria Crowther* sailed out through the Thames, and around the bend at Margate toward the English Channel. When Severn awoke at dawn, he climbed on deck to see the "glorious eastern gate" of sunrise. It was Milton's description that came to mind: "where heaven/With earth and ocean meets/ . . . /Conspicuous far, winding with one ascent/Accessible from earth, one entrance high;/The rest was craggy cliff."[7] The cliffs were craggy, and despite the glory of morning, the waters were rough. The interminable rise and fall of the waves made Severn sick.

As the ship approached Brighton, the white-capped breakers subsided. But John recognized the calm before the storm, and indeed, at two o'clock in the afternoon, the waves swelled to great heights threatening to engulf the boat. Water poured into the cabin from the skylight, and the passengers clung onto their berths for their lives. Trunks and furniture crashed against the sides of the ship, and whatever was not secured went crashing with it. Severn stumbled up to the deck to alert the captain that the cabin was flooded, and when he stepped on deck he saw the ship pitching and plunging in time with the giant blue waves that rolled around it like mountains. He rushed back to the cabin to reassure the ladies: the captain and his first mate had things under control. All through the night, as the sailors worked the pumps and the square-rigged sails of the *Maria Crowther,* the passengers in the cavernous space of the cabin could not sleep. Nor, for another sixteen hours, could anyone think of food.

On Thursday morning, September 21, the storm subsided. The battered ship with its beleaguered crew and passengers pulled into Portsmouth —only to face a new and opposite problem there: a lack of wind. "A Flat day," Severn noted, "waiting for a wind." He went ashore with the captain to discover a bleak and desolate scene: "a wide expanse of Gravel—2 houses in about 6 miles—and a solitary yard of furze."[8]

Time dragged on in the punitive crypt of the cabin, and eventually John decided to spend one last night in England. With the captain's permission, he and Severn escaped their nautical prison and traveled seven miles inland to the millhouse where Charles Dilke's sister, Letitia, and her husband, John Snook, lived with their two boys. Severn entertained himself by painting a spiked acacia tree, and John learned that his friend Brown was only ten miles away visiting Charles Dilke's father in Chichester. John had been waiting five months to see Brown, but he dared not venture farther. Any step he took in that direction might lead all the way to Hampstead. And then what? Wherever the poet went now, he would have to drag his dysfunctional anatomy—lungs, corrupted stomach, and other worse things —with him. Better to accept his fate with dignity. His insides were blasted, and unless some Italian miracle could restore him, his time on the British Isles had run out.

John and Severn had been traveling for two weeks, and they had made it no farther than the area around Southampton. The captain and crew were fatigued, and the passengers ill tempered. But physical discomfort was nothing compared to the emotional anguish John was feeling. When he returned to the brig, he sat down and broke his epistolary silence in a letter to Brown. "I wish for death every day and night to deliver me from these pains, and then I wish death away, for death would destroy even those pains which are better than nothing. Land and Sea, weakness and decline are great separators, but death is the great divorcer for ever." He confessed that the thought of Fanny Brawne now swallowed everything else. He seldom even thought of George in America. "The thought of leaving Miss Brawne is beyond every thing horrible," he wrote. He sensed darkness coming on. He hoped that Brown would surmount his aversion and become a friend to her after his death. "Is there another Life? Shall I awake and find all this a dream? There must be[;] we cannot be created for this sort of suffering."[9]

As they crept along the coast of Devonshire, the captain dropped anchor at Dorchester. Severn, who was always at his best exploring new places, convinced John to come ashore and show him the caverns and grottoes that he knew so well. John came back to life momentarily, as he led Severn through the secret hollows of his old stomping grounds. But this would be his last taste of England, for after that the *Maria Crowther* turned out of the English Channel into the Bay of Biscay.

Due to political unrest in Spain and Portugal, ships of war were patrolling the waters that the ship would have to pass though. Carlos María Isidro
de Borbón, the younger brother of King Ferdinand VII, sought the Spanish
Crown, and the country was in a state of civil war. "The *mighty* King of
Spain has applied to the Kings of France and England for assistance, to enable him to govern his own people," as George would have read in Louisville. "There is now no doubt but the army of the Insurgents is formidable."
The rebels were on guard against the British. Portuguese sympathies lay
with the Spanish insurgents who had forced the absolutist King Ferdinand VII to accept the more liberal Constitution of 1812, which had been
abandoned under Napoleon. A revolutionary junta was now in charge until a similar constitution could be drafted for Portugal. Almost as alarming
as what his brother encountered in the Bay of Biscay was the explanation
that George would have encountered: "The 'contagion' which broke out in
Spain and spread to Naples, is now communicated to Portugal!"[10]

A quadruple-decker Portuguese man-of-war approached the *Maria
Crowther* and fired a shot as a signal to stop. Severn, who was attached
to life by a stronger cord than Keats, took fright. The sailors seemed to have
a menacing, piratical appearance: "a more infernal set" he could never
imagine.[11] The captain was concerned that the ship would be plundered.
Through a speaking trumpet, the Portuguese commander demanded in
English to know where the ship was headed, and for what purpose. The
captain responded to the inquisitor's questions, and the brig was allowed to
move on. Soon after, a British warship stopped the brig with a similar set of
questions. Where were they going? And why? Had they seen any other
ships? Captain Walsh described the Portuguese warship, and the English
turned in pursuit.

So far the passage had been anything but peaceful. The ship sailed
down the western coast of Portugal on the way to Gibraltar, where the waters became rough. Different wave patterns collided, and the boat turned in
circles. The passengers once more found themselves trapped "without food,
without aid & with the rebel sea squashing about the cabin to the clatter of
the chairs & trunks." At one point, no doubt to make sure that his friend
was still alive on the bunk above him, Severn asked: "Keats this is pretty
music, is it not." With an elasticity of spirit that the artist admired, Keats
shot back: yes, it was "Water parted from the sea" (the opening line of a
popular air). In the morning, the cabin boy tried to hold the breakfast table

steady, but a ham flew into Severn's lap, and the coffee pot into one of the ladies'—one prefers to think it was Pidgeon's.[12]

This was the low point of the journey for Keats. He ran a high fever and vomited blood. Severn's nerves were wrought to a high pitch, and he begged the captain to turn the ship around. But as history reveals, it kept its course. At dawn, Severn stood on deck to see the mountainous coast of northern Africa (the "coast of Barbary") come into view.[13] The great cliffs known as the Pillars of Hercules flanked the entrance to the nine-mile strait between the southern tip of Spain and the northern tip of Morocco, which divided Europe from the African continent, and the Atlantic Ocean from the Mediterranean Sea.

Once past Hercules's northern pillar—the Rock of Gibraltar—the ship was safely afloat in the Mediterranean Sea, and Severn wondered how any of them had survived. He had been doing his best to negotiate the clashing needs of the two invalids on board. Miss Cotterell, for instance, needed to have the windows of the cabin open in order not to faint, but Keats would start coughing violently whenever Severn opened them. Pidgeon was "a most consummate brute," who kept her distance from her sick bunkmate. "She would see Miss Cotterell stiffened like a corpse . . . nor ever lend the least aid—full a dozen times I have recovered this Lady and put her to bed—sometimes she would faint 4 times in a day."[14] More than once, Severn thought Cotterell dead.

Keats and Severn had endured six weeks of bad weather and worse accommodations, when they entered the Bay of Naples. The Spanish revolution had inspired the Neapolitans to rise up against *their* monarch, the Spanish King Ferdinand I, and the British fleet also was patrolling this bay. Thanks to a recent epidemic of typhus in London, moreover, another trial was in store for the weary travelers: "the loathsome misery of Quarantine."[15] The *Maria Crowther* would be confined for ten days in a throng of ships at the pier. To make matters worse, Lieutenant Sullivan of the British fleet boarded the ship with ten of his men to make inquiries—a foolish blunder, for in violating the rules of quarantine they too became trapped on board, further crowding the ship. The Neapolitans flocked to see the spectacle of the unfortunate English.

Miss Cotterell's brother, Charles E. Cotterell, lived in Naples and was doing some translating. John heard him say that one of the Neapolitans thought the cabin boy laughed like a beggar, and John ordered Cotterell to say that the Italian laughed like a damned fool. When Cotterell replied that the Italians had no word for "damn," John coughed up a wry and weary pun: the Italians were not *worth* a damn.[16] Not until John's twenty-fifth birthday, October 31, 1820, would Keats and Severn be released from their nauseating captivity at the pier.

From where the ship lay bobbing at anchor, in the meantime, John could see the terraced gardens and vineyards of Naples. Fruit-sellers came to the dock bearing the bounty of the land: watermelon, peaches, plums, and baskets of purple grapes. Mariners in red capes hawked *frutti di mare,* and boys with fishing poles pulled little silver fish that looked like anchovies out of the bay. Clouds of smoke billowed up from Vesuvius, suggesting the lingering presence of Vulcan.

At night, as the fishing boats illuminated the bay with their torches, flashes of fire shot forth from the mountaintop. The volcano erupted periodically. On December 7, 1819, powerful explosions from the crater—combined with an earthquake and a hurricane from the south—had terrified the city. The top of Vesuvius blazed in an immense conflagration, as the crater belched boiling lava in red currents down the dark side of the mountain. Henry Matthews, a consumptive Englishman traveling in Italy for his health that same year, described the hellish mouth of Vesuvius:

> When you arrive at the top, it is an awful sight, and much more like the infernal regions, than any thing that human imagination could suggest. As you approach the great crater, the crust upon which you tread becomes so hot, that you cannot stand long on the same place;—your progress is literally *"per ignes suppositos cineri doloso";* [Horace: "on fires beneath a treacherous crust of ashes"]—if you push your stick an inch below the surface, it takes fire, and you may light paper by thrusting it into any of the cracks of the crust. The craters of the late eruption were still vomiting forth flames and smoke, and when we threw down large stones into these fiery mouths, one might have thought they were replying to Lear's imprecation—*"Rumble thy belly full!—Spit fire!"*[17]

All of this had little effect on the poet. As John stared absently at the strange world around him, he felt the weight of his posthumous existence.

He had been thinking of Fanny Brawne constantly. He planned to enclose the lock of hair she had given him in a locket and her paper knife in a silver case. He would find a golden net for the pocketbook she had made for him as soon as he got to shore. After three days in quarantine, he summoned the energy to write to Mrs. Brawne to let her know that he had arrived, yet he could not bring himself to address her daughter directly. A postscript to his letter compressed his pent-up emotion: "Good bye Fanny! god bless you."[18]

Postal workers then took charge of the letter, as Charles Cotterell took charge of Keats and Severn. An expatriate wine merchant living in Naples, Cotterell worked as a banker and agent for foreigners at 10 Largo della Vittoria. Messrs. Cotterell, Iggulden & Company had, besides a bank, a reading room stocked with British and other European newspapers. His vineyards produced the best Falernian wine in Italy, and better than that of the ancient Romans. Softened by honey, it tasted like champagne. *Come, boy, you who serve out the old Falernian,* sang Catullus, *fill up stronger cups for me.* Three days before George's wedding, John had apologized to Benjamin Bailey for his delay in seeing him in an analogy to the rough, heady vintage that took ten years to reach maturity, and that preserved its flavor for another twenty years after that. "I will be to you wine in the cellar," he said, "and the more modestly or rather indolently I retire into the backward Bin, the more *falerne* will I be at the drinking."[19]

Charles Cotterell was an "extremely active little man," who seemed to know everyone.[20] Most important, he knew his way through the maze of fishermen, sailors, vendors, ballad singers, puppeteers, and beggars crowding the pier. His sister had told him how Keats and Severn—one with his medical knowledge, the other with his kind attentions—had taken care of her during the rough voyage, and he could not seem to do enough for them in return. He took them to the Villa da Londra, a hotel catering to English clients, and found them spacious rooms overlooking Vesuvius.

To Severn, Naples seemed like an enormous kitchen. Most of the cooking, like everything else, seemed to take place out of doors. At night, workmen fell asleep by the sides of the streets, on the steps of houses, by the church gates, under the columned porticos of palaces. "A partial observer might say that Naples was a truly jovial place; all seems mirth and uproar," wrote Henry Sass (an artist from the British Royal Academy traveling in Italy in 1818): "lords and lazzaroni, ladies and demireps, improvisatores, pickpockets, and punch, all jumbled together in a heterogeneous mass. The rattling of coaches, the bawling of coachmen, the various cries of the various trades, of basket-makers and knife-grinders, of sellers of lemonade, fruit, brooms, &c., conveyed in the highest key of the voice, assail the traveller from all quarters, and stun his ears. It is all confusion; and there is equal danger of being run over, jostled in a crowd, or tumbled into a stall of fruit, fish, or vegetables."[21] Like the rumbling of the volatile mountain hovering over the city, Naples never ceased its clamor.

Henry Matthews observed in his *Diary of an Invalid* that "the eternal bustle and worry of the streets" of Naples was "enough to drive a nervous man mad." People everywhere proffered their services—shining shoes, selling fruit, picking pockets. The women wore their hair long and loose, and children ran about in tunics hanging down to their knees. Most wore no shoes. To the English, the place seemed savage and wild. The hubbub was bad for the nerves, and unlike the "mild and soft" airs of Devonshire, those by the Bay of Naples were "keen and piercing." It was "one of the worst climates in Europe for complaints of the chest," and Matthews advised: "If a man be tired of the slow lingering progress of consumption, let him repair to Naples; and the *dénouement* will be much more rapid."[22]

Leigh Hunt had attacked the English Prince Regent for flouting his wealth in the midst of poverty, and the same kind of contrast, though even sharper, had caused the political unrest in Naples that John found disturbing. "Naples is a fine city," Henry Sass wrote, "but when I see people immersed in so much dirt and filth, and who have, altogether, so wretched an appearance, it is difficult to reconcile it with the splendid palaces around."[23] Every roll of bread fed the royal coffers. Property taxes were twenty-five percent. The people blamed the king and queen for hunger in a land of plenty.

King Ferdinand I, the third son of Charles III of Spain and formerly Ferdinand IV of the Kingdom of Naples, was now sovereign of the Kingdom of the Two Sicilies. He had ascended to the throne even before the late George III, at the age of eight, and was the oldest reigning sovereign in Europe. A few months before Keats and Severn arrived, he had been forced to accept a new constitution, one that was, like the Portuguese, modeled on the Spanish Constitution of 1812. His consort was Archduchess Maria Carolina of Austria, daughter of Empress Maria Theresa and sister of Marie Antoinette. Three hundred thousand citizen-soldiers were now stationed in and around the city, prepared to defend the Neapolitans against retaliation by the Austrian Empire. But John did not think that they looked ready to face the Austrians.[24]

People were wondering what would happen next, and during the few days that Keats and Severn spent in Naples, the king stole away and renounced the rebel constitution—to return, five months later, with the full might of the Austrian army behind him. Severn waited twenty minutes in the Palazzo Reale one day to catch sight of Ferdinand I, who turned out to be (as Sass put it) "a heavy slovenly sort of man." Severn thought he had the countenance of a goat.[25] John was determined to leave Naples as soon as he and Severn received their visas from the British Legation. If he was doomed to die, he said, he should be allowed to die comfortably. He would not leave his ashes in Naples.

Misery had deadened him to every novelty surrounding him. "I fear there is no one can give me any comfort," he wrote to Brown after his first night in Naples. But the very mention of "comfort" seems to have triggered a familiar association. In the next breath, he asked: "Is there any news of George? O, that something fortunate had ever happened to me or my brothers!—then I might hope,—but despair is forced upon me as a habit."[26] Like the sun in John's sonnet "To My Brother George," George had always been around to dissipate the vaporish dews of melancholy. But the sun was no longer shining; George was deep in the interior of another continent.

Perforce, Keats and Severn became closer. Although John had kept his secret grief from Severn throughout the ordeal of the sea voyage, once strength was no longer needed for survival, he broke down. Their first night in Naples was his birthday, and John knew that it would be his last. He had now lived a quarter of a century and accomplished nothing that he could feel proud of. He would expire, and it would be as if he had never been.

Before going to sleep in the Villa da Londra, Keats confessed to Severn that he could bear to die but that he could not bear to leave Fanny Brawne. "Oh, God! God! God! Every thing I have in my trunks that reminds me of her goes through me like a spear," he cried; "My imagination is horribly vivid about her—I see her—I hear her. There is nothing in the world of sufficient interest to divert me from her a moment."[27] Opening his heart to his friend helped him to get some rest, but he woke up the next morning to the same alienated reality.

Notwithstanding all this, Charles Cotterell showed up at the hotel brimming with ideas for diversion. The city was full of cafés serving fruit-flavored ices; and there was no other place in the world with improvisational street theater like Naples. The puppeteers acted out scenes from

Tasso and Ariosto, and the *improvisitori* made up verse with words suggested by the audience. At the other end of the cultural spectrum, the elaborate San Carlo Theater could not be missed. A spectacle of a thousand lights, it had six levels of balcony seating and a tiered stage as deep as the orchestra. The theater did not fail to impress Keats and Severn. They admired the extravagant painted sets, but when the two life-sized soldiers guarding the stage turned out to be real, John's loathing for Naples returned. Everything smacked of the city's miserable politics.

Cotterell proposed a day trip to the Bourbon Palace on the Capodimonte Hill. The ride through the country north of the city walls would be pleasant, and the museum housed thousands of treasures, ancient and modern. The collection included everyday objects from Herculaneum and Pompeii: locks, keys, scissors, needles, seals, rings, necklaces, combs, surgical instruments, cosmetic cases, kettles, saucepans, a theater ticket made of ivory displaying Aeschylus's name in Greek letters, a pig's-bottom sundial with a pig's tail to cast the shadow, and phallic ornaments from the Temple of Isis.

Severn should not miss the fine-arts collection. Many of the ancient pieces had not been identified, but among the gems was a first-century B.C. *Venus Kallipygos* and a third-century copy of Glykon's *Farnese Hercules*. The Renaissance rooms held such masterpieces as Michelangelo's sketch for *The Last Judgment*, Raphael's Holy Families, Parmigianino's portrait of Columbus and of the Spanish King Phillip II, Titian's *Danae and the Shower of Gold*, and several paintings by Correggio. There were landscapes by Salvador Rosa and historical paintings by the neoclassical painter Vincenzo Camuccini. One of the latter portrays Pericles's consort Aspasia, who brings Pericles, Socrates, and the Athenian general Alcibiades to admire the works of the Greek sculptor Phidias. Alcibiades may have lodged in Severn's mind, for Severn chose the general's assassination as the subject of his painting for the Royal Academy's annual competition for a traveling fellowship.

Keats wanted his friend to take advantage of the opportunity, and so they rode up the Via Ponti Rossi to the Bourbon Palace. On the way, their carriage passed a cottage covered with roses, and John cried out, "How late in the Year! What an exquisite climate!" Thrilled at this sudden display of interest from his melancholy guest, Cotterell jumped out of the carriage and came back with a bouquet of flowers. China roses, in vogue at the time, had the advantage of deepening rather fading with age, but they also had no smell. The magic disappeared once Keats put the bouquet to his nose: "Humbugs! they have no scent! What is a rose without its fragrance? I hate and abhor all humbug, whether in a flower or in a man or woman!"[28] Thus denouncing them, he threw the flowers into the road. Humbug had brought him to Italy.

The adventure had not gotten off to a good start, but on the way back from the Bourbon Museum John was in a better mood. He had communed with beauty. As the carriage passed under the Capuan Gate coming into the city, he saw a group of Neapolitans gathered around a large cauldron of spaghetti, "introducing it in long, unbroken strings into their capacious mouths, without the intermediary of anything but their hands." John had lost his taste for food, but he loved the gusto of the Italians who spurned "the humbug of knives and forks. Fingers were invented first. Give them some *carlini* that they may eat more!" he cried. "Glorious sight! How they take it in!"[29] Flowers with no scent were humbug. Money was humbug too. Gusto, John agreed with Hazlitt, was life. He would gladly spare a few coins stamped with the head of the late King Charles II of Naples to encourage the hearty Italians.

The road from Naples to Rome was supposed to be dangerous. Sass claimed that it was "the most dangerous of any in Italy, not only from the hordes of brigands which infest it, and by whom you are in danger of being attacked every moment, but also from the *mal aria,* or bad air, caused by the vapours arising from the Pomptine marshes." Pope Pius VI had drained the marshes south of Velletri on the ancient Roman road in order to reduce the threat of malaria, but the area was still unhealthy. According to Matthews, "the livid aspect of the miserable inhabitants of this region is a shocking proof of its unwholesomeness." Dr. James Clark, John's doctor in Rome, had recently met with two young men who had spent a night near the Pomptine marshes, to their own detriment: "One slept on the floor of a barn among some hay, with the door open. On his arrival at Florence, soon after, this gentleman was attacked by a violent fever. . . . His companion, who had slept in the carriage, probably owed his safety in great measure to his greater height above the surface of the ground placing him beyond the influence of the *aria cattiva* [bad air]."[30] But John was too sick to care about earthly danger.

A week in Naples was enough. It was time to embark on the final leg of his two-thousand-mile odyssey to Rome. Small carriages (*vetture*) were available to carry passengers up the Via Appia, along the western coast of Italy, to Rome. After thanking Cotterell and saying their goodbyes, the invalid and his friend bumped along the ancient road that so many others had taken. Severn bounded by the side of the carriage like an accessory sprite, stopping every so often to pick wildflowers and toss them in to Keats. But inside the carriage John was fading as quickly as his friend was returning to health outside in the fresh air. Beneath Severn's blanket of flowers, John may have been drowsed with the smell of poppies, but the season had come around once more—and his heart ached.

Beyond Capua, the road passed Marcus Tullius Cicero's estate near Mola di Gaeta, where, in 43 B.C., a centurion had put an end to the senatorial eloquence of Mark Antony's enemy. The villa was now in ruins, but the orange, lemon, and pomegranate trees were flourishing. In a haze off the shore of Terracina stood the Rock of Circe, home of the enchantress who turns Odysseus's men into swine. To the left of the road, the waves of the Tyrrhenian Sea crashed against the giant rocks. The woods gave way on the right to scorched fields where the authorities had driven the *banditti* from their lairs.

These roadside predators, as resilient as any bandit from Walter Scott's Highland tales, lurked in the hills hunting chamois, stags, and wild boar. At night, they came down to hunt wild duck and quail in the marshes, steal corn and cattle from the villages, and kidnap villagers for ransom. To venture out after dark was to put oneself in the hands of these "modern desperadoes," who would not hesitate to "commit the most barefaced outrages." Two hostages, as Matthews related in his *Diary of an Invalid,* had recently returned from their imprisonment in the hills. One of them, whose friends had sent most, but not all, of the ransom, had come back without his ears. The other, whose friends had refused to pay (as the authorities advised to discourage the practice), came back in eight pieces.[31]

In the Campagna, outside Rome, birds flocked above fields scattered with sheep and goats in numbers that would have thrilled Audubon. "Countless flocks of wild-fowl of every kind and description wheeled in the air within gun-shot of our carriage," observed Lady Frances Shelley (no direct relation to the poet) on her ride through the Campagna. "They seemed to cover the earth like flies upon a window; or—to employ a homely simile—like fleas upon a Roman bed." When Keats and Severn crossed the

Campagna, they saw a Catholic cardinal shooting down an astonishing quantity of small birds. He had an owl tied to a stick, plus a small mirror, to attract the birds. His two servants, in livery as bright as the cardinal's crimson cloak, kept themselves busy loading and reloading his fowling pieces. It seemed that his greatest challenge was to avoid shooting the owl.[32]

The poet and his friend at last passed under the Lateran Gate in the old city walls enclosing the Seven Hills of Rome. "A ruin—yet what a ruin!" Byron exclaimed upon seeing the Coliseum. "While stands the Coliseum, Rome shall stand;/When falls the Coliseum, Rome shall fall;/And when Rome falls—the World." When Shelley saw it in 1818, he thought it surpassed any work of human hands he had ever seen.

> It is of enormous height & circuit & the arches built of massy stones are piled on one another, & jut into the blue air shattered into the forms of overhanging rocks. It has been changed by time into the image of an amphitheatre of rocky hills overgrown by the wild-olive the myrtle & the fig tree, & threaded by little paths which wind among its ruined stairs & immeasurable galleries; the copse-wood overshadows you as you wander through its labyrinths & the wild weeds of this climate of flowers bloom under your feet. The arena is covered with grass, & pierces like the skirts of a natural plain the chasms of the broken arches around. But a small part of the exterior circumference remains, it is exquisitely light & beautiful, & the effect of the perfection of its architecture adorned with ranges of Corinthian pilasters supporting a bold cornice, is such as to diminish the effect of its greatness. The interior is all ruin. I can scarcely believe that when encrusted with Dorian marble & ornamented by columns of Egyptian granite its effect could have been so sublime & so impressive as in its present state.[33]

John Keats saw the Coliseum at about the same time of year that Shelley did, but unlike Shelley, John was not there as a tourist, and he kept going.

Dr. James Clark had been in the act of writing to Naples to check up on his patient when, in a remarkable coincidence, Keats knocked at the door of his house. Dr. Clark had taken rooms for him and Severn on the Spanish Piazza, the lively hub of the English community in Rome. Keats and Severn would spend the winter months at 26 Piazza di Spagna, to the right of the double flight of steps that led up to the Church of the Trinità dei Monti.

The French King Louis XII had commissioned the church to celebrate his triumph over Naples, and in escaping Naples, John may have felt a minor triumph of his own. His bedroom would be on the second floor, overlooking the Fontana della Barcaccia at the bottom of the Steps. *Barcaccia* "sinking boat." No auspicious omen.

Yet, the doctor thought Rome would be good for Keats. The Piazza di Spagna was the best place in the city for a consumptive patient. It was sheltered from the wind and had the advantage of being near the Pincian Mount, a delightful hill with prospects of the city and a park surrounding it full of pleasant, well-protected walks. The houses, however, were large and full of drafts, and the invalid would have to be careful. The stone staircases and marble floors, there as everywhere else in Italy, served as better protection from the heat of summer than the cold of winter. The stairwells were especially "subject to currents of air," Dr. Clark explained, "of which invalids not unfrequently feel the effects."[34] He recommended that John take the tiny enclosed bedroom with a fireplace, and let Severn sleep in the big living room of the apartment.

A well-educated, compassionate man, Dr. Clark had settled in Rome only the previous year, but he had already become the leading physician for the English community. He had gained some authority with respect to John's complaint, but, after a cursory examination of the patient, he produced what Keats had been expecting: more humbug. The case was not lost. The patient was merely worn down. The Roman air, combined with rest and light exercise, would cure him.

Life in Louisville

Louisville had been blanketed in snow during the winter of 1820–1821, and the weather had been even colder than it had been the previous winter: the coldest in living memory.[35] The river above and below the falls was frozen over, and the early budders had been kept back until late in the season. George was worried about his brother, and he did not need Charles Brown's insinuating letters to make him feel worse. Hadn't he tried to sell his share in the boat? What else could he do to raise money? Couldn't Brown read English?

George knew that John complained about him, but John had misgivings about everyone. "His nervous morbid temperament at times led him to misconstrue the motives of his best Friends." George had always worked hard to smooth things over between his brother and other people, and he had in fact "been instrumental times innumerable in correcting erroneous impressions."[36] Brown should be grateful.

"The coldness of your letter explains itself," George wrote in response to Brown's letter informing him that his brother was in Rome. "It may be an amiable resentment on your part and you are at liberty to cherish it; whatever errors you may fall into thro' kindness for my Brother however injurious to me, are easily forgiven. I might have reasonably hoped a longer siege of doubts would be necessary to destroy your good opinion of me. . . . I have a firm faith that John has every dependence on my honour and affection, and altho' the chances have gone against me, my disappointments having been just as numerous as my risques, I am still above water and hope soon to be able to relieve him."[37] George had failed to send the money that John needed, but John was in Rome. All would be well. Help would come.

Brown had honored John's last request to him from Rome, and let the poet's siblings know where he was, but it was clear that when he wrote to George a few days before Christmas he did so with great reluctance. When he returned from his Scottish tour and opened his mail to find no remittance from George, he was flabbergasted: "Not a penny remitted yet?" The family disease was laying bloody siege to his brother, and yet George had sent nothing but excuses. So much for the *"money brother."* He wrote to Haslam that "as for remittances from him,—we must dream about them." George Keats would "have to answer for the death of his brother, if it must be so," Brown announced. In a note on the margin of Brown's letter of January 15, 1821, Severn wrote: "Indeed I knew not, till after he quitted us the second time for America, how cruel he had been."[38] Selfish George.

Ever since George had arrived in America, he felt, misunderstanding pursued him. His friends back home misread his character, and his acquaintances in Kentucky withheld their sympathy. "Here we are not understood," George wrote to John in November. "If our conduct will bear two constructions, the worst is put upon it." While neither he nor Georgiana faced the challenge of other emigrants in having to communicate in a foreign tongue, the Western Country of the United States was foreign enough. They had connections, but "no genuine exercise of kindly feelings," except between themselves.[39] Neither felt fully at home in Louisville society.

Americans seemed provincial, and George refused to learn "the art of flattering the *egregious, excessive* vanity of the Americans at the expence of all other Countries in the world." A conversation between two young men in Natchez recorded by Henry Fearon in 1818 reflects the kind of egocentrism that George associated with the Americans. Leaning on a doorpost, one claims that Natchez is a sickly place. As proof, he points to the churchyard, where a quarter of the town's population had been buried in the span of five weeks. His interlocutor, unable to "endure so foul an aspersion upon his native town," threatens to *"call him out* for daring to say that *his* city was sickly; to be sure, five hundred people *had* died in a short time, but men did not live for ever. . . . 'I say, Sir, that there is not a more healthy place in the world than Natchez.'" Such obtuse chauvinism also struck George in Kentucky. As a result, he and Georgiana were "kept a little out of society, which however from its extreme dryness, and insipidity, is no great deprivation; we are looked upon as proud, and treated with consideration, and respect, but not with kindness or familiarity." Things could be worse: "all as it should be, if we had but a few Friends to enliven life's dull stream."[40] When he wrote this, George had been in Kentucky for more than six years.

George had only just turned twenty-one when he left England, but it had already been too late to assimilate to western ways:

> My character, manners, and habits were so completely formed, that my long residence in this country has failed to wean my mind from English associations as the most agreeable, or to give it that American tone which seems to have become engrafted on that of all my countrymen, who have been so long and so early exposed to the effects of the circumstances and opinions that here surround them. I feel myself an *Englishman,* and am looked upon as obstinately *such,* enjoying the respect of my neighbours and acquaintances, but unable to mix with them intimately, familiarly or unreservedly[;] whether the fault is in me or them, or both of us or neither, they seem as conscious as I am of our unamalgamating qualities and are likely to leave me in possession of my unpopular identity.

If George's reserve shielded him from a familiarity that did not ring true, Georgiana clung to her British past. According to her husband, she had "good taste enough to dislike this country."[41] Their granddaughter Alice Lee Keats recalled sitting on her grandmother's lap as a five-year-old child, while Georgiana taught her the lyrics to *God Save the Queen:*

> God save our gracious Queen,
> Long live our noble Queen,
> God save the Queen:
> Send her victorious,
> Happy and glorious,
> Long to reign over us:
> God save the Queen.

Independence, rather than a proper respect for authority, ruled in Kentucky. Reluctant to leave her granddaughter solely to the remedy of the queen, Georgiana also taught her the words to "The Ancient of Days." "She awed me completely," said Alice Lee Keats, "and I was much scared of her. She liked children to behave properly, and I suppose I had terrible manners."[42] George worried also about the effect of American manners on his family.

If George had had sons first, instead of daughters, he believed, he would not have stayed in Kentucky to raise them. And if he'd had his choice, he would rather have risked the latter "in the giddiest circles of London, the reputed hot bed of vice," than rear them in Louisville. He hoped, before they were "old enough to be irreclaimable, to be able to move them out of this vortex of petty meannessses and low vices." In 1824, he asked his sister to prepare some "elegant accomplishment . . . to help polish your beautiful nieces from their Kentucky rust." When Georgiana visited London four years later, George asked Dilke to observe any changes in his wife's "looks, manners and language." Although Dilke never would have said this to George, he did note, in his copy of Richard Monckton Milnes's *Life, Letters, and Literary Remains of John Keats,* that when Georgiana came from Louisville, she "brought with her a daughter as wild as a red Indian."[43]

Just as Georgiana had the habits and rituals of the old country to fall back on to combat cultural degeneration, George had his books. He was determined not to let his character become planed down to the standard of his surroundings and built a library of more than three hundred volumes. The titles in the collection reflect a general taste for self-improvement.

"This taste he preserved for years in a region, where scarcely another could be found who had so much as heard the names of his favorite authors," James Freeman Clarke recalled. "It was strange to find, on the banks of the Ohio, one who had successfully devoted himself to active pursuits, and who yet retained so fine a sensibility for the rarest and most evanescent beauties of ancient song." Clarke admired George Keats for remaining conscious of spiritual needs in such a remote outpost as Louisville, Kentucky. But George had his older brother to live up to; and like him, he was "full of inward aspiration."[44]

George also had his brother's copy of John Bonnycastle's *Introduction to Astronomy,* which John had earned in 1811 at Clarke's school as a "Reward of Merit." Its frontispiece was by Henry Fuseli, a painter who formed part of a circle of artists and intellectuals in London including William Blake, Mary Wollstonecraft, and William Godwin. The engraving featured an allegorical figure, crowned with stars, pointing out the constellations to a seated man. Suggesting the wonder of the unknown, it may have seemed to John an appropriate gift for his brother, as he set off under the wide blue sky across the Atlantic. George also had John's copy of Oliver Goldsmith's *History of Greece,* on which Benjamin Haydon had scrawled some human figures in ink. Haydon had given the book to John, inscribing it in keeping with his character: "To John Keats from his ardent friend, B. R. Haydon, 1817." John inscribed it to George the year that George left for America.[45]

Although George had come to America to make money, he differed from many of his peers in the business world in his tendency to see excess material accumulation as greed. Yet, as the years passed, he discovered that "a love of accumulation grows with success in its accomplishment; not to make money when its attainment seems certain, seems, to a man of business like throwing it away, and altho' one may be assured that more and more will not encrease our happiness or contentment, many arguments readily present themselves to satisfy the partial mind, that its pursuit is a duty we owe our children, and those we wish to serve."[46] The Cockney Pioneer had been financially shipwrecked once, and he knew how quickly it could happen again. Business demanded his constant attention, for he never considered himself in completely easy circumstances. Something on the horizon was always threatening destruction.

"In America it is hard for any man to keep out of the vortex created by the evervarying policy of the government," George complained. "No

amount of prudence and caution can altogether ensure a man of business
who has to earn a living, from being mixed up in the general tumult." People in Louisville considered him a Republican, but George's political sympathies were more in line with Coleridge's notion of a secular clerisy,
an educated elite that would be responsible for public decisions. "Altho' I
consider the American republic as the best possible for an intelligent and
virtuous people that has no prejudices in favour of other forms," George
claimed, "I do not consider the Americans either sufficiently virtuous or
intelligent to perpetuate their institutions unimpaired to a very remote posterity." Most were too ignorant not to "be easily misled by mean, artful, office seeking politicians."[47]

As a refuge from the fray, George joined James Freeman Clarke's Philosophical Society. He hosted meetings at his house for "the choice men of
Louisville Ky.—scholars, men of the learned professions, judges, states-
men, &c." (as George's friend the Reverend Samuel Osgood described the
club members). George did not find them original thinkers. They may not
have been "altogether uninformed, or unphilosophical, but [were] certainly
unpoetical." When George himself spoke up in his careful, understated
way, people listened. His remarks were, according to Osgood, "to the
purpose & alike judicious & modest." Yet, rather than *reading* the philosophical works they were supposed to be discussing, most society members
preferred to voice their own opinions. Clarke had to admit that "there was
not much reading done by the people." But, on the bright side, Kentuckians
were "independent thinkers," who liked to see things "from every point of
view."[48]

The local philosophers debated a variety of topics, from the relative
merits of the Ancients versus the Moderns, to phrenology. This popular
pseudoscience, attached certain functions of mind to particular "organs" of
the brain. Thus, when John Taylor, for example, described Richard Abbey
as "a large stout good natured looking Man with a great Piece of Benevolence standing out on the Top of his Forehead," he was interpreting a certain protrusion on the tea dealer's forehead as an extension of the "organ"
of benevolence. The Scottish phrenologist George Combe claimed that
George's friend Charles Caldwell (Chair of Medicine and Clinical Practice
at Transylvania University in Lexington, Kentucky, and later, Professor of
Medicine at the Medical Institute of Louisville) was an "early, persevering,
intrepid, and successful advocate of phrenology."[49]

Like phrenology, physiognomy relied on the basic principle that character can be interpreted through physical traits, whether the shape of the head or facial features. Before leaving London in 1818, George had invited Taylor to Judd Street to meet Georgiana and determine whether "the lines of her face answer to her spirit." Georgiana may not have had many lines in her face at that point, but when George met James Freeman Clarke fifteen years later, his own head arrested the minister's attention: "The striking height of the head, in the region assigned by phrenology to veneration, was a sign of nobility of sentiment, and the full development behind marked firmness and practical energy." George's capacity for veneration did not detract from his power of independent thinking. Clarke found no dogmatism in his energetic mind, no pietism in his taste for poetry: "It was a necessity of his nature to have his own thought on every subject; and when he assented to your opinion, it was not acquiescence but agreement."[50] The pioneer brother's tendency to think through most matters for himself was another trait he shared with the poet.

In his Phi Beta Kappa speech entitled "The American Scholar," Emerson urged Americans to think for themselves. One must start from the ground up with every question in order to resist the ideology of commercial capitalism and "the vulgar prosperity that retrogrades ever to barbarism." When George encountered American Transcendentalism in the second issue of the *Dial*—the journal in which Ralph Waldo Emerson, Henry David Thoreau, Amos Bronson Alcott, James Russell Lowell, and Margaret Fuller all published—he found much in it that he liked, but also much that he thought was "straining and worse than useless." He did not think, for instance, that one needed to retreat from society to find self-fulfillment. His brother might have done that at one time, but George did not have the option. When Fuller sent George a book of Emerson's essays, he read them with "great pleasure and perhaps some profit" (in Emerson's sense of "profit").[51]

Despite his association with the Louisville philosophers, George considered himself deficient in the higher faculties of philosophical reflection —and especially out of his league when it came to the sublimities of German idealism. Yet he bravely joined Clarke in following Emerson into the metaphysical labyrinth of Thomas Carlyle. At a board meeting of the Bank of Kentucky, where George found himself in a room full of commercial bankers, he tried to apply the advice of Carlyle's fictional philosopher,

Diogenes Teufelsdröckh, from *Sartor Resartus:* "to tear off the shows of things, and see their essence."[52] Had Teufelsdröckh been in the room with George, he might have recognized the futility of trying to see the essence of anything as spectral as credit. George himself saw little more than a heated debate about discount rates and bills of exchange.

When it came to history, George had more definite views. Carlyle's *The French Revolution: A History* seemed to him too radical. He thought (as Clarke informed Emerson) "that the poor aristocrats do not get any of the sympathy which all others receive, and that Carlyle seems even to enjoy their troubles." George was closer in this respect to the British politician and philosopher Edmund Burke, who defends the royal pomp and insignia of sovereignty in his *Reflections on the Revolution in France.* George might not have gone as far as Burke in defending the establishment, but nor did he go as far as the "Jacobinical" Carlyle.[53]

George did like Emerson's "Nature," an essay in which Emerson quotes a song from Shakespeare's *Measure for Measure:* "Take o take those lips away/that so sweetly were forsworn,/And those eyes, the break of day,/lights that do mislead the morn." George recognized the song from the volume of plays on his shelf by Francis Beaumont and John Fletcher, specifically *The Bloody Brother; or, Rollo, Duke of Normandy,* then attributed to Beaumont and Fletcher. After speaking with George, Clarke suggested to Emerson that he may have made a mistake, but Emerson replied that while he was aware of scholarly debate regarding the origin of the song, he did not think that "Beaumont and Fletcher, nor both together, were ever . . . visited by such a starry gleam as that stanza." There was no direct proof at the time, but "the internal evidence is all for one, none for the other"; if Shakespeare "did not write it, they did not."[54] As it turned out, Emerson's aesthetic intuition was correct. Fletcher and Philip Massinger had written the passage in *The Bloody Brother* where the song appeared, but Shakespeare had composed the song.

George did not earn any points from Emerson by doubting Shakespeare, but in the winter of 1820–1821, he had— far too literally—another "Bloody Brother" on his mind. In Kentucky, even by the end of March, everything still wore "the dreary aspect of winter," one paper reported; in recent days it had been "nearly as cold as any part of the last winter."[55] Spring took its time in coming, and when it came, it marked the second season since Tom's death. Nature would ring in the summer in triumphant splendor, and other budders would succeed the early ones that had been blighted, but would John be around to witness the change? In fact, by the time George sat down, on the third of March, to thank Brown for letting him know that his brother was in Rome, John was six feet underground.

Rome

Dr. Clark originally thought Joseph Severn an unsuitable companion for Keats. He seemed nervous, flighty even—incompatible with his intense, emaciated friend. It took the doctor only one look in the dark, knowing eyes of the poet to realize that he was dealing with an extraordinary case. Yet over the next several months, as Clark slowly realized the error of his original diagnosis, he would also change his opinion of Severn. The change would be almost as great as the one Severn himself would undergo, learning about life in the way one only can when faced with implacable death.

From the start, Dr. Clark could tell that there was something more than bodily illness plaguing his patient. He was not able to minister to a "mind diseased" any more than Lady Macbeth's physician; and so, knowing that financial worry was at least part of the problem, he wrote to ask Taylor's help. This patient was "too noble an animal to be allowed to sink without some sacrifice being made to save him."[56] If Clark could have afforded to support the patient himself, he would have. But he could not.

And there were expenses other than lodging and food to think of. The air along the ancient Flaminian Way, bordering the Tiber River, was healthy. His patient would need a horse to ride when weather permitted. But the monthly rate for hiring a horse was greater than John's rent at the Piazza di Spagna: £6 per month for the horse, £4.16 for the apartment. Music, too, would be helpful, to calm the patient's nerves and assist recovery. Dr. Clark could provide printed music, and Severn could play, but to rent a piano would cost another thirty-two shillings a month. Finding a piano that satisfied the sensitive ear of the music master's son would be another matter.[57]

Severn later confessed that he had come to Italy for selfish motives, believing that a closer attachment to Keats might help his career. Since his painting *The Cave of Despair* (an interpretation of the ninth canto of Spenser's *Faerie Queene*) had won the coveted gold medal from the Royal Academy of Arts, he was eligible to compete for their traveling scholarship, awarded annually on a rotating basis for painting, sculpture, or architecture. In 1820, the prize would be given for painting. Perhaps, Severn thought, in the style of Raphael's frescoes in the Stanza d'Eliodoro at the Vatican he might paint the court of Queen Elizabeth I in the Golden Age of England. He could include portraits of illustrious contemporaries, from Shakespeare to Sir Walter Raleigh, as the Italian masters had done. Perhaps he could find a patron in one of the English aristocrats living in Rome.

Severn had a letter of introduction to the Welsh sculptor John Gibson, who had moved to Rome in 1817 to study under Antonio Canova, the leading sculptor of the day. Gibson was currently at work on a statue titled *Mars Restrained by Cupid,* for the (sixth) Duke of Devonshire, and Severn inadvertently timed his call to coincide with a visit by Charles Abbot, Lord Colchester, a former Speaker of the House of Commons, who had stopped by to see the progress of the statue. When he knocked, Severn expected to be summarily dismissed. He had begun slinking away when Gibson took him by the arm and ushered him into his gallery, treating him—an unknown artist—with all the respect shown to Lord Colchester. Severn rushed back to tell Keats: "If Gibson who is a great artist can afford to do such a thing as this, then Rome is the place for me."[58] John was delighted. Severn set up his easel in the alcove off John's bedroom.

Except when it rained, there were few days when a walk through the grounds of the Monte Pincio was not advisable. The grounds of the park were shielded equally from cold winds and direct sunlight, and the promenade now attracted, as Dr. Clark explained, "all the beauty and fashion of Rome." They came "to parade, either in their equipages or on foot, and discuss the gossip and tittle-tattle of the town." The panoramic view from the terrace took in the basilica of Saint Peter's, where a hundred lights were kept burning around the tomb of the saint. Although the doctor did not normally recommend outings to churches or ruins, "both of which are frequently damp and always cold," at St. Peter's the invalid might find "both occupation for the mind, and a mild temperature to take exercise in." The English invalid Henry Matthews observed that "it is a luxury indeed to enjoy the mild and genial air in the interior of St. Peter's." The temperature was "delightful" and the church itself "a spectacle that never tires;—you may visit every day and always find something new to admire."[59] The thick walls kept the church cool in summer, warm in winter, and free from damp.

On the terrace at the top of the Pincian Mount, Keats and Severn met another invalid, Lieutenant Isaac Marmaduke Elton of the Royal Engineers. Like Keats, he was battling consumption, and he too had come to Rome for the mild air. A handsome man, Elton caught the eye of Princess Pauline Borghese, Napoleon Bonaparte's youngest sister, who was in the habit of strolling the promenade surrounded by "a bevy of admirers." In features and attitude, she bore a strong resemblance to her brother, who had laid out the grounds of the park. She lived apart from her husband and had caused a scandal by posing nude, from the waist up, lounging seductively on a one-armed settee as a Conquering Venus: Canova's *Venere Vincitrice.* The statue was kept under lock and key at the Borghese Palace, and could be seen only with permission from the princess. Keats and Severn went to see it, and Severn reported that "Keats was very severe in his satire on this famous Coquette." The poet had lost his taste for "woman merely as woman."[60]

He had also lost his taste for the meals that the local *trattoria* sent up to their rooms above the Spanish Steps in a tin-lined basket. The English were not admired for their culinary arts, and the Italians assumed that they were not fastidious eaters. According to an oft-repeated anecdote, Keats told Severn that he would stand it no longer. One afternoon, when the basket arrived with "the same horrid mess as usual, he opened the window & quietly & deliberately emptied out on the steps each plate. This done he closed the basket and pointed to the Porter to take it away— Sure enough this was a masterpiece more eloquent than words."[61] Within half an hour, another, more satisfactory meal arrived, and the pair fared better thereafter.

The doctor's wife also cooked for the invalid and his friend, preparing cabbage in the way that Severn's mother made it. On one occasion, the doctor searched all over Rome for a certain fish that he thought his patient might tolerate, though when he arrived with the fish, prepared by his wife, Keats was coughing too much to eat. Sometimes, in the afternoons while John slept, Severn would go out for dinner. For about ten pence, he could get a full meal: a plate of pasta and a main course of roast beef, mutton, pork cutlet, or wild boar with vegetables, typically broccoli or spinach. Dessert was usually plum or rice pudding.[62] But John was finding it harder every day to leave his bedroom.

He had been continuing to study Italian, but in reading Vittorio Alfieri's tragedy *Filippo,* he found that he had to toss the book aside when he came to the lines, "Misera me! Sollievo me non resta / Altro che il pianto—è delitto" ("Miserable me! No comfort remains to me / But crying, and that is a crime"). Tragedy, and even poetry in general, was no longer an option. He could not bear to see, or to have read to him, any letters from home, and though he could tolerate the news from the English papers, and comic scenes from *Don Quixote,* it was becoming difficult to find appropriate reading material. Severn read to him from Walter Scott's *The Monastery,* set in the days of Mary, Queen of Scots, and the novels of Maria Edgeworth. But it wasn't long before the artist realized that this episode in his life was going to be different from anything he had expected.

The turning point came on the tenth of December, when John vomited up a pint of blood that was malignantly dark and viscous in appearance. Severn ran for the doctor, who came and drew another sixteen ounces of blood from his patient. "Keats was much alarmed and dejected," Severn wrote. "O what an awful day I had with him!—he rush'd out of bed and said 'this day shall be my last'—and but for me most certainly it would."[63] The poet, determined to put an end to his existence, had seized the vial of laudanum from the small basket of medicines that Severn had purchased at Gravesend. But Severn had wrested it away, and fearing to trust himself with it, gave it to Dr. Clark. John's escape route was now gone, and to punish Severn he described in painstaking detail the ten-week ordeal they would both be facing. In the coming weeks, had the fatal vial been within reach, Severn, by his own admission, would have turned it over.

What followed the first flood of blood in mid-December became an all-too-familiar routine: John hemorrhaging blood, Severn rushing for the doctor, the doctor showing up and draining more blood from the patient. John was now on a starvation diet of milk and toast. The doctor warned Severn that if he gave Keats more food than prescribed, this would kill him. Keats cried that if Severn did not, he would die of hunger. Overwrought, persecuted from both sides as he felt, Severn stuck to his post, changing the sheets that the maid refused to touch, boiling the kettle for tea or coffee, and cleaning the rooms. He had grown used to the bleeding, which was "the lesser evil when compared with his Stomach—not a single thing will digest—the torture he suffers all and every night—and [the] best part of the day—is dreadful in the extreme."[64]

By this point, Dr. Clark realized that the disease was in its most advanced stages. John should never have left England. The patient was already too far gone for the trip to have made any difference, and had he remained at home, he might have lived a bit longer and died among friends. The doctor now checked in four or five times a day, and once he showed up with an Italian physician. The latter examined Keats and concluded that his chest was malformed. He announced, to the horror and indignation of Severn, that when Keats died the law would require an autopsy.

The holidays passed with little festivity. At night, Severn would cool his friend's fevered brow with a damp towel, as John's memories washed over him: thoughts of his good friend Brown, his lover, his sister, his brother George, Tom . . . Severn worked hard to keep back the tears that welled in his eyes. One day after Christmas, he went to the bank run by Giovanni Raimondo Torlonia and his son Alessandro Torlonia to withdraw money from the account that Taylor had set up for them. The Torlonias served the English community in Rome by exchanging pounds for Roman scudi. In exchange for administering the papal finances, the popes Pius VI and Pius VII had loaded the elder Torlonia with titles, and many complained that the ruin of the Roman nobility had made him rich. The Torlonias held lavish receptions for their clients, two-thirds of whom were English, at their palace in a suite of rooms adorned with giltwood and porphyry tables and statues such as Canova's *Hercules and Lichas*. The tables were piled high with delicacies—at least as high as Porphyro, in "The Eve of St. Agnes," ever thought of piling Madeline's bedside table.

Their rent was due in mid-January, but when Severn went to the Torlonias' bank to withdraw a hundred scudi from their account, he could not. Taylor had been expecting the money to be withdrawn in small installments as needed, and when faced with a draft for ninety-two scudi immediately after John's arrival in Rome, he had stopped payment. In order to save money on transaction fees, the bankers had advised Keats and Severn to withdraw the money in a lump sum. Not knowing this, Taylor may have feared that Keats was lending money to all the Haydons of Rome—or else that his expenses were going to be greater than expected. Taylor scrambled to raise money through subscription, but by the time the money reached Rome, it would be too late.

Severn had no idea how they would manage. While Keats slept, he brooded over the "monstrous business" of sanitizing the apartment, which Italian law would require after John's death. Those "brutal Italians" would scrape and repaint the walls, perhaps refinish the ceiling and the floors, and charge *him* for all their heartless industry. They would make a bonfire of the furniture, the sheets, the curtains, the towels, and anything else that the consumptive patient might have touched. No doubt Severn's view of these "cursed cruelties" was exacerbated by Dr. Clark's belief that tuberculosis was not contagious, and that the Italians were guided by superstition in these matters.[65]

Severn had particularly grown to detest the landlady, Anna Angeletti. Previous tenants had found the middle-aged widow attractive and tasteful, but to Severn she was an "old Cat" bent on cheating them.[66] She lived behind the main rooms of the house, on the mezzanine level, and on Christmas Eve she had provoked Severn's ire by reporting to the police that her tenant was dying of consumption: she seemed to have no sympathy for the wretched invalid or his friend.

Had Severn been able to leave the apartment, he could have made money by painting miniatures, which were highly in demand as the cheapest form of portraiture. He guessed that there were about five hundred British residents (actually, the number was closer to two thousand) in Rome, and they paid more for miniatures there than in London. But Severn could not bring himself to tell John why he needed to go out. The invalid looked anxiously at him every time he seemed about to leave. "Poor Keats keeps me by him—and shadows out the form of one solitary friend—he opens his eyes in great horror and doubt—but when they fall upon me—they close gently and open and close until he falls into another sleep—The very thought keep[s] me by him until he dies."[67]

Two days into the New Year, 1821, Keats ruptured another blood vessel in his chest, and Severn at last gave up on the idea of recovery. While Severn's religious faith would help to sustain him through the nightmare of the coming weeks, John had lost his belief in immortality—the common comfort of every rogue and fool, as he complained. Yet, even *with* his faith, it all seemed too much at times for Severn: "This noble fellow lying on the bed—is dying in horror—no kind hope smoothing down his suffering—no philosophy—no religion to support him—yet with all the most knawing [*sic*] desire for it—yet without the possibility of receiving it." John could not fool himself into believing in an afterlife, but he now felt "the horrible want of some faith—some hope—something to rest on."[68]

When read as allegory, the Book of Job made sense to him. But John could not accept the stories in Severn's Bible as scripture. "Severn I can see under your quiet look—immense twisting and contending—you dont know what you are reading—you are induring for me more than I'd have you—O! that my last hour was come." Severn would say that nothing was wrong: he was merely thinking about his family back in England, or how he might ship his painting to the Royal Academy. . . . But they were all lies, and his heart almost leapt to deny them.[69] John's suffering might have been in proportion with Job's, but Severn had given up the role of stubborn comforter that Job's friends did not.

Although the Bible could not offer relief, at John's suggestion, Severn searched for other books that might. He could not find either Anne Dacier's translation of Plato or Bunyan's *Pilgrim's Progress,* which Keats had recommended, but he did procure a copy of Jeremy Taylor's *Holy Living and Holy Dying,* which, as Benjamin Bailey was later gratified to find out, did provide some comfort. Severn held John's hand, and they prayed. "Thus he gained strength of mind from day to day just in proportion as his poor body grew weaker & weaker," Severn wrote, "& at last I had the consolation of finding him more prepared for his death than I was. He tranquilly detailed to me what would be the process of his dying, what I was to do & how I was *to bear it.*"[70]

Dr. Clark was becoming concerned about Severn's haggard appearance. He urged the artist to get out and breathe some fresh air, if only for an hour or so a day, if only to keep up his strength so that he could continue to nurse his sick friend. Severn proved reluctant, but John insisted that they find a nurse to relieve him, and he ultimately gave in. But the first experiment with the new system failed: Severn found the nurse who showed up on January 26 unacceptable, and he would leave John's bedside no more.

Severn was now on call day and night, and he began to imagine death in its most violent forms. He had decided to portray Plutarch's account of the assassination of Alcibiades, and he could see the finished painting in his head. As Alcibiades rushes from his burning house "like a whirlwind— naked—with his right hand grasping the sword," seven assassins appear before him. The first covers his own neck and face at the sight of Alcibiades's gleaming weapon. The second starts away with two blazing torches, his face full of horror. Three more dash into the shadow of some nearby trees. One draws a bow. Another, his face full of malicious disappointment, shoots an arrow that misses its mark and strikes the door of the house. The third hurls a dart. Two more in the distance draw bows.[71] Death was everywhere—and inevitable. Severn's painting would win the Royal Academy prize.

Another month passed, and John was now longing for death "with dreadful earnestness." He sent Severn to visit the Protestant (or English) Cemetery and asked him to describe the place where he would be buried. Severn reported that it was "in one of the most lovely retired spots in Rome."[72] It lay in a softly sloping meadow in which violets, daisies, and buttercups bloomed throughout the year. The poet was pleased. He imagined the soothing, cold earth pressed against him, and the flowers growing over him.

On the night of Wednesday, February 21, Severn heard a sound he had not heard before. Phlegm was gurgling loudly in John's throat, and he seemed about to suffocate. Relieved that death had finally come, John asked Severn to lift him so that he would not die in pain. He told his friend not to tremble, for he did not think he would die in convulsions. He then asked Severn whether he had ever seen anyone die, and when Severn said no, he replied: "Well then I pity you poor Severn—what trouble and danger you have got into for me—now you must be firm for it will not last long—I shall soon be laid in the quiet grave."[73] But when the sun came shining through the window the next morning, and he was still alive to see it, John dissolved in tears.

When Dr. Clark arrived, the patient stared up at him with the same melancholy question he asked every morning: "How long is this *posthumous* life of mine to last."[74] He peered into the lines of the doctor's face, as if to read the answer there. The doctor left, and another day, and then another night passed. The doctor came again for his morning call, and on the way out the door this time he pulled Severn aside. Keats would die in the evening.

At four o'clock in the afternoon, John became drenched in sweat, and he again asked Severn to lift him. The mucus seemed to be boiling in his throat, and his friend's breath felt like ice when it brushed against his skin: "don't breathe on me—it comes like Ice."[75] His eyes burned bright against his pale face as he looked into Severn's eyes without pain. At eleven P.M. he died in Severn's arms.

Severn collapsed. Dr. Clark took his pulse and ordered him to keep quiet and perfectly still. He sent an English nurse to take care of him, while he performed an autopsy of his patient, assisted by two other surgeons.

What the doctor found when he opened the body was the worst case of consumption he had ever seen: "the lungs were entirely destroyed."[76] He could not comprehend how John had lived as long as he had. *On the high couch he lay!—his friends came round—/Supported him—no pulse, or breath they found,/And, in its marriage robe, the heavy body wound.* Like Lycius at the end of *Lamia,* John's body was wrapped in a winding sheet. His unopened letters from Fanny Brawne and Fanny Keats were placed over his heart. Severn kept John's signet ring, his pocket watch, some books and papers.

Night-burial was standard procedure for non-Catholics, but Keats's funeral would take place at nine o'clock in the morning of Monday, February 26. Severn seemed obsessed with the "funeral beasts," and to alleviate his anxiety Dr. Clark convinced the landlady to postpone the process of sanitizing the apartment until after the funeral.[77] On Saturday, a mask-maker came to cast the emaciated face of the corpse. Sunday passed in blackness.

The first thing Monday morning, Severn, Dr. Clark, and the two surgeons who had helped with the autopsy led a handful of mourners to Keats's grave. Among them were the sculptors William Ewing and Richard Westmacott, whom Severn had befriended, and the architect Ambrose Poynter. Severn was "the only personal friend present from amongst the little band of devoted friends the poet had left behind," as he put it. The Reverend Wolff performed the Protestant service, and Keats's body was laid in its final resting place, near the pyramid of Caius Cestius and the grave of Shelley's three-year-old son, William. Shelley's elegy for Keats describes it best: "a slope of green access/Where, like an infant's smile, over the dead,/A light of laughing flowers along the grass is spread."[78] Within a year Shelley would join them. John would no longer be able to run from his well-meaning rival.

Severn worked through his grief by planning a monument for his friend, but in the end, respecting John's desire for anonymity, he kept only one element of his design: a Greek lyre with broken or untied strings, from John's signature Tassie gem. Severn wanted to make himself a matching brooch out of John's own hair, but he could find no craftsman to do it. *Qui me néglige me désole.* John had said that he did not want any announcements of his death in the press, or any engravings made from his portrait to circulate in print. He wrote a plain epitaph for himself, which Brown felt it prudent to preface with a few more words:

> This Grave
> contains all that was Mortal,
> of a
> Young English Poet,
> Who
> on his Death Bed,
> in the Bitterness of his Heart,
> at the Malicious Power of his Enemies,
> Desired
> these Words to be engraven on his Tomb Stone:
> *Here lies One*
> *Whose Name was writ in Water.*[79]

Poor George

Three days after John's corpse was lowered into the ground in Rome, George turned twenty-four. More than half of his life was over, and for the next twenty years he would live on his memories in Louisville. He could not help thinking that if he had remained with his brother, John might still be alive. "I almost believe that if I had remained his companion, and had had the means, as I had the wish to have devoted my life to his fame, and happiness, he might have been living at this hour," George confessed to his sister in 1825.[80] But George was not the only one to blame himself for his brother's death.

Charles Brown, in coping with his own demons, demonized George. John had begged Brown more than once to go with him to Italy, but Brown had not replied from Scotland, nor cut short his Scottish tour. "And so you still wish me to follow you to Rome?" Brown wrote to John when he got back, "and truly I wish to go,—nothing detains me but prudence." Going to Rome would have entailed setting up a separate establishment for his housekeeper, Abby (who, thanks to Brown's fear of producing another child, was no longer sharing his bed), and their son, Carlino, born in July. Brown did not think he could afford that. "Little could be gained, if any thing, by letting my house at this time of the year, and the consequence would be a heavy additional expence which I cannot possibly afford,—unless it were a matter of necessity, and I see none while you are in such good hands as Severn's." Rather than making the trip, Brown covered his sorrow

with the jocularity of tough love, teasing Keats for wanting to exchange
Severn—an indulgent, pliable nurse—for one who would be more strin-
gent in enforcing the doctor's orders: "If I were in Severn's place, & you insisted on ever gnawing a bone," he wrote, "I'd lead you the life of a dog.
What the devil should you grumble for?"[81] Behind the façade, both recognized the finality of the situation.

John's farewell letter from Rome disturbed and haunted Brown, and
Brown deflected that pain onto George. "You know much of his grief, but
do you know how George has treated him?" Brown demanded of Severn
in January: "I sit planning schemes of vengeance upon his head. Should his
brother die exposure and infamy shall consign him to perpetual exile. I will
have no mercy,—the world will cry aloud for the cause of their Keats's untimely death, and I will give it."[82] True to his word, Brown nurtured his
grudge and never forgave the money-brother.

Perhaps needing someone to blame for the suffering they had witnessed so closely at first hand in the final months of the poet's life, Severn,
Haslam, and Taylor all agreed with Brown that George was a scoundrel.
Only Dilke would become convinced of George's honor, and only after
many long, heartfelt letters from George. When Brown received word of
John's death, he wrote to Rice and Dilke; and he asked Haslam to go immediately to the home of Richard Abbey lest Fanny Keats should hear
about her brother's death from another source. He asked Taylor to make
the announcement to the papers. "Word it as *you* please," he said, "you will
do it better than I can,—in fact I can't do it."[83] But in all this there was no
mention of George.

As time wore on after John's death, George continued to toil at his mill
and dream of home. "I look to Mr Dilke as my anchor in my native sod," he
wrote to Maria Dilke, "and so long as my cable of love of Country, and
kindly feeling lasts, I shall cherish a hope that I shall one day haul my vessel
to his hearth." He prepared mental notes for a memoir of John, but did not
write them down, and as the years passed, those memories were lost—to
posterity, if not to George. By the spring of 1838, George had given up the
idea of writing a memoir of his brother. "I am entirely incompetent," he
wrote to Dilke, "wanting talent and experience in such matters."[84]

George saw himself as a husband and a father—a thinker and reader,
at times an eloquent and persuasive speaker, even a civic leader, but in the
final instance, not a writer. "I have not done well," he told his sister one year

after their brother's death, "but I have stemmed the torrent of bad success, obtained some experience, and am now sailing steadily towards success." By 1825, the American economy had begun to recover, and George was finally able to build a house for his family on the spot "prettily situated at the head of the Falls close to the Mills" that he had picked out.[85]

To his sawmill, he added a gristmill capable of grinding seventy-five barrels of flour a day. When combined, he boasted, his mill operations were the most extensive in the Western Country. He owned a third of the firm, George Keats & Company, and he kept twenty percent of its profit. Except when he and his partners settled the books together once a year, he was "the entire manager, viz., chief engineer, cashier, clerk, without the interference or controul of the other owners."[86] As the years slipped by, George kept putting off his trip to England, always finding excuses for why he could not leave his mill. But in 1828, when a bank draft bounced and George found himself faced with a choice of either selling his share of the business at a loss or ruining his credit, he did the next best thing: he sent Georgiana.

In the second week of May 1828, George escorted his wife, his nine-year-old daughter (Georgiana Emily), and his firstborn son (John Henry) to the South Street Seaport in New York. He had hoped that a friend with the comforting name of John Bull would escort them back. Bull was a merchant with a warehouse on Main Street, Louisville, stocked with Staffordshire pottery. George described him as "a plain straightforward, worthy, uneducated, sagacious, slow minded, spirited, brave native born Kentuckian, bred a builder."[87] While Bull and George were quite different, there was goodwill between them and George was convinced that Bull would go out of his way to serve him.

Traveling up the Mississippi from New Orleans one time, the Kentuckian and the Londoner had gotten lost together when their steamboat was blocked by ice. They went ashore to go "a gunning" and subsequently became entangled "in a cane brake, so high and so nearly impenetrable that we almost despaired of getting out of it." They knew which direction they needed to go in, but the thickets made it impossible for them to proceed. George climbed a tree to look around and discovered a less obstructed path. The next time they came to a standstill, George related, "it was Bull's turn to climb which did not prove to him so easy as it had done to me, for he lost his wind, and for a time could neither ascend or descend, while he was in momentary fear of falling it struck me what an odd thing it was to see a

Bull up in a tree, which he looked as much like as any thing else thro' the mass of foliage, when in the very midst of his trouble I cried out to him that I had heard of Bears climbing trees but I never expected to see a Bull at such an altitude."[88] Bull was not a quick wit, nor especially a man for a pun; but George's joke brought relief, and after a good laugh they thrashed their way back to the boat.

Yet George was alone at the South Street Seaport on November 5, 1828, when his family pulled up to the pier in the ship *Britannia*. Georgiana and the children had set out from Liverpool on October 3, on the Black Ball ship commanded by Captain Charles H. Marshall, and after thirty-three days at sea arrived looking better than they had done when they left. George attributed the improvement to the three months spent in the Old Country.[89] He had given his wife detailed instructions about business matters, but he had also been counting on Georgiana to brighten up his relationship with his sister.

Fanny had married the Spanish novelist Valentín María Llanos y Gutiérrez on March 30, 1826. Fanny Brawne had introduced them, circumventing the Argus-eyed Abbey, and Llanos had claimed the youngest Keats sibling's immediate affection by telling her that he had seen her favorite brother in Rome three days before he died. Dilke had helped Fanny to see George in a better light, in the meantime, and she now recalled him as "a considerate, good natured fellow." But by the time Fanny Keats Llanos finally met her sister-in-law, niece, and nephew, George no longer saw himself in that way. "I am not a good natured fellow," he insisted. "I used to be so both in fact and appearance, but now I am less so in fact, and if I may judge from the almost universal fear (or something like it) that People have of me, less so in appearance. I am enveloped in an atmosphere whether of pride, or reserve, or ill nature or all or neither, that keeps People at a distance."[90] But George's demeanor at age thirty-one was more than a legacy of Old England. It was the price of years of trial and hard-won independence.

From the time John died in 1821 until the Panic of 1837, which shattered the American economy for a second time, George made a fortune by dint of steady application and hard work. During those years, the population of his adopted country grew from 10 million to 16 million, the greatest percentage of that growth taking place in the West. In those same years, the population of Illinois swelled from 60,000 to 400,000; that of Indiana grew from 170,000 to 600,000; Mississippi's quadrupled; and the number of residents in Missouri increased five-fold. Even the more settled states in the Western Country, like Tennessee and Ohio, doubled their populations. Steamboat tonnage on the western waters increased nearly five-fold, and the gross national product doubled.[91] George's fortunes grew in proportion with those of his adopted country.

Until January 11, 1830, George was in business with a man named Richard Atkinson. "Good wages will be given for a Sawyer, who understands his business well," George advertised in 1823. When Keats & Atkinson was dissolved by mutual consent, Richard and John Atkinson took over the steam-powered sawmill and flour-mill on the riverbank at the corner of Eighth and Water Streets. Throughout the 1830s George was in the lumber business with Daniel Smith, on Main Street by Beargrass Creek, between First and Brook. Smith was also in business with John P. Young, another lumber merchant in Louisville, who lived above their offices on Fulton Street, while Smith lived on Fifth between Green and Walnut—around the corner from where George later built his mansion. Felix Smith, who lived above Smith, Keats & Company on Main Street, later became one of George's executors. By 1832, "George Keats & Company's Steam Planeing, Grooving, and Tongueing Mill" had two woodworking machines and two circular saws, each capable of producing two hundred feet of boards per day.[92]

If the Dilkes were George's anchor in his native sod, the Bakewells, for better or for worse, were his anchors in the American West. George seems to have partnered with Will Bakewell, after Tom Bakewell moved to Cincinnati in 1824, at his gristmill. James Freeman Clarke claimed that George convinced "Mr. W. Bakewell, of Cincinnati, an English gentleman of his acquaintance, to join him in the purchase of a grist-mill, to grind wheat into flour, and to make him the miller." This was in 1873, by which point Will Bakewell had likewise moved (for a while) to Cincinnati. George knew nothing of the business, but said: "Try me for three months, and then, if you are not satisfied, I will resign." In the months that followed, he "almost might be said to have watched every grain of wheat which came through the mill. From that time his success was assured." By 1833, when Clarke met him, he was still in the lumber business and "quite wealthy."[93]

Throughout the 1830s, George fantasized about selling his stock in the mills and retiring. But, as he found when he had quit Richard Abbey's tea business, he could not stay unemployed. "Altho' my business continues profitable and I have suffered considerable losses I am still 'encreasing my store,'" he wrote in 1833, with allusion to Shakespeare's sixty-fourth sonnet, on the folly of enslaving oneself to worldly possessions. George planned to continue his operations at the mills until he could "say—enough."[94] But of course he never said, "Enough."

To keep his sawmill running, George often had to hound his clients and bring those "scoundrels" who attempted "to conceal their property and avoid paying their debts" to court. A trail of paperwork at the Jefferson County Courthouse supports George's claim that he went to great lengths to get paid. "You may fancy me talking daily, coolly, calmly and familiarly, or warmly, harshly and angrily, with men who are doing their utmost to cheat and swindle me out of my just claims," he told Dilke, also in 1833. That same year, he and his partner Daniel Smith filed at least five lawsuits involving five times as many people accused of not paying their bills.[95] But justice was slow and the judge underpaid—and, George believed, incompetent. Rather than filing claims that would drag on through the court from month to month, draining his time and money, George often had to settle.

With persistence, as Louisville came into its own as a prosperous American city, George emerged as one of its wealthiest citizens. He helped to extend the town's infrastructure by serving on the Ohio River Bridge Commission, which planned the first bridge over the Ohio. He served on the board of directors for the Lexington and Ohio Railroad Company, whose line stopped at Louisville. And before his death in 1841, he was elected to Louisville's City Council, which drafted the charter for the city. George was, as he described himself, "a busy man of business, having extensive concerns, and responsibilities, with mind, looks and manners generally found with such an one, tempered perhaps a little with the character of a lover of books, who reads in preference to being idle."[96]

George did stay active on the cultural side of life. He served as a trustee of Louisville College, as treasurer of the Kentucky Historical Society, and as curator of the Louisville Lyceum, an association devoted to literature and scientific subjects that was part of a larger transatlantic effort in adult education. George was not the only one in the nineteenth century to believe that education was a lifelong endeavor. The Lyceum sponsored public lectures and concerts in buildings designed on the Aristotelian model. In 1837, he became chairman of the board of the Harlan Museum Company in Lou-

isville, where for twenty-five cents, visitors gained admission to the museum's collection of three thousand natural-historical curiosities, and its exhi-
bition of fine arts.[97]

In 1836, one year before the Panic, George moved his family from their
wooden home above the falls of the Ohio River into a columned stone-and-
brick mansion just outside the center of town, on the south side of Walnut
between Third and Fourth streets. Two white marble lions flanked the
doorway of the building known locally as the "Englishman's Palace." A
front walk bordered by four marble statues, representing the four seasons,
led up to the corniced, four-columned façade of the house. One Louisville
resident thought that the weather stains on the cheeks of "Spring" looked
like black tears.[98]

The design of the Englishman's Palace followed the plan of many colonial American homes. A hallway ran the length of the house from front
to back, dividing two suites of living rooms. Service stairs connected the
dining rooms on the ground floor to the upstairs bedrooms, and a central
stairway, in this case carpeted with mahogany railings, led from the main
hallway to the rooms on the second floor: a sitting room, a sewing room,
and six sleeping chambers. The bedrooms were airy, with high ceilings and
large windows draped with sheer white curtains. Silver locks and hinges
set off the mahogany woodwork. The washstands had marble slabs, and
the standing and wall mirrors had gold-leaf frames. Glass chandeliers hung
from the ceilings, and rockers, rush-bottomed chairs, wardrobes, bureaus,
and bedsteads furnished the rooms. A poplar clothing press kept the linen
and towels crisp.

Downstairs, upholstered sofas and settees in the living rooms came
from the best shops in Louisville. The rooms themselves were painted white
and trimmed with gold. They were also large enough that, after George
died, the new owner (Chapman Coleman) held a ball at the Englishman's
Palace in honor of General Zachary Taylor's victories in the Mexican-
American War.[99] Above one of the doors hung a mezzotint miniature of a
dog engraved by Henry Wylie. Next to the tall living-room windows,
cloaked with rich, heavy draperies, were two paintings: a battle scene featuring the Duke of Wellington and a cavalry scene whose focal point was
Napoleon. The family's other paintings included a portrait of George
Washington, a still life with game, landscapes, seascapes, and silhouettes of
the children. Clusters of carved grapes adorned the marble mantelpieces.

All bespoke a comfortable lifestyle. The poet John Howard Payne declared that he had "attended few parties in better taste" than those given by George and Georgiana Keats in Louisville. Even before moving into the Englishman's Palace, they had entertained with "cordiality and unpretending elegance." Now the large mahogany tables in the dining rooms below the main living quarters had dozens of matching chairs. Georgiana had spoons for every occasion: tea spoons, salt spoons, soup spoons, dessert spoons . . . She had different glasses for wine, champagne, lemonade, and jelly, and cups for tea and for custard. She also had celery dishes, fruit baskets, tumblers, decanters, water pitchers, a silver-plated tea set and a matching coffeepot. No longer could George say that his circumstances would not allow him "to associate with what is called the first or in other words the richest people here."[100]

On occasion, George retreated to his library, which was separated from the main living rooms by doors that slid up and down. He had no wish to give up "a taste for those occupations and pleasures, that are the only assurances out of rural life, of a respectable and pleasant old age." Surrounding his desk and lounge chair were hundreds of books ranging across the different genres, from biography to poetry, history, philosophy, fiction, home economics, travel literature, gastronomy, penny magazines, journals, and encyclopedias. According to James Freeman Clarke, George "liked nothing better than to find some one with whom to spend the evening, and read a play of Massinger or Fletcher." Georgiana may have had better luck finding companions at the card table, for "there were few persons in Louisville, at that time, who took an interest in such studies."[101]

The crown of George's collection was his six-volume edition of the *Works of Mr. Edmund Spenser,* printed for Jacob Tonson in 1715, which had once belonged to his brother. George spent many hours in Louisville with James Freeman Clarke reading Spenser in the light of John's "suggestive annotations." On the title page containing John's initials, and George's signature with the date 1816, a note in John's handwriting referred the reader to Joseph Addison's periodical, *The Spectator.* More specifically, it referred to essay No. 540, which opens with a letter from a fictitious correspondent to Mr. Spectator: "There is no part of your writings which I have in more esteem than your criticism upon *Milton.* . . . You will lose much of my kind inclination towards you, if you do not attempt the encomium of *Spencer* also." George studied his brother's annotations to Spenser, and he also copied John's notes on Milton onto the flyleaves of his own copy of *Paradise Lost*. Clarke later asked George's permission to transcribe the latter, and with George's permission he sent them to Emerson for publication in the *Dial*.[102]

Sometimes, George sent visitors away with John's poems. As "a very precious remembrancer," he copied some "unpublished treasures of his brother's poetry" into John Howard Payne's scrapbook, including John's sonnet on Paolo and Francesca and his sonnet beginning, "Fame, like a wayward girl will be coy." Payne sent the sonnet "On Fame" to Edgar Allan Poe for publication in the *Ladies' Companion,* where it appeared in print for the first time in August 1837. To James Freeman Clarke, George gave the holograph of his brother's ode to Apollo, "God of the Golden Bow." Yet, despite George's privileged relation to English literary tradition, visitors noticed that he avoided trading on his brother's reputation. He displayed "no ostentation of literature, no attempt at conversational parade," and he "disclaimed the least pretension to any regard, excepting as a mere man of business, and a person deeply devoted to the best interests of his adopted country." It was quite a while before Payne found out that the Kentucky pioneer was the brother of the poet. Even then, he learned of it from a third party.[103]

Between 1819, when his oldest child, Georgiana Emily, was born, and 1838, George and Georgiana had seven other children: Rosalind (b. 1821), Emma Frances (b. 1823), Isabel (b. 1825), John Henry (b. 1827), Clarence George (b. 1830), Ella (b. 1833), and Alice Ann (b. 1836). Their second daughter, little Rose, died at six. She had always been a *"peculiar"* girl, her father thought, but she "repayed all the *immense* trouble she imposed on us by an evident strength of affection." Until her untimely death, George had counted on her to be "a Family link to hold her more volatile sisters together in bond of amity when we are no longer with them or when we are too old to influence their affections." When little Rose died, George took solace in "the knowledge that her tender constitution would not in all probability have lasted to maturity. . . . Her indulged tender, reserved disposition was not calculated to make her happy in nine tenths of the situations that fall to the lot of mortals."[104] Whether he consoled himself with similar thoughts about his deceased older brother remains unknown.

Little Rose did not speak until the age of four, and when she did, she blurted out what has become not only an unfortunate legacy but a reminder that there was another side to the glamor of the Englishman's Palace: "Hoad yo' yaw!" she reputedly snapped at the child of the cook. "You're only a knobby-headed niggah anyway." The inventory that was made of George's estate at the time of his death lists two female slaves, Hannah and Lucy, valued at $400 and $250, respectively, and a male slave named Jesse, valued at $600. A third female slave, who appears on the census of 1840, does not show up on the inventory of his estate the following year.[105] Perhaps she was sold.

The factories, ropewalks, and mills of Louisville all employed slaves, and Dr. Urban Epinitis Ewing, a friend of George's who had more slaves than he needed, "hired out some slaves to Mr. Keats and was impressed by his kind treatment of the Negroes," according to George's granddaughter Emma Speed Simpson. Some argued that slaves were better fed, clothed, and lodged in Kentucky than white laborers in Britain. "Slavery is no doubt hurtful to society," John Melish wrote, but "the blacks are generally as well fed and nearly as well clothed as the white people; and it is questionable whether they work so hard." After sixteen years of living in Louisville, George admitted that he had become "a Kentuckian as far as any one can be made one in a commercial City."[106]

Like his friend John Speed, a plantation owner whose son would marry George and Georgiana's daughter Emma Frances, George may have fit the profile of a slaveholder who did not believe in slavery. James Freeman Clarke explained that Speed "thought it wrong in itself and injurious to the State, and expected, like most intelligent Kentuckians at that time, that Kentucky would before long emancipate its slaves. Meantime, he held them as a trust, and did everything he could to make them comfortable." George worked as hard as anyone he employed, and he, too, might have justified his use of slaves as a temporary measure. By 1828, he and his family were living "surrounded by numerous negroo [sic] servants and superfluous plenty; maintaining a general outline of economy that will insure our expences to be within our income, but careless of those trifling expenditures that surrounded by circumstances attending a dense population would be matters of serious consideration. Our servants impose upon us without fretting us, and we with a profusion quite congenial, scatter our dollars without sighing at their disappearance."[107] Like other slaveowners in Kentucky, George referred to his slaves as servants.

By the time the Panic of 1837 devastated the U.S. economy, George

had amassed a sizable nest egg and seemed well positioned to enjoy a pleasant retirement in the bosom of his large family. "I am getting balder and I
suppose I am in the course of nature gradually wearing away," he wrote
in 1836, at age thirty-nine, "but I feel vigorous and enjoy uninterrupted
health."[108] But with the Panic, George's fortunes began to unravel. Before
stepping down from the presidency, Andrew Jackson had vetoed the re-
newal for the charter of the Second Bank of the United States; and as one of
his last acts, he announced that the federal land office would thenceforth be
accepting only gold and silver in payment for government land. After fifteen years of virtually unregulated speculative growth, the bubble burst.
The state banks followed the federal bank, and the Panic of 1837 broke
out, causing stocks to plummet and paper fortunes to vanish. The Western
Country was especially affected. When a cotton glut saturated the market
two years later, and state banks continued to fail, a full-scale depression
swept over the West.

George was not the only one affected. Tom Bakewell, having withdrawn from George Keats & Company on February 1, 1823, moved to Cincinnati the next year and, with a man named Joseph Cartwright, opened a
foundry to cast steamboat engines. He designed his own steamboat, one
that could carry more freight in proportion to registered tonnage than other
boats on the western waters and whose finish cost less than that of boats
designed in the East. Bakewell's steamboat was also easier to navigate
through the river shoals. Between his foundry and his shipyards, which
built the hulls for the boats, his facilities prospered. But with the Panic of
1837, Tom wound up in debt to his suppliers.[109]

Will Bakewell, before moving to Cincinnati, had worked in Louisville
as a merchant under the name W. G. Bakewell & Company. He sold passage on steamboats and stocked the usual array of wholesale dry goods—
coffee, tea, sugar, molasses, tea kettles, Indian saltpeter, Turks' Island and
Lisbon salt, pepper, spice, indigo, mackerel, pig lead, Boston nails, shot,
rolls of brimstone, flint tumblers, decanters, window glass, sickles, scythes,
corn hoes, mattocks, shovels, axes . . . But Will was less of a hard-nosed
businessman than his older brother. One person who knew him described
him as "a true gentleman" who was "good and wise, and generous and
brave, tender and kind, and very just, and supremely honest, above all."
Will had endorsed notes for his brother, and he found himself in debt to the
tune of $125,000. By 1842, he had declared bankruptcy. When John James

Audubon saw Will in Louisville the following year, he reported: "William is in good spirits though deceived by his Brother."[110] George Keats also found himself ruined.

"At George Keats's death," George's grandson John Gilmer Speed wrote, "his executors found that he had endorsed Mr. Bakewell's paper to such an extent that the accumulations of an enterprising and thrifty lifetime were swept away in making good the endorsements." George, like Will Bakewell, may have endorsed the notes that Tom could not honor, or he might have found himself legally responsible through his partnership with Will. Hyder Edward Rollins claims that George's financial disaster "came from a note he had endorsed to enable William Bakewell, Audubon's brother-in-law, to buy a shipping business."[111] One way or another, George sunk with the Bakewells into bankruptcy. In the end, their friendship turned out to be as much of a curse as a blessing.

After the Panic, George struggled on in Louisville. But there was little he could do to keep his world from collapsing around him like a house of cards. He had sent his daughter Emma to school in New England to study with Margaret Fuller, an American counterpart of Mary Wollstonecraft, who promoted a rational education for women. Emma was reputedly the daughter who resembled her father most and "of more than ordinary intelligence." One year before his death, in 1840, she invited her school friend Ellen Kilshaw Fuller, Margaret Fuller's younger sister, to the Englishman's Palace for the holidays. Ellen had been offered a position at a girls' boarding academy in Cincinnati, which was due to start February 1, 1841. But she developed migraines that kept her confined to her bed through May. "Emma waits upon her so devotedly," complained George, "that we of the Family hardly consider her as returned home to us."[112] George had discerned the jealous, contrary nature of his daughter's friend before his daughter:

> It would not become me to detail the thousand occurrences in which Miss F forced upon poor Emma the performance of divided duties. Every thing that her Mother or Georgiana wished her to do Miss F begged, entreated, stormed, and shed tears to prevent her from doing. She ridiculed our acquaintances, found fault with dresses, discouraged the performance of all social duties by trying to prevent a return of visits, shed tears in streams to prevent Emma from going to parties given to celebrate her re-

turn home, and in fact threw a damp over the family reunion so completely by the ingenious and acute management of her influence over
Emma, that poor Emma was worried to a care worn appearance, and in
every respect except an occasional burst of heart feeling [was] totally unlike her former self.

When Emma married Philip Speed at the Unitarian Church on June 9, her
friend Ellen did not attend. According to George, she had not been "duly
consulted about the match, nor apprized early enough when it was to take
place, nor invited in a sufficiently special manner." Ellen moved to Cincinnati, where on September 24 she married the Transcendentalist poet William Ellery Channing, who was serving there as a Unitarian minister, and
Emma moved to Farmington, the Speed plantation six miles outside Louisville. At the end of the summer, Emma spent a few weeks with Abraham
Lincoln, who was visiting his friend Joshua Speed at Farmington.[113]

On Independence Day, 1841, George proudly reported that Emma
"conforms with much good sense, and discretion to the habits of the family,
and I fondly trust that the alliance will not only be the cause of much and
enduring happiness to the couple themselves but of satisfaction to both
families in every respect; I see no cause to fear any other result."[114] Yet stress
had weakened George, and while he may have had no reason to fear *that*
result, he did have reason to fear.

Before the year came to a close, the family destroyer that George had
staved off for so many years caught up with him. Dr. Coleman Rogers and
his son, Dr. Lewis Rogers, both leading physicians in Louisville, attended
him, but there was little they could do. "Mr. Keats, Dr. Rogers thinks, will
not live long," a friend wrote on Monday, December 20, 1821. The next day,
George made out his will. Like his brother's it was brief: a single sheet of
paper, written by himself, with no erasures or cancellations. George had not
much to leave. Like the weather stains on the statue of "Spring" in front of
the Englishman's Palace, the blotted ink on George's will, in places, resembled black tears.[115]

On Christmas Eve exactly twenty-four years earlier, John had stared
into the freshly laid coals in the brothers' apartment over Bird-in-Hand
Court in Cheapside. He had no desire to leave his fraternal hearth for a
cold and gloomy church service. The bells that beckoned from the Church
of St. Mary-le-Bow down the street had aroused no feelings other than dis-

gust. *The church bells toll a melancholy round, / Calling the people to some other prayers, / Some other gloominess, more dreadful cares* . . . Now, on Christmas Eve, twenty-four years later, the church bells at the First Unitarian Church in Louisville tolled for his brother. The Cockney Pioneer had survived the Cockney poet by nineteen years. But on Friday, December 24, 1841, George Keats, at age forty-four, having made a fortune and lost it, died.

The *Louisville Daily Journal* announced his death on Christmas Day:

> Mr. Keats was a younger brother of John Keats, the distinguished British poet, and possessed much of the genius, and all of the philosophy, benevolence, and enlarged philanthropy, of the lamented bard. The suavity of his manners and the charm of his conversation endeared him to all who knew him, and his enterprise and public spirit rendered him an inestimable member of society. There is not a man in our community whose death would be more deeply and universally mourned. When such a one passes away from among us, every heart feels a mysterious chill, as if touched by the awful shadow of the tomb.

George's obituary identified the two salient aspects of his character: he was an Englishman and the brother of John Keats. George had always defined his spiritual life by his brother, and while he flattered himself on having been "more free from national prejudices than most men," he also admitted that "what few I am stained withal are those of an Englishman."[116] He never thought the move to America would be permanent.

His brother had composed his own modest epitaph in Rome, and one wonders to what degree George's original gravestone in the Western Cemetery of Louisville, before his remains were moved to Cave Hill, reflected the last will of the man whom it memorialized: "In Memory of George Keats: a Native of England." His family knew that he had always dreamed of returning to the place of his birth, where he had hoped to find "more congenial people amongst whom to cherish my sociable virtues."[117] But George's social virtues went with him to the grave.

James Freeman Clarke had no doubt that George's "love for his brother, which continued through his life to be among the deepest affections of his soul, would be a pledge of their reunion again in the spirit-land." The minister proposed, quoting Spenser's "Tears of the Muses" in the *Dial,* that

George "had gone to find his brother again among 'The spirits and intelligences fair,/ And angels waiting on the Almighty's chair.'"[118] George never saw the land of his birth again, but he *did* go to his final rest having seen a flower from his brother's grave in Rome.

Three years before the family complaint seized the last Keats brother, Anna Hazard Barker, a young Bostonian on her way back from a tour of Europe, stopped in Louisville to visit her friend James Freeman Clarke. When she showed him her collection of pressed flowers, he cried out, "I have here a friend the brother of Keats, the Poet, who would be made perfectly happy, could he see the flowers that you have brought from his brother's grave." Barker begged to meet him, and when she did she found him to be "a very interesting man." George was visibly moved at the sight of the flower from John's grave, and when Barker cut it out of her book to give him, "he seemed profoundly grateful."[119]

Anna Barker then left Louisville for New Orleans. When she arrived, she was amazed to find waiting for her a thank-you note from George Keats that contained his brother's original handwritten copy of the ode "To Autumn."[120] Even then, the gift was priceless. George must have thought carefully about it. *Where are the songs of spring?* The question opens the final stanza of John's last Great Ode, which was written, unlike the others, in autumn. Between the Great Odes of the spring of 1819 and "To Autumn" came not only the loss of innocence in *The Fall of Hyperion,* but also the loss of George's fortune below the falls of the Ohio River. The poet and his pioneer brother had both grown up.

Where are the songs of spring? George had spent long years in Louisville, dreaming of those bygone days when, as boys, he and John had "loved, jangled, and fought alternately."[121] By the time George saw the flower from his brother's grave in Rome, he was a middle-aged man. *Where are the songs of spring?* The speaker of "To Autumn" replies:

> Ay, where are they?
> Think not of them, thou hast thy music too.

George may have heard these words as consolation from a brother somewhere beyond the grave. Like the poet, the pioneer had his music too.

EPILOGUE:
BLUE!

Georgiana Augusta Keats was forty-three years old when her husband died. One of her daughters was married and one had died. She still had six children, a large home, and no money. The women in Louisville were wondering what she would do. Her friend Mildred Ann Bullitt observed that "Mr. Keats died a bankrupt." Another acquaintance, Elizabeth Williams, remarked, "Since the death of Mr. K. the property is found to be scarcely enough to pay his debts." Georgiana was stranded and "of course obliged to do something for support; she . . . never looked forward to anything of the kind, doubtless."[1]

But Georgiana was nothing if not a consummate survivor. George called her his "piquant Wife" and said that she had an eye for character as painstaking in its attention to detail as that of any Dutch artist. "She claims that her sarcasms are so general that no one has a right to apply them to himself," he said, "and if any one finding the cap to fit so exactly his own case pleases to self appropriate it, he may thank himself for the sting it contains. And so she bullies herself into the notion of the perfect benevolence and justice of her conduct, when she gratifies herself in exercising a quality that is in almost all cases incompatible with a fair consideration for the sore or tender points (which such powers are very acute in discovering) of others." One of Georgiana's great-granddaughters swore that her "caustic wit" made even her sons and daughters afraid of her. Her obituary described her as "a woman of the most sprightly, and, in her later years, the most caustic wit," who "retained the unusual qualities of mind that made her famous among Kentucky women to the very last."[2]

John had once teased his sister-in-law for being as ridiculous in Louisville with its "threepenny parties" and "half penny Dances" as the ladies in London. Now, there seemed to be a party almost every evening, and notwithstanding her recent losses, Georgiana continued (in Mrs. Bullitt's words) "to give parties and dash about."[3] About three months after George's death, she was considering a move to Westport, Kentucky, two hours up the river where a friend of hers had a farm. But Georgiana did not move to Westport.

Instead, she stayed put at the Englishman's Palace, and married a handsome young Scottish engineer. John Jeffrey was twenty years younger than Georgiana when he met the quick-witted widow. He had been working in the gasworks business in Louisville and had known and respected George. In 1839, the city had formed a corporation to illuminate the streets, which had been "greatly infested by robbers, who favored by the darkness, made nightly attacks upon passengers through the streets, striking and disabling them with colts [revolvers], and in no few instances murdering them outright." By the time George died, "miles of brilliant lamps stretching away in the distance" had opened new sublime vistas in the valley between the plateaus.[4] Jeffrey helped to light up the town.

James Freeman Clarke's successor, the Reverend John Healy Heywood, officiated at the wedding of Georgiana Keats and John Jeffrey on January 5, 1843, at the same church (the First Unitarian) where Georgiana's daughter Emma had recently been married. But even after her marriage to Jeffrey, Georgiana remained, for many, the wife of George Keats. When John James Audubon ran into her a couple of months after her wedding, he noted, "Mrs Keats is remarried with her 6 children tacked to her." When she died, the Louisville *Courier-Journal* announced: "Mrs. Georgiana Jeffrey, wife of John Jeffrey . . . will be remembered by many of our citizens as Mrs. George Keats."[5]

After their wedding, John Jeffrey took over the Englishman's Palace, where before the year was out another momentous family event took place. On October 28, 1843, after a Saturday night spent singing, dancing, and socializing in the family's living rooms, Isabel Keats (who had just turned eighteen) came down from her bedroom with a toothache. She applied a hot poultice or some toothache drops, and sat down on the couch in the parlor. "Shortly afterwards," the *Louisville Daily Journal* reported, "a loud report and a scream were heard, and the family, on rushing into the room, found her weltering in her blood upon the floor, and a gun, which had stood in the room, lying near her. The discharge had lacerated her breast and neck dreadfully." Georgiana, assuming that her daughter had attempted suicide, exclaimed: "Oh, Isabel! what made you do it?" Isabel replied, "I did not mean to kill myself! Indeed, mother, I did not mean to kill myself!"[6] The doctors applied their medical skill, but in vain. She died within a few hours.

One week after Isabel's death, their neighbor Richard Jacob observed that he "could hardly think that one so gay and young could be guilty of so heinous a crime as suicide." Instead, he blamed her brother Clarence: "It appears that the unfortunate Clarence (for so I may now truly call him, for if you recollect that through his carelessness a few years since, he himself was the bloody victim of the same gun, but fortunately recovered,) had been hunting and when he returned home laid the gun on the sofa[;] it is supposed that her (Miss Keats) tooth getting easier, that she threw herself on the sofa it being near the fire and in doing so she accidentally raised the cock of the gun, which went off and occasioned the tragical scene; thus making the second but more fatal sacrifice to the carelessness of the unlucky Clarence." John Howard Payne, on the other hand, asserted that George's "very promising daughter . . . committed suicide through mortification" caused by her father's financial ruin.[7]

Isabel, like her uncle, was supposed to have had an unusual, poetic disposition. George's friend George Dennison Prentice composed some stanzas on her as a young girl:

That joyous little girl
  Is as wild as a gazelle,
Yet a poet's name and lineage,
  Are thine, sweet Isabel!
And although thy wild heart seemeth
  All-heedless of the lyre,
Within that young heart dwelleth
  The poet's gift of fire.

But 'twas a fearful gift
  To that noble child of song,

Whose glorious name and lineage
    To thee, bright one, belong;
For it turned his heart to ashes
    Where its centred light was flung,
And he perished in his morning—
    The gifted and the young.

Ay, he perished in his morning,
    That child of light and gloom,
But he left a name that glitters
    Like a star above his tomb;
And I deem *thou* hast a genius
    Like that which won *his* fame;
Thou hast his name and features—
    And why not his soul of flame?

If Isabel had her Uncle John's "gift of fire," it went out before she could give it lasting expression. Speculations about her passionate nature and the cause of her death revived years later, when an elderly gentleman rode into Louisville and showed up at the Englishman's Palace. He asked the present owner if he could spend some time alone in the parlor where Isabel had died, and on his way out he explained: "I parted from her in there, and have returned from California to visit the scene once more."[8] No one knew his name. He then made his way to the grave where Isabel had been buried. Ever since that time, Isabel's death has been shrouded in an aura of tragic romance.

Georgiana's second marriage seems to have been a good one, but it did have its challenges. John Jeffrey's work kept him on the road, and in Nashville he met a woman, a Mrs. Barrows, who turned his head. Georgiana could understand the attraction "of so beautiful and stylish a woman as he describes her," and she dismissed her rival as a "present fancy." She suspected that the woman thought Jeffrey wealthier than he was. But when an anonymous letter informing her "in the coarsest terms of the *too* great intimacy" between her husband and "that abominable woman" arrived, followed by another letter from the woman herself, Georgiana took to her bed in "the greatest agony both of *mind* and body." The doctor claimed that he could not minister to a mind diseased, and Georgiana wondered how he could have known of the affair. Jeffrey finished installing the lights in Nashville, and, as Georgiana predicted, the "fancy" passed.[9]

A few years later, Georgiana's eldest child, Georgiana Emily ("Georgy"), married Alfred Gwathmey. Georgy was "a gentle good spirit" who "never imagined harm to anyone." Gwathmey was the eldest son of George Clark Gwathmey, founder of the Bank of Kentucky. On his mother's side he was related to William Clark, of the Lewis and Clark expedition. But Alfred Gwathmey turned out to be a less fortunate scion of the old Virginia family. Shortly after marrying Georgy, he became "frightened by the cholera into the habit of getting drunk every day" and abusing his pregnant wife. Jeffrey was out of town at the time, but he thought that he might have to return to Louisville and "thrash the rascal into good behavior." When Georgy's son, George Keats Gwathmey, was born, the father fled to New Orleans, where, in a bizarre twist of fate, he died of cholera.[10]

George and Georgiana's seventh child, blue-eyed Ella, fared no better in the world of romance. Ella had married George Nicholas Peay, with whom she had seven children. One day, Peay went to the bank and emptied his safe-deposit box of $25,000. He was heading to New York to deliver a bank draft for $4,700 on behalf of a clothing manufacturer in Louisville. But in New York he cashed in the draft under a false name, and, equipped with a Derringer pistol and hunting knife, fled to Canada. Ella assumed that her husband had been robbed and put on mourning weeds. Her brother-in-law George Speed Peay hired a detective to search for her husband's body, and Peay's uncle filed a claim with his life insurance company on the widow's behalf. But the insurance agents investigating the case discovered Peay in Montreal, working as a faro dealer and living with a woman of ill repute. Ella went to Montreal to persuade her husband to return, but he refused. She came back to Louisville pregnant with their eighth child.[11]

The Keats boys had their own trials. When Georgiana and John Jeffrey sold the Englishman's Palace and moved to Cincinnati, Georgiana apprenticed her eldest son, John Henry Keats, to the pharmacist Charles Augustus Smith for a period of three years. If not an American poet, why not an American apothecary? When the term expired, however, Jeffrey took John Henry into the gasworks business. They traveled to Cuba, to install lights for the Havana Gas Light Company. John Henry enjoyed Havana, but

Jeffrey was lonely. "I have no letter from my wife yet," Jeffrey complained. "The Keats name has a reputation for writing, but that is not my experience." He later sent his son-in-law to Illinois to manage the Springfield Gas Company, but the poet's namesake found it to be "the most disagreeable place I ever got into." John Henry quit the business and wandered off, as his sister Emma put it, "an eccentric unbalanced genius."[12]

Clarence George likewise entered the gasworks business. Jeffrey sent him to troubleshoot operations in Cleveland, Wheeling, Memphis, and Vicksburg, Mississippi, and they kept in touch about such absorbing matters as valves, rafters, elbows, bolts, blackouts, lampposts, meters, and pipes. But when Clarence moved to Evansville, at the mouth of Pigeon Creek in Indiana, he contracted the family complaint. His business associate at the Evansville Gas Company lamented, "My partner is dying of consumption which will give me endless trouble." Since neither Clarence nor John Henry had sons, the Keats family name in America died with them.[13]

Georgiana survived her youngest son by eighteen years, but Jeffrey, despite the difference in their ages, did not long survive Georgiana. She died on April 3, 1879, and he passed away on February 18, 1881. According to the *Kentucky Gazette,* he had been "in bad health since the death of his wife," an event that "greatly depressed and grieved him."[14]

By the time of her death, Georgiana Keats Jeffrey had lived through the most formative periods in American history. She had seen the dream of Manifest Destiny become a reality, as the First Transcontinental Railroad connected the eastern states to California. She had experienced the era of Jacksonian Democracy, when Native Americans were shoved west of the Mississippi, and the extravagancies of life in the antebellum Old South. She had seen the horrors of the American Civil War, and the changes that came with Reconstruction. She died in the Gilded Age. From the perspective of English literary history, the sister-in-law of John Keats expired in the Age of Mark Twain. Had she lived another three years, she might have met Oscar Wilde in Louisville.

The literary celebrity and leader of the fin-de-siècle Cult of Beauty worshipped John Keats almost as much as Keats had worshipped beauty. "A thing of beauty is a joy for ever," John had written in the opening line of *Endymion:* "Its loveliness increases; it will never / Pass into nothingness." Ever since childhood, Wilde had adored Keats, "the real Adonis of our age," who had "heard in Hyperion's vale the large utterance of the early gods" and seen "Madeline at the painted window, and Lamia in the house at Corinth, and Endymion ankle-deep in lilies of the vale." He had revered that glorious poet who knew both the Apollonian "secret of the morning" and "the silver-footed messages of the moon."[15]

When Wilde visited the city at the falls of the Ohio on Tuesday, February 21, 1882, a crowd of admirers thronged the Masonic Grand Lodge in the center of Louisville. Some of the young men in the crowd had come wearing green carnations—the Victorian harbinger of the pink triangle, symbol of gay rights—not to be outdone, it seems, by the Harvard students who had attended Wilde's lecture in Cambridge, Massachusetts, wearing knee breeches, and carrying lilies and long-stemmed sunflowers.

Wilde had come to speak about the mission of art in the nineteenth century. During his lecture, he quoted John's "Sonnet on Blue" as an example of "color harmony." The idea was not new. In the Age of Enlightenment, Louis Bertrand Castel, inspired by the color scheme of Sir Isaac Newton, had constructed a device known as a color organ, or ocular harpsichord *(clavecin oculaire),* designed to produce "ocular harmony." Unlike the French mathematician, however, John Keats was no great fan of Newton's *Optics.* By refracting light and quantifying its spectrum, Newton had destroyed all the magic of the rainbow, reducing beauty to physics. Keats had his own method of producing color harmony, which unlike Castel's could not be calculated or predicted.

After the lecture, a woman from the audience approached the speaker. Although nearing sixty, she seemed much younger. She had a gentle, unassuming manner, and her voice sounded sweet. She introduced herself as Emma Keats Speed, the poet's niece. Wilde thought she resembled her "marvellous kinsman," that "godlike boy," and in that he wasn't alone. When the American Transcendentalist poet Christopher Pearse Cranch visited the Englishman's Palace in 1837, he could hardly keep his eyes off Emma, "so striking was the likeness." She seemed a living image of the engraved portrait of her uncle that Cranch had seen in *The Poetical Works of Coleridge, Shelley and Keats* (a pirated edition of 1829 in which many Americans first encountered the poetry of Keats).[16]

Emma invited Oscar Wilde to her house to see her uncle's manuscripts, and, despite the whirlwind pace of his tour through America, Wilde spent the next day on First Street in Louisville, poring over the carefully preserved, yet well-worn pages of John's journal-letters to George and Georgiana. He handled the faded scraps of poems that the poet's brother had treasured for so many years. Among them was the draft of the very sonnet that Wilde had read at the Masonic Lodge the previous evening:

> Blue!—'Tis the life of heaven—the domain
>   Of Cynthia:—the wide palace of the sun;
> The tent of Hesperus and all his train;
>   The bosomer of clouds gold, grey, and dun.
> Blue!—'Tis the life of waters—Ocean,
>   And all its vassal streams, pools numberless,
> May rage, and foam, and fret, but never can
>   Subside, if not to dark blue nativeness.
> Blue!—gentle cousin to the forest green,
>   Married to green in all the sweetest flowers—
> Forget-me-not—the blue-bell—and, that queen
>   Of secrecy, the violet:—What strange powers
> Hast thou, as a mere shadow?—But how great,
> When in an eye thou art, alive with fate!

John had written the "Sonnet on Blue" twenty days before George's twenty-first birthday, a coming-of-age that would forever divide the brothers across a sea of blue. Perhaps it was the poet's spirit of prophecy at work in the sonnet. *What strange powers, / Hast thou, as a mere shadow! But how great, / When in an Eye thou art alive with fate!*

Wilde had always thought there was something not quite right about the published version of the "Sonnet on Blue" that he had read in the *Athenaeum* of June 3, 1876. Two extra syllables in the sixth line, caused by the substitution of "tributary" for "vassal," disrupted the flow of the verse. "Vassal" was the word Keats had chosen. Wilde had used John's sonnet to illustrate Keats's particular skill for painting with words in such a way that they appealed to more than one sense. And unlike earlier versions of color harmony, their synthetic—in Keats's case, synaesthetic—effect could not reduce to formula. *There was an awful rainbow once in heaven.* But now: "We know her woof, her texture; she is given / In the dull catalogue of common things. / Philosophy will clip an Angel's wings, / Conquer all mysteries by rule and line, / Empty the haunted air, and gnomed mine—Unweave a rainbow, as it erewhile made / The tender-person'd Lamia melt into a shade." John's arguably most human character was, herself, "rainbow-sided."

As Wilde pondered the crossed-out words and substitutions in the draft of the "Sonnet on Blue," it occurred to him that the secret of style was in selection. Keats had mastered the technicalities of craft, but it was his *spirit of selection* that distinguished his genius, the "workings of that spirit" which guided his choice of one word over another. Wilde concluded that "the technicalities of method are in their essence spiritual, not mechanical."[17]

From Louisville, Oscar Wilde traveled west. In Omaha, Nebraska, he paused to thank Emma Keats Speed for having given him the holograph of her uncle's "Sonnet on Blue." Somewhere on the railway between Louisville and Omaha, this leader of the nineteenth-century Aesthetic Movement had become enamored of the very paper that John's hand—his *living hand* —had touched, the ink that had done his bidding. He loved "the sweet comeliness of his charactery" especially. Of course, in his letter to George's daughter, Wilde's own spirit of selection was at work in calling John's handwriting "charactery," an archaic term that even the *Oxford English Dictionary* associates with Keats: "When I have fears that I may cease to be/Before my pen has glean'd my teeming brain,/Before high piled books, in charactry . . ." John had expressed those fears in a sonnet written only days before his "Sonnet on Blue."[18]

In return for her gift, Wilde sent Emma his sonnet, "The Grave of Keats," which he had composed on John's grave in Rome stretched out on the grass *I have had much calm enjoyment,/Stretch'd on the grass at my best lov'd employment/Of scribbling lines for you.* So John had once written to George. When Wilde wrote his lines to Keats "beneath God's veil of blue," he did not know that soon he too would follow the "youngest of the martyrs," a victim (as in *Lamia*) of the "gossip rout." In the meantime, Wilde asked the poet's niece to place his sonnet near her uncle's papers. Perhaps there, it might "keep some green of youth caught from those withered leaves in whose faded lines eternal summer dwells."[19] *Some green of youth . . .*

As early as his sonnet "To My Brother George," John had noticed the kinship of blue and its derivative, green. "Many the wonders I this day have seen," he began in the summer of 1816. "The ocean with its vastness, its blue green." *The ocean with its vastness.* George could never quite get the sonnet out of his head. *The ocean with its vastness, its blue green.* Even more than the opening, the last couplet hung over his life in Louisville like an echo. *But what, without the social thought of thee, / Would be the wonders of the sky and sea?* Ultimately, like that mysterious quality animating blue, the spirit that led the two eldest Keats brothers on their separate paths in life turned out to be as expansive, in its differing legacies, as the blue abyss that came between them.

ABBREVIATIONS

NOTES

ACKNOWLEDGMENTS

INDEX

ABBREVIATIONS

Amphlett's Directory	William Amphlett, *The Emigrant's Directory to the Western States of North America; Including A Voyage Out from Liverpool; The Geography and Topography of the Whole Western Country, According to Its Latest Improvements; with Instructions for Descending the Rivers Ohio and Mississippi; also, A Brief Account of a New British Settlement on the Head-waters of the Susquehanna, in Philadelphia* (London: Longman, Hurst, Rees, Orme, and Brown, 1819).
Bakewell Family Book	B. G. Bakewell, *The Family Book of Bakewell, Page, Campbell: Being Some Account of the Descendants of John Bakewell, of Castle Donington, Leicestershire, England, Born in 1638; Benjamin Page, Born in 1765, at Norwich, England; William Campbell, Born July 1, 1766, at Mauchline, Ayrshire, Scotland; John Harding, of Leicester* (Pittsburgh: W. M. G. Johnston & Co., 1896).
Birkbeck's Letters	Morris Birkbeck, *Letters from Illinois* (Philadelphia: M. Carey and Son, 1818).
Birkbeck's Notes	Morris Birkbeck, *Notes on a Journey in America, from the Coast of Virginia to the Territory of Illinois,* 4th ed. (London: James Ridgway, 1818).
Bradbury's Travels	John Bradbury, *Travels in the Interior of America in the Years 1809, 1810, and 1811; Including a Description of Upper Louisiana, Together with the States of Ohio, Kentucky, Indiana, and Tennessee, with the Illinois and Western Territories, and Containing Remarks and Observations Useful to Persons Emigrating to Those Countries* (London: Sherwood, Neely, and Jones, 1817).
Clarke's Autobiography	James Freeman Clarke, *Autobiography, Diary, and Correspondence,* ed. Edward Everett Hale (Boston and New York: Houghton Mifflin and Co., 1899).
Clarke's Recollections	Charles Cowden Clarke and Mary Cowden Clarke, *Recollections of Writers,* 2nd ed. (London: Sampson Low, Marston, Searle, and Rivington, 1878).

Clarke's Sketches	James Freeman Clarke, *Memorial and Biographical Sketches* (Boston: Houghton, Osgood and Company, 1878).
Collins' Guide	S. H. Collins, *The Emigrant's Guide to and Description of the United States of America; Including Several Authentic and Highly Important Letters from English Emigrants Now in America, to Their Friends in England,* 4th ed. (Hull: Joseph Noble, [1830]).
CP	John Keats, *Complete Poems,* ed. Jack Stillinger (Cambridge, Mass.: Harvard University Press, 1978).
Errors of Emigrants	George Flower, *The Errors of Emigrants: Pointing Out Many Popular Errors Hitherto Unnoticed; With a Sketch of the Extent and Resources of the New States of the North American Union, and a Description of the Progress and Present Aspect of the English Settlement in Illinois, Founded by Morris Birkbeck and George Flower in the Year 1817* (London: Cleave, 1841).
Fearon's Sketches	Henry Bradshaw Fearon, *Sketches of America: A Narrative of a Journey of Five Thousand Miles through the Eastern and Western States of America; Contained in Eight Reports Addressed to Thirty-Nine English Families by Whom the Author Was Deputed, in June 1817, to Ascertain Whether Any and What Part of the United States Would be Suitable for Their Residence; With Remarks on Mr. Birkbeck's "Notes" and "Letters,"* 2nd ed. (London: Longman, Hurst, Rees, Orme, and Brown, 1818).
Flower's History	George Flower, *History of the English Settlement in Edwards County, Illinois, Founded in 1817 and 1818, by Morris Birkbeck and George Flower,* ed. E. B. Washburne (Chicago: Fergus, 1882).
Fordham's Narrative	Elias Pym Fordham, *Personal Narrative of Travels in Virginia, Maryland, Pennsylvania, Ohio, Indiana, Kentucky, and of a Residence in the Illinois Territory, 1817–1818,* ed. Frederic Austin Ogg (Cleveland: Arthur H. Clark, 1906).
George's Letters	Appendix in Naomi J. Kirk, "Shared Porridge: The Life of George Keats," unpublished manuscript [undated], Filson Historical Society, Louisville, Kentucky.
Hall's Journal	William Hall, "From England to Illinois in 1821: The Journal of William Hall," ed. Jay Monaghan, *Journal of the Illinois State Historical Society* 39, no. 1 (March 1946), 21–67; and 39, no. 2 (June 1946), 208–253.
Harris's Remarks	William Tell Harris, *Remarks Made during a Tour through the United States of America in the Years 1817, 1818, and 1819, in a Series of Letters to Friends in England* (London: Sherwood, Neely, and Jones, 1821).
Howitt's Letters	Emanuel Howitt, *Selections from Letters Written during a Tour through the United States in the Summer and Autumn of 1819; Illustrative of the Character of the Native Americans, and of Their Descent from the Lost Ten Tribes of Israel, as well as Descriptive of the Present Situation and Suffering of Emigrants, and of the Soil and State of Agriculture* (Nottingham: J. Dunn & Co., 1820).

Hulme's Journal	Thomas Hulme, *Journal of a Tour in the West (Ohio, Indiana, and Illinois) in 1818*, in the series *Early Western Travels, 1748–1846*, ed. Reuben Gold Thwaites, vol. 10 (Cleveland: Arthur H. Clark, 1904), 19–84.
KC	*The Keats Circle*, ed. Hyder Edward Rollins, 2nd ed., 2 vols. (Cambridge, Mass.: Harvard University Press, 1965).
Keats Family	Lawrence M. Crutcher, *The Keats Family* (Louisville: Butler Books, 2009).
KL	John Keats, *The Letters of John Keats,* ed. Hyder Edward Rollins, 2 vols. (Cambridge, Mass.: Harvard University Press, 1958).
Melish's Travels	John Melish, *Travels through the United States of America in the Years 1806 and 1807, and 1809, 1810, and 1811; Including an Account of Passages betwixt America and Britain, and Travels through Various Parts of Britain, Ireland, and Canada,* 2 vols. (Philadelphia: John Melish, 1815).
Memorable Days	William Faux, *Memorable Days in America: Being a Journal of a Tour to the United States, Principally Undertaken to Ascertain, by Positive Evidence, the Condition and Probable Prospects of British Emigrants, Including Accounts of Mr. Birkbeck's Settlement in the Illinois: And Intended to Shew Men and Things as They Are in America* (London: W. Simpkin and R. Marshall, 1823).
ML	Hyder Edward Rollins, *More Letters and Poems of the Keats Circle* (Cambridge, Mass.: Harvard University Press, 1965).
New States	Andrew Miller, *New States and Territories; or, The Ohio, Indiana, Illinois, Michigan, North-Western, Missouri, Louisiana, Mississippi, and Alabama in their Real Characters, in 1818,* &c. ([Keene, N.H.: John Prentiss], 1819).
Pedestrious Tour	Estwick Evans, *A Pedestrious Tour of Four Thousand Miles, through the Western States and Territories, during the Winter and Spring of 1818* (Concord, N.H.: Joseph C. Spear, 1819).
Severn's Letters	Joseph Severn, *Letters and Memoirs,* ed. Grant F. Scott (Aldershot, U.K.: Ashgate, 2005).
Shared Porridge	Naomi J. Kirk, "Shared Porridge: The Life of George Keats," unpublished manuscript [undated], Filson Historical Society, Louisville, Kentucky.
Welby's Visit	Adlard Welby, *A Visit to North America and the English Settlements in Illinois, with a Winter Residence in Philadelphia; Solely to Ascertain the Actual Prospects of the Emigrating Agriculturalist, Mechanic, and Commercial Speculator* (London: J. Drury, 1821).
Western Gazetteer	Samuel R. Brown, *The Western Gazetteer, or Emigrant's Directory, Containing a Geographical Description of the Western States and Territories, viz. the States of Kentucky, Indiana, Louisiana, Ohio, Tennessee and Mississippi, and the Territories of Illinois, Missouri, Alabama, Michigan, and North-Western* (Auburn, N.Y.: H. C. Southwick, 1817).

Woods' Residence   John Woods, *Two Years' Residence on the English Prairie of
                            Illinois,* in the series *Early Western Travels, 1748–1846,* ed.
                            Reuben Gold Thwaites, vol. 10 (Cleveland: Arthur H. Clark,
                            1904), 171–357.

Wright's Views   Frances Wright, *Views of Society and Manners in America, in a
                            Series of Letters from That Country to a Friend in England, during
                            the Years 1818, 1819, and 1820* (New York: E. Bliss and E. White,
                            1821).

NOTES

Prologue

 1. Walter Jackson Bate, *John Keats* (Cambridge, Mass.: Harvard University Press, 1963), 2.

 2. *KC,* 2:313.

 3. "Recollections sent by Alice L. Keats to Maurice Buxton Forman," undated MS 215, University of Delaware Library, Newark, Delaware.

 4. Earle Balch to Naomi Joy Kirk, July 26, 1943. Blanche Colton Williams to Naomi Joy Kirk July 17, 1943. Naomi Joy Kirk Collection, Filson Historical Society, Louisville, Kentucky.

 5. Philip S. Tuley to Naomi Joy Kirk, May 12, 1943. Naomi Joy Kirk Collection, Filson Historical Society, Louisville, Kentucky.

1. To My Brother George

 1. William Turton, *A Treatise on Cold and Hot Baths, with Directions for Their Application in Various Diseases,* 2nd ed. (Swansea: printed by the author, 1803), 35.

 2. *KL,* 1:238–239.

 3. Ibid., 1:114.

 4. *KC,* 1:277.

 5. Ibid., 1:314.

 6. *KL,* 2:46. Compare *KL,* 1:314. On the description of Edmonton, see Marie Adami, *Fanny Keats* (New Haven: Yale University Press, 1938), 23.

 7. *ML,* 11.

 8. Ibid., 21, 34.

 9. Ibid., 20–21, 13.

10. *The Poetical Works of William Collins: With the Life of the Author and Critical Observations by Dr. Langhorne* (London: Suttaby, Evance, and Fox, 1815), Keats Collection (Keats EC8 K2262 Zy815c), Houghton Library, Harvard University.

11. Adami, *Fanny Keats,* 46–47n. Mary Ann Tuckey, *Assisting Questions on English Grammar, with Answers, Comprising an Explanation of Etymology and the Principal Rules of Syntax* (London: Boosey and Sons, 1829), v–vi.

12. *KC,* 2:185.

13. Ibid., 2:184, 186.

14. Ibid., 2:198. Mathew, "Of Solitude," quoted in Edmund Blunden, "Keats's Friend Mathew," *English* 1 (1936–1937), 50.

15. *KC,* 2:185, 1:325. See, too, *Clarke's Recollections,* 143–144.

16. *KC,* 2:211.

17. William Hazlitt, *The Fight and Other Writings,* ed. Tom Paulin and David Chandler (Harmondsworth: Penguin, 2000), 147.

18. Hazlitt, *The Fight and Other Writings,* 152. *Clarke's Recollections,* 145.

19. *Clarke's Recollections,* 146. *KC,* 2:163–164.

20. John Hamilton Reynolds, "Preface" to *The Fancy: A Selection from the Poetical Remains of the Late Peter Corcoran, of Gray's Inn, Student at Law; with a Brief Memoir of His Life* (London: Taylor and Hessey, 1820), xv.

21. Ibid., 91.

22. Shakespeare, *Henry VI,* Part III, 2.1.16–17.

23. *Clarke's Recollections,* 145.

24. *KL,* 1:392.

25. *KL,* 2:60.

26. *ML,* 30. *KL,* 1:293.

27. Richard Woodhouse records that the poem "was written by the author at the request of his brother George, to be sent by the latter to Miss Georgiana." *CP,* 424.

28. *KL,* 1:303. *ML,* 22.

29. Scrapbook compiled by Georgiana Augusta Wylie Keats and others (MS Keats 3.4), Houghton Library, Harvard University.

30. *KC,* 1:314.

31. *KL,* 1:341.

32. On Tom's plea for money, see Amy Lowell, *John Keats,* 2 vols. (Boston: Houghton Mifflin, 1929), 1:173. George writes: "he advanced some when Tom went to Lyons"; *KC,* 1:301.

33. *KC,* 1:307–308.

34. Andrew Johnstone lists "Abbey & Cocks"; *London Commercial Guide, and Street Directory: On a New and More Efficient Principle Than Any Yet Established,*

Corrected to August 31, 1817 (London: Barnard and Farley, 1817), 545. Rollins points out variants of the partnership; *KL,* 1:62n. See, too, Joanna Richardson, "New Light on Mr. Abbey," *Keats-Shelley Memorial Bulletin* 5 (1953), 26–31 (26).

35. *KC,* 1:304.

36. Ibid., 2:149, 2:209. *Clarke's Recollections,* 132.

37. *KC,* 2:208.

38. Stuart M. Sperry, "Isabella Jane Towers, John Towers, and John Keats," *Keats-Shelley Journal* 28 (1979), 35–58 (38–39). Johnstone, *London Commercial Guide,* 291.

39. *KL,* 2:207–208.

40. Compare Shakespeare, *Hamlet,* 4.5.72–73.

41. Leigh Hunt, "The Prince on St. Patrick's Day," *Examiner* 221 (March 22, 1812), 177–180 (179).

42. George Gordon, Lord Byron to Thomas Moore, May 19, 1813, in *Byron's Letters and Journals,* ed. Leslie A. Marchand, vol. 3, 1813–1814 (London: John Murray, 1974), 49.

43. Leigh Hunt, *The Autobiography of Leigh Hunt,* rev. ed. (London: Smith, Elder, and Co., 1891), 217. Z, "On the Cockney School of Poetry, No. 1," *Blackwood's Edinburgh Magazine* 2, no. 7 (October 1817), 38–41 (39).

44. *Clarke's Recollections,* 127.

45. Hunt, "To Thomas Moore," in *Foliage: Poems Original and Translated* (London: C. and J. Ollier, 1818), lxxx. Scrapbook compiled by Tom Keats, July–August 1814 (MS Keats 3.5), Houghton Library, Harvard University.

46. Carlyle quoted in James Anthony Froude, *Thomas Carlyle: A History of the First Forty Years of His Life, 1795–1835,* 2 vols. (London: Longmans, Green, and Co., 1882), 2:439.

47. *KL,* 1:416, 1:203.

48. Haydon to John Keats, May 11, 1817, in Benjamin Robert Haydon, *Correspondence and Table-Talk,* ed. Frederic Wordsworth Haydon, 2 vols. (London: Chatto and Windus, 1876), 2:3. *KL,* 1:124.

49. *KL,* 1:124. *KC,* 1:4.

50. Byron quoted in John Clubbe, "The Reynolds-Dovaston Correspondence," *Keats-Shelley Journal* 30 (1981), 152–181 (155).

51. *KL,* 1:118n.

52. Leigh Hunt, "Young Poets," *Examiner* 466 (December 1, 1816), 761–762 (761); *KC,* 2:211.

53. *KC,* 1:288, 1:304. *Clarke's Recollections,* 121.

54. Jean Haynes, "John Jennings: Keats's Grandfather," *Keats-Shelley Memorial Bulletin* 13 (1962), 18–23 (18–19). See also Jean Haynes, "At the Swan and Hoop," *Keats-Shelley Memorial Bulletin* 22 (1971), 52.

55. "Robert Mathews, Theft: Animal Theft," February 16, 1803, *Proceedings of the Old Bailey,* Ref. t18030216–31.

56. *KC,* 1:288, 1:314, 1:303.

57. Ibid., 1:303.

58. Benjamin Robert Haydon, *Autobiography and Journals,* ed. Malcolm Elwin (London: Macdonald, 1950), 297. Andrew Motion identifies "Mrs Frances Grafty"; *Keats* (London: Faber and Faber, 1997), 20; however, the merchant Samuel "Graffty" lived at 28 Walbrook Street, near the London Wall; Johnstone, *London Commercial Guide,* 694.

59. Jean Haynes, "Elizabeth Keats," *Keats-Shelley Memorial Bulletin* 9 (1958), 21. *KC,* 1:303.

60. Quoted in Richardson, "New Light on Mr. Abbey," 28.

61. *Clarke's Recollections,* 124.

62. *KC,* 1:304.

63. Haynes, "Elizabeth Keats," 21.

64. *KC,* 1:305.

65. *KC,* 1:279. Phyllis G. Mann, "New Light on Keats and His Family," *Keats-Shelley Memorial Bulletin* 11 (1960), 33–38 (33).

66. *KL,* 2:186; emphasis added.

67. Ibid., 1:401. See, too, Walter Jackson Bate, *John Keats* (Cambridge, Mass.: Harvard University Press, 1963), 10.

68. On John Clarke's pedagogy, see Nicholas Roe, "John Keats at Enfield School," *Keats-Shelley Review* 10 (1996), 13–29.

69. "Note on the School House at Enfield by Charles Cowden Clarke," quoted in Adami, *Fanny Keats,* 26–27. *Clarke's Recollections,* 120.

70. *KC,* 1:327–328. *Clarke's Recollections,* 123.

71. *Clarke's Recollections,* 123. *KC,* 1:325. Kenyon West, "Keats in Hampstead," *Century Illustrated Magazine* 50, no. 6 (October 1895), 898–910 (905). *KL,* 2:61.

72. *KC,* 2:165, 1:284.

73. Haynes, "John Jennings," 21; Richardson, "New Light on Mr. Abbey," 27.

74. Norman Kilgour, "Mrs. Jennings' Will," *Keats-Shelley Memorial Bulletin* 13 (1962), 24–27 (25). Last will and Testament of John Henry Powell Schneider, March 14, 1846, Public Record Office (Prob 11/2148), The National Archives, London.

75. *KL,* 1:141.

76. *KC,* 1:307–308.

77. Robert Gittings, *John Keats* (Boston: Little, Brown, 1968), 443. Jean Haynes, "Keats's Paternal Relatives," *Keats-Shelley Memorial Bulletin* 15 (1964),

27–28 (27). *Shared Porridge,* 19. Johnstone lists the hatter as "Keates," a common variant of the surname; *London Commercial Guide,* 116.

    78. *KC,* 1:308–309.

    79. See John's "Sleep and Poetry," lines 264–266.

2. What Mad Pursuit?

    1. *KL,* 2:60.

    2. Ibid., 2:253.

    3. Charles Brown, Florence, to Charles Wentworth Dilke, London, January 20, 1830, in *George's Letters,* 87. *Clarke's Sketches,* 224.

    4. *Clarke's Sketches,* 224. *KL,* 2:117–118.

    5. On May 13, 1833, Cadman Hodgkinson claimed that he had been in the tea trade for twenty-four years; see *First Report of Inquiry into the Excise Establishment, and into the Management and Collection of the Excise Revenue throughout the United Kingdom: Tea Permits and Surveys,* Appendix 44 (London: William Clowes, 1833), 143–145 (143). Sampson Hodgkinson, in a court case against a man accused of stealing beeswax, swears, "I am a druggist, in partnership with Thomas Wilson and William Minshull"; see *Proceedings of the Old Bailey,* "James Busby, Theft: Grand Larceny, 15 April 1801," Ref. t18010415–28, www.oldbaileyonline.org (accessed July 9, 2010). See, too, Records of Sun Fire Office, Guildhall Library (MS 11936/426/745713), April 1, 1803, and (MS 11936/464/885324) August 12, 1813, National Archives, London. The Merchant Taylors' School register lists Cadman Hodgkinson, born December 19, 1819, and Harry, born October 15, 1821, as the sons of Susan and Cadman Hodgkinson, tea dealer, at Dowgate Hill; see Charles J. Robinson, *A Register of the Scholars Admitted into Merchant Taylors' School, from A.D. 1562 to 1874,* vol. 2 (Lewes: Farncombe and Co., 1883), 251.

    6. Joanna Richardson, "New Light on Mr. Abbey," *Keats-Shelley Memorial Bulletin* 5 (1953), 26–31 (29–30). *Mechanics' Magazine, Museum, Register, Journal, and Gazette* 15, no. 395 (March 5, 1831), 476.

    7. *Clarke's Sketches,* 224.

    8. Robert Gittings, *John Keats* (Harmondsworth: Penguin, 1979), 132n. Andrew Johnstone, *London Commercial Guide, and Street Directory: On a New and More Efficient Principle Than Any Yet Established, Corrected to August 31, 1817* (London: Barnard and Farley, 1817), 64. On George Keats's lodging: Mary Cowden Clarke to W. Phillips, March 10, 1876, Folger Shakespeare Library (Y.c.970, no. 40). See also Charles Tilly, comp., *Kent's Directories of Business in London, 1759–1828* (Ann Arbor, Mich.: University of Michigan, Center for Research on Social Organization [producer], 1983, ICPSR [distributor], 1985); Edward

Baines, *History, Directory & Gazetteer of the County of York: With Select Lists of the Merchants & Traders of London, and the Principal Commercial and Manufacturing Towns of England,* 2 vols. (Leeds: E. Baines, 1822), 1:lxix.

9. *ML,* 28. *KC,* 1:299–300. On Wilkinson, see Aileen Ward, *John Keats: The Making of a Poet* (New York: Viking, 1963), 119; Gittings, *John Keats,* 132n; *KL,* 1:129n; Johnstone, *London Commercial Guide,* 64.

10. *KC,* 1:286.

11. *KL,* 1:193, 2:213.

12. *KC,* 1:318. *ML,* 20. Sir Charles W. Dilke, *The Papers of a Critic,* 2 vols. (London: John Murray, 1875), 1:8, 11.

13. *KC,* 1:lv; Amy Lowell, *John Keats,* 2 vols. (Boston: Houghton Mifflin, 1929), 1:470; Gillian Iles, "New Information on Keats's Friend Charles 'Armitage' Brown and the Brown Family," *Keats-Shelley Journal* 40 (1991), 146–166 (156–157, 161–162).

14. *KC,* 2:57. Kenyon West, "Keats in Hampstead," *Century Illustrated Magazine* 50, no. 6 (October 1895), 906.

15. *Clarke's Recollections,* 137–138.

16. Byron to John Murray, in George Cheatham, "Byron's Dislike of Keats's Poetry," *Keats-Shelley Journal* 32 (1983), 20–25 (23).

17. Z [John Gibson Lockhart], "On the Cockney School of Poetry, No. 1," *Blackwood's Edinburgh Magazine* 2, no. 7 (October 1817), 38–41 (39). John Wilson, review in the *Anti-Gallician Monitor,* quoted in Lewis M. Schwartz, "Keats's Critical Reception in Newspapers of His Day," *Keats-Shelley Journal* 21–22 (1973), 170–187 (173).

18. Z [John Gibson Lockhart], "On the Cockney School of Poetry, No. 6," *Blackwood's Edinburgh Magazine* 6, no. 31 (October 1819), 70–76 (75).

19. Hunt, *Foliage; or, Poems Original and Translated* (London: C. and J. Ollier, 1818), 9.

20. *Clarke's Recollections,* 140. Robert Underwood Johnson, "Note on Some Volumes Now in America, Once Owned by Keats," *Bulletin and Review of the Keats-Shelley Memorial* 2 (1913), 20–29 (23). George thought his birthday to be March 1, but it was actually February 28.

21. *KC,* 1:308.

22. George Felton Mathew, review of Keats's *Poems,* in *European Magazine, and London Review* 71 (May 1817), 434–437 (434). [John Hamilton Reynolds], review in the *Champion* (March 9, 1817), 78.

23. *KL,* 1:377.

24. Maurice Buxton Forman, ed., *The Letters of John Keats,* 4th ed. (London: Oxford University Press, 1952), 100–101n. The phrase "take in" here means deceit: the publishers have cheated the public.

25. *KC,* 1:cxxxix, 1.69.

26. *KC,* 1:54–55; or *KL,* 1:383–384, 2:151, 2:180.

27. *KL,* 1:125, 1:136. John Bunyan, *The Pilgrim's Progress,* ed. Cynthia Wall (New York: W. W. Norton, 2009), 13. Luke 14:26.

28. *KL,* 1:125.

29. Ibid., 1:154.

30. Ibid., 1:170.

31. *The Works of Thomas Love Peacock,* ed. H. E. B. Brett-Smith and C. E. Jones, 10 vols. (London: Constable, 1934), 8:107.

32. *KL,* 1:383, or *KC,* 1:54.

33. *KL,* 1:128.

34. Ibid., 1:128–129.

35. Ibid., 1:130. Shakespeare, *The Tempest,* 2.2.44 and 2.2.54.

36. *KL,* 1:415.

37. Ibid., 2:142.

38. Henry Irwin Jenkinson, *Jenkinson's Smaller Practical Guide to the Isle of Wight,* 2nd ed. (London: Edward Stanford, 1879), 185.

39. *KL,* 1:132.

40. Ibid., 1:131.

41. Ibid., 1:130–131.

42. Shakespeare, *King Lear,* 4.6.34–36. John uses the phrase "sublime pathetic" in relation to John Milton's *Paradise Lost;* see Beth Lau, *Keats's Paradise Lost* (Gainesville: University Press of Florida, 1998), 28.

43. *KL,* 1:139.

44. Ibid., 1:133, 1:173, 1:142.

45. Ibid., 1:132.

46. Ibid.

47. Ibid., 1:129.

48. Ibid., 1:135.

49. Ibid., 1:135, 1:142.

50. Ibid., 1:140–141. Compare Shakespeare, *Love's Labour's Lost,* 1.1.1–7.

51. Ibid., 1:143.

52. Ibid., 1:147, 1:142, 1:148.

53. *KC,* 2:15.

54. *KL,* 1:137.

55. *The Life of Benjamin Robert Haydon, Historical Painter, from His Autobiography and Journals,* ed. Tom Taylor, 2nd ed., 3 vols. (London: Longman, Brown, Green, and Longmans, 1853), 1:286.

56. *KL,* 1:403. See Robert Gittings, *John Keats,* 139–140, on Isabella Jones and her consort.

57. Shakespeare, *King Lear,* 4.1.166–169 (above). John Howard Payne, "Random Scraps and Recollections, from the Note Book of a Wanderer at Home and Abroad, No. 1," *Ladies' Companion: A Monthly Magazine Embracing Literature and the Fine Arts* 7 (August 1837), 185–187 (187).

58. *KL,* 2:64–65, 1:138. *KC,* 1:318.

59. *CP,* 453.

60. Charlotte Cox Reynolds to John F. M. Dovaston, November ? and 26, 1808, quoted in John Clubbe, "The Reynolds-Dovaston Correspondence," *Keats-Shelley Journal* 30 (1981), 152–181 (155, 159–160). Thomas Hood, "Fragment (Evidently Supposed to be Spoken by Mrs. Reynolds, Mother of the Poet's Wife)," in *The Complete Poetical Works of Thomas Hood,* ed. Walter Jerrold (London: Henry Frowde, 1906), 661.

61. *KC,* 2:15, 1:319.

62. Clayton E. Hudnall, "John Hamilton Reynolds, James Rice, and Benjamin Bailey in the Leigh Browne-Lockyer Collection," *Keats-Shelley Journal* 19 (1970), 11–39 (22, 13).

63. *KC,* 1:19; 2:267, 1:9. *KL,* 1:156–157, 2:67.

64. *KL,* 1:160, 1:374.

65. *KC,* 2:283. *KL,* 1:154, 1:162.

66. *KC,* 1:35.

67. *KL,* 1:351, 1:186, 1:171. Solomon Sawrey quoted in C. T. Andrews, "Keats and Mercury," *Keats-Shelley Memorial Bulletin* 20 (1969), 37–43 (41).

68. *KC,* 2:271. Compare Milton, *Paradise Regained,* 3.310.

69. *KL,* 1:154–155.

70. John Scott, *A Visit to Paris in 1814: Being a Review of the Moral, Political, Intellectual, and Social Condition of the French Capital* (London: Longman, Hurst, Rees, Orme, 1815), 16. See John's "Song about Myself" ("There was a naughty boy"), sent to Fanny Keats from Scotland.

71. *KL,* 1:217, 2:364.

72. Ibid., 2:364–365. John Taylor to his father, March 28, 1821, in Olive M. Taylor, "John Taylor: Author and Publisher, 1781–1864," *London Mercury* 12 (1925), 258–267 (260). *Severn's Letters,* 615.

73. Thomas Brown, pseud., *The Englishman in Paris: A Satirical Novel, with Sketches of the Most Remarkable Characters That Have Recently Visited That Celebrated Capital,* 3 vols. (London: Sherwood, Neely, and Jones, 1819), 1:21. *KL* 1:154–155.

74. Scott, *A Visit to Paris,* 24.

75. Ibid., 60–62.

76. John Scott, *The House of Mourning, a Poem: With Some Smaller Pieces* (London: Taylor and Hessey, 1817), 3, x.

77. Commonplace book compiled by Tom Keats, Keats Collection, Houghton Library, Harvard University; Caroline Scott sends respects to George and Tom through John on February 14, 1818; on March 18, 1818, to John and Tom through George; on March 25, to John through Haydon; *KL* 1:227, 1:247, 1:258.

78. Scott, *A Visit to Paris,* 121; Brown to Dilke, January 20, 1830, in *George's Letters,* 87.

79. Scott, *A Visit to Paris,* 117; Brown to Dilke, January 20, 1830, in *George's Letters,* 87.

80. *KL,* 1:169.

81. Ibid.

82. Ibid., 2:61.

83. Ibid., 1:197.

84. See George Cheyne, *The English Malady; or, A Treatise on Nervous Diseases of all Kinds, as Spleen, Vapours, Lowness of Spirits, Hypochondriacal, and Hysterical Distempers, &c.* (London: G. Strahan, 1733). Ibid., 1:172.

85. *KC,* 2:58. N. T. Carrington, et al., *The Teignmouth, Dawlish, and Torquay Guide: With an Account of the Surrounding Neighbourhood, Its Scenery, Antiquities, &c.* (Teignmouth: E. Croydon, 1810), 40–41.

86. G. D. Griffiths and E. G. C. Griffiths, *History of Teignmouth* (Teignmouth: Brunswick Press, 1965), 46. William Turton, *A Treatise on Cold and Hot Baths: With Directions for Their Application in Various Diseases* (Swansea: printed at the author's private press, 1803), 34.

87. *KL,* 1:188.

88. Z [John Gibson Lockhart], "On the Cockney School of Poetry, No. 4," *Blackwood's Edinburgh Magazine* 3, no. 17 (August 1818), 519–524 (522, 524).

89. *KL,* 1:184.

90. Ibid., 1:188. Compare Shakespeare's Sonnet 17, as quoted by Keats: "a poets rage / And stretched metre of an antique song."

91. *KL,* 1:225. Mary Cowden Clarke, "The Life and Labours of Vincent Novello," *Musical Times* 10, no. 227 (January 1, 1826), 169–172 (172).

92. [Edward Croydon], *Guide to Watering Places on the Coast between the Exe and the Dart, Including Teignmouth, Dawlish and Torquay* (Teignmouth: E. Croydon, 1817), 20–22.

93. Winthrop Mackworth Praed quoted in Griffiths and Griffiths, *History of Teignmouth,* 43.

94. Carrington, *The Teignmouth, Dawlish, and Torquay Guide,* 51. Griffiths and Griffiths, *History of Teignmouth,* 47.

95. Mrs. I. S. Prowse [Mary Ann Jeffery], *Poems* (London: Smith, Elder, and Co., 1830), 101.

96. *KC,* 1:13–15; letter formatted as dialogue with George's spelling of Marianne retained.

97. *KL,* 1:285. Mary Ann married Isaac Sparke Prowse on June 21, 1829, and her son William Jeffery was born May 6, 1836. On Kean: Griffiths and Griffiths, *History of Teignmouth,* 44.

98. See the obituary of Sir Warwick Hele Tonkin, dated September 11, 1863, in *The Gentleman's Magazine and Historical Review* 215 (October 1863), 521–522.

99. *KL,* 1:290. "Provincial Occurrences in the Counties of England," *New Monthly Magazine and Universal Register* 10, no. 57 (October 1818), 279–288 (281). Will of Eliza Jane Squarey Periman Tonkin, transcribed by Judy Bensen and Ivy F. Benoit from the *Newfoundland Will Books,* 2:272–286; see www.rootsweb.ances try.com/~cannf/unknown_wills_elizatonkin.htm. The probate year ("1870?") for Eliza Jane Squarey Periman's will appears incorrect, for according to Tonkin's obituary of September 11, 1863, his wife died about 1858; Obituary of Sir Warwick Hele Tonkin, 522.

3. Man of Genius and Man of Power

1. *KL,* 1:198.
2. *KL,* 1:286–287.
3. *Birkbeck's Letters,* 47. *Birkbeck's Notes,* 8.
4. *Birkbeck's Letters,* 64. Peacock to Percy Bysshe Shelley, Marlow, September 15, 1818, in *The Letters of Thomas Love Peacock,* ed. Nicolas A. Joukovsky, 2 vols. (Oxford: Clarendon, 2001), 1:152.
5. *Flower's History,* 27–29.
6. *Fordham's Narrative,* 121.
7. *The Complete Poetry and Prose of William Blake,* ed. David V. Erdman, rev. ed. (New York: Doubleday, 1988), 473.
8. *KL,* 1:397. *Birkbeck's Letters,* 144.
9. *Fearon's Sketches,* vii–viii.
10. [John Barrow and William Gifford], review of *Notes on a Journey in America,* in *Quarterly Review* 19, no. 37 (April 1818), 54–78 (78). [Barrow and Gifford], "Views, Visits, and Tours in North America," *Quarterly Review* 27, no. 53 (April 1822), 71–99 (99).
11. Francis Jeffrey, Review of *Radical Reform* and *The Democratic Recorder,* in *Edinburgh Review* 32, no. 64 (October 1819), 293–309 (293–294).
12. *Hall's Journal,* 1:23. John Ingle, Somersham, to John Ingle, Jr., at Morris Birkbeck's settlement, Princeton, Indiana, October 3, 1818; John Ingle Papers, 1813–1868, Indiana Historical Society, Collection no. M0167, Box 1, Folder 12, Indianapolis, Indiana.

13. *Memorable Days,* 298.

14. *Flower's History,* 94, 64.

15. Ibid., 93–94. John Melish, *Information and Advice to Emigrants to the United States: And from the Eastern to the Western States* (Philadelphia: printed by John Melish, 1819), 5.

16. *The Writings of Thomas Jefferson,* ed. Andrew A. Lipscomb, vol. 15 (Washington, D.C.: Thomas Jefferson Memorial Association, 1904), 141.

17. "Indenture made by James Peachey on leaving Clarke's school at Enfield, agreeing to be of good conduct"; Accounts, correspondence, and personal papers relating to the Peachey family of London, London Metropolitan Archives, F/PEY/001.

18. *Flower's History,* 96. On Lawrence and Trimmer's ship: *Boston Daily Advertiser* 21, no. 40 (May 18, 1818), 2. On Flower's ship: [William Ogden Niles], *Niles' Weekly Register* 14, no. 353 (June 6, 1818), 256. *New-York Gazette and General Advertiser* 28, no. 11370 (May 27, 1818), 2.

19. John James Audubon quoted in *Clarke's Sketches,* 226.

20. William Cobbett, *A Year's Residence in the United States of America* (Carbondale: Southern Illinois University Press, 1964; orig. pub. 1819), 287.

21. *KC,* 2:15.

22. *Keats Family,* 14–15. J. H. Dorwin, "Montreal in 1816: Reminiscences of Mr. J. H. Dorwin," *Montreal Daily Star* 13, no. 30 (February 5, 1881), 2.

23. Merrill Denison, *Canada's First Bank: A History of the Bank of Montreal,* 2 vols. (Toronto-Montreal: McClelland and Stewart, 1966), 1:101, 6, 230, 191. Denison's identification of Henry as Robert's brother, rather than son, is in error. See G. Blaine Baker, "Ordering the Urban Canadian Law Office and Its Entrepreneurial Hinterland, 1825 to 1875," *University of Toronto Law Journal* 48, no. 2 (1998), 175–251 (184–185), which draws on Henry Griffin's notarial minute books in the *Archives nationales du Québec à Montréal* (CN1–187).

24. Lawrence M. Crutcher, "Finding the Keats Family," *The Keats-Shelley Review* 25, no. 1 (April 2011), 3–9 (5). On Georgiana's birthdate, see *Keats Family,* 48–50, and Phyllis G. Mann, "More Keatsiana: George's Marriage," *Keats-Shelley Memorial Bulletin* 13 (1962), 37–38 (38).

25. *KL,* 1:293, 1:392.

26. Ibid., 1:273, 1:239, 1:246.

27. Ibid., 1:245.

28. Ibid., 1:284.

29. Ibid., 1:196–197.

30. Priscilla Johnston, "Charles Jeremiah Wells: An Early Keatsian Poet," *Keats-Shelley Journal* 26 (1977), 72–87 (78). *KL,* 1:245.

31. Commonplace book compiled by Tom Keats, MS Keats 3.5, Houghton Library, Harvard University.

32. *The Complete Works of William Hazlitt,* ed. P. P. Howe, 21 vols. (London: J. M. Dent), 5:122–123.

33. John Keats to George and Tom Keats, January 30, 1818, in Dearing Lewis, "A John Keats Letter Rediscovered," *Keats-Shelley Journal* 47 (1998), 14–18 (16).

34. *KL,* 1:234.

35. "Incidents, Promotions, Births, Marriages, Deaths, &c." *New Monthly Magazine and Universal Register* 9, no. 51 (April 1818), 264–270 (264–265).

36. *KL,* 1:244–245, 1:249, 1:258.

37. Ibid., 1:247.

38. Ibid., 1:369, 1:241.

39. Marginalia in Keats's copy of Hazlitt's *Characters of Shakespeare's Plays* (London: Printed by C. H. Reynall for R. Hunter and C. and J. Ollier, 1817), 125 (EC8 K2262 Zz817h), Houghton Library, Harvard University.

40. *KL,* 1:241–242.

41. *Complete Prose Works of John Milton,* vol. 4, pt. 1, 1650–1655, ed. Don M. Wolfe (New Haven: Yale University Press, 1966), 323–534. *KL,* 1:254.

42. *KL,* 1:267, 1:281.

43. *CP,* 64.

44. Ibid.

45. *KL,* 1:286.

46. Ibid., 1:281.

47. *KC,* 1:15. *KL,* 1:340.

48. *KL,* 1:284–285.

49. *KC,* 1:16.

50. Ibid., 2:15.

51. *Welby's Visit,* 259. John Jeffrey, "George Keats," *The Athenaeum* no. 2358 (January 4, 1873), 17–18 (18).

52. Georgiana's chain and the information relating to it are on display in the Keats Room (75Z-3), Houghton Library, Harvard University.

53. *KL,* 1:287.

54. Ibid. Wordsworth used the phrase "Moods of My Own Mind" to label a category of poetry in his *Poems in Two Volumes* (1807).

55. *KL,* 1:293.

56. Ibid., 1:184, 1:387.

57. Ibid., 1:403, 1:387.

58. *Clarke's Sketches,* 224–225. The age that Clarke gives for Georgiana is un-likely. The "Burden of the Mystery," which John spoke about to Reynolds after Tom's hemorrhage on May 3, 1818, is from Wordsworth, "Lines Composed a Few Miles above Tintern Abbey."

59. *KL,* 1:299.

60. Ibid., 2:138.

61. Mann, "More Keatsiana," 38.

62. *KL,* 2:207.

63. Charles's traveling papers are in Georgiana's Scrapbook (MS Keats 3.4), Keats Collection, Houghton Library, Harvard University. "Bankrupts," *Law Advertiser* 9, no. 52 (December 29, 1831), 490. Information for George Keats Wylie's birth (March 4, 1829) and Charles Wylie's death (June 5, 1839), courtesy of Lawrence M. Crutcher.

64. *KL,* 2:68–69. Shakespeare, *Merry Wives of Windsor,* 4.5.22.

65. *KL,* 2:247, 2:242. Henry Wylie is listed as a bankrupt merchant prior to 1830; *Law Advertiser* 8 (1830), xxxii, 218ff.

66. *KL,* 2:207, 2:29, 1:393.

67. *Letters from Illinois,* 116. *KL,* 1:295.

68. *KL,* 1:397–398.

69. Leigh Hunt, *The Autobiography of Leigh Hunt, with Reminiscences of Friends and Contemporaries,* 3 vols. (London: Smith, Elder, 1850), 1:195–196. The second two comments are from later editions of Hunt's *Autobiography.*

70. *KL,* 1:287, 1:398. See John's "'Tis the 'witching time of night,'" *KC,* 2:224–225.

71. [Sydney Smith], "Travellers in America," *Edinburgh Review* 31 (December 1818), 132–150 (144). James Fenimore Cooper, *Notions of the Americans: Picked Up by a Travelling Bachelor,* ed. Gary Williams (Albany: State University of New York Press, 1991; orig. pub. 1828), 348.

72. Robert Gittings, *The Keats Inheritance* (London: Heinemann, 1964), 38, 46ff. *KC,* 1:278.

73. *KL,* 2:230.

74. Charles Brown to Charles Dilke, Florence, January 20, 1830, in *George's Letters,* 87.

75. *KL,* 1:295.

76. Ibid., 1:342, 1:333.

77. Ibid., 2:253.

78. Ibid., 1:293.

79. "There was a naughty boy"; compare, *KL,* 1:312–313.

80. *KC,* 2:212. *KL,* 1:395.

81. Compare Aileen Ward's account of the trip in *John Keats: The Making of a Poet: A Biography* (New York: Viking Press, 1963), 188–189.

82. *Amphlett's Directory,* 1.

83. *KL,* 1:351.

84. Ibid., 1:237.

85. Ibid., 1:358.

86. *KC,* 1:285.

87. [Classified], *Franklin Gazette* 1, no. 41 (April 11, 1818), 4. Carol Kyros Walker, *Walking North with Keats* (New Haven: Yale University Press, 1992), 8.

88. "Shipping News," *New York Daily Advertiser* 2, no. 313 (April 13, 1818), 2. For an itemized list of cargo, see "Imports Entered at the Custom House Philadelphia, March 23, 1818," *Franklin Gazette* 1, no. 25 (March 24, 1818), 3. On George's trip: "Ship News," *Franklin Gazette* 1, no. 103 (June 23, 1818), 3; *New-York Evening Post* 4999 (June 22, 1818), 2. *Grotjan's Philadelphia Public Sale Report* 7, no. 18 (August 31, 1818), 143. *Franklin Gazette* 2, no. 157 (August 26, 1818), 3, Report and Manifest of the cargo laden on board of the *Telegraph;* The Passenger Lists of Vessels arriving at Philadelphia, 1800–1882, National Archives and Records Administration M425, roll no. 27.

89. On the fifty-two-day round trip following George's: "Ship Telegraph," *Poulson's American Daily Advertiser* 47, no. 13082 (October 27, 1818), 3; and "Ship News," *Franklin Gazette* 3, no. 335 (March 24, 1819), 3, which includes an itemized passenger list. On the winter crossing before the Keatses sailed: "Ship Telegraph, Coffin, was at Liverpool 27th Jan. wind bound, and probably sailed for Philadelphia with the fleet on the 30th"; "Ship News," *Franklin Gazette* 1, no. 22 (March 19, 1818), 3. [New York] *Commercial Advertiser* 21, no. 60 (March 24, 1818), 2. "Ship News," *Poulson's American Daily Advertiser* 47, no. 12895 (March 23, 1818), 3; "Ship News," *Franklin Gazette* 1, no. 25 (March 24, 1818), 3. "Arrivals and Abstract of Merchandise Entered at the Custom House at Philadelphia," *Grotjan's Philadelphia Public Sale Report* 6, no. 48 (March 30, 1818), 383.

90. On Walter Conyers: "Report and Manifest of the . . . *Telegraph,*" Passenger Lists of Vessels Arriving at Philadelphia, 1800–1882 (M425-27). John Adems Paxton, *The Philadelphia Directory and Register for 1818* (Philadelphia: John Adems Paxton, 1818), 88. On the court case: Samuel Hazard, ed., *Register of Pennsylvania Devoted to the Preservation of Facts and Documents and Every Other Kind of Useful Information Respecting the State of Pennsylvania* 1, no. 9 (March 1, 1828), 140. On the marriage: *Atkinson's Saturday Evening Post* 14, no. 703 (January 3, 1835), 3.

91. Albert Hale, *Old Newburyport Houses* (Boston: W. B. Clarke, 1912), 21. W. S. Appleton, *Gatherings toward a Genealogy of the Coffin Family* (Boston: David Clapp and Son, 1896), 20, 36. Hermann Bokum, *The Tennessee Hand-Book and Immigrant's Guide* (Philadelphia: J. B. Lippincott and Co., 1868), 160; *General Catalogue of the Officers and Students of the Phillips Exeter Academy, 1783–1903* (Exeter, N.H.: News-Letter Press, 1903), 8. *Newburyport Herald* 18, no. 26 (June 28, 1814), 3. Charles Dexter Allen, *American Book-Plates: A Guide to Their Study with Examples* (New York: Macmillan, 1894), 186.

92. Charles Coffin, Newbury, July 23, 1817, to his son at Knoxville, Coffin Family Papers, bMS Am2046 (7), Houghton Library, Harvard University. [Shipping News], *New York Evening Post* 5112 (November 2, 1818), 2. Hector Coffin to

Captain William Sturgis, Boston, November 2, 1818; Hooper-Sturgis Papers, 1798–1857, Box 9; Massachusetts Historical Society, Boston, Mass.

93. "The fine Packet ship Telegraph, Capt. Coffin, sailed for Liverpool on Sunday [May 29] with the following passengers Mrs. McMahon, Mrs. Coffin, Miss O'Brien, Miss Fitzgerald, Miss Simonds, Messrs. Fairman, J. Perkins, G. Perkins, Short, Whittle, Spencer, Tappan, Dr. Darrach, and 15 in the steerage"; "Ship News," *Franklin Gazette* 3, no. 394 (June 1, 1819), 2. On the experiment: *The New-York Columbian* 10, no. 2842 (June 29, 1819), 2. Greville Bathe and Dorothy Bathe, *Jacob Perkins: His Inventions, His Times, and His Contemporaries* (Philadelphia: Historical Society of Philadelphia, 1943), 75–81.

94. "Ship Telegraph," *Poulson's American Daily Advertiser* 47, no. 13082 (October 27, 1818), 3.

95. Charles Dickens, *American Notes,* ed. Christopher Hitchens (New York: Modern Library, 2000; orig. pub. 1842), 3–4.

96. "Report and Manifest of the . . . *Telegraph,*" Passenger Lists of Vessels Arriving at Philadelphia, 1800–1882 (M425-27).

97. *Hall's Journal,* 1:31.

98. Gilbert Imlay, *A Description of the Western Territory of North America, Containing a Succinct Account of Its Soil, Climate, Natural History, Population, Agriculture, Manners and Customs,* 3rd ed. (New York: August M. Kelley, 1969; orig. pub. 1797), 203.

99. *Howitt's Letters,* 2.

100. Dickens, *American Notes,* 22–23.

101. On the druggists: *The Commercial Directory, for 1818–19–20* (Manchester: R. and W. Dean, 1818), 247. *KC,* 1:6.

102. Walker, *Walking North with Keats,* 8–9.

103. [Advertisement], *Liverpool Mercury* 367 (July 3, 1818), 1.

104. *Welby's Visit,* 156.

105. "Ship News," *Franklin Gazette* 2, no. 157 (August 26, 1818), 3, which reports the ship's arrival from Liverpool after forty-seven days at sea, marking its departure around July 10. *Flower's History,* 31.

106. Henry Irving, *The Sketch-Book of Geoffrey Crayon, Gent.* (New York: Charles E. Merrill Co. Sons, 1911; orig. pub. 1819), 36.

107. Charles Brown, in his life of the poet, describes the conditions of composition of the sonnet, "Read me a lesson Muse, and speak it loud"; *CP,* 450.

4. The Mountains of Tartary and of Allegheny

1. *KC,* 1:315.

2. *ML,* 21. James Freeman Clarke to John Jeffrey, December 12, 1872, in John Jeffrey, "George Keats," *Athenaeum* 2358 (January 4, 1873), 17–18 (18).

3. *KL,* 2:243.

4. *ML,* 25. *KC,* 1:284, 1:328. *Birkbeck's Letters,* vii.

5. *ML,* 25. *KC,* 1:328.

6. *Welby's Visit,* 156–157.

7. Ibid., 160. See John's verse epistle written to John Hamilton Reynolds from Teignmouth, "Dear Reynolds"; compare *KL,* 1:262.

8. Hunt, To Kosciusko," *Examiner* 412 (November 19, 1815), 746. Hunt, "Impossibility of the Continuance of the Present State of Things in Europe," *Examiner* 472 (January 12, 1817), [17]–18 (18).

9. "State of the Thermometer," *Poulson's American Daily Advertiser* 47, no. 13027 (August 24, 1818), 3, and 47, no. 13033 (August 31, 1818), 2.

10. "Health Office, August 29, 1818," *Philadelphia Magazine and Weekly Repository* 1, no. 30 (September 5, 1818), 240; "Shipping News," *Franklin Gazette* 2, no. 157 (August 26, 1818), 3.

11. *Wright's Views,* 13. Wright is speaking here of her arrival in New York, but she felt the same way, like most visitors, about Philadelphia.

12. *Amphlett's Directory,* 65. Foster quoted in Edgar P. Richardson, "The Athens of America, 1800–1825," in *Philadelphia: A 300-Year History,* ed. Russell F. Weigley (New York: W. W. Norton, 1982), 208–257 (220).

13. *Wright's Views,* 12. *Errors of Emigrants,* 57. *Melish's Travels,* 1:153.

14. Richardson, "Athens of America," 254.

15. On Olympe: *Franklin Gazette* 2, no. 157 (August 26, 1818), 3. On the male slave Henry Manly Dules: *Poulson's American Daily Advertiser* 47, no. 13028 (August 25, 1818), 3. On Daniel Dick & Co.: John Adems Paxton, *Philadelphia Directory and Register, for 1819* ([Philadelphia]: author, [1819]), preliminary advertisements. On family tradition: *Shared Porridge,* 52.

16. American National Archives (5416-K and 5417-K), in Carol Kyros Walker, *Walking North with Keats* (New Haven: Yale University Press, 1992), 10.

17. *Collins's Guide,* 29.

18. Leigh Hunt to Lydia Shewell, July 20, 1791, Special Collections, University of Iowa Libraries; digital.lib.uiowa.edu/u?/leighhunt,6798. *The Autobiography of Leigh Hunt,* rev. ed. (London: Smith, Elder, and Co., 1891), 19–20.

19. *Autobiography of Leigh Hunt,* 19–20.

20. *KL,* 1:403.

21. *ML,* 73–74. *George's Letters,* 65.

22. Michael Drury was christened on March 22, 1791, at St. Peter's at Arches, Lincoln; his mother, Jane Wold, married John Drury on May 27, 1782, in Lincoln. John Taylor's father, James Taylor, married Sarah Drury on September 29, 1788, in Newark, Nottinghamshire. Family tree and church records courtesy of Martin Burnell.

23. John Clare quoted in a review of *Poems, Descriptive of Rural Life and Scenery,* in *The Analectic Magazine* 2, no. 3 (September 1820), 255–261 (255). James Hessey to John Taylor, November 15, 1820, in Olive M. Taylor, "John Taylor: Author and Publisher, 1781–1864," *London Mercury* 12 (1925), 258–267 (260).

24. Review of *Poems, Descriptive of Rural Life,* 259–260. *KC,* 1:100.

25. [Drury & Tallant advertisements], *Poulson's American Daily Advertiser* 47, no. 12831 (January 7, 1818), 4: and 47, no. 12849 (January 28, 1818), 4; and 47, no. 12965 (June 12, 1818), 1.

26. "Provincial Occurrences in the County of England," *New Monthly Magazine and Universal Register* 10, no. 57 (October 1818), 279–288 (284). On William Tallant's marriage, see "Provincial Occurrences, with All the Marriages and Deaths"; *Monthly Magazine; or, British Register* 32, no. 219 (November 1811), 391–413 (401). For further information on Michael Drury and his family, see Michael Burnell, *The Burnell Family History,* burnelluk.info/dft.html. *KC,* 1:215.

27. Michael Drury would not make it back to England, as he may have originally intended. He visited, but returned in 1823, having decided to become a naturalized American citizen, and declared that intention on April 8 in the Court of Common Pleas, Philadelphia; see William Filby, ed., *Philadelphia Naturalization Records* (Detroit: Gale Research, 1982). In 1834, he and his wife, Susan Drury, a Scottish emigrant, had a daughter, Isabella, who married David L. Wallace in New York. *KC,* 1:101, 1:215.

28. [Drury & Tallant advertisements], *Poulson's American Daily Advertiser* 47, no. 13070 (October 13, 1818), 2; *Franklin Gazette* 3, no. 338 (March 27, 1819), 4; *Poulson's American Daily Advertiser* 48, no. 13349 (September 7, 1819), 2. *Welby's Visit,* 197.

29. *Fearon's Sketches,* 172. *The Cincinnati Directory for the Year 1829* (Cincinnati: Robinson and Fairbank, 1829), 119.

30. Unnamed Lincoln paper reprinted in the London *Courier,* June 19, 1819, quoted in Stanley Jones, "A Glimpse of George Keats in Philadelphia," *Keats-Shelley Memorial Bulletin* 28 (1977), 29–31 (30).

31. [For the *Evening Post,* by An Illinoian], *New York Evening Post* 5533 (March 14, 1820), 2. "Emigration Anecdote," *Franklin Gazette* 2, no. 158 (August 27, 1818), 2.

32. *Errors of Emigrants,* 28.

33. *Flower's History,* 100.

34. Ibid., 192. The passenger list published in the *New York Gazette and General Advertiser* 28, no. 11370 (May 27, 1818), 2, lists "J. Tilder," which is probably a mistake. Charlotte Chambers to Sarah Bella Ludlow, September 26, 1820, in Lewis H. Garrard, *Memoir of Charlotte Chambers* (Philadelphia: printed for the author, 1856), 123.

35. Isabella Jane Towers, *Perils in the Woods; or, The Emigrant Family's Return: A Tale* (London: [Effingham Wilson], 1835), 114–115. *Welby's Visit*, 211.

36. *KL*, 2:60. *Fearon's Sketches*, 64–65. Morris Birkbeck, *Extracts from a Supplementary Letter from the Illinois . . . Address to British Emigrants Arriving in the Eastern Ports . . . Reply to William Cobbett, Esq.* (New York: C. Wiley and Co., 1819), 10.

37. C. B. Johnson, *Letters from the British Settlement in Pennsylvania* (Philadelphia: H. Hall; and London: John Miller, 1819), iv–v.

38. Richard Flower, *Letters from Lexington and the Illinois, Containing a Brief Account of the English Settlement in the Latter Territory, and a Refutation of the Misrepresentations of Mr. Cobbett,* in *Early Western Travels,* ed. Reuben Gold Thwaites, 32 vols. (Cleveland: Arthur H. Clark, 1904), 10:93. Carolyn E. DeLatte, *Lucy Audubon: A Biography,* rev. ed. (Baton Rouge: Louisiana State University Press, 2008), 39–40. *Birkbeck's Letters,* 33.

39. *Fordham's Narrative,* 61.

40. *Fearon's Sketches,* 189.

41. *Clarke's Sketches,* 225.

42. *Bradbury's Travels,* 315.

43. *Melish's Travels,* 1:164.

44. *Fearon's Sketches,* 156–157.

45. *Howitt's Letters,* 64.

46. "Peale's Museum in the State House," in Paxton, *Philadelphia Directory,* preliminary advertisement. *Wright's Views,* 63.

47. *Melish's Travels,* 2:134–137. Hunt is quoted in *Clarke's Recollections,* 148.

48. *Melish's Travels,* 2:135–136.

49. *Howitt's Letters,* 135. Hunt, *The Autobiography of Leigh Hunt,* 22.

50. *Fearon's Sketches,* 154.

51. *KC,* 2:17.

52. Ibid., 2:17, 2:6.

53. Ibid., 2:5–26.

54. *Amphlett's Directory,* 63. *Howitt's Letters,* 70. See Thomas Moore's "Lines Written on Leaving Philadelphia."

55. *Bakewell Family Book,* 25–26.

56. Ibid., 41, 27. Sarah Bakewell married Alexander M. Anderson on March 20, 1825, and Ann Bakewell married Alexander Gordon on May 3, 1823, in Louisville. The quotation below is from John's ode "To Autumn."

57. *Birkbeck's Notes,* 30. *Fearon's Sketches,* 196.

58. *KC,* 1:22, 1:33. *KL,* 1:372.

59. *KL,* 1:392, 1:364.

60. *KL,* 1:364n, 2:321.

61. Joseph Mercola and Dietrich Klinghardt, "Mercury Toxicity and Systemic Elimination Agents," *Journal of Nutritional and Environmental Medicine* 11, no. 11 (March 2001), 53–62; Renata E. Bluhm, Robert G. Bobbitt, et al., "Elemental Mercury Vapour Toxicity, Treatment, and Prognosis after Acute, Intensive Exposure in Chloralkali Plant Workers," Part I, *Human and Experimental Toxicology* 11, no. 3 (1992), 201–210. Susan L. Davis, "John Keats and 'The Poison': Venereal or Mercureal?" *Keats-Shelley Journal* 53 (2004), 86–96. Cooper quoted in C. T. Andrews, "Keats and Mercury," *Keats-Shelley Memorial Bulletin* 20 (1969), 37–43 (40). *KL,* 1:369.

62. *KC,* 1:285. "Y" [Edward Holmes], "John Keats, the Poet," *Morning Chronicle* 16309 (July 27, 1821), 4.

63. *KL,* 2:17, 2:5.

64. Ibid., 1:370, 2:9.

65. Milton, *Paradise Lost,* 12.41–42. *KL,* 1:369.

66. *ML,* 30. *KL,* 2:8.

67. *KL,* 1:403.

68. Ibid., 1:395.

69. John used the phrase "Poor Tom" repeatedly (e.g., *KL,* 1:375, 377, 391, 400, 406, 2:4). *KL,* 1:395, 1:404, 2:19.

70. *ML,* 72–73.

71. Z [John Gibson Lockhart], "On the Cockney School of Poetry, No. 4," *Blackwood's Edinburgh Magazine* 3, no. 17 (August 1818), 519–524 (520).

72. *KL,* 2:13.

73. Priscilla Johnston, "Charles Jeremiah Wells: An Early Keatsian Poet," *Keats-Shelley Journal* 26 (1977), 72–87 (79–80); punctuation added for the sake of clarity.

74. *KL,* 1:245. Johnston, "Charles Jeremiah Wells," 81.

75. *KL,* 1:405–406, 1:408.

76. Ibid., 1:391, 2:16, 2:9.

77. Ibid., 2:5, 2:9.

78. DeLatte, *Lucy Audubon,* 77–78.

79. *KL,* 2:46.

80. *KC,* 1:314, 1:325–326.

81. *KL,* 2:17. Sidney Colvin, *John Keats: His Life and Poetry, His Friends, Critics, and After-Fame* (New York: Charles Scribner's Sons, 1917), 31.

82. *KC,* 2:212.

83. *KL,* 1:404.

84. Z, "On the Cockney School of Poetry. No. 4," 524.

85. *KL,* 2:18. William Shakespeare, *King Lear,* 2.4.56–57.

86. *Flower's History,* 91.

87. Garrard, *Memoir of Charlotte Chambers,* xxxii.

88. See John Mitchell, "Report on the Susquehanna and Potomac Route," *Journal of the Senate, of the Commonwealth of Pennsylvania* 37 (1826–1827), 424–487 (425).

89. *Harris's Remarks,* 81–82.

90. *Hall's Journal,* 1:39. *Fearon's Sketches,* 187, 192.

91. *KL,* 1:361.

92. *Fearon's Sketches,* 191–192, formatted as dialogue. *Howitt's Letters,* 202–203.

93. *Amphlett's Directory,* 73–75.

94. *Welby's Visit,* 164. *Collins's Guide,* 28.

95. *Bradbury's Travels,* 305.

96. *Fearon's Sketches,* 189.

97. *Welby's Visit,* 195.

98. *Harris's Remarks,* 81.

99. Ibid., 85. *Pedestrious Tour,* 247. Calvin Colton, *Manual for Emigrants to America* (London: F. Westley and A. H. Davis, 1832), 105–106.

100. *Harris's Remarks,* 79.

101. See the article by R., "Inland Trade," *Franklin Gazette* 2, no. 158 (August 27, 1818), 2.

102. *Woods' Residence,* 218.

103. *Melish's Travels,* 2:55–56. *Hulme's Journal,* 37.

104. *KL,* 2:210.

105. "The Merchants," *Poulson's American Daily Advertiser* 47, no. 13028 (August 25, 1818), 3.

106. *Pedestrious Tour,* 248. Lucy Audubon to Miss Gifford, May 27, 1808, quoted in DeLatte, *Lucy Audubon,* 45.

107. John Milton, *Paradise Lost,* 12.38–42.

108. *Fearon's Sketches,* 204, 206.

109. Unnamed poem quoted from a manuscript in the possession of Captain J. G. Barker, Marietta, Ohio, in Archer B. Hulbert, "Western Ship-building," *The American Historical Review* 21, no. 4 (1916), 720–733 (732).

110. *Bakewell Family Book,* 47–48. Thomas W. Bakewell, "Audubon & Bakewell, Partners: Sketch of the Life of Thomas W. Bakewell, Written by Himself," *Cardinal* 4, no. 2 (1935), 34–42 (36).

111. Arlene M. Palmer, "American Heroes in Glass: The Bakewell Sulphide Portraits," *American Art Journal* 11, no. 1 (1979), 5–26. On Tassie's shop as a "fascinating place," see Mary Cowden Clarke, *Letters to an Enthusiast* (Chicago: A. C. McClurg & Co., 1902), 47.

112. John Curtis Franklin, "Once More the Poet: Keats, Severn, and the Grecian Lyre," *Memoirs of the American Academy in Rome* 48 (2003), 227–240 (230).

113. *KL,* 2:74.

5. Circumstances Gathering Like Clouds

1. *KC,* 2:223.

2. *KL,* 1:279. Walter Pater is representative in this respect: "A counted number of pulses only is given to us of a variegated, dramatic life"; see Pater, *The Renaissance: Studies in Art and Poetry* (London: Macmillan, 1888; orig. pub. 1973), 249.

3. *KL,* 2:69. The "pet-lamb" is from John's "Ode on Indolence."

4. Z [John Gibson Lockhart], "On the Cockney School of Poetry. No. 4," *Blackwood's Edinburgh Magazine* 3, no. 17 (August 1818), 519–524 (520). *KC,* 1:285, 1:280.

5. *KL,* 2:112–113.

6. Ibid., 2:209, 2:113. *KC,* 2:165.

7. *KC,* 2:65.

8. These lines begin another poem that Jack Stillinger dates to 1819.

9. *KL,* 1:286. For "idle days," see (appropriately) John's "Ode on Indolence."

10. Matthew 6:24.

11. *KL,* 2:113. Matthew 6:25, 28–29.

12. *KL,* 2:79–80.

13. Alexander Pope, *Essay on Man,* 1.3.24.

14. Shakespeare, *A Midsummer Night's Dream,* 5.1.7 8.

15. Jervis Cutler, *A Topographical Description of the State of Ohio, Indiana Territory, and Louisiana* (Boston: Charles Williams, 1812), 14.

16. *Clarke's Sketches,* 225–226. John Jeffrey, "George Keats," *Athenaeum* 2358 (January 4, 1873), 17–18 (18).

17. *Woods' Residence,* 228.

18. *Melish's Travels,* 2:88. *Harris's Remarks,* 93.

19. *Melish's Travels,* 2:94, 2:112. *Woods' Residence,* 221. Cf. Revelation 3:17.

20. *Fearon's Sketches,* 224.

21. John James Audubon, *Ornithological Biography; or, An Account of the Habits of the Birds of the United States of America,* 5 vols. (Edinburgh: Adam and Charles Black, 1831–1849), 1:31–32.

22. *Hulme's Journal,* 38. General William O. Butler, "O, Boatman!" in Leland D. Baldwin, *The Keelboat Age on Western Waters* (Pittsburgh: University of Pittsburgh Press, 1941), 94.

23. James Hall, *Letters from the West: Containing Sketches of Scenery, Manners,*

and Customs, and Anecdotes Connected with the First Settlements of the Western Sections of the United States (London: Henry Colburn, 1828), 48.

24. Ibid., 87. *ML,* 14.

25. On river conditions described here, see Charles Frederic Goss, *Cincinnati, the Queen City, 1788–1912,* 2 vols. (Chicago: S. J. Clarke, 1912), 2:96–100. River chantey quoted in Hall, *Letters from the West,* 94.

26. Classic river song quoted in Baldwin, *The Keelboat Age,* 92. Read "shot" for shote.

27. *Fordham's Narrative,* 196.

28. Audubon quoted in Goss, *Cincinnati,* 2:97.

29. *Hulme's Journal,* 69.

30. Gilbert Imlay, *A Description of the Western Territory of North America, Containing a Succinct Account of Its Soil, Climate, Natural History, Population, Agriculture, Manners and Customs,* 3rd ed. (New York: August M. Kelley, 1969; orig. pub. 1797), 21. John Melish, *Information and Advice to Emigrants to the United States: And from the Eastern to the Western States, Illustrated by a Map of the United States, and a Chart of the Atlantic Ocean* (Philadelphia: printed by John Melish, 1819), 3.

31. *Fearon's Sketches,* 222.

32. Ibid., 222–223.

33. *Harris's Remarks,* 34.

34. *Flower's History,* 129–130.

35. *New States,* 38. *Hulme's Journal,* 79.

36. *Woods' Residence,* 284. *Birkbeck's Notes,* 83. *KL,* 2:211.

37. *Clarke's Autobiography,* 55.

38. *Western Gazetteer,* 300.

39. *Woods' Residence,* 227, 230.

40. *KL,* 2:88.

41. James Freeman Clarke, "George Keats," *The Dial: A Magazine of History, Philosophy, and Religion* 3, no. 4 (April 1843), 495–500 (495).

42. Thomas Smith, *The Emigrant's Guide to the United States of America, Including the Substance of the Journal of Thomas Hulme, Esq.,* 2nd ed. (London: Sherwood, Neely, and Jones, 1818), 45.

43. James Fenimore Cooper discusses the cost of postage in *Notions of the Americans: Picked Up by a Travelling Bachelor,* ed. Gary Williams (Albany: State University of New York Press, 1991), 522–523. *ML,* 14.

44. *ML,* 20, 14. *KC,* 1:111.

45. *KC,* 1:284. *KL,* 1:104. *ML,* 22.

46. *KC,* 1:283–284. *Bakewell Family Book,* 23, 27.

47. John Adems Paxton, *The Philadelphia Directory and Register for 1818*

(Philadelphia: John Adems Paxton, 1818), xxi. The "Will of John Warder," executed in Philadelphia, Pa., May 17, 1828, and in Russell County, Va., June 8, 1847; Russell County Will Book 6, 68–78 (Reel No. 12), 68–78. "Imports, Entered at the Custom House, Philadelphia," *Franklin Gazette* 1, no. 25 (March 24, 1818), 3.

48. *KL,* 2:229.

49. Ann Head Warder, Philadelphia, to John Warder, 25 Martin's Lane, Cannon Street, London, July 3, 1794, Ann Head Warder Papers (1758–1829), Collection 2175, Historical Society of Pennsylvania, Philadelphia. Mary Capper, *A Memoir of Mary Capper, Late of Birmingham, England, a Minister of the Society of Friends* (Philadelphia: Friends Book Store, 1888), 76.

50. "Suicide—from Blair," *Poulson's American Daily Advertiser* 47, no. 13028 (August 25, 1818), 3. *KC,* 2:12.

51. *KL,* 2:92.

52. Georgiana Keats to Maria Dilke, undated, in *George's Letters,* 65.

53. *KL,* 2:4.

54. Ibid., 2:102. Psalms 84:6.

55. *KL,* 1:202, 2:81.

56. Ibid., 2:102.

57. Ibid., 2:79, 2:115.

58. Ibid., 2:103.

59. Ibid., 2:82, 2:90.

60. I rely here and in what follows on Robert Gittings, *The Keats Inheritance* (London: Heinemann, 1964). See, too, Walter Jackson Bate, *John Keats* (Cambridge, Mass.: Harvard University Press, 1963), 705–712.

61. *KL,* 2:121, 2:206. Norman Kilgour questions the role of the two trustees, Richard Abbey and John Nowland Sandell, in distributing the legacies; see Kilgour, "Mrs. Jennings' Will," *Keats-Shelley Memorial Bulletin* 13 (1962), 24–27. See, too, Kilgour, "Keats and the Abbey Cocks 'Account,'" *Keats-Shelley Memorial Bulletin* 14 (1963), 34–36.

62. *KL,* 2:121.

63. Ibid., 2:81.

64. Ibid.

65. Ibid., 2:91. See John's "As Hermes once took to his feathers light."

66. Ibid., 2:88.

67. John Keats to George and Georgiana Keats, May 3, 1819, in Grant F. Scott, "New Keats Letters: An Update," *Keats-Shelley Journal* 51 (2002), 21–29 (24).

68. Ibid.

69. Mrs. I. S. Prowse [Mary Ann Jeffery], "Ada," in Prowse, *Poems* (London: Smith, Elder, 1830), 47–53 (50).

70. *KL,* 2:115. Rollins's letter no. 164 was meant for Mary Ann, with whom

the poet was closer. Fanny was Sarah's nickname, and John says, "Fanny must by this time have altered her name—perhaps you have also"; *KL,* 2:113. No. 166, a continuation of no. 164, was also presumably to Mary Ann.

71. *Western Gazetteer,* 276. Frances Milton Trollope, *Domestic Manners of the Americans* (New York: Dodd, Mead, 1901), 49.

72. *Birkbeck's Notes,* 66. Farnsworth, *The Cincinnati Directory* (Cincinnati: Oliver Farnsworth, 1819), 29, 32.

73. *Fearon's Sketches,* 231.

74. Ibid., 230. Farnsworth, *Cincinnati Directory,* 30. Charlotte Chambers quoted in Lewis H. Garrard, *Memoir of Charlotte Chambers* (Philadelphia: printed for the author, 1856), 99.

75. Garrard, *Memoir of Charlotte Chambers,* 99, 21. John Filson, *The Discovery, Settlement, and Present State of Kentucky,* rev. ed. (London: J. Stockdale, 1793), 49.

76. Charlotte Chambers, in Garrard, *Memoir of Charlotte Chambers,* 22.

77. *Fearon's Sketches,* 234.

78. Farnsworth, *Cincinnati Directory,* 35–36. *Flower's History,* 29.

79. *New States,* 16. *Western Gazeteer,* 277–278. Farnsworth, *Cincinnati Directory,* 36.

80. Ross Thompson, *Structures of Change in the Mechanical Age: Technological Innovation in the United States, 1790–1865* (Baltimore: The Johns Hopkins University Press, 2009), 33–35, 347–348.

81. Oliver Evans, *The Abortion of the Young Steam Engineer's Guide* (Philadelphia: printed for the author, 1805), 1. Evans had planned to publish his book under the title *The Young Engineer's Guide,* but when his petition to Congress to extend the patent of his flour-milling machinery failed in 1804, he was forced to scale back production of the book, cutting a number of illustrations, and he retitled it accordingly.

82. Harvey Hall, *The Cincinnati Directory for 1825* (Cincinnati: Samuel J. Brown, 1825), 95. *The Cincinnati Directory for the Year 1829* (Cincinnati: Robinson and Fairbank, 1829), 119.

83. James Tallant quoted in Branch W. Miller, *Report of Cases Argued and Determined in the Supreme Court of the State of Louisiana,* vol. 5 (New Orleans: Gaston Brusle, 1834), 296–310 (296); subsequent information about the case derives from this source.

84. "An Act to Incorporate and Establish the Commercial Bank of Cincinnati" (February 10, 1829), in *The Statutes of Ohio and of the Northwestern Territory, Adopted or Enacted from 1788 to 1833 Inclusive,* vol. 3, ed. Salmon Portland Chase (Cincinnati: Corey and Fairbank, 1835), 2059–2064 (2063). *The Cincinnati Directory, for the Year 1831* (Cincinnati: Robinson and Fairbank, 1831), 152; *The Cincinnati Directory, for the Year 1834* (Cincinnati: E. Deming, 1834), 170. Alice Drury quoted by permission of Anne Wallbank, who holds the original document.

85. Julius Tallant's uncles were William Tallant and Joseph Prince, husband of Charlotte Tallant, James and William's sister, who also lived in Cincinnati. Mary Tallant married Edmonds in the third quarter of 1841 in Brixworth, near Guilsborough, where she ran a school. After her death in 1864, Sarah and Alice took over the school with their sister-in-law, Sarah A. Tallant. By 1850, their oldest brother, Julius Ferdinand, had moved to Des Moines, Iowa, where he worked as a druggist, married, and had six children. Census data and family records for the Drury-Tallant family, courtesy of Martin Burnell.

86. *Woods' Residence*, 255. *Welby's Visit*, 220 (on the trophies). *Harris's Remarks*, 64. *Melish's Travels*, 2:180 (on the punishment).

87. *Birkbeck's Letters*, 138. *Woods' Residence*, 265. *Howitt's Letters*, xi.

88. *Melish's Travels*, 2:206. Compare Revelation 14:11.

89. *Fearon's Sketches*, 249.

6. Backwoods and Blind Alleys

1. *KL*, 2:135–136.

2. Ibid., 2:137. See John's poem "What can I do to drive away."

3. Ibid., 2:186, 2:131.

4. Ibid., 2:137.

5. Ibid., 2:166.

6. Ibid., 2:189, 2:186.

7. [Leigh Hunt], "Disturbances at Manchester," *Examiner* 608 (August 22, 1819), 529–531 (529, 531).

8. *KL*, 2:146, 2:144. The description of Chatterton is from Wordsworth's "Resolution and Independence."

9. *KL*, 2:150.

10. Ibid., 2:164.

11. As quoted in John's letter to John Taylor, September 5, 1819; *KL*, 2:158. Compare *CP*, 355, in which John is easier on Lycius: "O senseless Lycius! Madman! wherefore flout . . ."

12. Bailey quoted in C. E. Hudnall, "John Hamilton Reynolds, James Rice, and Benjamin Bailey in the Leigh Browne-Lockyer Collection," *Keats-Shelley Journal* 19 (1970), 11–39 (27). See John's "Welcome joy, and welcome sorrow."

13. *KL*, 2:206. John Keats to William Haslam, Frampton & Co., Leadenhall Street, November 2, 1819, in Grant F. Scott, "New Keats Letters: An Update," *Keats-Shelley Journal* 51 (2002), 21–29 (26).

14. *Fordham's Narrative*, 120. *Woods' Residence*, 247.

15. Charles Dickens, *The Life and Adventures of Martin Chuzzlewit* (London: Oxford University Press, 1951), 375–376.

16. Ibid., 377–378.

17. Charles Dickens, *American Notes* (New York: Modern Library, 1996), 225.

18. *Birkbeck's Notes,* 122.

19. Quoted in George H. Yater, *Two Hundred Years at the Falls of the Ohio: A History of Louisville and Jefferson County* (Louisville: Heritage Corporation of Louisville and Jefferson County, 1979), 26.

20. [Classified advertisement], *Louisville Public Advertiser* 2, no. 155 (April 1, 1820), 1, 3.

21. "The Canal," *Louisville Public Advertiser* 2, no. 129 (January 1, 1820), 2. "Lottery & Canal," *Louisville Public Advertiser* 2, no. 155 (April 1, 1820), 2.

22. *The Louisville Directory for the Year 1832* (Louisville: Richard W. Otis, 1832), 59, 89. *Harris's Remarks,* 143.

23. [Classified advertisement], *Louisville Public Advertiser* 2, no. 111 (October 30, 1819), 1.

24. *Hulme's Journal,* 44.

25. John James Audubon, *Ornithological Biography; or, An Account of the Habits of the Birds of the United States of America,* 5 vols. (Edinburgh: Adam and Charles Black, 1831–1849), 1:29–31.

26. *KL,* 2:242.

27. *Flower's History,* 112. *Memorable Days,* 294. See, too, *Errors of Emigrants,* 51.

28. In April 1825, Birkbeck served as the foreman of the grand jury that indicted George and Eliza Flower for adultery; Mary Ann Salter, "Quarreling in the English Settlement: The Flowers in Court," *Journal of the Illinois State Historical Society* 75, no. 1 (Spring 1982), 101–114 (112).

29. *Fordham's Narrative,* 213. *Welby's Visit,* 229. *KL,* 2:243.

30. John E. Inglehart, "The Coming of the English to Indiana in 1817 and Their Hoosier Neighbors," *Indiana Magazine of History* 15, no. 2 (1919), 89–178 (92–93). NB: Inglehart reports the maximum amount of land that Birkbeck was selling at 320 acres. Perhaps this was true by the time Hornbrook Junior arrived, but Birkbeck promised a full section to each settler in *Letters from Illinois,* 116.

31. Inglehart, "The Coming of the English," 94–95.

32. Ibid., 138–140.

33. Ibid., 164.

34. Edward F. Madden, "The Poet Keats," *Harper's New Monthly Magazine* 55, no. 327 (August 1877), 357–361 (357). *Clarke's Sketches,* 226.

35. *Hall's Journal,* 1:52, 54. Richard Flower, *Letters from Lexington and the Illinois: Containing a Brief Account of the English Settlement in the Latter Territory, and a Refutation of the Misrepresentations of Mr. Cobbett,* in *Early Western Travels,* ed. Reuben Gold Thwaites (Cleveland: Arthur H. Clark, 1904), 85–109 (98).

36. *Flower's History,* 278.

37. *Melish's Travels,* 2:72.

38. *Hulme's Journal,* 60.

39. *Woods' Residence,* 246.

40. *Hulme's Journal,* 53, 59.

41. *Melish's Travels,* 2:69.

42. Ibid., 2:73–74. Flower, *Letters from Lexington,* 99.

43. *Harris's Remarks,* 134.

44. *Hall's Journal,* 2:243.

45. *Errors of Emigrants,* 58 (on the man from Guernsey). *Woods' Residence,* 318 (on Birkbeck's reading the service). Richard Flower, *Letters from Illinois, 1820–21,* in *Early Western Travels,* ed. Reuben Gold Thwaites, vol. 10 (Cleveland: Arthur H. Clark, 1904), 124–125, 131.

46. [John Barrow], "Views, Visits, and Tours in North America," *Quarterly Review* 27, no. 53 (April 1822), 71–99 (94, 98).

47. *The Book of Common Prayer, and Administration of the Sacraments, and Other Rites and Ceremonies of the Church, According to the Use of the Protestant Episcopal Church in the United States of America, Together with the Psalter, or Psalms of David* (Baltimore: Joseph N. Lewis, 1817), signed on the fly-leaf "Georgiana Augusta Keats 1826," EC8 K2262 Zy817p, Houghton Library, Harvard University. James Craik, *Historical Sketches of Christ Church, Louisville, Diocese of Kentucky* (Louisville: John P. Morton, 1862), 33, 12.

48. *Clarke's Sketches,* 228. Emma Speed Simpson to Naomi Kirk, December 13, 1933; Naomi Kirk Collection, Folder 2, Filson Historical Society, Louisville, Kentucky.

49. *Fordham's Narrative,* 214–216.

50. Carolyn DeLatte, *Lucy Audubon: A Biography,* rev. ed. (Baton Rouge: Louisiana State University Press, 2008), 76. The description here and elsewhere of the Audubons' cabin is indebted to DeLatte.

51. *Memorable Days,* 317. *Woods' Residence,* 249.

52. *Memorable Days,* 310. *Birkbeck's Notes,* 87.

53. *Hall's Journal,* 1:64. *Memorable Days,* 232.

54. *Clarke's Sketches,* 226–227.

55. *Memorable Days,* 309.

56. Ibid., 236.

57. Ibid. John Ingle to John Ingle, Jr., October 3, 1818; Collection no. M0167, Box 1, Folder 12, Indiana Historical Society.

58. *Memorable Days,* 309.

59. *Birkbeck's Letters,* 62.

60. *Flower's History,* 36. *Memorable Days,* 316.

61. Eliza Birkbeck, April 17, 1818, in Gladys Scott Thomson, *A Pioneer Family: The Birkbecks in Illinois, 1818–1827* (London: Jonathan Cape, 1953), 47–48.

62. Ibid., 46–47.

63. *Memorable Days,* 312, 222–223. *Hulme's Journal,* 46.

64. *Fordham's Narrative,* 97.

65. Ibid., 213.

66. *Fearon's Sketches,* 261.

67. *Fordham's Narrative,* 224.

68. *Hulme's Journal,* 47.

69. James Hall, *Letters from the West: Containing Sketches of Scenery, Manners, and Customs, and Anecdotes Connected with the First Settlements of the Western Sections of the United States* (London: Henry Colburn, 1828), 227. *Woods' Residence,* 258. *Harris' Remarks,* 137.

70. *Birkbeck's Letters,* 116.

71. *Fordham's Narrative,* 218. *Memorable Days,* 287–288.

72. On Fordham's activities, see Walter Colyer, "The Fordhams and La Serres of the English Settlement in Edwards County," *Transactions of the Illinois State Historical Society for the Year 1911* (Springfield: Illinois State Journal Co., 1913), 43–54 (44–45). *Birkbeck's Notes,* 149. *Fordham's Narrative,* 136, 204, 226–228.

73. *KC,* 2:5. *KL,* 2:5, 2:243.

74. *Hulme's Journal,* 50.

75. *KL,* 2:5.

76. Ibid., 2:230.

77. Quoted from George Henry Warren in Henry A. Ford and Kate B. Ford, *History of Cincinnati, Ohio* (Cleveland: L. A. Williams and Co., 1881), 71.

78. *The Letters of John Keats,* ed. John Gilmer Speed, 3 vols. (New York: Dodd Mead, 1883), 1:79n.

79. Francis Hobart Herrick, *Audubon the Naturalist: A History of His Life and Time,* 2 vols. (New York: D. Appleton and Company, 1917), 1:253. Herrick provides information for what follows.

80. Washington Irving, *A Tour on the Prairies,* ed. John Francis McDermott (Norman: University of Oklahoma Press, 1956), 21.

81. Herrick, *Audubon the Naturalist,* 1:248–249.

82. *Bakewell Family Book,* 35. Thomas W. Bakewell, "Audubon & Bakewell, Partners," *Cardinal* 4, no. 2 (1935), 34–42 (42).

83. John James Audubon and Maria Rebecca Audubon, *Audubon and His Journals,* ed. Elliott Coues, vol. 1 (New York: Charles Scribner's Sons, 1899), 33. Bakewell, "Audubon & Bakewell Partners," 37.

84. Sarah Pears to Benjamin Bakewell, January 28, 1826, in Thomas Clinton Pears, Jr., ed., *New Harmony: An Adventure in Happiness: Papers of Thomas and Sarah Pears* (Indianapolis: Indiana Historical Society, 1933), 60.

85. DeLatte, *Lucy Audubon,* 87.

86. Bakewell, "Audubon & Bakewell, Partners," 39–40.

87. Ibid. Audubon, *Audubon and His Journals,* 34.

88. Audubon, *Audubon and His Journals,* 33–34.

89. Bakewell, "Sketch of the Life of Thomas Woodhouse Bakewell," *Filson Club Historical Quarterly* 40 (1966), 240–248 (244). On the *Pike,* also see Ben Casseday, *The History of Louisville, from Its Earliest Settlement till the Year 1852* (Louisville: Hull and Brother, 1852), 131.

90. Audubon, *Audubon and His Journals,* 34.

91. [James Freeman Clarke], "George Keats," *Athenaeum* 2358 (January 4, 1873), 17–18 (18).

92. Stanley Clisby Arthur, *Audubon: An Intimate Life of the American Woodsman* (Louisiana: Pelican, 1962), 85–86, here and following.

93. *KL,* 2:185–186.

94. Herrick, *Audubon the Naturalist,* 1:258. Audubon, *Audubon and His Journals,* 34–35.

95. *KC,* 1:168–169. *Louisville Public Advertiser* 5, no. 451 (February 1, 1823), 3. *Louisville Public Advertiser* 8, no. 789 (April 29, 1826), 3. Case no. 2875, November 30, 1830; Archives Division, Jefferson County Court, Louisville, Kentucky.

96. *KL,* 2:226. Thomas H. Greer, "Economic and Social Effects of the Depression of 1819 in the Old Northwest," *Indiana Magazine of History* 44, no. 3 (September 1948), 227–243 (230).

97. *Memoirs of John Quincy Adams, Comprising Portions of His Diary from 1795 to 1848,* ed. Charles Francis Adams, 12 vols. (Philadelphia: J. B. Lippincott and Co., 1874–1877 [1875]), 4:375. George Warren quoted in Ford and Ford, *History of Cincinnati,* 71.

98. Notice of death dated August 2, *Louisville Public Advertiser* 2, no. 129 (January 1, 1820), 4.

99. Arthur, *Audubon,* 87–88. Audubon, *Audubon and His Journals,* 35.

100. DeLatte, *Lucy Audubon,* 98; see also Alice Ford, *John James Audubon: A Biography* (New York: Abbeville, 1988), 105–106.

101. DeLatte, *Lucy Audubon,* 74. Audubon, *Audubon and His Journals,* 36.

102. *KL,* 2:244, 2:242, 2:210 and 2:210n.

103. Ibid., 2:231, 2:229.

104. Ibid., 2:212.

7. Back across the Atlantic

1. *KL,* 2:210, 2:178–179.

2. Ibid., 2:229.

3. Ibid., 2:211.

4. Ibid., 2:223.

5. Samuel Taylor Coleridge, *Table Talk,* ed. Carl Woodring, vol. 14, in *The Collected Works of Samuel Taylor Coleridge,* ed. Kathleen Coburn (Princeton: Princeton University Press, 1990), 1:325.

6. Ibid., 1:325–326n.

7. *KL,* 2:208, 1.86.

8. *KC,* 1:328.

9. *KL,* 2:208–209.

10. Ibid., 2:241. Audubon to his family, March 23, 1843, in John Francis McDermott, ed., *Audubon in the West* (Norman: University of Oklahoma Press, 1965), 29. Ben Casseday, *The History of Louisville, from Its Earliest Settlement till the Year 1852* (Louisville: Hull and Brother, 1852), 134.

11. *ML,* 20. *KL,* 2:239.

12. Charles Dilke to Charles Brown, July 31, 1824, in *George's Letters,* 78. See, too, Robert Gittings, *The Keats Inheritance* (London: Heinemann, 1964), 51.

13. Anonymous verse letter quoted in Casseday, *The History of Louisville,* 157. *KC,* 1:290.

14. Brown to Dilke, January 20, 1830, *George's Letters,* 87.

15. *KL,* 2:145.

16. Brown to Dilke, September 6, 1824, in *George's Letters,* 80. Dilke to Brown, July 31, 1824, in *George's Letters,* 77.

17. *KC,* 1:278–279.

18. Brown to Dilke, September 6, 1824, in *George's Letters,* 80. The ledger: Charles Brown to Charles W. Dilke, May 15, 1826, in *George's Letters,* 81. On John's capacity in "money affairs": Brown to Dilke, Florence, January 20, 1830, in *George's Letters,* 85.

19. Brown to Dilke, January 20, 1830, in *George's Letters,* 88.

20. *KC,* 1:328–329, 1:201.

21. Brown to Dilke, January 20, 1830, in *George's Letters,* 88.

22. *KL,* 2:331.

23. Ibid., 2:283. 2:210. Dilke to Brown, July 31, 1824, in *George's Letters,* 77. *KC,* 2:102.

24. *KC,* 2:102. Brown to Dilke, September 6, 1824, in *George's Letters,* 79.

25. "Severity of the Weather," *Poulson's Daily American Advertiser* 49, no. 13507 (March 10, 1820), 2. *KL,* 2:243.

26. "Latest from Europe," reprinted from *Liverpool Price Current,* February 1, 1820, quoted in *New-York Daily Advertiser* 904 (March 11, 1820), 2. *New-York Commercial Advertiser* 23, no. 60 (March 11, 1820), 2.

27. Miscellaneous news items reprinted from London papers, this one headlined "London, January 22," *New-York Evening Post* 5533 (March 14, 1820), 2.

28. Arthur Fisher, *The Register of Blundell's School,* Part I, the Register, 1770–1882 (Exeter, U.K.: J. G. Commin, 1904), 13. Morris Lawdon Banks lists the Reverend Phillip Keats as headmaster, 1775–1797, in *Blundell's Worthies* (New York: Chatto & Windus, 1904), 82. However, the school's oldest prize, the "Keats Medal," is given every year in honor of Richard Keats, Master, 1775–1797, for rhetoric on biblical and English texts; see the program for "Blundell's Speech Day," July 9, 2010, posted at www.blundells.org. Sidney Colvin, *John Keats: His Life and Poetry, His Friends, Critics, and After-Fame* (New York: Charles Scribner's Sons, 1917), 4. On the ubiquity of the Keats name in Devonshire, see Gittings, *John Keats,* 441, and Dwight E. Robinson, "Notes on the Antecedents of John Keats: The Maritime Hypothesis," *Keats-Shelley Journal* 34 (1985), 25–52.

29. "Death of the Duke of Kent, London, January 24," *New-York Evening Post* 5531 (March 11, 1820), 2; *New-York Daily Advertiser* 904 (March 11, 1820), 2.

30. *New-York Commercial Advertiser* 23, no. 60 (March 11, 1820), 2.

31. *KL,* 2:251, 2:267. *KC,* 2.74.

32. *KC,* 2:73.

33. Ibid., 2:73–74.

34. The company's advertisement ran regularly, as in "Liverpool Packets," *New-York Gazette & General Advertiser* 29, no. 11843 (December 17, 1819), 1. In Liverpool, the wealthy Quaker merchants James Cropper and Robert Rathbone Benson listed the *Albion,* the *Amity,* the *James Monroe,* and the *Nestor* (rather than the *Courier*) as the ships in the line; [Cropper & Benson's advertisement], *Liverpool Mercury* of December 1, 1820, which incorrectly advertises the *Albion* at a capacity of 500 tons.

35. "Liverpool Packets," *New-York Gazette & General Advertiser,* 1.

36. "Port of New York," *New-York Columbian* 10, no. 2954 (November 9, 1819), 2. The arrival of the *Albion* in Liverpool by December 8 is indicated by an advertisement for beeswax and other cargo brought over in the ship from New York; *Liverpool Mercury* 496 (December 8, 1820), [188]. On Georgiana's trip: Passenger Lists of Vessels Arriving at New York, 1820–1897, No. 649; National Archives and Record Administration, Washington D.C.

37. "Blow the Man Down," *Outing Magazine* 61 (1912–1913), 547.

38. James Lindridge, ed., *Tales of Shipwrecks and Adventures at Sea* (London: William Mark Clark, 1846), 329.

39. List or Manifest, Ship Courier, March 13, 1820, National Archives and Records Administration (M2371).

40. *KL,* 2:240. *KC,* 1:110.

41. *KL,* 2:205–206, formatted here as dialogue.

42. List or Manifest, Ship Courier, March 13, 1820.

43. *KL,* 2:229.

44. *ML,* 12–13.

45. *KL,* 2:329.

46. Ibid., 2:248; also in *ML,* 12.

47. *ML,* 12. *KC,* 2:102.

48. *KL,* 2:357.

49. *KC,* 1:311. *KL,* 2:17.

50. *KL,* 2:250.

51. "Marine List," *New-York Gazette and General Advertiser* 30, no. 11915 (March 11, 1820), 2. The paper lists the cabin passengers of the *Albion.*

52. Ibid.

53. James Fenimore Cooper, *Notions of the Americans: Picked Up by a Travelling Bachelor* (Albany: State University of New York Press, 1991), 103–104.

54. "Death of the King," *New-York Gazette and General Advertiser* 30, no. 11915 (March 11, 1820), 2. "Death of the King of England," *National Advocate* [New York] 8, no. 2210 (March 11, 1820), 2. Among other reiterations: "From English Papers Received by the *Courier:* Death of the King," *New-York Columbian* 11, no. 2967 (March 11, 1820), 2; "Death of the King," *Rhode-Island American, and General Advertiser* 12, no. 46 (March 14, 1820), 3; "Late and Important from Europe," *Edwardsville Spectator* [Illinois] 1, no. 46 (April 11, 1820), 2. [Untitled, column 1], *Louisville Public Advertiser* 2, no. 155 (April 1, 1820), 2, emphasis added for clarity.

55. "Liverpool Packets," *New-York Gazette and General Advertiser* 30, no. 11915 (March 11, 1820), 3.

56. *KL,* 2:217.

57. "Era of Good Feelings," [Boston] *Columbian Centinel* no. 3471 (July 12, 1817), 2.

58. Matthew Arnold, "John Keats," in *The Complete Prose Works of Matthew Arnold,* ed. R. H. Super, vol. 9 (Ann Arbor: University of Michigan Press, 1973), 205–216 (206). *KL,* 2:282–283.

59. "Concert," *New-York Daily Advertiser* 903 (March 10, 1820), 2. [Announcement], *National Advocate* [New York] 8, no. 2210 (March 11, 1820), 2.

60. *KL,* 2:322.

61. Andrew Motion, *Keats* (London: Faber and Faber, 1997), 496–497. Robert Gittings, *John Keats* (Boston: Little, Brown, 1968), 496–497.

62. *KL,* 2:287.

63. Ibid., 2:291.

64. Richard Woodhouse identifies the profile on the title page of John's 1817 *Poems* as Shakespeare's; John Keats, *Poems (1817): A Facsimile of Richard Woodhouse's Annotated Copy in the Huntington Library,* ed. Jack Stillinger (New York: Garland Publishing, 1985), 17. George Keats to Joseph Severn, 120 Goswell Street,

May 22, 1817, in *George's Letters,* 1; also published in *Bulletin and Review of the Keats-Shelley Memorial* 1 (1910), 45–47 (46).

65. George Keats to Joseph Severn, undated, in *George's Letters,* 2.

66. Shelley, "Letter to Maria Gisborne, Leghorn, July 1, 1820," lines 79–83.

67. William Lambe, *Water and Vegetable Diet in Consumption, Scrofula, Cancer, Asthma, and Other Chronic Diseases* (New York: Fowlers and Wells, 1850), 170. In 1815, the title read: *Additional Reports on the Effects of a Peculiar Regimen in Cases of Cancer, Scrofula, Consumption, Asthma, and Other Chronic Diseases. KL,* 2:306.

68. Lord Byron to Mary Shelley, quoted in Barnette Miller, *Leigh Hunt's Relations with Byron, Shelley and Keats* (New York: Columbia University Press, 1910), 108. Marianne Hunt, "Unpublished Diary of Mrs. Leigh Hunt (Pisa, September 18, 1822–Genoa, October 24, 1822), *Bulletin and Review of the Keats-Shelley Memorial* 2 (1913), 69–77 (73).

69. *KL,* 2:309.

70. Leigh Hunt, *The Wishing-Cap Papers* (Boston: Lee and Shepard, 1888), 239.

71. *KL,* 2:310.

72. Ibid., 2:309.

73. John Reynolds to Francis Jeffrey, July 13, 1820, in Leonidas M. Jones, "Reynolds and Keats," *Keats-Shelley Journal* 7 (1958), 47–59 (52). *KL,* 2:315.

74. *KL,* 1:394. Review of "Lamia, and Other Poems," *New Monthly Magazine and Universal Register* 14, no. 80 (September 1, 1820), 245–248 (245).

75. "Modern Periodical Literature," reprinted from the London *New Monthly Magazine,* in *New York Literary Journal and Belles-Lettres Repository* 4, no. 1 (November 1, 1820), 49–56 (51). "Poetry," *Norwich Courier* 35, no. 6 (December 13, 1820), 4. "Poetry," *Rhode-Island American, and General Advertiser* 13, no. 29 (January 12, 1821), 1.

76. "Various Prospects of Mankind, Nature, and Providence," *Literary and Scientific Repository, and Critical Review* 2, no. 3 (January 1, 1821), 150–170 (167–168).

77. *KL,* 2:295.

78. Ibid. Quoted in Casseday, *The History of Louisville,* 156.

79. *Clarke's Autobiography,* 68.

80. *KL,* 2:239.

81. *Fearon's Sketches,* 248. *Harris's Remarks,* 66.

82. *Fearon's Sketches,* 247.

83. Ibid., 247–249. *Fordham's Narrative,* 158.

84. Frances Milton Trollope, *Domestic Manners of the Americans* (New York: Dodd, Mead, 1901), 48.

85. Jervis Cutler, *A Topographical Description of the State of Ohio, Indiana Territory, and Louisiana* (Boston: Charles Williams, 1812), 17.

86. *Clarke's Autobiography*, 52.

87. Robert Southey, *Madoc*, 5th ed., 2 vols. (London: Longman, Hurst, Rees, Orme, Brown, and Green, 1825), 1:viii. *Harris's Remarks*, 110.

88. *KC*, 1:331. "Snow," *Kentucky Reporter* 13, no. 14 (April 5, 1820), 3.

89. Phyllis G. Mann, "New Light on Keats and His Family," *Keats-Shelley Memorial Bulletin* 11 (1960), 33–38 (33).

90. *ML*, 19–20.

91. On George's notebook see John Keats, *Manuscript Poems in the British Library: Facsimiles of the Hyperion Holograph and George Keats's Notebook of Holographs and Transcripts*, ed. Donald H. Reiman (New York: Garland Publishing, 1988), xiii.

92. *KC*, 1:284.

93. *KL*, 2:296.

94. Ibid.

95. Ibid., 2:229, 2:296.

96. Ibid., 2:357.

97. Cutler, *A Topographical Description*, 82. *Fearon's Sketches*, 267.

98. Thomas H. Greer, "Economic and Social Effects of the Depression of 1819 in the Old Northwest," *Indiana Magazine of History*, 44, no. 3 (September 1948), 227–243. "Pointed Puns," *Louisville Public Advertiser* 2, no. 210 (October 11, 1820), 2.

99. George Warren quoted in Henry A. Ford and Kate B. Ford, *History of Cincinnati, Ohio, with Illustrations and Biographical Sketches* (Cleveland: L. A. Williams and Co., 1881), 71. Greer, "Economic and Social Effects," 231–232.

100. [Untitled news item, column 1], *Louisville Public Advertiser* 2, no. 208 (October 4, 1820), 2.

101. Thomas W. Bakewell, "Audubon & Bakewell, Partners: Sketch of the Life of Thomas W. Bakewell Written by Himself," *Cardinal* 4, no. 2 (1935), 34–42 (42). John E. Kleber, *The Encyclopedia of Louisville* (Lexington: University Press of Kentucky, 2001), 422.

102. *KC*, 1:287.

103. *KL*, 2:356–357.

104. *Fearon's Sketches*, 271.

105. Audubon quoted in Ruthven Deane, "Extracts from an Unpublished Journal of John James Audubon," *Auk* 21, no. 3 (July 1904), 334–338 (335).

106. Bakewell, "Audubon & Bakewell, Partners," 42. Case no. 982, *Thomas W. Bakewell vs. John J. Audubon and Nicholas Berthoud*, April 1, 1820, Archives Division, Jefferson County Court, Louisville, Kentucky. Case no. 1021, *William*

Bakewell vs. John J. Audubon and Nicholas Berthoud, April 1, 1820, Archives Division, Jefferson County Court, Louisville, Kentucky.

107. *KL,* 2:210.

108. *KC,* 1:329. *KL,* 2:356. "Bitter chill" is from the opening line of "The Eve of St. Agnes."

8. Posthumous Lives

1. *KL,* 2:359. See John's sonnet composed in 1819, "The day is gone, and all its sweets are gone!" Below see John's "Ode on Innocence."

2. Quoted in Kenyon West, "Keats in Hampstead," *Century Illustrated Magazine* 50, no. 6 (October 1895), 898–910 (906).

3. Leigh Hunt to Joseph Severn, March 8, 1821, in *The Correspondence of Leigh Hunt,* ed. Thornton Leigh Hunt, 2 vols. (London: Smith, Elder, 1862), 1:107–108.

4. *KL,* 2:337.

5. Sue Brown, *Joseph Severn, A Life: The Rewards of Friendship* (Oxford: Oxford University Press, 2009), 51.

6. *KL* 2:339.

7. Milton, *Paradise Lost,* 4.540–547.

8. Severn, "Leaf from Severn's Journal," *Bulletin and Review of the Keats-Shelley Memorial* 1 (1910), 41.

9. *KL,* 2:345–346.

10. *Louisville Public Advertiser* 2, no. 155 (April 1, 1820), 2; and ibid., 3, no. 216 (November 1, 1820), 3.

11. *KL,* 2:355.

12. *Severn's Letters,* 641.

13. Ibid., 642.

14. *KL,* 2:354–355.

15. Ibid., 2:353.

16. *Severn's Letters,* 643.

17. "Naples, December 7," *New-York Commercial Advertiser* 23, no. 60 (March 3, 1820), 2. Henry Matthews, *The Diary of an Invalid: Being the Journal of a Tour in Pursuit of Health; in Portugal, Italy, Switzerland, and France, in the Years 1817, 1818, and 1819,* 2nd ed. (London: John Murray, 1820), 219–220.

18. *KL,* 2:350.

19. Mariana Starke, *Travels in Europe, for the Use of Travellers on the Continent, Likewise in the Island of Sicily: Where the Author Had Never Been, till the Year 1834,* 9th ed. (Paris: A. and W. Galignani, 1836), 579. "Minister uetuli puer Falerni/inger mi calices amariores": Gaius Valerius Catullus, Poem 27. *KL,* 1:288, emphasis added.

20. *The Diary of James Minet* (1837), quoted in *The Letters of Charles Dickens,* vol. 4: 1844–1846, ed. Kathleen Tillotson (Oxford: Clarendon, 1977), 274n.

21. Henry Sass, *A Journey to Rome and Naples, Performed in 1817* (London: Longman, Hurst, Rees, Orme, and Brown, 1818), 160–161.

22. Matthews, *Diary of an Invalid,* 175, 173, 205.

23. Sass, *A Journey to Rome and Naples,* 160.

24. *Severn's Letters,* 644.

25. Sass, *A Journey to Rome and Naples,* 165. *Severn's Letters,* 644.

26. *KL,* 2:352.

27. As John expressed it in his letter of November 1, 1820, to Charles Brown; *KL,* 2:351.

28. Charles MacFarlane, *Reminiscences of a Literary Life* (New York: Charles Scribner's Sons, 1917), 14.

29. Ibid., 15.

30. Sass, *A Journey to Rome and Naples,* 138. James Clark, *Medical Notes on Climate, Diseases, Hospitals, and Medical Schools, in France, Italy, and Switzerland* (London: T. and G. Underwood, 1820), 83.

31. Matthews, *Diary of an Invalid,* 168–169.

32. Frances (Winckley) Shelley, *The Diary of Lady Frances Shelley,* vol. 1, ed. Richard Edgcumbe (New York: Scribner's, 1912), 362. *Severn's Letters,* 644–645.

33. Byron, *Childe Harold's Pilgrimage,* 4.142, 4.145. *The Letters of Percy Bysshe Shelley,* ed. Frederick L. Jones, 2 vols. (Oxford: Clarendon, 1964), 2:58–59.

34. Clark, *Medical Notes,* 74, 76.

35. "The Weather," *Louisville Public Advertiser* 3, no. 241 (January 27, 1821), 2.

36. *KC,* 1:284.

37. Ibid., 1:222.

38. Ibid., 1:201, 1:187, 1:201n.

39. Ibid., 1:169.

40. *Fearon's Sketches,* 270. *KC,* 1:289.

41. *ML,* 44. *KC,* 1:110.

42. "Recollections Sent by Alice L. Keats to Maurice Buxton Forman," undated MS 215, University of Delaware Library, Newark, Delaware.

43. *KC,* 1:289. *The Life, Letters, and Literary Remains of John Keats,* ed. Richard M. Milnes, 2 vols. (London, 1848), 1:142; Morgan Library and Museum (PML 16759–60), New York. The daughter was Georgiana Emily. *KL,* 1:316.

44. James Freeman Clarke, "George Keats," *Dial* 3, no. 4 (April 1843), 495–500 (495–496).

45. Robert Underwood Johnson, "Note on Some Volumes now in America once owned by Keats," *Bulletin and Review of the Keats-Shelley Memorial* 2 (1913), 20–29 (23–24, 28–29).

46. *KC,* 2:3–4.

47. Ibid., 2:31, 2:5–6.

48. Ibid., 2:348, 1:291. *Clarke's Autobiography,* 73.

49. *KC,* 1:308. George Combe, *Notes on the United States of North America, during a Phrenological Visit in 1838–9–40,* 2 vols. (Philadelphia: Carey and Hart, 1841), 2:293.

50. *KL,* 1:295. James Freeman Clarke, "George Keats," 495.

51. *Essays and Poems by Ralph Waldo Emerson,* ed. Peter Norberg (New York: Barnes and Noble Classics, 2004), 60. *KC,* 2:43, 2:112.

52. *Clarke's Autobiography,* 121.

53. Ibid.

54. Emerson, *Essays,* 35. See Shakespeare, *Measure for Measure,* 4.1.1–4. Emerson to Clarke, December 7, 1838, quoted in *Clarke's Autobiography,* 123.

55. "The Weather," *Argus of Western America* [Frankfort] 14, no. 5 (March 29, 1821), 2.

56. *KL,* 2:358.

57. *Severn's Letters,* 119. Emilio Cecciti, "Notes: Keats's Roman Piano," *Bulletin and Review of the Keats-Shelley Memorial* 2 (1913), 95–96 (96).

58. *Severn's Letters,* 645.

59. Clark, *Medical Notes,* 71, 75–76. Matthews, *Diary of an Invalid,* 128.

60. Matthews, *Diary of an Invalid,* 83. *Severn's Letters,* 647. *KL,* 2:345.

61. *Severn's Letters,* 647–648.

62. Ibid., 128.

63. *KL,* 2:361.

64. Ibid., 2:362.

65. Ibid., 2:377. Clark, *Medical Notes,* 94*n (the asterisk distinguishes 94* from 94, since signature sheet M was mistakenly numbered with duplicate page numbers).

66. *Severn's Letters,* 120.

67. *KC,* 1:221.

68. *KL,* 2:368.

69. Ibid., 2:367–368.

70. *Severn's Letters,* 614.

71. Ibid., 146.

72. *KL,* 2:373. *KC,* 1:238.

73. *KL,* 2:378.

74. *Severn's Letters,* 614.

75. *KL,* 2:378.

76. Ibid., 2:379.

77. *Severn's Letters,* 139.

78. *Severn's Letters,* 650; also see *KL,* 2:379. Shelley, "Adonais," lines 439–441.

79. Brooch: *Severn's Letters,* 188–189. On the effort of Keats's friends to honor his memory, see H. Nelson Gay, "The Protestant Burial-Ground in Rome: A Historical Sketch," *Keats-Shelley Memorial Bulletin* 2 (1913), 33–58. On the classical heritage of Keats's epitaph, Oonagh Lahr, "Greek Sources of 'Writ in Water,'" *Keats-Shelley Journal* 21–22 (1972–1973), 17–18; A. J. Woodman, "Greek Sources of 'Writ in Water': A Further Note," *Keats-Shelley Journal* 24 (1975), 12–13.

80. *KC,* 1:284.

81. *KL,* 2:364, 2:366.

82. *KC,* 1:201.

83. Ibid., 1:230.

84. Ibid., 1:318–319, 2:30.

85. *ML,* 15. *KC,* 1:290.

86. *KC,* 1:290.

87. *ML,* 49.

88. Ibid., 49–50.

89. Ibid., 51. Passenger Lists of Vessels Arriving at New York, 1820–1897, no. 649; National Archives and Record Administration, Washington, D.C. See also: *National Gazette* (Philadelphia) 9, no. 1187 (November 8, 1828), 3.

90. Marie Adami, *Fanny Keats* (New Haven: Yale University Press, 1938), 123, 111–112. *ML,* 42.

91. Wilbur Fisk Gordy, *A History of the United States for Schools,* new ed. (New York: Charles Scribner's Sons, 1911), 258–259. Susan B. Carter et al., eds., *Historical Statistics of the United States: Earliest Times to the Present,* millennial ed., 5 vols. (New York: Cambridge University Press, 2006), 3:23–24. Louis C. Hunter, *Steamboats on the Western Rivers: An Economic and Technological History* (Cambridge, Mass.: Harvard University Press, 1949), 33.

92. Notice, "Steam Flour and Saw Mills," *Louisville Public Advertiser* 12, no. 1257 (March 23, 1830), 1 (and subsequent issues). [Classified ad by George Keats], *Louisville Public Advertiser* 451 (February 1, 1823), 4. *Louisville Directory for the Year 1832* (Louisville, Kentucky: R. W. Otis, 1832). On February 7, 1842, the Commonwealth of Kentucky, Jefferson County, ordered Felix Smith, Francis E. Goddard, William G. Bakewell, and Fortunatus Cosby, Jr., or any three of them, to appraise the slaves and real estate of George Keats, deceased. On February 2, Goddard, Smith, and Cosby did the appraising.

93. James Freeman Clarke quoted in John Jeffrey, "George Keats," *Athenaeum* 2358 (January 4, 1873), 17–18 (18).

94. *KC,* 2:13, 2:3.

95. Ibid., 2:13. See Jefferson County Court Cases No. 2774 (October 1, 1833), No. 3082 (July 19, 1833), No. 3083 (June 15, 1833), No. 3084 (February 14, 1833), and No. 3086 (June 14, 1833).

96. *KC,* 2:3. On George's activities in Louisville, see *KC,* 1:cvii; Naomi J. Kirk, "Memoir of George Keats," in *The Poetical Works and Other Writings of John Keats,* ed. H. Buxton Foreman, rev. Maurice Buxton Forman, 8 vols. (New York: Charles Scribner's Sons, 1938), 1:lxxiii–xcviii; Jonathan Clark Smith, "George Keats: The 'Money Brother' of John Keats and His Life in Louisville," *Register of the Kentucky Historical Society* 106, no. 1 (2008), 43–68.

97. "Kentucky Historical Society," *Western Messenger Devoted to Religion Life, and Literature* 5, no. 1 (April 1838), 70. Harlan Museum Company Minute Book, 1837–1838; Filson Historical Society (BA/H283), Louisville, Kentucky.

98. *Shared Porridge,* 185. The description of the Keats mansion in Louisville, here and subsequent, derives from *Shared Porridge* and its appendix, "Appraiser's List of Furniture, Books, Banks Stock, Slaves, etc."

99. "The Keats Mansion," [Louisville] *Courier-Journal* (November 9, 1890), 5.

100. John Howard Payne, "Random Scraps and Recollections, from the Note Book of a Wanderer at Home and Abroad: No. 1," *Ladies' Companion: A Monthly Magazine Embracing Literature and the Fine Arts* (August 1837), 185–187 (186). George's statement to his sister of February 1824 in *ML,* 17.

101. *KC,* 2:3. James Freeman Clarke quoted in Jeffrey, "George Keats," 18.

102. Clarke quoted in Jeffrey, "George Keats," 17. John Keats's copy of Spenser, Keats Collection (EC8.K2262.Zz715a), Houghton Library, Harvard University. [Richard Steele, Joseph Addison], *Spectator,* 8 vols. (London: J. and R. Tonson, 1749), 7:247.

103. Payne, "Random Scraps and Recollections," 186.

104. *KC,* 1:xcvii (on the children's birthdates). *ML,* 35 (George on Rose).

105. Rosalind Keats quoted in *Shared Porridge,* 204. George's slaves are listed in Kirk, "Appraiser's List"; Sixth Census of the United States, 1840, National Archives and Record Administration (M704), Washington, D.C.

106. Emma Speed Simpson to Naomi Kirk, December 13, 1933, Naomi Kirk Collection, Filson Historical Society, Louisville, Kentucky. *Melish's Travels,* 2:206–207. *KC,* 2:30.

107. Clarke, *Autobiography,* 78. *ML,* 45.

108. *KC,* 2:24.

109. [Advertisement by Thomas W. Bakewell announcing the dissolution of his partnership with George Keats], *Louisville Public Advertiser* 5, no. 451 (February 1, 1823), 3. *Bakewell Family Book,* 35–36.

110. [Advertisements by W. G. Bakewell & Co.], *Louisville Public Advertiser* 9, no. 900 (May 23, 1827), 1, and 12, no. 1499 (December 31, 1830), 1. *Bakewell Family Book,* 44. Audubon to his family, March 19, 1843, from Louisville, in John Francis McDermott, ed., *Audubon in the West* (Norman: University of Oklahoma Press, 1965), 25.

111. *The Letters and Poems of John Keats,* ed. John Gilmer Speed, 3 vols. (New York: Dodd, Mead and Company, 1883), 1:102n. *KC,* 1:cviii.

112. Edward F. Madden, "The Poet Keats," *Harper's New Monthly Magazine* 55, no. 327 (1877), 357–361 (357). *KC,* 2:45.

113. *KC,* 2:110–111. Lincoln's thank-you letter to the Speed family, including a mention of "Aunt Emma," is on display at the Farmington residence, now a museum; *Keats Family,* 71.

114. *KC,* 2:110.

115. On the nature of George's disease, Naomi Joy Kirk remarks: "The family disease, tuberculosis, developed with startling suddenness" ("Memoir of George Keats," xcv); and "'Quick consumption' had fulfilled John's prophecy that they would 'all die young'"; see Naomi J. Kirk, "George Keats," *Filson Club Historical Quarterly* 8 (April 1934), 88–96 (92). Alice Lee Keats heard that her grandfather died of "some sudden malady" ("Recollections of Alice Lee Keats"), perhaps the "rapid consumption" to which (she claimed) Clarence George Keats succumbed; see Alice Lee Keats to Maurice Buxton Forman, Urbana, Ohio, undated, University of Delaware Library (MS 215), Newark, Delaware. Mrs. William C. [Mildred Ann] Bullitt to John C. Bullitt, December 20, 1841; Filson Historical Society, Louisville, Kentucky. For a description of George Keats's will, see *Shared Porridge,* 224.

116. "Died," *Louisville Daily Journal* 12, no. 22 (December 25, 1841), 3. *ML,* 44–45.

117. *Shared Porridge,* 224. *ML,* 45.

118. James Freeman Clarke, "George Keats," *Dial* 3, no. 4 (April 1843), 495–500 (499).

119. [Anna Hazard Barker Ward], fragment of unsigned letter, in *George's Letters,* 63.

120. Now in the Keats Collection (MS 1.64), Houghton Library, Harvard University. The poem was acquired by Amy Lowell from her friend Elizabeth Ward Perkins, a friend of Anna Hazard Barker Ward, who obtained it from George.

121. *KC,* 1:284.

Epilogue

1. Mrs. William C. [Mildred Ann] Bullitt to John C. Bullitt, December 20, 1841; Filson Historical Society, Louisville, Kentucky. Elizabeth Williams to Eleanor Green, c/o Hector Green, Esq., March 27, 1842; Filson Historical Society, Louisville, Kentucky.

2. *KC,* 2:48. Emma Speed Simpson to Naomi Kirk, December 13, 1933;

Naomi Kirk Collection, Folder 2, Filson Historical Society, Louisville, Kentucky. Obituary quoted in *KC,* 1:cii–ciii.

3. *KL,* 2:242. Mrs. William C. [Mildred Ann] Bullitt to John C. Bullitt, December 20, 1841. Elizabeth Williams to Eleanor Green, March 27, 1842.

4. Ben Casseday, *The History of Louisville, from Its Earliest Settlement till the Year 1852* (Louisville: Hull and Brother, 1852), 202–203.

5. John James Audubon to his family, March 19, 1843, from Louisville, in John Francis McDermott, ed., *Audubon in the West* (Norman: University of Oklahoma Press, 1965), 26. *KC,* 1:cii.

6. *KC,* 1:xcix.

7. Richard Jacob Taylor to Thomas P. Jacob, November 8, 1843; John Jeremiah Jacob Papers, 1778–1852, Filson Historical Society, Louisville, Kentucky. *KC,* 2:224.

8. *KC,* 1:c–ci. Lucien V. Rule, "Louisville: The Gateway to the South," in *Historic Towns of the Southern States,* ed. Lyman P. Powell (New York: G. B. Putnam's Sons, 1904), 503–535 (528).

9. Georgiana Augusta Wylie Keats, Louisville, to [Alexander Jeffrey]; undated. MS Keats 4.10.28, Houghton Library, Harvard University.

10. *Keats Family,* 60–61.

11. Ibid., 188–190.

12. Ibid., 57, 181–182. Emma Keats Speed quoted in *ML,* 43n.

13. Clarence G. Keats to the Governor of Indiana, April 1, 1859, Evansville, Indiana, John Jeffrey Collection (AJ 46j, Folder 32), Filson Historical Society, Louisville, Kentucky.

14. *KC,* 1:cii–ciii.

15. Oscar Wilde, "Keats's Sonnet on Blue," *Century Guild Hobby Horse* 1 (July 1886), 83–86 (83). Oscar Wilde to Emma Keats Speed, March 21, 1882, in *The Complete Letters of Oscar Wilde,* ed. Merlin Holland and Rupert Hart-Davis (London: Fourth Estate, 2000), 157.

16. *The Life and Letters of Christopher Pearse Cranch,* ed. Leonora Cranch Scott (Boston: Houghton Mifflin, 1917), 38.

17. Wilde, "Keats's Sonnet on Blue," 85. The lines on the rainbow are from "Lamia."

18. Wilde, *Complete Letters,* 157.

19. Ibid., 158. See John's verse epistle "To My Brother George."

ACKNOWLEDGMENTS

In doing research for this book I was fortunate to cross paths with Lawrence M. Crutcher, an American descendant of George Keats from Louisville, Kentucky. We spent much time in discussion about the Keats brothers, most of it in virtual reality, some at Stanford University, the rest while watching the seals at Stinson Beach, California, where George's legacy still survives in his family Bible and his great-great-great grandson. Crutcher's intelligence, amiability, and persistence make him the spitting image of his ancestor. He has been a vital interlocutor on *The Keats Brothers,* and his study *The Keats Family* (2009) will be useful to anyone interested in George's descendants in America.

Martin Burnell, a great-great grandson of Edward Bell Drury, generously helped to unravel the tangled lives of the Drury family in England, Philadelphia, and Cincinnati. Edward's brother Michael was a cousin of John Taylor (John Keats's publisher). Michael's sister, Mary Drury, married his business partner, James Tallant, two days before George and Georgiana Keats landed in Philadelphia. The Drurys are a helpful family, and I am grateful to Burnell for information relating to them and to James Tallant. For further details see Burnell's webpage, The Burnell Family History.

John Kulka at Harvard University Press, the best of editors, recognized when I first called him from the Filson Historical Society in Louisville, Kentucky, years ago that the narrative presented here needed to be about *both* John and George Keats. I thank him for that, and for his ongoing wisdom, guidance, and patience over the years. I would also like to thank Matthew Hills and Maria Ascher at HUP for their help in the production of this book.

Harold Bloom, my spiritual father, is the person from whom I have learned most about how to read and think about literature, and I am grateful to him for the ongoing inspiration that has motivated this book. Stanley Plumly's formal challenge to the standard linearity of biographical narrative in *Posthumous Keats* helped me to give shape to the story presented here, and I have consistently relied upon Jack Stillinger's superb editorial work in writing it. I thank all three scholars for their generosity in reading the manuscript of *The Keats Brothers* and for their comments on it.

One would be hard pressed to write about either John or George Keats without the work of generations of scholars—above all, Hyder Edward Rollins, who edited *The Keats Letters* and the letters included in *The Keats Circle;* Jack Stillinger, who edited John's *Complete Poems;* biographers Amy Lowell, Walter Jackson Bate, Robert Gittings, and Andrew Motion; and those who have published their work over the years in the *Keats-Shelley Memorial Bulletin,* the *Keats-Shelley Review,* and the *Keats-Shelley Journal.* They are pioneers—some of them poets—from whom I have learned much.

John Keats once said that his great misfortune in life was, from an early age, to have had no mother; but he found a surrogate in Mrs. Brawne, just as George found a surrogate in Mrs. Wylie. Far be it for me to put my excellent colleague Jennifer Summit in a similar position, but she is a model academic and mother (no easy combination), and without her support as Chair of the Department of English at Stanford University, I could not have completed this book. I also warmly thank the School of Humanities and Sciences at Stanford University, and the Filson Historical Society, for funding research for *The Keats Brothers.*

I have learned much since my undergraduate days at Yale University from Gordon Turnbull, who offered many meticulous comments on the manuscript of this book, and I am grateful to him and to Erik Johnson, who performed Herculean labors with hundreds of facts. For help with research, I would like to thank Carol Brobeck, at the Folger Shakespeare Library; Delinda S. Buie, at Special Collections, Ekstrom Library, University of Louisville; Lawrence M. Crutcher for his help at the Massachusetts Historical Society, Boston, and at Houghton Library, Harvard University; Inge Dupont, at the Morgan Library, New York; Dennis Harrell, at Christ Church Cathedral, Cincinnati; Jillian Hess for her help at the British Library; James J. Holmberg and Robin Lynn Wallace, at the Filson Historical Society, Louisville; Christoph Irmscher, for help in seeking William Bakewell, Sr.'s, journal, reputedly in a private collection; Tamara A. Measler, at the Historical Society of Pennsylvania; Leslie Morris, at Houghton Library, Harvard University; the indefatigable Mary Louise Munill at Green Library, Stanford University; Ken Page, at the Keats House, City of London; David Riggs, at the Jefferson Judicial Center, Louisville; Samantha Sachs and Joe Shapiro for their help at Stanford University; and Kelly Swartz for help at Princeton University Library. I thank the institutions named above, as well as the Indiana Historical Society, the University of Delaware Library, and the University of Iowa Libraries, for permission to quote from their collections.

Images can be a challenge. For help with artwork and permissions, I wholeheartedly thank Alyce Boster. I would also like to thank Melissa Atkinson at the National Portrait Gallery; Katherine Dunill at the Westcountry Studies Library, Exeter; Josephine Greywood and Louise McCourt at the Keats-Shelley House, Rome; Mary Haegart at Houghton Library, Harvard University; Matthew Hills at Harvard University Press; Matthew Jockers at Stanford University; AnnaLee Pauls at Firestone Library, Princeton University; Adrienne Sharpe at the Beinecke Rare Book and Manuscript Library, Yale University; Jeremy Smith at the London Metropolitan Archives; and for photos of the author, Raul Diaz.

Throughout the writing of this book, Amy Kohrman has been more than a sister to me—she has been my greatest friend. And I claim being the affectionate friend of Thomas J. Kealey, who taught me a few things I needed to know, although not about the Keats brothers. The book is dedicated to him, not to Tom Keats. For their kind support, I would also like to thank Nancy Witt and Fred Porta. My most enormous debt of gratitude is to my son, Julian Rovee, who at age eleven has sat through more than one lecture on Keats and intervened at so many key moments during the lives of the brothers—and of my own—that I really do not know how to thank him.

INDEX

JK, GK, and TK refer to John Keats, George Keats, and Tom Keats, respectively.

Abbey, Eleanor (née Jones), 23, 111
Abbey, Miss, 23
Abbey, Richard, 216, 267; and Abbey, Cock, & Company, 35; and Abbey, Cocks & Gullet, 35; and Abbey & Cock, 35; and Abbey & Cocks, 35; background of, 35; as churchwarden at St. Stephen, 51; and Clarke's school, 48; debts of, 60; delayed remittance from, 238–239, 241; and Don Quixote, 162; dress of, 53; and Fanny Keats, 4, 12, 23, 24, 25, 148, 239, 247, 328; and GK, 12, 20–21; GK respected by, 61, 111; and GK's deposit at Abbey & Cocks, 317–318; and GK's emigration, 40, 146; and GK's finances, 320, 330; and GK's inheritance, 124, 146; GK's inquiries about associates with, 62; and GK's move to Cheapside, 52–53; GK's quitting job with, 56–57, 59; GK's trust in, 328; and GK's wedding, 146; on indulgence, 47; JK as taking over tea business for, 311–312; and JK quitting medical profession, 41, 52, 53–54, 61; and JK's attitudes toward trade, 34–35; JK's attitude toward, 12; and JK's biography, 4; and JK's character, 21; and JK's inheritance, 246–247; and JK's letters to Fanny Keats, 239; and JK's medical training, 22, 25; and JK's petition for money for GK, 307–308; and JK's *Poems* (1817), 68; and JK's poetic ambition, 55; JK's proximity to, 321; and JK's Scotland trip, 149; and JK's studies, 34; and JK's travels to Italy, 320; and JK's work, 146; on Thomas Keats, 35, 44, 48; on Keats family, 20–21, 46, 48–49, 53; made guardian by Alice Jennings, 51, 52; public service of, 51; reputation of, 34; residence of, 21, 23; Taylor on, 378; and tea trade, 31, 60, 311–312; and TK, 34, 53, 56, 146, 308
Abbey & Cocks, 21, 35, 44, 56–57, 59, 60, 61, 146, 317–318
Abbot, Charles, Lord Colchester, 382
Absolutism, 117, 363

Achilles, 120

Act for the Gradual Abolition of Slavery, 168

Adami, Marie, *Fanny Keats,* 6

Adams, John Quincy, 306

Addison, Joseph, 207, 397

Adonis, 49, 410

Aeneas, 220

African Americans, 168–169. *See also* Slavery

Albion, 276, 277, 279, 284, 285, 289, 295

Albion, 325, 326, 331

Alcott, Amos Bronson, 379

Alexandria. *See* Gallipolis

Alfieri, Vittorio, *Filippo,* 383–384

Alfred, king of England, 210

Allan, Archibald, 345

Allegheny Mountains, 2, 120, 180, 198; inns of, 200–203, 205; landscape of, 200, 203, 204; numbers of emigrants crossing, 186; poverty in, 203

Allegheny Ridge, 204

Allegheny River, 205, 206

All Hallow's Eve, 44

America: Birkbeck on, 112–113; British attitudes toward, 145; commerce in, 207–208; domestic servants in, 289–290; economy of, 175, 305, 306, 317, 352–353, 392, 393, 394, 399–400; financial markets in, 241–242; financial speculation in, 241, 242, 251, 297, 305, 306; and free press, 115; GK and news about, 111; and Hazlitt, 170; and Hunt, 67, 144, 170–171; inns in, 180, 200–203, 205, 259; JK on, 143–145; land in, 203; merchants in, 175; port cities of, 181; and self-sufficiency, 203; and Shelley, 114; social status in, 203; speculators in, 238; taxes in, 113–114; titles in, 203; travel in, 179–180

American Civil War, 410

American Declaration of Independence, 165, 179, 323

American Revolution, 2, 67, 165, 171, 236, 241, 274, 323, 332

American Transcendentalism, 284, 379

American Western Country, 2, 115, 143, 175, 225; Birkbeck on, 113; and Cincinnati, 251; condition in, 179; Dickens's depictions of, 268–269, 270–271; disease in, 271; economic depression in, 400; as Eden, 270; farming in, 120; fortunes in, 297; and Hall, 230; indolence in, 231, 237; intoxication and brawls in, 258–259; justice in, 286–287; land clearing in, 236, 278; life in, 296; and Panic of 1837, 400; and Pittsburgh, 206; population of, 394; prairie fires in, 287; travel writers on, 271; uncertain fortunes in, 242; women's fashions in, 243. *See also* Illinois; Indiana; Kentucky; Missouri; Ohio; Virginia

Amicable Society for a Perpetual Assurance, 43

Amity, 325

Amphlett, William, 151, 167, 202–203

Anderson, Alexander M., 438

Anderson's Creek, 278

André, John, 184

Andrews, Elizabeth Rutt, 276

Andrews, Eliza Julia, 113. *See also* Flower, Eliza Julia Andrews

Andrews, Mordecai, 276

Angeletti, Anna, 386

Ann Maria, 120, 160, 278

Apollo, 1, 39, 190, 221

Apothecary Act of 1815, 25

Appalachian Mountain Range, 201

Apperson, David, 302

April Fool, 348

Arks, 229–230, 231, 278

Arnold, Benedict, 184

Arnold, Matthew, 337

Athenaeum, 62, 412

Atkins, Mrs., 135

Atkinson, John, 394

Atkinson, Richard, 394
Audubon, John Gifford, 196
Audubon, John James, 3, 180, 371, 400–401;
  and Benjamin Bakewell, 298; and
  Thomas Woodhouse Bakewell, 299–302,
  354–355; and barges, 233–234; and
  Berthoud family, 273, 274; and Samuel
  Bowen, 303–305, 306; and explorations in
  Mississippi River Valley, 299; finances of,
  279, 298, 302, 303, 304, 306–307; and
  Fordham, 285–286; and Georgiana
  Keats, 274, 279, 406; and GK, 196, 274,
  279, 286, 288, 302, 307, 321; and GK's investments, 297–298, 303, 304; and GK's
  losses, 296; on GK's perseverance, 121;
  and grist- and sawmill, 257–258, 279,
  298, 300–302; and *Henderson,* 303–304;
  home in Red Banks, 285–286; hunting
  by, 298–299; in Louisville, 307; and Louisville general store, 298; marriage to
  Lucy, 186, 298; move from Louisville to
  Cincinnati, 354; on Ohio River scenery,
  274–275; on Ohio River Valley, 228; and
  Red Banks general store, 299, 300;
  sketches by, 299, 300, 307, 354; tried for
  assault, 306
Audubon, Lucy Green Bakewell, 285, 286,
  305, 306; boards with Rankin family, 299;
  and Georgiana Keats, 279, 288, 307; and
  GK, 196, 279; marriage of, 186, 273, 298;
  and Pittsburgh, 208; and travel hazards,
  180
Audubon, Victor Woodhouse, 196
Audubon & Bakewell, 300, 301, 302
Augustan Age, 43
Augustan verse, 26
Austen, Jane, 266, 291; *Emma,* 100; *Pride
  and Prejudice,* 75–76, 317

Backwoodsmen, 292, 293–294
Bailey, Benjamin, 5, 163, 366; character of,
  87; and JK, 87; with JK at Oxford, 87, 88;

and JK's depression, 138; and JK's ideas
  on soul, 244–245; and JK's venereal disease, 89; and letters from JK, 112; and
  pleasure and pain, 266–267; as quitting
  poetry, 215; and Marianne Reynolds, 86;
  and Rice, 97; on sexuality in *Endymion,*
  89; on Shelley, 89; and Jeremy Taylor,
  387; and TK, 187; and TK's illness, 99
Bakewell, Ann. *See* Gordon, Ann (née
  Bakewell)
Bakewell, Anne, 300
Bakewell, Benjamin, 185, 186, 301; and
  Audubon, 298; and Thomas Woodhouse
  Bakewell, 299; death of, 300; and glassware, 208, 209–210; and Gordon, 240;
  and Thomas Pears, 301; and *Pike,* 303
Bakewell, Elizabeth Rankin Page, 301
Bakewell, John Palmer (son of Benjamin
  Bakewell), 210
Bakewell, Rebecca (née Smith), 300
Bakewell, Sarah, 186, 438
Bakewell, Thomas (son of Benjamin
  Bakewell), 210
Bakewell, Thomas Woodhouse, 305, 394;
  and Audubon, 257–258, 279, 299–302;
  and GK, 186, 258, 305, 307; and glass-
  ware, 210, and William Gordon, 240; and
  grist- and sawmill, 257–258, 300–302;
  and marriage, 301; and mechanical engi-
  neering, 300; and Panic of 1837, 400; and
  steamboats, 258, 302–303, 351, 353; suit
  against Audubon, 354–355
Bakewell, William, Sr. (Squire), 185–186,
  208, 300
Bakewell, William Gifford (son of Squire
  William Bakewell), 186, 258, 300, 301,
  305, 307, 355, 394, 400–401, 458
Bakewell family: and GK, 321; and Unitarianism, 284
Bakewell, Page, & Bakewell, 210
Balboa, Vasco Núñez de, 40, 243
Balch, Earl, 6

Baltimore, 199, 325

Bank failures, 400

Bank of Kentucky, 301, 379–380, 409

Bank of Louisville, 273

Bank of the United States, 305, 400

Barbers, 134–135

Barber-surgeons, 135

Bargemen, 233–234

Barges, 233–234

Barker, Anna Hazard, 404

Barrow, John, 115–116

Barrows, Mrs., 408

Basilica of Saint-Denis, 93

Bastille, 117

Bate, Walter Jackson, 4, 5, 6

Bathing machines, 12, 13, 99, 133

Battery of New York, 333, 334

Bay of Biscay, 4

Bay of Naples, 364, 365, 367

Bay of New York, 325, 331

Bearbaiting, 28, 30–31

Beargrass Creek, 272

Beaumont, Francis, 1; *The Bloody Brother,*
     380

Beaver Creek, 227

Beaverstown, 227

Beckford, William, 43

Beckwith, Jacob, 353

Beilby, 62

Belcher, Jem, 28

Benjamin Bakewell & Company, 210

Bentley, Benjamin, 58

Bentley family, 58, 84, 147, 340, 341

Berthoud, Eliza Bakewell, 186, 273, 306

Berthoud, James (Hervé de Belisle, Marquis
     de Saint-Pié), 273–274, 305, 306

Berthoud, Marie-Anne-Julia, 274

Berthoud, Nicholas Augustus, 186, 273–
     274, 302, 306–307, 354

Bible, 219, 386–387

Big Bone Valley, Kentucky, 183, 195, 349

Big Prairie, 288, 289, 294–295

Big Scioto River, 237, 270

Birkbeck, Bradford, 113, 291, 292

Birkbeck, Charles, 113, 291, 292

Birkbeck, Elizabeth, 113, 277, 291–292

Birkbeck, Morris: and Andrews, 276–277;
     attacks on, 115–116, 178; "British Emi-
     grants Arriving in the Eastern Ports,"
     179; and Cobbett, 121; and conditions on
     English Prairie, 177; death of, 282–283;
     effect on emigration, 117; and *The Fall of
     Hyperion,* 221; as farmer, 236; on finan-
     cial gain, 251; and free press, 115; GK's
     letter of introduction to, 143; and Indiana
     forest, 291; and infrastructure vs. cultiva-
     tion, 296; on intoxication and brawls, 258;
     and justice, 287; *Letters from Illinois,* 112,
     142, 163, 168, 180, 284; and life on fron-
     tier, 296; and maple syrup, 291; *Notes on a
     Journey in America,* 112–113, 115, 120,
     163, 296; *Notes on a Journey through
     France,* 113; and numbers of emigrants,
     186; preparation of home by, 291; and re-
     ligion, 284; rift with Flower, 275–277; on
     Shawneetown, 271; and sheep, 236–237;
     skepticism about, 3; on stagecoach travel,
     180; and Wanborough, 295; and Wash-
     ington, 255

Birkbeck, Prudence, 113, 277, 291, 292

Birkbeck, Richard, 248–249

Birks, Jeremiah, 293

Black Ball Line, 324–325, 332, 393

Black Bull Inn, 150

Blackwood's Edinburgh Magazine, 39, 66, 91,
     100, 121, 198, 217

Blair, Robert, *The Grave,* 242

Blake, William, 42, 62, 114, 222, 377

Bloody Run, 204

Blue Ridge, 204

Bly, James, 46

Boatmen, 231–234, 242–243, 272

Boiardo, Matteo Maria, 245

Boltenhouse Prairie. *See* English Prairie

Bonaparte, Pauline, Princess Borghese,
     383

Bond, William, 337

Bonnycastle, John, *Introduction to Astronomy,* 377

Bon Pas River, 280, 288, 289, 294, 295

Boone, Daniel, 183, 195, 274, 299, 346, 347

Bo Peep, 81–84

Borough-mongering, 113, 283

Bourbon Palace, 369–370

Bowcombe Down, 76

Bowen, Samuel Adams, 303–305, 306, 348

Bowen, William Russell, 304

Boxing matches, 28–29

Bradbury, Cornelius S., 255

Bradbury, John, 181, 203

Braddock, Edward, 205

Brawne, Frances (Fanny): and Campion, 6; character of, 191; and father's tuberculosis, 358; and GK, 191, 315; JK's description of, 194; JK's desire to be near, 341; JK's distance from, 336–337; JK's early relationship with, 191–194; after JK's hemorrhage, 335; JK's letters to, 140, 262, 264, 312, 336–337; JK's love for, 140, 194, 247, 248, 261, 267, 312; JK's need to be with, 317; and JK's trip to Italy, 356, 357, 358, 362, 365–366, 368; JK's understanding with, 315, 316; and Fanny Keats, 393; letters to JK, 341, 389; literary tastes of, 192; lock of hair of, 358, 365–366; and Reynolds sisters, 317; and "This living hand, now warm and capable," 313; as trap, 220; at Wentworth Place, 220, 248

Brawne, Mrs. Frances, 191, 341–342, 357, 366

Brawne, Margaret, 191, 315

Brawne, Sam, 191, 315

Bree, Robert, 334

Brent, George, 304

Bridport, 134

Briggs, Charles, 240, 316

Bright Star, 6

Britannia, 393

Broadnax, Henry P., 306

Brooklyn, 331, 332

Brown, Charles (Carlino), 64, 390

Brown, Charles Armitage, 4, 62, 191–192, 215; as bastion of strength, 147; and Fanny Brawne, 362; and Mrs. Brawne, 191; and Channel crossing, 75; character of, 63–65; charity of, 267; as enforcing doctors' orders, 335; finances of, 318, 319; and GK, 315, 373–374; and GK and TK in Paris, 95; and GK as dismissed by Abbey, 59; GK blamed by, 319–320, 390, 391; GK disliked by, 196–197, 321, 350, 374; GK on character of, 197; and GK's deposit at Abbey & Cocks, 318; and GK's emigration, 146–147; JK as partner on *Otho the Great,* 65, 260–262, 267, 314, 318; JK left homeless by, 247; and JK's composition habits, 217–218; and JK's death, 390; and JK's epitaph, 389–390; JK's farewell letter from Rome to, 391; as JK's friend, 163; and JK's hemorrhage, 324, 335; and JK's illness, 335; JK's last leavetaking with, 336; JK's letters to, 368; JK's loans from, 247, 318, 319–320, 335; JK's residence with, 196–197, 334; JK's surrogate fraternal bond with, 315, 316; and JK's "The Jealousies," 313; JK's travels to Scotland with, 133, 147, 149, 152, 197, 201; and JK's trip to Italy, 335, 357–358, 362, 390–391; letter to GK about JK's hemorrhage, 343–344; letter to GK about JK's trip to Italy, 351; letter to Haslam, 374; *Narensky,* 65; and "Ode to a Nightingale," 218–219; and Abigail O'Donhague, 64, 390; on John Scott, 91; and Severn, 391; and Snook family, 262; summer rental by, 65, 335; and TK's death, 99, 196; and travel to Scotland, 187, 335, 390; and Wentworth Place, 62–63, 335; and Richard Woodhouse, 70

Brown, James, 64

Brown, John Armitage, 64

Brown, Samuel, *Western Gazetteer,* 237

Brown, Thomas, *The Englishman in Paris,*
    91–92
Brownsville (Old Fort), 205
Brunswick, Duke of, 140
Brunswick Square, 148
Bryant, William Cullen, 144
Buffalo, 195
Buffalo trails, 228
Bull, John, 392–393
Bullitt, Mildred Ann, 405, 406
Bunyan, John, 70–71
Burford Bridge, 4, 100
Burge, Sir James Bland, *Riches,* 101
Burke, Edmund, *Reflections on the Revolu-*
    tion in France, 380
Burns, Robert, 173
Buzzards, 275
Byron, Clara Allegra, 72
Byron, George Gordon, Lord, 3, 68, 70; and
    Allegra, 72; and boxing, 29; *Childe Har-*
    old's Pilgrimage, 28; and Coliseum, 372;
    education of, 49; *Hours of Idleness,* 27;
    and Leigh Hunt, 38; and Leigh Hunt's
    children, 340; and JK and Fanny
    Brawne, 192; and JK and Leigh Hunt,
    66; letter to Thomas Moore, 38; and
    Reynolds, 43; skepticism of, 266
Byronic hero, 28

Cairo, Illinois, 271
Caldwell, Charles, 378
California, 410
Calypso, 220
Campbell, Thomas, *Gertrude of Wyoming,*
    163, 296
Campion, Jane, 6
Canova, Antonio, 382; *Hercules and Lichas,*
    385; *Venere Vincitrice,* 383
Capper, Harry, 241–242, 257
Capper, John, 240
Capper, Mary, 241
Capper, Mrs. Harry, 241
Capper & Haslewood, 240, 241

Carisbrooke Castle, 4, 75, 76
Carlos María Isidro de Borbón, 363
Carlyle, Thomas, 41; *The French Revolu-*
    tion, 380; *Sartor Resartus,* 379–380
Carneal, Thomas, 256
Cartwright, Joseph, 400
Castel, Louis Bertrand, 411
Castlereagh, Lord, 117
Catullus, 366
Cavalier lyric, 33
Cave Hill Cemetery, 403
Cervantes, Miguel de, 162, 317; *Don Quix-*
    ote, 384
Chambers, Benjamin, 199
Chambers, Charlotte, 199
Chambers, Sir William, 159
Chambersburg, 186, 198–200
Champion, 68, 90, 91, 101
Chancery. *See* Court of Chancery
Channing, William Ellery, 402
Chapman, George, 39–40
Charles I, 131
Charles II, 44
Charles III, 367
Charles X, 106
Charles II of Naples, 370
Chatterton, Thomas, 70, 126–127, 130, 265
Chaucer, Geoffrey, 68, 80, 265
Cherokee Nation, 274
Cheshire, 150
Chester, 165
Chestnut Ridge, 204
Chiabrera, Gabriello, 94
Chillicothe, Ohio, 347
Christie, Jonathan Henry, 91
Christ's Hospital, 43
Church of England, 56, 86, 113, 116, 284
Church of St. Mary-le-Bow, 56, 402–403
Church of St. Stephen's, 350
Church of the Trinità dei Monti, 372–373
Cicero, Marcus Tullius, 371
Cincinnati, 175, 183, 206, 238, 250–260, 352
Cincinnati Manufacturing Company, 254

Civil unrest, 116, 117

Clairmont, Claire, 72

Clare, John, *Poems Descriptive of Rural Life and Scenery,* 173

Clark, Charles, 327

Clark, James, 360, 382; first meeting with JK, 372, 373; and JK's death, 388; and JK's diet, 383; and JK's hemorrhaging, 384; opinion of JK, 381; opinion of Severn, 381; and Pomptine marshes, 370; and prognosis of JK, 373, 384–385; and Severn, 387; on tuberculosis as not contagious, 386

Clark, John W., 326

Clark, Molly, 326–327

Clark, William, 327

Clark, William (of Lewis and Clark expedition), 409

Clarke, Charles Cowden, 35, 50, 177, 210; and bearbaiting, 30; and Leigh Hunt, 39; and JK and boxing, 29; and JK at Novellos's, 101; and JK's *Poems* (1817), 65, 67–68; and "On First Looking into Chapman's Homer," 39–40; opinion of Thomas Keats, 44; "Recollections of Keats," 4, 61; and "To Charles Cowden Clarke," 36–38

Clarke, Isabella Jane. *See* Towers, Isabella Jane (née Clarke)

Clarke, James Freeman, 406; and Emerson, 380; and flower from JK's grave, 404; on forests, 237; and Georgiana's age, 123; and GK, 379, 394; on GK, 61; on GK and Abbey, 59; and GK and Georgiana on Ohio River, 226; and GK as successful businessman, 238; and GK's investment in *Henderson,* 303; on GK's love for JK, 403–404; on GK's marriage, 139; on GK's reading, 377, 397; and holograph of JK's "God of the Golden Bow," 398; Philosophical Society of, 378; and Spenser, 397; on stagecoach to Louisville, 347; and Unitarianism, 284–285

Clarke, John, 36, 39; school of, 47–48, 49–51, 60, 119, 240, 249, 316, 377

Clarke, Mary Cowden (née Novello), 61, 210. *See also* Novello, Mary

Cobbett, William, 121, 178–179

Cobbett's Weekly Register, 178

Cock, The, and The Bull (inns), 150

Cockney Pioneers, 117, 146, 163, 227; and Birkbeck-Flower rift, 275–277; Birkbeck's failed preparations for, 276; and conditions on English Prairie, 176–179, 292; and Dickens, 269; disparate religious beliefs of, 283–284; emigration plans of, 117; and Evansville, Indiana, 275–276; and *The Fall of Hyperion,* 221; and Filder, 177; and Fordham, 233; and German settlers at Harmony, 279; and GK, 238; and Harmony, 280; and land sales, 143, 277–278; and profit from land, 118–120; satirization of, 115–116; travel to Philadelphia, 153. *See also* Emigration; English Prairie

Cockney Poets, 56, 67, 115, 144, 145, 193, 314

Cockneys, 44

Cody, Horace, 157

Coffee houses, 239

Coffee Island Swamp, 288

Coffin, Charles, Jr., 154

Coffin, Charles, Sr., 154–155

Coffin, Francis Vergnies, 155

Coffin, Hector, 153–154, 159, 160, 169, 239, 241

Coffin, Mary Caswell (née Cook), 154, 155

Coffin, Tristram, Jr., 154

Cold Bath Fields Prison, 38

Coleridge, Samuel Taylor, 43, 185–186, 284; and America, 115; "Frost at Midnight," 55; and GK, 378; JK's meeting with, 313; "The Nightingale," 218; on reviews of *Endymion,* 314; and "To Charles Cowden Clarke," 37; "To Kosciusko," 165

Coles, Edward, 113

Coles, John, 113

Collins, S. H., 170, 203

Collins, William, *The Poetical Works of William Collins,* 24, 35

Colton, Calvin, *Manual for Emigrants,* 205

Columbus, Christopher, 348

Colvin, Sir Sidney, 5

Combe, George, 378

Comerford, Frederick William, 155

Company of Apothecaries, 25

Conecocheague Creek, 199

Continental Congress, 165, 182

Conyers, John, 154

Conyers, Walter, 154

Cook, Mrs., 78, 84

Cooper, James Fenimore, 145

Cooper, Sir Astley, 188

Corcoran, Peter, 29

Corneille, Pierre, 67

Corn Laws, 116

Cortez, Hernando, 40, 243

Cosby, Fortunatus, Jr., 306, 458

Cotterell, Charles E., 364–365, 366, 368, 369, 371

Cotterell, Miss, 359, 360, 364, 366

Cotton, 228, 240, 352, 354, 400

Courier, 325, 326, 331, 332, 333, 334, 348

Court of Chancery, Kentucky, 256, 355

Court of Chancery, London, 246, 247

Covent Garden Theatre, 31, 126, 267

Coventry, 150

Cove Ridge, 204

Coverly, 253

Cowley, Hannah, *The Belle's Stratagem,* 159

Cox, Jane, 192

Cranch, Christopher Pearse, 411

Croker, John Wilson, 115

Crown Inn, 151, 161

Croydon, Edward, 101–102, 131

Crutcher, Lawrence M., 123

Cutler, Jervis, 352

Cynthia (moon goddess), 100. *See also* Moon goddess

Daniel Dick & Company, 169

Dante, 165, 221; *Divine Comedy,* 149; *Inferno,* 248, 273

Darling, George, 341

Darwin, Charles, 185

Darwin, Erasmus, 185

Day after the Wedding, The, 159

Deer Creek, 250

Delaware Bay, 3, 165

Delaware River, 165, 167–168, 174

De Wint, Peter, 101

Dial, 379, 398

Dickens, Charles, 2, 62, 155–156, 158; *American Notes,* 271; *Martin Chuzzlewit,* 3, 268–269, 270–271

Dido, 220

Dilke, Charles Wentworth, 87, 220; and America, 114–115; change in residence of, 262; as congenial spirit to GK, 62; father of, 362; and GK, 296, 391, 395; and GK's finances, 318, 320; GK's letters to, 240; as JK's friend, 163; JK's residence near, 311; and marriage, 62, 64, 80, 84, 215, 362; personality of, 62, 63; profession of, 62; and support for GK's emigration plans, 297

Dilke, Charley, 63

Dilke, Maria, 64, 84, 87, 220; Georgiana's letters to, 243; GK's letter to, 391; and GK's return to London, 316; on JK's return from Scotland, 188; personality of, 62–63

Dodgson, Joseph, 157

Don Quixote, 162–163, 197

Drake, Daniel, 354

Drew family, 157

Drewe, Eliza Powell, 68, 69, 86

Drury, Alice, 257

Drury, Edward Bell, 173

Drury, Helen, 257

Drury, Isabella, 437

Drury, John, Sr., 173

Drury, Mary. *See* Tallant, Mary Drury

Drury, Michael, 168, 207, 242, 255; background of, 143, 173–174; business of, 174; and GK, 179; and GK and Georgiana Keats, 175; GK's visit to, 173; mail for, 154; residence at 14 South Front Street, 174

Drury, Sarah, 436

Drury, Susan, 437

Drury Lane Theatre, 31, 65, 216, 267, 318

Drury & Tallant, 174, 175, 241

Dry Ridge, 204

Dyer, John, 208

Eagle Works foundry, 301

East India Company, 64

Edgeworth, Maria, 384

Edinburgh Review, 116, 145

Edmonds, Isaac, 257

Edmonds, John, 257, 445

Edmonson, Francis H., 256–257

Edmonton, 20, 22, 25, 49

Edward, Duke of Kent and Strathearn, 322–323

Eldridge, Jonathan, 326, 328, 331–332, 333

Elizabeth I, 382

Elton, Isaac Marmaduke, 383

Embargo Act of 1807, 209

Emerson, Ralph Waldo, 144, 284, 380, 398; "The American Scholar," 379; "Nature," 3, 380

Emigration, 2; and Allegheny Mountains, 186; and Birkbeck, 117; and Cincinnati, 253–254; and conditions in America, 176–184; enthusiasm for, 112–119; and Evansville, 275–276; and Lawrence, 117; money needed for, 118; and port cities, 181. *See also* Cockney Pioneers; Keats, George

Englishman's Palace, 396–397, 402, 406, 408, 409, 411

English Prairie, 111, 113, 157, 169, 227, 271; and Audubon, 286; and Richard Birkbeck, 249; Birkbeck on, 113; Cobbett vs.

Birkbeck on life on, 121; conditions on, 176–179, 292; depictions of, 269–270; and desire for freedom, 116–117; and Fordham, 295–296; and GK, 238; GK's account of, 163; GK's travel to, 287–297; and Harmony, 279, 280; and Hulme, 207; life of inhabitants on, 295–297; and Maidlow, 278; and Native Americans, 293; and profit from land, 118–119; religious beliefs of settlers in, 283–284; sale of land limited on, 143; satirization of, 115. *See also* American Western Country; Cockney Pioneers

Era of Good Feelings, 333

Eton, 49

Evans, Estwick, 208; *A Pedestrious Tour,* 205

Evans, George, 254

Evans, Oliver, 254–255, 258, 444

Evansville, Indiana, 275, 278, 286, 288, 291, 410

Evansville Gas Company, 410

Ewing, Urban Epinitis, 399

Ewing, William, 389

Examiner, 19, 38, 43, 248

Exchange Coffee House, 345

Farmers, 113, 235–236, 237, 238, 278

Farnsworth, Oliver, 252, 254

Fatland Ford, 185, 186

Faux, William, 289, 291, 293; and Birkbeck, 117; and law and justice, 286–287; and life on English Prairie, 295; and prairie fires, 287; and servants, 290; and wildlife, 286

Fearon, Henry Bradshaw, 178, 180, 181, 200, 201, 204, 354, 375; on backwoodsmen, 294; and Bakewell, 208–209; on farmers, 235; on Louisville, 259; on Louisville taverns, 345, 346; and merchants, 175; and numbers of emigrants, 186; *Sketches of America,* 115; and slavery, 227–228; visit to Cincinnati, 251–252

Ferdinand I of the Kingdom of the Two Sicilies, 364, 367–368
Ferdinand VII of Spain, 363
Fiesole, 4
Fifeshire, Scotland, 123–124
Filder, J., 177
Filson, John, 253
First Transcontinental Railroad, 410
First Unitarian Church, Louisville, 402, 403, 406
First Unitarian Church, Philadelphia, 185
Fives Court, 28
Flagstaff Fort, 332
Flatboats, 229–230, 256, 272
Flaubert, Gustave, 266
Fletcher, John, 1; *The Bloody Brother,* 380
Florida, 243
Flower, Eliza Julia Andrews, 199, 276–277
Flower, George, 3, 180, 278; and Albion, 295; and Andrews, 277; and Atlantic crossing, 160; and Birkbeck, 113, 275–277; and Chambersburg, 199; emigration plans of, 117, 118; *Errors of Emigrants,* 176; and *The Fall of Hyperion,* 221; on farmers, 236; and Filder, 177; and Fordham, 233, 285; and frontier life, 176; and GK, 279; and Harmony, 280; and Indiana forest, 291; and land sale restrictions, 119; as leading emigrants, 120; and leaving Liverpool, 160; marriage of, 199, 277; on Philadelphia, 168; and prosperity, 254; travel to Philadelphia, 153
Flower, Jane Dawson, 277
Flower, Richard, 276–277, 280, 282, 284
Forbes, John, 200
Fordham, Elias Pym, 113, 180, 268; and Audubon, 285–286; and backwoodsmen, 294; on boatmen, 233; and life on English Prairie, 295–296; and Native Americans, 293; and Village Prairie cabin, 295; on Washington Hall in Louisville, 346
Forstall, Edmond Jean, 240
Fort Billings, 165

Fort Duquesne, 205
Fort Greenville, 253
Fort Jefferson, 253
Fort Pitt, 205, 206
Fort St. Clair, 253
Fort Washington, 253
Foster, Charles, 255
Foster, Sir Augustus, 167
Foster, William R., 255
Foster & Company, 255
Fountain Inn, 201
Fox River, 283
Frampton & Sons, 31
France, 59, 75; Birkbeck and Flower in, 113; GK and TK in, 90–95
Franklin, Benjamin, 143, 145, 165, 170
Franklin Gazette, 168, 176, 206
French and Indian War, 183, 200, 205, 206, 237
French neoclassical school, 67
French Revolution, 2, 67, 92, 93, 116, 117, 274
Frith, 62
Frogley, Mary, 26, 33
Fuller, Ellen Kilshaw, 401–402
Fuller, Margaret, 379, 401
Fulton-Street Wharf, 332
Fuseli, Henry, 377

Galen, 134
Gallipolis (Alexandria), 237–238
Garskill, Augustus Thomas, 123
Garton, Elizabeth, 113
Gay rights, 411
George III, 123, 159, 165, 323, 332, 367
George IV, 323, 332. *See also* Prince Regent
George Keats & Company, 305, 350–351, 392, 394, 400
Georgetown, 227
Gibson, John, *Mars Restrained by Cupid,* 382
Gifford, William, 115–116
Gilded Age, 410

Girardon, François, 93
Gisborne, Maria Reveley, 339
Gittings, Robert, 5, 53, 61
Glassware, 208–210
Goadby, James, 45–46
Goddard, Francis E., 458
Godwin, William, 72, 377
Goldsmith, Oliver, *History of Greece,* 377
Goose Island, 272
Gordon, Alexander, 240, 438
Gordon, Ann (née Bakewell), 186, 240, 438
Gordon, William, 240
Gordon, Forstall, & Company, 240
Goswell Street, Islington, 25
Grafty, Frances, 47
Gray, Thomas, "Ode on a Distant Prospect of Eton College," 48
Great Appalachian Valley, 181, 187, 198, 199
Great Cumberland Gap, 347
Great Miami River, 253
Great National Road (United States Road), 347
Great Ouse River, 150
Great Wabash River, 288
Great Western Road, 187
Great Wilderness Road, 274, 347
Green, H. G., 85, 86
Green, Joseph Henry, 313
Griffin, Frederick, 122
Griffin, Henry, 122
Griffin, Mary (née Carr), 122
Griffin, Robert, 122
Grundy, Samuel, 326
Gwathmey, Alfred, 345, 409
Gwathmey, George Clark, 409
Gwathmey, George Keats, 409
Gwathmey, Georgiana Emily ("Georgy"; née Keats), 315, 392, 398; bilious fever of, 271; birth of, 271, 307, 398; illness of, 331, 344; and JK, 351; marriage of, 345, 409; and parents, 327
Gwathmey, John, 345

Hall, James, 230, 231
Hall, William, 279–280, 283, 287
Hammond, Thomas, 12, 21, 22, 36, 337
Hammond, Stocker & Joseph Keats, 53
Hampstead Heath, 41, 58, 59, 61, 65. *See also* Well Walk; Wentworth Place
Hanover Square, 46
Harlan Museum Company, 395–396
Harlequin and Don Quixote, 330
Harman family, 157
Harmony, Indiana, 279–285, 290
Harmony, Pennsylvania, 280
Harmony Hall, 345
Harris, William Tell, 348; and Allegheny forests, 200; and food for travelers, 294; and gouging, 258; and Harmony, 282; and Indian corn, 235; and Louisville, 273; and Monongahela River, 205; and New Lancaster, 348; on taverns, 345–346; and travel difficulties, 204
Harrow, 49
Hart, John de, 316
Hart, Samuel, 316
Haslam, William, 147, 163, 267, 321; and Brown, 374; and GK, 391; GK's borrowing from, 330; and JK's letters, 240; JK's loss of contact with, 315; and JK's trip to Italy, 359–360; Keats brothers' meeting with, 31; loss of father, 245; and news of TK's death, 243
Haslewood, William, 240
Haydon, Benjamin: and Bo Peep, 81; *Christ's Entry into Jerusalem,* 96; and Goldsmith, 377; and Hunt, 70, 80, 96; and JK, 52, 71; JK's early relationship with, 41–43; JK's letters to, 74, 79, 128; JK's loan to, 247, 327; and JK's *Poems* (1817), 70; letters from JK, 79; and Martello Towers, 81; requested sketches by, 78; and Shelley, 96; and TK, 187
Haynes, Jean, 53
Hazlitt, William, 28, 42, 126–127, 130, 170, 284, 370

Henderson, 303

Henderson, Richard, 274

Henderson, Kentucky. *See* Red Banks
(Henderson, Ky.)

Henderson Company, 303

Henry I, 76

Henry IV, king of France, 93

Henshaw, Samuel, 151

Herrick, Robert, 33

Hessey, James Augustus, 69–70, 88, 173

Hettick, Mrs., 199

Heywood, John Healy, 406

Hodgkinson, Cadman, 59–61, 62, 311, 425

Hodgkinson, Cadman, Jr., 60, 425

Hodgkinson, Harry, 60, 425

Hodgkinson, Sampson, 60, 425

Hodgkinson, Susan, 60, 425

Holmes, Edward, 29, 188, 217

Homer, 39–40

Hood, Thomas, 85–86

Hornbrook, Saunders, 277, 278

Hornbrook, Saunders, Jr., 277–278

Horsemonger Lane Prison. *See* Surrey Gaol

Hôtel Mayence, 91, 93

Howitt, Emanuel, 158, 185, 201–202, 258

Hulme, Thomas, 207, 229, 236, 274, 280–
281, 292, 294, 296

Humoral theory, 134

Hunt, Isaac, 170

Hunt, John, 38

Hunt, John Horatio, 38

Hunt, Leigh, 4, 52, 77, 248, 367; and aestheticism, 39; and America, 144; children
of, 340; "Christmas and Other Old National Merry-Makings Considered," 101;
and Cockney School of Poetry, 56, 66–67;
The Descent of Liberty, 38; and family in
America, 170–171; *Foliage,* 66–67; and
"Great spirits now on earth are sojourning," 43; and Benjamin Haydon, 42, 43,
70, 80, 96; and JK in Kentish Town, 335;
JK's disillusionment with, 96; JK's early
relationship with, 39–42, 44; and JK's

early reputation, 216; and JK's hemorrhage, 339, 340–341; and JK's *Hyperion,*
183; JK's opinion of, 79–80; and JK's trip
to Italy, 356–357; as King of the Cockneys, 39, 41, 42, 66, 70, 96; Lockhart's attacks on, 66, 67; mother of, 170, 183; and
Native Americans, 183; on Nature, 44;
and Novellos, 101; and "On First Looking into Chapman's Homer," 40–41; and
Peterloo Massacre, 263; and Philadelphia,
183; "The Political Examiner," 38, 263; in
prison, 38–39; published memories of JK,
4; and Joseph Severn, 357; and Shelley,
80, 96; and Shelley circle, 72; and Shelley-
JK meeting, 71; and Stephen Shewell,
144; and *Sleep and Poetry,* 54; "Sonnet to
Hampstead," 41, 94; *Story of Rimini,* 65,
248; "To Kosciusko," 165–166; and "To
Solitude," 19; and Vale of Health, 41,
216; Wilson's attacks on, 66; "Young Poets," 43–44, 67

Hunt, Marianne (née Kent), 38, 340, 341

Hunt, Mary Florimel, 38

Hunt, Percy Bysshe Shelley, 96

Hunt, Stephen (brother), 170–171

Hunt, Stephen (uncle), 171

Hunt, Swinburne Percy, 41

Hunt, Thornton Leigh, 38, 341

Hyacinth, 1

Hyde Park, Long Island, 178

Illinois, 119, 120, 169, 293; and Birkbeck,
112, 113, 117; conditions in, 178–179; de-
scriptions of, 118; and desire for freedom,
116; and *The Fall of Hyperion,* 221; and
fighting and gouging, 258; Flower on,
176; as free state, 120; and GK, 111; and
Great Wabash River, 288; population of,
393; satirization of, 116, 269–270. *See also*
English Prairie

Imlay, Gilbert, 235

Independence Day (Fourth of July), 183,
352

Indiana, 3, 118, 227, 278, 286, 291, 393–394

Indian corn, 235–236

Indian Queen Tavern, Louisville, 298, 345

Indian Summer, 226, 275, 287

Indian trails, 228. *See also* Red Banks Trail

Ingle, John, Jr., 278, 289, 291

Ingle, John, Sr., 290

Ingle, Mrs. John, 289

Inns, 150, 180, 199, 200–203, 259

Irish Sea, 153, 159, 161

Iroquois, 228

Irving, Washington, 299; "Rip Van Winkle," 160; "The Voyage," 160

Isle of Wight, 58, 73–79, 80, 84, 152, 215, 247, 250, 260

Jackson, Andrew, 184, 243, 307, 400

Jackson, John, 29

Jacksonian Democracy, 184, 410

Jacob, Richard, 344, 407

James Monroe, 325, 332–333

Jefferson, Thomas, 113, 119, 209

Jefferson County Courthouse, 306, 354, 395

Jeffersonville, Indiana, 272, 273, 316

Jeffery, Mary Ann, 103–106, 134, 135–136, 217, 250. *See also* Prowse, I. S.

Jeffery, Mrs. Sarah, 103, 133, 135, 136

Jeffery, Sarah Frances (Fanny), 103–106, 134, 135, 136, 357

Jeffrey, Francis, 116, 343

Jeffrey, John, 406, 408–410

Jennings, Alice (Whalley), 21, 46, 47, 49, 51, 52, 246

Jennings, Frances, 246. *See also* Keats, Frances Jennings

Jennings, John, 20, 44, 45, 46, 47, 49, 51, 246

Jennings, Margaret, 246–247, 307

Jennings, Margaret Alice, 246

Jennings, Mary Ann, 246

Jennings, Midgley John, 47–48, 49, 246, 348

Jennings, Midgley John, Jr., 246

Jennings, Thomas, 47–48, 49, 348

Jesus Christ, 219, 220, 222, 224

John James Audubon & Company, 302

John Schneider & Company, 52

Johnson, Charles Britten, 179

John Warder & Sons, 241

Jones, Isabella, 82, 84, 137, 192

Jones, T. M., 154

Jones, William, 327

Jones, William D., 256

Judd's Hotel, 169

Judd Street, 139, 140

Juniata River, 204

Juniata Valley, 204

Kauffman, C. H., *Dictionary,* 60

Kean, Edmund, 101, 106, 126, 261–262, 267

Keats, Alice Ann, 398

Keats, Alice Lee, 5, 376

Keats, Clarence George, 123, 398, 407, 410

Keats, Edward, 46

Keats, Elizabeth, 48, 322

Keats, Ella, 398

Keats, Emma Frances. *See* Speed, Emma Frances (née Keats)

Keats, Frances Jennings (mother), 48–49; Abbey on, 20; character of, 46; death of, 36, 49, 51, 52; as extravagant, 47; JK as favorite of, 33; marriage to Rawlings, 48; marriage to Thomas Keats, 46; and tuberculosis, 49, 348

Keats, Frances Mary (Fanny), 56; and Abbey, 4, 12, 21, 23, 24, 25; and Abbey family, 23, 148, 247, 328; Adami on, 6; birth of, 45, 46, 47; and Fanny Brawne, 393; and Collins, 35; and *Endymion,* 100; and GK, 62; GK as neglectful of, 328–329; and GK's emigration, 163, 391–392, 393; GK's remoteness from, 239; GK's strained communication with, 23–24; GK's visit with, 328; and GK's wedding, 141, 148; inheritance of, 246; and JK, 12, 23, 33, 73, 134, 239; and JK as child, 21–

Keats, Frances Mary (Fanny) *(continued)*
22; JK as responsible for, 103, 163; and JK
on *Endymion,* 71; and JK's death, 390; in
JK's journal-letter to GK and Georgiana,
250; and JK's finances, 247; and JK's letters to GK, 249; JK's reassurance about
health to, 334; JK's regret leaving, 341;
and JK's Scotland travels, 147–148; and
Georgiana Keats, 141, 148, 393; letters
from GK, 239, 327, 328, 329–330, 348–
349; letters from JK, 59, 239, 305; letters
to JK, 389; marriage of, 393; and mother's
death, 49; and portrait gems, 210; residence at Pindars, 23; residence with Alice
Jennings, 49; schooling of, 24–25; and
TK, 23, 92, 195, 317
Keats, George: and bearbaiting, 30; and billiards, 28; biographies of, 5, 6–7; birth of,
46; and boxing matches, 28; boyhood of,
28, 30; Christ Church, Louisville, 284;
Church of England, 284; and concerts at
Vauxhall Gardens, 31; death of, 176, 401,
403, 405, 406; education at Clarke's
school, 47–48, 49–51; epitaph of, 403; illness of, 323, 460; "The Influence of Tea
upon the *Ladies,*" 193; last will of, 402; library and reading, 376–377, 397; and
marriage, 33, 171–172; obituary of, 403;
"On Woman," 171–172, 193; and sports,
50; and theater, 31; and tuberculosis, 330,
402; twenty-first birthday of, 107, 127,
412; twenty-fourth birthday of, 390; wedding of, 124, 136, 140–141, 146
—Career: Abbey's tea business, 12, 20, 21,
56–57, 59, 61, 62, 298; Bank of Kentucky,
379–380; business letter at 62 Bread
Street, 61–62; fitness for farm labor, 120;
George Keats & Company, 392; gristmill,
4, 258, 392, 394; Harlan Museum Company, 395–396; *Henderson,* 303; Kentucky
Historical Society, 395; lawsuits by, 395;
letter of introduction to Birkbeck, 143;

Lexington and Ohio Railroad Company,
395; as linendraper, 144; in Louisville, 1,
305, 373–381; Louisville College, 395;
Louisville Lyceum, 395; Louisville's City
Council, 395; as novice at business, 238;
Ohio River Bridge Commission, 395;
Panic of 1837, 400; preparation for frontier life, 175–176; rejection of English
Prairie life, 296–297; sawmill, 4, 258, 305,
315, 317, 344, 350–351, 392, 394, 395; success of, 238, 391–392; Taylor's letters of
introduction, 142–143, 169; Wilkinson's
plan, 62, 78, 80
—Character, 143, 330, 338; ambitions, 80,
111, 210–211; Burden of Society, 1, 138,
139; common sense, 162; feelings of age,
327–328; friends, 12, 25, 106, 169; generous, 162; Man of Power, 139, 152, 193;
methodical, 77; need for occupation, 111;
optimistic, 143; people pleaser, 12; persevering, 121; poetry in soul of, 225; positive outlook, 121; promise of prosperity,
238; protective, 50; puns, 65, 172, 350,
393; relationships, 16; reputation in Kentucky, 162–163; reserve, 375; satirist, 193;
self-image as gentleman vs. merchant, 60;
at thirty-one, 393
—Finances, 405; and Audubon, 296, 297–
298, 302, 303, 304, 305, 306, 307–308; deposit for brothers at Abbey & Cocks, 146,
317–318; economy, 353; estate of, 405,
458; fortune of, 393, 394; gambling, 80;
inheritance, 61, 117, 118, 124, 146, 246;
inheritance from TK's estate, 241, 317;
investment plans, 238, 288; investments,
279, 297–298, 303, 304; JK's delayed
money draft, 308, 317; land purchases,
120–121, 143, 277; loan from William
Haslam, 330; money taken back to
America, 318, 320, 333, 334, 350; return
to England, 317–321, 330; ruin of, 401,
404, 407; squaring accounts and paying

debts, 146; steamboat investment, 351,
352, 353–354, 355, 373; Wilkinson's plan,
78, 80
—Ideas and opinions of: American democracy, 184–185, 377–378; American Transcendentalism, 379; Birkbeck's *Letters
from Illinois,* 163; Edmund Burke, 380;
business, 377–378; Carlyle, 379–380;
Coleridge, 378; commerce in Pittsburgh,
207; commercial capitalism, 162; Don
Quixote, 162–163; egocentrism of Americans, 375; Ralph Waldo Emerson, 380;
government, 377–378; greed, 377; Andrew Jackson, 184; Milton, 208, 398; philosophical reflection, 379; Philosophical
Society, 378; Pittsburgh's appearance,
208; Shakespeare, 395; shipwrecked
among Americans, 321; slavery, 4, 169,
399; sublimity, 15–16; Unitarianism, 284–
285; voting rights, 184
—Letters: to Charles Armitage Brown, 373,
374; concerning arrival in America, 171;
and delayed remittance from Abbey,
238–239, 241; to Charles Wentworth
Dilke, 240; to Charles Wentworth and
Maria Dilke, 62; to Jeffery sisters, 104;
from JK, 115, 125, 133–134, 141, 189,
192, 196, 198, 211, 216, 220, 240–241,
242–245, 247–250, 262, 264, 297, 307, 316,
411–412; to JK, 90, 276, 277, 297, 304,
343, 350, 351, 353–354, 355; to Fanny
Keats, 239, 327, 328, 329–330, 348–349;
from Louisville, 240; and private merchant shipping companies, 239; to Ann
Amelia Wylie, 333
—Relationships: Richard Abbey, 12, 20–21,
34, 40, 51, 52–53, 61, 107, 124, 146, 320,
328, 330; Richard Atkinson, 394; John
James Audubon, 196, 279, 286, 288, 296,
302, 307, 321; Benjamin Bailey, 86;
Thomas Woodhouse Bakewell, 186, 240,
258, 300, 307, 401; William Gifford

Bakewell, 186, 394, 401; Bakewell family,
321; Anna Hazard Barker, 404; Benjamin Bentley, 58; Fanny Brawne, 191, 315;
Charles Briggs, 240, 316; Charles Armitage Brown, 59, 64, 65, 196–197, 315, 319–
320, 321, 350, 373–374, 390, 391; John
Bull, 392–393; Charles Cowden Clarke,
36; James Freeman Clarke, 285, 378, 379;
Charles Wentworth Dilke, 62, 80, 115,
163, 240, 296, 391, 395; Maria Dilke, 62–
63; Michael Drury, 143, 173, 179; George
Flower, 113, 279; Mary Frogley, 26; William Haslam, 31, 391; Cadman Hodgkinson, 59–60; Mary Ann Jeffery, 103–
106, 134, 136; Sarah Frances Jeffery,
103–106, 134, 136; John Jeffrey, 406;
Fanny Keats, 23–24, 62, 148, 163, 239,
328–329, 391–392, 393; Frances Jennings
Keats, 14, 20–21, 46, 49, 51; Georgiana
Keats, 31, 32, 33, 103, 105, 107, 124, 133–
134, 136, 140–141, 146, 171; Georgiana
Emily Keats, 315, 327, 344; Rose Keats,
398; Thomas Keats, 14, 20–21, 44; David
Prentice, 258; Charlotte Cox Reynolds,
86, 121–122; John Hamilton Reynolds,
30, 85; Marianne Reynolds, 86; James
Rice, 97; John Scott, 91; Joseph Severn,
55, 338, 374, 391; Daniel Smith, 394;
Mary Drury Tallant, 174–175; John Taylor, 142–143, 173, 379, 391; TK, 95–96,
128, 163, 189, 195, 196, 243–244, 344, 350;
Warwick Hele Tonkin, Jr., 106; Ann
Amelia Wylie, 121, 122, 330, 333
—Relationship *with John Keats:* GK and
JK's annotations to Spenser, 397; GK as
distant but sympathetic to JK, 17, 163–
164; GK as distant in America, 195; GK
as JK's anchor, 14; GK as unheard by JK,
218; and GK's knowledge of TK's death,
243–244; GK's planned memoir of JK, 4,
391; GK's sadness over JK, 349–350;
GK's separation from JK, 152; GK's

Keats, George *(continued)*
  worry over JK, 163–164; and JK and
  Fanny Brawne, 193–194; JK and GK's
  social thought, 14, 20, 139; JK and GK's
  spiritual life, 403; and JK and Lockhart,
  216–217; and JK and Olliers, 69; JK as
  altered after emigration of GK, 314–315;
  JK as chastising GK, 210–211; JK as
  cheered by GK, 134; JK as estranged
  from GK, 316, 349; JK as reading Shakespeare with GK, 196, 198; JK as worshipped by GK, 36; and JK in Italy, 368;
  JK needed by GK, 311, 312, 315; JK's
  childhood quarrels with GK, 50; JK's
  communication of spirit with GK, 196,
  297; JK's complaints to Brown about GK,
  373–374; and JK's deal with Taylor &
  Hessey, 70; and JK's "Dear Reynolds, as
  last night I lay in bed," 164; and JK's
  death, 381, 390; JK's distance from GK,
  247; and JK's emotions, 26; and JK's
  Endymion, 348–349; and JK's finances,
  318–321; and JK's friends, 163; and JK's
  genius, 163; and JK's grave, 404; JK's
  heart as closed to GK, 315–316; and JK's
  hemorrhage, 343–344; and JK's "Hither,
  hither, love" manuscript, 84; JK's imagined reunion with GK, 161; and JK's
  itinerary, 74; JK's loss of GK, 138; and
  JK's melancholy, 51, 188, 368; and JK's
  moods, 12; and JK's pain of separation from
  GK, 152; and JK's *Poems* (1817), 68, 69;
  and JK's poems to GK, 2, 77; and JK's
  portrait of Shakespeare, 79; and JK's reputation, 398; and JK's *Sleep and Poetry,*
  54; and JK's "Stay, ruby breasted warbler,
  stay," 27; and JK's "'Tis the 'witching
  time of night'" ("Child, I see thee!"), 145;
  and JK's "To My Brothers," 55; and JK's
  travels to compose, 71; JK's travel to Liverpool with GK, 147, 148–151; and JK's
  trip to Italy, 362; and JK's trip to Rome,
  374; JK's warnings about America to

  GK, 237, 238; and Severn's miniature of
  JK, 1, 337
—Residences, 139; Cheapside, 44, 52; Englishman's Palace, 394, 396–397; home
  above Ohio River falls, 1, 392, 396; honeymoon suite at Judd Street, 139; Louisville, 79, 241; Pancras Lane, 20, 25, 44;
  Red Banks, Kentucky, 279, 298; The
  Strand, Teignmouth, 103; Well Walk, 58,
  62
—Travels: on *Albion,* 325; in America, 3–4;
  to America, 40; arrival in Philadelphia,
  166–167; by carriage and horses, 180–181;
  to Cincinnati, 251; on *Courier,* 324, 325,
  326–327, 331; to Devonshire, 58, 100, 125,
  126, 127; to Dieppe, 92; and emigration,
  1–4, 111–112, 120, 125, 147; and emigration plans, 115, 118, 120–122, 124, 133–
  134, 136, 139, 297; and emigration record
  by Coffin, 169; to English Prairie, 279,
  287–297; from Evansville to Red Banks,
  278–279; to France, 58; to Harmony, Indiana, 279; to Liverpool, 147, 148–151; to
  Louisville, 273, 333, 334, 347; and luggage, 148–149, 157; and news of land in
  America, 111–112; to Normandy, 58; on
  Ohio River, 225–238, 267–279; to Ohio
  River Valley, 114; to Paris, 58, 87, 90–95;
  to Philadelphia, 152–155, 156, 157, 159,
  160, 162–166; to Pittsburgh, 186, 187,
  198–206; to prairie, 287–288; to Red
  Banks, 279; and Red Banks Trail, 286,
  288, 289, 290; return from Teignmouth,
  112, 117, 119; return to America, 319–
  321, 323, 324–334; return to England,
  308, 315, 325, 349; return to Hampstead,
  95, 315; to Rouen, 93; to Saint-Denis, 93;
  stay in Philadelphia, 166–187; to Teignmouth, 58, 101–107, 126; on *Telegraph,*
  152–155, 156, 157, 159, 160, 162–166; to
  Western Country, 179
Keats, Georgiana Augusta Wylie: and
  American history, 410; and Lucy Audu-

bon, 279, 288, 307; and Audubon family, 279; bilious fever of, 271, 331; bridal trousseau of, 136; British past of, 375–376; character of, 31, 32, 405; and Church of England, 284; Coffin's emigration record of, 169; and culture in Western Country, 268; death of, 410; domestic skills of, 136; dress of, 136, 226; and Englishman's Palace, 406; entertainment in Louisville by, 397; and fashion, 243; father of, 123; and frontier life, 136, 175–176; GK's courtship of, 31, 33; and GK's death, 405, 406; GK's engagement to, 103, 105; GK's marriage with, 107, 171; and honeymoon suite at Judd Street, 139; as illegitimate, 123; and imported carpets, 136; and John Jeffrey, 406, 408–409; and JK and Fanny Brawne, 194; JK and GK linked by, 34, 137; JK needed by, 311, 312; JK's acrostic poem for, 137; JK's attitude toward, 31, 32, 124, 150, 192; and JK's death announcements, 33; JK's early relationship with, 33; JK's imagined reunion with, 161; JK's letters to, 141, 216, 242–245, 247–250, 264, 276, 277, 307, 321, 411–412; and JK's *Poems* (1817), 68; and JK's portrait, 1; and JK's portrait of Shakespeare, 79; JK's sonnet for, 32; JK's teasing of, 406; and JK's "To My Brother George" (verse letter), 33; JK's wedding present to, 137; Alice Lee Keats on, 376; and Fanny Keats, 141, 148; and Georgiana Emily Keats, 327; and Isabel Keats's death, 407; and land purchases from Birkbeck, 277; letter to Maria Dilke, 243; Louisville as unhappy place for, 344, 346; and Amelia Millar's death, 344; obituary of, 405–406; and parties, 397, 406; and physiognomy, 379; pregnancy of, 181, 288; and 3 Romney Street, Westminster, 31; scrapbook of, 27, 33, 122–123; and Henry Stephens, 150; and Mary Drury Tallant, 174–175; and TK's portrait, 1; and Unitarianism, 284; and wedding, 124, 136, 141
—Travels: by carriage and horses, 180–181; to Cincinnati, 251; and emigration, 2, 120, 123, 124, 147; from Evansville to Red Banks, 278–279; with JK to Liverpool, 147, 148–151; by keelboat, 136; to London, 376; to Louisville, 136, 273; and luggage, 148–149, 157; move to Cincinnati, 409; on Ohio River, 136, 225–238, 267–279; to Philadelphia by *Telegraph*, 152–155, 156, 157, 159, 160, 161, 162–166; and Philadelphia stay, 166–187; to Pittsburgh, 186, 187, 198–206; return from England, 393; return to England, 325, 392; by stagecoach, 180; to Western Country, 179

Keats, Georgiana Emily ("Georgy"). *See* Gwathmey, Georgiana Emily ("Georgy"; née Keats)

Keats, Isabel, 398, 406–408

Keats, John: and adolescence, 132; and Adonis, 49, 410; *annus mirabilis* of, 219, 224, 225; audience of, 266, 267; and bear-baiting, 30–31; and billiards, 28; biographical accounts of, 4–6; birth of, 46; and boxing matches, 28–29; and Campion, 6; and C. H. Kauffman's *Dictionary*, 60; copyright of, 358–359; and distance and disease, 138; dress of, 28, 49; education at Clarke's school, 47–48, 49–51; and Greek, 133; international audience of, 343; and Italian, 133; and Kean, 261–262, 267; and Land of the Harpsicols, 101; and leave-taking, 152; miniature painting of, 1; and portrait gems, 210; publishers of, 69–70, 80, 127, 132, 321, 358–359; resemblance to parents, 21; and rhyming, 47; and slang, 97; social status of, 198, 314; and sublimity, 189; and synaesthesia, 412; Tassie signature gem of, 210, 240, 389; twenty-fifth birthday of, 365, 368; twenty-first birthday of, 43; twenty-fourth birthday of, 312; twenty-second

Keats, John (continued)
   birthday of, 97; at twenty-one, 44, 52;
   voice of, 77; and winter of 1819–1820,
   321–322
—Career: ambition to become poet, 52;
   book trade, 146; considerations of options
   for, 215; decision to quit medicine, 41, 52,
   53–54, 61; medical education, 11–12, 20,
   21, 22, 25, 34, 35, 36, 39, 41, 50, 57;
   planned work reviewing for journals,
   311; as taking over Abbey's tea business,
   311–312; United Hospitals of St. Thomas
   and Guy's, 11, 20, 25, 39; vocation of,
   220–222
—Character, 147, 217, 250; childhood temper, 50; defense of weaker persons, 50–51;
   depression, 217–218; despair, 12, 78;
   fears, 79; fighting, 29; friendships, 163,
   197–198, 321; intense relationships, 16;
   loneliness, 2, 73, 76; loss of brothers, 2,
   223–224; loyalty, 50–51; Man of Genius,
   197; melancholy, 11, 13–14, 49, 128, 134,
   138, 188, 218, 311, 368; moods, 338; morbid temperament, 163; parody of self as
   Cockney Poet, 216; reserve, 197, 198;
   skepticism, 266
—Death, 2, 11, 91, 388; announcements of,
   33; apartment sanitized after, 385–386,
   389; autopsy after, 385, 388–389; burial,
   390; burial arrangements, 388; death
   mask, 389; epitaph, 389–390; flower from
   the grave of, 404; funeral, 389; grave, 413
—Finances, 312; Abbey's concerns about,
   34; Charles Armitage Brown's loans to,
   247, 318, 319–320, 335; career plans, 215,
   216; delayed money sent to GK, 308;
   fears of Hunt's situation, 80; GK's deposit
   at Abbey & Cocks, 146, 317–318; and
   GK's finances, 146, 147, 312, 318–321,
   373; Haydon loan, 247; and inheritance,
   216, 246–247; and Italy trip, 320, 342, 350,
   351, 353–354, 355, 359, 374, 381, 385; and
   Otho the Great, 261–262, 267, 314, 318; in

Rome, 385; and John Taylor, 265, 318,
   385; Woodhouse's support, 70, 359
—Ideas and opinions of: afterlife, 358, 386;
   Albany army barracks, 75–76; America,
   143, 242–243; Balboa vs. Cortez, 40, 243;
   beauty, 370; bells, 44; Bible, 219, 386–387;
   Morris Birkbeck, 163, 178; Boiardo, 245;
   Brunswick Square, 139–140; Burden of
   the Mystery, 139; Chamber of Maiden-
   Thought, 132; Christmas holidays, 56;
   Church of England, 56; commerce and
   trade, 34–35, 61; commercialization of
   romance, 139–140; as Count de Cockaigne, 216, 220; and Cynthia, 4; death,
   132, 247, 368; Devonshire, 131; difficulty,
   52; disinterestedness, 220; English writers, 245; escape, 125; experience, 244–245;
   genius vs. material self-interest, 219; Gospel of Matthew, 219; Gospels, 223; gusto,
   370; and human consciousness, 2; human
   identity, 245; Human Nature vs. Men, 74;
   idling vs. wasting time, 219; imagination,
   198; immortality, 244, 386; Jesus Christ,
   219, 220, 224; Jonah, 222; Judd Street,
   140; and Locke, 244; Man of Genius, 222;
   Man of Genius vs. Man of Power, 138,
   219; marriage, 140, 171, 172; mastodons,
   183; meals in Rome, 383, 384; medical
   knowledge, 36; Milton in Devonshire,
   131–132; money, 210; Negative Capability, 62; pain, 245; permanent forms of nature, 14; personal character, 250; plays at
   Drury Lane and Covent Garden, 31;
   pleasure, 245; poetic pride, 265; poets,
   138; present moment, 198; pride, 61;
   Prime Objects, 52; reality, 244; reality as
   proved on pulses, 215, 220; rift among
   Cockney Pioneers, 276, 277; William
   Robertson's History of America, 40; roses,
   1, 370; sacred ties to siblings, 195; saying
   goodbye, 37; selection, 413; self, 138;
   sense of creative power, 13–14; sense of
   identity, 138–139; sentimental tokens, 27;

sexuality, 89; Socrates, 220, 223, 224; sorrow, 244; soul, 244–245, 249; spontaneous overflow of powerful emotion, 15; sports, 50; St. Mary-le-Bow Church, 44; sublimity, 143, 147, 190, 192; suffering, 245; Jeremy Taylor, 87; universal sympathy, 138; Vale of Soul-making, 244–245, 247, 248; Wellington boots, 140; women, 33, 191, 192–193, 337; World as full of Misery, 133
—Illness, 247; after nursing TK, 312–313; after Scotland trip, 187–188; Clark's prognosis, 373, 384–385; convalescence at Leigh Hunt's home, 340; desire for death, 362, 388; doctors' bleeding of, 324, 339, 384; feeling like walking corpse, 356; fever, 335, 364; hemorrhaging, 324, 338–340, 343–344, 364, 384, 386; JK's last will and testament, 342; knowledge of self as dying, 219, 221, 358; and laudanum, 361, 384; and medical diagnosis, 334–335; mercury treatments, 89, 98, 187–188; posthumous life, 388; return from London, 323–324; sore throat, 187, 215, 313, 335; tuberculosis, 188–189, 324, 334; venereal disease, 89, 187, 267
—Letters, 33, 71; and Audubon, 298; to Benjamin Bailey, 112; from Fanny Brawne, 341, 389; to Fanny Brawne, 140, 262, 264, 312, 336–337; to Mrs. Brawne, 366; to Charles Armitage Brown, 362, 368, 391; and delayed remittance from Abbey, 238–239; and Haslam, 240; from Benjamin Haydon, 79, 128; to Benjamin Haydon, 74, 79; to Mary Ann Jeffery, 217, 250; from Fanny Keats, 389; to Fanny Keats, 59, 239, 264, 305; to Georgiana, 276, 277, 321; from GK, 90, 276, 277, 297, 304, 343, 350, 351, 353–354, 355; to GK, 37, 115, 125, 133–134, 189, 192, 196, 198, 211, 220, 240–241, 262, 297, 316; to GK and Georgiana, 141, 191, 216, 242–245, 247–250, 264, 307, 411–412; and private merchant shipping companies, 239; to Jane and Marianne Reynolds, 88; to John Hamilton Reynolds, 101, 125, 126, 134; from Rome, 343; to John Taylor, 124, 265; to TK, 125, 151; as unbearable for JK to read, 384; to Ann Amelia Wylie, 333–334; to Mrs. James Wylie, 123
—Literary forms: allegory, 220, 266; apostrophe, 15; Augustan verse style, 266; ballad meter, 84; blazon, 26; Cavalier lyric, 33; dream vision, 221; ekphrasis, 210; epic, 72, 84, 147; heroic couplets, 37, 262; heroic meter, 84; iambic trimeter, 84; ode, 134; *ottava rima,* 82; Petrarchan sonnet, 32, 55; poetic romance, 18, 72, 147; satire, 140; Shakespearean sonnet, 15, 32, 101; sonnet, 15, 32, 55, 77, 85, 86, 101; verse epistle, 16, 36–37
—Literary relationships: Vittorio Alfieri, 383–384; Jane Austen, 100; Sir James Bland Burge, 101; Lord Byron, 27–28, 192, 266; Miguel de Cervantes, 384; Thomas Chatterton, 126, 130, 265; Geoffrey Chaucer, 265; Samuel Taylor Coleridge, 37, 313; William Collins, 35; Dante, 149, 221; English literary tradition, 265; John Milton, 18, 78, 143, 221, 223, 248, 398; Thomas Moore, 27; Alexander Pope, 150, 262, 266; William Shakespeare, 74, 76–77, 78–79, 83, 85, 89–90, 101, 131, 142, 192, 196, 198, 216, 225, 245, 337, 358; Sir Philip Sidney, 37; Edmund Spenser, 32, 132, 150, 217, 397; Jeremy Taylor, 387; Mary Tighe, 27; transatlantic context, 2; Oscar Wilde, 410–413; wisdom literature, 223; William Wordsworth, 15, 16, 37, 43, 101, 217, 245; Young Poets, 44
—Relationships: Richard Abbey, 4, 12, 21, 22, 34–35, 41, 51, 52, 61, 68, 146, 320, 321; Benjamin Bailey, 87, 138, 163, 215, 244–245, 366; Benjamin Bentley family, 58, 84, 341; Richard Birkbeck, 248–249;

Keats, John (*continued*)

Fanny Brawne, 191–194, 220, 247, 248, 261, 267, 312, 313, 315, 316, 317, 335, 336–337, 341, 356, 357, 358, 362, 365–366, 368; Frances Brawne, 341–342; Sam Brawne, 315; Charles Armitage Brown, 4, 62, 63–65, 75, 133, 147, 149, 163, 191–192, 215, 247, 260–262, 267, 315, 316, 318, 319–320, 335–336, 362, 390–391; James Clark, 372, 373, 381; Charles Cowden Clarke, 30–31, 36–38, 39–40, 65; Charles Cotterell, 366, 368, 369, 371; Miss Cotterell, 364–365; Jane Cox, 192; Peter De Wint, 101; Charles Wentworth Dilke, 63, 163, 311; Charles Wentworth Dilke family, 220; Maria Dilke, 63, 188; Isaac Marmaduke Elton, 383; Frances Grafty, 47; Thomas Hammond, 12, 21, 22, 36, 337; Hart, 316; William Haslam, 31, 163, 240, 245, 315, 359–360; Benjamin Haydon, 41–43, 52, 70, 71, 79, 81, 247; William Hazlitt, 126–127, 130, 370; James Hessey, 70; Cadman Hodgkinson, 60–61; Edward Holmes, 29, 188, 217; John Hunt, 38; Leigh Hunt, 4, 38, 39–42, 43–44, 52, 65–66, 77, 79–80, 96, 216, 339, 340–341, 356–357; Alice Jennings, 14, 27; John Jennings, 14; Isabella Jones, 82, 84, 192; Emily Keats, 351; Fanny Keats, 12, 21–22, 23, 33, 56, 71, 73, 134, 147–148, 163, 239, 247, 250, 334, 341, 390; Frances Jennings Keats, 14, 33, 36, 49, 51; Georgiana Keats, 1, 31, 32, 33, 34, 124, 137, 150, 161, 192, 311, 312, 406; Isabel Keats, 407, 408; Thomas Keats, 14, 21; John Landseer, 101; George Wilson Mackereth, 35; John Martin, 260; Ann Mathew, 26–27, 81; Caroline Mathew, 26–27, 81; George Felton Mathew, 25–26, 68; Mary Amelia Millar, 142; Richard Monckton Milnes, 4–5; Mary Novello, 101; Vincent Novello, 101; Amelia Opie, 101; James Peachey, 120, 249; Jane Reynolds, 85, 86, 192, 316–317; John Hamilton Reynolds, 29, 52, 69, 85, 89, 163, 215, 315; Marianne Reynolds, 192, 316–317; James Rice, 97, 163, 260, 314–315; Henry Crabb Robinson, 101; Solomon Sawrey, 89, 188, 267; John Scott, 91; Joseph Severn, 54–55, 125, 337–338, 359–366, 368, 384, 385, 386–389; Percy Bysshe Shelley, 71–72, 81, 96–97, 114, 341, 389; Horace Smith, 101, 127; Henry Stephens, 35–36, 44, 149–150, 152, 197; John Taylor, 4, 147, 342, 356, 359, 360; Warwick Hele Tonkin, Jr., 106; Charles Wells, 125–126, 194–195, 245–246; John Wolcot, 101; Richard Woodhouse, 70, 359, 360; Charles Gaskell Wylie, 141; Henry Robert Wylie, 141; Mary Ann Keysell Wylie, 141–142

—Relationship *with George Keats,* 1–2; childhood quarrels, 50; communication of spirit with GK, 196, 297; and deal with Taylor & Hessey, 70; and death of JK, 381, 390; estranged from, 315–316, 349; GK as anchor for JK, 14, 15; GK as chastised by JK, 210–211; GK as distant but sympathetic to, 17; GK as distant from, 195, 218; GK as needing JK, 311, 312, 315; GK as reading Shakespeare with, 196, 198; and GK in America, 195, 196, 211, 217, 237, 238, 247, 296, 368; and GK in trade, 144; and GK's affability, 12; and GK's and Georgiana's daughter Emily, 327; and GK's concern for JK, 163–164; and GK's deposit at Abbey & Cocks, 146, 317–318; and GK's emigration, 1, 112, 133–134, 314–315; and GK's financial accounts, 146–147; GK's help for JK's melancholy, 51, 134, 188, 368; and GK's honeymoon suite, 139; and GK's investment with Audubon, 304; and GK's knowledge of TK's death, 243–244; and GK's neglect of Fanny Keats, 328–329; and GK's obituary, 403; GK's opinions of JK, 26, 163, 197; and GK's reading in America, 377; GK's reunion with JK, 161; GK's

sadness over JK, 349–350; and GK's social thought, 14, 20, 139; GK's worship of
JK, 36; and JK and Fanny Brawne, 193–
194; and JK and Lockhart, 216–217; JK
as link between GK and Georgiana, 34;
JK on GK's generosity, 162; JK's concern
about GK's illness, 323; and JK's hemorrhage, 343–344; and JK's "Hither, hither,
love," 84; JK's loss of GK, 138, 152; and
JK's *Poems* (1817), 68; and JK's poems to
GK, 2, 55, 77; and JK's portrait of Shakespeare, 79; and JK's "Sleep and Poetry,"
54; and JK's "'Tis the 'witching time of
night'" ("Child, I see thee!"), 145; and
JK's travels to compose, 71, 74; and JK's
trip to Italy, 362; JK with GK at wedding, 140–141; and Olliers, 69; and
Severn's miniature of GK, 337
—Relationship *with Tom Keats:* JK as adrift
after TK's death, 312; JK as following
TK in death, 358; JK's dejection after
TK's death, 247; JK's loss of TK, 138; TK
and JK's travel to Scotland, 147; TK as
anchor for JK, 14; TK nursed by JK, 133,
188–189, 313, 361; and TK's death, 187,
188, 196, 198, 217, 218, 221, 245, 340;
TK's dying, 189, 191; and TK's estate,
317; TK's illness, 147; TK's love for JK,
19–20; TK's need for care, 11; TK's worsening condition, 95–96, 125, 128, 132;
Charles Wells's love letters to TK, 194–
195, 245–246
—Residences: with Brown at Wentworth
Place, 84–85, 196–197, 215, 312, 324, 334,
335, 341; Cheapside, 44, 52, 58, 148, 402;
Craven Street, Finsbury, 46–47; Dean
Street, 20, 35, 36, 44; Edmonton, 20, 22,
25; London, 19–20; Naples, 355; St.
Thomas Street, 20; Swan & Hoop, 46; Piazza di Spagna, 372, 373; Well Walk, 58,
62, 71, 188; Westminster, 311; Winchester, 312
—Reviews, 70, 100, 265, 266, 314–315, 342–

343, 413; and critics as not mattering, 132;
by Croker, 115; of *Endymion,* 3, 115, 127,
198, 215, 216, 314, 342; and Hunt, 66; and
JK belittled as "Johnny Keats," 100, 216–
217; by Lockhart, 67; of *Poems* (1817), 67–
68, 69, 90
—Travels, 4; across English Channel, 75; to
Ben Nevis, 161; to Bo Peep, 58, 81–84, 89;
and Bourbon Palace, 369–370; and Bowcombe Down, 76; to Box Hill, 4, 100; to
Burford Bridge, 100–101; to Canterbury,
58, 80–81; to Carisbrooke Castle, 75, 76;
and Coliseum, 372; to concerts at Vauxhall Gardens, 31; in Cumberland, 160–
161; at Derwent Water, 161; to Devonshire, 127–128, 131–134; to Dorchester,
362; to Dorking, 99–100; to Fox and
Hounds, 100–101; to Hampstead, 58, 59,
90, 134, 323–324, 341; to Island of Mull,
187; to Isle of Wight, 58, 73–79, 80, 84,
152, 215, 247, 250, 260; to Italy, 4, 334,
335, 342, 350, 351, 353–354, 355, 356–373;
to Kentish Town, 335–336, 338; to Lancaster, 147; to Liverpool, 147, 148–151; to
London, 101; from Margate, 29; to Margate, 11, 12–13, 18, 19, 20, 24, 36, 58, 77,
78, 79, 80, 126, 146–147, 240; on *Maria
Crowther,* 359–366; in Naples, 364–373; to
Newport, 75; to Oxford, 58, 87–90; and
River Mole, 100; to Rome, 370–373; to
Scotland, 89, 125, 133, 147, 149, 152, 187,
189, 197, 201, 215, 313; to Scottish Hebrides, 187; to Shanklin, 76, 77, 261, 262; to
Southampton, 58, 73–74; to St. Catherine's Hill, 76; to Stratford-upon-Avon,
89–90; to Teignmouth, 124–125, 131–134,
195; to Vale of Health, 58; to Well Walk
from Scotland, 188; to West Cowes, 75; to
Winchester, 262–265
—Works: "And what is Love?—It is a doll
dress'd up," 139–140; "Calidore," 18–19,
94; "The Cap and Bells," 313, 336; "Character of C. B.," 63–64, 249; "Chorus of

Keats, John (continued)
Fairies," 249; "The day is gone, and all its sweets are gone!" 356; "A Dream, after Reading Dante's Episode of Paulo and Francesca" ("As Hermes Once took to his Feathers Light"), 248, 249, 398; Endymion, 3, 15, 71, 72, 73, 77, 81–82, 84, 88, 89, 95, 96, 97, 98–99, 100, 101, 115, 126, 127, 132, 187, 198, 215, 216, 265, 266, 314, 342, 348–349, 358, 410; "Epistle to John Hamilton Reynolds," 164; "The Eve of St. Agnes," 265, 343, 355; The Fall of Hyperion, 71, 190, 210, 221–225, 262, 264, 266, 267, 349, 404; "For there's Bishop's Teign," 128–130; "Give me your patience, sister, while I frame," 137, 161; "God of the Golden Bow," 398; "The Gothic looks solemn," 87–88; Great Odes, 2, 218, 220, 221, 224, 245, 313, 356, 404; "Great spirits now on earth are sojourning," 43, 94; "Had I a Man's Fair Form," 94; "Hadst thou liv'd in days of old," 26; "Hither, hither, love," 83–84; "Hush, hush, tread softly," 82, 85, 328; Hyperion, 2, 183, 189–190, 221, 222, 223, 262, 267, 343, 349; "I cry your mercy—pity—love!—aye, love," 220, 336–337; "Imitation of Spenser," 94; "Isabella; or, The Pot of Basil," 61, 82, 130–131, 134, 265, 343; "I stood tip-toe upon a little hill," 71; "The Jealousies," 313, 336; "La Belle Dame sans Merci," 98, 249; Lamia, 262, 265–267, 343, 389, 412–413; Lamia, Isabella, The Eve of St. Agnes, and Other Poems, 342; "O come, dearest Emma!" 33–34; "Ode on a Grecian Urn," 210, 218–219, 224–225; "Ode on Indolence," 216, 218, 219, 220, 266, 356; "Ode on Melancholy," 17, 18, 218; "Ode to a Nightingale," 218–219; "Ode to Psyche," 27, 218, 249; "On a Leander Which Miss Reynolds, My Kind Friend, Gave Me," 210; "On Fame," 398; "On First Looking into Chapman's Homer," 39–41; "On Receiving a Curious Shell, and a Copy of Verses, From the Same Ladies," 27, 94; "On Receiving a Laurel Crown from Leigh Hunt," 66; "On Seeing the Elgin Marbles," 349; "On the Sea," 77; "O Solitude!" ("To Solitude," "Sonnet to Solitude"), 19–20; "O Sorrow," 97–98; Otho the Great, 65, 260–262, 267, 312, 314, 318; Poems (1817), 65, 67–68, 69, 70, 71, 87, 90; Poems (1820), 70; poems to GK, 77; preface to Endymion, 132–133, 140; "Read me a lesson, Muse, and speak it loud," 161; "Sleep and Poetry," 41, 53–54, 57; "Sonnet on Blue," 411, 412–413; "Spenser, a jealous honorer of thine," 85; "Stay, ruby breasted warbler, stay," 27; "Sweet sweet is the greeting of eyes," 161; "There is a joy in footing slow across a silent plain" ("Lines written in the highlands after a visit to Burns's Country"), 152, 350; "There was a naughty boy," 21, 22, 149, 335; "This living hand, now warm and capable," 313–314; "'Tis the 'witching time of night'" ("Child, I see thee!"), 144–145; "To ****," 32–33; "To a Friend Who Sent Me Some Roses" ("To Charles Wells on receiving a bunch of full blown roses"), 94, 126; "To Autumn," 186, 404, 460; "To Charles Cowden Clarke," 36–38; "To Fanny," 134–135, 336; "To G.A.W." ("Nymph of the downward smile, and sidelong glance"), 32–33, 94; "To George Felton Mathew," 16, 18, 25, 54, 56; "To Kosciusko," 165, 166; "To Leigh Hunt, Esq," 65–66; "To Lord Byron," 27–28; "To Mrs. Reynolds's Cat," 86; "To My Brother George" (sonnet), 14–16, 17, 19, 20, 27, 358, 368, 413; "To My Brother George" (verse epistle), 16, 17–18, 27, 33; "To My Brothers" ("Sonnet: Written to His Brother Tom on His Birthday") 55–56, 358; "To One Who

Has Been Long in City Pent," 94; "To Sleep," 249; "To Some Ladies," 27; "What can I do to drive away," 218, 261; "When I have fears that I may cease to be," 413; "Where be ye going, you Devon maid," 130–131; "Why did I laugh to-night?" 247–248; "Written in Disgust of Vulgar Superstition," 56, 94, 403; "Written on the Day that Mr. Leigh Hunt Left Prison," 39

Keats, John Henry, 142, 392, 398, 409–410

Keats, Joseph, 53

Keats, R., 322

Keats, Rosalind, 398

Keats, Rose, 398–399

Keats, Sir Richard Goodwin, 322

Keats, Thomas (father), 44–46, 47; Abbey's opinion of, 20, 35; death of, 21, 46, 48, 49; and horse thief, 45–46; marries Frances Jennings, 46

Keats, Thomas (Joseph's father), 53

Keats, Tom, 16; and bathing machines, 133; birth of, 46; and bloodletting, 134–135; buried at Church of St. Stephen's, 350; and "Calidore," 19; as clerk for Richard Abbey, 56; cuffed at school, 50–51; death of, 2, 4, 196, 198, 219, 221, 245, 380; and death of mother, 49; deaths of parents and grandparents, 14; estate of, 241, 308, 317; finances of, 34; and Leigh Hunt, 41; illness of, 12, 147; imminent death of, 187, 188, 189, 191, 194–195; inheritance of, 246–247; and Fanny Keats, 92; knowl-edge about, 6; letters from JK, 125, 151; letters to Jeffery sisters, 135; loss of, 196, 217; miniature painting of, 1; money re-quests of, 34; notebook of, 94; physique of, 21; plans for travel to Italy, 133; play-fulness of, 12; and Plutarch, 81; poor health of, 58; and John Scott, 91; sensi-tive, trusting nature of, 20; Severn on JK's resemblance to, 339–340; and *Sleep and Poetry,* 54; and "To My Brothers," 55;

and "To Solitude," 19–20; and Towers, 36; and tuberculosis, 4, 11, 13, 34, 348; at Wentworth Place, 84; worsening condi-tion of, 95–96, 125, 128, 132, 133, 134, 138

—Relationships: Richard Abbey, 21, 34, 53, 146; Benjamin Bentley, 58; Bentley fam-ily, 147; GK, 163, 195; GK and death of, 344, 350; and GK's accounts, 146–147; and GK's deposit at Abbey & Cocks, 146, 317–318; and GK's planned marriage and emigration, 133–134; William Haslam, 31; Sarah Jeffery, 357; Jeffery sisters, 103–106; and JK, 11; JK as adrift after death of, 312; JK as following, 358; JK as worshipped by, 36; and JK in Scot-land, 147; JK on death of, 340; as JK's an-chor, 14; JK's dejection after death of, 247; JK's loss of, 138, 218; JK's news of death of, 243–244; JK's nursing of, 188–189, 313, 361; and JK's travels to com-pose, 71; and JK's venereal disease, 89; and Isabella Jones, 192; Fanny Keats, 23, 195; love letters from Charles Wells, 194–195, 245–246

—Residences: Cheapside, 44, 52, 58, 148; Dean Street, 20, 35, 36, 44; with Alice Jennings on Church Street, Edmonton, 49; The Strand, Teignmouth, 103; Well Walk, Hampstead, 58, 62, 188

—Travels: to Canterbury, 58, 80–81; to De-vonshire, 58, 99, 100, 125, 126, 127; to Dieppe, 92; to France, 58; to Hampstead, 95, 134, 135; to Lyon, 34, 53; to Margate, 11, 12–13, 19, 20, 24, 34, 58, 78, 79, 81, 126, 146–147, 240; to Normandy, 58; to Paris, 58, 87, 90–95; to Rouen, 93; to Saint-Denis, 93; to Teignmouth, 58, 101–107, 125, 126, 131–134

Keats & Atkinson, 394

Keats & Company, 53

Keelboatmen, 231–233, 234

Keelboats, 231–233

Kent, Elizabeth, 72

Kent, Mr., 330
Kentucky, 186, 208, 227, 231, 236, 268, 293;
    as Dark and Bloody Ground, 346; and
    fighting and gouging, 258; opportunities
    in, 296; and slavery, 399; state elections in,
    184; work in, 176
Kentucky Gazette, 410
Kentucky Reporter, 348
Keysell, Mary Ann, 31, 141–142
Kinder, Thomas, 209
Kirk, Naomi Joy, 53; "The Life of George
    Keats," 6–7
Kitchen, Andrew and Walter, 326
Kosciusko, Tadeusz, 165–166

Lackington, James, 70
Ladies' Companion, 398
Lamb, Charles, 39, 43, 62, 101
Lambe, William, 339
Lancaster, 173
Land of Cockaigne, 114, 115, 117, 120, 177,
    187, 284
Landreth, Cuthbert, 326
Landseer, John, 101
Launey, Henry A., 326
Laurel Ridge, 204
Lawrence, James, 117, 119
Lazaretto (quarantine station), 165
Leigh, Mary, 86
Leigh, Sarah, 86
Leigh, Thomasine, 86
Letarts Rapids, 237
Lewis, David, 147
Lewis and Clark expedition, 409
Lexington and Ohio Railroad Company,
    395
Liddell family, 157
Limestone (Maysville), Kentucky, 347
Lincoln, Abraham, 278, 402
Lincoln, Nancy, 278
Lincoln, Thomas, 278
Linnaeus, Carl: *General System of Nature,*
    106; Linnaean system, 281

Lisbon, 96, 322
Little Britain, 85
Little Hampton, 87
Little Wabash River, 288
Liverpool, 3, 150–151, 159, 329, 330
Llanos, Frances Mary Keats, 393. *See also*
    Keats, Frances Mary
Llanos y Gutiérrez, Valentín María, 393
Locke, John, 244
Lockhart, John Gibson (Z), 67, 91, 193, 314;
    "On the Cockney School of Poetry," 66,
    91, 198, 216–217; "On the Cockney
    School of Prose Writers," 174
London Company of Girdlers, 4, 53
London Company of Innholders, 45
London Gazette, 332
Long Island, 331, 332
Looking Glass Prairie, 269
Lord Mayor's Day, 47
Louis XII, 373
Louis XIV, 67, 93
Louis XVI, 93
Louisville, 186, 256; appearance of, 344–345;
    and commerce, 206; distance from Pitts-
    burgh, 227; entertainment in, 345; fash-
    ion in, 346; gambling in, 259; gander-
    pulling in, 258–259; gasworks business
    in, 406; GK and Georgiana's life in, 373–
    381; GK settles in, 241; GK's letters from,
    240; leisure in, 259; and Ohio River, 271–
    272; population of, 273; required stop for
    pilot at, 272; sickness in, 271, 344; Wilde's
    visit to, 410, 411–413
Louisville Bathing House, 346
Louisville Daily Journal, 403
Louisville Lyceum, 395
Louisville Public Advertiser, 273, 332, 353
Lowell, Amy, 5
Lowell, James Russell, 144, 379
Luddites, 263
Ludlow, Charlotte, 252–253
Ludlow Station, 253
Lukens, Isaiah, 182

Mack, Andrew, 255

Mackereth, George Wilson, 35

Madison, James, 113

Madoc (Madog ab Owain Gynedd), 348

Maidlow, James, Jr., 278

Mail, 239; and Coffin, 154, 239, 241; and cost of postage, 239; and JK, 248–249; reliability of, 238–239; time lag in, 239, 241; transatlantic, 238–250

Mammoths, 183, 195

Manchester, 263

Manhattan, 209, 332–334

Manifest Destiny, 254, 410

Maple syrup, 290–291

Margate, 11, 12–13, 14, 18, 19, 20, 24, 36, 58, 77, 78, 79, 80, 101, 126, 146–147, 240

Maria Carolina, 367

Maria Crowther, 356, 359, 361, 363

Maria Theresa, 367

Marie Antoinette, 67, 93, 274, 367

Marshall, Bennett, 304

Marshall, Charles H., 393

Martello Towers, 81

Martin, John, 260

Marvell, Andrew, 33

Mary, Queen of Scots, 78

Massinger, Philip, *The Bloody Brother,* 380

Mathew, Ann Felton, 25, 26–27, 81

Mathew, Caroline, 25, 26–27, 81

Mathew, Felton, 25

Mathew, George Felton, 16, 18, 25, 68; "Of Solitude," 25–26; "To a Poetical Friend," 25

Mathew, Mary Strange, 27; *The Garland,* 25

Mathews, Robert, 45–46

Matthews, Henry, 365, 382; *Diary of an Invalid,* 367, 370, 371

McConnellsville, 200, 203

Mechanicsville, 291

Melish, John, 168, 235, 259, 281, 399

Mendoza, Daniel, 29, 30

Mercer River, 165

Merchants, 60–61, 114, 207–208, 346

Merchant's Coffee House, Philadelphia, 239

Merchant Taylors' School, 60

Mercury, 89, 98, 187–188, 191

Miami River. *See* Great Miami River

Millar, Amelia, 31, 344

Millar, Mary Amelia, 31, 142

Mill Creek, 250, 253, 254

Mills family, 157

Milnes, Richard Monckton, 4–5; *Life, Letters, and Literary Remains of John Keats,* 5, 376

Milton, John, 63, 70, 77, 78, 143, 197, 221; *Defence of the People of England,* 131–132; and Devonshire, 131–131; and JK's *Hyperion,* 189–191; JK's notes on, 398; "L'Allegro," 18; *Paradise Lost,* 189, 190, 191, 208, 223, 361, 398; and philosophy, 248; and Pittsburgh, 208; portrait gems of, 210; *Reason of Church Government,* 265

Minshull, William, 425

Misses Caley and Tuckeys' Boarding Academy, 24–25

Mississippi, 394

Mississippi River, 271, 275, 352

Missouri, 177, 394

Mitchell, Eliza Jane Squarey Periman, 106

Mitchell, Thomas, 106

Molière, 67

Molsom, John, 326

Monkeys, 243, 249

Monongahela Bridge, 206

Monongahela River, 205, 206, 208, 209, 280

Monroe, James, 184, 307, 333

Monroe Doctrine, 333

Monte Pincio, 382, 383

Montreal, 122

Moon goddess, 14–15, 71, 100

Moore, James Francis, 273

Moore, Thomas, 38, 68; "Lines Written on Leaving Philadelphia," 185; "The Wreath and the Chain," 27

Motion, Andrew, 5–6

Murray, John, 70
Muskingum River, 347

Naples, 364, 366–370
Napoleon I, 2, 38, 67, 93, 383
Napoleonic Wars, 1, 101, 151
Natchez, Mississippi, 228, 351, 352, 354, 375
National Advocate, 332
Native Americans, 170–171, 204, 221, 226, 228, 258, 286, 410; and Audubon, 299; and Big Bone Valley, 183; and Cincinnati, 253–254; displacement of, 234; and Fearon, 294; and Illinois Territory, 293; and Kentucky, 346, 347; and Northwest Territory, 183; and Ohio River, 225; and Pittsburgh, 206–207; and prairie fires, 287; tensions between settlers and, 293; tribes of, 234
Neoclassicism, 44. *See also* French neoclassical school
New Brunswick, 331
Newcastle, 165
New Cottage farm, 52
Newfoundland, 125
Newfoundland Fishery (inn), 125
New Harmony, Indiana, 282
New Lancaster, Ohio, 347–348
New Monthly Magazine and Universal Register, 174, 342, 343
New Orleans, 240, 300, 352
Newport army barracks, 253
Newton, Sir Isaac, 411
New York, 170, 324–326, 333, 392. *See also* Manhattan
New York Evening Post, 176
New-York Gazette and General Advertiser, 331
New York Harbor, 331, 332
New York Literary Journal, 343
Northamptonshire, 150
North Mountain, 198, 200

North Ridge, 204
Northwest Territory, 293
Norwich Courier, 343
Nova Scotia, 125
Novello, Mary, 101. *See also* Clarke, Mary Cowden (née Novello)
Novello, Vincent, 101
Nuttall, Sarah and William, 157

O'Callaghan, Donat, 82
Ocean travel, 155–160, 164, 165
O'Donhague, Abigail, 64, 390
Odysseus, 40, 220
Ohio, 208, 227, 234–235, 272, 293, 347, 394
Ohio Canal Company, 273
Ohio Insurance Company, 256–257
Ohio River, 3, 175, 205, 225–238, 347, 353; annual flooding of, 271; Audubon on scenery of, 274–275; birds along, 226; boats on, 229–231; and commerce, 272; course of, 226–227; fish in, 234; hazards of, 231; inns along, 259; landscape along, 225–226, 237; at Louisville, 271–272; and Mississippi River, 352; name of, 225; people living along, 268; primitive lands past falls of, 267–268; towns alongside, 227; traffic on, 227
Ohio River Bridge Commission, 395
Ohio River Valley, 114, 228, 235, 237, 296
Old Moore's Almanack, 131
Old Poets, 4
Ollier, Charles, 69, 70, 73
Ollier, James, 69, 70, 73
Omaha, Nebraska, 413
Opie, Amelia, 101
Osages, 299
Osgood, Samuel, 378
Oslow, Lord, 112
Otho the Great, 215–216
Owen, Robert, 282
Owen, Robert Dale, 282
Oxford, 4, 49, 88–90

Packet ships, 155–160

Page, Benjamin, 209, 302

Page, Elizabeth Rankin. *See* Bakewell,
Elizabeth Rankin Page

Palais-Royal, 58, 95

Palmer, John, 300

Palmer, Sarah White, 300

Panic of 1819, 252, 297, 305, 317, 330, 333

Panic of 1837, 393, 396, 399–400

Pantisocracy, 115, 348

Paolo and Francesca, 248

Paris, 58, 87, 90–95, 346

Parliament, 113, 121

Patmore, Peter George, 91

Patronage, 113, 184

Payne, John Howard, 84, 145, 397, 398, 407

Peachey, James, 119–120, 249

Peacock, Thomas Love, 72, 112–113

Peale, Charles Willson, Museum of, 182–184

Pears, Benjamin, 300–301

Pears, John Palmer, 300–301

Pears, Maria, 300–301

Pears, Sarah Ann, 300–301

Pears, Sarah Palmer, 300–301

Pears, Thomas, 300–301

Pearse, Maria, 86

Peay, Ella (née Keats), 409

Peay, George Nicholas, 409

Peay, George Speed, 409

Pekin, 155

Penn, William, 182, 183

Pennsylvania, 3, 168, 204, 205, 282, 347

Peona, 100

Perkins, Jacob, 155

Peterloo Massacre, 263

Petrarch, Francesco, 15

Petrarchan sonnet, 15, 32

Philadelphia, 143, 144, 165; architecture and
design of, 166–168, 206; boarding houses
in, 169; and Chambersburg, 199; cultural
aspects of, 181–184; GK's arrival in, 166;
Independence Hall, 182; Liberty Bell,
182; manufactures of, 170; population of,
168–169; prison in, 181–182; public library of, 181

Phlebotomy (bloodletting), 134–135

Phrenology, 378–379

Physiognomy, 379

Pidgeon, Mrs., 359, 360, 364

Pierce, Joseph, 256

Pigeon Creek, 275, 290, 410

Pike, Zebulon M., 303

Pike, 303

Pillars of Hercules, 364

Pindars, 23

Pitot, James, 303–304

Pittsburgh, 3, 175, 179, 186, 205–211, 280;
arks sold in, 229; as Birmingham of the
West, 208; business in, 207; and Chambersburg, 199; and Cincinnati, 251; and
coal, 208; design of, 206; distance to Louisville, 227; and GK's letters, 240; industry of, 208; manufacturing in, 206, 207;
population of, 206; road to, 199, 203–204;
and western market, 206

Pius VI, 370, 385

Pius VII, 385

Place Louis XV, 93

Place Vendôme, 93

Planters, 352

Plutarch, 81, 387

Poe, Edgar Allan, 398

*Poetical Works of Coleridge, Shelley and
Keats, The,* 411

Poor laws, 116

Pope, Alexander, 26, 40, 150, 193, 262, 266;
"Rape of the Lock," 26

Pope, Nathaniel, 302

Pope, Nathaniel Wells, 298–299, 302

Porter, Alexander, Jr., 256

Porte Saint-Denis, 93

Portland, 353

Port Penn, 165

Poynter, Ambrose, 389

Praed, Winthrop Mackworth, 102

Prentice, David, 258, 301, 302, 303, 305, 307, 351, 353

Prentice, George Dennison, "That joyous little girl," 407–408

Priestley, Joseph, 185–186, 284, 300

Prince, Joseph, 445

Prince Regent, 116, 322

Prince Saxe-Coburg stagecoach, 148, 150

Princeton, Indiana, 181, 283, 286, 288, 289, 290, 291, 292–293

Prowse, I. S. (Mary Ann Jeffery): "Ada," 250; "On Visiting a Cataract," 103–104. *See also* Jeffery, Mary Ann

Psalm 84, 244

Pymmes Brook, 50

Quakers, 168, 325; Birkbeck as, 113

Quarantine, 165, 331, 364

Quarterly Review, 115, 121

Queen's Head Tavern, 148

Racine, Jean, 67

Rackets, 28

Rafts, 230

Raleigh, Sir Walter, 382

Randall, Jack, 28–29, 30

Rankin, Adam, 299

Rankin, Elizabeth Speed, 299

Rapp, Frederick, 281

Rapp, Johann Georg, 280, 281–282

Raritan River, 331

Rawlings, William, 48

Reconstruction, 410

Red Banks (Henderson, Ky.), 257, 274, 275, 278–279, 285, 301

Red Banks Trail, 286, 288, 289

Redbourne, 150, 152

Red Lion Inn, 45, 46

Reform Act of 1832, 283

Regency England, 59, 101, 102, 198

Reveley, Henry, 339

Reynolds, Charlotte, 85, 89, 316–317

Reynolds, Charlotte Cox, 43, 85–86, 121–122

Reynolds, Eliza, 85, 89, 122, 316–317

Reynolds, George, 29, 43, 85, 86

Reynolds, Jane, 85, 86, 88, 89, 97, 122, 192, 316–317

Reynolds, John Hamilton, 42–43, 67, 260; and Benjamin Bailey, 86; and Jane Cox, 192; deterioration of, 315; and Devonshire, 97; and Eliza Powell Drewe, 68–69, 86; *The Fancy,* 29–30; and "The Gothic looks solemn," 88; and Hunt, 43–44; and JK, 52, 69; and JK at Oxford, 89; as JK's friend, 69, 163; and JK's letters, 101, 125, 126, 134; and JK's *Poems* (1817), 69; on JK's travel to Italy, 342; as quitting poetry, 215; review of JK's *Poems* (1817), 68; rheumatic fever of, 132; and Rice, 97; *Safie,* 43; and Shelley-Keats competition, 96; sisters of, 85; "Sonnet on the Nonpareil," 30; and Taylor & Hessey, 69–70; and TK's illness, 99

Reynolds, Marianne, 85, 86, 87, 88, 89, 192, 316–317

Reynolds family, 85, 87

Rhode-Island American, 343

Rice, James, 97, 99, 132, 163, 260, 314–315, 391

Ridgeway, William, 326

River Lea, 50

River Licking, 183, 253, 349

River Mersey, 150, 153

Robb, James, 326

Roberts, George and Charles, 141

Robertson, William, *History of America,* 40

Robinson, Henry Crabb, 101

Rock Island, 272

Rodd, George R., 334

Rogers, Coleman, 402

Rogers, Lewis, 402

Rollins, Hyder Edward, 401; *The Letters of John Keats,* 249, 307

Rome, 370–373

Rossetti, Christina, 5

Rossetti, Dante Gabriel, 5

Rossetti, William Michael, 5

Rouen, 93

Rousseau, Jean-Jacques, 50

Rozier, Claude François, 298

Rozier, Ferdinand, 298, 299

Saint-Denis, 93

Saint Peter's basilica, 382

Salmasius (Claude Saumaise), 131–132

Salmon's Brook, 21

Saltee Islands, 153

Sandell, John Nowland, 51–52

Sandy Hook, 331

Sans-culottes, 67

Sass, Henry, 366, 367, 368, 370

Saunders, Margaret, 157

Savage, Hannah, 157

Sawrey, Solomon, 188, 267; *An Inquiry,* 89

Schneider, John Henry Powell, 52

Schuylkill River, 167, 168, 185, 187

Scott, Caroline, 93, 94

Scott, John, 90–91, 95, 101; *The House of Mourning,* 93–94

Scott, Paul, 93

Scott, Sir Walter, 32, 293–294, 371; *The Monastery,* 384

Scottish Highlands, 147

Scrub Ridge, 200

Seminole Nation, 243

Sensibility: cult of, 28; poetry of, 26

Sentimental poetry, 26

Severn, Joseph, 54–55, 125; and Alcibiades, 369, 387–388; artistic reasons for Italy trip, 381–382; attendance to JK in Rome, 384, 385, 386–389; and Bible, 386–387; and Bourbon Palace, 369–370; and Charles Armitage Brown, 391; *The Cave of Despair,* 381; James Clark on, 381; and death of JK, 388; devotion to JK, 337–338; father of, 55, 359, 360; and food in

Rome, 383; and Gibson, 382; and GK, 338, 374, 391; *Hermia and Helena,* 337–338; and Leigh Hunt, 357; and JK's hemorrhaging, 339–340, 384, 386; JK's openness to, 368; miniature portraits of JK and GK by, 337; monument for JK, 389; moods of, 338; and Naples, 364–373, 366; and Raphael, 382; residence at Piazza di Spagna, 372–373; on John Scott, 91; and theater in Naples, 368–369; and travel from Naples to Rome, 370–373; and trip to Italy with JK, 359–366

Shakespeare, William, 68, 70, 216, 225, 395; birthplace of, 89–90; *Comedy of Errors,* 330; as good Genius, 79; grave of, 90; *Hamlet,* 245; Hazlitt on, 130; *Henry VI,* 30; heroines of, 85; and JK and Fanny Brawne, 192; JK's folio edition of, 131; and JK's *Poems* (1817), 337, 452; and JK's trip to Italy, 358; *King Lear,* 76–77, 83, 198; *Love's Labour's Lost,* 79; *Measure for Measure,* 380; *The Merry Wives of Windsor,* 142; *A Midsummer Night's Dream,* 338; portrait of, 1, 78–79; portrait gems of, 210; and Severn, 337–338, 382; sonnets of, 15, 32, 101; *The Tempest,* 74, 76, 130; "Venus and Adonis," 73

Shanklin, 76, 261, 262

Shawneetown, 271, 278, 288, 352

Sheep, 236–237

Shelley, Frances, 371

Shelley, Mary Wollstonecraft Godwin: *Frankenstein,* 3, 72; *Lodore,* 3; *Valperga,* 273

Shelley, Percy Bysshe, 15, 67; *Alastor; or, The Spirit of Solitude and Other Poems,* 72; and America, 114; and atheism, 96; and Benjamin Bailey, 89; and beauty, 221; and Birkbeck, 112; circle of, 72; and Coliseum, 372; competition with Keats, 72, 81, 96, 114; death of, 389; education of, 49; and epic, 72; and Maria Reveley Gisborne, 339; and Haydon, 96; and Leigh

Shelley, Percy Bysshe *(continued)*
  Hunt, 43–44, 80, 96; invitation to JK to
  Pisa, 341; and JK, 81, 96–97; and JK's
  hemorrhage, 341; and William Lambe,
  339; *Laon and Cythna (The Revolt of Is-
  lam),* 72–73, 114; meets with JK, 71–72;
  "Men of England," 263; and Novellos,
  101; and Olliers, 73; preface to "Alastor,"
  72; and society, 198
Shelley, William, 389
Sheridan, Richard Brinsley, *The School for
  Scandal,* 128
Shewell, Lydia, 170
Shewell, Stephen, Sr., 144, 171
Shippingport, 186, 272, 273, 274, 353
Sidling Hill, 200
Sidney, Sir Philip, 143; *Astrophel and Stella,*
  37
Simpson, Emma Speed, 285, 399
Slade House, 86
Slater family, 157
Slavery, 4, 168–169, 227, 285, 346, 399
Smith, Charles Augustus, 409
Smith, Daniel, 394
Smith, Felix, 394, 458
Smith, Horace, 101, 127
Smith, Obadiah, 304
Smith, Sydney, *Radical Reform,* 116
Smith, Thomas, *Emigrant's Guide,* 238
Smith, Keats & Company, 394
Smith, Payse, & Company, 48
Smyth family, 157
Snook, Henry, 262
Snook, John, 262, 362
Snook, John, Jr., 262
Snook, Letitia, 262, 362
Soames, William, 30–31
Social progress, 115
Socrates, 220, 222, 224
Socratic dialogues, 223
Somerset, New Jersey, 347
Sophocles, 134
Southampton, 73–74

Southey, Robert, 115, 185–186, 348
South/Southern Ridge, 204
South Street Seaport, 393–393. *See also*
  Fulton-Street Wharf
Southwark, 11, 28
Spa Fields, Islington, 117
Spanish Constitution of 1812, 363, 367
Spectator, The, 397
Speed, Emma Frances (née Keats), 279, 398,
  399, 401–402, 406, 410, 411, 413
Speed, John, 399
Speed, John Gilmer, 297, 298, 401
Speed, Joshua, 402
Speed, Philip, 402
Speed, Robert, 304
Spenser, Edmund, 32, 132, 150, 197, 217,
  397; *Faerie Queene,* 381; *Works of Mr. Ed-
  mund Spenser,* 397
Spofford, Reginald, "Julia to the Wood
  Robin," 27
Springfield Gas Company, 410
Squirrels, hunting of, 229
Stagecoach, travel by, 148, 180, 334, 347
Stark's Nest, 22
Staten Island, 331, 332
St. Catherine's Hill, 76
St. Clair, Arthur, 253
Steamboats, 233, 240, 256, 394; and Thomas
  Woodhouse Bakewell, 258, 302–303, 351,
  353, 400; and GK, 351, 352, 353–354, 355,
  373; and river hazards, 231
Steam power, 254–256, 258, 300. See also
  Bakewell, Thomas Woodhouse; Evans,
  Oliver; Perkins, Jacob
Steerage passengers, 155, 156–158
Stephens, Henry, 35–36, 44, 149–150, 152,
  197
Sterne, Laurence, *A Sentimental Journey,* 93
Steuben, Friedrich Wilhelm Augustus von,
  236
Steubenville, 236
St. George Church, 142
St. George's Church, 46

St. James's Church, 141

St. Leonard's Shoreditch, 284

St. Margaret's Church, 136, 140–141

St. Mary-le-Bow Church, 44, 56, 402–403

Stockdale, Hannah, 157

Stony-Stratford, 150

St. Peter's Field, 263

Sturgis, William, 155

Sublimity, 3, 11, 19, 143, 147, 189, 190, 192, 224; and GK, 15–16; in "To My Brother George" (sonnet), 14, 15–16; and Wordsworth, 15

Suicide, 241–242; and Henry Capper, 242–242, 257; and Isabel Keats, 407

Surrey Gaol, 38, 39, 41

Susquehanna County, 179

Susquehanna River, 185, 204

Swan & Hoop, 44–45, 46–47, 48, 70

Swan with Two Necks, Lad Lane, 148, 149

Swan with Two Necks (in America), 201

Sweetinburgh, Mary (née Jennings), 246

Tallant, Alice Gwynne, 257, 445

Tallant, Charlotte, 445

Tallant, Elizabeth Jane Drury, 174

Tallant, James, 174, 175, 207, 255–257

Tallant, Jane Drury, 174

Tallant, John, 174, 257

Tallant, Julius Ferdinand, 257, 445

Tallant, Mary Drury, 174–175, 257, 445

Tallant, Sarah A., 445

Tallant, Sarah Tuxford, 257, 445

Tallant, William, 174, 175, 257

Tarascon, John Anthony, 272, 274

Tarascon, Louis Anastasius, 274

Tassie, William, 210

Taverns, 345–346. See also Inns

Tawapatee Bottom, 299

Taxes, 112, 116, 121

Taylor, James, 173, 436

Taylor, Jeremy, 87; Holy Living and Holy Dying, 387

Taylor, John, 34, 147; and Richard Abbey, 378; and Birkbeck's Letters from Illinois, 163; and John Clare, 173; and James Clark, 381; and Michael Drury, 154, 168, 173; and father, 70, 173, 436; and GK, 173, 391; and GK's finances, 318; GK's letters of introduction from, 142–143, 169; and GK's marriage and emigration, 142–143; and JK's biography, 4; and JK's departure for Italy, 356; and JK's finances in Rome, 385; JK's letter to, 124; as JK's publisher, 69–70; and JK's travel to Italy, 342, 359, 360; and Frances Jennings Keats, 46; and money advances to JK, 265; and physiognomy, 379; and TK, 187

Taylor, Sarah (née Drury), 173

Taylor, W. G., 61

Taylor, Zachary, 396

Taylor & Hessey, 69–70, 93, 112, 142, 149, 265, 342–343

Tea trade, 60, 311–312

Teignmouth, 99, 101–107, 112

Teign River, 99, 103

Telegraph, 152–155, 156, 159–160, 164, 168, 176

Tennessee, 208, 274, 394

Textile workers, 263

Thompson, Captain. See Mathews, Robert

Thompson, Francis, 324–325, 332

Thompson, Judge, 294

Thompson family, 157

Thoreau, Henry David, 379

Tighe, Mary, Psyche, 27

Tobacco, 169, 279, 352

Tonkin, Letitia (née Spencer), 106

Tonkin, Warwick Hele, Jr., 106

Tonkin, Warwick Hele, Sr., 106

Torlonia, Alessandro, 385

Torlonia, Giovanni Raimondo, 385

Tower of London, 117

Towers, Isabella Jane (née Clarke), 36; Perils in the Woods, 177–178

Towers, John, 36

Transatlantic communication, 238–239

Transcendentalism. *See* American Transcendentalism

Treaty of Ghent, 2

Trimmer, Charles, 119, 249

Trollope, Frances Milton, 251, 346

Tuckey, Mary Ann, 24

Tuckey, Susanna, 24

Tuileries Palace, 93

Tuley, Philip Speed, 6

Turner, Ned, 28–29

Turtle Creek, 205

Turtle Hill, 205

Turton, William, 13, 99, 106–107, 133, 135; *Conchological Dictionary,* 107; *A Treatise,* 99

Twain, Mark, 410; *The Adventures of Huckleberry Finn,* 256

Union Town, Pennsylvania, 347

Unitarianism, 284–285

United Hospitals of St. Thomas and Guy's, 11, 20, 25, 39

Ure, Andrew, 326

U.S. Congress, 113, 119

U.S. Postal Service, 239

Vauxhall Gardens, 31

Venereal disease, 89, 187, 188, 267

Vesuvius, 365, 366

Victoria, 106, 322

Victorian fashion, 141

Victorian life writing, 4–5

Victorian poets, 98

Victorians, 215

Village Prairie, 295

Vincennes, Indiana, 177, 278, 286

Virginia, 113, 227, 345, 347

Wabash River, 183, 280, 281, 283, 286, 289, 293, 294

Waite, Isaac, 120

Waldegrave, Mary, 31, 142

Wall family, 157

Wallace, David L., 437

Walsh, Thomas, 359, 360–361, 362, 363

Walter Scott, 256–257

Walthamstow, 21, 23, 24, 52, 60, 247, 328

Walton, Newton, & Company, 61

Wanborough, Illinois, 276, 277, 283, 284, 288–289, 295

Ward, Aileen, 5

Warder, Ann (née Head), 241

Warder, Benjamin, 241

Warder, Jeremiah, 241

Warder, Jeremiah, Jr., 241

Warder, John, 241, 308

Warder, John, Jr., 241

Warder, William, 241

Warder & Brothers, 241

War of 1812, 1, 175, 300, 301, 305, 333

Warwickshire, 150

Washington, D.C., 181, 199

Washington, George, 143, 185, 205, 236, 240, 255, 332, 345, 396

Washington Hall, 169, 345

Waterloo, battle of, 2

Wayne, Anthony, 184, 253

Wedgwood, Josiah, 210

Welby, Adlard, 164, 175, 178, 203

Wellington, Duke of, 140

Wells, Charles, 125–126; *Joseph and His Brethren,* 195; and love letters to TK, 194–195, 245–246

Well Walk, 58, 62, 71, 187, 188. *See also* Bentley family

Wentworth, Sir Peter, 63

Wentworth Place, 62, 65, 84, 188, 191, 196, 220, 248, 312, 315, 324, 335, 336, 341, 342, 349, 357

West, Benjamin, *Christ Healing the Sick in the Temple,* 182

West, Rebecca K., 154

Western Cemetery of Louisville, 403

Western Country. *See* American Western Country

Westmacott, Sir Richard, 159, 389

W. G. Bakewell & Company, 400

Wheeling, Virginia, 237, 278, 347

Wiggin & Whitney, of Philadelphia, 152

Wiggin & Whitney's pier, 166, 169

Wilde, Oscar, 410–413; "The Grave of
    Keats," 413

Wilkinson, 62, 78, 80

Williams, Blanche Colton, *Forever Young,* 6

Williams, Elizabeth, 405

Williams, John ("Kicking Jack"), 325–326,
    331

Williams, Robert, 326

Wilmington, Delaware, 165

Wilson, James, 304

Wilson, John, 66

Wilson, Thomas, 425

Winchester, 262–265

Winn family, 157

Winter, of 1819–1820, 321–322

Wolcot, John, 101

Wold, Jane, 436

Wolff, Reverend, 389

Wollstonecraft, Mary, 235, 377, 401

Wood, John, Jr., 326

Wood, Thomas, 326

Wood construction, 290

Woodhouse, Richard, 70, 73, 96, 265, 266,
    321, 359, 360

Woods, John, 227, 237, 258, 268, 281, 286,
    294

Wool, 81, 236

Wordsworth, Dorothy, 15

Wordsworth, William, 42, 298; and Chat-
    terton, 126; confidence in, 15; and "Great
    spirits now on earth are sojourning," 43,
    94; and Hunt, 43, 44; and JK's dedicatory
    sonnet to Hunt, 65–66; "Lines Composed
    a Few Miles above Tintern Abbey," 15;
    meets JK, 101; misery of, 245; "Ode: Inti-
    mations of Immortality," 65–66; and
    philosophic mind, 217; and poetic dic-
    tion, 16; preface to *Lyrical Ballads,* 43;
    and Scott, 94; and "To Charles Cowden
    Clarke," 37

Worshipful Company of Pattenmakers,
    47

Wright, Frances, 167, 168, 182

Wright, Isaac, 324–325

Wylie, Ann Amelia (née Griffin), 31, 124,
    141, 152, 249, 330; and Mrs. Frances
    Brawne, 342; and Georgiana's emigra-
    tion, 121, 122; GK's letter to, 333; GK's
    visit with, 330; JK's letter to, 333–334

Wylie, Augusta Christina, 142

Wylie, Charles Gaskell, 31, 123, 141

Wylie, George Keats, 141, 142

Wylie, Henry, 31, 344, 396

Wylie, Henry Robert, 31, 123, 141, 142

Wylie, James, 123, 154

Wylie, Margaret Roberts, 141

Wylie family, 123–124

Yeatman, Griffin, 255

Yeatman's Cove, 255

Yellow fever, 331

Yohogany River, 204

Young, John P., 394

Young Poets, 67, 70

Zane, Ebenezer, 347

Zane's Trace, 347

Zanesville, Ohio, 347